The Handbook of Research on Scalable Computing Technologies

Kuan-Ching Li
Providence University, Taiwan

Ching-Hsien Hsu
Chung Hua University, Taiwan

Laurence Tianruo Yang
St. Francis Xavier University, Canada

Jack Dongarra
University of Tennessee, USA

Hans Zima
Jet Propulsion Laboratory, California Institute of Technology, USA
and University of Vienna, Austria

Volume II

Information Science REFERENCE

INFORMATION SCIENCE REFERENCE

Hershey · New York

Director of Editorial Content: Kristin Klinger
Senior Managing Editor: Jamie Snavely
Assistant Managing Editor: Carole Coulson
Publishing Assistant: Sean Woznicki
Typesetter: Carole Coulson, Dan Wilson, Daniel Custer, Kait Betz
Cover Design: Lisa Tosheff
Printed at: Yurchak Printing Inc.

Published in the United States of America by
Information Science Reference (an imprint of IGI Global)
701 E. Chocolate Avenue
Hershey PA 17033
Tel: 717-533-8845
Fax: 717-533-8661
E-mail: cust@igi-global.com
Web site: http://www.igi-global.com/reference

Library of Congress Cataloging-in-Publication Data

Handbook of research on scalable computing technologies / Kuan-Ching Li ... [et al.], editors.
p. cm.
Includes bibliographical references and index.
Summary: "This book presents, discusses, shares ideas, results and experiences on the recent important advances and future challenges on enabling technologies for achieving higher performance"--Provided by publisher.
ISBN 978-1-60566-661-7 (hardcover) -- ISBN 978-1-60566-662-4 (ebook) 1. Computational grids (Computer systems) 2. System design. 3. Parallel processing (Electronic computers) 4. Ubiquitous computing. I. Li, Kuan-Ching.
QA76.9.C58H356 2009
004--dc22

2009004402

British Cataloguing in Publication Data
A Cataloguing in Publication record for this book is available from the British Library.

Editorial Advisory Board

List of Contributors

Table of Contents

Section 6
Optimization Techniques

Section 7
Web Computing

Section 8
Mobile Computing and Ad Hoc Networks

Section 9
Fault Tolerance and QoS

Section 10
Applications

Detailed Table of Contents

information as an integral part to manage, control, adapt and optimize. However, the inherent scale and complexity of Pervasive Grid systems fundamentally impact how applications are formulated, deployed and managed, and presents significant challenges that permeate all aspects of systems software stack. In this chapter, the authors present some use-cases of Pervasive Grids and highlight their opportunities and challenges. They then present why semantic knowledge and autonomic mechanisms are seen as foundations for conceptual and implementation solutions that can address these challenges.

Desktop Grids, literally Grids made of Desktop Computers, are very popular in the context of "Volunteer Computing" for large scale "Distributed Computing" projects like SETI@home and Folding@home. They are very appealing, as "Internet Computing" platforms for scientific projects seeking a huge amount of computational resources for massive high throughput computing, like the EGEE project in Europe. Companies are also interested of using cheap computing solutions that does not add extra hardware and cost of ownership. A very recent argument for Desktop Grids is their ecological impact: by scavenging unused CPU cycles without increasing excessively the power consumption, they reduce the waste of electricity. This book chapter presents the background of Desktop Grid, their principles and essential mechanisms, the evolution of their architectures, their applications and the research tools associated with this technology.

Aim of this chapter is to guide developers and users through the most important stages of implementing software applications on Grid infrastructures, and to discuss important challenges and potential solutions. Those challenges come from the underlying grid infrastructure, like security, resource management, and information services; the application data, data management, and the structure, volume, and location of the data; and the application architecture, monolithic or workflow, serial or parallel. As a case study, we present the DEISA Distributed European Infrastructure for Supercomputing Applications and describe its DEISA Extreme Computing Initiative DECI for porting and running scientific grand challenge applications. The chapter concludes with an outlook on Compute Clouds, and suggests ten rules of building a sustainable grid as a prerequisite for long-term sustainability of the grid applications.

Application benchmarks can play a key role in analyzing and predicting the performance and scalability of Grid applications, serve as an evaluation of the fitness of a collection of Grid resources for running a specific application or class of applications (Tsouloupas & Dikaiakos, 2007), and help in implementing performance-aware resource allocation policies of real time job schedulers. However, application benchmarks have been largely ignored due to diversified types of applications, multi-constrained executions, dynamic Grid behavior, and heavy computational costs. To remedy these, we present an approach taken by the ASKALON Grid environment that computes application benchmarks considering variations in the problem size of the application and machine size of the Grid site. Our system dynamically controls the number of benchmarking experiments for individual applications and manages the execution of these experiments on different Grid sites. We present experimental results of our method for three real-world applications in the Austrian Grid environment.

In order to improve the scalability and reduce the traffic of Gnutella-like unstructured peer-to-peer networks, index caching and controlled flooding mechanisms had been an important research topic in recent years. In this chapter we will describe and present the current state of the art about index management schemes, interest groups and data clustering for unstructured peer-to-peer networks. Index caching mechanisms are an approach to reducing the traffic of keyword querying. However, the cached indices may incur redundant replications in the whole network, leading to the less efficient use of storage and the increase of traffic. We propose a multiplayer index management scheme that actively diffuses the indices in the network and groups indices according to their request rate. The peers of the group that have indices with higher request rate will be placed in layers that receive queries earlier. Our simulation shows that the proposed approach can keep a high success query rate as well as reduce the flooding size.

Structured peer-to-peer networks are scalable overlay network infrastructures that support Internet-scale network applications. A globally consistent peer-to-peer protocol maintains the structural properties of the network with peers dynamically joining, leaving and failing in the network. In this chapter, we discuss hierarchical distributed hash tables (DHT) as an approach to reduce the overhead of maintaining the overlay network. In a two-level hierarchical DHT, the top-level overlay consists of groups of nodes where each group is distinguished by a unique group identifier. In each group, one or more nodes are designated as supernodes and act as gateways to nodes at the second level. Collisions of groups occur when concurrent node joins result in the creation of multiple groups with the same group identifier. This has the adverse effects of increasing the lookup path length due to a larger top-level overlay, and the overhead of overlay network maintenance. We discuss two main approaches to address the group collision problem: collision detection-and-resolution, and collision avoidance. As an example, we describe an implementation of hierarchical DHT by extending Chord as the underlying overlay graph.

Structured peer-to-peer (P2P) overlay networks like Distributed Hash Tables (DHTs) map data items to the network based on a consistent hashing function. Such mapping for data distribution has an inherent load balance problem. Thus, a load balancing mechanism is an indispensable part of a structured P2P overlay network for high performance. The rapid development of P2P systems has posed challenges in load balancing due to their features characterized by large scale, heterogeneity, dynamism, and proximity. An efficient load balancing method should flexible and resilient enough to deal with these characteristics. This chapter will first introduce the P2P systems and the load balancing in P2P systems. It then introduces the current technologies for load balancing in P2P systems, and provides a case study of a dynamism-resilient and proximity-aware load balancing mechanism. Finally, it indicates the future and emerging trends of load balancing, and concludes the chapter.

This chapter describes Aneka-Federation, a decentralized and distributed system that combines enterprise Clouds, overlay networking, and structured peer-to-peer techniques to create scalable wide-area networking of compute nodes for high-throughput computing. The Aneka-Federation integrates numerous small scale Aneka Enterprise Cloud services and nodes that are distributed over multiple control and enterprise domains as parts of a single coordinated resource leasing abstraction. The system is designed with the aim of making distributed enterprise Cloud resource integration and application programming flexible, efficient, and scalable. The system is engineered such that it: enables seamless integration of existing Aneka Enterprise Clouds as part of single wide-area resource leasing federation; self-organizes the system components based on a structured peer-to-peer routing methodology; and presents end-users with a distributed application composition environment that can support variety of programming and execution models. This chapter describes the design and implementation of a novel, extensible and decentralized peer-to-peer technique that helps to discover, connect and provision the services of Aneka Enterprise Clouds among the users who can use different programming models to compose their applications. Evaluations of the system with applications that are programmed using the Task and Thread execution models on top of an overlay of Aneka Enterprise Clouds have been described here.

Section 3
Programming Models and Tools

Grid computing is a newly developed technology for complex systems with large-scale resource sharing, wide-area communication, and multi-institutional collaboration. It is hard to analyze and model the Grid reliability because of its largeness, complexity and stiffness. Therefore, this chapter introduces the Grid computing technology, presents different types of failures in grid system, models the grid reliability with star structure and tree structure, and finally studies optimization problems for grid task partitioning and allocation. The chapter then presents models for star-topology considering data dependence and tree-structure considering failure correlation. Evaluation tools and algorithms are developed, evolved from Universal generating function and Graph Theory. Then, the failure correlation and data dependence are considered in the model. Numerical examples are illustrated to show the modeling and analysis.

Parallel programming models using parallel tasks have shown to be successful for increasing scalability on medium-size homogeneous parallel systems. Several investigations have shown that these programming models can be extended to hierarchical and heterogeneous systems which will dominate in the future. In this article, we discuss parallel programming models with parallel tasks and describe these programming models in the context of other approaches for mixed task and data parallelism. We discuss compiler-based as well as library-based approaches for task programming and present extensions to the model which allow a flexible combination of parallel tasks and an optimization of the resulting communication structure.

In this chapter, we will describe today's technological trends on building a multi-core based microprocessor and its programmability and scalability issues. Ever since multi-core processors have been commercialized, we have seen many different multi-core processors. However, the issues related to how to utilize the physical parallelism of cores for software execution have not been suitably addressed so far. Compared to implementing multiple identical cores on a single chip, separating an original sequential program into multiple running threads has been an even more challenging task. In this chapter, we introduce several different software programs which can be successfully ported on the future multi-core based processors and describe how they could benefit from the multi-core systems. Towards the end, the future trends in the multi-core systems are overviewed.

The main ideas of the Assembly Technology (AT) in its application to parallel implementation of large scale realistic numerical models on a rectangular mesh are considered and demonstrated by the parallelization (fragmentation) of the Particle-In-Cell method (PIC) application to solution of the problem of energy exchange in plasma cloud. The implementation of the numerical models with the assembly technology is based on the construction of a fragmented parallel program. Assembling of a numerical simulation program under AT provides automatically different useful dynamic properties of the target program including dynamic load balance on the basis of the fragments migration from overloaded into underloaded processor elements of a multicomputer. Parallel program assembling approach also can be considered as combination and adaptation for parallel programming of the well known modular programming and domain decomposition techniques and supported by the system software for fragmented programs assembling.

This chapter uses two scientific computing kernels to illustrate challenges of designing parallel algorithms for one heterogeneous multi-core processor, the Cell Broadband Engine processor (Cell/B.E.). It describes the limitation of the current parallel systems using single-core processors as building blocks. The limitation deteriorates the performance of applications which have data-intensive and computation-intensive kernels such as Finite Difference Time Domain (FDTD) and Fast Fourier Transform (FFT). FDTD is a regular problem with nearest neighbour comminuncation pattern under synchronization constraint. FFT based on indirect swap network (ISN) modifies the data mapping in traditional Cooley-Tukey butterfly network to improve data locality, hence reducing the communication and synchronization overhead. The authors hope to unleash the Cell/B.E. and design parallel FDTD and parallel FFT based on ISN by taking into account unique features of Cell/B.E. such as its eight SIMD processing units on the single chip and its high-speed on-chip bus.

Section 4
Scheduling and Communication Techniques

The knowledge of application behavior allows predicting their expected workload and future operations. Such knowledge can be used to support, improve and optimize scheduling decisions by distributing data accesses and minimizing communication overheads. Different techniques can be used to obtain such knowledge, varying from simple source code analysis, sequential access pattern extraction, history-based approaches and on-line behavior extraction methods. The extracted behavior can be later classified into different groups, representing process execution states, and then used to predict future process events. This chapter describes different approaches, strategies and methods for application behavior extraction and classification, and also how this information can be used to predict new events, focusing on distributed process scheduling.

Task allocation and scheduling are essential for achieving the high performance expected of parallel computing systems. However, there are serious issues pertaining to the efficient utilization of computational resources in such systems that need to be resolved, such as, achieving a balance between system throughput and execution time. Moreover, many scheduling techniques involve massive task graphs with complex precedence relations, processing costs, and inter-task communication costs. In general, there are two main issues that should be highlighted: problem representation and finding an efficient solution in a timely fashion. In the work proposed here, we have attempted to overcome the first problem by using a structured model which offers a systematic method for the representation of the scheduling problem. The model used can encode almost all of the parameters involved in a scheduling problem in a very systematic manner. To address the second problem, a Tabu Search algorithm is used to allocate tasks to processors in a reasonable amount of time. The use of Tabu Search has the advantage of obtaining solutions to more general instances of the scheduling problem in reasonable time spans. The efficiency of the proposed framework is demonstrated by using several case studies. A number of evaluation criteria will be used to optimize the schedules. Communication- and computation-intensive task graphs are analyzed, as are a number of different task graph shapes and sizes.

C.E.R. Alves, Universidade Sao Judas Tadeu, Brazil
E. N. Cáceres, Universidade Federal de Mato Grosso do Sul, Brazil
F. Dehne, Carleton University, Canada
S. W. Song, Universidade de Sao Paulo, Brazil

In this book chapter, we discuss some important communication issues to obtain a highly scalable computing system. We consider the CGM (Coarse-Grained Multicomputer) model, a realistic computing model to obtain scalable parallel algorithms. The communication cost is modeled by the number of communication rounds and the objective is to design algorithms that require the minimum number of communication rounds. We discuss some important issues and make considerations of practical importance, based on our previous experience in the design and implementation of parallel algorithms. The first issue is the amount of data transmitted in a communication round. For a practical implementation to be successful we should attempt to minimize this amount, even when it is already within the limit allowed by the CGM model. The second issue concerns the trade-off between the number of communication rounds which the CGM attempts to minimize and the overall communication time taken in the communication rounds. Sometimes a larger number of communication rounds may actually reduce the total amount of data transmitted in the communications rounds. These two issues have guided us to present efficient parallel algorithms for the string similarity problem, used as an illustration.

Wanchun Dou, Nanjing University, P. R. China
Jinjun Chen, Swinburne University of Technologies, Australia

This chapter introduces a scheduling approach for cross-domain scientific workflow execution with time-related QoS evaluation. Generally, scientific workflow execution often spans self-managing administrative domains to achieving global collaboration advantage. In practice, it is infeasible for a domain-specific application to disclose its process details for privacy or security reasons. Consequently, it is a challenging endeavor to coordinate scientific workflows and its distributed domain-specific applications from service invocation perspective. Therefore, in this chapter, we aim at proposing a collaborative scheduling approach, with time-related QoS evaluation, for navigating cross-domain collaboration. Under this collaborative scheduling approach, a private workflow fragment could maintain temporal consistency with a global scientific workflow in resource sharing and task enactments. Furthermore, an evaluation is presented to demonstrate the scheduling approach.

Volume II

Data Grids provide services and infrastructure for distributed data-intensive applications that need to access, transfer and modify massive datasets stored at distributed locations around the world. For example, the next-generation of scientific applications such as many in high-energy physics, molecular modeling, and earth sciences will involve large collections of data created from simulations or experiments. The size of these data collections is expected to be of multi-terabyte or even petabyte scale in many applications. Ensuring efficient, reliable, secure and fast access to such large data is hindered by the high latencies of the Internet. The need to manage and access multiple petabytes of data in Grid environments, as well as to ensure data availability and access optimization are challenges that must be addressed.

This chapter first presents taxonomies on approaches for resource allocation across resource sharing networks such as Grids. It then examines existing systems and classifies them under their architectures, operational models, support for the life-cycle of virtual organisations, and resource control techniques. Resource sharing networks have been established and used for various scientific applications over the last decade. The early ideas of Grid computing have foreseen a global and scalable network that would provide users with resources on demand. In spite of the extensive literature on resource allocation and scheduling across organisational boundaries, these resource sharing networks mostly work in isolation, thus contrasting with the original idea of Grid computing. Several efforts have been made towards providing architectures, mechanisms, policies and standards that may enable resource allocation across Grids. A survey and classification of these systems are relevant for the understanding of different approaches utilised for connecting resources across organisations and virtualisation techniques. In addition, a classification also sets the ground for future work on inter-operation of Grids.

Integrated heterogeneous wireless and mobile network (IHWMN) is introduced by combing different types of wireless and mobile networks (WMNs) in order to provide more comprehensive service such as high bandwidth with wide coverage. In an IHWMN, a mobile terminal equipped with multiple network interfaces can connect to any available network, even multiple networks at the same time. The terminal also can change its connection from one network to other networks while still keeping its communication alive. Although IHWMN is very promising and a strong candidate for future WMNs, it brings a lot of issues because different types of networks or systems need to be integrated to provide seamless service to mobile users. In this chapter, we focus on some major issues in IHWMN. Several noel network selection strategies and resource management schemes are also introduced for IHWMN to provide better resource allocation for this new network architecture.

The evolution of Internet and its successful technologies has brought a tremendous growth in business, education, research etc. over the last four decades. With the dramatic advances in multimedia technologies and the increasing popularity of real-time applications, recently Quality of Service (QoS) support in the Internet has been in great demand. Deployment of such applications over the Internet in recent years, and the trend to manage them efficiently with a desired QoS in mind, researchers have been trying for a major shift from its Best Effort (BE) model to a service oriented model. Such efforts have resulted in Integrated Services (Intserv), Differentiated Services (Diffserv), Multi Protocol Label Switching (MPLS), Policy Based Networking (PBN) and many more technologies. But the reality is that such models have been implemented only in certain areas in the Internet not everywhere and many of them also faces scalability problem while dealing with huge number of traffic flows with varied priority levels in the Internet. As a result, an architecture addressing scalability problem and satisfying end-to-end QoS still remains a big issue in the Internet. In this Chapter we propose a policy based architecture which we believe can achieve scalability while offering end to end QoS in the Internet.

computer vision. This chapter presents a significant application of Spiral Architecture for distributed image processing. It demonstrates the impressive characteristics of spiral architecture for high performance image processing. The proposed method tackles several challenging practical problems during the implementation. The proposed method reduces the data communication between the processing nodes and is configurable. Moreover, the proposed partitioning scheme has a consistent approach: after image partitioning each sub-image should be a representative of the original one without changing the basic object, which is important to the related image processing operations.

This chapter studies a load scheduling strategy with near-optimal processing time that is designed to explore the computational characteristics of DNA sequence alignment algorithms, specifically, the Needleman-Wunsch Algorithm. Following the divisible load scheduling theory, an efficient load scheduling strategy is designed in large-scale networks so that the overall processing time of the sequencing tasks is minimized. In this study, the load distribution depends on the length of the sequence and number of processors in the network and, the total processing time is also affected by communication link speed. Several cases have been considered in the study by varying the sequences, communication and computation speeds, and number of processors. Through simulation and numerical analysis, this study demonstrates that for a constant sequence length as the numbers of processors increase in the network the processing time for the job decreases and minimum overall processing time is achieved.

Network security applications such as intrusion detection systems (IDSs), firewalls, anti-virus/spyware systems, anti-spam systems, and security visualisation applications are all computing-intensive applications. These applications all heavily rely on deep packet inspection, which is to examine the content of each network packet's payload. Today these security applications cannot cope with the speed of broadband Internet that has already been deployed, that is, the processor power is much slower than the bandwidth power. Recently the development of multi-core processors brings more processing power. Multi-core processors represent a major evolution in computing hardware technology. While two years ago most network processors and personal computer microprocessors had single core configuration, the majority of the current microprocessors contain dual or quad cores and the number of cores on die is expected to grow exponentially over time. The purpose of this chapter is to discuss the research on using multi-core technologies to parallelize deep packet inspection algorithms, and how such an approach will improve the performance of deep packet inspection applications. This will eventually provide a security system the capability of real-time packet inspection thus significantly improve the overall status of security on current Internet infrastructure.

Computation mobility enables running programs to move around among machines and is the essence of performance gain, fault tolerance, and system throughput increase. State-carrying code (SCC) is a software mechanism to achieve such computation mobility by saving and retrieving computation states during normal program execution in heterogeneous multi-core/many-core clusters. This chapter analyzes different kinds of state saving/retrieving mechanisms for their pros and cons. To achieve a portable, flexible and scalable solution, SCC adopts the application-level thread migration approach. Major deployment features are explained and one example system, MigThread, is used to illustrate implementation details. Future trends are given to point out how SCC can evolve into a complete lightweight virtual machine. New high productivity languages might step in to raise SCC to language level. With SCC, thorough resource utilization is expected.

Foreword

I am delighted to write the Foreword to this book, as it is a very useful resource in a time where change is dramatic and guidance on how to proceed in the development and use of scalable computing technology is in demand.

The book is timely, as it comes at the meeting point of two major challenges and opportunities. Information technology, having grown at an increasingly rapid pace since the construction of the first electronic computer, has now reached a point where it represents an essential, new and transformational enabler of progress in science, engineering, and the commercial world. The performance of today's computer hardware and the sophistication of their software systems yield a qualitatively new tool for scientific discovery, industrial engineering, and business solutions. The solutions complement and promise to go beyond those achievable with the classical two pillars of science - theory and real-world experiments. The opportunity of the third pillar is substantial; however, building it is still a significant challenge. The second challenge and opportunity lays is the current transformation that the computer industry is undergoing. The emergence of multicore processors has been called "the greatest disruption information technology has seen." As several decades of riding Moore's law to easily accelerate clock speeds have come to and end, parallel hardware and software solutions must be developed. While the challenge of creating such solutions is formidable, it also represents an opportunity that is sure to create food for thought and work for new generations of scientists, engineers, students, and practitioners. Scalable computing technologies are at the core of both challenges; they help create the hardware and software architectures underlying the third pillar of science and they help create the parallel computing solutions that will make or break the multicore revolution.

The book addresses many issues related to these challenges and opportunities. Among them is the question of the computer model of the future. Will we continue to obtain computer services from local workstations and personal computers? Will the compute power be concentrated in servers? Will these systems be connected in the form of Grids? The book also discusses the Cloud model, where the end user obtains all information services via networks from providers "out there" - possibly via small hand-held devices. Embedded and real-time computer systems are another factor in this equation, as information technology continues to penetrate all appliances, equipment, and wearables in our daily lives.

While computer systems evolve, the question of the relevant new applications continues to boggle our minds. Classical performance-thirsty programs are those in the area of science and engineering. Future scalable applications are likely to include business and personal software, such as web and mobile applications, tools running on ad-hoc networks, and a myriad of entertainment software.

Among the grandest challenges is the question of programming tools and environments for future, scalable software. In the past, parallel programming has been a niche for a small number of scientists and geeks. With multicores and large-scale parallel systems, this technology now must quickly be learned by masses of software engineers. Many new models are being proposed. They include those where multiple cores and computers communicate by exchanging messages as well as those that share a global address space. The book also discusses mixed models, which will likely have an important role in bridging and integrating heterogeneous computer architectures.

The book touches on both classical and newly emerging issues to reach for the enormous opportunities ahead. Among the classical issues are those of performance analysis and modeling, benchmarking, development of scalable algorithms, communication, and resource management. While many solutions to these issues have been proposed in the past, evolving them to true scalability is likely to lead to many more doctoral dissertations at universities and technologies in industries.

Among the chief pressing new issues is the creation of scalable hardware and software solutions. Tomorrow's high-performance computers may contain millions of processors; even their building blocks may contain tens of cores within foreseeable time. Today's hardware and software solutions are simply inadequate to deal with this sheer scale. Managing power and energy is another issue that has emerged as a major concern. On one hand, power dissipation of computer chips is the major reason that clock speeds can no longer increase; on the other hand, the overall consumption of information technology's power has risen to a political issue - we will soon use more energy for information processing than for moving matter! Furthermore, as computer systems scale to a phenomenal number of parts, their dependability is of increasing concern; failures and their tolerance may need to be considered as part of standard operating procedures. Among the promising principles underlying many of these technologies is that of dynamic adaptation. Future hardware and software systems may no longer by static. They many change, adapting to new data, environments, faults, resource availability, power, and user demands. They may dynamically incorporate newly available technology, possibly creating computer solutions that evolve continually.

The large number of challenges, opportunities, and solutions presented herein will benefit a broad readership from students, to scientists, to practitioners. I am pleased to be able to recommend this book to all those who are looking to learn, use, and contribute to future scalable computing technologies.

Rudolf Eigenmann
Professor of Electrical and Computer Engineering and
Technical Director for HPC, Computing Research Institute
Purdue University
November 2008

Rudolf Eigenmann *is a professor at the School of Electrical and Computer Engineering and Technical Director for HPC of the Computing Research Institute at Purdue University. His research interests include optimizing compilers, programming methodologies and tools, performance evaluation for high-performance computers and applications, and Internet sharing technology. Dr. Eigenmann received a Ph.D. in Electrical Engineering/Computer Science in 1988 from ETH Zurich, Switzerland.*

Preface

There is a constantly increasing demand for computational power for solving complex computational problems in science, engineering and business. The past decade has witnessed a proliferation of more and more high-performance scalable computing systems. The impressive progress is mainly due to the availability of enabling technologies in hardware, software or networks. High-end innovations on such enabling technologies have been fundamental and present cost-effective tools to explore the currently available high performance systems to make further progress.

To that end, this Handbook of Research on Scalable Computing Technologies presents, discusses, share ideas, results and experiences on the recent important advances and future challenges on such enabling technologies.

This handbook is directed to those interested in: developing programming tools and environments for academic or research computing, extracting the inherent parallelism, and achieving higher performance. This handbook will also be useful for upper-level undergraduate and graduate students studying this subject.

Main topics covered in this book are on scalable computing and cover a wide array of topics:

- Architectures and systems
- Software and middleware
- Data and resource management paradigms
- Programming models, tools, problem solving environments
- Trust and security
- Service-oriented computing
- Data-intensive computing
- Cluster and Grid computing
- Community and collaborative computing networks
- Scheduling and load balancing
- Economic and utility computing models
- Peer-to-Peer systems
- Multi-core/Many-core based computing
- Parallel and distributed techniques
- Scientific, engineering and business computing

This book is a valuable source targeted to those interested in the development of field of grid engineering for academic or enterprise computing, aimed for computer scientists, researchers and technical managers working all areas of science, engineering and economy from academia, research centers and industries.

Acknowledgment

Of course, the represented areas/topics in this handbook, are not an exhaustive representation of the world of current scalable computing. Nonetheless, they represent the rich and many-faceted knowledge, that we have the pleasure of sharing with the readers.

The editors would like to acknowledge all of the authors for their insights and excellent contributions to this handbook and the help of all involved in the collaboration and review process of the handbook, without whose support the project could not have been satisfactorily completed. Most of the authors of chapters included in this handbook also served as referees for chapters written by other authors. Thanks go to all those who provided constructive and comprehensive reviews.

Special thanks also go to the publishing team at IGI Global, whose contributions throughout the whole process from inception of the initial idea to final publication have been invaluable. In particular to, Rebecca Beistline, who continuously prodded via e-mail for keeping the project on schedule and to Joel A. Gamon who has been helping us to complete the book project's production professionally.

Kuan-Ching Li
Ching-Hsien Hsu
Laurence Tianruo Yang
Jack Dongarra
Hans Zima

Chapter 22
The State of the Art and Open Problems in Data Replication in Grid Environments

Mohammad Shorfuzzaman
University of Manitoba, Canada

Rasit Eskicioglu
University of Manitoba, Canada

Peter Graham
University of Manitoba, Canada

ABSTRACT

Data Grids provide services and infrastructure for distributed data-intensive applications that need to access, transfer and modify massive datasets stored at distributed locations around the world. For example, the next-generation of scientific applications such as many in high-energy physics, molecular modeling, and earth sciences will involve large collections of data created from simulations or experiments. The size of these data collections is expected to be of multi-terabyte or even petabyte scale in many applications. Ensuring efficient, reliable, secure and fast access to such large data is hindered by the high latencies of the Internet. The need to manage and access multiple petabytes of data in Grid environments, as well as to ensure data availability and access optimization are challenges that must be addressed. To improve data access efficiency, data can be replicated at multiple locations so that a user can access the data from a site near where it will be processed. In addition to the reduction of data access time, replication in Data Grids also uses network and storage resources more efficiently. In this chapter, the state of current research on data replication and arising challenges for the new generation of data-intensive grid environments are reviewed and open problems are identified. First, fundamental data replication strategies are reviewed which offer high data availability, low bandwidth consumption, increased fault tolerance, and improved scalability of the overall system. Then, specific algorithms for selecting appropriate replicas and maintaining replica consistency are discussed. The impact of data replication on job scheduling performance in Data Grids is also analyzed. A set of appropriate metrics including access latency, bandwidth savings, server load, and storage overhead for use in making critical

DOI: 10.4018/978-1-60566-661-7.ch022

comparisons of various data replication techniques is also discussed. Overall, this chapter provides a comprehensive study of replication techniques in Data Grids that not only serves as a tool to understanding this evolving research area but also provides a reference to which future e orts may be mapped.

INTRODUCTION

The popularity of the Internet as well as the availability of powerful computers and high-speed network technologies is changing the way we use computers today. These technology opportunities have also led to the possibility of using distributed computers as a single, unified computing resource, leading to what is popularly known as **Grid Computing** (Kesselman & Foster, 1998). Grids enable the sharing, selection, and aggregation of a wide variety of resources including supercomputers, storage systems, data sources, and specialized devices that are geographically distributed and owned by different organizations for solving large-scale computational and data intensive problems in science, engineering, and commerce (Venugopal, Buyya, & Ramamohanarao, 2006).

Data Grids deal with providing services and infrastructure for distributed data-intensive applications that need to access, transfer and modify massive datasets stored across distributed storage resources. For example, scientists working in areas as diverse as high energy physics, bioinformatics, and earth observations need to access large amounts of data. The size of these data is expected to be terabyte or even petabyte scale for some applications. Maintaining a local copy of data on each site that needs the data is extremely expensive. Also, storing such huge amounts of data in a centralized manner is almost impossible due to extensively increased data access time. Given the high latency of wide-area networks that underlie many Grid systems, and the need to access or manage several petabytes of data in Grid environments, data availability and access optimization are key challenges to be addressed.

An important technique to speed up data access for Data Grid systems is to replicate the data in multiple locations, so that a user can access the data from a site in his vicinity (Venugopal et al., 2006). Data replication not only reduces access costs, but also increases data availability for most applications. Experience from parallel and distributed systems design shows that replication promotes high data availability, lower bandwidth consumption, increased fault tolerance, and improved scalability. However, the replication algorithms used in such systems cannot always be directly applied to Data Grid systems due to the wide-area (mostly hierarchical) network structures and special data access patterns in Data Grid systems that differ from traditional parallel systems.

In this chapter, the state of the current research on data replication and its challenges for the new generation of data-intensive grid environments are reviewed and open problems are discussed. First, different data replication strategies are introduced that offer efficient **replica**[1] placement in Data Grid systems. Then, various algorithms for selecting appropriate replicas and maintaining replica consistency are discussed. The impact of data replication on job scheduling performance in Data Grids is also investigated.

The main objective of this chapter, therefore, is to provide a basis for categorizing present and future developments in the area of replication in Data Grid systems. This chapter also aims to provide an understanding of the essential concepts of this evolving research area and to identify important and outstanding issues for further investigation.

The remainder of this chapter is organized as follows. First, an overview of the data replication problem is presented, describing the key issues involved in data replication. In the following section, progress made to date in the area of replication in Data Grid systems is reviewed. Following this, a critical comparison of data placement strategies, probably the core issue affecting replication efficiency in Data Grids, is provided. A summary is then given and some open research issues are identified.

OVERVIEW OF REPLICATION IN DATA GRID SYSTEMS

The efficient management of huge distributed and shared data resources across Wide Area Networks (WANs) is a significant challenge for both scientific research and commercial applications. The Data Grid as a specialization and extension of the Grid (Baker, Buyya, & Laforenza, 2006) provides a solution to this problem. Essentially, Data Grids (Chervenak, Foster, Kesselman, Salisbury, & Tuecke, 2000) deal with providing services and infrastructure for distributed data-intensive applications that need to access, transfer and modify massive datasets stored in distributed storage resources. At the minimum, a **Data Grid** provides two basic functions: a high-performance, reliable data transfer mechanism, and a scalable replica discovery and management mechanism. Depending on application requirements, other services may also be needed (e.g. security, accounting, etc.).

Grid systems typically involve loosely coupled jobs that require access to a large number of datasets. Such a large volume of datasets has posed a challenging problem in how to make the data more easily and efficiently available to the users of the systems. In most situations, the datasets requested by a user's job cannot be found at the local nodes in the Data Grid. In this case, data must be fetched from other nodes in the grid which causes high access latency due to the size of the datasets and the wide-area nature of the network that underlies most grid systems. As a result, job execution time can become very high due to the delay of fetching data (often over the Internet).

Replication (Ranganathan & Foster, 2001b) of data is the most common solution used to address access latency in Data Grid systems. Replication results in the creation of copies of data files at many different sites in the Data Grid. Replication of data has been demonstrated to be a practical and efficient method to achieve high network performance in distributed environments, and it has been applied widely in the areas of distributed databases and some Internet applications (Ranganathan & Foster, 2001b; Chervenak et al., 2000). Creating replicas can effectively reroute client requests to different replica sites and offer remarkably higher access speed than a single server. At the same time, the workload of the original server is distributed across the **replica** servers and, therefore, decreases significantly. Additionally, the network load is also distributed across multiple network paths thereby decreasing the probability of congestion related performance degradation. In these ways, replication plays a key role in improving the performance of data-intensive computing in Data Grids.

The Replication Process and Components

The use of replication in Data Grid systems speeds up data access by replicating the data at multiple locations so that a user can access data from a site in his vicinity (Venugopal et al., 2006). Replication of data, therefore, aims to reduce both access latency and bandwidth consumption. Replication can also help in server load balancing and can enhance reliability by creating multiple copies of the same data. Replication is, of course, limited by the amount of storage available at each site in the Data Grid and

Figure 1. A replica management architecture

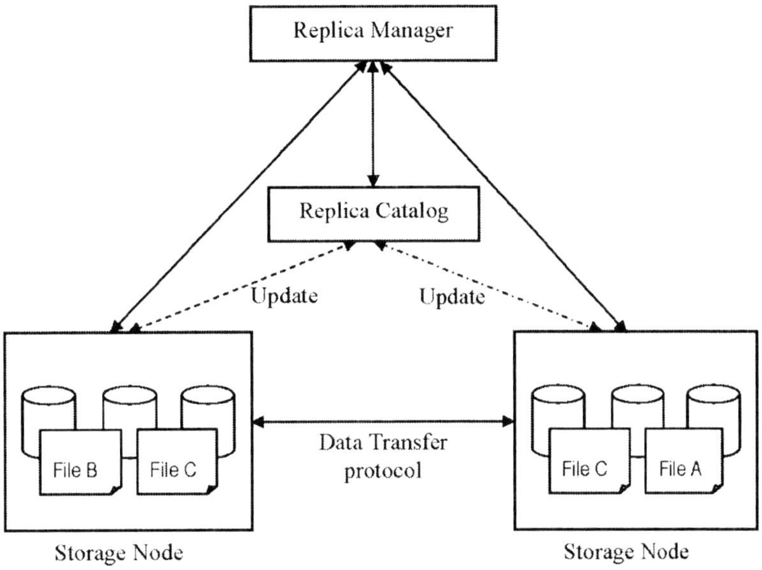

by the bandwidth available between those sites. A replica management system, therefore, must ensure access to the required data while managing the underlying storage and network resources.

A replica management system, shown in Figure 1, consists of storage nodes that are linked to each other via high-performance data transport protocols. The replica manager directs the creation and management of replicas according to the demands of the users and the availability of storage, and a catalog (or directory) keeps track of the replicas and their locations. The catalog can be queried by applications to discover the number and locations of available replicas of a given file.

Issues and Challenges in Data Replication

Although the necessity of replication in Data Grid systems is evident, its implementation entails several issues and challenges such as selecting suitable replicas, maintaining replica consistency, and so on. The following fundamental issues are identified:

a. Strategic placement of replicas is needed to obtain maximum gains from replication according to the objectives of applications.
b. The degree of replication must be selected to require the minimum number of replicas without reducing the performance of applications.
c. Replica selection identifies the replica that best matches the user's quality of service (QoS) requirements and, perhaps, achieves one or more system-wide management objectives.
d. Replica consistency management ensures that the multiple copies (i.e., replicas) of a given file are kept consistent in the presence of multiple concurrent updates.
e. The impact of replication on the performance of job scheduling must also be considered.

Figure 2. Taxonomy of the issues in data replication

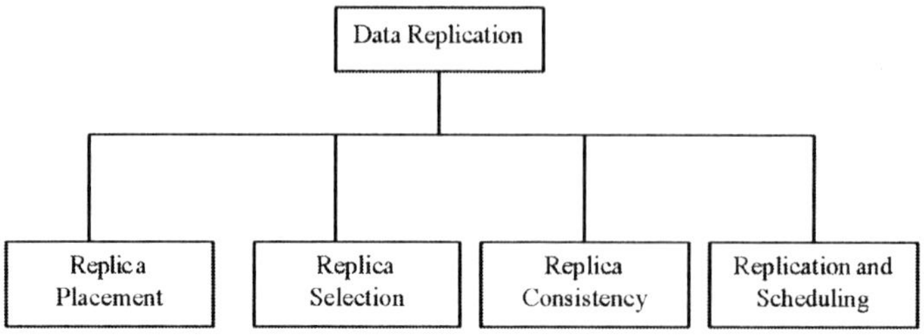

Figure 2 presents a visual taxonomy of these issues which will be used in the next subsections.

Replica Placement

Although, data replication is one of the major optimization techniques for promoting high data availability, low bandwidth consumption, increased fault tolerance, and improved scalability, the problem of replica placement has not been well studied for large-scale Grid environments. To obtain the maximum possible gains from file replication, strategic placement of the file replicas in the system is critical. The **replica placement** service is the component of a Data Grid architecture that decides where in the system a file replica should be placed. The overall file replication problem consists of making the following decisions (Ranganathan & Foster, 2001b): (1) which files should be replicated; (2) when and how many should replicas be created; (3) where should these replicas be placed in the system.

Replication methods can be classified as static or dynamic (M. Tang, Lee, Yeo, & Tang, 2005). For static replication, after a replica is created, it will exist in the same place until it is deleted manually by users or its "replica duration" expires. The drawback of static replication is evident – when client access patterns change greatly in the Data Grid, the benefits brought by replicas will decrease sharply. On the contrary, dynamic replication takes into consideration changes in the Data Grid environment and automatically creates new replicas for popular data files or moves the replicas to other sites when necessary to improve performance.

Replica Selection

A system that includes replicas also requires a mechanism for selecting and locating them at file access time. Choosing and accessing appropriate replicas are very important to optimize the use of grid resources. A **replica selection** service discovers the available replicas and selects the "best" replica given the user's location and quality of service (QoS) requirements. Typical QoS requirements when doing replica selection might include access time as well as location, security, cost and other constraints, The replica selection problem can be divided into two sub-problems (Rahman, Barker, & Alhajj, 2005): 1) discovering the physical location(s) of a file given a logical file name, and 2) selecting the best replica from a set based on some selection criteria.

Network performance can play a major role when selecting a replica. Slow network access limits the efficiency of data transfer regardless of client and server implementation. One optimization technique to select the best replica from different physical locations is by examining the available (or predicted) bandwidth between the requesting computing element and various storage elements that hold replicas. The best site, in this case, is the one that has the minimum transfer time required to transport the replica to the requested site. Although, network bandwidth plays a major role in selecting the best replica, other factors including additional characteristics of data transfer (most notably, latency), replica host load, and disk I/O performance are important as well.

Replica Consistency

Consistency and synchronization problems associated with replication in Data Grid systems are not well addressed in the existing research with files often being regarded as being read-only. However, as grid solutions are increasing used by a number of applications, requirements will arise for mechanisms that maintain the consistency of replicated data that can change over time. The **replica consistency** problem deals with concurrent updates made to multiple replicas of a file. When one file is updated, all other replicas then have to have the same contents and thus provide a consistent view. Consistency therefore requires some form of concurrency control.

Replica consistency is a traditional issue in distributed systems, but it introduces new problems in Data Grid systems. The traditional consistency implementations such as invalidation protocols, distributed locking mechanisms, atomic operations and two-phase commit protocols are not necessarily suitable for Data Grid environments because of the long delays introduced by the use of a wide-area network and the high degree of autonomy of Data Grid resources (Domenici, Donno, Pucciani, Stockinger, & Stockinger, 2004). For example, in a Data Grid, the replicas for a file may be distributed over different countries. So, if one node which holds a replica is not available when the update operation is working, the whole updating process could fail.

The Impact of Data Replication on Job Scheduling

Dealing with the large number of data files that are geographically distributed causes many challenges in a Data Grid. One that is not commonly considered is scheduling jobs to take data location into account when determining job placement. The locations of data required by a job clearly impact grid scheduling decisions and performance (M. Tang, Lee, Yeo, & Tang, 2006).

Traditional job schedulers for grid systems are responsible for assigning incoming jobs to compute nodes in such a way that some evaluative conditions are met, such as the minimization of the overall execution time of the jobs or the maximisation of throughput or utilisation. Such systems generally take into consideration the availability of compute cycles, job queue lengths, and expected job execution times, but they typically do not consider the location of data required by the jobs. Indeed, the impact of data and replication management on job scheduling behaviour has largely remained unstudied.

Data intensive applications such as High Energy Physics and Bioinformatics require both Computational Grid and Data Grid features. Performance improvements for these applications can be achieved by using a Computational Grid that provides a large number of processors and a Data Grid that provides efficient data transport and data replication mechanisms. In such environments, effective resource scheduling is a challenge. One must consider not only the abundance of computational resources but also data locations. A site that has enough available processors may not be the optimal choice for computation if it doesn't have the required data nearby. (Allocated processors might wait a long time to access the remote data.) Similarly, a site with local copies of required data is not a good place to compute if it doesn't have

Figure 3. Taxonomy of the replica placement algorithms

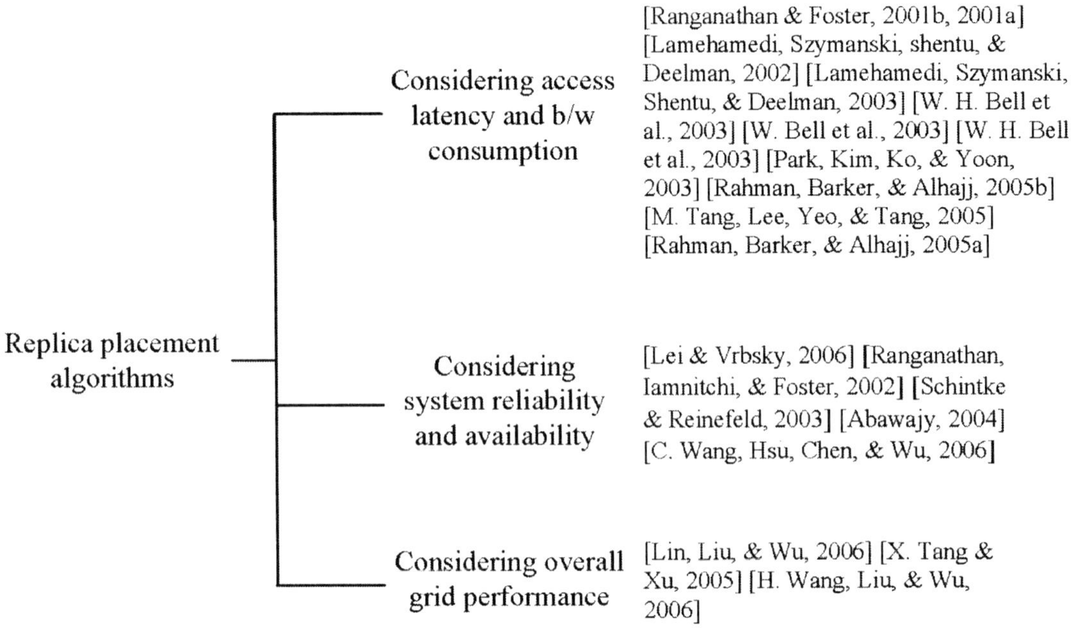

adequate computational resources.

An effective scheduling mechanism is required that will allow shortest access to the required data, thereby reducing the data access time. Since creating data replicas can significantly reduce the data access cost, a tighter integration of job scheduling and automated data replication can bring substantial improvement in job execution performance.

DATA REPLICATION: STATE OF THE ART

As mentioned earlier, data replication becomes more challenging because of some unique characteristics of Data Grid systems. This section surveys existing replication strategies in Data Grids and the issues involved in replication that will form a basis for future discussion of open issues in the next section.

Replica Placement Strategies

With the high latency of wide-area networks that underlies most Grid systems, and the need to access and manage multiple petabytes of data, data availability and access optimization become key challenges to be addressed. Hence, most of the existing **replica placement** algorithms focus on at least two types of objective functions for placing replicas in Data Grid systems. The first type of replica placement strategy looks towards decreasing the data access latency and the network bandwidth consumption. The other type of replica placement strategy focuses on how to improve system reliability and availability. Figure 3 shows a taxonomy of the replica placement algorithms based on the realized objective functions together with references to papers in each category.

Algorithms Focusing on Access Latency and Bandwidth Consumption

Ranganathan and Foster (Ranganathan & Foster, 2001b, 2001a) present and evaluate different replication strategies for a hierarchical Data Grid architecture. These strategies are defined depending on when, where, and how replicas are created and destroyed in a hierarchically structured grid environment. They test six different replication strategies: 1) No Replication: only root node holds replicas; 2) Best Client: replica is created for the client who accesses the file the most; 3) Cascading: a replica is created on the path from the root node to the best client; 4) Plain Caching: a local copy is stored upon initial request; 5) Caching plus Cascading: combines plain caching and cascading; 6) Fast Spread: file copies are stored at each node on the path from the root to the best client. They show that the cascading strategy reduces response time by 30% over plain caching when data access patterns contain both temporal and geographical locality. When access patterns contain some locality, Fast Spread saves significant bandwidth over other strategies. These replication algorithms assume that popular files at one site are also popular at others. The client site counts hops for each site that holds replicas, and the model selects the site that is the least number of hops from the requesting client; but it does not consider current network bandwidth and also limits the model to a hierarchical grid. The proposed replication algorithms can be refined so that time interval and threshold of replication change automatically based on user behaviour.

Lamehamedi et. al (Lamehamedi, Szymanski, shentu, & Deelman, 2002; Lamehamedi, Szymanski, Shentu, & Deelman, 2003) study replication strategies where the replica sites can be arranged in different topologies such as a ring, tree or hybrid. Each site or node maintains an index of the replicas it hosts and the other locations that it knows about that host replicas of the same files. Replication decisions are made based on a cost model that evaluates both the data access costs and performance gains of creating each replica. The estimation of costs and gains is based on factors such as run-time accumulated read/write statistics, response time, bandwidth, and replica size. The replication strategy places a replica at a site that minimises the total access costs including both read and write costs for the datasets. The write cost considers the cost of updating all the replicas after a write at one of the replicas. They show via simulation that the best results are achieved when the replication process is carried out closest to the users.

Bell et al. (W. H. Bell et al., 2003) present a file replication strategy based on an economic model that optimises the selection of sites for creating replicas. Replication is triggered based on the number of requests received for a dataset. Access mediators receive these requests and start auctions to determine the cheapest replicas. A Storage Broker (SB) participates in these auctions by offering a "price" at which it will sell access to a replica if it is available. If the replica is not available at the local storage site, then the broker starts an auction to replicate the requested file onto its storage if it determines that having the dataset is economically feasible. Other SBs then bid with the lowest prices that they can offer for the file. The lowest bidder wins the auction but is paid the amount bid by the second-lowest bidder.

In subsequent research, Bell et al. (W. Bell et al., 2003) describe the design and implementation of a Grid simulator, OptorSim. In particular, OptorSim allows the analysis of various replication algorithms. The goal is to evaluate the impact of the choice of an algorithm on the throughput of typical grid jobs. The authors implemented a simple remote access heuristic and two traditional cache replacement algorithms (oldest file deletion and least accessed file deletion).

Their simulation was constructed assuming that the grid consists of several sites, each of which may provide computational and data-storage resources for submitted jobs. Each site consists of zero or more Computing Elements and zero or more Storage Elements. Computing Elements run jobs, which use the data in files stored on Storage Elements. A Resource Broker controls the scheduling of jobs to Comput-

Figure 4. An example of the history and node relations

nodeID	*fileID*	*numOfAccesses*
N_1	A	5
N_2	B	4
N_3	B	3

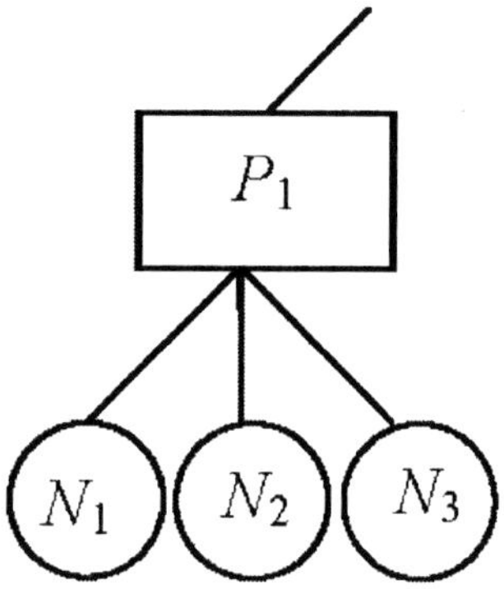

ing Elements. Sites without Storage or Computing Elements act as network routing nodes.

Various algorithms were compared to a novel algorithm (W. H. Bell et al., 2003) based on an economic model. The comparison was based on several grid scenarios with various workloads. The results obtained from OptorSim suggest that the economic model performs at least as well as traditional methods. However, the economic model shows marked performance improvements over other algorithms when data access patterns are sequential.

Sang-Min Park et al. (Park, Kim, Ko, & Yoon, 2003) propose a dynamic replication strategy, called BHR (Bandwidth Hierarchy based Replication), to reduce data access time by avoiding network congestion in a Data-Grid network. The BHR algorithm benefits from 'network-level locality', which indicates that the required file is located at the site that has the broadest bandwidth to the site of the job's execution. In Data Grids, some sites may be located within a region where sites are linked closely. For instance, a country or province/state might constitute a network region. Network bandwidth between sites within a region will be broader than bandwidth between sites across regions. That is, a hierarchy of network bandwidth may appear in the Internet. If the required file is located in the same region, less time will be consumed to fetch the file. Thus, the benefit of network-level locality can be exploited. The BHR strategy reduces data access time by maximizing this network-level locality.

Rahman et al. (Rahman, Barker, & Alhajj, 2005b) present a replica placement algorithm that considers both the current state of the network and file requests. Replication is started by placing the master files at one site. Then the expected "utility" or "risk index" is calculated for each site that does not currently hold a replica and then one replica is placed on the site that optimizes the expected utility or risk. The proposed algorithm based on utility selects a candidate site to host a replica by assuming that future requests and current load will follow current loads and user requests. Conversely, the algorithm using a risk index exposes sites far from all other sites and assumes a worst case scenario whereby future requests will primarily originate from that distant site thereby attempting to provide good access throughout the network. One major drawback of these strategies is that the algorithms select only one site per iteration and place a replica there. Grid environments can be highly dynamic and thus there might be a sudden burst of requests such that a replica needs to be placed at multiple sites simultaneously to quickly satisfy the large spike of requests.

Two dynamic replication mechanisms (M. Tang, Lee, Yeo, & Tang, 2005) are proposed for a multi-tier architecture for Data Grids: Simple Bottom-Up (SBU) and Aggregate Bottom-Up (ABU). The SBU algorithm replicates any data file that exceeds a pre-defined threshold of access rate as close as possible to the clients. The main shortcoming of SBU is the lack of consideration of the relationship with historical access records. To address this problem, ABU was designed which takes into account access histories of files used by sibling nodes and aggregates the access record of similar files so that these frequently accessed files are replicated first. This process is repeated until the root is reached. An example of a data file access history and the network topology of the related nodes is shown in Figure 4. The history indicates that node *N*1 has accessed file *A* five times, while *N*2 and *N*3 have accessed *B* four and three times, respectively. Nodes *N*1, *N*2 and *N*3 are siblings and their parent node is *P*1.

If we assume that the SBU algorithm is adopted and the given threshold is five, the last two records in the history will be skipped and only the first record will be processed. The result is that the file *A* will be created in node *P*1 if it has enough space, and file *B* will not be replicated. Considering this example it is clear that the decision of SBU is not optimal, because from the perspective of the whole system, file *B*, which is accessed seven times by node *N*2 and *N*3, is more popular than *A*, which is only accessed five times by node *N*1. Hence, the better solution is to replicate file *B* to *P*1 first, then replicate file *A* to *P*1 if it still has enough space available. The Aggregate Bottom-Up (ABU) algorithm works in a similar fashion. With a hierarchical topology, the client searches for files from a client to the root. In addition, the root replicates the needed data at every node. Therefore, access latency can be improved significantly. On the other hand, significant storage space may be used. Storage space utilization and access latency must be traded off against each other.

Rahman et al. (Rahman, Barker, & Alhajj, 2005a) propose a multi-objective approach to address the replica placement problem in Data Grid systems. A grid environment is highly dynamic, so predicting user requests and network load, a-priori, is difficult. Therefore, only considering a single objective, variations in user requests and network load will have larger impacts on system performance. Rahman et al. use two models: the *p*-median and *p*-center models (Hakami, 1999), for selecting the candidate sites at which to host replicas. The *p*-median model places replicas at sites that optimize the request-weighted average response time (which is the time required to transfer a file from the nearest replication site). The response time is zero if a local copy exists. The request-weighted response time is calculated by multiplying the number of requests at a particular site by the response time for that site. The average is calculated by averaging the request weighted response times for all sites. The *p*-center model selects candidate sites to host replicas by minimizing the maximum response time. Rahman et al consider a multi-objective approach that combines the p-center and p-median objectives to decide where to place replica.

Algorithms Focusing on System Reliability and Availability

Once bandwidth and computing capacity become relatively cheap, data access time can decrease dramatically. How to improve the system reliability and availability then becomes the focal point for replication algorithms. Lei and Vrbsky (Lei & Vrbsky, 2006) propose a replica strategy to improve availability when storage resources are limited without increasing access time.

To better express system data availability, Lei and Vrbsky introduce two new measures: the file missing rate and the bytes missing rate. The File Missing Rate (FMR) represents the number of files potentially unavailable out of all the files requested by all the jobs. The Bytes Missing Rate (BMR) represents the number of bytes potentially unavailable out of the total number of bytes requested by all jobs. Their replication strategy is aimed at minimizing the data missing rate. To minimize the FMR and BMR, their proposed strategy makes the replica and placement decisions based on the benefits received from replicating the file in the long term. If the requested file is not at a site, it is replicated at the site if there is enough storage space. If there is not enough free space to store the replica, an existing file must be replaced. Their replication algorithm can be enhanced by differentiating between the file missing rate and bytes missing rate in the grid when the file size is not unique.

Ranganathan et al. (Ranganathan, Iamnitchi, & Foster, 2002) present a dynamic replication strategy that creates copies based on trade-o s between the cost and the future benefits of creating a replica. Their strategy is designed for peer-to-peer environments where there is a high-degree of unreliability and hence, considers the minimum number of replicas that might be required given the probability of a node being up and the accuracy of information possessed by a site in a peer-to-peer network. In their approach, peers create replicas automatically in a decentralized fashion, as required to meet availability goals. The aim of the framework is to maintain a threshold level of availability at all times.

Each peer in the system possesses a model of the peer-to-peer storage system that it can use to determine how many replicas of any file are needed to maintain the desired availability. Each peer applies this model to the (necessarily incomplete and/or inaccurate) information it has about the system state and replication status of its files to determine if, when, and where new replicas should be created. The result is a completely decentralized system that can maintain performance guarantees. These advantages come at the price of accuracy since nodes make decisions based on partial information, which sometimes leads to unnecessary replication. Simulation results show that the redundancy in action associated with distributed authority is more evident when nodes are highly unreliable.

An analytical model for determining the optimal number of replica servers is presented by Schintke and Reinefeld (Schintke & Reinefeld, 2003) to guarantee a given overall reliability given unreliable system components. Two views are identified: the requester who requires a guaranteed availability of the data (local view), and the administrator who wants to know how many replicas are needed and how much disk space they would occupy in the overall system (global view). Their model captures the characteristics of peer-to-peer-like environments as well as that of grid systems. Empirical simulations confirm the accuracy of this analytical model.

Abawajy (Abawajy, 2004) addresses the file replication problem while focusing on the issue of strategic placement of the replicas with the objectives of increased availability of the data and improved response time while distributing load equally. Abawajy proposes a replica placement service called Proportional Share Replication (PSR). The main idea underlying the PSR policy is that each file replica should serve an approximately equal number of requests in the system. The objective is to place the replicas on a set of sites systematically in such a way that file access parallelism is increased while the access costs are decreased. Abawajy argues that no replication approach balances the load of data requests within the system both at the network and host levels. Simulation results show that file replication improves the performance of data access but the gains depend on several factors including where the file replicas are located, burstiness of the request arrivals, packet losses and file sizes.

To use distributed replicas efficiently and to improve the reliability of data transfer, Wang et al. (C. Wang, Hsu, Chen, & Wu, 2006) propose an efficient multi-source data transfer algorithm for data replication, whereby a data replica can be assembled in parallel from multiple distributed data sources in a fashion that adapts to various network bandwidths. The goal is to minimize the data transfer time by scheduling sub-transfers among all replica sites. All replica sites must deliver their source data continuously to maximize their aggregated bandwidth, and all sub-transfers of source data should, ideally, be fully overlapped throughout the replication. Experimental results show that their algorithm can obtain more aggregated bandwidth, reduce connection overheads, and achieve superior load balance.

Algorithms Focusing on Overall Grid Performance

Although a substantial amount of work has been done on data replication in Grid systems, most of it has focused on infrastructure for replication and mechanisms for creating and deleting replicas. However, to obtain the maximum benefit from replication, a strategic placement of replicas considering many factors is essential. Notably, different sites may have different service quality requirements. Therefore, quality of service is an important additional factor in overall system performance.

Lin et al. (Lin, Liu, & Wu, 2006) address the problem of data replica placement in Data Grids given traffic patterns and locality requirements. They consider several important issues. First, the replicas should be placed in proper server locations so that the workload on each server is balanced. Another important issue is choosing the optimal number of replicas when the maximum workload capacity for each replica server is known. The denser the distribution of replicas is, the shorter the distance a client site needs to travel to access a data copy. However, maintaining multiple copies of data in Grid systems is expensive, and therefore, the number of replicas must be bounded. Clearly, optimizing the access cost of data requests and reducing the cost of replication are two conflicting goals. Finding a balance between them is a challenging task. Lin et al. also consider the issue of service locality. Each user may specify the minimum distance he will accept to the nearest data server. This serves as a locality assurance that users may specify, and the system must make sure that within the specified range there is a server to answer any file request.

Lin et al. assume a hierarchical Data Grid model. In such a hierarchical Data Grid model, all the request traffic may reach the root, if not satisfied by a replica. This introduces additional complexity for the design of an efficient algorithm for replica placement in Grid systems when network congestion is one of the objective functions to be optimized.

Tang and Xu (X. Tang & Xu, 2005) suggest a QoS-aware replica placement approach to cope with quality-of-service issues. They provide two heuristic algorithms for general graphs, and a dynamic programming solution for a tree topology. Every edge uses the distance between the two end-points as a cost function. The distance between two nodes is used as a metric for quality (i.e. access time) assurance. A request must be answered by a server that is within the distance specified by the request. Every request knows the nearest server that has the replica and the request takes the shortest path to reach the server. Their goal has been to find a replica placement that satisfies all requests without violating any range constraint, and that minimizes the update and storage costs at the same time. They show that this QoS-aware replica placement problem is NP-complete for general graphs.

Wang et al. (H. Wang, Liu, & Wu, 2006) study the QoS-aware replica placement problem and provide a new heuristic algorithm to determine the positions of the replicas to improve system performance and satisfy the quality requirements specified by the users simultaneously. Their model is based on general graphs and their algorithm starts by finding the cover set (Revees, 1993) of every server in the network. In the second phase, the algorithm identifies and deletes super cover sets in the network. Finally, it inserts replicas into the network iteratively until all servers are satisfied. Experiment results indicate that the algorithm efficiently finds near-optimal solutions so that it can be deployed in various realistic environments. However, the study does not consider the workload capacity of the servers.

Figure 5. A taxonomy of replica selection algorithms and selected papers

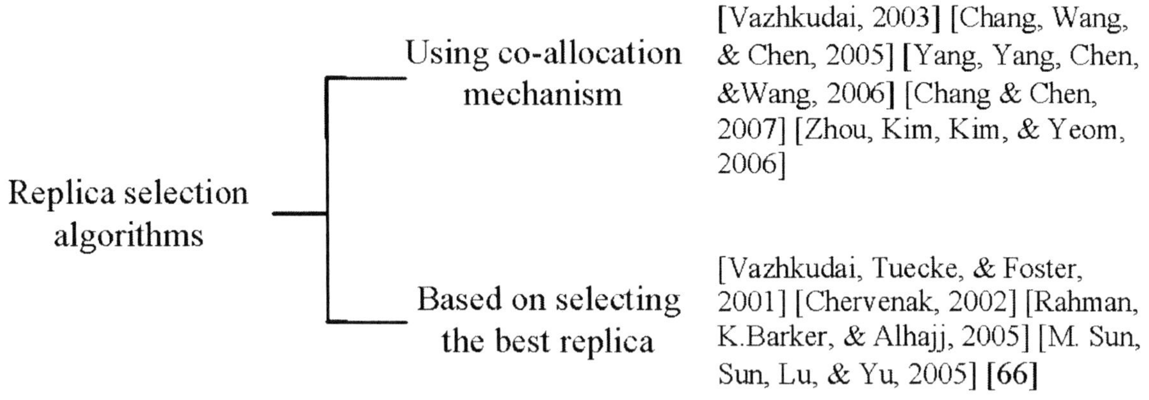

Replica Selection Algorithms

To improve replica retrieval we must determine the best replica location using a replica selection technique. Such techniques attempt to select the single best server to provide optimum transfer rates. This can be challenging because bandwidth quality can vary unpredictably due to the shared nature of the Internet. Another approach is to use co-allocation technology (Vazhkudai, 2003) to download data. Co-allocation of data transfers enables the clients to download data from multiple locations by establishing multiple connections in parallel. This can improve the performance compared to single-server approaches and helps to mitigate Internet congestion problems. Figure 5 shows a taxonomy of replica selection algorithms based on the method used for retrieving the replicas distributed in the system.

Algorithms Based on Selecting the Best Replica

Vazhkudai et al. (Vazhkudai, Tuecke, & Foster, 2001) discuss the design and implementation of a high-level replica selection service that uses information regarding replica location and user preferences to guide selection from among storage replica alternatives. An application that requires access to replicated data begins by querying an application specific metadata repository, specifying the characteristics of the desired data. The metadata repository maintains associations between representative characteristics and logical files, thus enabling the application to identify logical files based on application requirements rather than by a possibly unknown file name. Once the logical file has been identified, the application uses the replica catalog to locate all replica locations containing physical file instances of this logical file, from which it can choose a suitable instance for retrieval. Vazhkudai et al. use Globus (Foster, 2006) information service capabilities concerning storage system properties to collect dynamic information to improve and optimize the selection process.

Chervenak et al. (Chervenak, 2002) characterize the requirements for a Replica Location Service (RLS) and describe a Data Grid architectural framework, Giggle (GIGa-scale Global Location Engine), within which a wide range of RLSs can be defined. An RLS is composed of a Local Replica Catalog (LRC) and a Replica Location Index (RLI). The LRC maps logical identifiers to physical locations and vice versa. It periodically sends out information to other RLSs about its contents (mappings) via a soft-state propagation method. Collectively, the LRCs provide a complete and locally consistent record of global replicas. The RLI contains a set of pointers from logical identifier to LRC. The RLS uses the RLIs to find LRCs that contain the requested replicas. RLIs may cover a subset of LRCs or cover the entire set of LRCs.

To select the best replica Rahman et al. (Rahman, K.Barker, & Alhajj, 2005) design an optimization technique that considers both network latency and disk state. They present a model that uses a simple data mining approach to select the best replica from a number of sites that hold replicas. Previous history of data transfers can help in predicting the best site to hold a replica. Rahman et al's approach is one such predictive technique. In their technique, when a new request arrives for the best replica, all previous data are examined to find a subset of previous file requests that are similar and then they are used to predict the best site to hold the replica. The proposed model shows significant performance improvement for sequential and unitary random file access patterns. The client node always contacts the site found by the classifier and requests the file, regardless of the accuracy of the classification result. Switching from a classification method to a traditional one is not considered even when the classification result is far from ideal. Hence, the system performance will decrease for inaccurate file accesses. Future work could be done on designing an adaptive algorithm so that the algorithm can switch to a traditional approach for consecutive file transfers when it encounters misclassification.

Sun et al. (M. Sun, Sun, Lu, & Yu, 2005) propose an ant optimization algorithm for file replica selection in Data Grids. The general idea of the ant-based approach is to use an ant colony optimization algorithm to decide which data file replicas should be accessed when a job requires data resources. The ant algorithm (Dorigo, 1992) is a meta-heuristic method which mimics the behavior of how real ants find the shortest path from their nest to a food source. The main idea is to mimic the pheromone trail used by real ants as a medium for communication and feedback among ants. The goal of using the ant-based approach is to exploit the ant algorithm to decide which data file replicas should be accessed when a job requires data resources. For the selection of a data replica the ant uses pheromone information which reflects the efficiency of previous accesses. The algorithm has been implemented and the advantages of the new ant algorithm have been investigated using the grid simulator OptorSim (W. Bell et al., 2003). Their evaluation demonstrates that their ant algorithm can reduce data access latency, decrease bandwidth consumption and distribute storage site load.

Algorithms Using Co-Allocation Mechanism

Vazhkudai (Vazhkudai, 2003) developed several co-allocation mechanisms to enable parallel downloading of files. The most interesting one is called Dynamic Co-Allocation. The dataset that the client wants is divided into "*k*" disjoint blocks of equal size. Each available server is assigned to deliver one block in parallel. When a server finishes delivering a block, another block is requested, and so on, until the entire file is downloaded. Faster servers can deliver the data quickly, thus serving larger portions of the file requested when compared to slower servers. This approach exploits the partial copy feature of GridFTP (Allcock, 2003) provided by the Globus Toolkit (Foster, 2006) to reduce the total transfer time. One drawback of this approach is that faster servers must wait for the slowest server to deliver the final block. This 'idle-time drawback' is common to existing co-allocation strategies. It is important to reduce the differences in completion time among replica servers to achieve the best possible performance.

Chang et al. (Chang, Wang, & Chen, 2005) suggest an improvement to dynamic co-allocation to address the problem of faster servers waiting for slower ones. Their work is based on a co-allocation architecture coupled with prediction techniques. They propose two techniques: (1) abort and retransfer, and (2) one by one co-allocation. These techniques can increase the volume of data requested from faster servers and reduce the volume of data fetched from slower servers thereby balancing the load and individual completion times.

The Abort and Retransfer scheme allows the aborting of the slowest server transfer so the work can be moved to faster servers. This can dynamically change the allocation condition based on the dynamic conditions of the transfer. When all data blocks are assigned, the procedure will check the remaining transfer time of the slowest server. If the remaining time is longer than the time of transferring the last data block from the fastest server, the final data block will be re-assigned to the fastest server.

One by one co-allocation focuses on preventing the problematic allocation to the slowest server a-priori. One by one co-allocation is a pre-scheduling method used to allocate the data blocks to be transferred to the available servers. By using a prediction technique, the transfer time of each server is estimated. The data blocks are then assigned to the fastest server with the lowest transfer time in each round. Further, if one server is assigned to transfer more than one data block in an earlier round, its total transfer time is accumulated.

Yang et al. (Yang, Yang, Chen, & Wang, 2006) propose a dynamic co-allocation scheme based on a co-allocation grid data transfer architecture called the Recursive-Adjustment Co-Allocation scheme that reduces the idle time spent waiting for the slowest server and improves data transfer performance. Their co-allocation scheme works by continuously adjusting each replica server's workload to correspond to its real-time bandwidth during file transfers. Yang et al. also provide a function that enables users to define a "final block threshold", according to the characteristics of their Data Grid environment to avoid continuous over adjustment.

Usually, a complete file is replicated to many Grid sites for local access (including when co-allocation is used). However, a site may only need certain parts of a given replica. Therefore, to use the storage system efficiently, it may be desirable for a grid site to store only part(s) of a replica.

Chang and Chen (Chang & Chen, 2007) propose a concept called fragmented replicas where, when doing replication, a site can store only those partial contents that are needed locally. This can greatly reduce the storage space wasted in storing unused data. Chang and Chen also propose a block mapping procedure to determine the distribution of blocks in every available server for later replica retrieval. Using this procedure, a server can provide its available partial replica contents to other members in the grid system since clients can retrieve a fragmented replica directly by using the block mapping procedure. Given the block mapping procedure, co-allocation schemes (Vazhkudai, 2003; Chang et al., 2005) can be used to retrieve data sets from the available servers given the added constraint that only specific servers will hold a particular fragment. Simulation results show that download performance is improved in their fragmented replication system.

Chang and Chen (Chang & Chen, 2007) assume that the blocks in a fragmented replica are contiguous. If they were not, then the data structure to represent the fragmented replica and the algorithm for retrieval would be more complicated. Also, the proposed algorithms do not always find an optimal solution as explained by the authors. It would be interesting to determine if a worst case performance bound exists for these algorithms.

When multiple replicas exist, a client uses a replica selection mechanism to find the "best" source from which to download. However, this simple approach may not yield the best performance and reliability because data is received from only one replica server. To avoid this problem, Zhou et al. (Zhou, Kim, Kim, & Yeom, 2006) developed ReCon, a fast and reliable replica retrieval system for Data Grids that acquires data not only from the best source but from other sources as well. Through concurrent transfer, they are able to achieve significant performance improvement when retrieving a replica. ReCon also provides fault-tolerant replica retrieval since multiple replication sites are employed.

For fast replica retrieval, Zhou et al considered various fast retrieval algorithms, among which probe-based retrieval appears to be the best approach, providing twice the transfer rate of the best replica server chosen by the replica selection service. Probe-based retrieval predicts the future network throughput of the replica servers by sending probing messages to each server. This allows them to select replicas which will provide fast access. For reliable replica retrieval, they introduce a recursive scheduling mechanism, which provides fault-tolerant retrieval by rescheduling failed sub-transfers.

Replica Consistency Algorithms

As mentioned earlier, the replica consistency problem in Data Grid systems deals with the update synchronization of multiple copies (replicas) of a file. When one file is updated, all other replicas have to be synchronized to have the same contents and thus provide a consistent view. Different algorithms for maintaining such consistency have been proposed in the literature.

Replication consistency algorithms have traditionally been classified into strong and weak consistency. A **strong consistency** algorithm (Duvvuri, Shenoy, & Tewari, 2000) ensures that all the replicas have exactly the same content (synchronized systems) before any transaction is carried out. In an unreliable network like the Internet, with a large number of replicas, latency can become high so it becomes impractical to use such systems. Strong consistency algorithms are suitable for systems with few replicas, and on a reliable, low latency network where a large amount of bandwidth is available.

In contrast, **weak consistency** algorithms (Golding, 1992) maintain approximate consistency of the replicas sacrificing data freshness in a controlled way to improve availability and performance. They are very useful in systems where it is not necessary for all the replicas to be totally consistent for carrying out transactions (systems that can withstand a certain degree of inconsistency).

In the context of weak consistency, the fast consistency algorithm (Elias & Moldes, 2002b) prioritizes replicas with high demand in such a way that a large number of clients receive fresh content. As described by Elias and Moldes (Elias & Moldes, 2002a), this algorithm gives high performance in one zone of high demand, but in multiple zones the performance may become poor. To improve this poor performance, Elias and Moldes (Elias & Moldes, 2003) propose an election algorithm based on demand, whereby the replicas in each zone of high demand select leader replicas that subsequently construct a logical topology, linking all the replicas together. In this way, changes are able to reach all the high demand replicas without the low demand zones forming a barrier to prevent this from happening.

Two coherence protocols for Data Grids were introduced by Sun and Xu (Y. Sun & Xu., 2004) called lazy-copy and aggressive-copy. In the lazy-copy based protocol, replicas are only updated as needed if someone accesses them. This can save network bandwidth by avoiding transferring up-to-date replicas every time some modifications are made. However, the lazy-copy protocol has to pay penalties in terms of access delay when inter-site updating is required. For the aggressive-copy protocol, replicas are always updated immediately when the original file is modified. In other words, full consistency for replicas is guaranteed in aggressive-copy, whereas partial consistency is applied to lazy-copy. Compared with lazy-copy, access delay time can be reduced by an aggressive-copy based mechanism without suffering from long update time during each replica access. Nevertheless, full consistency with frequent replica updates could consume a considerable amount of network bandwidth. Furthermore, some updates may be unnecessary because it is probable that they will never be used.

Chang and Chang (Chang & Chang, 2006) propose an innovative and effective architecture called the Adaptable Replica Consistency Service (ARCS) which has the capability of dealing with the replica consistency problem to provide better performance and load balance for file replication in Data Grids. The ARCS architecture works by modifying the two previously described distinct coherence protocols. Chang and Chang make use of the concept of network regions in (Park et al., 2003) to develop the scheme. Several grid sites located closely together are organized into a grid group called a grid region. A 'Region Server' is responsible for the consistency service within a region. Each region is connected via the Internet.

Each grid region has at most zero or one master replica and multiple master replicas are distributed over grid regions. A region server must be aware of the location of other master replicas to maintain full consistency among all master replicas. Update modifications are propagated to other connected region servers for their master replicas with the aid of a file locking mechanism whenever a master replica is modified in a certain grid region. Thus, a master replica within a grid region has the latest information all the time. Each secondary replica can update its contents more efficiently in accordance with the master replica if the region has a master replica. Simulation results show that ARCS is superior to the coherence protocols described in (Y. Sun & Xu., 2004).

Belalem and Slimani (Belalem & Slimani, 2006, 2007) proposed a hybrid model to manage the consistency of replicas in large scale systems. The model combines two existing approaches (optimistic and pessimistic (Saito & Levy, 2000; Saito & Shapiro, 2005)) to consistency management. The pessimistic approach prohibits any access to a replica unless it is provably up to date. The main advantage of this approach is that all replicas converge at the same time, a fact that guarantees high consistency of data. Hence, any problem of divergence is avoided. On the contrary, the optimistic approach allows access to any replica at any time regardless of the state of the replica sets, which might be incoherent. This also means that the approach can cause replica contents to diverge. Optimistic techniques require a follow-up phase to detect and correct divergences among replicas by converging them toward a coherent state.

Pessimistic replication and optimistic replication are two contrasting replication models. The work of Belalem and Slimani tries to benefit from the advantages of both approaches. Optimistic principals are used to ensure replica consistency within each site in the grid individually. Global consistency, i.e., consistency between sites, is covered by the application of algorithms inspired by the pessimistic approach. Their model aims to substantially reduce the communication time between sites to achieve replica consistency, increase the effectiveness of consistency management, and more importantly, be adaptive to changes in large systems.

Domenici et al. (Domenici, Donno, Pucciani, & Stockinger, 2006) propose a Replica Consistency Service, CONStanza, that is general enough to be suitable for most types of applications in a grid environment and which meets the general requirements for grid middleware, such as performance, scalability, reliability, and security. Their proposed replica consistency service allows for replica updates in a single-master scenario with lazy update synchronization. Two types of replicas are maintained which have different semantics and access permissions for end-users. The first is a master replica that can be updated by end-users of the system. The master replica is the one that is, by definition, always up-to-date. The other is a secondary replica (also referred to as secondary copy) that is updated/synchronized by CONStanza with a certain delay to eventually have the same contents as the master replica. Obviously, the longer the update propagation delay is, the more unsynchronized the master and the secondary replica are, and the higher is the probability of experiencing stale reads on secondary replicas. This service

Figure 6. A taxonomy of algorithms considering data scheduling and associated papers

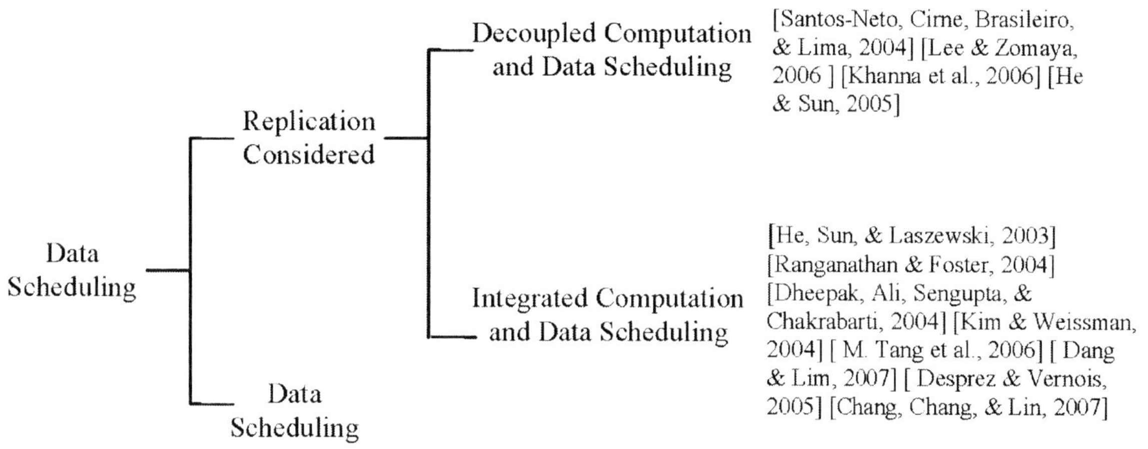

provides users with the ability to update data using a certain consistency delay parameter (hence relaxed consistency) to adapt to specific application requirements and tolerances.

Impact of Data Replication on Job Scheduling

Effective scheduling can reduce the amount of data transferred across the Internet by dispatching a job to where the needed data files are available. Assume a job is scheduled to be executed at a particular compute node. When job scheduling is coupled to replication and the data has to be fetched from remote storage, the scheduler can create a copy of the data at the point of computation so that future requests for the same file that come from the neighborhood of the compute node can be satisfied more quickly. Further, in the future, any job dealing with that particular file can be preferentially scheduled at that compute node if it is available. In a decoupled scheduler, the job is scheduled to a suitable computational resource and a suitable replica location is then identified to request the required data from. In this case, the storage requirement is transient, that is, disk space is required only for the duration of execution. Figure 6 shows a taxonomy of replication algorithms considering data scheduling. A comparison of decoupled against coupled strategies by Ranganathan and Foster (Ranganathan & Foster, 2002) has shown that decoupled strategies promise increased performance and reduce the complexity of designing algorithms for Data Grid environments.

He et al. (He, Sun, & Laszewski, 2003) deal with the problem of Integrated Replication and Scheduling (IRS). They couple job scheduling and data scheduling. At the end of periodic intervals when jobs are scheduled, the popularity of required files is calculated and then used by the data scheduler to replicate data for the next set of jobs. While these may or may not share the same data requirements as the previous set there is often a high probability that they will.

The importance of data locality in job scheduling was also realized by Ranganathan and Foster (Ranganathan & Foster, 2004). They proposed a Data Grid architecture based on three main components: External Scheduler (ES), Local Scheduler (LS) and Dataset Scheduler (DS). An ES receives job submissions from the user, then it decides the remote site to which the job should be sent depending on its scheduling strategy. The LS of each site decides how to schedule all the jobs assigned to it, using its local resources. The DS keeps track of the popularity of each dataset currently available and makes data replication decisions. Using this architecture, Ranganathan and Foster developed and evaluated various replication and scheduling strategies. Their results confirmed the importance of data locality in scheduling jobs.

Dheepak et al. (Dheepak, Ali, Sengupta, & Chakrabarti, 2005) have created several scheduling techniques based on a developed replication strategy. The scheduling strategies are Matching based Job Scheduling (MJS), Cost base Job Scheduling (CJS) and Latency based Job Scheduling (LJS). In MJS, the jobs are scheduled to those sites that have the maximum match in terms of data.

For example, if a job requests '*n*' files, and in a site, all those files are already present, then the amount of data in bytes corresponding to those 'n' files represents the match corresponding to the job request. In CJS, the cost of scheduling a job onto a site is defined as the combined cost of moving the data to the site, the time to compute the job at the site, and the wait time in the queue at the site. The job is scheduled onto the site which has the minimum cost. Finally, LJS takes the latency experienced into account before taking the scheduling decision. The cost of scheduling in this case includes the latency involved in scheduling the current job based on the current data locations, and also the latency involved due to the current queue. Simulation results show that among the strategies, LJS and CJS perform similarly and MJS performs less well.

Venugopal et al. (Venugopal & Buyya, 2005) propose a scheduling algorithm that considers two cost metrics: an economic budget and time. The algorithm tries to optimize one of them given a bound on the other, e.g., spend a budget as small as possible, while not missing any deadline. The incoming applications consist of a set of independent tasks each of which requires a computational resource and accesses a number of data sets located on different storage sites. The algorithm assumes every data set has only one copy in the Grid, so that the resource selection is only for computational resources, taking into account the communication costs from data storage sites to different computation sites as well as the actual computation costs. Instead of doing a thorough search in a space whose size is exponential in the number of data sets requested by a task, the resource selection procedure simply performs a local search which only guarantees that the current mapping is better than the previous one. In this way, the cost of the search procedure is linear. The drawback of this strategy is that it is not guaranteed to find a feasible schedule even if there is one.

As we have seen, data can be decomposed into multiple independent sub datasets and distributed for parallel execution and access. Most of the existing studies on scheduling in Data Grids do not consider this possibility which is typical in many data intensive applications. Kim and Weissman (Kim & Weissman, 2004), however, exploit such parallelism to achieve desired performance levels when scheduling large Data Grid applications. When parallel applications require multiple data files from multiple data sources, the scheduling problem is challenging in several dimensions; how should data be decomposed, should data be moved to computation or vice-versa, and which computing resources should be used. The problem can be optimally solved by adding some constraints (e.g., decomposing data into sub datasets of only the same size). Another approach is to use heuristics such as those based on optimization techniques (e.g. genetic algorithms, simulated annealing, and tabu search). Kim and Weissman propose a novel genetic algorithm (GA) based approach to address the scheduling of decomposable Data Grid applications, where communication and computation are considered at the same time. Their proposed algorithm is novel in two ways. First, it automatically balances load, that is, data in this case, onto communication/computation resources while generating a near optimal schedule. Second, it does not require a job to be pre-decomposed. This algorithm is a competitive choice for scheduling large Data Grid applications in terms of both scheduling overhead and the quality of solutions when compared to other algorithms. However, this work does not consider the case of multiple jobs competing for shared resources.

Tang et al. (M. Tang, Lee, Tang, & Yeo, 2005; M. Tang et al., 2006) propose a Data Grid architecture supporting efficient data replication and job scheduling. The computing sites are organized into individual domains according to the network structure, and a replica server is placed in each domain. Two centralized dynamic replication algorithms with different replica placement methods and a distributed dynamic replication algorithm are proposed. At regular intervals, the dynamic replication algorithms exploit the data access history for popular data files and compute the replication destinations to improve data access performance for grid jobs.

Coupled with these replication algorithms, the grid scheduling heuristics of Shortest Turnaround Time (STT), Least Relative Load and Data Present are proposed. For each incoming job, the STT heuristic estimates the turnaround time on every computing site and assigns a new job to the site that provides the shortest turnaround time. The Least Relative Load heuristic assigns a new job to the computing site that has the least relative load. This scheduling heuristic attempts to balance the workloads for all computing sites in the Data Grid. Finally, the Data Present heuristic considers the data location as the major factor when assigning the job. Simulation results demonstrate that the proposed algorithms can shorten the job turnaround time greatly.

Analyzing earlier work, Dang and Lim (Dang & Lim, 2007) identified two shortcomings in earlier work. The first is not considering the relationships among data file and between the data files and jobs. By replicating a set of files that has high probability to be used together on nearby resources, they expect that the jobs using these files will be scheduled to that small area. The second is a limitation in the use of the Dataset Scheduler (DS) (Ranganathan & Foster, 2004). Instead of just tracking data popularity, the DS plays the role of an independent scheduler. They propose a tree of data types in which the relationship between data in the same category and relationship between nearby categories are defined. By means of this, a correlation between data is extracted. The idea is then to gather data that is 'related' to a small region so that any job requiring such data will be executed inside that region. This reduces the cost to transfer data to the job execution site, therefore, improves the job execution performance.

Desprez et al. (Desprez & Vernois, 2006) describe an algorithm that combines data management and scheduling via a steady state approach. Using a model of the grid platform, the number of requests as well as their distribution, and the number and size of data files, they define a linear programming problem to satisfy the constraints at every level of the platform in steady-state. The solution of this linear program provides a placement for the data files on the servers as well as, for each kind of job, the server on which they should be executed. However, this heuristic approach for approximating an integer solution to the linear program does not always give the best mapping of data and can potentially give results that are far from the optimal value of the objective function.

Chang et al. (Chang, Chang, & Lin, 2007) developed a job scheduling policy, called Hierarchical Cluster Scheduling (HCS), and a dynamic data replication strategy, called Hierarchical Replication Strategy (HRS), to improve data access efficiency in a cluster structured grid. Their HCS scheduling policy considers the locations of required data, the access cost and the job queue length of a computing node. HCS uses hierarchical scheduling that takes cluster information into account to reduce the search time for an appropriate computing node. HRS integrates the previous replication strategy with the job scheduling policy to increase the chance of accessing data at a nearby node. The probability of scheduling the same type of job to the same cluster will be rather high in their proposed scheduling algorithm, leading to possible load balancing problems. The consideration of system load balancing with other scheduling factors will be an important direction for future research. In addition, balancing between data access time, job execution time, and network capabilities also needs to be studied further.

Some recent work has addressed data movement in task scheduling. The current research has developed along two directions: allocating the task to where the data is, and moving the data to where the task is. He and Sun (He & Sun, 2005) incorporate data movement into task scheduling using a newly introduced data structure called the Data Distance Table (DDT) to measure the dynamic data movement cost, and integrate this cost into an extended Min-Min (He et al., 2003) scheduling heuristic. A data replica based algorithm is dynamically adjusted to place data on under-utilized sites before any possible load imbalance occurs. Based on DDT, a data-conscious task scheduling heuristic is introduced to minimize data access delay. Experimental results show that their data-conscious dynamic adjusting scheduling heuristics outperforms the general Min-Min technique significantly for data intensive applications, especially when the critical data sets are unevenly distributed.

Khanna et al. (Khanna et al., 2006) address the problem of efficient execution of a batch of data-intensive tasks with batch-shared I/O behavior, on coupled storage and compute clusters. They approach the problem in three stages. The first stage, called sub-batch selection, partitions a batch of tasks into sub-batches such that the total size of the files required for a sub-batch does not exceed the available aggregate disk space on the compute cluster. The second stage accepts a sub- batch as input and yields an allocation of the tasks in the sub-batch onto the nodes of the compute cluster to minimize the sub-batch execution time. The third stage orders the tasks allocated to each node at runtime and dynamically determines what file transfers need to be done and how they should be scheduled to minimize end-point contention on the storage cluster.

Two scheduling schemes are proposed to solve this three stage problem. The first approach formulates the sub-batch selection problem using a 0-1 Integer Programming (IP) formulation. The second stage is also modeled as a 0- 1 IP formulation to determine the mapping of tasks to nodes, source and destination nodes for all replications, and the destination nodes for all remote transfers. The second approach, called BiPartition, employs a bi-level hypergraph partitioning based scheduling heuristic that formulates the sharing of files among tasks as a hypergraph. The BiPartition approach results in slightly longer batch execution times, but is much faster than the IP based approach. Thus, the IP based approach is attractive for small workloads, while the BiPartition approach is preferable for large scale workloads.

Lee and Zomaya (Lee & Zomaya, 2006) propose a novel scheduling algorithm called the Shared Input data based Listing (SIL) algorithm for Data intensive Bag-of-Tasks (DBoT) applications on grids. The algorithm uses a set of task lists that are constructed taking data sharing patterns into account and that are reorganized dynamically based on the performance of resources during the execution of the application. The primary goal of this dynamic listing is to minimize data transfers thus leading to shortening the overall completion time of DBoT applications.

The SIL algorithm also attempts to reduce serious schedule increases (that occur because of inefficient task/host assignments) by using task duplication. The SIL algorithm consists of two major phases. The task grouping phase groups tasks into a set of lists based on their data sharing patterns, associates these task lists with sites, and further breaks and/or associates them with hosts. Then the scheduling phase assigns tasks to hosts dynamically reorganizing task lists and duplicates tasks once all tasks are scheduled but while some tasks are still running.

Additionally, Santos-Neto et al. (Santos-Neto, Cirne, Brasileiro, & Lima, 2004) have developed a Storage Affinity (SA) algorithm which tries to minimize data transfers by making scheduling decisions incorporating the location of data previously transferred. In addition, they consider task replication as soon as a host becomes available –between the time the last unscheduled task gets assigned and the time the last running task completes its execution. The SA algorithm determines task/host assignments based on a "storage affinity metric". The storage affinity of a task to a host is the amount of the task's input data already stored at the site to which the host belongs. Although the scheduling decision SA makes is between task and host, storage affinity is calculated between task and site. This is because in the grid model used for SA, each site in the grid uses a single data repository that is accessed by all the hosts in the site.

For each scheduling decision, the SA algorithm calculates storage affinity values for all unscheduled tasks and dispatches the task with the largest storage affinity value. If none of the tasks has a positive storage affinity value one of them is scheduled at random. By the time this initial scheduling is completed, all the hosts will be busy in running the same number of tasks. On the completion of any of the running tasks, the SA algorithm starts task replication. Then each of the remaining running tasks is considered for replication and the best one is selected. The selection decision is based on the storage affinity value and the number of replicas available.

COMPARISON OF REPLICA PLACEMENT STRATEGIES

In this section, we summarize current and past research on different replica placement techniques for Data Grid environments. Several important factors such as grid infrastructure, data access patterns, network traffic conditions, and so on are taken into account when choosing a replica placement strategy. In the presence of diverse and varying grid characteristics it is difficult to create a common ground for comparison of different strategies. To gain insight into the effectiveness of different replication strategies, we compare them by considering metrics including access latency, bandwidth savings, and server work load.

Response Time: This is the time that elapses from when a node sends a request for a file until it receives the complete file. If a local copy of the file exists, the response time is assumed to be zero.

Bandwidth Consumption: This includes the bandwidth consumed for data transfers occurred when a node requests a file and when a server creates a replica at another node.

Server Work Load: This is the amount of work done by the servers. Ideally, the replicas should be placed so that the workload on each server is balanced.

Comparison of Replica Placement Algorithms

We start with the initial work (Ranganathan & Foster, 2001b) on replication strategies proposed for hierarchical Data Grids. Among these strategies, Fast Spread shows relatively consistent performance and is best both in terms of access latency and bandwidth consumption given random access patterns. The disadvantage is that it has high storage requirements. The entire storage space at each tier is fully utilized by Fast-Spread. If, however, there is sufficient locality in the access patterns, Cascading would work better than the others in terms of both access latency and bandwidth consumption. The Best Client algorithm is naive and illustrates the worst case performance among those presented in (Ranganathan & Foster, 2001b).

An improvement to the Cascading technique is the Proportional Share Replica policy (Abawajy, 2004). The method is a heuristic one that places replicas at the "optimal" locations by assuming that the number of sites and the total number of replicas to be distributed are already known. Firstly, an ideal load distribution is calculated and then replicas are placed on candidate sites that can service replica requests slightly greater than or equal to that ideal load. This technique was evaluated based on mean response time (mean access latency). Simulation results show that it performs better than the cascading technique with increased availability of data and considers load sharing among replica servers. Unfortunately, the approach is unrealistic for most scenarios and is inflexible once placement decisions have been made.

With the aim of improving the performance of data access given varying workloads, dynamic replication algorithms were presented by Tang et al. (M. Tang, Lee, Yeo, & Tang, 2005). In their paper, two dynamic replication algorithms, Simple Bottom-Up (SBU) and Aggregate Bottom-Up (ABU), were proposed for a multi-tier Data Grid. Their simulation results show that both algorithms can reduce the average response time of data access significantly compared to static replication methods. ABU can achieve great performance improvements for all access patterns even if the available storage size of the replication server is relatively small. Comparing the two algorithms to Fast Spread, the dynamic replication strategy ABU proves to be superior. As for SBU, although the average response time of Fast Spread (Ranganathan & Foster, 2001b) is better in most cases, Fast Spread's replication frequency may be too high to be useful in the real world.

A multi-objective approach to dynamic replication placement exploiting operations research techniques was proposed in (Rahman, Barker, & Alhajj, 2005a). In this method, replica placement decisions are made considering both the current network status and data request patterns. Dynamic maintainability is achieved by considering replica relocation cost. Decisions to relocate are made when a performance metric degrades significantly in the last specific number of time periods. Their technique was evaluated in terms of request-weighted average response time, but the performance results were not compared to any of the other existing replication techniques.

The BHR (Park et al., 2003) dynamic replication strategy focuses on 'network-level locality' by trying to place the targeted file at a site that has broad bandwidth to the site of job execution. The BHR strategy was evaluated in term of job execution time (which includes access latency) with varying bandwidths and storage spaces using the OptorSim (W. Bell et al., 2003) simulator.

The simulation results show that it can even outperform aggressive replication strategies like LRU Delete and Delete Oldest (W. Bell et al., 2003) in terms of data access time especially when grid sites have relatively small storage capacity and a clear hierarchy of bandwidths.

Lin et al. (Lin et al., 2006) is one of the relatively few replication efforts that focus on overall grid performance. Their proposed placement algorithm, targeted for a tree-based network model, finds optimal locations for replicas so that the workload among the replicas is balanced. They also propose a new algorithm to determine the minimum number of replicas required when the maximum workload capacity of each replica server is known. All these algorithms ensure that QoS requirements from the users are satisfied. Subsequent work by Wang et al. (H. Wang et al., 2006) addresses the replica placement problem when the underlying network is a general graph, instead of a tree. Their experimental results indicate that their proposed algorithm efficiently finds near-optimal solutions.

SUMMARY AND OPEN PROBLEMS

This survey has reviewed data replication in grid systems, considering the issues and challenges involved in replication with a primary focus on replica placement which is at the core of all replication strategies.

Although replication in parallel and distributed systems has been intensively studied, new challenges in grid environments make replication an interesting ongoing topic and many research e orts are underway in this area. We have identified heterogeneity, dynamism, system reliability and availability, and the impact of data replication on scheduling as the primary challenges addressed by current research in grid replication. We also find that the evolution of Data Grid architectures (e.g., support for a variety of grid structure models, fragmented replicas, co-allocation mechanisms and data sharing) provide an opportunity to implement sophisticated data replication algorithms providing specific benefits. In addition to enhancements to classic replication algorithms, new methodologies have been applied, such as grid economic models and nature inspired heuristics (e.g., genetic and ant algorithms).

Due to the characteristics of grid systems and the challenges involved in replication, there are still many open issues related to data replication on the grid. Without any specific assumptions, we find the following general issues deserving of additional/future exploration.

Fragmented Replication

Focusing on the concept of using fragmented replicas in replica placement and selection is a recent research trend. As mentioned when discussing algorithms that use co-allocation methods, the problem with current strategies that deal with fragmented replicas is increased complexity. Usually, the blocks in a fragmented replica are considered to be contiguous. If they were not, then the data structure to represent the fragmented replica and the algorithm for retrieval would be more complicated. Also, the proposed algorithms (Chang & Chen, 2007) do not always find an optimal solution. It would be interesting to find whether a worst case performance bound exists for the algorithms. Finding efficient ways to handle fragmented replica updates would also be an interesting area for future research.

Algorithms that are Adaptive to Performance Variation

It will likely be important to come up with a suite of adaptive job placement and data movement algorithms that can dynamically selecting strategies depending on current and predicted grid conditions. The limitations of current rescheduling algorithms for Data Grids are high cost and lack of consideration of dependent tasks. For jobs whose turn-around times are large, rescheduling can improve performance dramatically. However, rescheduling is itself costly, especially when there are extra data dependencies among tasks compared to independent applications. In addition, many related problems also must be considered. For example, when the rescheduling mechanisms should be invoked, what measurable parameters should be used to decide whether rescheduling will be profitable, and where tasks should be migrated to. Research on rescheduling for Data Grids is largely an open field for future work.

Enhanced Algorithms Combining Computation and Data Scheduling

Only a handful of current research e orts consider the simultaneous optimization of computation and data transfer scheduling, which suggests possible opportunities for future work. Consideration of data staging in grid scheduling has an impact on the choice of a computational node for a task. The situation could be far more complex if there were multiple copies of data, and data dependencies among the tasks were considered. As discussed, in the work in (Kim & Weissman, 2004), scheduling decomposable Data Grid applications does not consider the case of multiple jobs competing for shared resources which would be an interesting topic for future research. Also, combined computation and data scheduling may lead to possible load balancing problems (e.g., the probability of scheduling the same type of job to the same cluster is high in the scheduling algorithm proposed in (Chang et al., 2007)). Thus, consideration of system load balancing with different scheduling factors will be an important future research direction.

New Models of Grid Architecture

Grid-like complex distributed environments cannot always be organized and controlled in a hierarchical manner. Any central directory service would inevitably become a performance bottleneck and a single point of failure. Rather, in the future, many of these systems will likely be operated in a self-organizing way, using replicated catalogs and a mechanism for the autonomous generation and placement of replicas at different sites. As discussed earlier, one open question for replica placement in such environments is how to determine replica locations when the network is general graph, instead of a tree. It is important to consider the properties of such other graphs and derive efficient algorithms for use with them. The design of efficient algorithms for replica placement in grid systems when network congestion is one of the objective functions to be optimized also needs to receive further consideration.

Increased Collaboration Using VO-based Data Grids

Foster et al. (Foster, Kesselman, & Tukcke, 2001) have proposed a grid architecture for resource sharing among different entities based around the concept of **Virtual Organizations** (VOs). A VO is formed when different organizations pool resources and collaborate to achieve a common goal. A VO defines the resources available for the participants and the rules for accessing and using the resources and the conditions under which the resources may be used. A VO also provides protocols and mechanisms for applications to determine the suitability and accessibility of available resources. The existence of VOs impacts the design of Data Grid architectures in many ways. For example, a VO may be stand alone or may be composed of a hierarchy of regional, national and international VOs. In the latter case, the underlying Data Grid may have a corresponding hierarchy of repositories and the replica discovery and management system might be structured accordingly. More importantly, sharing of data collections is guided by the relationships that exist between the VOs that own each of the collections.

While Data Grids may be built around VOs, current technologies do not provide many of the capabilities required for enabling collaboration between participants. For example, the tree structure of many replication mechanisms inhibits direct copying of data between participants that reside on different branches. Replication systems, therefore, will likely need to follow hybrid topologies that involve peer-to-peer links between different branches for enhanced collaboration.

With the use of VOs, efforts have moved towards community-based scheduling in which schedulers follow policies that are set at the VO level and enforced at the resource level through service level agreements and allocation quotas (Dumitrescu & Foster, 2004). Since communities are formed by pooling of resources by participants, resource allocation must ensure fair shares to everyone. This requires community-based schedulers that assign quotas to each of the users based on priorities and resource availability. Individual user schedulers should then submit jobs taking into account the assigned quotas and could negotiate with the central scheduler for a quota increase or change in priorities. It could also be possible to swap or reduce quotas to gain resource share in the future. Users are able to plan ahead for future resource requirements by advance reservation of resources. This community-based scheduling combined with enhanced Data Grid capabilities for collaboration will introduce new challenges to efficient replica placement in Data Grids and also the need to reduce replication cost.

CONCLUSION

Data Grids are being adopted widely for sharing data and collaboratively managing and executing large-scale scientific applications that process large data sets, some that are distributed around the world. However, ensuring efficient and fast access to such huge and widely distributed data is hindered by the high latencies of the Internet upon which many Data Grids are built. Replication of data is the most common solution to this problem. In this chapter, we have studied, characterized, and categorized the issues and challenges involved in such data replication systems. In doing so, we have tried to provide insight into the architectures, strategies and practices that are currently used in Data Grids for data replication. Also, through our characterization, we have been attempted to highlight some of the shortcomings in the work done and identify gaps in the current architectures and strategies. These represent some of the directions for future research in this area. This paper provides a comprehensive study of replication in Data Grid that should not only serve as a tool for understanding this area but also present a reference by which future efforts can be classified.

REFERENCES

Abawajy, J. (2004). Placement of file replicas in data grid environments. In *Proceedings of international conference on computational science* (Vol. 3038, pp. 66-73).

Allcock, W. (2003, Mar). *GridFTP protocol specification*. Global Grid Forum Recommendation GFD.20.

Baker, M., Buyya, R., & Laforenza, D. (2002). Grids and grid technologies for wide-area distributed computing. *Software* [SPE]. *Practice and Experience*, *32*, 1437–1466. doi:10.1002/spe.488

Belalem, G., & Slimani, Y. (2006). A hybrid approach for consistency management in large scale systems. *In Proceedings of the international conference on networking and services* (pp. 71–76).

Belalem, G., & Slimani, Y. (2007). Consistency management for data grid in optorsim simulator. In *Proceedings of the international conference on multimedia and ubiquitous engineering* (pp. 554–560).

Bell, W., Cameron, D., Capozza, L., Millar, P., Stockinger, K., & Zini, F. (2003). Optorsim - A grid simulator for studying dynamic data replication strategies. *International Journal of High Performance Computing Applications*, *17*, 403–416. doi:10.1177/10943420030174005

Bell, W. H., Cameron, D. G., Carvajal-Schiaffino, R., Millar, A. P., Stockinger, K., & Zini, F. (2003). Evaluation of an economy-based file replication strategy for a data grid. In *Proceedings of the 3rd IEEE/ACM international symposium on cluster computing and the grid.*

Chang, R., & Chang, J. (2006). Adaptable replica consistency service for data grids. In *Proceedings of the third international conference on information technology: New generations* (ITNG'06) (pp. 646–651).

Chang, R., Chang, J., & Lin, S. (2007). Job scheduling and data replication on data grids. *Future Generation Computer Systems*, *23*(7), 846–860. doi:10.1016/j.future.2007.02.008

Chang, R., & Chen, P. (2007). Complete and fragmented replica selection and retrieval in data grids. *Future Generation Computer Systems*, *23*(4), 536–546. doi:10.1016/j.future.2006.09.006

Chang, R., Wang, C., & Chen, P. (2005). Replica selection on co-allocation data grids. In *Proceedings of the second international symposium on parallel and distributed processing and applications* (Vol. 3358, pp. 584–593).

Chervenak, A. (2002). Giggle: A framework for constructing scalable replica location services. In *Proceedings of the IEEE supercomputing* (pp. 1–17).

Chervenak, A., Foster, I., Kesselman, C., Salisbury, C., & Tuecke, S. (2000). The Data Grid: Towards an architecture for the distributed management and analysis of large scientific datasets. *Journal of Network and Computer Applications*, *23*, 187–200. doi:10.1006/jnca.2000.0110

Dang, N. N., & Lim, S. B. (2007). Combination of replication and scheduling in data grids. *International Journal of Computer Science and Network Security*, *7*(3).

Desprez, F., & Vernois, A. (2006). Simultaneous scheduling of replication and computation for data-intensive applications on the grid. *Journal of Grid Computing*, *4*(1), 66–74. doi:10.1007/s10723-005-9016-2

Dheepak, R., Ali, S., Sengupta, S., & Chakrabarti, A. (2005). Study of scheduling strategies in a dynamic data grid environment. In *Distributed Computing - IWDC 2004* (Vol. 3326). Berlin: Springer.

Domenici, A., Donno, F., Pucciani, G., & Stockinger, H. (2006). Relaxed data consistency with CONStanza. In *Proceedings of the sixth IEEE international symposium on cluster computing and the grid* (pp. 425–429).

Domenici, A., Donno, F., Pucciani, G., Stockinger, H., & Stockinger, K. (2004, Nov). *Replica consistency in a Data Grid. Nuclear Instruments and Methods in Physics Research*, *534*, 24–28. doi:10.1016/j.nima.2004.07.052

Dorigo, M. (1992). *Optimization, learning and natural algorithms* (Tech. Rep.). Ph.D. Thesis, Politecnico di Milano, Milan, Italy.

Dumitrescu, C., & Foster, I. (2004). Usage policy-based CPU sharing in virtual organizations. In *Proceedings of the fifth IEEE/ACM international workshop on grid computing* (pp. 53–60).

Duvvuri, V., Shenoy, P., & Tewari, R. (2000). Adaptive leases: A strong consistency mechanism for the World Wide Web. *In Proceedings of IEEE INFOCOM* (pp. 834–843).

Elias, J. A., & Moldes, L. N. (2002a). Behaviour of the fast consistency algorithm in the set of replicas with multiple zones with high demand. In *Proceedings of symposium in informatics and telecommunications*.

Elias, J. A., & Moldes, L. N. (2002b). A demand based algorithm for rapid updating of replicas. In *Proceedings of IEEE workshop on resource sharing in massively distributed systems* (pp. 686– 691).

Elias, J. A., & Moldes, L. N. (2003). Generalization of the fast consistency algorithm to a grid with multiple high demand zones. *In Proceedings of international conference on computational science (ICCS 2003)* (pp. 275–284).

Foster, I. (2006). Globus toolkit version 4: Software for service-oriented systems. In *Proceedings of the international conference on network and parallel computing* (pp. 2–13).

Foster, I., Kesselman, C., & Tukcke, S. (2001). The anatomy of the grid: Enabling scalable virtual organizations. *International Journal of High Performance Computing Applications*, *15*(3), 200–222. doi:10.1177/109434200101500302

Golding, R. A. (1992, Dec). *Weak-consistency group communication and membership* (Tech. Rep.). Computer and Information Sciences, University of California, Ph.D. Thesis.

Hakami, S. (1999). Optimum location of switching centers and the absolute centers and medians of a graph. *Operations Research*, *12*, 450–459. doi:10.1287/opre.12.3.450

He, X., & Sun, X. (2005). Incorporating data movement into grid task scheduling. In *Proceedings of grid and cooperative computing* (pp. 394–405).

He, X., Sun, X., & Laszewski, G. (2003). QoS guided Min-Min heuristic for grid task scheduling. *Journal of Computer Science and Technology, Special Issue on Grid Computing, 18* (4).

Kesselman, C., & Foster, I. (1998). *The Grid: Blueprint for a new computing infrastructure*. San Francisco: Morgan Kaufmann Publishers.

Khanna, G., Vydyanathan, N., Catalyurek, U., Kurc, T., Krishnamoorthy, S., Sadayappan, P., et al. (2006). Task scheduling and file replication for data-intensive jobs with batch-shared I/O. In *Proceedings of high-performance distributed computing (HPDC)* (pp. 241–252).

Kim, S., & Weissman, J. B. (2004). A genetic algorithm based approach for scheduling decomposable data grid applications. In *Proceedings of international conference on parallel processing* (Vol. 1, pp. 405–413).

Lamehamedi, H., & Szymanski, B. shentu, Z., & Deelman, E. (2002). Data replication strategies in grid environments. In *Proceedings of the fifth international conference on algorithms and architectures for parallel processing* (pp. 378–383).

Lamehamedi, H., Szymanski, B., Shentu, Z., & Deelman, E. (2003). Simulation of dynamic data replication strategies in data grids. *In Proceedings of the international parallel and distributed processing symposium* (pp. 10–20).

Lee, Y. C., & Zomaya, A. Y. (2006). Data sharing pattern aware scheduling on grids. In *Proceedings of International Conference on Parallel Processing*, (pp. 365–372).

Lei, M., & Vrbsky, S. V. (2006). A data replication strategy to increase data availability in data grids. In *Proceedings of the international conference on grid computing and applications* (pp. 221–227).

Lin, Y., Liu, P., & Wu, J. (2006). Optimal placement of replicas in data grid environments with locality assurance. In *Proceedings of the 12th International Conference on Parallel and Distributed Systems* (*ICPADS*'06), *01*, 465–474.

Park, S., Kim, J., Ko, Y., & Yoon, W. (2003). Dynamic data grid replication strategy based on Internet hierarchy. In *Proceedings of the second international workshop on grid and cooperative computing* (*GCC*'2003).

Rahman, R. M., Barker, K., & Alhajj, R. (2005). Replica selection in grid environment: A data-mining approach. In *Proceedings of the ACM symposium on applied computing* (pp. 695–700).

Rahman, R. M., Barker, K., & Alhajj, R. (2005a). Replica placement in data grid: A multi-objective approach. In *Proceedings of the international conference on grid and cooperative computing* (pp. 645–656).

Rahman, R. M., Barker, K., & Alhajj, R. (2005b). Replica placement in data grid: Considering utility and risk. In *Proceedings of the international conference on information technology: Coding and computing* (*ITCC*'05) (Vol. 1, pp. 354–359).

Ranganathan, K., & Foster, I. (2001a). Design and evaluation of dynamic replication strategies for a high performance data grid. *In Proceedings of the international conference on computing in high energy and nuclear physics* (pp. 260-263).

Ranganathan, K., & Foster, I. (2002). Decoupling computation and data scheduling in distributed data intensive applications. In *Proceedings of the 11th international symposium for high performance distributed computing* (*HPDC*) (pp. 352–358).

Ranganathan, K., & Foster, I. (2003). Simulation studies of computation and data scheduling algorithms for data grids. *Journal of Grid Computing, 1*(1), 53–62. doi:10.1023/A:1024035627870

Ranganathan, K., & Foster, I. T. (2001b). Identifying dynamic replication strategies for a high-performance data grid. In *Proceedings of the International Workshop on Grid Computing* (*GRID*'2001) (pp. 75–86).

Ranganathan, K., Iamnitchi, A., & Foster, I. (2002). Improving data availability through dynamic model-driven replication in large peer-to-peer communities. In *Proceedings of the 2nd IEEE/ACM international symposium on cluster computing and the grid* (*CCGRID*'02) (pp. 376–381).

Revees, C. (1993). *Moderm heuristic techniques for combinatorial problems*. Oxford, UK: Oxford Blackwell Scientific Publication.

Saito, Y., & Levy, H. M. (2000). Optimistic replication for internet data services. *In Proceedings of international symposium on distributed computing* (pp. 297–314).

Saito, Y., & Shapiro, M. (2005). Optimistic replication. *ACM Computing Surveys*, 37(1), 42–81. doi:10.1145/1057977.1057980

Santos-Neto, E., Cirne, W., Brasileiro, F., & Lima, A. (2004). Exploiting replication and data reuse to efficiently schedule data-intensive applications on grids. In *Proceedings of 10th workshop on job scheduling strategies for parallel processing* (Vol. 3277, pp. 210–232).

Schintke, F., & Reinefeld, A. (2003). Modeling replica availability in large data grids. *Journal of Grid Computing, 1*(2), 219–227. doi:10.1023/B:GRID.0000024086.50333.0d

Sun, M., Sun, J., Lu, E., & Yu, C. (2005). Ant algorithm for file replica selection in data grid. In *Proceedings of the first international conference on semantics, knowledge, and grid* (*SKG 2005*) (pp. 64–66).

Sun, Y., & Xu, Z. (2004). Grid replication coherence protocol. In *Proceedings of the 18th international parallel and distributed processing symposium* (pp. 232–239).

Tang, M., Lee, B., Tang, X., & Yeo, C. K. (2005). Combining data replication algorithms and job scheduling heuristics in the data grid. In *Proceedings of European conference on parallel computing* (pp. 381–390).

Tang, M., Lee, B., Yeo, C., & Tang, X. (2005). Dynamic replication algorithms for the multi-tier data grid. *Future Generation Computer Systems, 21*(5), 775–790. doi:10.1016/j.future.2004.08.001

Tang, M., Lee, B., Yeo, C., & Tang, X. (2006). The impact of data replication on job scheduling performance in the data grid. *Future Generation Computer Systems, 22*(3), 254–268. doi:10.1016/j.future.2005.08.004

Tang, X., & Xu, J. (2005). QoS-aware replica placement for content distribution. *IEEE Transactions on Parallel and Distributed Systems, 16*(10), 921–932. doi:10.1109/TPDS.2005.126

Vazhkudai, S. (2003, Nov). Enabling the co-allocation of grid data transfers. In *Proceedings of the fourth international workshop on grid computing* (pp. 41–51).

Vazhkudai, S., Tuecke, S., & Foster, I. (2001). Replica selection in the globus data grid. *In Proceedings of the first IEEE/ACM international conference on cluster computing and the grid* (*CCGRID* 2001) (pp. 106–113).

Venugopal, S., & Buyya, R. (2005, Oct). A deadline and budget constrained scheduling algorithm for escience applications on data grids. In *Proceedings of the 6th international conference on algorithms and architectures for parallel processing* (ICA3PP-2005) (pp. 60–72).

Venugopal, S., Buyya, R., & Ramamohanarao, K. (2006). A taxonomy of data grids for distributed data sharing, management, and processing. *ACM Computing Surveys, 1*, 1–53.

Wang, C., Hsu, C., Chen, H., & Wu, J. (2006). Efficient multi-source data transfer in data grids. In *Proceedings of the sixth IEEE international symposium on cluster computing and the grid* (CCGRID'06) (pp. 421–424).

Wang, H., Liu, P., & Wu, J. (2006). A QoS-aware heuristic algorithm for replica placement. *Journal of Grid Computing*, 96–103.

Yang, C., Yang, I., Chen, C., & Wang, S. (2006). Implementation of a dynamic adjustment mechanism with efficient replica selection in data grid environments. In *Proceedings of the ACM symposium on applied computing* (pp. 797–804).

Zhou, X., Kim, E., Kim, J. W., & Yeom, H. Y. (2006). ReCon: A fast and reliable replica retrieval service for the data grid. *In Proceedings of IEEE international symposium on cluster computing and the grid* (pp. 446–453).

KEY TERMS AND THEIR DEFINITIONS

Access Latency: Access latency is the time that elapses from when a node sends a request for a file until it receives the complete file.

Data Grids: Data Grids primarily deal with providing services and infrastructure for distributed data-intensive applications that need to access, transfer and modify massive datasets stored in distributed storage resources.

Job Scheduling: Job scheduling assigns incoming jobs to compute nodes in such a way that some evaluative conditions are met, such as the minimization of the overall execution time of the jobs.

Replica Consistency: The replica consistency problem deals with the update synchronization of multiple copies (replicas) of a file.

Replica Placement: The replica placement service is the component of a Data Grid architecture that decides where in the system a file replica should be placed.

Replica Selection: A replica selection service discovers the available replicas and selects the best replica that matches the user's location and quality of service (QoS) requirements.

Replication: Replication is an important technique to speed up data access for Data Grid systems by replicating the data in multiple locations, so that a user can access the data from a site in his vicinity.

ENDNOTE

[1] A replica may be a complete or a partial copy of the original dataset.

Chapter 23
Architectural Elements of Resource Sharing Networks

Marcos Dias de Assunção
The University of Melbourne, Australia

Rajkumar Buyya
The University of Melbourne, Australia

ABSTRACT

This chapter first presents taxonomies on approaches for resource allocation across resource sharing networks such as Grids. It then examines existing systems and classifies them under their architectures, operational models, support for the life-cycle of virtual organisations, and resource control techniques. Resource sharing networks have been established and used for various scientific applications over the last decade. The early ideas of Grid computing have foreseen a global and scalable network that would provide users with resources on demand. In spite of the extensive literature on resource allocation and scheduling across organisational boundaries, these resource sharing networks mostly work in isolation, thus contrasting with the original idea of Grid computing. Several efforts have been made towards providing architectures, mechanisms, policies and standards that may enable resource allocation across Grids. A survey and classification of these systems are relevant for the understanding of different approaches utilised for connecting resources across organisations and virtualisation techniques. In addition, a classification also sets the ground for future work on inter-operation of Grids.

INTRODUCTION

Since the formulation of the early ideas on meta-computing (Smarr & Catlett, 1992), several research activities have focused on mechanisms to connect worldwide distributed resources. Advances in distributed computing have enabled the creation of Grid-based resource sharing networks such as TeraGrid (Catlett, Beckman, Skow, & Foster, 2006) and Open Science Grid (2005). These networks, composed of multiple resource providers, enable collaborative work and sharing of resources such as computers,

DOI: 10.4018/978-1-60566-661-7.ch023

storage devices and network links among groups of individuals and organisations. These collaborations, widely known as Virtual Organisations (VOs) (Foster, Kesselman, & Tuecke, 2001), require resources from multiple computing sites. In this chapter we focus on networks established by organisations to share computing resources.

Despite the extensive literature on resource allocation and scheduling across organisational boundaries (Butt, Zhang, & Hu, 2003: Grimme, Lepping, & Papaspyrou, 2008; Iosup, Epema, Tannenbaum, Farrellee, & Livny, 2007; Ranjan, Rahman, & Buyya, 2008; Fu, Chase, Chun, Schwab, & Vahdat, 2003; Irwin et al., 2006; Peterson, Muir, Roscoe, & Klingaman, 2006; Ramakrishnan et al., 2006; Huang, Casanova, & Chien, 2006), existing resource sharing networks mostly work in isolation and with different utilisation levels (Assunção, Buyya, & Venugopal, 2008; Iosup et al., 2007), thus contrasting with the original idea of Grid computing (Foster et al., 2001). The early ideas of Grid computing have foreseen a global and scalable network that would provide users with resources on demand.

We have previously demonstrated that there can exist benefits for Grids to share resources with one another such as reducing the costs incurred by over-provisioning (Assunção & Buyya, in press). Hence, it is relevant to survey and classify existing work on mechanisms that can be used to interconnect resources from multiple Grids. A survey and classification of these systems are important in order to understand the different approaches utilised for connecting resources across organisations and to set the ground for future work on inter-operation of resource sharing networks, such as Grids. Taxonomies on resource management systems for resource sharing networks have been proposed (Iosup et al., 2007; Grit, 2005). Buyya et al. (2000) and Iosup et al. (2007) have described the architectures used by meta-scheduler systems and how jobs are directed to the resources where they execute. Grit (2005) has classified the roles of intermediate parties, such as brokers, in resource allocation for virtual computing environments.

This chapter extends existing taxonomies, thus making the following contributions:

- It examines additional systems and classifies them under a larger property spectrum namely resource control techniques, scheduling considering virtual organisations and arrangements for resource sharing.
- It provides classifications and a survey of work on resource allocation and scheduling across organisations, such as centralised scheduling, meta-scheduling and resource brokering in Grid computing. This survey aims to show different approaches to federate organisations in a resource sharing network and to allocate resources to its users. We also present a mapping of the surveyed systems against the proposed classifications.

BACKGROUND

Several of the organisational models followed by existing Grids are based on the idea of VOs. The VO scenario is characterised by resource providers offering different shares of resources to different VOs via some kind of agreement or contract; these shares are further aggregated and allocated to users and groups within each VO. The life-cycle of a VO can be divided into four distinct phases namely creation, operation, maintenance, and dissolution. During the creation phase, an organisation looks for collaborators and then selects a list of potential partners to start the VO. The operation phase is concerned with resource management, task distribution, and usage policy enforcement (Wasson & Humphrey, 2003; Dumitrescu & Foster, 2004). The maintenance phase deals with the adaptation of the VO, such as allocation of additional resources according to its users' demands. The VO dissolution involves legal and economic issues such as determining the success or failure of the VO, intellectual property and revocation of access and usage privileges.

The problem of managing resources within VOs in Grid computing is further complicated by the fact that resource control is generally performed at the job level. Grid-based resource sharing networks have users with units of work to execute, also called jobs; some entities decide when and where these jobs will execute. The task of deciding where and when to run the users' work units is termed as scheduling. The resources contributed by providers are generally clusters of computers and the scheduling in these resources is commonly performed by Local Resource Management Systems (LRMSs) such as PBS (2005) and SGE (Bulhões, Byun, Castrapel, & Hassaine, 2004). Scheduling of Grid users' applications and allocation of resources contributed by providers is carried out by Grid Resource Management Systems (GRMSs). A GRMS may comprise components such as:

- Meta-schedulers, which communicate with LRMSs to place jobs at the provider sites;
- Schedulers that allocate resources considering how providers and users are organised in virtual organisations (Dumitrescu & Foster, 2005); and
- Resource brokers, which represent users or organisations by scheduling and managing job execution on their behalf.

These components interact with providers' LRMSs either directly or via interfaces provided by the Grid middleware. The Grid schedulers can communicate with one another in various ways, which include via sharing agreements, hierarchical scheduling, Peer-to-Peer (P2P) networks, among others.

Recently, utility data centres have deployed resource managers that allow the partitioning of physical resources and the allocation of raw resources that can be customised with the operating system and software of the user's preference. This partitioning is made possible by virtualisation technologies such as Xen (Barham et al., 2003; Padala et al., 2007) and VMWare[1]. The use of virtualisation technologies for resource allocation enables the creation of customised virtual clusters (Foster et al., 2006; Chase, Irwin, Grit, Moore, & Sprenkle, 2003; Keahey, Foster, Freeman, & Zhang, 2006). The use of virtualisation technology allows for another form of resource control termed containment (Ramakrishnan et al., 2006), in which remote resources are bound to the users' local computing site on demand. The resource shares can be exchanged across sites by intermediate parties. Thereby, a VO can allocate resources on demand from multiple resource providers and bind them to a customised environment, while maintaining it isolated from other VOs (Ramakrishnan et al., 2006).

In the following sections, we classify existing systems according to their support to the life-cycle of VOs, their resource control techniques and the mechanisms for inter-operation with other systems. We also survey representative work and map them according to the proposed taxonomies.

CLASSIFICATIONS FOR GRID RESOURCE MANAGEMENT SYSTEMS

Buyya et al. (2000) and Iosup et al. (2007) have classified systems according to their architectures and operational models. We present their taxonomy in this section because it classifies the way that schedulers can be organised in a resource sharing network. We have included a new operational model to the taxonomy (i.e. hybrid of job routing and job pulling). Moreover, systems with similar architecture may

Figure 1. Taxonomy on Grid resource management systems

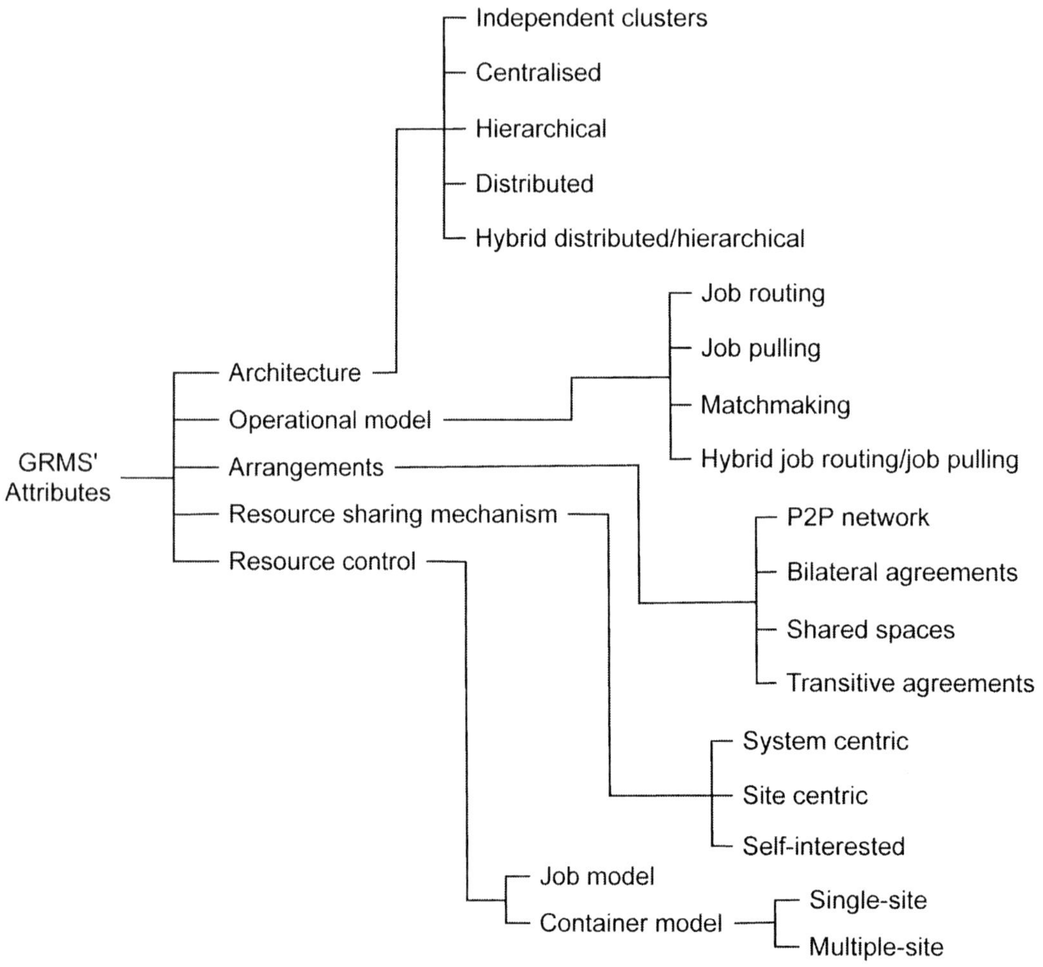

still differ in terms of the mechanisms employed for resource sharing, the self-interest of the system's participants, and the communication model. A Grid system can use decentralised scheduling wherein schedulers communicate their decisions with one another in a co-operative manner, thus guaranteeing the maximisation of the global utility of the system. On the other hand, a broker may represent a particular user community within the Grid, can have contracts with other brokers in order to use the resources they control and allocate resources that maximise its own utility (generally given by the achieved profit). We classify the arrangements between brokers in this section. Furthermore, systems can also differ according to their resource control techniques and support to different stages of the VO life-cycle. This section classifies resource control techniques and the systems' support for virtual organisations. The attributes of GRMSs and the taxonomy are summarised in Figure 1.

Architecture and Operational Models of GRMSs

This section describes several manners in which schedulers and brokers can be organised in Grid systems. Iosup et al. (2007) considered a multiple cluster scenario and classified the architectures possibly used as Grid resource management systems. They classified the architectures in the following categories:

- **Independent clusters** - each cluster has its LRMS and there is no meta-scheduler component. Users submit their jobs to the clusters of the organisations to which they belong or on which they have accounts. We extend this category by including single-user Grid resource brokers. In this case, the user sends her jobs to a broker, which on behalf of the user submits jobs to clusters the user can access.
- **Centralised meta-scheduler** - there is a centralised entity to which jobs are forwarded. Jobs are then sent by the centralised entity to the clusters where they are executed. The centralised component is responsible for determining which resources are allocated to the job and, in some cases, for migrating jobs if the load conditions change.
- **Hierarchical meta-scheduler** - schedulers are organised in a hierarchy. Jobs arrive either at the root of the hierarchy or at the LRMSs.
- **Distributed meta-scheduler** - cluster schedulers can share jobs that arrive at their LRMSs with one another. Links can be defined either in a static manner (i.e. by the system administrator at the system's startup phase) or in a dynamic fashion (i.e. peers are selected dynamically at runtime). Grit (2007) discusses the types of contracts that schedulers (or brokers) can establish with one another.
- **Hybrid distributed/hierarchical meta-scheduler** - each Grid site is managed by a hierarchical meta-scheduler. Additionally, the root meta-schedulers can share the load with one another.

This classification is comprehensive since it captures the main forms through which schedulers and brokers can be organised in resource sharing networks. However, some categories can be further extended. For example, the site schedulers can be organised in several decentralised ways and use varying mechanisms for resource sharing, such as a mesh network in which contracts are established between brokers (Irwin et al., 2006; Fu et al., 2003) or via a P2P network with a bartering-inspired economic mechanism for resource sharing (Andrade, Brasileiro, Cirne, & Mowbray, 2007).

Iosup et al. also classified a group of systems according to their operational model; the operational model corresponds to the mechanism that ensures jobs entering the system arrive at the resource in which they run. They have identified three operational models:

- **Job routing**, whereby jobs are routed by the schedulers from the arrival point to the resources where they run through a push operation (scheduler-initiated routing);
- **Job pulling**, through which jobs are pulled from a higher-level scheduler by resources (resource-initiated routing); and
- **Matchmaking**, wherein jobs and resources are connected to one another by the resource manager, which acts as a broker matching requests from both sides.

We add a fourth category to the classification above in which the operational model can be a **hybrid of job routing and job pulling**. Examples of such cases include those that use a job pool to (from) which jobs are pushed (pulled) by busy (unoccupied) site schedulers (Grimme et al., 2008). (See Figure 2).

Figure 2. Architecture models of GRMSs

System	Architecture	Example Systems
Independent clusters	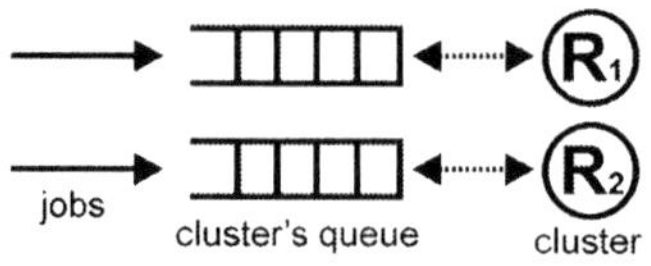	Portable Batch Scheduler (PBS), Sun Grid Engine (SGE)
Centralised meta-scheduler	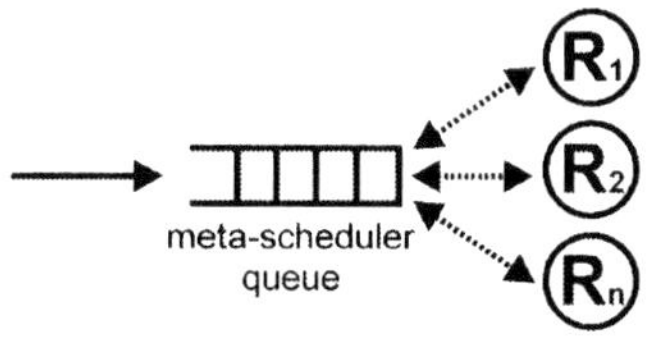	EGEE Workload Management Service (WMS), KOALA, PlanetLab
Hierarchical meta-scheduler	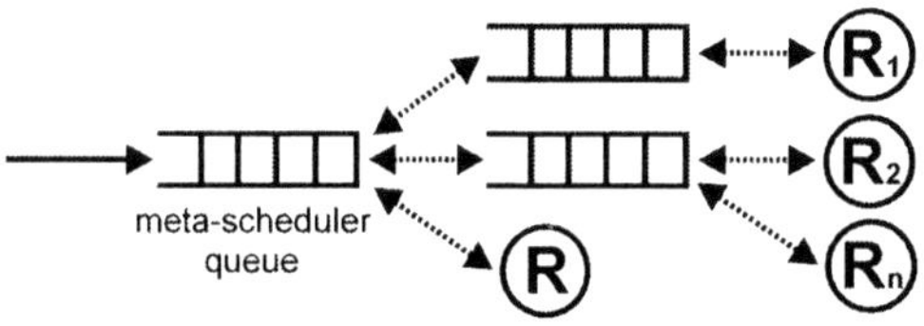	Computing Center Software (CCS)
Decentralised	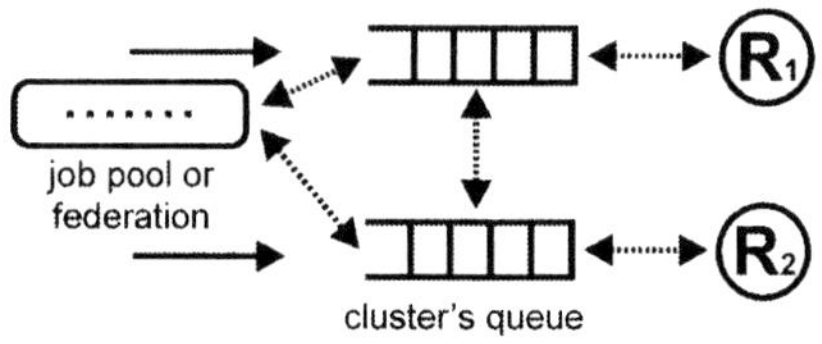	OurGrid, Askalon, Shirako
Hybrid of decentralised and hierarchical	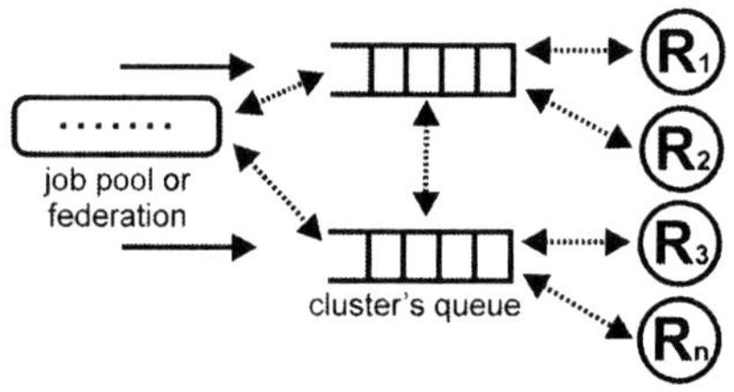	Delegated Matchmaking, InterGrid

Arrangements Between Brokers in Resource Sharing Networks

This section describes the types of arrangements that can be established between clusters in resource sharing networks when decentralised or semi-decentralised architectures are in place. It is important to distinguish between the way links between sites are established and their communication pattern; from the mechanism used for negotiating the resource shares. We classify the work according to the communication model in the following categories:

- **P2P network** - the sites of the resource sharing network are peers in a P2P network. They use the network to locate sites where the jobs can run (Butt et al., 2003; Andrade, Cirne, Brasileiro, & Roisenberg, 2003).
- **Bilateral sharing agreements** - sites establish bilateral agreements through which a site can locate another suitable site to run a given job. The redirection or acceptance of jobs occurs only

between sites that have a sharing agreement (Epema, Livny, Dantzig, Evers, & Pruyne, 1996).

- **Shared spaces** - sites co-ordinate resource sharing via shared spaces such as federation directories and tuple spaces (Grimme et al., 2008; Ranjan et al., 2008).
- **Transitive agreements** - this is similar to bilateral agreements. However, a site can utilise resources from another site with which it has no direct agreement (Fu et al., 2003; Irwin et al., 2006).

Although existing work can present similar communication models or similar organisational forms for brokers or schedulers, the resource sharing mechanisms can differ. The schedulers or brokers can use mechanisms for resource sharing from the following categories:

- **System centric** - the mechanism is designed with the goal of maximising the overall utility of the participants. Such mechanisms aim to, for example, balance the load between sites (Iosup et al., 2007) and prevent free-riding (Andrade et al., 2007).
- **Site centric** - brokers and schedulers are driven by the interest of maximising the utility of the participants within the site they represent without the explicit goal of maximising the overall utility across the system (Butt et al., 2003; Ranjan, Harwood, & Buyya, 2006).
- **Self-interested** - brokers act with the goal of maximising their own utility, generally given by profit, yet satisfying the requirements of their users. They do not take into account the utility of the whole system (Irwin et al., 2006).

Resource Control Techniques

The emergence of virtualisation technologies has resulted in the creation of testbeds wherein multiple-site slices (i.e. multiple-site containers) are allocated to different communities (Peterson et al., 2006). In this way, slices run concurrently and are isolated from each other. This approach, wherein resources are bound to a virtual execution environment or workspace where a service or application can run, is termed here as a container model. Most of the existing Grid middleware employ a job model in which jobs are routed until they reach the sites' local batch schedulers for execution. It is clear that both models can co-exist, thus an existing Grid technology can be deployed in a workspace enabled by container-based resource management (Ramakrishnan et al., 2006; Montero, Huedo, & Llorente, 2008). We classify systems in the following categories:

- **Job model** - this is the model currently utilised by most of the Grid systems. The jobs are directed or pulled across the network until they arrive at the nodes where they are finally executed.
- **Container-based** - resource managers in this category can manage a cluster of computers within a site by means of virtualisation technologies (Keahey et al., 2006; Chase et al., 2003). They bind resources to virtual clusters or workspaces according to a customer's demand. They commonly provide an interface through which one can allocate a set of nodes (generally virtual machines) and configure them with the operating system and software of choice.
    - **Single-site** - these container-based resource managers allow the user to create a customised virtual cluster using shares of the physical machines available at the site. These resource managers are termed here as single-site because they usually manage the resources of one administrative site (Fontán, Vázquez, Gonzalez, Montero, & Llorente, 2008; Chase et al.,

2003), although they can be extended to enable container-based resource control at multiple sites (Montero et al., 2008).

- **Multiple-site** - existing systems utilise the features of single-site container-based resource managers to create networks of virtual machines on which an application or existing Grid middleware can be deployed (Ramakrishnan et al., 2006). These networks of virtual machines are termed here as multiple-site containers because they can comprise resources bound to workspaces at multiple administrative sites. These systems allow a user to allocate resources from multiple computing sites thus forming a network of virtual machines or a multiple-site container (Irwin et al., 2006; Shoykhet, Lange, & Dinda, 2004; Ruth, Jiang, Xu, & Goasguen, 2005; Ramakrishnan et al., 2006). This network of virtual machines is also referred to as virtual Grid (Huang et al., 2006) or slice (Peterson et al., 2006).

Some systems such as Shirako (Irwin et al., 2006) and VioCluster (Ruth, McGachey, & Xu, 2005) provide container-based resource control. Shirako also offers resource control at the job level (Ramakrishnan et al., 2006) by providing a component that is aware of the resources leased. This component gives recommendations on which site can execute a given job.

Taxonomy on Virtual Organisations

The idea of user communities or virtual organisations underlies several of the organisational models adopted by Grid systems and guides many of the efforts on providing fair resource allocation for Grids. Consequently, the systems can be classified according to the VO awareness of their scheduling and resource allocation mechanisms. One may easily advocate that several systems, that were not explicitly designed to support VOs, can be used for resource management within a VO. We restrict ourselves to provide a taxonomy that classifies systems according to (i) the VO awareness of their resource allocation and scheduling mechanisms; and (ii) the provision of tools for handling different issues related to the VO life-cycle. For the VO awareness of scheduling mechanisms we can classify the systems in:

- **Multiple VOs** - those scheduling mechanisms that perform scheduling and allocation taking into consideration the various VOs existing within a Grid; and
- **Single VO** - those mechanisms that can be used for scheduling within a VO.

Furthermore, the idea of VO has been used in slightly different ways in the Grid computing context. For example, in the Open Science Grid (OSG), VOs are recursive and may overlap. We use several criteria to classify VOs as presented in Figure 3.

With regard to dynamism, we classify VOs as static and dynamic (Figure 3). Although Grid computing is mentioned as the enabler for dynamic VOs, it has been used to create more static and long-term collaborations such as APAC (2005), EGEE (2005), the UK National e-Science Centre (2005), and TeraGrid (Catlett et al., 2006). A static VO has a pre-defined number of participants and its structure does not change over time. A dynamic VO presents a number of participants that changes constantly as the VO evolves (Wesner, Dimitrakos, & Jeffrey, 2004). New participants can join, whereas existing participants may leave.

A dynamic VO can be stationary or mobile. A stationary VO is generally composed of highly specialised resources including supercomputers, clusters of computers, personal computers and data resources. The

Figure 3. Taxonomy on Grid facilitated VOs

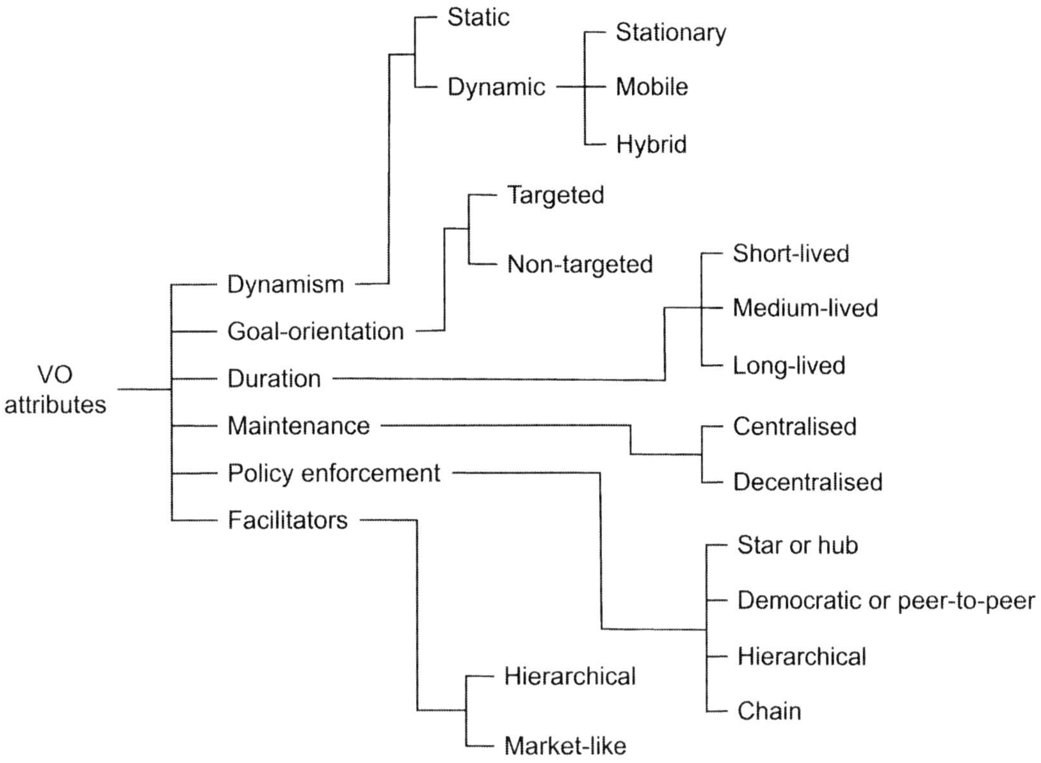

components of the VO are not mobile. In contrast, a mobile VO is composed of mobile resources such as Personal Digital Assistants (PDAs), mobile phones. The VO is highly responsive and adapts to different contexts (Wesner et al., 2004). Mobile VOs can be found in disaster handling and crisis management situations. Moreover, a VO can be hybrid, having both stationary and mobile components.

Considering goal-orientation, we divide VOs into two categories: targeted and non-targeted (Figure 3). A targeted VO can be an alliance or collaboration created to explore a market opportunity or achieve a common research goal. A VO for e-Science collaboration is an example of a targeted VO as the participants have a common goal (Hey & Trefethen, 2002). A non-targeted VO is characterised by the absence of a common goal; it generally comprises participants who pursue different goals, yet benefit from the VO by pooling resources. This VO is highly dynamic because participants can leave when they achieve their goals.

VOs can be short-, medium- or long-lived (Figure 3). A short-lived VO lasts for minutes or hours. A medium-lived VO lasts for weeks and is formed, for example, when a scientist needs to carry out experiments that take several days to finish. Data may be required to carry out such experiments. This scenario may be simplified if the VO model is used; the VO may not be needed as soon as the experiments have been carried out. A long-lived VO is formed to explore a market opportunity (goal-oriented) or to pool resources to achieve disparate objectives (non-targeted). Such endeavours normally last from months to years; hence, we consider a long-lived VO to last for several months or years.

As discussed in the previous section, the formation and maintenance of a VO present several challenges. These challenges have been tackled in different ways, which in turn have created different formation and maintenance approaches. We thus classify the formation and membership, or maintenance, as centralised and decentralised (Figure 3). The formation and membership of a centralised VO is controlled by a trusted third party, such as Open Science Grid (2005) or the Enabling Grids for E-SciencE (2005). OSG provides an open market where providers and users can advertise their needs and intentions; a provider or user may form a VO for a given purpose. EGEE provides a hierarchical infrastructure to enable the formation of VOs. On the other hand, in a decentralised controlled VO, no third party is responsible for enabling or controlling the formation and maintenance. This kind of VO can be complex as it can require multiple Service Level Agreements (SLAs) to be negotiated among multiple participants. In addition, the monitoring of SLAs and commitment of the members are difficult to control. The VO also needs to self-adapt when participants leave or new participants join.

Regarding the enforcement of policies, VOs can follow different approaches, such as hub or democratic. This is also referred to as topology. Katzy et al. (2005) classify VOs in terms of topology, identifying the following types: chain, star or hub, and peer-to-peer. Sairamesh et al. (2005) identify business models for VOs; the business models are analogous to topologies. However, by discussing the business models for VOs, the authors are concerned with a larger set of problems, including enforcement of policies, management, trust and security, and financial aspects. In our taxonomy, we classify the enforcement and monitoring of policies as star or hub, democratic or peer-to-peer, hierarchical, and chain (Figure 3).

Some projects such as Open Science Grid (2005) and EGEE (2005) aim to establish consortiums or clusters of organisations, which in turn allow the creation of dynamic VOs. Although not very related to the core issues of VOs, they aim to address an important problem: the establishment of trust between organisations and the means for them to look for and find potential partners. These consortiums can be classified as hierarchical and market-like (Figure 3). A market-like structure is any infrastructure that offers a market place, which organisations can join and present interests in starting a new collaboration or accepting to participate in an ongoing collaboration. These infrastructures may make use of economic models such as auctions, bartering, and bilateral negotiation.

A SURVEY OF EXISTING WORK

This section describes relevant work of the proposed taxonomy in more detail. First, it describes work on a range of systems that have a decentralised architecture. Some systems present a hierarchy of scheduling whereby jobs are submitted to the root of the hierarchy or to their leaves; in either case, the jobs execute at the leaves of the hierarchical structure. Second, this section presents systems of hierarchical structure, resource brokers and meta-scheduling frameworks. During the past few years, several Grid-based resource sharing networks and other testbeds have been created. Third, we discuss the work on inter-operation between resource sharing networks. Finally, this section discusses relevant work focusing on VO issues.

Distributed Architecture Based Systems

Condor Flocking: The flocking mechanism used by Condor (Epema et al., 1996) provides a software approach to interconnect pools of Condor resources. The mechanism requires manual configuration of sharing agreements between Condor pools. Each pool owner and each workstation owner maintains full control of when their resources can be used by external jobs.

The developers of Condor flocking opted for a layered design for the flocking mechanism, which enables the Condor's Central Manager (CM) (Litzkow, Livny, & Mutka, 1988) and other Condor machines to remain unmodified and operate transparently from the flock.

The basis of the flocking mechanism is formed by Gateway Machines (GW). There is at least one GW in each Condor pool. GWs act as resource brokers between pools. Each GW has a configuration file describing the subset of connections it maintains with other GWs. Periodically, a GW queries the status of its pool from the CM. From the list of resources obtained, the GW makes a list of those resources that are idle. The GW then sends this list to the other GWs to which it is connected. Periodically, the GW that received this list chooses a machine from the list, and advertises itself to the CM with the characteristics of this machine. The flocking protocol (which is a modified version of the normal Condor protocol) allows the GWs to create shadow processes that so that a submission machine is under the impression of contacting the execution machine directly.

Self-Organizing Flock of Condors: The original flocking scheme of Condor has the drawback that knowledge about all pools with which resources can be shared need to be known a priori before starting Condor (Epema et al., 1996). This static information poses limitations regarding the number of resources available and resource discovery. Butt et al. (2003) introduced a self-organising resource discovery mechanism for Condor, which allows pools to discover one another and resources available dynamically. The P2P network used by the flocking mechanism is based on Pastry and takes into account the network proximity. This may result in saved bandwidth in data transfer and faster communications. Experiments with this implementation considering four pools with four machines each were provided. Additionally, simulation results demonstrated the performance of the flocking mechanism when interconnecting 1,000 pools.

Shirako: Shirako (Irwin et al., 2006) is a system for on-demand leasing of shared networked resources across clusters. Shirako's design goals include: autonomous providers, who may offer resources to the system on a temporary basis and retain the ultimate control over them; adaptive guest applications that lease resources from the providers according to changing demand; pluggable resource types, allowing participants to include various types of resources, such as network links, storage and computing; brokers that provide guest applications with an interface to acquire resources from resource providers; and allocation policies at guest applications, brokers and providers, which define the manner resources are allocated in the system.

Shirako utilises a leasing abstraction in which authorities representing provider sites offer their resources to be provisioned by brokers to guest applications. Shirako brokers are responsible for coordinating resource allocation across provider sites. The provisioning of resources determines how much of each resource each guest application receives, when and where. The site authorities define how much resource is given to which brokers. The authorities also define which resources are assigned to serve requests approved by a broker. When a broker approves a request, it issues a ticket that can be redeemed for a lease at a site authority. The ticket specifies the type of resource, the number of resource units granted and the interval over which the ticket is valid. Sites issue tickets for their resources to brokers; the brokers' polices may decide to subdivide or aggregate tickets.

A service manager is a component that represents the guest application and uses the lease API provided by Shirako to request resources from the broker. The service manager determines when and how to redeem existing tickets, extend existing leases, or acquire new leases to meet changing demand. The system allows guest applications to renew or extend their leases. The broker and site authorities match accumulated pending requests with resources under the authorities' control. The broker prioritises requests and selects resource types and quantities to serve them. The site authority assigns specific resource units from its inventory to fulfill lease requests that are backed by a valid ticket. Site authorities use Cluster on Demand (Chase et al., 2003) to configure the resources allocated at the remote sites.

The leasing abstraction provided by Shirako is a useful basis to co-ordinate resource sharing for systems that create distributed virtual execution environments of networked virtual machines (Keahey et al., 2006; Ruth, Rhee, Xu, Kennell, & Goasguen, 2006; Adabala et al., 2005; Shoykhet et al., 2004).

Ramakrishnan et al. (2006) used Shirako to provide a hosting model wherein Grid deployments run in multiple-site containers isolated from one another. An Application Manager (AM), which is the entry point of jobs from a VO or Grid, interacts with a Grid Resource Oversight Coordinator (GROC) to obtain a recommendation of a site to which jobs can be submitted. The hosting model uses Shirako's leasing core. A GROC performs the functions of leasing resources from computing sites and recommending sites for task submission. At the computing site, Cluster on Demand is utilised to provide a virtual cluster used to run Globus 4 along with Torque/MAUI.

VioCluster: VioCluster is a system that enables dynamic machine trading across clusters of computers (Ruth, McGachey, & Xu, 2005). VioCluster introduces the idea of virtual domain. A virtual domain, originally comprising its physical domain of origin (i.e. a cluster of computers), can grow in the number of computing resources, thus dynamically allocating resources from other physical domains according to the demands of its user applications.

VioCluster presents two important system components: the creation of dynamic virtual domains and the mechanism through which resource sharing is negotiated. VioCluster uses machine and network virtualisation technology to move machines between domains. Each virtual domain has a broker that interacts with other domains. A broker has a borrowing policy and a lending policy. The borrowing policy determines under which circumstances the broker will attempt to obtain more machines. The lending policy governs when it is willing to let another virtual domain make use of machines within its physical domain.

The broker represents a virtual domain when negotiating trade agreements with other virtual domains. It is the broker's responsibility to determine whether trades should occur. The policies for negotiating the resources specify: the reclamation, that is, when the resources will be returned to their home domain; machine properties, which represent the machines to be borrowed; and the machines' location as some applications require communication. The borrowing policy must be aware of the communication requirements of user applications.

Machine virtualisation simplifies the transfer of machines between domains. When a machine belonging to a physical domain B is borrowed by a virtual domain A, it is utilised to run a virtual machine. This virtual machine matches the configuration of the machines in physical domain A. Network virtualisation enables the establishment of virtual network links connecting the new virtual machine to the nodes of domain A. For the presented prototype, PBS is used to manage the nodes of the virtual domain. PBS is aware of the computers' heterogeneity and never schedules jobs on a mixture of virtual and physical machines. The size of the work queue in PBS was used as a measure of the demand within a domain.

OurGrid: OurGrid (Andrade et al., 2003) is a resource sharing system organised as a P2P network of sites that share resources equitably in order to form a Grid to which they all have access. OurGrid was designed with the goal of easing the assembly of Grids, thus it provides connected sites with access to the Grid resources with a minimum of guarantees needed. OurGrid is used to execute Bag-of-Tasks (BoT) applications. BoT are parallel applications composed of a set of independent tasks that do not communicate with one another during their execution. In contrast to other Grid infrastructures, the system does not require offline negotiations if a resource owner wants to offer her resources to the Grid.

OurGrid uses a resource exchange mechanism termed network of favours. A participant A is doing a favour to participant B when A allows B to use her resources. According to the network of favours, every participant does favours to other participants expecting the favours to be reciprocated. In conflicting situations, a participant prioritises those who have done favours to it in the past. The more favours a participant does, the more it expects to be rewarded. The participants locally account their favours and cannot profit from them in another way than expecting other participants to do them some favours. Detailed experiments have demonstrated the scalability of the network of favours (Andrade et al., 2007), showing that the larger the network becomes, the more fair the mechanism performs.

The three participants in the OurGrid's resource sharing protocol are clients, consumers, and providers. A client requires access to the Grid resources to run her applications. The consumer receives requests from the client to find resources. When the client sends a request to the consumer, the consumer first finds the resources able to serve the request and then executes the tasks on the resources. The provider manages the resources shared in the community and provides them to consumers.

Delegated Matchmaking: Iosup et al. (2007) introduced a matchmaking protocol in which a computing site binds resources from remote sites to its local environment. A network of sites, created on top of the local cluster schedulers, manages the resources of the interconnected Grids. Sites are organised according to administrative and political agreements so that parent-child links can be established. Then, a hierarchy of sites is formed with the Grid clusters at the leaves of the hierarchy. After that, supplementary to the hierarchical links, sibling links are established between sites that are at the same hierarchical level and operate under the same parent site. The proposed delegated matchmaking mechanism enables requests for resources to be delegated up and down the hierarchy thus achieving a decentralised network.

The architecture is different from work wherein a scheduler forwards jobs to be executed on a remote site. The main idea of the matchmaking mechanism is to delegate ownership of resources to the user who requested them through this network of sites, and add the resources transparently to the user's local site. When a request cannot be satisfied locally, the matchmaking mechanism adds remote resources to the user's site. This simplifies security issues since the mechanism adds the resources to the trusted local resource pool. Simulation results show that the mechanism leads to an increase in the number of requests served by the interconnected sites.

Grid Federation: Ranjan et al. (2005) proposed a system that federates clusters of computers via a shared directory. Grid Federation Agents (GFAs), representing the federated clusters, post quotes about idle resources (i.e. a claim stating that a given resource is available) and, upon the arrival of a job, query the directory to find a resource suitable to execute the job. The directory is a shared-space implemented as a Distributed Hash Table (DHT) P2P network that can match quotes and user requests (Ranjan et al., 2008).

An SLA driven co-ordination mechanism for Grid superscheduling has also been proposed (Ranjan et al., 2006). GFAs negotiate SLAs and redirect requests through a Contract-Net protocol. GFAs use a greedy policy to evaluate resource requests. A GFA is a cluster resource manager and has control over the cluster's resources. GFAs engage into bilateral negotiations for each request they receive, without considering network locality.

Askalon: Siddiqui et al. (2006) introduced a capacity planning architecture with a three-layer negotiation protocol for advance reservation on Grid resources. The architecture is composed of allocators that make reservations of individual nodes and co-allocators that reserve multiple nodes for a single Grid application. A co-allocator receives requests from users and generates alternative offers that the user can utilise to run her application. A co-allocation request can comprise a set of allocation requests, each allocation request corresponding to an activity of the Grid application. A workflow with a list of activities is an example of Grid application requiring co-allocation of resources. Co-allocators aim to agree on Grid resource sharing. The proposed co-ordination mechanism produces contention-free schedules either by eliminating conflicting offers or by lowering the objective level of some of the allocators.

GRUBER/DI-GRUBER: Dumitrescu et al. (2005) highlighted that challenging usage policies can arise in VOs that comprise participants and resources from different physical organisations. Participants want to delegate access to their resources to a VO, while maintaining such resources under the control of local usage policies. They seek to address the following issues:

- How usage policies are enforced at the resource and VO levels.
- What mechanisms are used by a VO to ensure policy enforcement.
- How the distribution of policies to the enforcement points is carried out.
- How policies are made available to VO job and data planners.

They have proposed a policy management model in which participants can specify the maximum percentage of resources delegated to a VO. A VO in turn can specify the maximum percentage of resource usage it wishes to delegate to a given VO's group. Based on this model above, they have proposed a Grid resource broker termed GRUBER (Dumitrescu & Foster, 2005). GRUBER architecture is composed of four components, namely:

- Engine: which implements several algorithms to detect available resources.
- Site monitoring: is one of the data providers for the GRUBER engine. It is responsible for collecting data on the status of Grid elements.
- Site selectors: consist of tools that communicate with the engine and provide information about which sites can execute the jobs.
- Queue manager: resides on the submitting host and decides how many jobs should be executed and when.

Users who want to execute jobs, do so by sending them to submitting hosts. The integration of existing external schedulers with GRUBER is made in the submitting hosts. The external scheduler utilises GRUBER either as the queue manager that controls the start time of jobs and enforces VO policies, or as a site recommender. The second case is applicable if the queue manager is not available.

DI-GRUBER, a distributed version of GRUBER, has also been presented (Dumitrescu, Raicu, & Foster, 2005). DI-GRUBER works with multiple decision points, which gather information to steer resource allocations defined by Usage Service Level Agreements (USLAs). These points make decisions on a per-job basis to comply with resource allocations to VO groups. Authors advocated that 4 to 5 decision points are enough to handle the job scheduling of a Grid 10 times larger than Grid3 at the time the work was carried out (Dumitrescu, Raicu, & Foster, 2005).

Other important work: Balazinska et al. (2004) have proposed a load balancing mechanism for Medusa. Medusa is a stream processing system that allows the migration of stream processing operators from overloaded to under-utilised resources. The request offloading is performed based on the marginal cost of the request. The marginal cost for one participant is given by the increase (decrease) in the cost curve given by the acceptance (removal) of the request from the requests served by the participant.

NWIRE (Schwiegelshohn & Yahyapour, 1999) links various resources to a metacomputing system, also termed meta-system. It also enables the scheduling in these environments. A meta-system comprises interconnected MetaDomains. Each MetaDomain is managed by a MetaManager that manages a set of ResourceManagers. A ResourceManager interfaces the scheduler at the cluster level. The MetaManager permanently collects information about all of its resources. It handles all requests inside its MetaDomain and works as a resource broker to other MetaDomains. In this way, requests received by a MetaManager can be submitted either by users within its MetaDomain or by other MetaManagers. Each MetaManager contains a scheduler that maps requests for resources to a specific resource in its MetaDomain.

Grimme et al. (2008) have presented a mechanism for collaboration between resource providers by means of job interchange though a central job pool. According to this mechanism, a cluster scheduler adds to the central pool jobs that cannot be started immediately. After scheduling local jobs, a local scheduler can schedule jobs from the central pool if resources are available.

Dixon et al. (2006) have provided a tit-for-tat or bartering mechanism based on local, non-transferable currency for resource allocation in large-scale distributed infrastructures such as PlanetLab. The currency is maintained locally within each domain in the form of credit given to other domains for providing resources in the past. This creates pair-wise relationships between administrative domains. The mechanism resembles OurGrid's network of favours (Andrade et al., 2003). The information about exchanged resources decays with time, so that recent behaviour is more important. Simulation results showed that, for an infrastructure like PlanetLab, the proposed mechanism is more fair than the free-for-all approach currently adopted by PlanetLab.

Graupner et al. (2002) have introduced a resource control architecture for federated utility data centres. In this architecture, physical resources are grouped in virtual servers and services are mapped to virtual servers. The meta-system is the upper layer implemented as an overlay network whose nodes contain descriptive data about the two layers below. Allocations change according to service demand, which requires to the control algorithms to be reactive and deliver quality solutions. The control layer performs allocation of services to virtual server environments and its use has been demonstrated by a capacity control example for a homogeneous Grid cluster.

Hierarchical Systems, Brokers and Meta-Scheduling

This section describes some systems that are organised in a hierarchical manner. We also describe work on Grid resource brokering and frameworks that can be used to build meta-schedulers.

Computing Center Software (CCS): CCS (Brune, Gehring, Keller, & Reinefeld, 1999) is a system for managing geographically distributed high-performance computers. It consists of three components, namely: the CCS, which is a vendor-independent resource management software for local HPC systems; the Resource and Service Description (RSD), used by the CCS to specify and map hardware and software components of computing environments; and the Service Coordination Layer (SCL), which co-ordinates the use of resources across computing sites.

The CCS controls the mapping and scheduling of interactive and parallel jobs on massively parallel systems. It uses the concept of island, wherein each island has components for user interface, authorisation and accounting, scheduling of user requests, access to the physical parallel system, system control, and management of the island. At the meta-computing level, the Center Resource Manager (CRM) exposes scheduling and brokering features of the islands. The CRM is a management tool atop the CCS islands. When a user submits an application, the CRM maps the user request to the static and dynamic information on resources available. Once the resources are found, CRM requests the allocation of all required resources at all the islands involved. If not all resources are available, the CRM either re-schedules the request or rejects it. Center Information Server (CIS) is a passive component that contains information about resources and their statuses, and is analogous to Globus Metacomputing Directory Service (MDS) (Foster & Kesselman, 1997). It is used by the CRM to obtain information about resources available.

The Service Co-ordination Layer (SCL) is located one level above the local resource management systems. The SCL co-ordinates the use of resources across the network of islands. It is organised as a network of co-operating servers, wherein each server represents one computing centre. The centres determine which resources are made available to others and retain full autonomy over them.

EGEE Workload Management System (WMS): EGEE WMS (Vázquez-Poletti, Huedo, Montero, & Llorente, 2007) has a semi-centralised architecture. One or more schedulerscan be installed in the Grid infrastructure, each providing scheduling functionality for a group of VOs. The EGEE WMS components are: The User Interface (UI) from where the user dispatches the jobs; the Resource Broker (RB), which uses Condor-G (Frey, Tannenbaum, Livny, Foster, & Tuecke, 2001); the Computing Element (CE), which is the cluster front-end; the Worker Nodes (WNs), which are the cluster nodes; the Storage Element (SE), used for job files storage; and the Logging and Bookkeeping service (LB) that registers job events.

Condor-G: Condor-G (Frey et al., 2001) leverages software from Globus and Condor (Frey et al., 2001) and allows users to utilise resources spanning multiple domains as if they all belong to one personal domain. Although Condor-G can be viewed as a resource broker itself (Venugopal, Nadiminti, Gibbins, & Buyya, 2008), it can also provide a framework to build meta-schedulers.

The GlideIn mechanism of Condor-G is used to start a daemon process on a remote resource. The process uses standard Condor mechanisms to advertise the resource availability to a Condor collector process, which is then queried by the Scheduler to learn about available resources. Condor-G uses Condor mechanisms to match locally queued jobs to the resources advertised by these daemons and to execute them on those resources. Condor-G submits an initial GlideIn executable (a portable shell script), which in turn uses GSI-authenticated GridFTP to retrieve the Condor executables from a central repository. By submitting GlideIns to all remote resources capable of serving a job, Condor-G can guarantee optimal queuing times to user applications.

Gridbus Broker: Gridbus Grid resource broker (Venugopal et al., 2008) is user-centric broker that provides scheduling algorithms for both computing- and data-intensive applications. In Gridbus, each user has her own broker, which represents the user by (i) selecting resources that minimise the user's quality of service constraints such as execution deadline and budget spent; (ii) submitting jobs to remote resources; and (iii) copying input and output files. Gridbus interacts with various Grid middleware's (Venugopal et al., 2008).

Gridway: GridWay (Huedo, Montero, & Llorente, 2004) is a Globus based resource broker that provides a framework for execution of jobs in a 'submit and forget' fashion. The framework performs job submission and execution monitoring. Job execution adapts itself to dynamic resource conditions and application demands in order to improve performance. The adaptation is performed through application migration following performance degradation, sophisticated resource discovery, requirements change, or remote resource failure.

The framework is modular wherein the following modules can be set on a per-job basis: resource selector, performance degradation evaluator, prolog, wrapper and epilog. The name of the first two modules or steps are intuitive, so we describe here only the last three. During prolog, the component responsible for job submission (i.e. submission manager) submits the prolog executable, which configures the remote system and transfers executable and input files. In the case of restart of an execution, the prolog also transfers restart files. The wrapper executable is submitted after prolog and wraps the actual job in order to obtain its exit code. The epilog is a script that transfers the output files and cleans the remote resource.

GridWay also enables the deployment of virtual machines in a Globus Grid (Rubio-Montero, Huedo, Montero, & Llorente, 2007). The scheduling and selection of suitable resources is performed by GridWay whereas a virtual workspace is provided for each Grid job. A pre-wrapper phase is responsible for performing advanced job configuration routines, whereas the wrapper script starts a virtual machine and triggers the application job on it.

KOALA: Mohamed and Epema (in press) have presented the design and implementation of KOALA, a Grid scheduler that supports resource co-allocation. KOALA Grid scheduler interacts with cluster batch schedulers for the execution of jobs. The work proposes an alternative to advance reservation at local resource managers, when reservation features are not available. This alternative allows processors to be allocated from multiple sites at the same time.

SNAP-Based Community Resource Broker: The Service Negotiation and Acquisition Protocol (SNAP)-based community resource broker uses an interesting three-phase commit protocol. SNAP is proposed because traditional advance reservation facilities cannot cope with the fact that information availability may change between the moment at which resource availability is queried and the time when the reservation of resources is actually performed (Haji, Gourlay, Djemame, & Dew, 2005). The three phases of SNAP protocol consist of (i) a step in which resource availability is queried and probers are deployed, which inform the broker in case the resource status changes; (ii) then, the resources are selected and reserved; and (iii) after that, the job is deployed on the reserved resources.

Platform Community Scheduler Framework (CSF): CSF (2003) provides a set of tools that can be utilised to create a Grid meta-scheduler or a community scheduler. The meta-scheduler enables users to define the protocols to interact with resource managers in a system independent manner. The interface with a resource manager is performed via a component termed Resource Manager (RM) Adapter. A RM Adapter interfaces a cluster resource manager. CSF supports the GRAM protocol to access the services of the resource managers that do not support the RM Adapter interface.

Platform's LSF and MultiCluster products leverage the CSF to provide a framework for implementing meta-scheduling. Grid Gateway is an interface that integrates Platform LSF and CSF. A scheduling plug-in for Platform LSF scheduler decides which LSF jobs are forwarded to the meta-scheduler. This decision is based on information obtained from an information service provided by the Grid Gateway. When a job is forwarded to the meta-scheduler, the job submission and monitoring tools dispatch the job and query its status information through the Grid Gateway. The Grid Gateway uses the job submission, monitoring and reservation services from the CSF. Platform MultiCluster also allows multiple clusters using LSF to forward jobs to one another transparently to the end-user.

Other important work: Kertész et al. (2008) introduced a meta-brokering system in which the meta-broker, invoked through a Web portal, submits jobs, monitors job status and copies output files using brokers from different Grid middleware, such as NorduGrid Broker and EGEE WMS.

Kim and Buyya (2007) tackle the problem of fair-share resource allocation in hierarchical VOs. They provide a model for hierarchical VO environments based on a resource sharing policy; and provide a heuristic solution for fair-share resource allocation in hierarchical VOs.

Inter-Operation of Resource Sharing Networks

Relevant work on the attempts to enable inter-operation between resource sharing networks is discussed in this section.

PlanetLab: PlanetLab (Peterson et al., 2006) is a large-scale testbed that enables the creation of slices, that is, distributed environments based on virtualisation technology. A slice is a set of virtual machines, each running on a unique node. The individual virtual machines that make up a slice contain no information about the other virtual machines in the set and are managed by the service running in the slice. Each service deployed on PlanetLab runs on a slice of PlanetLab's global pool of resources. Multiple slices can run concurrently and each slice is like a network container that isolates services from other containers.

The principals in PlanetLab are:

- **Owner:** organisation that hosts (owns) one or more PlanetLab nodes.
- **User:** researcher who deploys a service on a set of PlanetLab nodes.
- **PlanetLab Consortium (PLC):** centralised trusted intermediary that manages nodes on behalf of a group of owners and creates slices on those nodes on behalf of a group of users.

When PLC acts as a Slice Authority (SA), it maintains the state of the set of system-wide slices for which the PLC is responsible. The SA provides an interface through which users register themselves, create slices, bind users to slices, and request the slice to be instantiated on a set of nodes. PLC, acting as a Management Authority (MA), maintains a server that installs and updates the software running on the nodes it manages and monitors these nodes for correct behavior, taking appropriate action when anomalies and failures are detected. The MA maintains a database of registered nodes. Each node is affiliated with an organization (owner) and is located at a site belonging to the organization. MA provides an interface used by node owners to register their nodes with the PLC and allows users and slices authorities to obtain information about the set of nodes managed by the MA.

PlanetLab's architecture has evolved to enable decentralised control or federations of PlanetLabs (Peterson et al., 2006). The PLC has been split into two components namely the MA and SA, which allow PLC-like entities to evolve these two components independently. Therefore, autonomous organisations can federate and define peering relationships with each other. For example, peering relationships with other infrastructure is one of the goals of PlanetLab Europe (2008). A resource owner may choose a MA to which it wants to provide resources. MAs, in turn, may blacklist particular SAs. A SA may trust only certain MAs to provide it with the virtual machines it needs for its users. This enables various types of agreements between SAs and MAs.

It is also important to mention that Ricci et al. (2006) have discussed issues related to the design of a general resource allocation interface that is sufficiently wide for allocators in a large variety of current and future testbeds. An allocator is a component that receives as input the users' abstract description for the required resources and the resource status from a resource discoverer and produces allocations performed by a deployment service. The goal of an allocator is to allow users to specify characteristics of their slice in high-level terms and find resources to match these requirements. Authors have described their experience in designing PlanetLab and Emulab and among several important issues, they have advocated that:

- In future infrastructures, several allocators may co-exist and it might be difficult for them to co-exist without interfering into one another;
- With the current proportional-share philosophy of PlanetLab, where multiple management services can co-exist, allocators do not have guarantees over any resources;
- Thus, co-ordination between the allocators may be required.

Grid Interoperability Now - Community Group (GIN-CG): GIN-CG (2006) has been working on providing interoperability between Grids by developing components and adapters that enable secure and standard job submissions, data transfers, and information queries. These efforts provide the basis for load management across Grids by facilitating standard job submission and request redirection. They also enable secure access to resources and data across Grids. Although GIN-CG's efforts are relevant, its members also highlight the need for common allocation and brokering of resources across Grids.[2]

InterGrid: Assunção et al. (2008) have proposed an architecture and policies to enable the interoperation of Grids. This set of architecture and policies is termed as the InterGrid. InterGrid is inspired by the peering agreements between Internet Service Providers (ISPs). The Internet is composed of competing ISPs that agree to allow traffic into one another's networks. These agreements between ISPs are commonly termed as peering and transit arrangements (Metz, 2001).

In the InterGrid, a Resource Provider (RP) contributes a share of computational resources, storage resources, networks, application services or other type of resource to a Grid in return for regular payments. An RP has local users whose resource demands need to be satisfied, yet it delegates provisioning rights over spare resources to an InterGrid Gateway (IGG) by providing information about the resources available in the form of free time slots (Assunção & Buyya, 2008). A free time slot includes information about the number of resources available, their configuration and time frame over which they will be available. The control over resource shares offered by providers is performed via a container model, in which the resources are used to run virtual machines. Internally, each Grid may have a resource management system organised in a hierarchical manner. However, for the sake of simplicity, experimental results consider that RPs delegate provisioning rights directly to an IGG (Assunção & Buyya, in press).

A Grid has pre-defined peering arrangements with other Grids, managed by IGGs and, through which they co-ordinate the use of resources of the InterGrid. An IGG is aware of the terms of the peering with other Grids; provides Grid selection capabilities by selecting a suitable Grid able to provide the required resources; and replies to requests from other IGGs. The peering arrangement between two Grids is represented as a contract. Request redirection policies determine which peering Grid is selected to process a request and at what price the processing is performed (Assunção & Buyya, in press).

Other important work: Boghosian et al. (2006) have performed experiments using resources from more than one Grid for three projects, namely Nektar, SPICE and Vortonics. The applications in these three projects require massive numbers of computing resources only achievable through Grids of Grids. Although resources from multiple Grids were used during the experiments, they emphasised that several human interactions and negotiations are required in order to use federated resources. The authors highlighted that even if interoperability at the middleware level existed, it would not guarantee that the federated Grids can be utilised for large-scale distributed applications because there are important additional requirements such as compatible and consistent usage policies, automated advanced reservations and co-scheduling.

Caromel et al. (2007) have proposed the use of a P2P network to acquire resources dynamically from a Grid infrastructure (i.e. Grid'5000) and desktop machines in order to run compute intensive applications. The communication between the P2P network and Grid'5000 is performed through SSH tunnels. Moreover, the allocation of nodes for the P2P network uses the deployment framework of ProActive by deploying Java Virtual Machines on the allocated nodes.

In addition to GIN-CG's efforts, other Grid middleware interoperability approaches have been presented. Wang et al. (2007) have described a gateway approach to achieve interoperability between gLite (2005) (the middleware used in EGEE) and CNGrid GOS (2007) (the middleware of the Chinese National Grid (2007)). The work focuses on job management interoperability, but also describes interoperability between the different protocols used for data management as well as resource information. In the proposed interoperability approach, gLite is viewed as a type of site job manager by GOS, whereas the submission to GOS resources by gLite is implemented in a different manner; an extended job manager is instantiated for each job submitted to a GOS resource. The extended job manager sends the whole batch job to be executed in the CNGrid.

Virtual Organisations

We have also carried out a survey on how projects address different challenges in the VO life-cycle. Two main categories of projects have been identified: the facilitators for VOs, which provide means for building clusters of organisations hence enabling collaboration and formation of VOs; and enablers for VOs, which provide middleware and tools to help in the formation, management, maintenance and dissolution of VOs. The classification is not strict because a project can fall into two categories, providing software for enabling VOs and working as a consortium, which organisations can join and start collaborations that are more dynamic. We divide our survey into three parts: middleware and software infrastructure for enabling VOs; consortiums and charters that facilitate the formation of VOs; and other relevant work that addresses issues related to a VO's life-cycle.

Enabling Technology

Enabling a VO means to provide the required software tools to help in the different phases of the life-cycle of a VO. As we present in this section, due to the complex challenges in the life-cycle, many projects do not address all the phases. We discuss relevant work in this section.

The CONOISE Project: CONOISE (Patel et al., 2005) uses a marketplace (auctions) for the formation of VOs (Norman et al., 2004). The auctions are combinatorial; combinatorial auctions allow a good degree of flexibility so that VO initiators can specify a broad range of requirements. A combinatorial auction allows multiple units of a single item or multiple items to be sold simultaneously. However, combinatorial auctions lack on means for bid representation and efficient clearing algorithms to determine prices, quantities and winners. As demonstrated by Dang (2004), clearing combinatorial auctions is an NP-Complete problem. Thus, polynomial and sub-optimal auction clearing algorithms for combinatorial auctions have been proposed.

Stakeholders in VOs enabled by CONOISE are called agents. As example of VO formation, a user may request a service to an agent, who in turn verifies if it is able to provide the service requested at the time specified. If the agent cannot provide the service, it looks for the Service Providers (SPs) offering the service required. The Requesting Agent (RA) then starts a combinatorial auction and sends call for bids to SPs. Once RA receives the bids, it determines the best set of partners and then, starts the formation of the VO. Once the VO is formed, RA becomes the VO manager.

An agent that receives a call for bids has the following options: (a) she can decide not to bid for the auction; (b) she can bid considering its resources; (c) she may bid using resources from an existing collaboration; (d) she may identify the need to start a new VO to provide the extra resources required. Note that call for bids are recursive. CONOISE uses a cumulative scheduling based on a Constraint Satisfaction Program (CSP) to model the decision process of an agent.

CONOISE also focuses on the operation and maintenance phases of VOs. Once a VO is formed, it uses principles of coalition formation for distributing tasks amongst the member agents (Patel et al., 2005). An algorithm for coalition structure generation, which is bound from the optimal, is presented and evaluated (Dang, 2004). Although not very focused on authorisation issues, the CONOISE project also deals with issues regarding trust and reputation in VOs by providing reputation and policing mechanisms to ensure minimum quality of service.

The TrustCoM Project: TrustCoM (2005) addresses issues related to the establishment of trust throughout the life-cycle of VOs. Its members envision that the establishment of Service Oriented Architectures (SOAs) and the dynamic open electronic marketplaces will allow dynamic alliances and VOs among enterprises to respond quickly to market opportunities. The establishment of trust, not only at a resource level but also at a business process level, is hence of importance. In this light, TrustCoM aims to provide a framework for trust, security and contract management to enable on-demand and self-managed dynamic VOs (Dimitrakos, Golby, & Kearley, 2004; Svirskas, Arevas, Wilson, & Matthews, 2005).

The framework extends current VO membership services (Svirskas et al., 2005) by providing means to: (i) identify potential VO partners through reputation management; (ii) manage users according to the roles defined in the business process models that VO partners perform; (iii) define and manage the SLA obligations on security and privacy; (iv) enable the enforcement of policies based on the SLAs and contracts. From a corporate perspective, Sairamesh et al (2005) provide examples of business models on the enforcement of security policies and the VO management.

While the goal is to enable dynamic VOs, TrustCoM focuses on the security requirements for the establishment of VOs composed of enterprises. Studies and market analysis to identify the main issues and requirements to build a secure environment in which VOs form and operate have been performed.

Facilitators or Breeding Environments

In order to address the problem of trust between organisations, projects have created federations and consortiums which physical organisations or Grids can join to start VOs based on common interests. We describe the main projects in this field and explain some of the technologies they use.

Open Science Grid (OSG): OSG (2005) can be considered as a facilitator for VOs. The reason is that the project aims at forming a cluster or consortium of organisations and suggests them to follow a policy that states how collaboration takes place and how a VO is formed. To join the consortium and consequently form a VO, it is necessary to have a minimum infrastructure and preferably use the middleware suggested by OSG. In addition, OSG provides tools to check the status and monitor existing VOs. OSG facilitates the formation of VOs by providing an open-market-like infrastructure that allows the consortium members to advertise their resources and goals and establish VOs to explore their objectives. The VO concept is used in a recursive manner; VOs may be composed of sub-VOs. For more information we refer to the Blueprint for the OSG (2004).

A basic infrastructure must be provided to form a VO, including a VO Membership Service (VOMS) and operation support. The operation support's main goal is to provide technical support services at the request of a member site. As OSG intends to federate across heterogeneous Grid environments, the resources of the member sites and users are organised in VOs under the contracts that result from negotiations among the sites, which in turn have to follow the consortium's policies. Such contracts are defined at the middleware layer and can be negotiated in an automated fashion; however, thus far there is no easily responsive means to form a VO and the formation requires complex multilateral agreements among the involved sites.

OSG middleware uses VOMS to support authorisation services for VO members hence helping in the maintenance and operation phases. Additionally, for the sake of scalability and easiness of administration, Grid User Management System (GUMS) facilitates the mapping of Grid credentials to site-specific credentials. GUMS and VOMS provide means to facilitate the authorisation in the operation and maintenance phases. GridCat provides maps and statistics on jobs running and storage capacity of the member sites. This information can guide schedulers and brokers on job submission and in turn facilitate the operation phase. Additionally, MonALISA (MONitoring Agents using a Large Integrated Services Architecture) (Legrand et al., 2004) has been utilised to monitor computational nodes, applications and network performance of the VOs within the consortium.

Enabling Grids for E-sciencE (EGEE): Similarly to OSG, EGEE (2005) federates resource centres to enable a global infrastructure for researchers. EGEE's resource centres are hierarchically organised: an Operations Manager Centre (OMC) located at CERN, Regional Operations Centres (ROC) located in different countries, Core Infrastructures Centres (CIC) and Resource Centres (RC) responsible for providing resources to the Grid. A ROC carries out activities as supporting deployment and operations; negotiating SLAs within its region and organising certification authorities. CICs are in charge of providing VO-services, such as maintaining VO-Servers and registration; VO-specific services such as databases, resource brokers and user interfaces; and other activities such as accounting and resource usage. The OMC interfaces with international Grid efforts. It is also responsible for activities such as approving connection with new RCs, promoting cross-trust among CAs, and enabling cooperation and agreements with user communities, VOs and existing national and regional infrastructures.

To join EGEE, in addition to the installation of the Grid middleware, there is a need for a formal request and further assessment from special committees. Once the application is considered suitable to EGEE, a VO will be formed. Accounting is based on the use of resources by members of the VO. EGEE currently utilises LCG-2/gLite (2005).

Other Important Work

Resource allocation in a VO depends on, and is driven by, many conditions and rules: the VO can be formed by physical organisations under different, sometimes conflicting, resource usage policies. Participating organisations provide their resources to the VO, which can be defined in terms of SLAs, and agree to enforce VO level policies defining who has access to the resources in the VO. Different models can be adopted for negotiation and enforcement of SLAs. One model is by relying on a trusted VO manager. Resource providers supply resources to the VO according to SLAs established with the VO manager. The VO manager in turn assigns resource quotas to VO groups and users based on a commonly agreed VO-level policy. In contrast, a VO can follow a democratic or P2P sharing approach, in which "you give what you can and get what others can offer" or "you get what give" (Wasson & Humphrey, 2003).

Elmroth and Gardfj¨all (2005) presented an approach for enabling Grid-wide fair-share scheduling. The work introduces a scheduling framework that enforces fair-share policies in a Grid-wide scale. The policies are hierarchical in the sense that they can be subdivided recursively to form a tree of shares. Although the policies are hierarchical, they are enforced in a flat and decentralised manner. In the proposed framework, resources have local policies and split the available resources to given VOs. These local policies have references to the VO-level policies. Although the proposed framework and algorithm do not require a centralised scheduler, it may impose certain overhead in locally caching global usage information.

MAPPING OF SURVEYED WORK AGAINST THE TAXONOMIES

This section presents the mapping of the surveyed projects against the proposed taxonomies. For simplicity, the mapping only considers selected work from those surveyed to be included in the tables presented in this section.

Table 1 classifies existing work according to their architectures and operational models. Gridbus Broker, GridWay, and SNAP-based community resource broker are resource brokers that act on behalf of users to submit jobs to Grid resources to which they have access. They follow the operational model based on job routing. Although GridWay provides means for the deployment of virtual machines, this deployment takes place on a job basis (Rubio-Montero et al., 2007). DI-GRUBER, VioCluster, Condor flocking and CSF have a distributed-scheduler architecture in which brokers or meta-schedulers have bilateral sharing agreements between them (Table 2). OurGrid and Self-organising flock of Condors utilise P2P networks of brokers or schedulers, whereas Grid federation uses a P2P network to build a shared space utilised by providers and users to post resource claims and requests respectively (Table 2). VioCluster and Shirako enable the creation of virtualised environments in which job routing or job pulling based systems can be deployed. However, in these last two systems, resources are controlled at the level of containment or virtual machines.

Table 2 summarises the communication models and sharing mechanisms utilised by distributed-scheduler based systems. Shirako uses transitive agreements in which brokers can exchange claims of resources issued by site authorities who represent the resource providers. It allows brokers to delegate access to resources multiple times.

The resource control techniques employed by the surveyed systems are summarised in Table 3. As described beforehand, VioCluster and Shirako use containment based resource control, whereas the remaining systems utilise the job model. EGEE WMS and DI-GRUBER take into account the scheduling of jobs according to the VOs to which users belong and the shares contributed by resource providers. The other systems can be utilised to form a single VO wherein jobs can be controlled on a user basis.

The support of various works to the VO life-cycle phases is depicted in Table 4. We select a subset of the surveyed work, particularly the work that focuses on VO related issues such as their formation and operation. DI-GRUBER and gLite schedule jobs by considering the resource shares of multiple VOs. EGEE and OSG also work as facilitators of VOs by providing consortiums to which organisations can join and start VOs (Table 5). However, the process is not automated and requires the establishment of contracts between the consortium and the physical resource providers. Shirako enables the creation of virtualised environments spanning multiple providers, which can be used for hosting multiple VOs (Ramakrishnan et al., 2006).

The systems characteristics and the VOs they enable are summarised in Table 5. Conoise and Akogrimo allow the formation of dynamic VOs in which the VO can be started by a user utilising a mobile

Table 1. GRMSs according to architectures and operational models

System	Architecture	Operational Model
SGE and PBS	Independent clusters	Job routing
Condor-G	Independent clusters*	Job routing
Gridbus Broker	Resource Broker	Job routing
GridWay	Resource Broker	Job routing**
SNAP-Based Community Resource Broker	Resource Broker	Job routing
EGEE WMS	Centralised	Job routing
KOALA	Centralised	Job routing
PlanetLab	Centralised	N/A***
Computing Center Software (CCS)	Hierarchical	Job routing
GRUBER/DI-GRUBER	Distributed/static	Job routing
VioCluster	Distributed/static	N/A***
Condor flocking	Distributed/static	Matchmaking
Community Scheduler Framework	Distributed/static	Job routing
OurGrid	Distributed/dynamic	Job routing
Self-organising flock of Condors	Distributed/dynamic	Matchmaking
Grid federation	Distributed/dynamic	Job routing
Askalon	Distributed/dynamic	Job routing
SHARP/Shirako	Distributed/dynamic	N/A***
Delegated Matchmaking	Hybrid	Matchmaking

*	Condor-G provides software that can be used to build meta-schedulers.
**	GridWay also manages the deployment of virtual machines.
***	PlanetLab, VioCluster and Shirako use resource control at the containment level, even though they enable the creation of virtual execution environments on which systems based on job routing can be deployed.

Table 2. Classification of GRMSs according to their sharing arrangements

System	Communication Pattern	Sharing Mechanism
GRUBER/DI-GRUBER	Bilateral agreements	System centric
VioCluster	Bilateral agreements	Site centric
Condor flocking	Bilateral agreements	Site centric
OurGrid	P2P network	System centric
Self-organising flock of Condors	P2P network	Site centric
Grid federation	Shared space	Site centric
Askalon	Bilateral agreements	Site centric
SHARP/Shirako	Transitive agreements	Self-interest
Delegated MatchMaking	Bilateral agreements	Site centric

Table 3. Classification of GRMSs according to their support for VOs and resource control

System	Support for VOs	Resource Control
EGEE WMS	Multiple VO	Job model
KOALA	Single VO	Job model
GRUBER/DI-GRUBER	Multiple VO	Job model
VioCluster	Single VO	Container model/multiple site*
Condor flocking	Single VO	Job model
OurGrid	Single VO	Job model
Self-organising flock of Condors	Single VO	Job model
Grid federation	Single VO	Job model
Askalon	Single VO	Job model
SHARP/Shirako	Multiple VO**	Container model/multiple site***
Delegated MatchMaking	Single VO	Job model

*	VioCluster supports containment at both single site and multiple site levels.
**	Shirako enables the creation of multiple containers that can in turn be used by multiple VOs, even though it does not handle issues on job scheduling amongst multiple VOs.
***	Shirako supports containment at both (i) single site level through Cluster on Demand and (ii) multiple-site level. Shirako also explores resource control at job level by providing recommendations on the site in which jobs should be executed.

Table 4. Support to the phases of the VO's lifecycle by the projects analysed

Project Name	Support to the phases of the VO life-cycle				Support for short term collaborations
	Creation	Operation	Maintenance	Dissolution	
OSG*	Partial	Partial	Not available	Not available	Not available
EGEE/gLite*	Partial	Available	Not available	Not available	Not available
CONOISE	Available	Available	Available	Not available	Available
TrustCoM	Mainly related to security issues	Mainly related to security issues	Not available	Not available	Not available
DI-GRUBER	Not available	Available	Partial**	Not available	Not available
Akogrimo***	Partial	Partial	Partial	Partial	Partial
Shirako	Not available	Available	Available	Not available	Not available

*	OSG and EGEE work as consortiums enabling trust among organisations and facilitating the formation of VOs. They also provide tools for monitoring status of resources and job submissions. EGEE's WMS performs the scheduling taking into account multiple VOs.
**	DI-GRUPER's policy decision points allow for the re-adjustment of the VOs according to the current resource shares offered by providers and the status of the Grid.
***	Akogrimo aims at enabling collaboration between doctors upon the patient's request or in case of a health emergency.

Table 5. Mapping of the systems against the propsed VO taxonomies

System	Dynamism	Goal Orientation	Duration	Control	Policy Enforcement	Facilitators
Conoise*	Dynamic/Hybrid	Targeted	Medium-lived	Decentralised	Democratic	N/A
TrustCoM**	Static	Targeted	Long-lived	N/A	N/A	N/A
GRUBER/DI-GRUBER	Static	Targeted	Long-lived	Decentralised	Decentralised***	N/A
gLite/EGEE	Static	Targeted	Long-lived	Centralised	Centralised	Centralised+
Open Science Grid	Static	Targeted	Long-lived	Hierarchical	Centralised	Market-like
Akogrimo	Dynamic/Hybrid	Targeted	Short or Medium-lived	Decentralised	Democratic	N/A
Shirako	Dynamic	Non-targeted	Medium-lived	Decentralised	Democratic	N/A

*	Conoise and Akogrimo allow a client using a mobile device to start a VO, thus the VO can comprise fixed and mobile resources.
**	TrustCoM deals with security issues and does not provide tools for the management and policy enforcement in VOs.
***	DI-GRUBER uses a network of decision points to guide submitting hosts and schedulers about which resources can execute the jobs.
+	EGEE Workload Management System is aware of the VOs and schedules jobs accordingly to the VOs in the system.

device. The virtual environments enabled by Shirako can be adapted by leasing additional resources or terminating leases according to the demands of the virtual organisation it is hosting (Ramakrishnan et al., 2006). Resource providers in Shirako may offer their resources in return for economic compensation meaning that the resource providers may not have a common target in solving a particular resource challenge. This makes the VOs non-targeted.

FUTURE TRENDS

Over the last decade, the distributed computing realm has been characterised by the deployment of large-scale Grids such as EGEE and TeraGrid. Such Grids have provided the research community with an unprecedented number of resources, which have been used for various scientific research. However, the hardware and software heterogeneity of the resources provided by the organisations within a Grid have increased the complexity of deploying applications in these environments. Recently, application deployment has been facilitated by the intensifying use of virtualisation technologies.

The increasing ubiquity of virtual machine technologies has enabled the creation of customised environments atop a physical infrastructure and the emergence of new business models such as virtualised data centres and cloud computing. The use of virtual machines brings several benefits such as: server consolidation, the ability to create VMs to run legacy code without interfering in other applications' APIs, improved security through the creation of application sandboxes, dynamic provisioning of virtual machines to services, and performance isolation.

Existing virtual-machine based resource management systems can manage a cluster of computers within a site allowing the creation of virtual workspaces (Keahey et al., 2006) or virtual clusters (Foster et al., 2006; Montero et al., 2008; Chase et al., 2003). They can bind resources to virtual clusters or workspaces according to a customer's demand. These resource managers allow the user to create customised virtual clusters using shares of the physical machines available at the site. In addition, current data centres are using virtualisation technology to provide users with the look and feel of taping into a dedicated computing and storage infrastructure for which they are charged a fee based on usage (e.g. Amazon Elastic Computing Cloud[3] and 3Tera[4]).

These factors are resulting in the creation of virtual execution environments or slices that span both commercial and academic computing sites. Virtualisation technologies minimise many of the concerns that previously prevented the peering of resource sharing networks, such as the execution of unknown applications and the lack of guarantees over resource control. For the resource provider, substantial work is being carried out on the provisioning of resources to services and user applications. Techniques such as workload forecasts along with resource overbooking can reduce the need for over-provisioning a computing infrastructure. Users can benefit from the improved reliability, the performance isolation, and the environment isolation offered by virtualisation technologies.

We are likely to see an increase in the number of virtual organisations enabled by virtual machines, thus allocating resources from both commercial data centres and research testbeds. We suggest that emerging applications will require the prompt formation of VOs, which are also quickly responsive and automated. VOs can have dynamic resource demands, which are quickly responded by data centres relying on virtualisation technologies. There can also be an increase in business workflows relying on globally available messaging based systems for process synchronisation[5]. Our current research focuses on connecting computing sites managed by virtualisation technologies for creating distributed virtual environments which are used by the user applications.

CONCLUSION

This chapter presents classifications and a survey of systems that can provide means for inter-operating resource sharing networks. It also provides taxonomies on Virtual Organisations (VOs) with a focus on Grid computing practices. Hence, we initially discussed the challenges in VOs and presented a background on the life-cycle of VOs and on resource sharing networks. This chapter suggests that future applications will require the prompt formation of VOs, which are also quickly responsive and automated. This may be enabled by virtualisation technology and corroborates the current trends on multiple site containers or virtual workspaces. Relevant work and technology in the area were presented and discussed.

ACKNOWLEDGMENT

We thank Marco Netto, Alexandre di Costanzo and Chee Shin Yeo for sharing their thoughts on the topic and helping in improving the structure of this chapter. We are grateful to Mukaddim Pathan for proof reading a preliminary version of this chapter. This work is supported by research grants from the Australian Research Council (ARC) and Australian Department of Innovation, Industry, Science and Research (DIISR). Marcos' PhD research is partially supported by NICTA.

REFERENCES

A Blueprint for the Open Science Grids. (2004, December). Snapshot v0.9.

Adabala, S., Chadha, V., Chawla, P., Figueiredo, R., Fortes, J., & Krsul, I. (2005, June). From virtualized resources to virtual computing Grids: the In-VIGO system. *Future Generation Computer Systems*, *21*(6), 896–909. doi:10.1016/j.future.2003.12.021

Andrade, N., Brasileiro, F., Cirne, W., & Mowbray, M. (2007). Automatic Grid assembly by promoting collaboration in peer-to-peer Grids. *Journal of Parallel and Distributed Computing*, *67*(8), 957–966. doi:10.1016/j.jpdc.2007.04.011

Andrade, N., Cirne, W., Brasileiro, F., & Roisenberg, P. (2003). OurGrid: An approach to easily assemble Grids with equitable resource sharing. In *9th Workshop on Job Scheduling Strategies for Parallel Processing* (Vol. 2862, pp. 61–86). Berlin/Heidelberg: Springer.

Australian Partnership for Advanced Computing (APAC) Grid. (2005). Retrieved from http://www.apac.edu.au/programs/GRID/index.html.

Balazinska, M., Balakrishnan, H., & Stonebraker, M. (2004, March). Contract-based load management in federated distributed systems. In *1st Symposium on Networked Systems Design and Implementation (NSDI)* (pp. 197-210). San Francisco: USENIX Association.

Barham, P., Dragovic, B., Fraser, K., Hand, S., Harris, T., Ho, A., et al. (2003). Xen and the art of virtualization. In *19th ACM Symposium on Operating Systems Principles (SOSP '03)* (pp. 164–177). New York: ACM Press.

Boghosian, B., Coveney, P., Dong, S., Finn, L., Jha, S., Karniadakis, G. E., et al. (2006, June). Nektar, SPICE and vortonics: Using federated Grids for large scale scientific applications. In *IEEE Workshop on Challenges of Large Applications in Distributed Environments (CLADE)*. Paris: IEEE Computing Society.

Brune, M., Gehring, J., Keller, A., & Reinefeld, A. (1999). Managing clusters of geographically distributed high-performance computers. *Concurrency (Chichester, England)*, *11*(15), 887–911. doi:10.1002/(SICI)1096-9128(19991225)11:15<887::AID-CPE459>3.0.CO;2-J

Bulhões, P. T., Byun, C., Castrapel, R., & Hassaine, O. (2004, May). *N1 Grid Engine 6 Features and Capabilities* [White Paper]. Phoenix, AZ: Sun Microsystems.

Butt, A. R., Zhang, R., & Hu, Y. C. (2003). A self-organizing flock of condors. In *2003 ACM/IEEE Conference on Supercomputing (SC 2003)* (p. 42). Washington, DC: IEEE Computer Society.

Buyya, R., Abramson, D., & Giddy, J. (2000, June). An economy driven resource management architecture for global computational power grids. In *7th International Conference on Parallel and Distributed Processing Techniques and Applications (PDPTA 2000)*. Las Vegas, AZ: CSREA Press.

Caromel, D., di Costanzo, A., & Mathieu, C. (2007). Peer-to-peer for computational Grids: Mixing clusters and desktop machines. *Parallel Computing*, *33*(4–5), 275–288. doi:10.1016/j.parco.2007.02.011

Catlett, C., Beckman, P., Skow, D., & Foster, I. (2006, May). Creating and operating national-scale cyberinfrastructure services. *Cyberinfrastructure Technology Watch Quarterly*, *2*(2), 2–10.

Chase, J. S., Irwin, D. E., Grit, L. E., Moore, J. D., & Sprenkle, S. E. (2003). Dynamic virtual clusters in a Grid site manager. In *12th IEEE International Symposium on High Performance Distributed Computing (HPDC 2003)* (p. 90). Washington, DC: IEEE Computer Society.

Chinese National Grid (CNGrid) Project Web Site. (2007). Retrieved from http://www.cngrid.org/

CNGrid GOS Project Web site. *(2007).* Retrieved from http://vega.ict.ac.cn

Dang, V. D. (2004). *Coalition Formation and Operation in Virtual Organisations.* PhD thesis, Faculty of Engineering, Science and Mathematics, School of Electronics and Computer Science, University of Southampton, Southampton, UK.

de Assunção, M. D., & Buyya, R. (2008, December). Performance analysis of multiple site resource provisioning: Effects of the precision of availability information [Technical Report]. In *International Conference on High Performance Computing (HiPC 2008)* (Vol. 5374, pp. 157–168). Berlin/Heidelberg: Springer.

de Assunção, M. D., & Buyya, R. (in press). Performance analysis of allocation policies for interGrid resource provisioning. *Information and Software Technology*.

de Assunção, M. D., Buyya, R., & Venugopal, S. (2008, June). InterGrid: A case for internetworking islands of Grids. [CCPE]. *Concurrency and Computation*, *20*(8), 997–1024. doi:10.1002/cpe.1249

Dimitrakos, T., Golby, D., & Kearley, P. (2004, October). Towards a trust and contract management framework for dynamic virtual organisations. In *eChallenges*. Vienna, Austria.

Dixon, C., Bragin, T., Krishnamurthy, A., & Anderson, T. (2006, September). Tit-for-Tat Distributed Resource Allocation [Poster]. *The ACM SIGCOMM 2006 Conference*.

Dumitrescu, C., & Foster, I. (2004). Usage policy-based CPU sharing in virtual organizations. In *5th IEEE/ACM International Workshop on Grid Computing (Grid 2004)* (pp. 53–60). Washington, DC: IEEE Computer Society.

Dumitrescu, C., & Foster, I. (2005, August). GRUBER: A Grid resource usage SLA broker. In J. C. Cunha & P. D. Medeiros (Eds.), *Euro-Par 2005* (Vol. 3648, pp. 465–474). Berlin/Heidelberg: Springer.

Dumitrescu, C., Raicu, I., & Foster, I. (2005). DI-GRUBER: A distributed approach to Grid resource brokering. In *2005 ACM/IEEE Conference on Supercomputing (SC 2005)* (p. 38). Washington, DC: IEEE Computer Society.

Dumitrescu, C., Wilde, M., & Foster, I. (2005, June). A model for usage policy-based resource allocation in Grids. In *6th IEEE International Workshop on Policies for Distributed Systems and Networks* (pp. 191–200). Washington, DC: IEEE Computer Society.

Elmroth, E., & Gardfjäll, P. (2005, December). Design and evaluation of a decentralized system for Grid-wide fairshare scheduling. In *1st IEEE International Conference on e-Science and Grid Computing* (pp. 221–229). Melbourne, Australia: IEEE Computer Society Press.

Enabling Grids for E-sciencE (EGEE) project. (2005). Retrieved from http://public.eu-egee.org.

Epema, D. H. J., Livny, M., van Dantzig, R., Evers, X., & Pruyne, J. (1996). A worldwide flock of condors: Load sharing among workstation clusters. *Future Generation Computer Systems*, *12*(1), 53–65. doi:10.1016/0167-739X(95)00035-Q

Fontán, J., Vázquez, T., Gonzalez, L., Montero, R. S., & Llorente, I. M. (2008, May). OpenNEbula: The open source virtual machine manager for cluster computing. In *Open Source Grid and Cluster Software Conference – Book of Abstracts*. San Francisco.

Foster, I., Freeman, T., Keahey, K., Scheftner, D., Sotomayor, B., & Zhang, X. (2006, May). Virtual clusters for Grid communities. In *6th IEEE International Symposium on Cluster Computing and the Grid (CCGRID 2006)* (pp. 513–520). Washington, DC: IEEE Computer Society.

Foster, I., & Kesselman, C. (1997, Summer). Globus: A metacomputing infrastructure toolkit. *The International Journal of Supercomputer Applications*, *11*(2), 115–128.

Foster, I., Kesselman, C., & Tuecke, S. (2001). The anatomy of the Grid: Enabling scalable virtual organizations. *The International Journal of Supercomputer Applications*, *15*(3), 200–222.

Frey, J., Tannenbaum, T., Livny, M., Foster, I. T., & Tuecke, S. (2001, August). Condor-G: A computation management agent for multi-institutional Grids. In *10th IEEE International Symposium on High Performance Distributed Computing (HPDC 2001)* (pp. 55–63). San Francisco: IEEE Computer Society.

Fu, Y., Chase, J., Chun, B., Schwab, S., & Vahdat, A. (2003). SHARP: An architecture for secure resource peering. In *19th ACM Symposium on Operating Systems Principles (SOSP 2003)* (pp. 133–148). New York: ACM Press.

gLite - Lightweight Middleware for Grid Computing. (2005). Retrieved from http://glite.web.cern.ch/glite.

Graupner, S., Kotov, V., Andrzejak, A., & Trinks, H. (2002, August). *Control Architecture for Service Grids in a Federation of Utility Data Centers* (Technical Report No. HPL-2002-235). Palo Alto, CA: HP Laboratories Palo Alto.

Grid Interoperability Now Community Group (GIN-CG). (2006). Retrieved from http://forge.ogf.org/sf/projects/gin.

Grimme, C., Lepping, J., & Papaspyrou, A. (2008, April). Prospects of collaboration between compute providers by means of job interchange. In *Job Scheduling Strategies for Parallel Processing* (Vol. 4942, p. 132-151). Berlin / Heidelberg: Springer.

Grit, L. E. (2005, October). *Broker Architectures for Service-Oriented Systems* [Technical Report]. Durham, NC: Department of Computer Science, Duke University.

Grit, L. E. (2007). *Extensible Resource Management for Networked Virtual Computing.* PhD thesis, Department of Computer Science, Duke University, Durham, NC. (Adviser: Jeffrey S. Chase)

Haji, M. H., Gourlay, I., Djemame, K., & Dew, P. M. (2005). A SNAP-based community resource broker using a three-phase commit protocol: A performance study. *The Computer Journal, 48*(3), 333–346. doi:10.1093/comjnl/bxh088

Hey, T., & Trefethen, A. E. (2002). The UK e-science core programme and the Grid. *Future Generation Computer Systems, 18*(8), 1017–1031. doi:10.1016/S0167-739X(02)00082-1

Huang, R., Casanova, H., & Chien, A. A. (2006, April). Using virtual Grids to simplify application scheduling. In *20th International Parallel and Distributed Processing Symposium (IPDPS 2006)*. Rhodes Island, Greece: IEEE.

Huedo, E., Montero, R. S., & Llorente, I. M. (2004). A framework for adaptive execution in Grids. *Software, Practice & Experience, 34*(7), 631–651. doi:10.1002/spe.584

Iosup, A., Epema, D. H. J., Tannenbaum, T., Farrellee, M., & Livny, M. (2007, November). Inter-operating Grids through delegated matchmaking. In *2007 ACM/IEEE Conference on Supercomputing (SC 2007)* (pp. 1–12). New York: ACM Press.

Irwin, D., Chase, J., Grit, L., Yumerefendi, A., Becker, D., & Yocum, K. G. (2006, June). Sharing networked resources with brokered leases. In *USENIX Annual Technical Conference* (pp. 199–212). Berkeley, CA: USENIX Association.

Katzy, B., Zhang, C., & Löh, H. (2005). Virtual organizations: Systems and practices. In L. M. Camarinha-Matos, H. Afsarmanesh, & M. Ollus (Eds.), (p. 45-58). New York: Springer Science+Business Media, Inc.

Keahey, K., Foster, I., Freeman, T., & Zhang, X. (2006). Virtual workspaces: Achieving quality of service and quality of life in the Grids. *Science Progress, 13*(4), 265–275.

Kertész, A., Farkas, Z., Kacsuk, P., & Kiss, T. (2008, April). Grid enabled remote instrumentation. In F. Davoli, N. Meyer, R. Pugliese, & S. Zappatore (Eds.), *2nd International Workshop on Distributed Cooperative Laboratories: Instrumenting the Grid (INGRID 2007)* (pp. 303–312). New York: Springer US.

Kim, K. H., & Buyya, R. (2007, September). Fair resource sharing in hierarchical virtual organizations for global Grids. In *8th IEEE/ACM International Conference on Grid Computing (Grid 2007)* (pp. 50–57). Austin, TX: IEEE.

Legrand, I., Newman, H., Voicu, R., Cirstoiu, C., Grigoras, C., Toarta, M., et al. (2004, September-October). Monalisa: An agent based, dynamic service system to monitor, control and optimize Grid based applications. In *Computing in High Energy and Nuclear Physics (CHEP)*, Interlaken, Switzerland.

Litzkow, M. J., Livny, M., & Mutka, M. W. (1988, June). Condor – a hunter of idle workstations. In *8th International Conference of Distributed Computing Systems* (pp. 104–111). San Jose, CA: Computer Society.

Metz, C. (2001). Interconnecting ISP networks. *IEEE Internet Computing, 5*(2), 74–80. doi:10.1109/4236.914650

Mohamed, H., & Epema, D. (in press). KOALA: A co-allocating Grid scheduler. *Concurrency and Computation.*

Montero, R. S., Huedo, E., & Llorente, I. M. (2008, September/October). Dynamic deployment of custom execution environments in Grids. In *2nd International Conference on Advanced Engineering Computing and Applications in Sciences (ADVCOMP '08)* (pp. 33–38). Valencia, Spain: IEEE Computer Society.

National e-Science Centre. (2005). Retrieved from http://www.nesc.ac.uk.

Norman, T. J., Preece, A., Chalmers, S., Jennings, N. R., Luck, M., & Dang, V. D. (2004). Agent-based formation of virtual organisations. *Knowledge-Based Systems, 17*, 103–111. doi:10.1016/j.knosys.2004.03.005

Open Science Grid. (2005). Retrieved from http://www.opensciencegrid.org

Open Source Metascheduling for Virtual Organizations with the Community Scheduler Framework (CSF) (Tech. Rep.) (2003, August). Ontario, Canada: Platform Computing.

OpenPBS. *The portable batch system software.* (2005). Veridian Systems, Inc., Mountain View, CA. Retrieved from http://www.openpbs.org/scheduler.html

Padala, P., Shin, K. G., Zhu, X., Uysal, M., Wang, Z., Singhal, S., et al. (2007, March). Adaptive control of virtualized resources in utility computing environments. In *2007 Conference on EuroSys (EuroSys 2007)* (pp. 289-302). Lisbon, Portugal: ACM Press.

Patel, J., Teacy, L. W. T., Jennings, N. R., Luck, M., Chalmers, S., & Oren, N. (2005). Agent-based virtual organisations for the Grids. *International Journal of Multi-Agent and Grid Systems, 1*(4), 237–249.

Peterson, L., Muir, S., Roscoe, T., & Klingaman, A. (2006, May). *PlanetLab Architecture: An Overview* (Tech. Rep. No. PDN-06-031). Princeton, NJ: PlanetLab Consortium.

PlanetLab Europe. (2008). Retrieved from http://www.planet-lab.eu/.

Ramakrishnan, L., Irwin, D., Grit, L., Yumerefendi, A., Iamnitchi, A., & Chase, J. (2006). Toward a doctrine of containment: Grid hosting with adaptive resource control. In *2006 ACM/IEEE Conference on Supercomputing (SC 2006)* (p. 101). New York: ACM Press.

Ranjan, R., Buyya, R., & Harwood, A. (2005, September). A case for cooperative and incentive-based coupling of distributed clusters. In *7th IEEE International Conference on Cluster Computing*. Boston, MA: IEEE CS Press.

Ranjan, R., Harwood, A., & Buyya, R. (2006, September). SLA-based coordinated superscheduling scheme for computational Grids. In *IEEE International Conference on Cluster Computing (Cluster 2006)* (pp. 1–8). Barcelona, Spain: IEEE.

Ranjan, R., Rahman, M., & Buyya, R. (2008, May). A decentralized and cooperative workflow scheduling algorithm. In *8th IEEE International Symposium on Cluster Computing and the Grid (CCGRID 2008)*. Lyon, France: IEEE Computer Society.

Ricci, R., Oppenheimer, D., Lepreau, J., & Vahdat, A. (2006, January). Lessons from resource allocators for large-scale multiuser testbeds. *SIGOPS Operating Systems Review, 40*(1), 25–32. doi:10.1145/1113361.1113369

Rubio-Montero, A., Huedo, E., Montero, R., & Llorente, I. (2007, March). Management of virtual machines on globus Grids using GridWay. In *IEEE International Parallel and Distributed Processing Symposium (IPDPS 2007)* (pp. 1–7). Long Beach, USA: IEEE Computer Society.

Ruth, P., Jiang, X., Xu, D., & Goasguen, S. (2005, May). Virtual distributed environments in a shared infrastructure. *IEEE Computer*, *38*(5), 63–69.

Ruth, P., McGachey, P., & Xu, D. (2005, September). VioCluster: Virtualization for dynamic computational domain. In *IEEE International on Cluster Computing (Cluster 2005)* (pp. 1–10). Burlington, MA: IEEE.

Ruth, P., Rhee, J., Xu, D., Kennell, R., & Goasguen, S. (2006, June). Autonomic live adaptation of virtual computational environments in a multi-domain infrastructure. In *3rd IEEE International Conference on Autonomic Computing (ICAC 2006)* (pp. 5-14). Dublin, Ireland: IEEE.

Sairamesh, J., Stanbridge, P., Ausio, J., Keser, C., & Karabulut, Y. (2005, March). *Business Models for Virtual Organization Management and Interoperability* (Deliverable A - WP8&15 WP - Business & Economic Models No. V.1.5). Deliverable document 01945 prepared for TrustCom and the European Commission.

Schwiegelshohn, U., & Yahyapour, R. (1999). Resource allocation and scheduling in metasystems. In *7th International Conference on High-Performance Computing and Networking (HPCN Europe '99)* (pp. 851–860). London, UK: Springer-Verlag.

Shoykhet, A., Lange, J., & Dinda, P. (2004, July). *Virtuoso: A System For Virtual Machine Marketplaces* [Technical Report No. NWU-CS-04-39]. Evanston/Chicago: Electrical Engineering and Computer Science Department, Northwestern University.

Siddiqui, M., Villazón, A., & Fahringer, T. (2006). Grid capacity planning with negotiation-based advance reservation for optimized QoS. In *2006 ACM/IEEE Conference on Supercomputing (SC 2006)* (pp. 21–21). New York: ACM.

Smarr, L., & Catlett, C. E. (1992, June). Metacomputing. *Communications of the ACM*, *35*(6), 44–52. doi:10.1145/129888.129890

Svirskas, A., Arevas, A., Wilson, M., & Matthews, B. (2005, October). Secure and trusted virtual organization management. *ERCIM News* (63).

The TrustCoM Project. (2005). Retrieved from http://www.eu-trustcom.com.

Vázquez-Poletti, J. L., Huedo, E., Montero, R. S., & Llorente, I. M. (2007). A comparison between two grid scheduling philosophies: EGEE WMS and Grid Way. *Multiagent and Grid Systems*, *3*(4), 429–439.

Venugopal, S., Nadiminti, K., Gibbins, H., & Buyya, R. (2008). Designing a resource broker for heterogeneous Grids. *Software, Practice & Experience*, *38*(8), 793–825. doi:10.1002/spe.849

Wang, Y., Scardaci, D., Yan, B., & Huang, Y. (2007). Interconnect EGEE and CNGRID e-infrastructures through interoperability between gLite and GOS middlewares. In *International Grid Interoperability and Interoperation Workshop (IGIIW 2007) with e-Science 2007* (pp. 553–560). Bangalore, India: IEEE Computer Society.

Wasson, G., & Humphrey, M. (2003). Policy and enforcement in virtual organizations. In *4th International Workshop on Grid Computing* (pp. 125–132). Washington, DC: IEEE Computer Society.

Wesner, S., Dimitrakos, T., & Jeffrey, K. (2004, October). Akogrimo - the Grid goes mobile. *ERCIM News,* (59), 32-33.

ENDNOTES

1. http://www.vmware.com/
2. The personal communication amongst GIN-CG members is online at: http://www.ogf.org/pipermail/gin-ops/2007-July/000142.html
3. http://aws.amazon.com/ec2/
4. http://www.3tera.com/
5. http://aws.amazon.com/sqs/

Section 6
Optimization Techniques

Chapter 24
Simultaneous MultiThreading Microarchitecture

Chen Liu
Florida International University, USA

Xiaobin Li
Intel® Corporation, USA

Shaoshan Liu
University of California, Irvine, USA

Jean-Luc Gaudiot
University of California, Irvine, USA

ABSTRACT

Due to the conventional sequential programming model, the Instruction-Level Parallelism (ILP) that modern superscalar processors can explore is inherently limited. Hence, multithreading architectures have been proposed to exploit Thread-Level Parallelism (TLP) in addition to conventional ILP. By issuing and executing instructions from multiple threads at each clock cycle, Simultaneous MultiThreading (SMT) achieves some of the best possible system resource utilization and accordingly higher instruction throughput. In this chapter, the authors describe the origin of SMT microarchitecture, comparing it with other multithreading microarchitectures. They identify several key aspects for high-performance SMT design: fetch policy, handling long-latency instructions, resource sharing control, synchronization and communication. They also describe some potential benefits of SMT microarchitecture: SMT for fault-tolerance and SMT for secure communications. Given the need to support sequential legacy code and emerge of new parallel programming model, we believe SMT microarchitecture will play a vital role as we enter the multi-thread multi/many-core processor design era.

INTRODUCTION

Ever since the first integrated circuits (IC) were independently invented by Jack Kilby (Nobel Prize Laureate in Physics in 2000) from Texas Instruments and Robert Noyce (co-founder of Intel®) around 50 years ago, we have witnessed an exponential growth of the whole semiconductor industry.

DOI: 10.4018/978-1-60566-661-7.ch024

Figure 1. Moore's Law: Transistor count increase

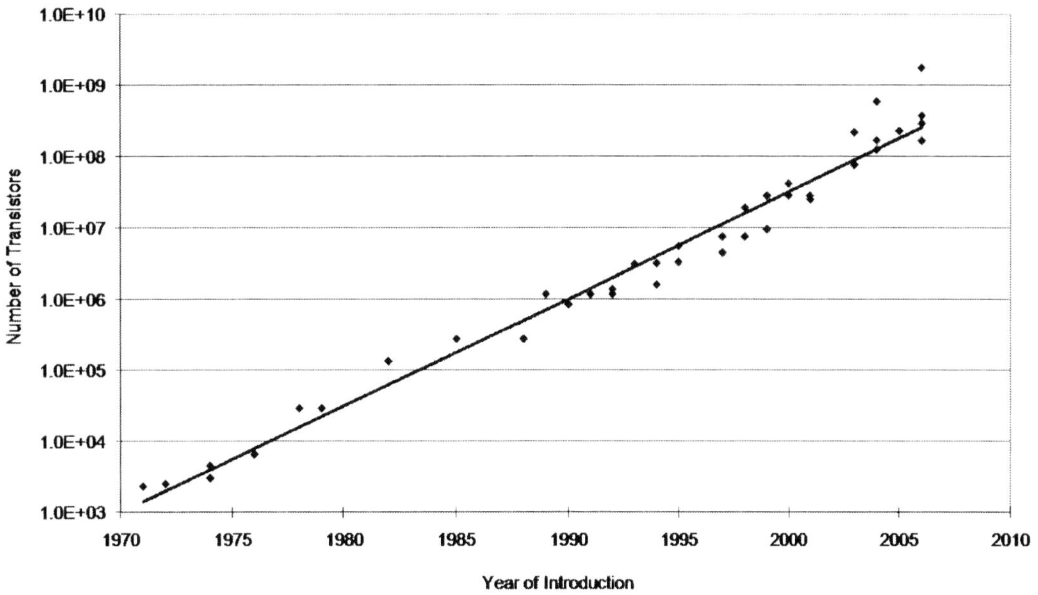

Moore's Law and Memory Wall

The semiconductor industry has been driven by Moore's law (Moore, 1965) for about 40 years with the continuing advancements in VLSI technology. Moore's law states that the number of transistors on a single chip doubles every TWO years, as shown in Figure 1[1], which is based on data from both Intel® and AMD. A corollary of Moore's law states that the feature size of chip manufacturing technology keeps decreasing at the rate of one half approximately every FIVE years (a quarter every two years), based on our observation shown in Figure 2.

As the number of transistors on a chip grows exponentially, we have reached the point where we could have more than one billion transistors on a single chip. For example, the Dual-Core Itanium® 2 from Intel® integrates more than 1.7 billion transistors (Intel, 2006). How to efficiently utilize this huge amount of transistor estate is a challenging task which has recently preoccupied many researchers and system architects from both academia and industry.

Processor and memory integration technologies both follow Moore's law. Memory latency, however, is drastically increasing relatively to the processor speed. This is often referred to as the "Memory Wall" problem (Hennessy, 2006). Indeed, Figure 3 shows that CPU performance increases at an average rate of 55% per year, while the memory performance increases at a much lower 7% per year average rate. There is no sign this gap will be remedied in the near future. Even though the processor speed is continuously increasing, and processors can handle increasing numbers of instructions in one clock cycle, however, we will continue experiencing considerable performance degradation each time we need to access the memory. Pipeline stalls will occur when the data does not arrive soon enough after it has been requested from the memory.

Figure 2. Moore's Law: Feature size decrease

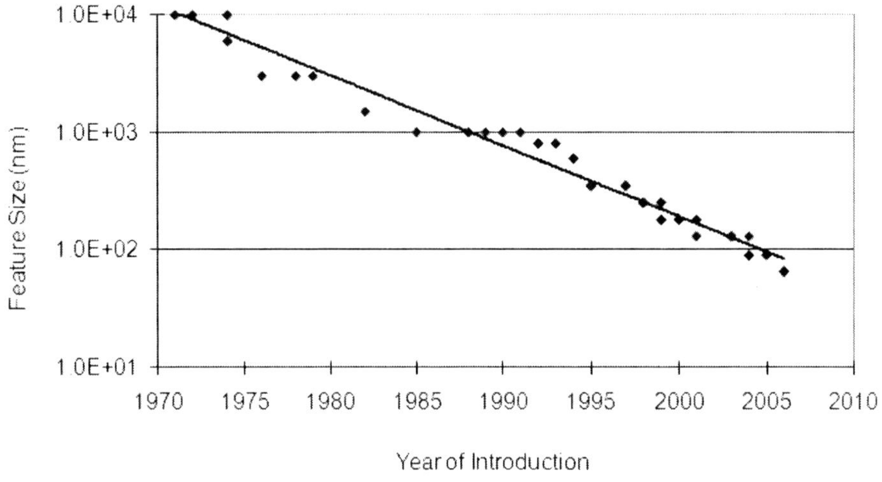

Figure 3. Memory wall

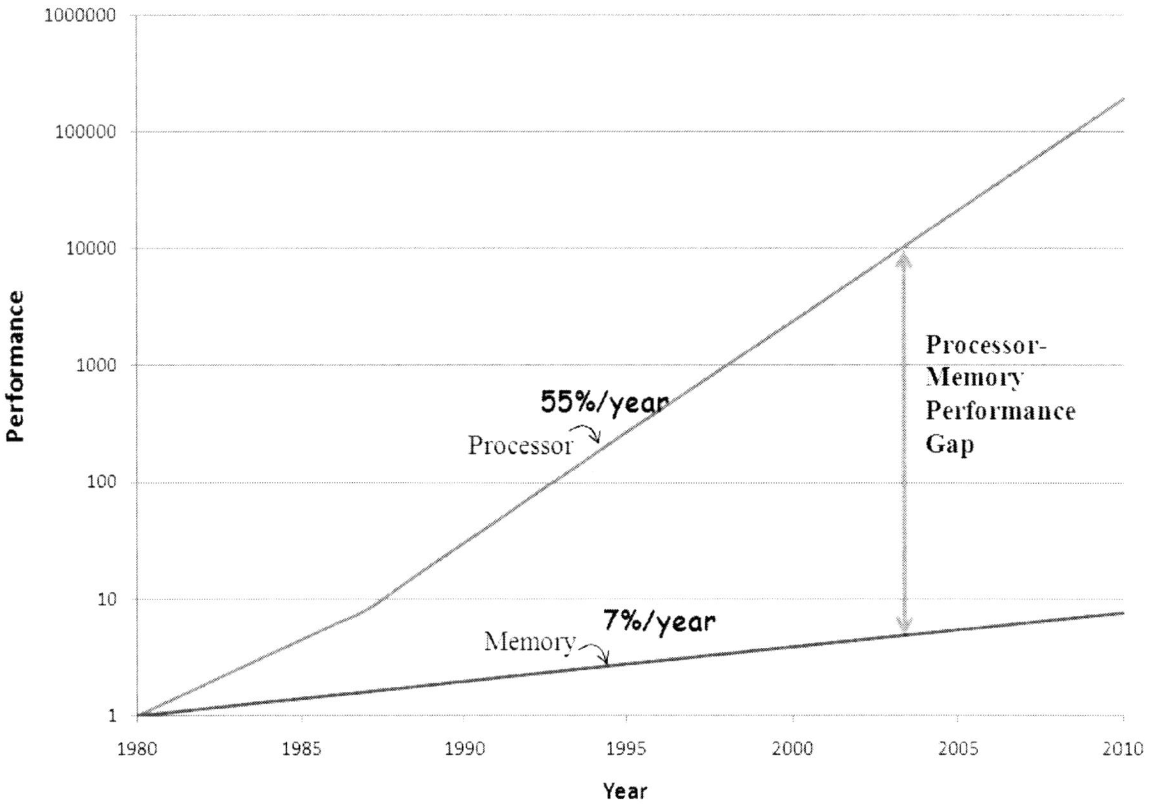

Overcoming the Limits of Instruction-Level Parallelism

Modern superscalar processors are capable of fetching multiple instructions at the same time and execute as many instructions as there are functional units, exploiting the Instruction-Level Parallelism (ILP) that inherently exists even in otherwise sequential programs. Furthermore, in order to extract more instructions that can be executed in parallel, these processors have employed dynamic instruction scheduling and have been equipped with larger instruction window than ever.

Even though increasing the size of the instruction window would increase to some extent the amount of ILP that a superscalar processor can deliver, control and data dependencies among the instructions, branch mispredictions, and long-latency operations such as memory accesses limit the effective size of the instruction window. For SPEC benchmark programs (http://www.spec.org/), a basic instruction block typically consists of up to 25 instructions (Huang, 1999). However, the average block size for integer programs has remained small (Mahadevan, 1994), around 4-5 instructions (Marcuello, 1999). Wall (1991) also pointed out that most representative application programs do not have an intrinsic ILP higher than 7 instructions per cycle even with unbounded resources and optimistic assumptions. Hence, if many slots in the instruction window are occupied by those depending on a preceding instruction suffering from a cache miss for the input operands, the effective size of the instruction window is quite small: only a few instructions can be issued due to the lack of Instruction-Level Parallelism. Therefore, the performance achieved by such processors is far below the theoretical peak as a result of poor resource utilization. For example, even a superscalar processor with a fetch width of eight instructions, derived from the MIPS R10000 processor (Yeager, 1996), equipped with out-of-order execution and speculation, provided an Instruction Per Cycle (IPC) reading of only 2.7 for a multi-programming workload (multiple independent programs), and 3.3 for a parallel-programming workload (one parallelized program), despite a potential of eight (Eggers, 1997).

BACKGROUND

As the design of modern microprocessors, either of superscalar or Very Long Instruction Word (VLIW) architectures, has been pushed to its limit, the performance gain that could be achieved is diminishing due to limited Instruction-Level Parallelism, even with deeper (in terms of pipeline stages), wider (in terms of the fetch/execute/retire bandwidth) pipeline design (Culler, 1998; Eggers, 1997; Hennessy, 2006). Needless to say, the performance of a superscalar processor depends on how many independent instructions are delivered to both the front-end (all the stages before execution) and the back-end stages of the pipeline. Due to the sequential programming model, most of the software programs are written without giving consideration to parallelizing the code. This introduces practical problems when it comes to executing those programs because of many control and data dependencies. This has compelled hardware architects to focus on breaking the barriers introduced by limited ILP:

- One approach entails performing speculative execution in order to deliver more Instruction-Level Parallelism. Many techniques for speculative execution have been studied to alleviate the impact of control dependencies among instructions. As the pipeline of microprocessors becomes wider and deeper, however, the penalty of incorrect speculation increases significantly.

- The other approach entails exploiting Thread-Level Parallelism (TLP) as well as ILP. If we can break the boundary among threads and execute instructions from multiple threads, there is a better chance to find instructions ready to execute.

Multithreading Microarchitectures

Multithreading microarchitectures can be classified by their method of thread switching: coarse-grain multithreading, fine-grain multithreading, Chip Multi-Processing (CMP) and Simultaneous MultiThreading (SMT). Different implementation methods can significantly affect the behavior of the application. In coarse-grain multithreading and fine-grain multithreading, at each cycle, we still execute instructions from a single thread only. In Chip Multi-Processing and Simultaneous MultiThreading, at each cycle we execute instructions from multiple threads concurrently.

Hardware-Supported Multithreading

The original idea of hardware-supported multithreading was to increase the performance through overlapping communication operations with computation operations in parallel architectures, without any intervention from the software (Culler 1998). Based on the frequency of thread swapping operations, hardware-supported multithreading can be divided into two categories:

- *Coarse-grain multithreading* (or *blocked multithreading*), a new thread is selected for execution only when a long-latency event occurs for the current thread, such as an L2 cache miss or a remote communication request. The advantage of coarse-grain multithreading is that it masks the otherwise wasted slots with the execution of another thread. The disadvantage is that when there are multiple short-latency events, the context switch overhead is high. Due to the limited ILP, the issue slot is not fully utilized when executing one thread. The MIT Alewife is implemented using this technique (Agarwal, 1995).
- *Fine-grain multithreading* (or *interleaved multithreading*), a new thread is selected for execution at every clock cycle, compared with coarse-grain multithreading which only switches context on long-latency events. The advantage is that it does not require extra logic to detect the long-latency events and it handles both long-latency and short-latency events because the context switch will happen anyway. The disadvantage is also the context switch overhead. Due to the single-thread execution at every clock cycle, the issue slot is not fully utilized either. HEP (Smith, 1981), HORIZON (Thistle, 1988) and TERA (Alverson, 1990) all belong to this category.

Chip Multi-Processing

A CMP processor normally consists of multiple single-thread processing cores. As each core executes a separate thread, concurrent execution of multiple threads, hence TLP, is realized (Hammond, 1997). However, the resources on each core are not shared with others, even though a shared L2 cache (or L3 cache if there is one) is common in CMP designs. Each core is relatively simpler than a heavy-weight superscalar processor.

The width of the pipeline of each core is smaller so that the pressure to explore Instruction-Level Parallelism is reduced. Because of the simpler pipeline design, each core does not need to run at a high frequency, directly leading to a reduction in power consumption. Actually this is one of the reasons why the industry shifted from single-core processor to multi-core processor design: because of the "Power Wall" problem. We cannot include more transistors into the processor and rely solely on raw frequency increase to claim it as the next-generation processor, simply because the power density is just prohibitive. On the other hand, with multi-core design, we avoid the "Power Wall" because we can now operate at a lower frequency while the power consumption increases linearly with the number of cores. For a CMP processor, however, if the application program cannot be effectively parallelized, the cores will be under-utilized because we can not find enough threads to keep all the cores busy at one time. In the worst case, only one core is working and we cannot execute across the cores to utilize the idle functional units of other cores.

There are actually two categories of CMP design: homogeneous multi-core and heterogeneous multi-core. In homogeneous multi-core, we have identical cores on the same die. For example, the Stanford Hydra (Hammond, 2000) integrates four MIPS-based processor on a single die. The IBM POWER4 (Tendler, 2002) is a 2-way CMP design. Intel® Core™2 duo processor series, Core™2 Extreme Quad-Core processors and AMD Opteron™ Quad-Core processors are the new generation CMP design. Heterogeneous multi-core is an asymmetric design: there is normally one or more general-purpose processing core(s) and multiple specialized, application-specific processing units. The IBM Cell/B.E.™ belongs to this category.

Simultaneous MultiThreading

Superscalar or VLIW architectures are often equipped with more functional units than the width of the pipeline, because of a more aggressive execution type. Often, not all functional units are active at the same time because of an insufficient number of instructions to execute due to limited ILP. Simultaneous MultiThreading has been proposed as an architectural technique whose goal is to efficiently utilize the resources of a superscalar machine without introducing excessive additional control overhead. An SMT processor is still one physical processor, but it is made to appear like multiple logical processors. In an effort to reduce hardware implementation overhead, most of the pipeline resources are shared, including instruction queues and functional units. Only hardware parts necessary to retain the thread context are duplicated, *e.g.*, program counter (PC), register files and branch predictors, as shown in Figure 4 (Kang, 2004). By allowing one processor to execute two or more threads concurrently, a Simultaneous MultiThreading microarchitecture can exploit both Instruction-Level Parallelism and Thread-Level Parallelism, accordingly achieving improved instruction throughput (Burns, 2002; Lee, 2003; Nemirovsky, 1991; Shin, 2003; Tullsen, 1995; Tullsen, 1996; Yamamoto, 1995). The multiple threads can come either from a parallelized program (parallel-programming workload) or from multiple independent programs (multi-programming workload). With the help of multiple thread contexts that keep track of the dynamic status of each thread, SMT processors have the ability to fetch, issue and execute instructions from multiple threads at every clock cycle, taking advantage of the vast number of functional units that neither superscalar nor VLIW processors can absorb. Also because of TLP, the pressure on exploring ILP within a single thread is reduced and we do not need aggressive speculative execution any longer. This reduces the chances of wrong-path execution. Hence, Simultaneous MultiThreading is one of the most efficient architecture to utilize the vast computing power that such a microprocessor would have, achieving optimal system resource utilization and higher performance.

Figure 4. SMT vs. CMP

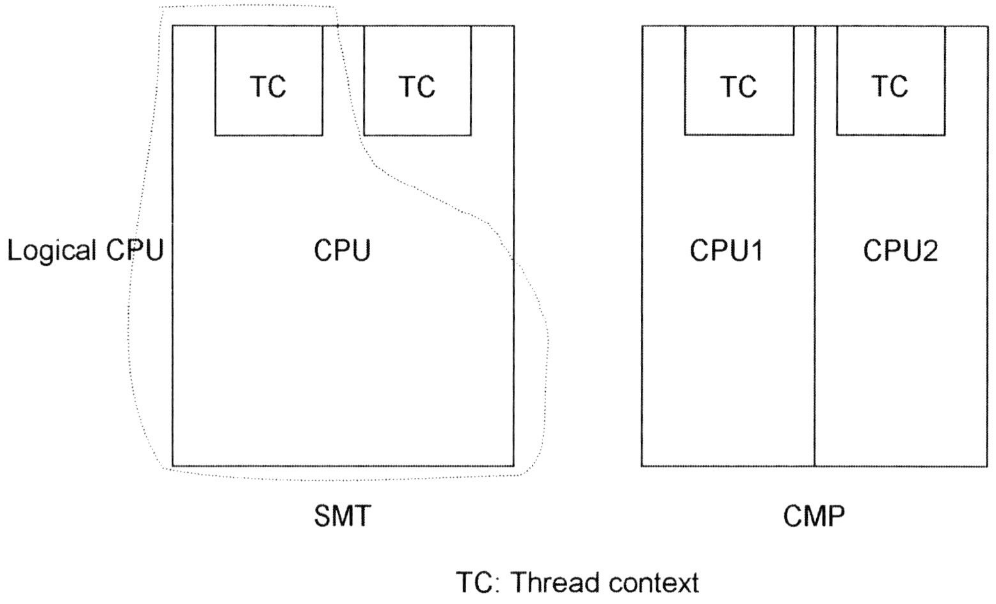

The difference in scheduling among Superscalar, CMP and SMT is shown in Figure 5: CMP exploits TLP by executing different threads in parallel on different processing cores while SMT exploits TLP by simultaneously issuing instructions from different threads with a large issue width on a single processor.

Figure 5. Resource utilization comparison of different microarchitectures

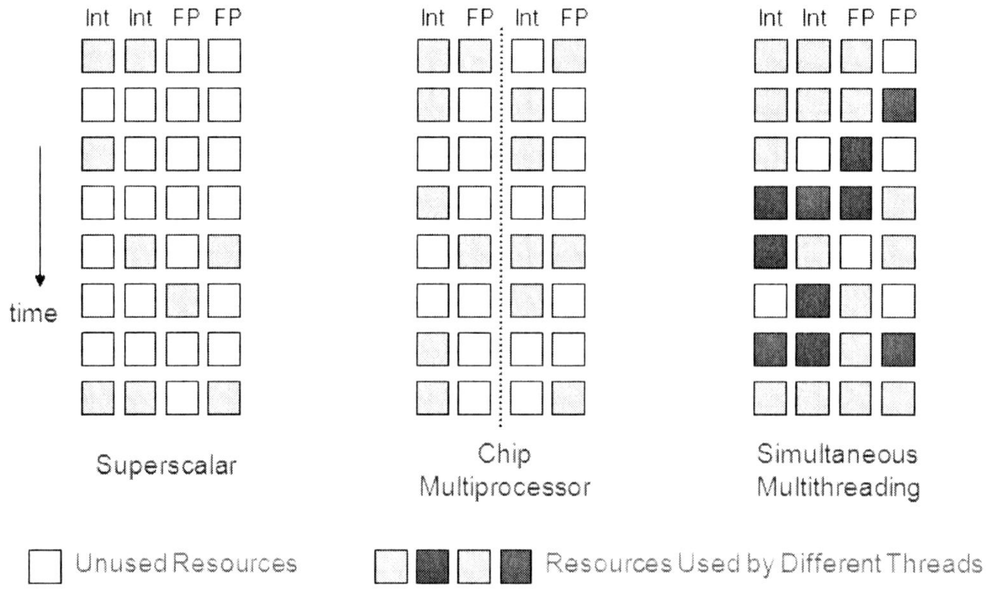

From the graph we can see that SMT processors inherently decrease the horizontal and vertical waste by executing instructions fetched from different threads (Eggers, 1997). They can provide enhanced performance in terms of instruction throughput as a result of taking better usage of the resources.

Commercial Implementation of SMT

SMT has been an active research area for more than one decade and has also met with some commercial success. Among others, embryonic implementations can be found in the design of the CDC 6600 (Thornton, 1970), the HEP (Smith, 1981), the TERA (Alverson, 1990), the HORIZON (Thistle, 1988), and the APRIL (Agarwal, 1990) architectures, in which there exists some concept of multithreading or Simultaneous MultiThreading. The first major commercial development of SMT was embodied in the DEC 21464 (EV-8) (Preston, 2002). However, it never made it into production line after DEC was acquired by Compaq. The Intel® Pentium® 4 processor 3.06GHz or higher (Hinton, 2001) and Intel® Xeon® processor families (Marr, 2002) are the first modern desktop/server processor implemented SMT, with a basic 2-thread SMT engine (named Hyper-Threading (HT) technology by Intel®). When multiple threads are available, two threads can be executed simultaneously; if there is only one thread to execute, the resources can be combined together as if it were one single processor. Intel® claims its Hyper-Threading technology implementation only requires 5% hardware overhead, while provides up to a 65% performance improvement (Marr, 2002). This matches exactly the stated implementation goal of Hyper-Threading: smallest hardware overhead and high enough performance gain (Marr, 2002).

Recently we see a trend to blur the boundary between CMP and SMT, which is multi-core multi-thread processor. For example, IBM POWER5 (Sinharoy, 2005) is such an implementation, with multi-core on a single chip and each core is a 2-thread SMT engine. MIPS Technology designed an SMT system called "MIPS MT". One implementation of this architecture has 8 cores and each core is a 4-thread SMT engine. All these examples demonstrate the power and popularity of SMT.

SMT DESIGN ASPECTS

With the concept of SMT in mind, this section will dive into the unique design aspects of this microarchitecture. The techniques used to boost the performance of SMT processors can be roughly divided into the following categories: fetch policy, handling long-latency instructions, active resource allocation and cache coherence communication.

Thread Selection Policy

Just like superscalar machines, the performance of an SMT processor is affected by the "quality" of the instructions injected into the pipeline. There are two critical aspects to this observation:

- First, if the instructions fetched and/or executed have dependencies among each other or if they have long latencies, the ILP and TLP which can be exploited will be limited. This will result in a clogging of the instruction window and a stalling of the front-end stages.
- Second, if the instructions fetched and/or executed belong to the wrong path, these instructions would compete with the instructions from the correct path for system resources in both the front-end and the back-end, which would degrade the overall performance and power efficiency.

Therefore, how to fill the front-end stages of an SMT processor with "high-quality" instructions from multiple threads is a critical decision which must be made at each cycle. Tullsen *et al.* (1996) suggested the following priority-based thread-scheduling policies for SMT microarchitectures that surpass the simple Round-Robin policy:

- BRCOUNT policy, which prioritizes the threads according to the number of unresolved branches in the front-end of the pipeline.
- MISSCOUNT policy, which prioritizes the threads according to the number of outstanding D-Cache misses.
- ICOUNT policy, which prioritizes the threads according to the number of instructions in the front-end stages.
- IQPOSN policy, which prioritizes the threads according to which one has the oldest instruction in the instruction queue.

Among those, ICOUNT policy was found to provide the best performance in terms of overall instruction throughput. The reason is that the ICOUNT variable can indicate the current performance of the thread to some extent. However, the ICOUNT policy does not take speculative execution into account because it does not consider that after an instruction has been injected into the pipeline, it may be discarded whenever a conditional branch preceding the instruction has been determined to have been incorrectly predicted. ICOUNT fails to distinguish between the instructions discarded in the intermediate stages due to incorrect speculation and the ones normally retired from the pipeline. Furthermore, the ICOUNT policy does not handle long-latency instructions well. If one thread has a temporarily low ICOUNT, it does not necessarily mean that a cache miss will not happen to the current instructions from that thread. As a result, the ICOUNT variable may incorrectly reflect the respective activities of the threads. This is one of the reasons why the sustained instruction throughput obtained under the ICOUNT-based policy still remains significantly lower than the possible peak.

Sometimes, a priority-based fetch policy could cause uneven execution of the threads, considering the case that one thread has very few cache misses while the other one has frequent misses. In an effort to avoid biased execution so that all the threads can progress equally, Raasch *et al.* (1999) proposed a priority-rotating scheme in an attempt to increase the execution of instructions from less efficient threads when threads are of equal priority. However, the performance of this scheme is not as good as anticipated: the throughput falls short of ICOUNT policy, sometimes even Round-Robin policy. The authors suggested enforcing the scheme by including branch confidence estimator into the process of fetch decision making.

Handing Long-Latency Instructions

Due to the "Memory Wall" problem, there is a major factor that affects resource distribution in SMT microarchitectures: long-latency instructions such as load misses. These instructions will clog the pipeline, unless the data can be pre-fetched from the memory. When one thread has injected many instructions into the pipeline and a load miss happens, the miss instruction and the instructions depending on it would not be able to move forward at all. Thus, the residency of those instructions in the pipeline does not necessarily translate into an increased overall instruction throughput. On the contrary, they pollute the instruction window and waste system resources which could otherwise be utilized by instructions from other threads. Taking into consideration the severe "damage" these instructions could cause, this means that an SMT processor must be aware of the execution of long-latency instructions.

Since ICOUNT does not handle long-latency instructions well, Tullsen *et al.* (2001) proposed two fetch policies that can better deal with those instructions. One is STALL, which immediately stops fetching from a thread once a cache miss has been detected. The other is FLUSH, which flushes the instructions from those threads with long-latency loads out of the pipeline, rather than occupying system resources while waiting for the completion of the long-latency operations. In both schemes, however, the detection of long-latency operations comes too late (after an L2 miss), and flushing out all the instructions already fetched into the pipeline is not a power-efficient solution.

There are several other techniques that attempt to advance the handling of those long-latency instructions, hence improving SMT performance. In DG (El-Moursy, 2003), when the number of outstanding L1 data cache misses from a thread is beyond a preset threshold, fetching from that thread is prohibited. However, L1 cache misses do not necessarily lead to L2 cache misses. Therefore, stalling a thread in such a case may be too severe and would cause an unnecessary stall and resource under-use. It has thus been proposed in DWarn (Cazorla, IPDPS, 2004) to use L1 cache misses as an indicator of L2 cache misses and give those threads with cache misses a lower fetch priority instead of stalling them. This allows DWarn to act in a controlled manner on L1 misses before L2 misses even happen so as to reduce resource under-use and avoid harming a thread when L1 misses do not lead to L2 misses.

Resource Partitioning among Multiple Threads

If we want to exploit more TLP, we need multiple threads to co-exist in the pipeline. At the same time, competition for system resources among these threads is also introduced. The overall performance of an SMT processor depends on many factors. How to distribute the resources among multiple threads is certainly one of the key issues in order to achieve better performance. Nevertheless, there are different opinions when it comes to this specific problem. Sometimes a dynamic sharing method can be applied to the system resources at every pipeline stage in SMT microarchitectures (Eggers, 1997; Tullsen, 1995; Tullsen, 1996), which means threads can compete for the resources and there is no quota on the resources that one single thread could utilize. Some other times, all the major queues can be statically partitioned (Koufaty, 2003; Marr, 2002), so that each thread has its own portion of the resources and there is no overlap. In most of the fetch policy studies, dynamic sharing was normally used and assumed to be capable of maximizing the resource utilization and corresponding performance.

Fetch policy alone achieves the resource distribution function in an extremely indirect and limited way. Upon a load miss, the pipeline of a superscalar processor will simply stall after running out of instructions before the operand from memory returns. For SMT processors on a load miss, other thread(s) can still proceed because of the TLP, but in a "handicapped" way. This is due to the fact that the instructions from the thread with a cache miss will occupy system resources in the pipeline. It directly translates into a reduction in the amount of system resources that other thread(s) can utilize. This is what we call "mutual-hindrance" execution. Hence, we do need direct control over system resources in order to achieve what we call "mutual-benefit" execution. This would allow us to avoid the resource being unevenly distributed among threads, which could cause pipeline clogging.

An investigation of the impact of different system resource partitioning mechanisms on SMT processors was performed by Raasch *et al.* (2003). Various system resources, like instruction queue, ReOrder Buffer (ROB), issue bandwidth, and commit bandwidth are studied under different partitioning mechanisms.

Figure 6. Fetch prioritizing and throttling scheme

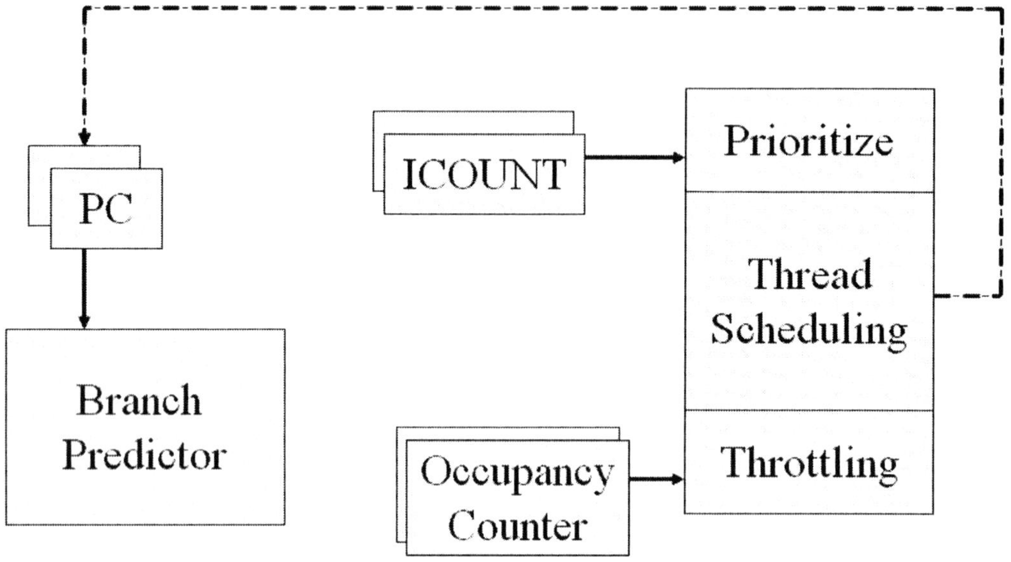

The authors concluded that the true power of SMT lies in its ability to issue and execute instructions from different threads at every clock cycle. If those resources are partitioning among threads, it would severely impair the ability of SMT to exploit TLP. Hence, the issue bandwidth has to be shared all the time. They also observed that partitioning the storage queues, like ROB, has little impact on the overall system performance. DCRA (Cazorla, MICRO, 2004) is proposed in an attempt to dynamically allocate the resources among threads by dividing the execution of each thread into different phases, using instruction and cache miss count as indicators. The study shows that DCRA achieves around 18% performance gain over ICOUNT in terms of harmonic mean. Hill-Climbing (Choi, 2006) dynamically allocates the resources based on the current performance of each thread and feedback into the resource-allocation engine. It uses its hill-climbing algorithm to sample some different resource distributions first to find out the local optimum and then adopt that distribution. It achieves a slightly higher performance (2.4%) than DCRA but is certainly the most expensive one in terms of execution overhead when it comes to finding the local optimum. There is also concern with how to justify the local optimum is the global optimum.

Liu C. *et al.* (2008) extended their work by proposing several different resource sharing control schemes and combining them with the front-end fetch policy to enforce the resource distribution. They also studied the impact on the overall performance caused by enforcing resource sharing control on both the front-end and the back-end of the pipeline. They introduced a two-level decision making process. The widely accepted ICOUNT policy is still used for thread prioritizing in order to select the candidate thread to fetch instructions from in the next clock cycle. On top of the ICOUNT policy, another variable, the Occupancy Counter, is adopted. Each thread occupying a resource currently monitored is associated with a designated Occupancy Counter. At every clock cycle, more instructions from a given thread are fed into the queue. Also some instructions from the thread leave the queue and are passed onto the next stage of the pipeline or retire. The value of the Occupancy Counter is updated after comprehensively evaluating the number of instructions from the certain thread in the specific queue every cycle. If after updating, the value of the Occupancy Counter of a running thread is greater than its assigned resource cap, the fetching of instructions from that thread will be stalled next clock cycle, even if it is of highest priority from ICOUNT policy. This allows the throttling of selected thread(s) after prioritizing, which enforces the resource sharing control schemes among multiple threads, as shown in Figure 6.Four different resource sharing control mechanisms have been proposed:

- D-Share: Both Instruction Fetch Queue (IFQ) and ROB are in the dynamic sharing mode, just like other system resources. No throttling.
- IFQ-Fen[2]: Enforcing the sharing control on IFQ. Cap is set to be half of the IFQ entries, and other system resources are in the dynamic sharing mode. Throttling based on Occupancy Counter of IFQ.
- ROB-Fen: Enforcing the sharing control on ROB, Cap is set to be half of the ROB entries, while other system resources are in the dynamic sharing mode. Throttling based on Occupancy Counter of ROB.
- Dual-Fen: Enforcing the sharing control on both IFQ and ROB, Cap is set to be half of the IFQ or ROB entries, and other system resources are in the dynamic sharing mode. Throttling based on Occupancy Counters of either IFQ or ROB.

It is found that controlling the resource sharing of either IFQ or ROB is not sufficient if implemented alone. However, when controlling the resource sharing of both IFQ and ROB, the Dual-Fen scheme can yield an average performance gain of 38% when compared with the dynamic sharing case. The average L1 D-Cache miss rate has been reduced by 33%. The average time during which an instruction resides in the pipeline has been reduced by 34%. This demonstrates the power of the resource sharing control mechanism for SMT microarchitectures.

SMT Synchronization and Communication

When multiple processes share data, their accesses to the shared data must be serialized according to the program semantics so as to avoid errors caused by non-deterministic data access behavior. Conventional synchronization mechanisms in Symmetric MultiProcessing (SMP) designs are constrained by long synchronization latency, resource contention, as well as synchronization granularity. Synchronization latency is determined by where synchronization operations take place. For conventional SMP machines that perform synchronization operations in memory, it can take hundreds of cycles to complete one synchronization operation. Resource contention exists in many of the existing synchronization operations, *e.g.*, test-and-set and compare-and-swap. These operations utilize polling mechanism which introduces serious contention problems. When multiple processes are attempting to lock a shared variable in memory, only one process will succeed, while all other attempts are strictly overheads. In addition, contention may lead to deadlock situations that require extra mechanisms for deadlock prevention, which further degrade system performance. Furthermore, due to the long-latency associated with each synchronization operation, most synchronization operations in SMP designs are coarse-grained. Thus, a data structure such as an array needs to be locked for synchronization although only one array element is under synchronization at any instance of parallel execution. This results in unnecessary serialization of the access to data structures, and restricts the parallelization of programs (Liu, 2007).

Figure 7. Microarchitecture of the Godson-2 SMT processor

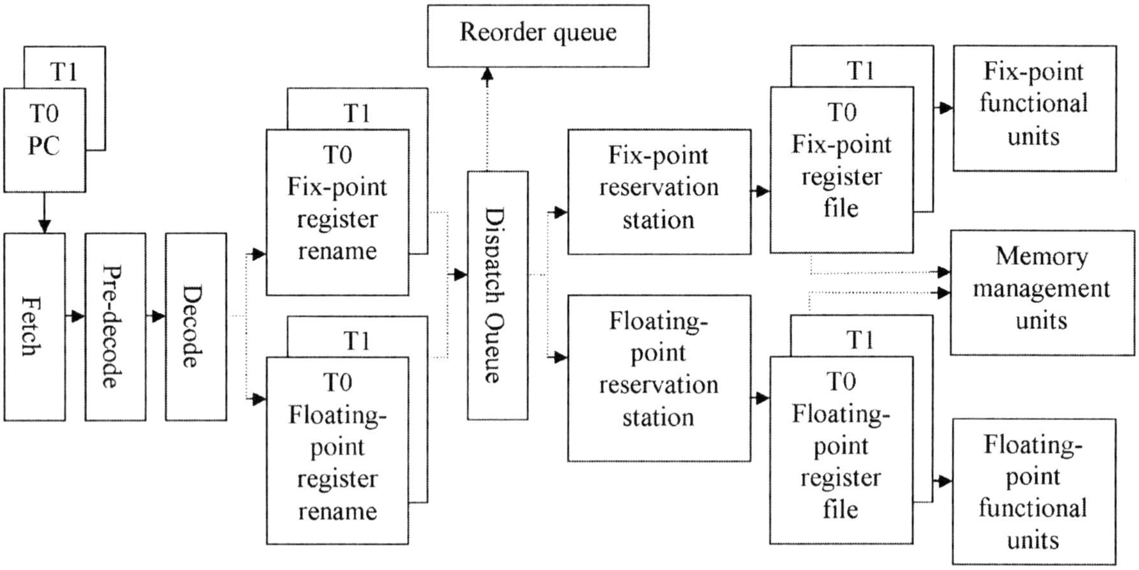

The granularity and performance of synchronization operations determine the degree of parallelism that can be extracted from a program. Hence the conventional coarse-grained synchronization operations cannot exploit the fine-grained parallelism which is required for SMT designs. As demonstrated by Tullsen *et al.* (1999), an SMT processor differs from a conventional multiprocessor in several crucial ways which influence the design of SMT synchronization:

- Threads share data in L1 cache, instead of in memory as in SMP designs, implying a much lower synchronization latency.
- Hardware thread contexts on an SMT processor share functional units, thus synchronization and communication of data can be much more effective than through memory. Based on this characteristic, one possible way of synchronization is through direct register access between two threads.
- Threads on an SMT processor compete for all fetch and execution resources each cycle, thus synchronization mechanisms that consume any shared resources without making progress can impede other threads. In the extreme case, when one thread demands blocking synchronization while holding all the resources such as all instruction window entries, a deadlock would occur.

Based on these differences between SMT and conventional multiprocessor designs, the synchronization operations for SMT designs should possess the following properties:

- *Low Latency*: this can be easily achieved because threads in SMT share data in the L1 cache. As mentioned before, one possibility of synchronization is through direct register access, but this may complicate the hardware design to avoid deadlock situations.
- *Fine-Grained*: the degree of parallelism that can be exploited in a parallel computing system is limited by the granularity of synchronization. To achieve high performance, the SMT design must

be capable to handle fine-grained synchronization.

- *Minimum Contention*: conventional synchronization mechanism such as spin locks requires either spinning or retrying, thus consuming system resources. This effect is highly undesirable. To achieve high performance, stalled threads must use zero processor resources.
- *Deadlock Free*: blocked threads must release processor resources to allow execution progress.

One interesting SMT synchronization mechanism is implemented in the Godson-2 SMT processor. As shown in Figure 7 (Li, 2006), Godson-2 SMT processor supports the simultaneous execution of two threads, and each thread owns its individual program counter, logical registers, and control registers. Other system resources, including various queues, pipeline path, functional units, and caches are shared between the two threads.

The Godson-2 SMT processor implements full/empty synchronization to pass messages between threads at the register level. Each register has an associated full/empty bit and each register can be read and written by synchronized read and write instructions. Communication and synchronization through registers meets the goal of low latency; also, the granularity of synchronization in this case is at the single register level, which meets the goal of fine granularity. On the other hand, full/empty scheme may result in deadlock. After being decoded, a synchronized read instruction is in the register renaming stage and the register it reads is empty (not ready or not produced). If this instruction waits for the register it reads to be set to full in the register renaming stage, it will block the pipeline and result in a deadlock. One solution to this problem is to block synchronized read/write instructions in the instruction buffer in the decode stage and rename the register to get the correct physical register number only after the register is full (ready or produced). This approach avoids blocking the whole pipeline and thus prevents deadlocks. Furthermore, this synchronization mechanism is contention-free because once a synchronized read operation is issued, the thread is blocked and not consuming any processor resources until the operation is retired.

Another interesting SMT synchronization approach has been proposed by Tullsen *et al.* (1999). This approach uses hardware-based blocking locks such that a thread which fails to acquire a lock, blocks and frees all resources it is using except for the hardware context itself: Further, a thread that releases a lock causes the blocked thread to be restarted. The implementation of this scheme consists of two hardware primitives, *Acquire* and *Release*, and one hardware data structure, a *lock box*. The *Acquire* operation acquires a memory-based lock and does not complete until the lock has been acquired. The *Release* operation releases the lock if no other thread is waiting; otherwise, the next waiting thread is unblocked. The *lock box* contains one entry per context and each entry contains the address of the lock, a pointer to the lock instruction that blocked and a valid bit. The scheme works as follows: when a thread fails to acquire a lock, the lock address and instruction pointer are stored in the *lock box* entry, and the thread is flushed from the processor after the lock instruction. When another thread releases the lock, the blocked thread is found in the *lock box* and its execution is resumed. In the meantime, this thread's *lock box* entry is invalidated. This approach has low-latency and is fine-grained because synchronization takes place at the level of the L1 cache and the size of the data can be adjusted. Also, when a thread is blocked, all its instructions are flushed from the instruction queue, thus guaranteeing execution progress and freedom from deadlock. In addition, this approach imposes minimal contention because once *Acquire* fails, the thread is blocked and consumes no processor resources.

As indicated by Liu S. *et al.* (2008), modern applications may not contain enough ILP due to data dependencies among instructions. Nevertheless, value prediction techniques are able to exploit the inherent data redundancy in application programs. Specifically, value prediction techniques are able to predict the value to be produced before the instruction executes, therefore the execution can move on with the correctly predicted value. Value prediction techniques require extra hardware resources and it also requires a recovery mechanism when the value is not correctly predicted. SMT is a perfect platform for value prediction because the system is underutilized only when there is not enough ILP. When this happens, a speculative thread can be triggered to perform value prediction on the underutilized resources, which allows the execution to proceed if the value is correctly predicted. Value prediction techniques in the context of SMT architecture have been studied by Gontmakher *et al.* (2006) and Tuck *et al.* (2005). In (Tuck, 2005), it shows that by allowing the value-speculative execution to proceed in a separate thread, value prediction is able to overcome data dependencies presented in traditional computing paradigms. With value prediction techniques, 40% performance gain has been reported. In (Gontmakher, 2006), it examines the interaction of speculative execution with the thread-related operations and develops techniques to allow thread-related operations to be speculative executed. The results demonstrate 25% performance improvement.

POTENTIAL BENEFITS OF SMT

We have discussed a number of design issues. We will now address some potential incidental benefits of SMT microarchitectures beyond strict performance improvement.

SMT for Fault-Tolerance

One possible SMT application is to design microprocessors resistant to transient faults (Li X., 2006). The multi-thread execution paradigm inherently provides the spatial and temporal redundancy necessary for fault-tolerance. We can run two copies of the same threads on an SMT processor and compare the results in order to detect any transient fault which would have occurred in the meantime. This allows, upon detection of an error, to roll back the processor state to a known safe point, and then retry the instructions, thereby resulting in an error-free execution. This means that temporal redundancy is inherently implemented by SMT: for instance, assume a soft error occurred in a functional unit (FU) when executing an instruction from thread #1. Even though the FUs are typically shared between active threads, since the soft error is assumed to be transient, as long as the same instruction from thread #2 is executed at a different moment, the results of the redundant execution from the two copied threads would not match. Furthermore, if any fault in the pipeline is detected, the checkpoint information can then be used to return the processor to a state corresponding to a fault-free point. After that, the processor can retry the instructions from the point of recovery.

Nevertheless, this basic idea comes at a cost. Generally speaking, it requires the redundant execution from the two copied threads to have appropriate fault detection coverage for a given processor component. Hence, the higher the desired fault detection coverage, the more redundant the required execution. However, redundant execution inevitably comes at the cost of performance overhead, added hardware, increased design complexity, *etc*. Consequently, how to trade the fault detection coverage off the added costs is essential for the practicality of the basic idea. Specifically, consider the need to generate redundant executing threads: given a general five-stage pipeline which is comprised of instruction fetch, decode, issue, execute and retire stages, all stages can be exploited for that requirement. Take the fetch stage as

Figure 8. Functional diagram of the fault-tolerant SMT data path

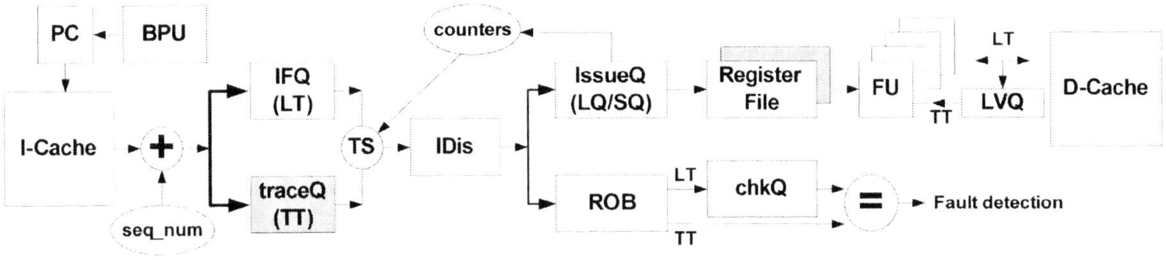

an example; we can generate the redundant threads by fetching instructions twice. Since the instruction fetch stage is the first pipeline stage, the redundant execution would then cover all the pipeline stages, thus, the largest possible fault detection coverage could be achieved. However, allowing two redundant threads to fetch instructions would possibly end up halving the effective fetch bandwidth. Consequently, that halved fetch bandwidth would be an upper bound for the maximum pipeline throughput. Additionally, the redundant thread generated in the fetch stage would then compete not only for the decode bandwidth, the issue bandwidth, and the retire bandwidth, but also for Issue Queue (IssueQ) and ROB capacity, which are all identified as key factors that affect the performance of the redundant execution. Conversely, we can re-issue the retired instructions from ROB back to the functional units for redundant execution. In doing so, the bandwidth and spatial occupancy contention at IssueQ and ROB can be relieved, thus the performance overhead can be lowered. However, this retire-stage-based design comes at the price of smaller fault detection coverage: only the execution stage would be covered.

Given these trade-off considerations, we can simply fetch the instructions once and then immediately copy the instructions fetched to generate the redundant thread. In doing this, there is no need for partitioning the fetch bandwidth between the redundant threads. Moreover, we can rely on the dispatch thread scheduling and redundant thread reduction to relieve the contention in the IssueQ and ROB. Both techniques lower the performance overhead.

Other than the design trade-off, another issue associated with the basic idea is the need to prevent deadlocks. In a fault-tolerant SMT design, two copies of the same thread are now cooperating with each other. Such cooperation could cause deadlocks. We present a systematic deadlock analysis and conclude that as long as ROB, Load Queue (LQ) and Store Queue (SQ) (the instruction issue queues for load and store instructions, separately) have allocated some dedicated entries to the trailing thread, the deadlock situations identified can be prevented. Based on this conclusion, we propose two ways for the prevention of any deadlock situation: one is to statically allocate entries in ROB, LQ, and SQ for the redundant thread copy; the other is to dynamically monitor for deadlocks.

Lowering the Performance Overhead

As discussed, to lower the performance overhead, we can simply fetch the instructions once and then immediately copy the instructions fetched in order to generate the redundant thread. However, in doing so, faults in three major components in the fetch stage: I-Cache, Program Counter, and Branch Prediction Units (BPU) might not be covered. In particular, any transient faults which would happen inside the I-Cache might not be detected. However, to protect the I-Cache, we can implement Error Correcting Code (ECC)-like mechanisms that are very effective at handling transient faults in memory structures.

Further, the fault occurring in the BPUs will have no effect on the functional correctness of program execution; however, the critical component PCs must also be protected by ECC-like mechanisms. As shown in Figure 8, the instruction copy operation is simple: just buffer the instructions fetched into two instruction queues, hence, the copy operation would not enlarge the pipeline cycle frequency, nor would another pipeline stage be added. To be specific, each instruction fetched can be bound to a sequential number and a unique thread ID. For instructions that are stored in IFQ, the "leading thread" (LT) is used as their thread ID, whereas for those stored in another IFQ, called trace queue (traceQ), the "trailing thread" (TT) is used. It should be noted that traceQ also serves in the two performance overhead lowering techniques which will be described in detail in the following subsections.

Focusing on our redundant execution mode, the key factors that affect the performance of redundant execution can be identified as: contention for bandwidth as far as issue, execution, and retire operations are concerned, as well as the capacity contention in IssueQ and ROB. We now address these types of resource contention by introducing four schemes to reduce TT to be as lightweight as possible (remember that executing TT is merely for fault detection purposes). In doing so, the competition between IssueQ, ROB, and FUs could then be reduced.

The first scheme we propose is to prevent the mispredicted TT instructions from being dispatched for execution. This is based on the observation that the number of dynamic mispredicted instructions might be a significant portion of the total fetched instructions. For example, Kang *et al.* (2008) observed that nearly 16.2% to 28.8% of the instructions fetched would be discarded from the pipeline even with high branch prediction accuracy. Hence, if we could prevent mispredicted instructions in TT from being dispatched, the effective utilization of IssueQ, ROB, and FUs would be accordingly improved. Based on this observation, we leverage LT branch resolution results to completely prevent the mispredicted instructions in TT from being dispatched. It should also be noted that in this design neither a branch outcome queue nor a branch prediction queue is needed. Specifically, when encountering a branch instruction in traceQ, the dispatch operation will check its prediction status: if its prediction outcome has been resolved by its counterpart from LT, we continue its dispatch operation; otherwise, the TT dispatch operation will be paused. In order not to pause the TT dispatch operation, LT must be executed ahead of TT. The LT ahead of TT execution mode is called staggered execution. To set up the TT branch instruction status (the initial status is set as "unresolved"), every completed branch instruction from LT will search traceQ to match its TT counterpart. We should note here that the sequential numbers provide the mean for matching two redundant threads instructions. As we have seen, each instruction fetched is associated with a sequential number at first, and then the fetched instruction is replicated to generate the redundant thread. In doing so, two copied instructions will have the same sequential numbers in different threads. It should also be noted that such a sequential number feature has been implemented, for example, in the Alpha and PowerPC processors. If the branch has been correctly predicted, the status of the matched counterpart TT branch instruction will be assured as "resolved". Conversely, if the branch has been mispredicted, LT will perform its usual branch misprediction recovery, while at the same time it will flush all those instructions inside traceQ that are located behind the matched counterpart branch instruction. In other words, LT performs the branch misprediction recovery for both LT and TT. Thus, TT does not recover any branch misprediction by itself. After recovery, the status of the TT branch instruction will be set up as "resolved".

In the second scheme, we adopt the Load Value Queue (LVQ) design (Reinhardt, 2000) and include it in our design as shown in Figure 8. Basically, when an LT load fetches data from the cache (or the main memory), the data fetched and the matching tag associated are also buffered into the LVQ. Instead of accessing the memory hierarchy, the TT loads simply check and match the LVQ for the data fetched. In doing so, TT might reduce the D-Cache miss penalties and in turn improve its performance. It should be noted here that in order to fully benefit from the LT data prefetching, we must guarantee that LT is always ahead of TT, which requires a staggered execution mode.

The third scheme consists in applying the dispatch thread scheduling. A well-known fact is that there are many idle slots in the execution pipeline. Hence, we must make sure that the redundant execution will exploit those idle slots as much as possible in order to circumvent the identified performance affecting contentions. To exploit the idle slots, we must ensure that whenever one thread is idle for any reason, the execution resources can be promptly allocated to another thread that can utilize them more efficiently. Based on this observation, the ICOUNT policy (Tullsen, 1996) was proposed to schedule threads in order to fill IssueQ with issuable instructions, *i.e.*, restrict threads from clogging IssueQ. However, we argue that it is the dispatch stage that directly feeds IssueQ with useful instructions. Hence, scheduling threads in the dispatch stage level would react more promptly to the thread idleness in IssueQ. Therefore, we modify the ICOUNT policy as follows (also see in Figure 8): at each clock cycle, we count the number of instructions that are still waiting in the IssueQ from LT and TT. A higher dispatch priority is assigned to the thread with the lower instruction count. More specifically, when the dispatch rate is eight instructions per cycle, the selected thread is allowed to dispatch as many instructions as possible (up to eight). If any dispatch slot is left from the selected thread, the alternate thread would consume the remaining slots. The above policy is denoted as "ICOUNT.2.8.dispatch".

While developing techniques to make TT as simple as possible, we found that a staggered execution mode is beneficial for those techniques. To that end, the fourth scheme, the "slack dispatch" scheme is proposed: in the instruction dispatch stage, if the selected thread is TT, we check the instruction distance between LT and TT. If the distance is less than a predefined threshold, we skip the TT dispatch operation and continue buffering TT in traceQ. This means that the size of traceQ (the entry number of traceQ) must meet the following requirement: sizeof (traceQ) > sizeof (IFQ) + predefined distance. Moreover, for the purposes of fault-detection, all retired LT instructions and their execution results are buffered into the checking queue (chkQ), as shown in Figure 8. Hence, TT is responsible for triggering the result comparison. We further assume the register file of TT is protected by ECC-like mechanisms. This means that, if any fault is detected, the register file state of TT could be used to recover that of LT.

Deadlock Analysis and Prevention

As pointed out before, the two copies of a thread cooperate with each other for fault checking and recovering. However, if not carefully synchronized, such cooperation could result in deadlock situations where neither copy could make any progress. To prevent this, a detailed analysis and appropriate synchronization mechanisms are necessary.

Resource sharing is one of the underlying conditions of deadlocks. Indeed, it should be noted that there is much resource sharing between the two thread copies. For example, IssueQ is a shared hardware resource and both thread copies contend for it. The availability of instructions being issued is another type of resource sharing: the issue bandwidth is dynamically partitioned between the two thread copies.

Take chkQ as an example, only if there is a free entry in chkQ could LT retire its instruction and back up the retiring instructions and execution results there. On the other hand, the entry in chkQ can only be freed by TT: only after an instruction has been retired and compared, can the corresponding entry in chkQ be released. Further, due to the similarity between dispatch and issue operations, we combine

Figure 9. Resource allocation graph for the fault-tolerant SMT deadlock analysis

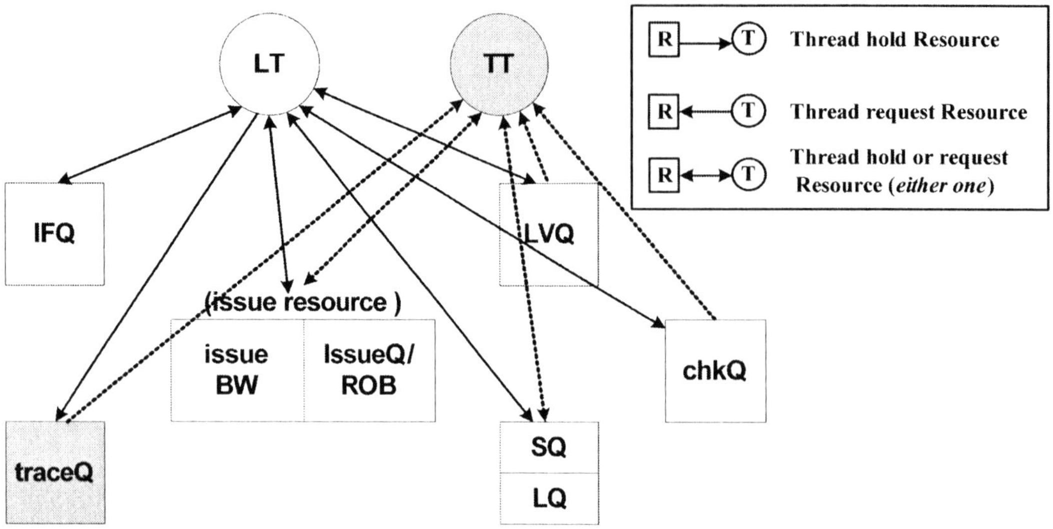

them under the term "issue resource" in the discussion which follows.

Based on Figure 9, we can list all possible circular wait conditions. However, some conditions obviously do not end up in a deadlock (*e.g.*, "LT → traceQ → TT → SQ → LT"). After exhausting the list, we describe all the possible deadlock scenarios as follows:

1. LT → chkQ → TT → issue resource → LT

Scenario: When chkQ is full, LT cannot retire its instructions. Then, those instructions ready to retire from LT are simply stalled in ROB. If that stalling ends with an ROB full of instructions from LT (the case in which ROB is full of instructions from LT could be exacerbated by the fact that LT is favored by the dispatch thread scheduling policy for the stagger execution mode), the instruction dispatch operation will be blocked, thus, TT will be stalled in traceQ. Consequently, no corresponding instructions from TT can catch up to release the chkQ entries and then a deadlock can happen. In summary, the condition for this deadlock situation is derived from the following:

Observation 1: When chkQ is full and ROB is full of instructions from LT, a deadlock happens.

2. LT → LVQ → TT → issue resource → LT

Observation 2: When LVQ is full and LQ is full of instructions from LT, a deadlock happens.

Similarly, the stalled load instructions could end up in a full ROB, thus, the instruction dispatch operation will be blocked. Hence, the deadlock observation follows:

Observation 3: When LVQ is full and ROB is full and no load instructions from TT in ROB, a deadlock happens.

3. LT → SQ → TT → issue resource → LT

Observation 4: When SQ is full of instructions from LT, a deadlock happens.

Based on the above systematic deadlock analysis, we propose two mechanisms to handle the possible deadlock situations: static hardware resource partitioning and dynamic deadlock monitoring.

In static hardware resource partitioning, *i.e.,* each thread has its own allocated resources, the deadlock conditions identified can be broken such that we can prevent the deadlock. For example, we can partition the ROB in order to prevent the possible deadlock situation identified in Observation 1: if some entries of the ROB are reserved for TT, TT dispatch operations could continue since, when chkQ is full, the partitioned ROB cannot be full of instructions from LT. Subsequently, those dispatched TT instructions will be issued and their execution completed afterwards. After completion, they will trigger the result comparison and then free the corresponding chkQ entries if the operation was found to be fault-free. After some chkQ entries have been freed, LT is allowed to make progress.

Moreover, we find that only three hardware resources (ROB, LQ, and SQ) need to be partitioned in order to prevent all the deadlock situations that we identified: Partitioning the ROB to break the deadlock situation identified in Observation 1: ROB will never be full of instructions from LT such that TT will be dispatched and then chkQ will be released. Similarly, partitioning LQ to break the deadlock situation identified in Observation 2; Partitioning SQ to break the deadlock situation identified in Observation 4.

Now considering Observation 3, when LVQ is full, an LT load instruction *LD_k* in LQ cannot be issued. However, since ROB is now partitioned between LT and TT, the stalled load instruction *LD_k* in ROB will only block LT from being dispatched. In other words, the TT dispatch operation will not be blocked by the stalled load instruction *LD_k*, thus, for example, another load instruction *LD_i* from TT will be dispatched which will then release the LVQ entry occupied by the counterpart load instruction *LD_i* from LT. Once free LVQ entries are made available, the stalled LT load instruction *LD_k* can be issued. In summary, we have the following observation:

Observation 5: For each ROB, LQ, and SQ, allocating some dedicated entries for TT will prevent the deadlock situations identified.

It should be noted, however, that static hardware resource partitioning has some performance impact on the SMT, particularly when partitioning ROB, LQ, and SQ. To mitigate this performance impact, we allocate some minimum number entries for TT to prevent deadlocks and the remainder of the queue is shared between LT and TT. Hence, the maximum available entry number for LT is the total queue entry number minus the reserved entry number whereas the maximum available entry number for TT is the total queue entry number.

From the deadlock analysis, we can also conclude that if we could dynamically regulate the progress of LT such that neither ROB nor LQ and SQ can be filled with instructions only from LT, the deadlock situations identified can be prevented. As illustrated in Figure 10, we can dynamically count the number of instructions from LT in ROB, LQ, and SQ, respectively, and then a caution signal is generated if at least one of the numbers of counted instructions exceeds the corresponding predefined occupancy threshold. Furthermore, as long as the caution signal is generated, the dispatch thread scheduling policy will hold on LT from being dispatched.

Algorithm 1. Dispatch threads scheduling policy (with dynamic deadlock monitoring)

```
Apply ICOUNT.2.8.dispatch policy;
If ((selected thread is LT) AND
(IFQ not empty) AND
```

Figure 10. Dynamic monitoring for the deadlock prevention

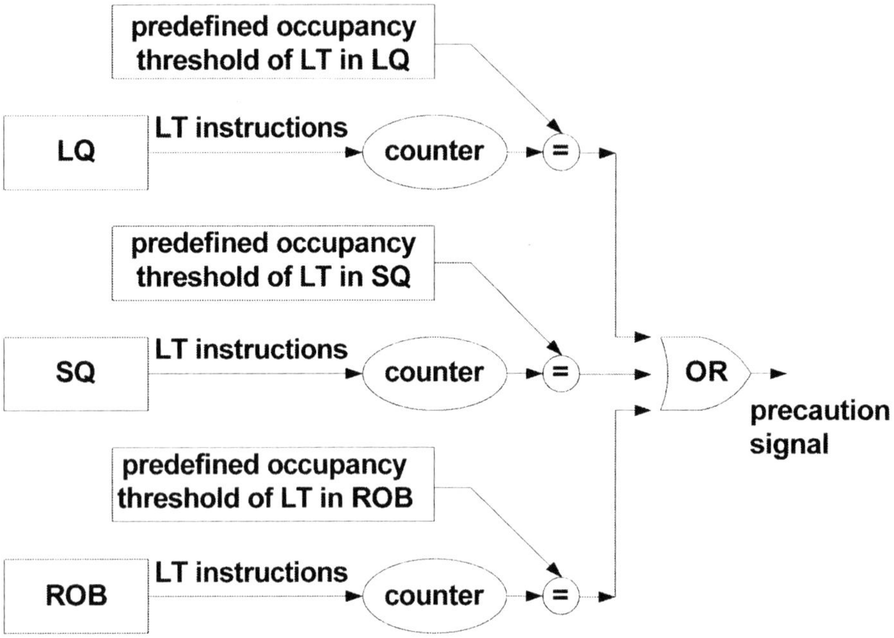


```
(no precaution signal))
Dispatch from IFQ;
else if ((distance between LT and TT meets predefined stagger execu-
tion mode) AND
(traceQ is not empty) AND
(not an unresolved branch instruction))
Dispatch from traceQ;
else
Nothing to be dispatched.
```

To be specific, the comprehensive dispatch thread scheduling policy we developed is listed in Algorithm1: first, we apply the ICOUNT.2.8. Dispatch policy. If the selected thread is LT, we must then check whether IFQ is empty since no instruction can be dispatched in the case of an empty IFQ. Furthermore, we need to make sure no caution signal has been generated. If there is one such signal, we must stop dispatching from LT. On the other hand, if the selected thread is TT, we check the following conditions before dispatch TT: (1) the staggered execution mode requirement; (2) traceQ not empty; (3) not encountering an unresolved branch instruction.

It should be noted that the dynamic deadlock monitoring approach offers higher design flexibility than the static resource partitioning. By adjusting the predefined occupancy thresholds, we can manipulate the resource allocation between the cooperating threads. However, this flexibility comes at the cost of additional hardware as well as a more complicated thread scheduling policy.

SMT for Secure Communication

Another possibility is to exploit SMT microarchitectures for secure communication. Traditionally, computer security focuses on the prevention and avoidance of software attacks. Nevertheless, the PC architecture is too trusting of its code environment, which makes PCs vulnerable to hardware attacks (Huang, 2003). For instance, to take control of a processor, a hacker can initiate a man-in-the-middle attack that injects malicious code into a system bus that connects the processor and the memory module. One approach to counter these attacks is memory authentication, which guarantees data integrity. Memory authentication normally needs to be performed in three steps (Yan, 2006). First, all memory lines have to be brought to the processor for authentication tag computation. Then, these lines are sent back to memory. At last, each time a line is brought to the processor at run-time, the authentication tag is recomputed and compared. This approach takes extra CPU cycles for authentication, generates extra bus traffic, and is vulnerable at system start time. To compensate the performance overhead, many propose extra pipeline stages or hardware units for authentication (Shi, 2004). However, the extra hardware overhead involved makes trusted systems only affordable to high-end users.

Is it worth the hardware overhead? Financial institutions can afford spending hundreds of thousands dollars on trusted systems but this is too much for ordinary PC users. Is it worth the performance overhead? Large trusted systems can afford spending 60% of its cycle time scrutinizing every instruction received but this is certainly not acceptable for ordinary PC users either. To address these issues, we propose Patrolling Thread (PT) for instruction memory authentication in an SMT microarchitecture. We choose to only authenticate instruction memory because the most common attack is malicious code injection and thus instruction memory is the "*Achilles' heel*" in computer (hardware) security. Also, instruction memory is one-way traffic (read-only), which makes security schemes easier to implement. In our proposed scheme, little performance overhead is incurred because it utilizes idle resources for authentication computation through employing SMT technique. What's more, since PT uses only existing pipeline stages/resources, little hardware overhead is necessary. In addition, by dedicating a hardware thread for system security, our approach provides tunable security levels for the system to operate under different requirements and environments.

Even though SMT exploits TLP in addition to ILP, the pipeline utilization still can not reach 100%. Thus the patrolling thread can take advantage of unused pipeline resources to execute instruction memory authentication algorithm, by which means to minimize the impact on regular program execution. If one incoming instruction does not pass the authentication test, then a warning would be issued and the system stops taking in any more instructions from memory until recovery.

To accommodate different security requirements and performance overhead, we have proposed three different schemes to implement patrolling thread:

i. *Regular-checking scheme*: served as the baseline scheme, *e.g.*, check one in every ten incoming instruction lines. This approach introduces some performance overhead and can secure the system when utilization is high, but a small number of malicious instructions could still sneak in. In most situations, this approach is secure enough because one malicious instruction is usually not enough to cause disastrous effects to the system. For instance, if n instructions are required to hack the system, then as long as the patrolling thread can catch one line of malicious instructions before all n instructions enter the processor, the system is safe.

ii. *Self-checking scheme*: the patrolling thread examines the incoming instruction lines only if there are free pipeline slots available. This scheme incurs no performance overhead but it becomes vulnerable when the system utilization is kept high.
iii. *Secured-checking scheme*: schedule the patrolling thread to authenticate every incoming instruction line regardless of the system utilization.

For authentication algorithm, we choose the One-Key CBC MAC (OMAC), which is a block-cipher-based message authentication algorithm for messages of any bit length (Iwata, 2003). Using this algorithm, a block cipher and a tag length need to be specified, and then both parties (Memory Management Unit (MMU) and Processor in our case) share the same secret key for tag generation and tag verification. In the proposed PT approach, when a memory line is requested, MMU generates a tag for the line, and the processor can check the line authenticity by verifying its tag. We assume that MMU is able to generate authentication tag on-the-fly since it has been demonstrated that MMU can be modified to carry out more sophisticated security operations, such as encryption and decryption (Gilmont, 1999).

Here is a brief analysis of the probability of detecting malicious code using patrolling thread scheme. The question can be summarized as follow: if we have *m* lines of instructions coming in, *n* of which are malicious codes, and we perform memory authentication on *k* lines of instructions, what would be the probability of catching one line of malicious code *P(detection)*[3]? The probability that the first line we authenticate is malicious code can be written as:

$$P(Detection1) = \frac{n}{m}$$

If the first memory line passes the authentication, then we choose the second memory line to check,

$$P(Detection2) = \frac{m-n}{m} \cdot \frac{n}{m-1}$$

The first term represents the first memory line is from the *m-n* genuine lines, and then the second time we pick one from the remaining *m-1* memory lines to authenticate.The probability that we catch the malicious code at the third time is:

$$P(Detection3) = \frac{m-n}{m} \cdot \frac{m-n-1}{m-1} \cdot \frac{n}{m-2}$$

Until the kth time,

$$P(Detectionk) = \frac{m-n}{m} \cdot \frac{m-n-1}{m-1} \cdot \cdots \cdots \frac{n}{m-(k-1)}$$

Figure 11. P(Detection) with m = 10

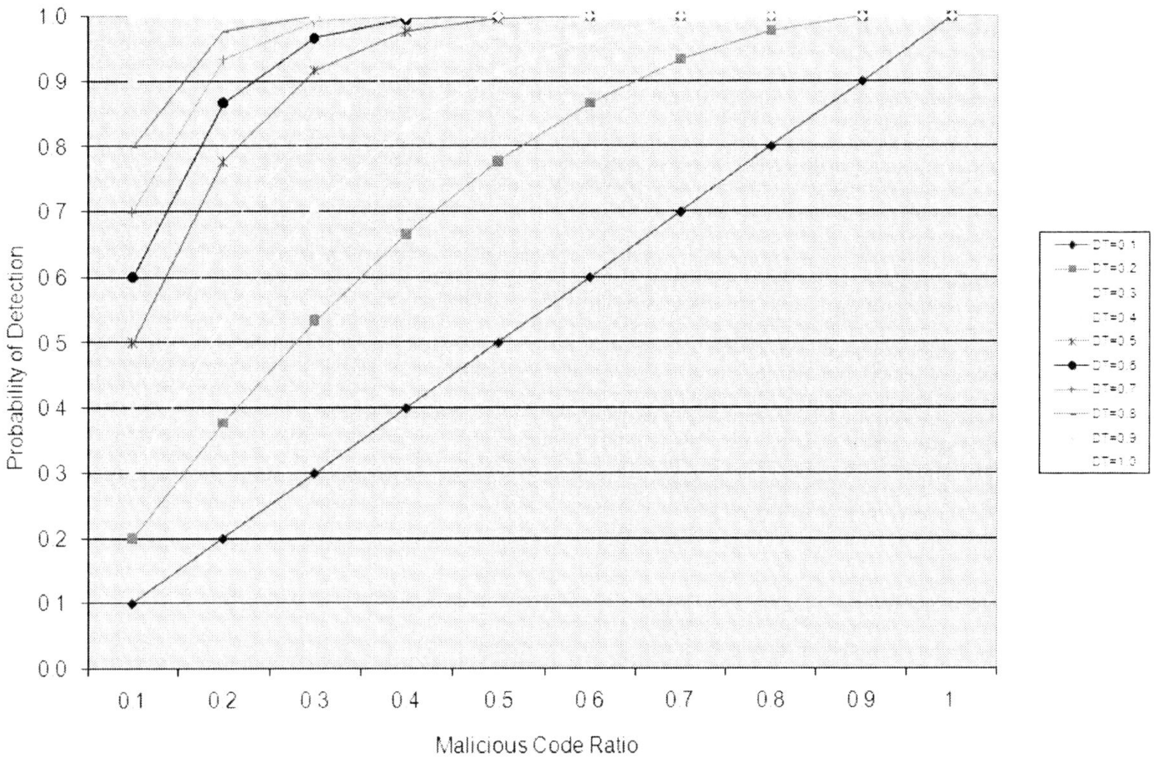

Figure 12. Pipeline with patrolling thread

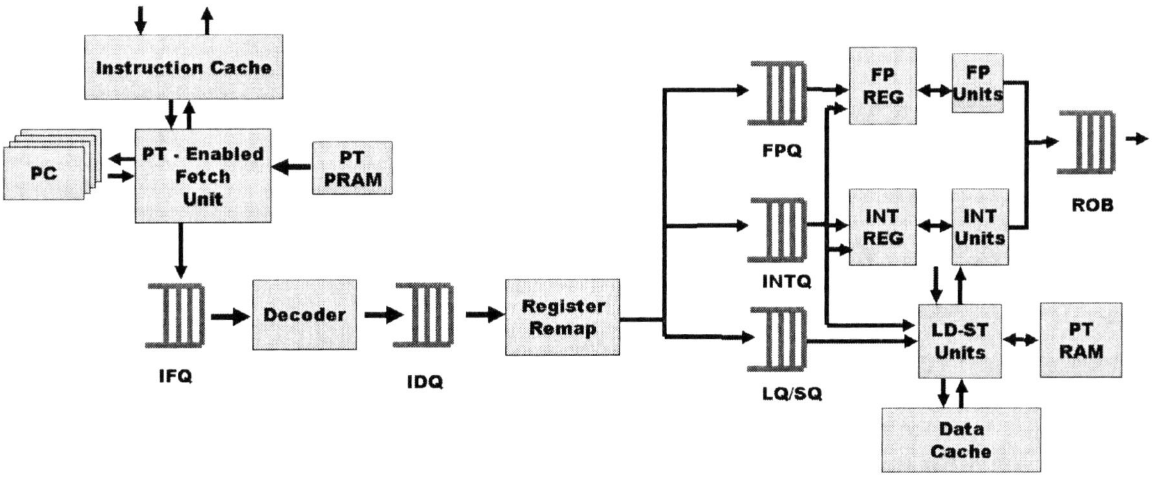

P(Detection) is the summation of all above terms, which we could write as:

$$P(Detection) = \sum_{i=1}^{k} \frac{\binom{m-i}{n} \cdot n}{\binom{m}{n} \cdot (m-i-n+1)}$$

Here $\binom{m}{n}$ represents the binomial coefficient.

Based on this equation, we plotted *P(Detection)* for the scenario where we perform memory authentication on 10 memory lines with the malicious code ratio and detection ratio varies, as shown in Figure 11. As we can see, if detection rate (DT) is 0.1 (corresponding to the regular-checking scheme), then the probability of detecting the malicious code is directly corresponding to the Malicious code ratio. On the other hand, if DT is 1 (corresponding to the secured-checking scheme), then we will always be able to detect the malicious code, hence for the *P(Detection)* we have a horizontal line here. At last, for the self-checking scheme we proposed, its *P(Detection)* would be in between of the previous two schemes.

PT is designed in a similar fashion to the detector thread proposed by Shin *et al.* (2006). As shown in Figure 12, PT's initial program image is loaded via DMA to PT PRAM by the OS during the boot. Once loaded, PT can start running from its own reset address depending on the patrolling scheme we choose. Whenever we have a cache miss for instructions, MMU would send in the instruction line with authentication tag. Then the instructions are sent to the instruction caches as normal, while its corresponding security tag is sent to the PT RAM. The tag and the instructions share the same memory address while PT RAM and Instruction Cache use the same cache indexing algorithm. This is to make sure that the tag and its corresponding instructions are related with each other. The PT-enabled fetch unit decides which thread to fetch from, the patrolling thread or the regular thread(s).

Whenever patrolling thread finishes the authentication process and it is a pass, nothing will happen and pipeline continues to flow. If, however, the authentication fails, then an alert would be raised and the whole pipeline would be flushed. Program counter(s) would be rolled back to the last known good position and restart execution.

TRENDS AND CONLUSIONS

With major general-purpose processor manufacturers transiting from single-core to multi-core processor production, one basic obstacle is lying before us: *are we truly ready for the multi-core era?*

With most programs still developed under sequential programming model, the extent of the Instruction-Level Parallelism we can exploit is very limited. Many resources on chip just remain idle and we are considerably short of fully utilizing the vast computing power of those chips. To solve this problem, we need to revolutionize the whole computing paradigm, from incorporating parallel programming into the application program development, to hardware design that could better facilitate the program for parallel execution. On the other hand, the Simultaneous MultiThreading microarchitecture model has proven to be capable of maximizing the utilization of on-chip resources and hence achieve improved performance.

Here we see a perfect match through utilizing the multi-thread microarchitecture to harness the computing power of multi-core, exploiting Thread-Level Parallelism (TLP) in addition to ILP.

We expect near-future processors to be of the multi-thread, multi/many-core kind. SMT would fit into the both homogeneous and heterogeneous multi/many-core system case, with one or many cores running multiple threads. Because of limited ILP, the main thread normally cannot use all the system resources. On the other hand, we have the demand from all those "house-keeping" functions such as on-chip resource usage analysis, data synchronization and routing decision making to assist the execution of the main thread. With SMT microarchitecture, we could achieve better system utilization when running those multiple threads together, hence achieve overall performance improvement.

According to the "Refrigerator Theory" of Professor Yale Patt from the University of Texas at Austin, another trend for future heterogeneous multi/many-core processor design is to include some application specific cores, in additional to the general-purpose processing cores. For example, AMD's vision on "fusion" (AMD, 2008) and the next generation Intel® "Larrabee" processor (Seiler, 2008), are both targeting a GPU/CPU combined design. These specific cores can be used as performance boosters for specific applications to achieve an overall performance improvement. In order to utilize these specific cores effectively, we need:

- An instruction set enhancement, to add dedicated instructions to best exploit these special cores.
- Improvement from the compiler, to extract more that can be run in these special cores.
- Operating system assistance, to be aware of these special cores for a better job scheduling.

For some power-constrained applications, we may need to put those specific cores into sleep mode in order to reduce the power consumption during normal execution and then power them back on when the need arises. If that is the case, however, the sleep state enter/exit latency would be a factor that should not be overlooked. Unless the core will be idle for considerably extended period of time, the gain you could get from running the specific core(s) may not justify the latency you need for the core mode change (from active to sleep/deep sleep or vice versa). What's more, put a core into deep sleep is not of trivial job in terms of hardware overhead. Due to these limiting factors, this approach needs to be considered cautiously by system architect.

SMT technology has been one of the de facto features of modern microprocessors. In this chapter, we examined this important technology from its motivation, design aspects, and applications. We strongly believe that, if we can utilize effectively, SMT will continue playing a critical role in future multi/many-core processor design.

REFERENCES

Agarwal, A., Bianchini, R., Chaiken, D., Johnson, K. L., Kranz, D., Kubiatowicz, J., et al. (1995). The MIT Alewife machine: architecture and performance. In *Proceedings of the 22nd Annual International Symposium on Computer Architecture* (ISCA'95), S. Margherita Ligure, Italy, (pp. 2-13). New York: ACM Press.

Agarwal, A., Lim, B.-H., Kranz, D., & Kubiatowicz, J. (1990). *April: a processor architecture for multiprocessing*. In Proceedings of the 17th Annual International Symposium on Computer Architecture (ISCA'90), (pp. 104-114), Seattle, WA: ACM Press.

Alverson, R., Callahan, D., Cummings, D., Koblenz, B., Porterfield, A., & Smith, B. (1990) *The Tera computer system*. In Proceedings of the 4th International Conference on Supercomputing (ICS'90), (pp. 1-6). Amsterdam: ACM Press.

Burns, J., & Gaudiot, J.-L. (2002). SMT layout overhead and scalability. *IEEE Transactions on Parallel and Distributed Systems, 13*(2), 142–155. doi:10.1109/71.983942

Cazorla, F. J., Ramirez, A., Valero, M., & Fernandez, E. (2004). Dcache Warn: an I-fetch policy to increase SMT efficiency. In *Proceedings of the 18th International Parallel & Distributed Processing Symposium* (IPDPS'04), (pp. 74-83). Santa Fe, NM: IEEE Computer Society Press.

Cazorla, F. J., Ramirez, A., Valero, M., & Fernandez, E. (2004). Dynamically controlled resource allocation in SMT processors. In *Proceedings of the 37th Annual IEEE/ACM International Symposium on Microarchitecture* (MICRO'04), (pp. 171-182). Portland, OR: IEEE Computer Society Press.

Choi, S., & Yeung, D. (2006). Learning-based SMT processor resource distribution via hill-climbing. In *Proceedings of the 33rd Annual International Symposium on Computer Architecture* (ISCA'06), (pp. 239-251), Boston: IEEE Computer Society Press.

Culler, D. E., Singh, J. P., & Gupta, A. (1998) *Parallel computer architecture: a hardware/software approach,* (1st edition). San Francisco: Morgan Kaufmann.

Eggers, S. J., Emer, J. S., Levy, H. M., Lo, J. L., Stamm, R. L., & Tullsen, D. M. (1997). Simultaneous multithreading: a platform for next-generation processors. *IEEE Micro, 17*(5), 12–19. doi:10.1109/40.621209

El-Moursy, A., & Albonesi, D. H. (2003). Front-end policies for improved issue efficiency in SMT processors. In *Proceedings of the 9th International Symposium on High-Performance Computer Architecture* (HPCA'03), (pp. 31-40). Anaheim, CA: IEEE Computer Society Press.

Gilmont, T., Legat, J.-D., & Quisquater, J.-J. (1999). Enhancing the security in the memory management unit. In *Proceedings of the 25th EuroMicro Conference* (EUROMICRO'99). *1*, 449-456. Milan, Italy: IEEE Computer Society Press.

Gontmakher, A., Mendelson, A., Schuster, A., & Shklover, G. (2006) *Speculative synchronization and thread management for fine granularity threads.* In Proceedings of the 12th International Symposium on High-Performance Computer Architecture (HPCA'06), (pp. 278-287). Austin, TX: IEEE Computer Society Press.

Hammond, L., Hubbert, B. A., Siu, M., Prabhu, M. K., Chen, M., & Olukotun, K. (2000). The Stanford Hydra CMP. *IEEE Micro, 20*(2), 71–84. doi:10.1109/40.848474

Hammond, L., Nayfeh, B. A., & Olukotun, K. (1997). A single-chip multiprocessor. *IEEE Computer, 30*(9), 79–85.

Hennessy, J., & Patterson, D. (2006). *Computer architecture: a quantitative approach* (4th Ed.). San Francisco: Morgan Kaufmann.

Hinton, G., Sager, D., Upton, M., Boggs, D., Carmean, D., Kyker, A., & Roussel, P. (2001). The microarchitecture of the Pentium 4 processor. *Intel® Technology Journal, 5*(1), 1-13.

Huang, A. (2003) *Hacking the Xbox: an introduction to reverse engineering*, (1st Ed.). San Francisco: No Starch Press.

Huang, J., & Lilja, D. J. (1999). Exploiting basic block value locality with block reuse. *Proceedings of 5th International Symposium on High-Performance Computer Architecture* (HPCA'99), (pp. 106-114). Orlando, FL: IEEE Computer Society Press.

Intel News Release. (2006). *New dual-core Intel® Itanium® 2 processor doubles performance, reduces power consumption*. Santa Clara, C: Author.

Iwata, T., & Kurosawa, K. (2003). OMAC: One-Key CBC MAC. In *10th International Workshop on Fast Software Encryption* (FSE'03), (LNCS Vol. 2887/2003, pp. 129-153), Lund, Sweden. Berlin/Heidelberg: Springer.

Kang, D.-S. (2004) *Speculation-aware thread scheduling for simultaneous multithreading.* Doctoral Dissertation, University of Southern California, Los Angeles, CA.

Kang, D.-S., Liu, C., & Gaudiot, J.-L. (2008). The impact of speculative execution on SMT processors. [IJPP]. *International Journal of Parallel Programming, 36*(4), 361–385. doi:10.1007/s10766-007-0052-3

Koufaty, D., & Marr, D. (2003). Hyperthreading technology in the Netburst microarchitecture. *IEEE Micro, 23*(2), 56–65. doi:10.1109/MM.2003.1196115

Lee, S.-W., & Gaudiot, J.-L. (2003). Clustered microarchitecture simultaneous multithreading. In *9th International Euro-Par Conference on Parallel Processing* (Euro-Par'03), (LNCS Vol. 2790/2004, pp. 576-585), Klagenfurt, Austria. Berlin/Heidelberg: Springer.

Li, X., & Gaudiot, J.-L. (2006). Design trade-offs and deadlock prevention in transient fault-tolerant SMT processors. In *Proceedings of 12th Pacific Rim International Symposium on Dependable Computing* (PRDC'06), (pp. 315-322). Riverside, CA: IEEE Computer Society Press.

Li, Z., Xu, X., Hu, W., & Tang, Z. (2006). Microarchitecture and performance analysis of Godson-2 SMT processor. In *Proceedings of the 24th International Conference on Computer Design* (ICCD'06), (pp. 485-490). San Jose, CA: IEEE Computer Society Press.

Liu, C., & Gaudiot, J.-L. (2008). Resource sharing control in simultaneous multithreading microarchitectures. In *Proceedings of the 13th IEEE Asia-Pacific Computer Systems Conference* (ACSAC'08), (pp. 1-8). Hsinchu, Taiwan: IEEE Computer Society Press.

Liu, S., & Gaudiot, J.-L. (2007). Synchronization mechanisms on modern multi-core architectures. In *Proceedings of the 12th Asia-Pacific Computer Systems Architecture Conference* (ACSAC'07), (LNCS Vol. 4697/2007), (pp. 290-303), Seoul, Korea. Berlin/Heidelberg: Springer.

Liu, S., & Gaudiot, J.-L. (2008). The potential of fine-grained value prediction in enhancing the performance of modern parallel machines. *In Proceedings of the 13th IEEE Asia-Pacific Computer Systems Conference* (ACSAC'08), (pp. 1-8). Hsinchu, Taiwan: IEEE Computer Society Press.

Mahadevan, U., & Ramakrishnan, S. (1994) *Instruction scheduling over regions: A framework for scheduling across basic blocks*. In *Proceedings of the 5th International Conference on Compiler Construction* (CC'94), Edinburgh, (LNCS Vol. 786/1994, pp. 419-434). Berlin/Heidelberg: Springer.

Marcuello, P., & Gonzalez, A. (1999) *Exploiting speculative thread-level parallelism on a SMT processor*. In *Proceedings of the 7th International Conference on High-Performance Computing and Networking* (HPCN Europe'99), Amsterdam, the Netherlands, (LNCS Vol. 1593/1999, pp. 754-763) Berlin/Heidelberg: Springer.

Marr, D.T., Binns, F., Hill, D.L., Hinton, G., Koufaty, D.A, Miller, J.A., & Upton, M. (2002). Hyper-threading technology architecture and microarchitecture. *Intel® Technology Journal, 6*(1), 4-15.

Moore, G. E. (1965). Cramming more components onto integrated circuits. *Electronics Magazine, 38*(8).

Nemirovsky, M. D., Brewer, F., & Wood, R. C. (1991). DISC: dynamic instruction stream computer. In *Proceedings of the 24th Annual International Symposium on Microarchitecture* (MICRO'91), Albuquerque, NM (pp. 163-171). New York: ACM Press.

Preston, R. P., Badeau, R. W., Bailey, D. W., Bell, S. L., Biro, L. L., Bowhill, W. J., et al. (2002). Design of an 8-wide superscalar RISC microprocessor with simultaneous multithreading. In *Digest of Technical Papers of the 2002 IEEE International Solid-State Circuits Conference* (ISSCC'02), San Francisco, CA (Vol. 1, pp. 334-472). New York: IEEE Press.

Raasch, S. E., & Reinhardt, S. K. (1999). Applications of thread prioritization in SMT processors. In *Proceedings of the 3rd Workshop on Multithreaded Execution and Compilation* (MTEAC'99), Orlando, FL.

Raasch, S. E., & Reinhardt, S. K. (2003). The impact of resource partitioning on SMT processors. In *Proceedings of the 12th International Conference on Parallel Architectures and Compilation Techniques* (PACT'03), (pp. 15–25). New Orleans, LA: IEEE Computer Society.

Reinhardt, S., & Mukherjee, S. (2000). Transient fault detection via simultaneous multithreading. In *ACM SIGARCH Computer Architecture News: Special Issue: Proceedings of the 27th Annual International Symposium on Computer Architecture* (ISCA'00), (pp. 25-36). Vancouver,Canada: ACM Press

Seiler, L., Carmean, D., Sprangle, E., Forsyth, T., Abrash, M., & Dubey, P. (2008). Larabee: a many-core x86 architecture for visual computing. [TOG]. *ACM Transactions on Graphics, 27*(3). doi:10.1145/1360612.1360617

Shi, W., Lee, H.-H., Ghosh, M., & Lu, C. (2004). Architectual support for high speed protection of memory integrity and confidentiality in multiprocessor systems. In *Proceedings of the 13th International Conference on Parallel Architectures and Computation Techniques* (PACT'04), Antibes Juan-les-Pins, France (pp.123-134). New York: IEEE Computer Society.

Shin, C.-H., & Gaudiot, J.-L. (2006). Adaptive dynamic thread scheduling for simultaneous multithreaded architectures with a detector thread. *Journal of Parallel and Distributed Computing*, *66*(10), 1304–1321. doi:10.1016/j.jpdc.2006.06.003

Shin, C.-H., Lee, S.-W., & Gaudiot, J.-L. (2003). Dynamic scheduling issues in SMT architectures. In *Proceedings of the 17th International Symposium on Parallel and Distributed Processing* (IPDPS'03), Nice, France, (p. 77b). New York: IEEE Computer Society.

Sinharoy, B., Kalla, R. N., Tendler, J. M., Eickemeyer, R. J., & Joyner, J. B. (2005). Power5 system microarchitecture. *IBM Journal of Research and Development*, *49*(4/5), 505–521.

Smith, B. J. (1981). Architecture and applications of the HEP multiprocessor computer system. In *SPIE Proceedings of Real Time Signal Processing IV, 298*, 241-248.

Tendler, J. M., Dodson, J. S. Jr, Fields, J. S., Le, H., & Sinharoy, B. (2002). Power4 system microarchitecture. *IBM Journal of Research and Development*, *46*(1), 5–25.

Thistle, M. R., & Smith, B. J. (1988). A processor architecture for Horizon. In *Proceedings of the 1988 ACM/IEEE conference on Supercomputing* (SC'88), Orlando, FL, (pp. 35-41). New York: IEEE Computer Society Press.

Thornton, J. E. (1970). *Design of a computer - the Control Data 6600*. Upper Saddle River, NJ: Scott Foresman & Co.

Tuck, N., & Tullsen, D. M. (2005). Multithreaded value prediction. In *Proceedings of the 11th International Symposium on High-Performance Computer Architecture* (HPCA'05), (pp. 5-15), San Francisco: IEEE Computer Society.

Tullsen, D. M., & Brown, J. A. (2001). Handling long-latency loads in a simultaneous multithreading processor. In *Proceedings of the 34th Annual ACM/IEEE International Symposium on Microarchitecture* (MICRO'01), (pp. 318–327). Austin, TX: IEEE Computer Society.

Tullsen, D. M., Eggers, S. J., Emer, J. S., Levy, H. M., Lo, J. L., & Stamm, R. L. (1996). Exploiting choice: instruction fetch and issue on an implementable simultaneous multithreading processor. In *Proceedings of the 23rd Annual International Symposium on Computer Architecture* (ISCA'96), Philadelphia, (pp. 191–202). New York: ACM Press.

Tullsen, D. M., Eggers, S. J., & Levy, H. M. (1995). Simultaneous multithreading: maximizing on-chip parallelism. In *Proceedings of the 22nd Annual International Symposium on Computer Architecture* (ISCA'95), Santa Margherita Ligure, Italy (pp. 392-403). New York: ACM Press.

Tullsen, D. M., Lo, J. L., Eggers, S. J., & Levy, H. M. (1999). Supporting fine-grained synchronization on a simultaneous multithreading processor. In *Proceedings of the 5th International Symposium on High Performance Computer Architecture* (HPCA'99), Orlando, FL (pp. 54-58). New York: IEEE Computer Society.

Wall, D. W. (1991). Limits of instruction-level parallelism. In *Proceedings of the 4th International Conference on Architectural Support for Programming Languages and Operating Systems,* Santa Clara, CA (ASPLOS-IV), (pp. 176-188). New York: ACM Press.

White Paper, A. M. D. (2008). *The industry-changing impact of accelerated computing.*

Yamamoto, W., & Nemirovsky, M. (1995). Increasing superscalar performance through multistreaming. In *Proceedings of the IFIP WG10.3 Working Conference on Parallel Architectures and Compilation Techniques* (PACT'95), (pp. 49-58). Limassol, Cyprus: IFIP Working Group on Algol.

Yan, C., Rogers, B., Englender, D., Solihin, Y., & Prvulovic, M. (2006). Improving cost, performance, and security of memory encryption and authentication. In *Proceedings of 33rd Annual International Symposium on Computer Architecture* (ISCA'06), (pp. 179-190). Boston: IEEE Computer Society Press.

Yeager, K. C. (1996). The MIPS R10000 superscalar microprocessor. *IEEE Micro*, *16*(2), 28–40. doi:10.1109/40.491460

KEY TERMS AND DEFINITIONS

Cache Coherence: The integrity of the data stored in local caches of a shared resource.

Fault Tolerance: The property that enables a system (often computer-based) to continue operating properly in the event of the failure of (or one or more faults within) some of its components.

Fetch Policy: A mechanism which allows the determination of which thread(s) to fetch instructions from, when executing multiple threads.

Instruction-Level Parallelism: A measure of how many of the operations in a computer program can be performed simultaneously.

Simultaneous Multithreading: A technique to improve the overall efficiency by executing instructions from multiple threads simultaneously to better utilize the resources provided by modern processor architecture.

Microarchitecture: A description of the electrical circuits of a processor that is sufficient to completely describe the operation of the hardware.

Resource Sharing Control: A mechanism which allows the distribution of various resources in the pipeline among multiple threads.

Secure Communication: Means by which information is shared with varying degrees of certainty so that third parties cannot know what the content is.

Synchronization: Timekeeping which requires the coordination of events to operate a system in unison.

Thread-Level Parallelism: A measure of how many of the operation across multiple threads can be performed simultaneously.

ENDNOTES

1. Some literature refers to 18 months. However, the official Moore's law website of Intel®, and even an interview with Dr. Gordon Moore, confirms the two year figure.
2. In Chinese, Fen means "Divide" or "Partition".
3. As long as we detect one line of malicious code, we will trigger an alert.

Chapter 25
Runtime Adaption Techniques for HPC Applications

Edgar Gabriel
University of Houston, USA

ABSTRACT

This chapter discusses runtime adaption techniques targeting high-performance computing applications. In order to exploit the capabilities of modern high-end computing systems, applications and system software have to be able to adapt their behavior to hardware and application characteristics. Using the Abstract Data and Communication Library (ADCL) as the driving example, the chapter shows the advantage of using adaptive techniques to exploit characteristics of the network and of the application. This allows to reduce the execution time of applications significantly and to avoid having to maintain different architecture dependent versions of the source code.

INTRODUCTION

High Performance Computing (HPC) has reshaped science and industry in many areas. Recent groundbreaking achievements in biology, drug design and medical computing would not have been possible without the usage of massive computational resources. However, software development for HPC systems is currently facing significant challenges, since many of the software technologies applied in the last ten years have reached their limits. The number of applications being capable of efficiently using several thousands of processors or achieving a sustained performance of multiple teraflops is very limited and is usually the result of many person-years of optimizations for a particular platform. These optimizations are however often not portable. As an example, an application optimized for a commodity PC cluster performs (often) poorly on an IBM Blue Gene or the NEC Earth Simulator. Among the problems application developers face are the wide variety of available hardware and software components, such as

DOI: 10.4018/978-1-60566-661-7.ch025

- Processor type and frequency, number of processor per node and number of cores per processor,
- Size and performance of the main memory, cache hierarchy,
- Characteristics and performance of the network interconnect,
- Operating system, device drivers and communication libraries,

and the influence of each of these components on the performance of their application. Hence, an end-user faces a unique execution environment on each parallel machine he uses. Even experts struggle to fully understand correlations between hardware and software parameters of the execution environment and their effect on the performance of a parallel application.

Motivating Example

In the following, we would like to clarify the dilemma of an application developer using a realistic and common example. Consider a regular 3-dimensional finite difference code using an iterative algorithm to solve the resulting system of linear equations. The parallel equation solver consists of three different operations requiring communication: scalar products, vector norms and matrix-vector products. Although the first two operations do have an impact on the scalability of the algorithm, the dominating operation from the communication perspective is the matrix-vector product. The occurring communication pattern for this operation is neighborhood communication, i.e. each process has to exchange data with its six neighboring processes multiple times per iteration of the solver. Depending on the execution environment and some parameters of the application (e.g. problem size), different implementations for the very same communication pattern can lead to optimal performance. We analyze the execution times for 200 iterations of the equation solver applied for a steady problem using 32 processes on the same number of processors on a state-of-the-art PC cluster for two different problem sizes ($32\times32\times32$ and $64\times32\times32$ mesh points per process) and two different network interconnects (4xInfiniBand and Gigabit Ethernet). The neighborhood communication has been implemented in four different ways, named here *fcfs, fcfs-pack, ordered, overlap*. While the nodes/processors have been allocated exclusively for these measurements using a batch-scheduler, the network interconnect was shared with other applications using the same PC cluster.

The results indicate, that already for this simple test-case on a single platform three different implementations of the neighborhood communication lead to the best performance of this application: although the differences between the different implementations are not dramatic over this network interconnect, *fcfs* shows the best performance for both problem sizes when using the InfiniBand interconnect. This implementation is initiating all required communications simultaneously using asynchronous communication followed by a Waitall operation on all pending messages. However, for the Gigabit Ethernet interconnect the *fcfs* approach seems to congest the network. Instead, the implementation which is overlapping communication and computation (*overlap*), is showing the best performance for the small problem size (6.2 seconds for *overlap* vs. 6.6 seconds for *fcfs*, 7.5 seconds for *fcfs-pack*, 8.1 seconds for *ordered*) while the *ordered* algorithm, which limits the number of messages concurrently on the fly, is the fastest implementation for the large problem size for this network interconnect (14.7 seconds for *ordered* vs. 26.9 seconds for *fcfs*, 19.9 for *fcfs-pack* and 23.4 seconds for *overlap*). The implementation considered to be the fastest one over the InfiniBand network leads thus to a performance penalty of nearly

80% over Gigabit Ethernet. An application developer implementing the neighborhood communication using a particular, fixed algorithm will inevitably give up performance on certain platforms.

Problem Description

As demonstrated above, the wide variety in hardware and software leads to the inherent limitation that any code sequence or communication operation which contributes (significantly) towards the overall execution time of an application will inevitably give up performance, if the operation is hard-coded in the source code, i.e. the code sequence or communication operation does not have the ability to adapt its behavior at runtime due to changing conditions. Traditional tuning approaches have their fundamental limitations, and are not capable to solve the problem in a satisfactory manner.

Specific Goals

The goal of this chapter therefore is to present dynamic runtime optimization techniques applied in high performance computing. Runtime adaption in HPC serves two purposes: first it allows tweaking the performance of a code in order to exploit the capabilities of the hardware. At the same time it simplifies software maintenance, since an application developer does not have to maintain multiple different versions of his code for different platforms.

The chapter focuses on one specific project, the Abstract Data and Communication Library (ADCL). ADCL enables the creation of self-optimizing applications by allowing an application to register alternative versions of a particular function. Furthermore, ADCL offers several pre-defined operations allowing for seamless optimization of often occurring communication patterns in MPI parallel application. Although not fundamentally restricted to collective communication operations, most operation optimized through ADCL are collective in nature. In the following we discuss the related work in that area, present the concept of ADCL and give performance results obtained in three different scenarios using ADCL.

BACKGROUND

In the last couple of years many projects have been dealing with optimizing collective operations in High Performance Computing. For the subsequent discussion, projects are categorized as approaches which are applying either static tuning, i.e. projects which typically lead to software components that cannot alter their behavior during execution, or dynamic tuning, in which the software/application does adapt at runtime its behavior as a reaction to varying conditions.

Static Tuning of Applications

Most projects applying static tuning focus on one of two approaches to determine the best performing implementation for a particular operation: they either apply a pre-execution tuning step by testing the performance of different versions for the same operation for various message length and process counts; alternatively, some projects rely on performance prediction using sophisticated communication models to compare different algorithms. We will discuss representatives, advantages and disadvantages for both approaches in the next paragraphs.

Among the best known projects representing the first approach are the Automatically Tuned Linear Algebra Software (ATLAS) (Whaley, 2005) and the Automatically Tuned Collective Communications (ATCC) (Pjesivac-Grbovic, 2007) framework. ATLAS is a library providing optimized implementations of the Basic Linear Algebra Software (BLAS) library routines. As one of the very first projects acknowledging the wide variety of hardware and software components, ATLAS uses an extensive configuration step to determine the best performing implementation from a given pool of available algorithms on a specific platform and a given compiler for each operation. Furthermore, based on additional information such as cache sizes, ATLAS determines optimal, internal parameters such as the blocking factor for blocked algorithms. As a result of the configuration step, the ATLAS library will only contain the routines known to deliver the best performance on that platform.

Similarly to ATLAS, ATCC determines the optimal algorithms for MPI's collective operations on a given platform by using a parallel configuration step. During this configure step, several implementations for each collective operations are being tested and the fastest algorithm for each message length is stored in a configuration file. The resulting set of algorithms and parameters for this platform are then used during the execution of the application. In order to minimize the size of the configuration file, ATCC uses quad-tree encoding to represent the overall decision tree. This is also used to conclude which algorithm to use for message sizes/process counts which have not been tested in the parallel configure step.

Projects such as ATLAS and ATCC face a number of fundamental drawbacks. First, the tuning procedure itself often takes more time than running an individual application. Thus, in case the system administrators of a cluster do not reserve the according time slots to tune these libraries in advance – and typically they will only reserve limited time and not multiple days to tune e.g. the MPI collective operations exhaustingly on a multi-thousand node cluster - end-users themselves will very probably not use their valuable compute time to perform these time consuming operations. Additionally, several factors influencing the performance of the application can only be determined while executing the application. These factors include process placement by the batch scheduler due to non-uniform network behavior (Evans, 2003), resource utilization due to the fact that some resources such as the network switch or file systems are shared by multiple applications, operating system jitter leading to slow-down of a subset of processes utilized by a parallel job (Petrini, 2003) and application characteristics such as communication volume and frequencies. Furthermore, some projects have also highlighted the influence of process arrivals patterns to the performance of collective communication operations: depending on the work that each process has to perform, the order in which processes start to execute a collective operation varies strongly depending on the application. Thus, the algorithm determined to lead to the best performance using a synthetic benchmark might in fact be suboptimal in a real application (Faraj, 2007).

The second common approach used e.g. by the MagPIe project (Kielmann, 1999) compares the predicted execution time of various algorithms for a given operation using performance models. Although some of the communication models used such as LogP (Culler, 1993) and LogGP (Alexandrov, 1995) are highly sophisticated, these projects ultimately suffer from three limitations. Firstly, it is often hard to determine some parameters of (sophisticated) communication models. As an example, no approach is published as of today which derives a reasonable estimate of the receive-overhead in the LogGP model (Hoefler, 2007). Second, while it is possible to develop a performance model for a simple MPI-level communication operation, more complex functions involving alternating and irregular sequences of computation and communication have hardly been modeled as of today. Lastly, all models have their fundamental limitations and break-down scenarios, since they represent simplifications of the real world behavior of the machines. Thus, while modeling collective communication operations can improve the understanding of performance characteristics for various algorithms, tuning complex operations based on these models is fundamentally limited.

Dynamic Tuning of Applications

The dynamic optimization and tuning problem can be related to multiple research areas in various domains. Starting from the lower level of the software hierarchy, most runtime optimization problems are represented as empirical search procedure, having the boundary condition that any evaluation of the results has to be computationally inexpensive to minimize the overhead introduced by the runtime optimization itself. Depending on the type of the parameters tuned during the runtime optimization, various approaches from optimizations theory (Gill 1993) can be applied as well, e.g. the method of steepest decent in case of a contiguous, real-valued parameter. Vuduc (Vuduc, 2004) provides an excellent overview of various algorithms.

On top of the search algorithms are often statistical methods used to remove outliers and analyze the performance results of the various alternatives tested during the search space. These algorithms can vary in their complexity and range from simple inter-quartile range methods to sophisticated algorithms from cluster analysis and robust statistics. Benkert (Benkert, 2008) gives a good overview and a performance comparison of different approaches.

Finally, since most approaches used in runtime optimization are separated into an evaluation phase, where the runtime library uses certain events or instances in order to learn the best approach for those operations, and a phase applying the knowledge determined earlier, theories from machine learning (Witten, 2005) can often be applied as well. Once again, the main constraint for applying machine learning algorithms is due to the fact that the overhead introduced by the learning algorithm itself has to be inevitable cheap for a runtime library.

A vast body of research for code optimizations is furthermore available in the field of compilers. As an example ADAPT (Voss, 2000) introduces runtime adaption and optimization by having different variants of a code sequence. During a sampling phase, the runtime environment explores the performance of the different versions and decides which one performs best. The runtime environment can furthermore invoke a separate dynamic code generator, which delivers new alternative code versions which can be loaded dynamically.

Despite of the significant progress in these areas, the number of projects applying automated (runtime) tuning techniques in HPC is still very limited. Among those projects are FFTW (Fringo, 2005), PhiPAC (Vuduc, 2004), STAR-MPI (Faraj, 2006), and SALSA (Dongarra, 2003). In the following, we detail three of these projects which utilize advanced adaptation techniques, and compare them to various aspects of ADCL (Gabriel, 2007).

FFTW

The FFTW (Fastest Fourier Transform in the West) library optimizes sequential and parallel Fast Fourier Transform (FFT) operations. To compute an FFT, the application has to invoke first a 'planner' step specifying a problem which has to be solved. Depending on an argument passed by the application to the planner routine, the library measures the actual runtime of many different implementations and selects the fastest one (FFTW_MEASURE). In case many transforms of the same size are executed in an application, this 'plan' delivers the optimal performance for all subsequent FFTs. Since creating a plan can be time consuming, FFTW also provides a mode of operation where the planner comes up quickly with a good estimate, which might however not necessarily be the optimal one (FFTW_ESTIMATE). The decision procedure is initiated just once by the user. Thus, FFTW makes the runtime optimization upfront in the planner step without performing any useful work. In contrary to the approach taken by FFTW, ADCL integrated the runtime selection logic into the regular execution of the applications. Thus, the ADCL approach enables the library to restart the runtime selection logic in case the performance deviates significantly from the performance measured during the tuning step is observed, e.g. due to changing network conditions.

FFTW has also the notion of historic learning, namely using a feature called *Wisdom*. The user can export experiences gathered in previous runs into a file, and reload it at subsequent executions. However, the wisdom concept in FFTW lacks any notion of related problems, i.e. wisdom can only be reused for exactly the same problem size that was used to generate it. Furthermore, the wisdom functionality also does not include any mechanism which helps to recognize outdated or invalid wisdom, e.g. if the platform used for collecting the wisdom is significantly different than the platform used while reloading the wisdom.

STAR-MPI

STAR-MPI incorporates runtime optimization of collective communication operations providing a similar API as defined in the MPI specifications. Using an Automatic Empirical Optimization Software (AEOS), the library performs dynamic tuning of each collective operation by determining the performance of all available algorithms in a repository. Once performance data for all available algorithms have been gathered, STAR-MPI determines the most efficient algorithm.

STAR-MPI tunes different instances/call-sites for each operation separately. In order to achieve this goal, the prototypes of the STAR-MPI collective operations have been extended by an additional argument, namely an integer value uniquely identifying each call-site. This is however hidden from applications by using pre-processor directives to redirect the MPI calls to their STAR-MPI.

Similarly to all projects focusing on runtime adaption techniques, the largest overhead in STAR-MPI comes from the initial evaluation of the underperforming algorithms and the distributed decision logic, which is necessary to ensure that all processes agree on the final 'winner'. While STAR-MPI does a good job of minimizing the latter one by only introducing a single collective global reduction, the first item, i.e. testing of underperforming implementations is highly evident in STAR-MPI, due to the independent optimization of all operations per call-site. In contrary to that, ADCL allows for both, per-call site optimization and concatenating performance data of multiple call-sites for the same operation and message length.

One approach used in STAR-MPI to minimize the problem outlined in the previous paragraph is to introduce grouping of algorithms. STAR-MPI initially compares a single algorithm from all available groups. After the winner group has been determined, the library does a fine-tuning of the performance by evaluating all other available algorithms within the winner group. As described later, ADCL further extends the notion of grouping implementations using an attribute concept, which allows characterizing algorithms and alternative implementations without enforcing the participation of an algorithm in a single group.

SALSA

The Self-Adapting Large-scale Solver Architecture (SALSA) aims at providing the best suitable linear and non-linear system solver to an application. Using the characteristics of the application matrix, the solver contacts a knowledge database and provides an estimate on the best solver to use. Among the characteristics used for choosing the right solver are structural properties of the matrix (e.g. maximum and minimum number of non-zeros per row), matrix norms such as the 1- or the Frobenius-norm, and spectral properties.

Recently, the authors have applied algorithms from machine learning such as boosting algorithms and alternating decision trees to improve the prediction quality of the system (Bhowmick, in press). The decision algorithm has been trained by using a large set of matrices from various application domains. Among the interesting features of this approach is, that the algorithm is capable of handling missing features for the prediction, e.g. in case some norms are considered too expensive to be calculated at runtime. The main drawback of the approach within the context of this chapter lies in the fact that the training steps have to be executed before running the application, due to the computation complexity of the according operations. The problem is however softened by the fact that the knowledge data base is per design reusable across multiple runs/executions.

THE ABSTRACT DATA AND COMMUNICATION LIBRARY

The Abstract Data and Communication Library (ADCL) enables the creation of self-optimizing applications by either registering alternative versions of a particular function or use predefined operations capable of self-optimization. ADCL uses the initial iterations of the application to determine the fastest available code version. Once performance data on a sufficient number of versions is available, the library makes a decision on which alternative to use throughout the rest of the execution.

From the conceptual perspective, ADCL takes advantage of two characteristics of most scientific applications:

1. Iterative execution: most parallel, scientific applications are centered around a large loop, and execute therefore the same code sequence over and over again. Consider for example an application which solves a time dependent partial differential equation (PDE). These problems are often solved by discretizing the PDE in space and time, and by solving the resulting system of linear equations for each time step. Depending on the application, iteration counts can reach six digit numbers.
2. Collective execution: most large scale parallel applications are based on data decomposition, i.e. all processes execute the same code sequence on different data items. Processes are typically also synchronized, i.e. all processes are in the same loop iteration. This synchronization is often required for numerical reasons and is enforced by communication operations.

Description of the ADCL API

The ADCL API offers high level interfaces of application level collective operations. These are required in order to be able to switch the implementation of the according collective operation within the library without modifying the application itself. The main objects within the ADCL API are:

- **ADCL_Topology**: provides a description of the process topology and neighborhood relations within the application.
- **ADCL_Vector**: specifies the data structures to be used during the communication. The user can for example register a data structure such as a matrix with the ADCL library, detailing how many dimensions the object has, the extent of each dimension, the number of halo-cells, and the basic datatype of the object.
- **ADCL_Function**: each ADCL function is the equivalent to an actual implementation of a particular operation.
- **ADCL_Fnctset**: a collection of ADCL functions providing the same functionality. ADCL provides pre-defined function-sets, such as for neighborhood communication (ADCL_FNCTSET _NEIGHBORHOOD). The user can however also register its own functions in order to utilize the ADCL runtime selection logic.
- **ADCL_Attribute**: abstraction for a particular characteristic of a function/implementation. Each attribute is represented by the set of possible values for this characteristic.
- **ADCL_Attrset**: an ADCL Attribute-set is a collection of ADCL attributes. An ADCL Function-set can have an ADCL Attribute-set attached to it, in which case all functions in the function-set have to provide valid values for each attribute in the attribute-set.
- **ADCL_Request**: combines a process topology, a function-set and a vector object. The application can initiate a communication by *starting* a particular ADCL request.

The following code sequence gives a simple example for an ADCL code, using a 2-D neighborhood communication on a 2-D process topology. This application first generates a 2-D process topology using an MPI Cartesian communicator. By registering a multi-dimensional matrix with ADCL, the library generates a vector-object. Combining the process topology, the vector object and the predefined function set ADCL_FNCTSET_NEIGHBORHOOD allows the library to determine automatically which portions of the vector have to be transferred to which process. Afterwards, each call to ADCL_Request_start initiates a neighborhood communication.

```
double vector[...][...];
ADCL_Vector vec;
ADCL_Topology topo;
ADCL_Request request;
/* Generate a 2-D process topology */
MPI_Cart_create (MPI_COMM_WORLD, 2, cart_dims, periods,
0, &cart_comm);
ADCL_Topology_create (cart_comm, &topo);
/* Register a 2D vector with ADCL */
ADCL_Vector_register (ndims, vec_dims, NUM_HALO_CELLS,
MPI_DOUBLE, vector, &vec);
/* Combine description of data structure and process topology */
ADCL_Request_create (vec, topo, ADCL_FNCTSET_NEIGHBORHOOD, &re-
quest);
/* Main application loop */
```

```
for (i=0; i<NIT; i++) {
    ...
   /* Initiate neighborhood communication */
   ADCL_Request_start (request);
   ...
}
```

Technical Concept

Two key components of ADCL are the algorithm used to determine, which versions of a particular operation shall be tested, and how to decide efficiently across multiple process on the best performing version. In the following, we give some details on both components.

Distributed Decision Logic

A fundamental assumption within ADCL is, that the library has multiple alternative versions for a particular functionality available to choose from. These alternatives will be stored as different functions in the same function-set. The number of alternatives can reach from a few, (e.g. the user providing three different version of a parallel matrix-multiply operation) to many millions, in case the user is exploring different values for internal or external parameters, such as various buffer sizes, loop unroll depth etc. As of today, ADCL incorporates two different strategies for version selection at runtime. The first version incorporates a simple brute-force search, which evaluates all available alternatives. An alternative version selection algorithm is used, if the user annotates the implementations by a set of attributes/attribute values. These attributes are used to reduce the time taken by the runtime selection procedure, by tuning each attribute separately.

Independently of the version selection approach used by the library, the collective decision logic of ADCL will have to compare performance data of multiple functions gathered on different processes. The challenge lies in the fact, that in the most general case, processes only have access to their own performance data and performance data for the same code version might in fact differ significantly across multiple processes. Distributing the performance data of all processes for all versions to all other processes is however not feasible, since the costs for communicating these large volumes of data would often offset the performance benefits achieved by runtime tuning. The approach taken by the library relies therefore on data reduction, i.e. each process provides only a single value for each alternative version of the code section being optimized. In order to detail the algorithm let's assume ADCL gather n measurements/data points for each version i on each process j. Let us denote the execution time of the kth measurement by $t(I, j, k)$. In an initial step, the library removes outliers, i.e. measurements not fulfilling a condition $C = t(i, j, k) \mid t(i, j, k) < b \cdot \min_k t(i, j, k)$ with b being a well defined constant, from the data set. This leads to a filtered subset$M^f(i, j) = \{t(i, j, k) \mid t(i, j, k)$ fulfills $C\}$of measurements with cardinality $n_f(i, j)$. Then, the performance measurements for each version are analyzed locally on each process and characterized by the local average execution time

$$m(i,j) = \frac{1}{n}\sum_{k} t(i,j,k)$$

and its filtered counterpart

$$m_f(i,j) = \frac{1}{n_f}\sum_{k \in M^f(i,j)} t(i,j,k)$$

as estimates of the mean value. In a global reduction operation, the library determines for each version the maximum average execution time across all processes

$$m(i) = \max_j m(i,j)$$

$$m_f(i) = \max_j m_f(i,j)$$

considering all respectively only filtered data, and the maximum number of outliers $n_o(i)$ over all processes

$$n_o(i) = \max_j n_o(i,j)$$

This reduction is motivated by a fundamental law in parallel computing, which states, that the performance of a (synchronous) application is determined by the slowest process/ processor. Finally, the library selects the maximum execution time including or excluding outliers by

$$r(i) = \begin{cases} m_f(i) & \textit{if} \quad n_o(i) \le nm_o \\ m(i) & \textit{else} \end{cases}$$

depending on whether the maximum number of outliers allowed is exceeded or not. The algorithm i' fulfilling $r(i') = \min_i r(i)$ is chosen as the best one. Assuming that the runtime environment produces reproducible performance data over the lifetime of an application, this algorithm is guaranteed to find the fastest of available implementations for the current tuple of {problem size, runtime environment, versions tested}.

Attribute Based Tuning

ADCL extends the algorithm grouping concept used in STAR-MPI by introducing the formal notion of attributes. The main idea behind that concept is, that any implementation of a collective communication operation has certain implicit requirements to the hardware and software environment in order to achieve the expected performance. As an example, ADCL uses as of today three attributes in order to characterize an implementation for the neighborhood communication function-set:

1. Number of simultaneous communication partners: this attribute characterizes how many communication operations are initiated at once. For neighborhood communication, the currently supported values by ADCL are all (ADCL attribute value *aao*) and one (*pair*). This parameter is typically bound by the network/switch.
2. Handling of non-contiguous messages: supported values are MPI derived data types (*ddt*) and pack/unpack (*pack*). The optimal value for this parameter will depend on the MPI library and some hardware characteristics.
3. Data transfer primitive: a total of eight different data transfer primitives are available in ADCL as of today, which can be categorized as either blocking communication (e.g. MPI_Send, MPI_Recv), non-blocking/asynchronous communication (e.g. MPI_Isend, MPI_Irecv), or one-sided operations (e.g. MPI_Put, MPI_Get). Which data transfer primitive will deliver the best performance depends on the implementation of the according function in the MPI library and potentially some hardware support (e.g. for one-sided communication).

Please note that not all combinations of attributes might really lead to feasible implementations. As an example, implementations using a blocking data transfer primitives such as MPI_Send/Recv cannot be applied for implementations having more than one simultaneous communication partner, since this would potentially result in a deadlock. Therefore, a total of 20 implementations are currently available within ADCL for the n-dimensional neighborhood communication. Further attributes such as the capability of the library/environment to overlap communication and computation will be added in the near future.

In order to speed up the selection logic, an alternative runtime heuristic based on the attributes characterizing an implementation has been developed. The heuristic is based on the assumption, that the fastest implementation for a given problem size on a given execution environment is also the implementation having 'optimal' values for the attributes in the given scenario. Therefore, the algorithm tries to determine the optimal value for each attribute used to characterize an implementation. Once the optimal value for an attribute has been found, the library removes all implementations not having the required value for the according attribute and thus shrinks the list of available implementations.

In order to explain the approach in more details, let's assume that an implementation is characterized by N attributes. Each attribute has $n_v(i),\ i = 1,N$ possible values $v(i, j), j = 1, n_v(i)$. The library assumes that the optimal value $k_{opt}(i)$ for an attribute i has been found, if $rc(i)$ measurements confirm this hypothesis. In order to be able to deduct from a set of measurements towards the optimal value of a single attribute, the library only compares the execution times of implementations whose attributes differ only in the according attribute. To clarify this approach, please assume that we have to deal with four different attributes $(N = 4)$, and want to determine the best value for the second attribute. We assume that this attribute has three distinct values $(n_v(2) = 3)$), e.g. $v(2, 1) = 1$, $v(2, 2) = 2$, and $v(2, 3) = 3$. Since the values of all attributes except for the second one are being constant we assume that any performance differences between the three implementations can be accredited to the second attribute. The library determines collectively across all processes which of the three implementations has the lowest average execution time, using the same approach as outlined in the section 0. If we assume as an example, that the implementation with the attribute values $[v(1, j'), 3, v(3, j''), v(4, j''')]$ has the lowest average execution time, the library would develop the hypothesis that 3 is the optimal value for the second attribute. At this point, only one set of measurement confirms the hypothesis that 3 is the optimal value for the second attribute. Thus, the confidence value in this hypothesis is set to 1. Typically, a hypothesis has to be confirmed by more than one set of measurements before ADCL considers this hypothesis to be probably correct. Thus, an additional set of measurements with differing (but constant) values for one of the other attributes has to be gathered, e.g by using $v(3, j''+1)$ as the value for the third attribute. If the new set of measurements confirms the result of the previous set, the confidence value for the hypothesis is increased. If another attribute value is determined for this set of measurements to be the best one, the confidence value for the original performance hypothesis is decreased by one. Once a hypothesis reaches the required number of confirmations, the library removes all implementations which do not have the optimal value for the according attribute and shrinks the list of available implementations. Please note that if the measurements do not converge toward an optimal value for an attribute, no implementation will be removed based on this attribute.

Ongoing Research

Additionally to the topics described so far, active research is currently being performed in multiple areas. In this subsection we would like to highlight some of the topics.

The first research direction is related to the version management and selection within ADCL. As described in the previous paragraphs, ADCL utilizes as of today either a brute force search strategy, which is applied in case a function-set is not characterized by any attributes. Alternatively, ADCL can utilize the per-attribute based search strategy. Both approaches can however further be improved. The brute force search can be extended by algorithm containing early stopping criteria, as described in (Vuduc, 2004). This approach helps to reduce the number of alternative versions tested by randomly selecting versions to test and giving a measure, when the worst implementations have been excluded with a certain probability.

The main restriction of the per-attribute based search strategy as of today is that it assumes that attributes are fundamentally not correlated. Depending on the usage scenario and attributes defined by the application, this assumption is not necessarily correct. However, there is a broad body of work known in experimental design theory, namely the 2k factorial design algorithms, which provide an excellent framework for version management of correlated attributes. ADCL is currently being extended to include 2k factorial design algorithms for correlated attributes.

A second active research area is to introduce the notion of historic learning in ADCL, i.e. develop mechanism to propagate results of various optimizations from one run to another run. Historic Learning in ADCL extends the Wisdom concept of FFTW in multiple areas: first, the historic data in ADCL is always accompanied by a high level description of the architecture used to determine the results of the optimization. This is necessary in order to develop mechanisms which can discard automatically data in the historic data base, e.g. in case an application is run on a different network than the machine had when a particular optimization has been performed. Discarding historic data is furthermore supported by introducing the notion of expected performance. In case the historic data suggests a particular version of a function-set to lead to the optimal performance, ADCL can also generate an estimate of the execution time for that operation. If the measured execution time for the operation deviates from the predicted execution time by a given threshold, the library automatically discards the results and starts a new optimization, assuming that the runtime conditions have changed compared to the original assumptions.

Lastly, ADCL introduces the notion of related problems, in order to have the ability to deduct results from similar problems solved on similar machines. Related problems in that are defined by introducing a function-set specific distance measure. As an example, for the neighborhood communication the library uses a Euclidean distance between two problems using the vector of the data sizes transmitted to each process as the base measure.

PERFORMANCE EVALUATION

In the following, we present performance results of three different scenarios. The first one discusses the optimization of the three-dimensional neighborhood communication as often occurring in scientific applications. The second scenario describes the results achieved for tuning a parallel matrix-matrix multiply kernel. Finally, the third scenario describes the usage of ADCL within the context of a tool optimizing the system parameters of the Open MPI library.

Optimizing 3-D Nearest Neighbor Communication

In the following, we will analyze the effect of using different implementations for the neighborhood communication on the performance of a parallel, iterative solver as often applied in scientific application. The software used in this section solves a set of linear equations that stem from discretization of a partial differential equation (PDE) using center differences. The parallel implementation subdivides the computational domain into subdomains of equal size. The processes are mapped onto a regular three-dimensional Cartesian topology. Due to the discretization scheme, a processor has to communicate with at most six processors to perform a matrix-vector product. For the subsequent analysis, the code has been modified such that it makes use of the ADCL library, i.e. the sections of the source code which established the 3-D process topology and the neighborhood communication routines have been replaced by the according ADCL counterparts.

In order to evaluate the 'correct' decision of the runtime selection logic, we additionally executed the same application using one single implementation at a time by circumventing the runtime selection logic of ADCL. In order to make the conditions as comparable as possible, the reference data was produced within the same batch scheduler allocation and thus had the same node assignments. We will refer to these measurements as verification runs throughout the rest of this section. During each verification run, the execution times of 700 iterations per implementation were stored and subsequently averaged over all three runs. Depending on the machine, we have executed three different problem sizes, namely a small test case with (32 x 32 x 32) mesh points per process, a medium test case with (64 x 32 x 32) mesh points per process, and a large test case with (64 x 64 x 32) mesh point per process. Since most MPI libraries do not show performance advantages for MPI put/get operations compared to two-sided communication on a typical PC cluster and in order to simplify our analysis, we have configured ADCL for the following tests without the one-sided data transfer primitives. This leaves twelve implementations for the 3-D neighborhood communication for the runtime selection logic to choose from. The number of tests required to evaluate an implementation has been set to 30.

Tests have been executed on six platforms all in all:

Table 1. Best performing implementation on different architectures and for different problem sizes

Architecture	# of proc	Pb Size/Proc	Best implementation
DataStar p655 (DS)	64	64x32x32	Sendlrecv_aao
		64x64x32	Sendlrecv_aao
	128	64x32x32	Sendlrecv_pair_pack
		64x64x32	Isendlrecv_aao
	256	64x32x32	Isendlrecv_aao
		64x64x32	Isendlrecv_aao
	512	64x32x32	Sendlrecv_pair_pack
		64x64x32	Isendlrecv_aao
IBM Blue Gene/L (BG)	128	64x32x32	Sendlrecv_pair_pack
		64x64x32	Isendlrecv_aao_pack
	256	64x32x32	Sendlrecv_pair_pack
		64x64x32	Isendlrecv_aao_pack
	512	64x32x32	Sendlrecv_pair_pack
		64x64x32	Isendlrecv_aao_pack
NEC SX8 (SX)	16	64x32x32	Sendrecv_pair
		64x64x32	Sendrecv_pair
	32	64x32x32	Sendlrecv_pair_pack
		64x64x32	Sendlrecv_pair_pack
	64	64x32x32	Sendrecv_pair_pack
		64x64x32	Sendlrecv_pair_pack
SharkIB (ShIB)	32	32x32x32	Isendlrecv_aao
		64x64x32	Sendlrecv_pair_pack
	48	32x32x32	Sendlrecv_aao
		64x64x32	Isendlrecv_aao
SharkGE (ShGE)	32	32x32x32	Isendlrecv_aao
		64x64x32	Isendlrecv_aao_pack
	48	32x32x32	Isendlrecv_aao
		64x64x32	Sendrecv_pair
CacauGE (CGE)		64x32x32	SendRecv_pair_pack

1. **IBM Blue Gene/L**: The Blue Gene system at the San Diego Supercomputing Center consists of 3,072 compute nodes with 6,144 processors. Each node consists of two PowerPC processors that run at 700 MHz and share 512 MB of memory. All compute nodes are connected by two high-speed networks: a 3-D torus for point-to-point message passing and a global tree for collective message passing. We ran tests using 128, 256 and 512 processes.
2. **NEC SX8**: the installation at the High Performance Computing Center in Stuttgart, Germany (HLRS) consists of 72 nodes, each node having 8 vector processors of 16 GOPS peak (2Ghz) and 128 GB of main memory. The nodes are interconnected by an IXS switch. Each node can send and receive data with 16 GB/s in each direction. We executed tests with 16, 32 and 64 processes.

Figure 1. Performance overhead of the slowest vs. fastest implementation on each platform and for each problem size

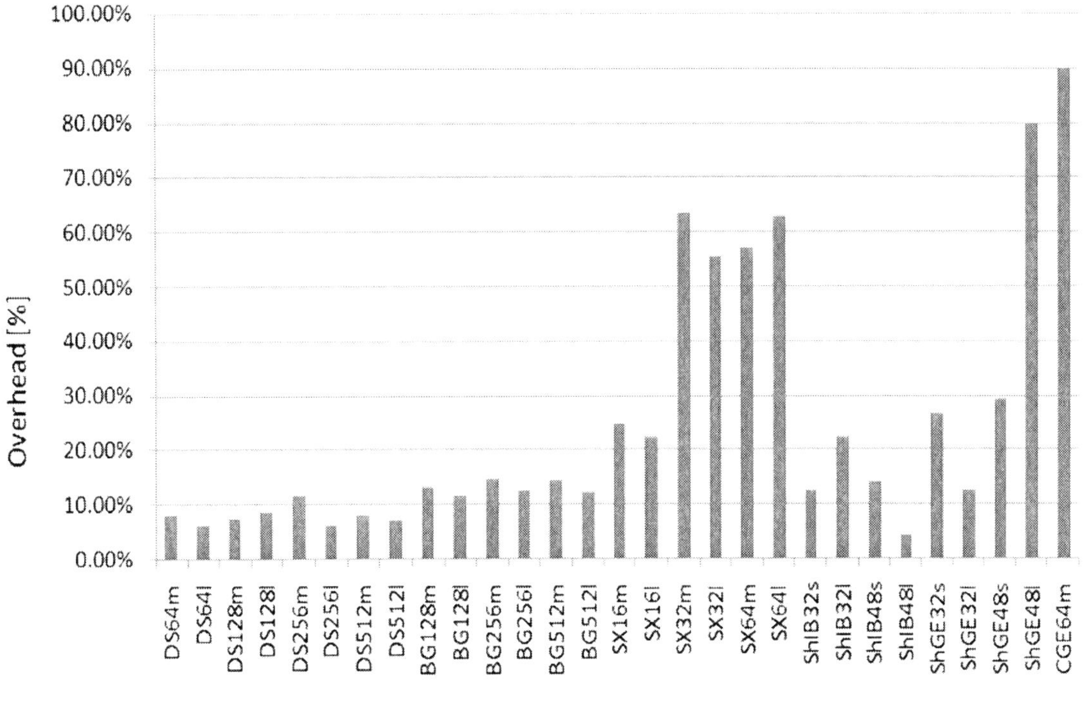

3. **DataStar p655**: the p655 partition of DataStar cluster at San Diego Supercomputing Center has 272 8-way compute nodes 176 nodes with 1.5-GHz Power4+ CPUs and 16 GB of memory, and 96 with 1.7 GHz Power4+ CPUs and 32 GB of memory. The nodes are connected by an IBM high-speed Federation switch. The tests executed and presented in this subsection include 64, 128, 256 and 512 processes runs.
4. **SharkIB**: this cluster consists of 24 nodes, each node having a dual core AMD Opteron processor and 2 GB of main memory. The nodes are interconnected by a 4xInfiniBand network. We present results for 32 and 48 processes on 16 respectively 24 nodes.
5. **SharkGE:** This is same cluster as described in the previous bullet, using however the Gigabit Ethernet network interconnect.
6. **CacauGE**: Cacau is a 200 node, dual processor Intel EM64T cluster at the HLRS. Although the main network of the cluster is a 4xInfiniBand interconnect, we used for the subsequent analysis the secondary network of the cluster, namely a hierarchical Gigabit Ethernet network. This network consists of six 48-port switches, each 48-port switch has four links to the upper level 24 port Gigabit Ethernet switch. Thus, this network has a 12:1 blocking factor. We have executed tests using 64 processors on 64 nodes in order to ensure that communication between the processes has to use two or more of the 48-port switches.

Figure 2. Comparison of the largest problems run on each patform (left) and of various platforms and problem sizes (right)

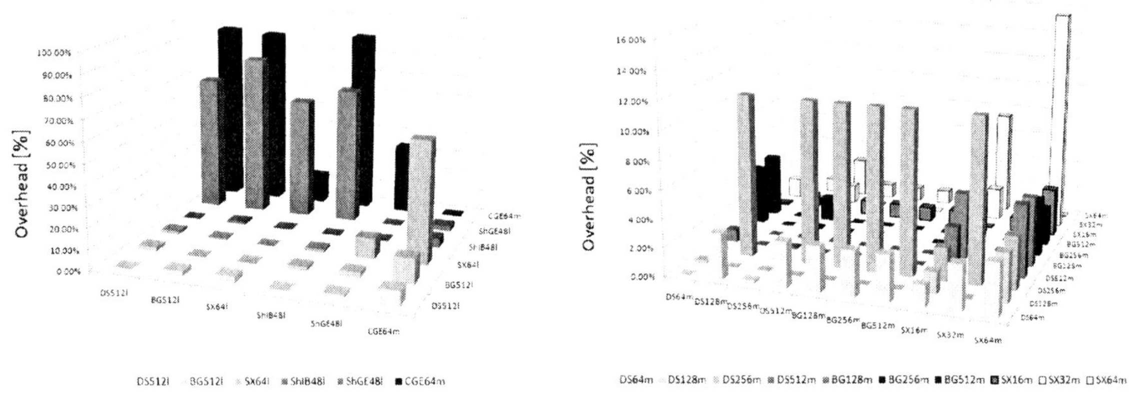

Table 1 summarizes for each platform and problem size the implementation of the neighborhood communication which leads to the overall best performance. In the 29 different test cases presented here, seven out of the twelve implementations available in ADCL for that communication pattern turn out to lead to the minimal execution time of the application. Most notably, there are changes for the best performing implementation depending on both, the number of processors and the problem size per process for basically all platforms tested.

In the following, we show that (1) hard coding a particular code sequence can lead to a significant performance penalty on any platform; (2) pre-tuning the code on a platform does not lead to portable performance on other platforms and (3) that ADCL is capable of generating portable code with minimal overhead compared to manually tuned versions.

Since most applications hard-code the neighborhood communication using a sequence of Send/Receive operations, we show in the following diagram the performance implication of potentially using a suboptimal code version for the neighborhood communication on the overall performance of the code. For this, we show in Figure 1 the maximum performance penalty that an application code could face for that scenario by comparing the performance of the best vs. the worst performing implementation. The penalty an application faces in this scenario does depend on the platform used. While most of the platforms analyzed show a performance penalty in the range of 5-20% in this test, some platforms show also more dramatic variability to the implementation, such as both platforms using Gigabit Ethernet networks, for which the execution time nearly doubles in the worst case. The NEC SX8 also shows a significant sensitivity to the implementation with an additional overhead of more than 60% depending on the number of processes and the problem size.

Next, we would like to quantify the penalty an application would pay by using a code version which has been tuned on one platform on another platform. We detail two scenarios. First, for each platform we choose the largest problem on the largest number of processors that we ran, and evaluate what the performance penalty would be to use an implementation, which has been determined to be the winner on any of the other platforms. In Figure 2, each entry represents the performance penalty of the application running on the platform shown on the x-axis when using the implementation determined to be the winner on the platform shown in the according y-axis. As an example, the bar in the first row, third column

Figure 3. Performance difference between the manually tuned and an automatically tuned code version using ADCL

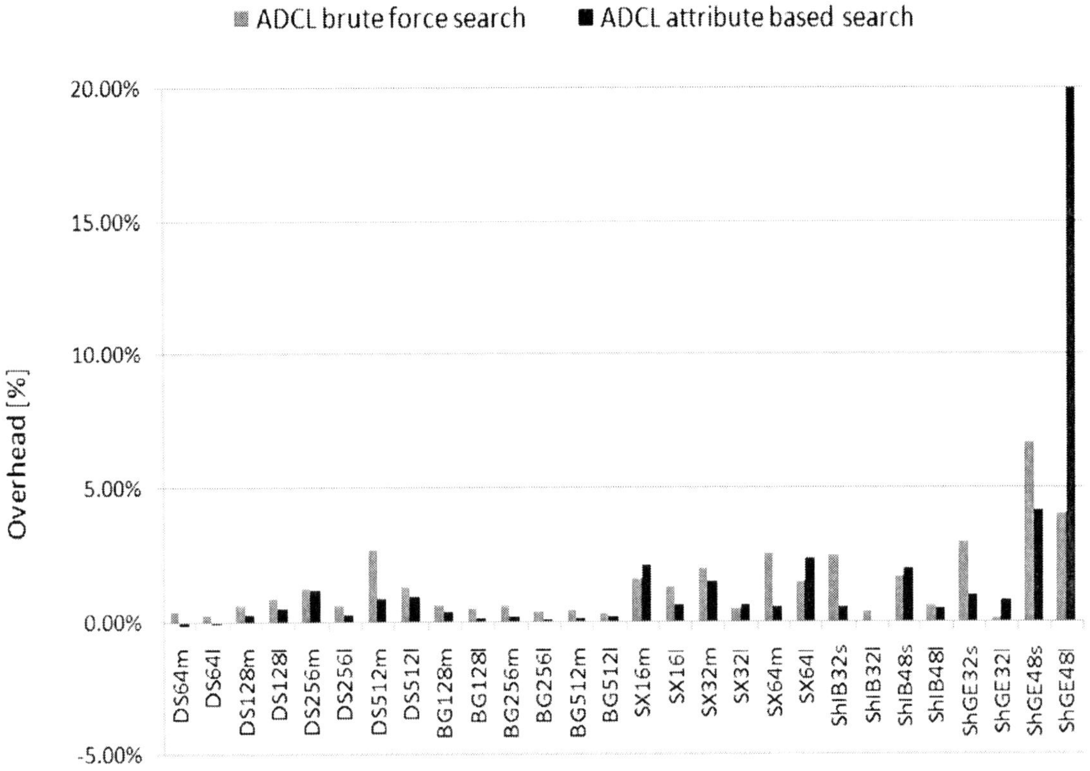

shows the performance penalty for the application running the large problem size on the Datastar cluster using the 'winner' function determined by the SX8 using 64 processes.

The most remarkable result of Figure 2 (left) is, that the winner functions of the SharkGE and CacauGE cause significant performance penalties on the high performance interconnects used on Datastar, IBM Blue Gene and NEC SX 8. The performance penalty ranges from 1.74% up to 58.99%. Vice versa, the implementation chosen by these machines lead to significant performance penalties on SharkGE and CacauGE, increasing the execution time up to 90% compared to their fastest implementation. This result is especially relevant, since many large-scale scientific applications are originally developed and tuned on a smaller cluster within the institute where the authors reside. Typically, these smaller clusters utilize Gigabit Ethernet network interconnects. Our results indicate, that when moving to a large-scale system at a remote site, the code tuned for the Gigabit Ethernet network might in-fact pay a significant performance penalty when run without modifications.

In the second scenario, we focus on only three architectures, namely Datastar, IBM Blue Gene and the NEC SX8. We analyze the execution times for the medium problem size for all available number of processes. The results are presented using same format as previously. Although the performance penalty for many scenarios shown in the right part of Figure 2 is negligible, there are notable exceptions. As an example, applying the winner function of the 64 processes case on Datastar onto the 128 processes case on Blue Gene/L leads to a 5% increase in the execution time of that simulation. Similarly, the best performing implementation in the 256 processes test case on the Blue Gene would lead to a 11.49% increase in the execution time for the 256 processes test case on the Datastar architecture. Last but not least, the implementation leading to the best performance on the 64 processes test case on the SX8 would lead to a performance penalty of more than 15% on the same architecture for the same problem size per processes but for the 32 processes test case.

ADCL Performance Results

As of now, we have documented the fact that the performance of an application does depend on the implementation of the neighborhood communication, the hardware architecture, the application problem size, and the number of processes. In the following, we would like to show that using the ADCL runtime selection logic leads in most cases to a close-to-optimal performance. Figure 3 documents the average overhead of the application when using ADCL compared to the performance of the application using the fastest implementation for that particular scenario. Figure 3 distinguishes between the two runtime selection logics of ADCL, namely the brute force search strategy, and the attribute based search strategy.

The main result of Figure 3 is that the execution time of the application when using ADCL with its runtime adaption features is in fact very close the optimal performance determined in the verification runs. The overhead introduced by ADCL is in the vast majority of the test cases below 1%. This (minimal) overhead stems from two facts: first, during the initial iterations of the application, ADCL evaluates some of the implementations, which show a suboptimal performance on that platform for that particular problem size. Second, ADCL incorporates a distributed decision algorithm in order for all processes to agree on the same implementation as the 'winner'. This distributed decision algorithm requires one all-reduce operation per implementation. Furthermore, the attribute based search strategy shows in virtually all test scenarios a lower overhead due to the reduced number of implementations being tested.

There are two notable exceptions to the results above: firstly, for the hierarchical Gigabit Ethernet network used on Cacau and secondly, for the 48 processes test case on SharkGE when using the attributes based search strategy and the large problem size. In the first problem scenario, despite of the fact that the ADCL runtime selection logic did determine in all three runs the correct implementation as the winner, the performance penalty for using a suboptimal implementation during the learning phase turned out to be tremendous: the overall execution time of the application increased by 72% compared to using the optimal implementation from the very beginning. This result only highlights the necessity for additional, improved runtime selection algorithms which can further reduce the time required to determine the fastest algorithm.

For the second problem scenario, a more detailed analysis shows, that in two out of the three runs which have been used to calculate the average overhead in Figure 3, the parameter based search strategy did reveal a very good performance, showing only a minor overhead compared to the optimal execution time. However, in the third run, the system seemed to face some perturbations which lead to a wrong decision by the ADCL runtime selection logic. Using a suboptimal implementation for that test case resulted in a significant overhead. ADCL as of today relies on the fact, that the data gathered during the training phase is representative for the overall execution. In case this assumption turns out to be wrong, as happened in the third run, the runtime selection logic will make a suboptimal decision. In order to handle this scenario, ADCL will be extended by a monitoring subsystem in the near future. In case the performance data of the 'winner' implementation deviates significantly from the performance data

Figure 4. Performance of various algorithms for parallel matrix-matrix multiply operation and the according ADVL results

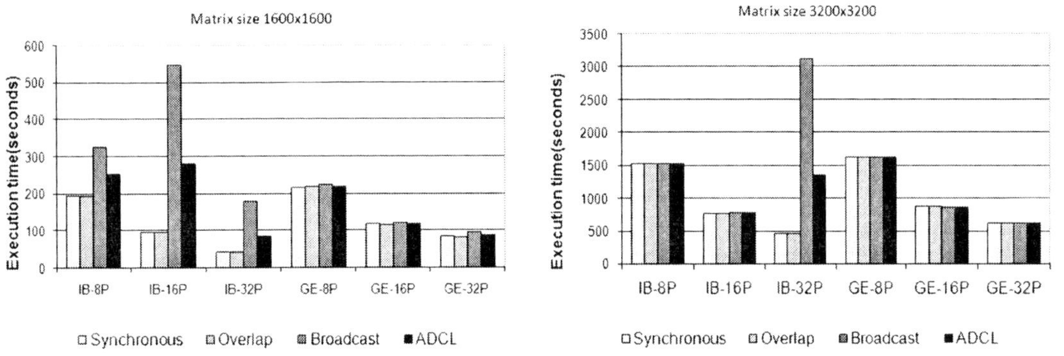

gathered during the learning phase, ADCL will be able to re-start the runtime selection logic and thus correct an erroneous decision. However, this component is not yet available as of today.

Tuning a Parallel Matrix-Matrix Multiply Kernel

Matrix-matrix multiplication is a common operation in many applications from graph theory, numerical algorithms, digital control, and signal processing. Within the frame of a master thesis (Huang, 2007), three different kernels for a parallel matrix-matrix multiply operation have been implemented. The code used as the basis for this analysis assumed that matrices are decomposed among the processes using 1-D decomposition, i.e. each process holds a certain number of columns of the overall matrix. During execution, a process calculates a partial result using the sub-matrices it currently has access to. Using some form of communication, the processes then exchange their sub-matrices and successively perform the same calculation on new sub-matrices, adding the new results to the previous ones. From the computational perspective, Cannon's algorithm is used to implement the parallel matrix-matrix multiplication. The main difference between the versions is the approach taken for communication between the processes.

The three communication patterns explored within the thesis can be described as follows:

- **Synchronous**: In this version, the algorithm performs the computation on the local part of the matrices, followed by a circular shift of the sub-matrices of B. Thus, after the first communication step, process 1 holds the sub-matrices of B which has originally been assigned to process 0, process 2 holds the sub-matrices of B originally assigned to process 1 etc. This sequence of computation and communication is repeated p times for a p processes scenario. After the final computation, an additional shift operation is required in order to have the original assignment of the sub-matrices of B in place. This implementation is called synchronous, since there is no overlap between the communication and the computation.
- **Overlapping:** The main difference of this version to the previous one is, that the code tries to overlap the communication occurring in the shift operations, and the computation. For this, an additional temporary buffer is required to hold a sub-matrix. Using a double-buffering concept, the buffer given by the sub-matrix B and the temporary buffer are used in an alternating fashion for

communication and computation.

- **Broadcast:** this implementation avoids the circular shift operations for transferring sub-matrices of B. Instead, process *i* broadcasts its sub-matrix in iteration *i* to all other processes, and each process performs the corresponding part of the computation

The three versions of the matrix-matrix multiplication described in this section have been integrated with ADCL in order to let the ADCL runtime selection logic decide dynamically, which algorithm performs best for a given application and hardware configuration. Note, that ADCL deals in this subsection with user-defined function-set in contrary to the pre-defined function-set used in the previous subsection.

For our tests, we used the SharkIB and SharkGE cluster described in the previous subsection. We show here performance results for matrix sizes of 1600x1600 and 3200x3200, using 8, 16 and 32 processes. (Figure 4)

The results obtained indicate, that the algorithm using the broadcast operation for disseminating the sub-matrices is performing significantly slower than the implementations entitled *synchronous* or *overlap*. Over InfiniBand, *synchronous* typically achieves a slightly better performance than *overlap*, while over Gigabit Ethernet *overlap* is somewhat faster. ADCL chose for all instances the right implementation. The execution time of the operations when using ADCL is however somewhat slower than the according implementation, due to the fact that the library has to test also the under-performing *broadcast* version. This is especially evident for the 32 process test case over Gigabit Ethernet, where the penalty for using the *broadcast* versions is tremendous.

Using ADCL to Tune System Parameters of Open MPI

The last usage scenario of ADCL described in this chapter deals with tuning runtime parameters of a communication library such as Open MPI (Gabriel, 2004). Open MPI supports a large number of runtime parameters, which allow an end-user or system administrator to tune specifics of the library, such as network parameters, settings for collective operations or processor affinity options, without having to recompile the library. The Open Tool for Parameter Optimization (OTPO) (Chaarawi, 2008), the result of a joint project between Cisco Systems and the University of Houston, allows the user to specify a certain number of Open MPI parameters, desired values or ranges of values to be explored, and the benchmark to be executed with each run. The result of an OTPO run is a collection of Open MPI parameters and the according optimal values, which lead to the minimal execution time of the benchmark previously specified.

Internally, OTPO maps Open MPI parameters to ADCL attributes, and creates an ADCL function set. Each function in the function set executes the same sequence, namely spawning a new process which starts an MPI job with the according Open MPI parameters. This allows OTPO to take advantage of the regular ADCL mechanisms to determine the best performing function in the function set.

In (Chaarawi, 2008) we demonstrated how this tool can be used to tune the InfiniBand parameters of Open MPI. Two separate set of tests have been executed, one exploiting the shared-receive queue feature of InfiniBand, the second using a separate receive queue per process. For the sake of clarity, we focused on tuning only four parameters, which lead to 825 possible combinations for the first scenario, and 275 possible combinations of for the second scenario. The test code executed for both scenarios consisted of the NetPipe (Turner, 2002) benchmark.

The results reveal a small number of parameter sets that resulted in the lowest latency (3.77μs and 3.78μs), namely four parameter sets for shared receive queues and six parameter sets for per peer receive queues. However, there were a significant number of parameter combinations leading to results within 0.05μs of the best latency. These results highlight, that typically, the optimization process using OTPO will not deliver a single set of parameters leading to the best performance, but will result in groups of parameter sets leading to similar performance

CONCLUSION

This chapter presented a library capable of adapting the behavior of an application at runtime, which allows for tuning the performance of a particular code section by switching between different implementations. The library has been used in various scenarios, such as for tuning the neighborhood communication of scientific applications, tuning parallel matrix-matrix multiply operations, or adjusting the InfiniBand parameters of the Open MPI library. ADCL does not only allow for seamless tuning of an application at runtime, but also helps from the software engineering perspective since it avoids having to maintain different code version for different platforms. These two features combined make us believe, that runtime adaptation techniques such as used in ADCL are one of the most promising approaches in order to successfully use and exploit Petascale architectures.

REFERENCES

Alexandrov, A. Ionescu, M. F. Schauser, K. E. & Scheiman, C. (1995). LogGP: Incorporating long messages into the LogP model. In *Proceedings of the seventh annual ACM symposium on Parallel algorithms and architectures,* (pp. 95–105). New York: ACM Press.

Benkert, K. Gabriel, E. & Resch, M. M. (2008). *Outlier Detection in Performance Data of Parallel Applications*. In the 9th IEEE International Workshop on Parallel Distributed Scientific and Engineering Computing (PDESC), Miami, Florida, USA.

Bhowmick, S. Eijkhout, V. Freund, Y. Fuentes, E. & Keyes, D. (in press). Application of Machine Learning in Selecting Sparse Linear Solver. Submitted for publication to the *International Journal on High Performance Computing Applications.*

Chaarawi, M. Squyres, J. Gabriel, E. & Feki, S. (2008). A Tool for Optimizing Runtime Parameters of Open MPI. Accepted for publications in *EuroPVM/MPI, September 7-10*, Dublin, Ireland.

Culler, D., & Karp, R. Patterson, D. Sahay, A. Schauser, K. E. Santos, E. Subramonian, R. & von Eicken, T. (1993). LogP: Towards a realistic model of parallel computation. In *Proceedings of the fourth ACM SIGPLAN symposium on Principles and practice of parallel programming*, (pp. 1–12). New York: ACM Press.

Dongarra, J. J., & Eijkhout, V. (2003). Self-Adapting Numerical Software for Next-Generation Applications. *International Journal of High Performance Computing Applications, 17*(2), 125–131. doi:10.1177/1094342003017002002

Evans, J. J. Hood, C. S.& Gropp, W. D. (2003). Exploring the Relationship Between Parallel Application Run-Time Variability and Network Performance. In *Proceedings of the Workshop on High-Speed Local Networks (HSLN), IEEE Conference on Local Computer Networks (LCN)*, (pp. 538-547).

Faraj, A. Yuan, X. & Lowenthal, D. (2006). STAR-MPI: self tuned adaptive routines for MPI collective operations. In *ICS '06: Proceedings of the 20th Annual International Conference on Supercomputing*, (pp. 199-208). New York: ACM Press.

Faraj, A. Patarasuk, P. & Yuan, X. (2007). A Study of Process Arrival Patterns for MPI Collective Operations. *International Conference on Supercomputing*, (pp.168-179).

Frigo, M., & Johnson, S. (2005). The Design and Implementation of FFTW3. *Proceedings of the IEEE, 93*(2), 216–231. doi:10.1109/JPROC.2004.840301

Gabriel, E. Fagg, G. Bosilca, G. Angskun, T. Dongarra, J. J. Squyres, J. M., et al. (2004). Open MPI: Goals, Concept, and Design of a Next Generation MPI Implemention. In D. Kranzlmueller, P. Kacsuk, J. J. Dongarra (Eds.), *Recent Advances in Parallel Virtual Machine and Message Passing Interface*, (LNCS, Vol. 3241, pp. 97-104). Berlin: Springer.

Gabriel, E., & Huang, S. (2007). Runtime optimization of application level communication patterns. In *Proceedings of the 2007 International Parallel and Distributed Processing Symposium, 12th International Workshop on High-Level Parallel Programming Models and Supportive Environments*, (p. 185).

Gill, P. E. Murray, W. & Wright, M. H. (1993). *Practical Optimization*. London: Academic Press Ltd.

Hoefler, T. Lichei, A. & Rehm, W. (2007). Low-Overhead LogGP Parameter Assessment for Modern Interconnect Networks. *Proceedings of the IPDPS*, Long Beach, CA, March 26-30. New York: IEEE.

Huang, S. (2007). *Applying Adaptive Software Technologies for Scientific Applications.* Master Thesis, Department of Computer Science, University of Houston, Houston, TX.

Jain, R. K. (1991). *The Art of Computer Systems Performance Analysis: Techniques for Experimental Design, Measurement, Simulation, and Modeling*. New York: Wiley.

Kielmann, T. Hofman, R. F. H. Bal, H. E. Plaat, A. & Bhoedjang, R. A. F. (1999). MagPIe: MPI's collective communication operations for clustered wide area systems. *ACM SIGPLAN Symposium on Principles and Practice of Parallel Programming (PPoPP'99), 34*(8),131-140.

Petrini, F. Kerbyson, D. J. & Pakin, S. (2003). The Case of the Missing Supercomputer Performance: Achieving Optimal Performance on the 8,192 Processors of ASCI Q. *Proceedings of the 2003 ACM/IEEE Conference on Supercomputing.*

Pjesivac-Grbovic, J., Bosilca, G., Fagg, G. E., Angskun, T., & Dongarra, J. J. (2007). MPI Collective Algorithm Selection and Quadtree Encoding. *Parallel Computing, 33*(9), 613–623. doi:10.1016/j.parco.2007.06.005

Turner, D., & Chen, X. (2002). Protocol-dependent message-passing performance on linux clusters. *Proceedings of the 2002 IEEE International Conference on Linux Clusters, pp. 187-194.* New York: IEEE Computer Society.

Voss, M. J., & Eigenmann, R. (2000). ADAPT: Automated De-coupled Adaptive Program Transformation. *International Conference on Parallel Processing,* Toronto, Canada, (pp. 163).

Vuduc, R., Demel, J., & Bilmes, J. A. (2004). Statistical Models for Empirical Search-Based Performance Tuning. *International Journal of High Performance Computing Applications, 18*(1), 65–94. doi:10.1177/1094342004041293

Whaley, R. C., & Petite, A. (2005). Minimizing development and maintenance costs in supporting persistently optimized BLAS. *Software, Practice & Experience, 35*(2), 101–121. doi:10.1002/spe.626

Witten, I. H., & Frank, E. (2005). *Data Mining: Practical Machine Learning Tools and Techniques* (2nd Ed.). San Francisco: Morgan Kaufmann.

KEY TERMS AND DEFINITIONS

Adaptive Applications: Application capable of changing its behavior, switch to alternate code sections or change to different values for certain parameters at runtime as a response to different input data or changing conditions.

Decision Algorithms: algorithms used to compare different versions of the same unctionalitywhile executing the application with respect to a particular metric such as execution time.

Dynamic Tuning: Tuning of a code sequence or function during the execution of the real application.

Static Tuning: Tuning of a code sequence or function before executing the real application.

Chapter 26
A Scalable Approach to Real-Time System Timing Analysis

Alan Grigg
Loughborough University, UK

Lin Guan
Loughborough University, UK

ABSTRACT

This chapter describes a real-time system performance analysis approach known as reservation-based analysis (RBA). The scalability of RBA is derived from an abstract (target-independent) representation of system software components, their timing and resource requirements and run-time scheduling policies. The RBA timing analysis framework provides an evolvable modeling solution that can be instigated in early stages of system design, long before the software and hardware components have been developed, and continually refined through successive stages of detailed design, implementation and testing. At each stage of refinement, the abstract model provides a set of best-case and worst-case timing 'guarantees' that will be delivered subject to a set of scheduling 'obligations' being met by the target system implementation. An abstract scheduling model, known as the rate-based execution model then provides an implementation reference model with which compliance will ensure that the imposed set of timing obligations will be met by the target system.

INTRODUCTION

A key requirement in the development of a real-time system is the ability to demonstrate that the final target system has met its specified timing requirements. This can be carried out by constructing a model of system timing behaviour that can be used to make predictions about worst-case performance in terms of maximum response times, communication delays, delay variations and resource utilisation. In order to develop a modelling solution that is scalable, however, the timing analysis model must be constructed with this goal specifically in mind.

DOI: 10.4018/978-1-60566-661-7.ch026

Scalability of the timing analysis solution can ultimately be achieved by meeting two key modelling objectives:

- **Partitionable analysis:** The ability to model the timing behaviour of parts of the system independently from other parts and, correspondingly, limit the scope of re-analysis required in the event of localised changes;
- **Evolvable analysis:** The ability to assess the timing behaviour of the system incrementally throughout the development process (and through later modifications), based on the information available at each stage of development.

Partitionable Analysis

It was recognised by Audsley *et al* (1993) that the holistic nature of timing analysis models for distributed real-time systems (the inability to analyse the system in part due to circular inter-dependencies in the model) arises due to a combination of functional and physical integration effects. It therefore follows that the model could be partitioned by placing appropriate restrictions on the manner in which integration of the system software and hardware components is performed as follows:

- **Functional partitioning:** Constraints on data communication and ordering/ precedence relationships between related software components;
- **Physical partitioning:** Constraints on resource sharing policies (scheduling and communication protocols).

Functional partitioning can be implemented by breaking up end-to-end *transactions* (sequences of processing and communication activities required to meet some higher level system objective) into individual components based purely on knowledge of the end-to-end timing requirements of the system (and the transaction topology). The net result is that the timing behaviour of groups of software components allocated to individual processors (and other resources) can potentially be analysed independently.

Functional partitioning, in its extreme, results in a 'federated' timing analysis model where resource boundaries in the physical architecture dictate the partitions in the timing model. The resulting model can only be applied/evaluated after the physical integration stage of system development has been performed, *i.e.* the allocation of software components to hardware processors (and other resources) has been defined and the details of the scheduling solution and communication protocols have been finalised.

Physical partitioning can be implemented by applying resource scheduling mechanisms that support temporal partitioning between the components being scheduled. The net result is that the timing behaviour of functionally-dependent groups of components, *ie.* end-to-end transactions, can be analysed independently. This offers some key advantages over functional partitioning. Firstly, for systems that embody a degree of safety-critical functionality, this means that there is inherent temporal isolation between safety-critical and non-safety-critical software components that share processing resources and/or communication media. Secondly, and more generally from the perspective of an overall system engineering process, there is potential for supporting independent development and verification of groups of functionally-related components for a target computing environment that is physically integrated. Moreover, the analysis can potentially be applied before the physical integration stage of development has been performed, *i.e.* much earlier in the development life of the system.

The *Reservation-Based Analysis* (RBA) method described in this chapter uses a physical partitioning approach throughout but also supports functional partitioning with the guideline that this is to be used sparingly. Before going on to describe RBA, the second of the two key modelling requirements is discussed below.

Evolvable Analysis

No particular form of development life-cycle is assumed here, merely the notion that requirements, design, implementation/integration and testing/verification stages are involved, where these stages may be performed with a degree of concurrency and iteration. More specifically, it is assumed that the following activities are involved in the process:

- Definition of system-level timing requirements;
- Decomposition and refinement of these requirements during system design and implementation;
- Development/acquisition and integration of software and hardware components;
- Verification of systems timing properties against stated requirements.

Timing analysis models are normally developed in a 'bottom-up' manner, *i.e.* the model is not finalised until after the implementation and integration details of the system have been decided. Hence, it is not possible to assess the timing behaviour of the system until late in the development process. Furthermore, subsequent changes to the implementation or integration details of the system, particularly changes to the scheduling or communication protocols involved, are likely to impact on the details of the timing model. The results of analysis performed at this late stage of development are, of course, essential to support final verification of the system timing requirements. Any deficiencies discovered at this late stage, however, can give rise to significant re-work, involving possible re-consideration of the artefacts produced from the integration, implementation, design or even requirements phases of development, depending on the severity of the problem. The costs associated with re-work can be a major factor in the overall development cost of industrial real-time systems.

The amount of re-work associated with the development and verification of the timing properties of the system could be reduced by making the notion of timing analysis more integral to the systems engineering process as a whole, allowing it to be applied throughout the development of the system, starting much earlier in the process. This would allow an ongoing assessment of emerging system timing properties relative to specified timing requirements and also provide progressive guidance on the selection of future design/implementation details at successive stages of development. Two fundamental issues can be identified regarding the provision of an evolvable timing analysis model through the system life-cycle:

- How to perform timing analysis with a lack of system integration and implementation details during the earlier stages of development;
- How to deal with a continually evolving definition of the system, with different parts of the system evolving at different rates.

Timing Analysis without System Integration and Implementation Details

In the earlier stages of development, the timing-related information for all parts of the system will be scarce. Whilst the system level timing requirements may be reasonably well understood and decomposed to varying extent during design stages, the ability to perform timing analysis relies fundamentally on the notion of *resources* - some media through which the functions of the system can be performed. Processing resource details are used as a basis for calculating worst-case execution times of software components. Similarly, details of the communication media (and associated protocols) are used to characterise worst-case communication delays.

In order to perform timing analysis prior to the system implementation stage, therefore, it is therefore necessary to work with an implementation-independent, *abstract* model of system resources. Such a model could provide a means to perform timing analysis in the earlier stages of system development using estimations or assumptions about system integration and implementation details that will not become concrete until a later date. This abstract model must be defined to provide a sufficient (although pessimistic) basis for performing timing analysis but without over-constraining the final implementation of the system. When implementation details are eventually finalised, the results of timing analysis performed via the abstract model could then be verified. This gives rise to a two-stage approach to timing analysis:

- **Abstract timing analysis:** Performed during the definition and decomposition stages of development on the basis of the abstract resource model; the net result is a set of worst-case (and best-case) *guarantees* regarding the timing behaviour of the system that are subject to a set of *obligations* being met by the final implementation of the system;
- **Target-specific timing analysis:** Performed during the system implementation and integration stages of system development, the aim being to demonstrate that the set of obligations imposed during the abstract timing analysis phase have actually been met.

By appropriate construction of the timing model, the guarantees generated during the abstract timing analysis phase can be inferred automatically at the target-specific analysis stage, *i.e.* there should be no need to reconstruct the results of the system-wide abstract analysis after the target-specific details have been finalised and verified.

Significantly, the opportunity can be taken here to define a consistent (unified) model for system-wide analysis, i.e. for end-to-end timing analysis across all system resources. *This is a key attribute of the RBA framework.* It is normally the case that different types of system resources (processing and communication media) and resource access policies (scheduling and communication protocols) are modelled in different ways. The use of consistent abstractions improves the composability and ultimately scalability of the system-wide timing analysis model.

Timing Analysis for an Evolving System Definition

The development of a timing analysis model for application through the system life-cycle must inherently address the problem of dealing with an evolving definition of the system. Throughout the development process, different parts of the system will mature at different rates, leading to an inconsistent level of detail regarding the timing properties of the system. The timing model must not only be able to represent the various parts of the system at different levels of detail but also still be evaluated to determine system timing behaviour based on such information.

This can be achieved by structuring the real-time transaction model as a hierarchy, where successive levels of the hierarchy capture the results of successive stages of system evolution. At any given stage of development, the hierarchy needs to capture all known ordering/precedence relationships between the entities that describe the system at that stage and all known resource requirements (if any). Ideally, the nodes of the hierarchy should be of a form that is consistent throughout the development of the system in order to avoid any problems associated with transforming the timing properties of the system between different representations at different stages of development. The proposal to partition the timing model in the physical domain, as described above, suggests that the nodes of the hierarchy should be characterised by indivisible resource usage requirements (and the corresponding delay/response times) associated with computational and communication elements within the system.

In this way, functionally unrelated parts of the system can potentially be modelled, analysed and modified independently and therefore allowed to evolve at different rates throughout the development process. Similarly, in the later stages of system development, the analysis should be applicable to partially integrated subsets of the system in order that verification of system timing properties can occur in step with the integration process itself, rather than waiting for the complete system to be finalised before the timing behaviour of any one part of it can be verified.

In terms of the two-stage approach described above, the timing guarantees generated from the *abstract* timing analysis model at successive stages of refinement can be taken to represent timing obligations on subsequent stages of development. As the model is evolved, timing obligations are refined to generate increasingly detailed implementation constraints on the final system.

Abstract Timing Analysis Model

The system level, end-to-end timing characteristics are captured, developed and analysed in terms of *transactions*. A transaction captures the temporal relationship between:

- A set of *input events* from the external environment of the system (or from other transaction(s));
- A set of *output events* to the external environment of the system (or to some other transaction(s)).

In the true sense, transaction input and output events correspond to the arrival or dispatch of control signals and/or information from or to the external interfaces of the system. In order to better support the engineering of large-scale real-time systems, however, such events can relate to other transactions within the system as well as the external environment of the system. This allows particular end-to-end requirements of the system to be modelled as multiple transactions where practical engineering constraints dictate, such as the need to allocate responsibilities across industrial partnerships and sub-contractors. This practical concern is supported without compromising the system timing model due to the uniform nature adopted for expressing transaction structural and timing properties, as explained below.

Real-Time Transaction Topology

For reasons of supporting an evolving definition of the system during development, the structure of the transaction model is hierarchical. The body of a transaction at any stage in its development is expressed in the form of an acyclic, directed, nested graph whose leaf nodes capture the concurrent processing and communication elements of the transaction, termed *activities*. Non-leaf nodes in the hierarchy are referred to as *nested transactions*. The edges (or arcs) of the graph capture the precedence (ordering) and nesting relationships within the transaction:

- Precedence relationships describe the required order of execution of activities and nested transactions;
- Nesting relationships capture strict refinement (specification-implementation) relationships that arise during the evolution of the transaction model.

Consider the transaction λ depicted in Figure 1. This illustrates the evolving definition of a transaction from an initial system level description (referred to as the *level 0* model) through two successive stages/levels of refinement. At the first stage of refinement, the level 0 nested transaction λ_1 is implemented via three level 1 nested transactions, each of which is implemented as a set of level 2 activities at the second stage of refinement.

In the general case, let $\lambda_{i,...,k}$ denote any arbitrarily nested transaction or activity within transaction λ. This notation is sufficient to define the topology of the transaction for the purpose of performing timing analysis (once the timing characteristics of the individual activities have been defined - see section 2.2).

Figure 1. Example transaction topology

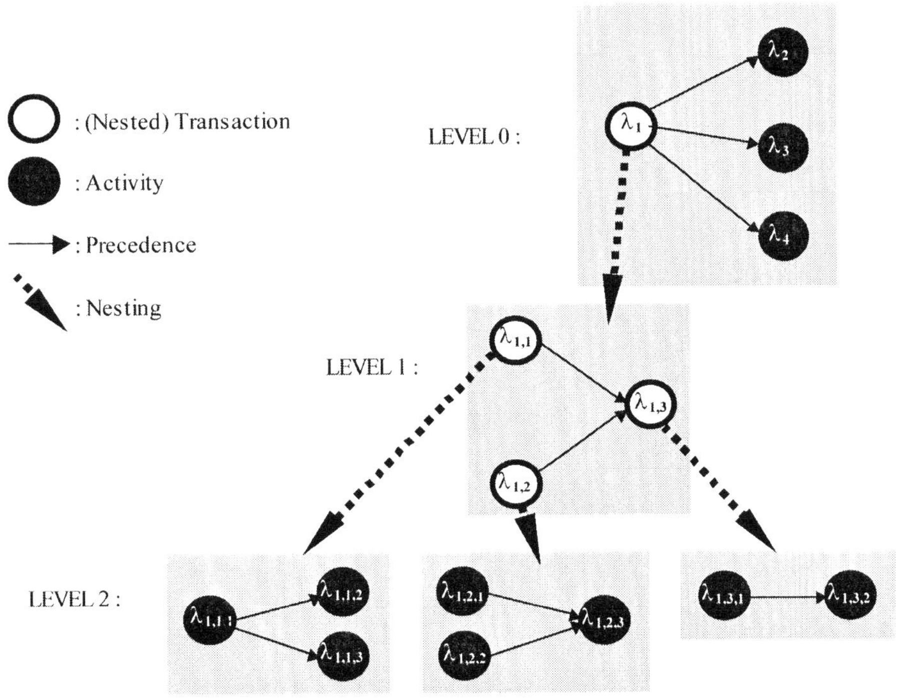

Further structural information, however, can optionally be provided regarding the nature of precedence and nesting relationships as a means of reducing the pessimism in the analysis. This is achieved via the association of a *guard* function $Q_{i,...,k}$ with each node $\lambda_{i,...,k}$ describing the conditions that trigger its arrival for execution. In many cases, $Q_{i,...,k}$ is implicit given the form of relationship involved. For example, the arrival of $\lambda_{i,...,k}$ dependent on completion of a single predecessor does not require $Q_{i,...,k}$ to be defined at all since the constraint is wholly described by topology of the directed graph. In other cases, however, $Q_{i,...,k}$ is not sufficiently defined from the graph topology alone and can, if required, be expressed explicitly. For example, $Q_{1,3}$ could be defined such that the arrival of $\lambda_{1,3}$ is triggered only upon completion of the two predecessors, $\lambda_{1,1}$ and $\lambda_{1,2}$ or, alternatively, on completion of either one of those predecessors. The choice of guard functions will have an impact on the timing analysis in terms of improving accuracy of the model.

To this end, a basic categorisation of precedence and nesting relationships, from which more complex transaction topologies can be constructed, is given below. Consider first the case of precedence relationships, which can be categorised as follows:

- **One-to-many:** Where the completion of a single activity or nested transaction triggers the arrival of one or more successors (as illustrated in Figure 1 within the level 0 model);
- **Many-to-one:** Where the completion of one or more concurrent activities or nested transactions is required to trigger the arrival of a single successor (as illustrated in Figure 1 within the level 1 model).

The simple case of *one-to-one* precedence, where the completion of a single activity or nested transaction triggers the arrival of a single successor, is a special case of each of these classes and actually represents the intersection between the two.

An analogous categorisation can be defined for nesting relationships as follows, observing that these relationships involve successive (referred to as parent and child) levels of the transaction hierarchy:

- **One-to-many:** Where the arrival of a single nested transaction at the parent level triggers the arrival of one or more concurrent activities at the child level (as illustrated in Figure 1 in the transition from the level 1 to the 2 model at $\lambda_{1,2}$) or, traversing the hierarchy in the opposite direction, where the completion of a single activity at the child level triggers the completion of one or more concurrent nested transactions at the parent level;
- **Many-to-one:** Where the arrival of one or more concurrent nested transaction at the parent level triggers the arrival of a single activity at the child level or, traversing the hierarchy in the opposite direction, where the completion of one or more concurrent activities at the child level triggers the completion of a single nested transaction at the parent level (as illustrated in Figure 1 in the reverse transition from the level 2 to the 1 model at $\lambda_{1,1}$).

For ease of future reference, nesting relationships that are directed from parent to child will be referred to as *descending* and those that are directed from child to parent will be referred to as *ascending*.

The purpose of the nesting relationships in the transaction topology is to reflect the ongoing evolution of the system during development and later in service. For convenience, transactions can also be visualised at any stage of refinement in an equivalent 'flat' form, *i.e.* with nesting relationships transformed into precedence relationships. This is achieved by performing a depth-first traversal of the nested transaction graph and successively replacing each nested transaction with its lower level sub-graph; the sub-graph inheriting all higher level nesting and precedence relationships from the nested transaction that it replaces. For example, Figure 2 illustrates the example transaction with the nesting relationship that stems from $\lambda_{1,1}$ resolved.

Applying this process repeatedly to resolve all nesting relationships for the example transaction gives the resultant flat topology illustrated in Figure 3.

Note that this flattening of the transaction hierarchy is merely for user visualisation purposes and does not affect the transaction from the perspective of the timing model.

Figure 2. Example transaction with nesting partially resolved

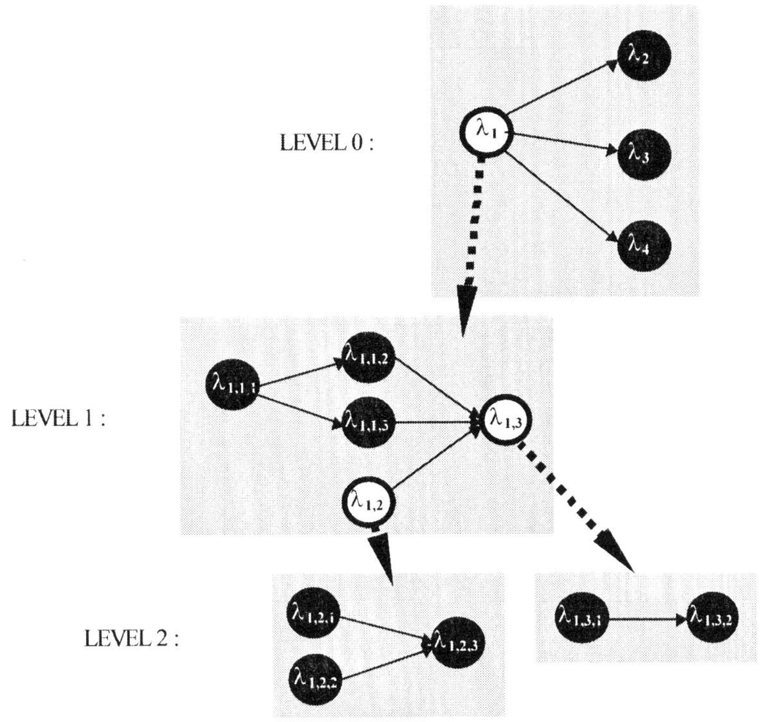

Figure 3. Example transaction with nesting fully resolved

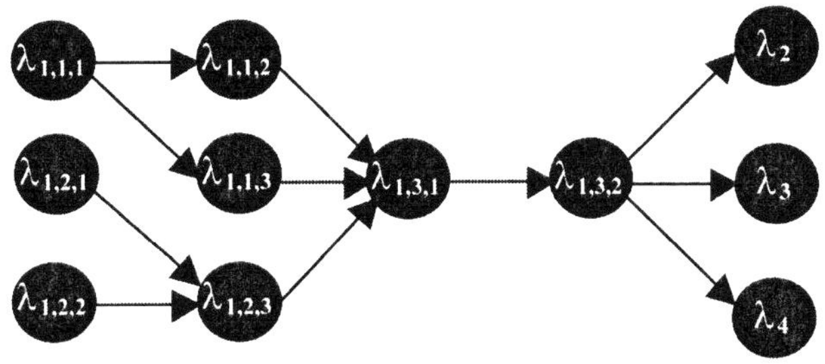

Real-Time Transaction Properties

A set of timing parameters must be assigned for each transaction in order to perform timing analysis. A key consideration here is the need for the timing model to be evolvable and, to this end, the timing parameters that represent the nested transaction and the activity are defined such that these objects are interchangeable. In other words, any nested transaction can be implemented in terms of activities (and further nested transactions) and, *vice versa*, an activity can be replaced by a nested transaction and become the subject of further evolution. In this way, the same timing analysis approach can be applied to predict the behaviour of a transaction throughout its evolution.

The only distinction between activities and nested transactions is that activities, since these represent leaf nodes of the transaction graph, must define their resource requirements directly, whereas nested transactions inherit such characteristics from the activities they embody. Otherwise, the parameters via which timing behaviour is represented and observed are the same for a single activity, a group of activities, a nested transaction and all the way up the hierarchy to a level 0 transaction.

In the general case, for any arbitrarily nested transaction or activity, $\lambda_{i,...,k}$, with level 0 'parent' λ_i, the timing properties are captured as follows:

- *input jitter*, $J^{in}_{i,...,k}$ - the maximum width of the time window that spans the arrival of all input events associated with $\lambda_{i,...,k}$;
- *output jitter*, $J^{out}_{i,...,k}$ - the maximum width of the time window that spans the deliverance of all output events associated with $\lambda_{i,...,k}$;
- *minimum I/O separation*, $d_{i,...,k}$ - the minimum separation in time (delay) between the input and output event windows of $\lambda_{i,...,k}$;
- *minimum inter-arrival time*, $a_{i,...,k}$ - the minimum separation in time between the input event windows associated with successive instances of $\lambda_{i,...,k}$.

The relationships between these parameters are depicted in Figure 4.

In Figure 4, the minimum inter-arrival time of $\lambda_{i,...,k}$ is shown to be greater than the latest completion time of any $\lambda_{i,...,k}$ output event, corresponding to the case where any one instance of $\lambda_{i,...,k}$ will always complete before the next instance arrives. This is merely to keep the illustration simple and is not actually a constraint on the model. For example, a pilot display generation application is likely to require

Figure 4. Timing properties of transaction/Activity $\lambda_{i,...,k}$

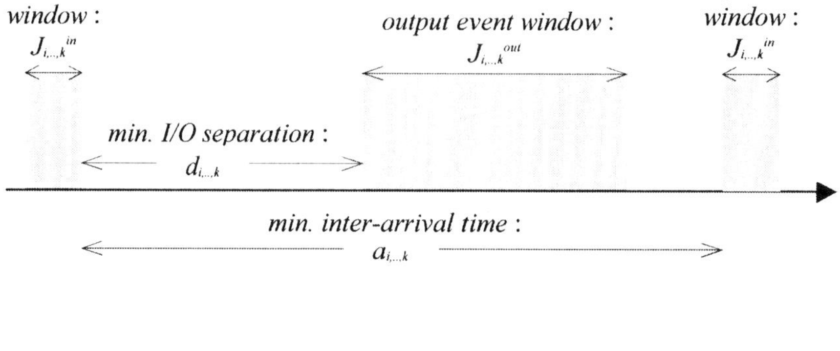

a minimum frame update time that is significantly less than the worst-case latency of the data being displayed. The model supports this type of behaviour, though there *are* some other constraints imposed on model parameters as follows, for reasons as given:

- $d_{i,\dots,k} > -J^{in}_{i,\dots,k}$: A necessary condition arising from the basic restriction that, for any given instance of $\lambda_{i,\dots,k}$, the output event window cannot begin before the input event window begins;
- $a_{i,\dots,k} > 0$: A constraint imposed to ensure that the input event windows associated with successive instances of $\lambda_{i,\dots,k}$ are totally ordered.

End-to-End Timing Analysis

End-to-end timing analysis can be performed at *any* stage of evolution of the transaction model, based on the information specified at that stage. Clearly, the analysis results will become more accurate as the definition of the model/system is evolved during development. The starting point for describing this timing analysis is to express the relationship between the basic timing parameters as specified and the overall delays accrued, at each level of nesting in the transaction definition. Let $r_{i,\dots,k}$ and $R_{i,\dots,k}$ denote the minimum and maximum accrued delays (response times) associated with any nested transaction or activity $\lambda_{i,\dots,k}$. The following relationships are observed:

$$d_{i,\dots,k} = r_{i,\dots,k} - J^{in}_{i,\dots,k} \tag{1}$$

$$J^{out}_{i,\dots,k} = J^{in}_{i,\dots,k} + (R_{i,\dots,k} - r_{i,\dots,k}) \tag{2}$$

These relationships are clarified by the illustration in Figure 5.

The values $r_{i,\dots,k}$ and $R_{i,\dots,k}$ must then be specified for each leaf node of the hierarchy, *i.e.* for each activity - these activity level delays are referred to as localised delays. The end-to-end analysis can then proceed by recursively descending the nested transaction topology/graph definition, accounting at each stage for the impact of nesting relationships, precedence relationships and localised delays on the overall end-to-end delays. The same approach can be taken to determining accrued delay variation, *i.e.* jitter. This will be illustrated by example later in the section.

Ultimately, all accrued delay and jitter values relate back to the input event window for the level 0 transaction, λ. That said, the end-to-end timing model is constructed such that the delays and jitter accrued across any nested transaction or activity can be calculated relative to those inherited at its time

Figure 5. Delay relationships for transaction/activity $\lambda_{i,\dots,k}$

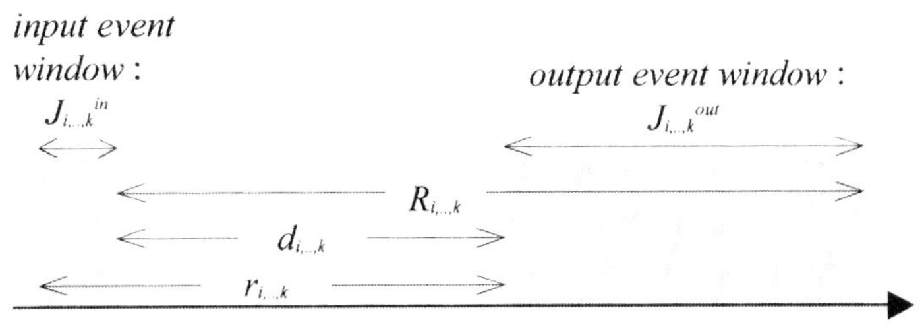

of arrival, *i.e.* the relative impact of a given stage in the transaction can be observed. In the transaction depicted in Figure 1, for example, the activities $\lambda_{1,2,1}$ and $\lambda_{1,2,2}$ will each inherit accrued delay and jitter values on their arrival via a nesting relationship from their parent transaction $\lambda_{1,2}$. In the general case, let $d^{in}_{i,\ldots,k}$ denote the accrued delay inherited by $\lambda_{i,\ldots,k}$ upon its arrival and, in turn, let $d^{out}_{i,\ldots,k}$ denote the accrued delay that $\lambda_{i,\ldots,k}$ exports to its successors upon completion. These values are related as follows:

$$d^{out}_{i,\ldots,k} = d^{in}_{i,\ldots,k} + r_{i,\ldots,k} \tag{3}$$

This relationship is illustrated in Figure 6. Notice in the diagram that the term $d^{in}_{i,\ldots,k}$ actually represents the separation in time between two *input* windows, rather than one input and one output window. This is consistent with the use of d to denote minimum I/O separation since the input event window of activity $\lambda_{i,\ldots,k}$ is equivalent to the output window that describes the combined output jitter of it predecessors.

Equation *(3)* provides a means by which *minimum* localised delay values calculated at the activity level can be consolidated into the end-to-end delay calculation. The consolidation of *maximum* local delays is taken care of by the output jitter calculation given in Equation *(2)*.

The manner in which accrued delays and jitter are inherited (and exported) for any particular $\lambda_{i,\ldots,k}$ depends on the form of precedence or nesting relationships involved. In the previous section, a number of fundamental forms of such relationships were identified. In the following circumstances, accrued delays and jitter are directly inherited (unchanged) in the direction of the relationship:

- *one-to-many precedence relationship:* When $\lambda_{i,\ldots,k}$ is one of many successors to $\lambda_{i,\ldots,j}$: (Figure 7)

$$d^{in}_{i,\ldots,k} = d^{out}_{i,\ldots,j} \tag{4}$$

$$J^{in}_{i,\ldots,k} = J^{out}_{i,\ldots,j} \tag{5}$$

- *One-to-many nesting relationship (descending):* When $\lambda_{i,\ldots,k}$ is one of many child activities whose arrival is triggered by that of the parent transaction $\lambda_{i,\ldots,j}$: (Figure 8)

$$d^{in}_{i,\ldots,k} = d^{in}_{i,\ldots,j} \tag{6}$$

$$J^{in}_{i,\ldots,k} = J^{in}_{i,\ldots,j} \tag{7}$$

- *One-to-many nesting relationship (ascending):* When $\lambda_{i,\ldots,k}$ is one of many parent transactions whose completion is triggered by that of the child activity $\lambda_{i,\ldots,j}$: (Figure 9)

$$d^{out}_{i,\ldots,k} = d^{out}_{i,\ldots,j} \tag{8}$$

Figure 6. Accrued delay relationships for transaction/activity $\lambda_{i,...,k}$

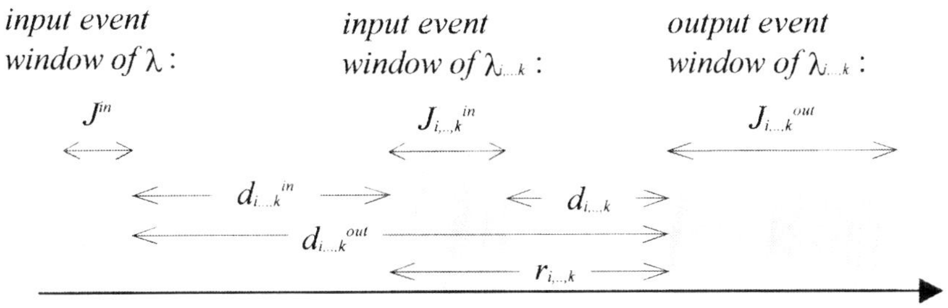

Figure 7. Delay inheritance - one-to-many precedence relationship

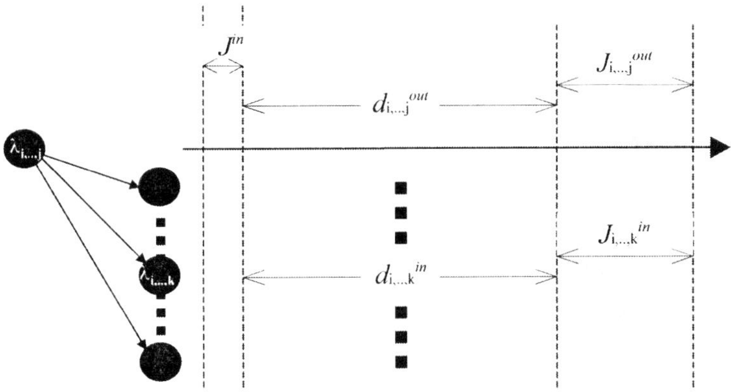

Figure 8. Delay inheritance - one-to-many nesting relationship (descending)

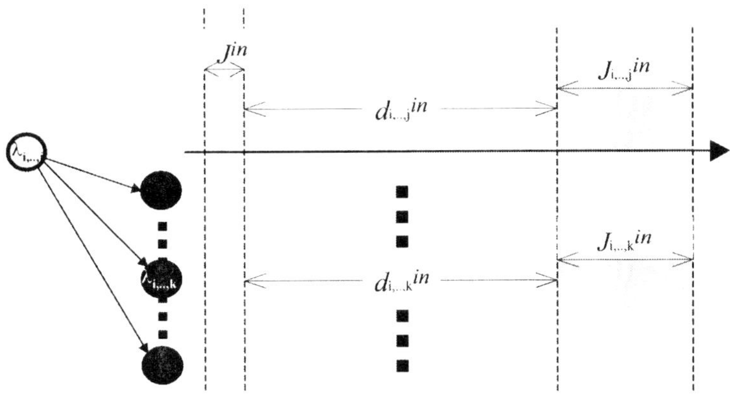

$$J^{out}_{i,..,k} = J^{out}_{i,..,j} \tag{9}$$

In circumstances other than those cases illustrated above, however, delay and jitter inheritance is less straight forward, depending ultimately on the form of guard function $Q_{i,..,k}$ that resides over the arrival of $\lambda_{i,...,k}$. Without knowledge of $Q_{i,...,k}$, the exact values for the inherited delay and jitter parameters cannot be determined, but the smallest 'safe' range of values can be stated as follows:

- *many-to-one precedence relationship:* When $\lambda_{i,...,j}$ is one of many predecessors to $\lambda_{i,...,k}$: (Figure 10)

$$\min_j(d^{out}_{i,...,j}) \leq d^{in}_{i,...,k} \leq \max_j(d^{out}_{i,...,j}) \tag{10}$$

$$\min_j(d^{out}_{i,...,j} + J^{out}_{i,...,j}) - d^{in}_{i,...,k} \leq J^{in}_{i,...,k} \leq \max_j(d^{out}_{i,...,j} + J^{out}_{i,...,j}) - d^{in}_{i,...,k} \tag{11}$$

- *many-to-one nesting relationship (descending):* When $\lambda_{i,...,j}$ is one of many parent transactions whose arrival is required to trigger that of the child activity $\lambda_{i,...,k}$: (Figure 11)

$$\min_j(d^{in}_{i,...,j}) \leq d^{in}_{i,...,k} \leq \max_j(d^{in}_{i,...,j}) \tag{12}$$

$$\min_j(d^{in}_{i,...,j} + J^{in}_{i,...,j}) - d^{in}_{i,...,k} \leq J^{in}_{i,...,k} \leq \max_j(d^{in}_{i,...,j} + J^{in}_{i,...,j}) - d^{in}_{i,...,k} \tag{13}$$

- *many-to-one nesting relationship (ascending):* When $\lambda_{i,...,j}$ is one of many child activities whose completion is required to trigger that of the parent transaction $\lambda_{i,...,k}$: (Figure 12)

$$\min_j(d^{out}_{i,...,j}) \leq d^{out}_{i,...,k} \leq \max_j(d^{out}_{i,...,j}) \tag{14}$$

$$\min_j(d^{out}_{i,...,j} + J^{out}_{i,...,j}) - d^{out}_{i,...,k} \leq J^{out}_{i,...,k} \leq \max_j(d^{out}_{i,...,j} + J^{out}_{i,...,j}) - d^{out}_{i,...,k} \tag{15}$$

Note again that these bounds are derived without knowledge of $Q_{i,...,k}$ and are 'safe' but pessimistic:

- The stated lower bounds correspond to the case where $Q_{i,...,k}$ is defined such that the arrival of $\lambda_{i,...,k}$

Figure 9. Delay inheritance - one-to-many nesting relationship (ascending)

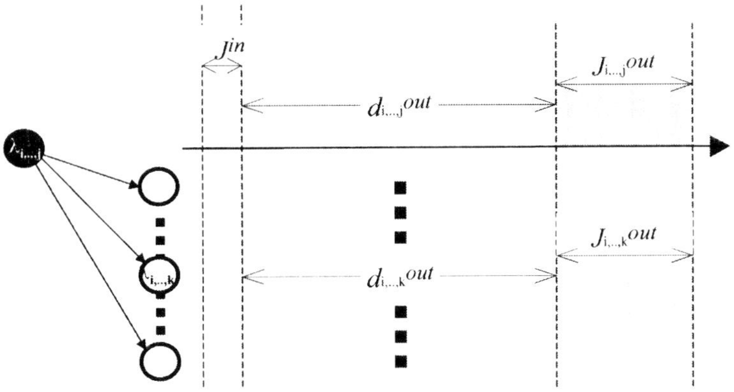

Figure 10. Delay inheritance - many-to-one precedence relationship

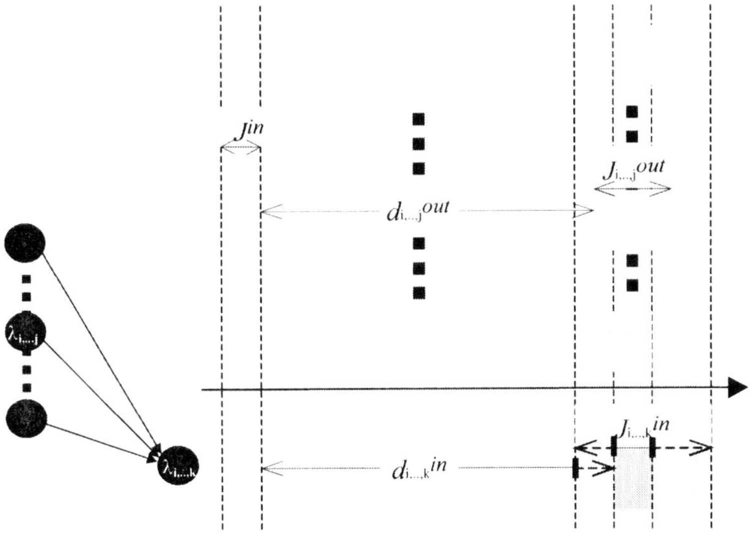

is triggered upon completion of *any one* $\lambda_{i,...,j}$;

- The stated upper bounds correspond to the case where $Q_{i,...,k}$ is defined such that the arrival of $\lambda_{i,...,k}$ is triggered upon completion of *all* $\lambda_{i,...,j}$.

In practice, the form of $Q_{i,...,k}$ could be defined and refined in line with the development of the associated transaction and this information can be used to reduce the pessimism of the accrued delay and jitter bounds compared to those determined by Equations *(10)* to *(15)*. This can be illustrated by considering the two extreme cases that are used as the basis for deriving those equations, as given below.

In the first case, where $Q_{i,...,k}$ is defined such that the arrival of $\lambda_{i,...,k}$ is triggered upon completion of *any one* $\lambda_{i,...,j}$, Equations *(10)* to *(15)* can be reduced as follows:

Figure 11. Delay inheritance - many-to-one nesting relationship (descending)

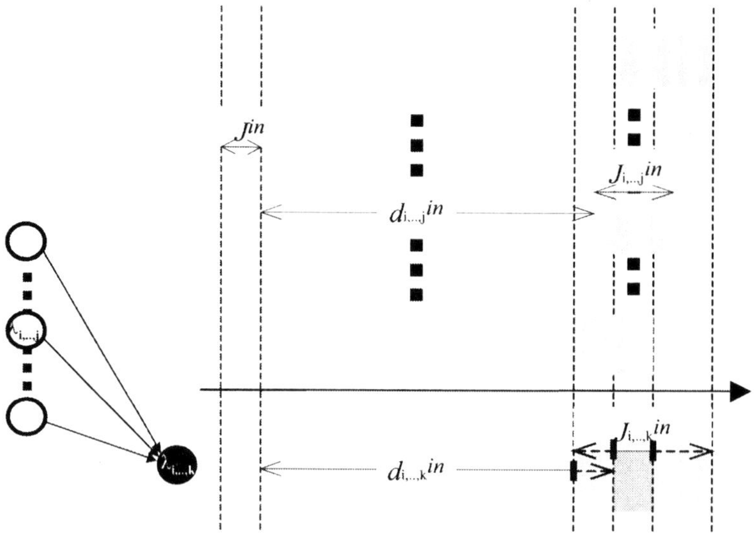

Figure 12. Delay inheritance - many-to-one nesting relationship (ascending)

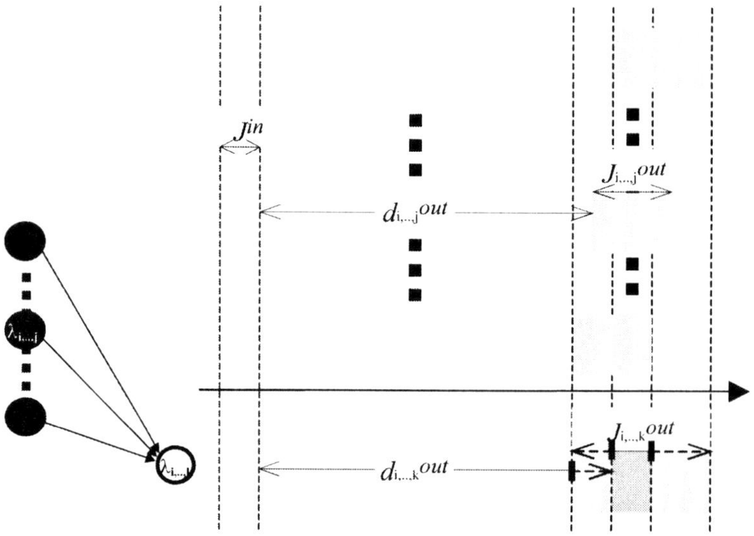

- *many-to-one precedence relationship:* When $\lambda_{i,\dots,j}$ is one of many predecessors to $\lambda_{i,\dots,k}$:

$$d^{in}_{i,\dots,k} = \min_{j}(d^{out}_{i,\dots,j}) \tag{10a}$$

$$J^{in}_{i,\dots,k} = \min_{j}(d^{out}_{i,\dots,j} + J^{out}_{i,\dots,j}) - d^{in}_{i,\dots,k} \tag{11a}$$

- *many-to-one nesting relationship (descending)* - when $\lambda_{i,\ldots,j}$ is one of many parent transactions whose arrival is required to trigger that of the child activity $\lambda_{i,\ldots,k}$:

$$d^{in}_{i,\ldots,k} = \min_{j}(d^{in}_{i,\ldots,j}) \tag{12a}$$

$$J^{in}_{i,\ldots,k} = \min_{j}(d^{in}_{i,\ldots,j} + J^{in}_{i,\ldots,j}) - d^{in}_{i,\ldots,k} \tag{13a}$$

- *many-to-one nesting relationship (ascending):* When $\lambda_{i,\ldots,j}$ is one of many child activities whose completion is required to trigger that of the parent transaction $\lambda_{i,\ldots,k}$:

$$d^{out}_{i,\ldots,k} = \min_{j}(d^{out}_{i,\ldots,j}) \tag{14a}$$

$$J^{out}_{i,\ldots,k} = \min_{j}(d^{out}_{i,\ldots,j} + J^{out}_{i,\ldots,j}) - d^{out}_{i,\ldots,k} \tag{15a}$$

In the second case, where $Q_{i,\ldots,k}$ is defined such that the arrival of $\lambda_{i,\ldots,k}$ is triggered only upon completion of *all* $\lambda_{i,\ldots,j}$, Equations *(10)* to *(15)* can be reduced as follows:

- *many-to-one precedence relationship:* When $\lambda_{i,\ldots,j}$ is one of many predecessors to $\lambda_{i,\ldots,k}$:

$$d^{in}_{i,\ldots,k} = \max_{j}(d^{out}_{i,\ldots,j}) \tag{10b}$$

$$J^{in}_{i,\ldots,k} = \max_{j}(d^{out}_{i,\ldots,j} + J^{out}_{i,\ldots,j}) - d^{in}_{i,\ldots,k} \tag{11b}$$

- *many-to-one nesting relationship (descending):* When $\lambda_{i,\ldots,j}$ is one of many parent transactions whose arrival is required to trigger that of the child activity $\lambda_{i,\ldots,k}$:

$$d^{in}_{i,\ldots,k} = \max_{j}(d^{in}_{i,\ldots,j}) \tag{12b}$$

$$J^{in}_{i,\ldots,k} = \max_{j}(d^{in}_{i,\ldots,j} + J^{in}_{i,\ldots,j}) - d^{in}_{i,\ldots,k} \tag{13b}$$

- *many-to-one nesting relationship (ascending):* When $\lambda_{i,\ldots,j}$ is one of many child activities whose completion is required to trigger that of the parent transaction $\lambda_{i,\ldots,k}$:

$$d^{out}_{i,..,k} = \max_{j}(d^{out}_{i,...,j}) \tag{14b}$$

$$J^{out}_{i,..,k} = \max_{j}(d^{out}_{i,...,j} + J^{out}_{i,...,j}) - d^{out}_{i,...,k} \tag{15b}$$

Timing Model Initialisation and Finalisation

Initialisation of the end-to-end timing analysis model involves the assignment of input jitter and minimum I/O separation parameters for all nested transactions and activities that directly service the input events of the transaction. For example, for the transaction depicted in Figure 1, this relates to the nested transaction λ_1. In the general case, the following assignments are made for each level 0 λ_i whose arrival is triggered directly by some transaction input event:

$$d^{in}_{i} = -J^{in} \tag{16}$$

$$J^{in}_{i} = J^{in} \tag{17}$$

where J^{in} is the transaction level input jitter, *i.e.* the maximum variation in arrival time over *all* transaction input events.

Finalisation of the end-to-end analysis involves the assignment of transaction level minimum I/O separation and output jitter values. Transaction level values are determined by consolidating the values of the same parameters for all nested transactions and activities that directly service the output events of the transaction. For example, for the transaction depicted in Figure 1, this relates to the activities λ_2, λ_3 and λ_4. In the general case, the following expressions are evaluated over all level 0 λ_i that relate directly to transaction output events:

$$\min_{i}(d^{out}_{i}) \leq d \leq \max_{i}(d^{out}_{i}) \tag{18}$$

$$\min_{i}(d^{out}_{i} + J^{out}_{i}) - d \leq J^{out} \leq \max_{i}(d^{out}_{i} + J^{out}_{i}) - d \tag{19}$$

where d and J^{out} are the transaction level minimum I/O separation and output jitter, respectively.

Example Transaction Definition and Decomposition

In order to evaluate the end-to-end timing model at any stage of refinement, values must be assigned to the localised (activity level) delay parameters $r_{i,...,k}$ and $R_{i,...,k}$ for each activity $\lambda_{i,...,k}$. In general terms, this can be done in one of two ways:

- By assigning *budgeted* values for each $r_{i,\dots,k}$ and $R_{i,\dots,k}$, *e.g.* based on knowledge of the transaction timing requirements;
- By assigning *actual* values for each $r_{i,\dots,k}$ and $R_{i,\dots,k}$, *e.g.* based on actual measurement or static analysis of code.

The latter approach is clearly only applicable when the target hardware and software implementation are complete (or at least underway). The former approach is what is required during the early stages of system development and evolution and is used in the example that follows.

To start, consider the assignment of the following end-to-end timing properties to the example transaction - in practice, such details could be extracted from an overall statement of system level end-to-end timing requirements. (Figure 13 and Figure 14)

The initial level 0 model of the transaction is depicted in Figure 15 - in practice, this information could be extracted from the top level software architecture design.

From the set of boundary conditions given in Equations *(16)* to *(19)*, it is straight forward to assign a set of values to the corresponding level 0 timing attributes. Firstly, from the transaction input conditions given in Equations *(16)* and *(17)*, values are directly inferred for the input jitter and initial accrued delay of λ_1:

$$d_1^{in} = -5 \quad d_1^{in} = -5 \quad J_1^{in} = 5 \quad J_1^{in} = 5$$

Figure 13. Example - transaction timing requirements

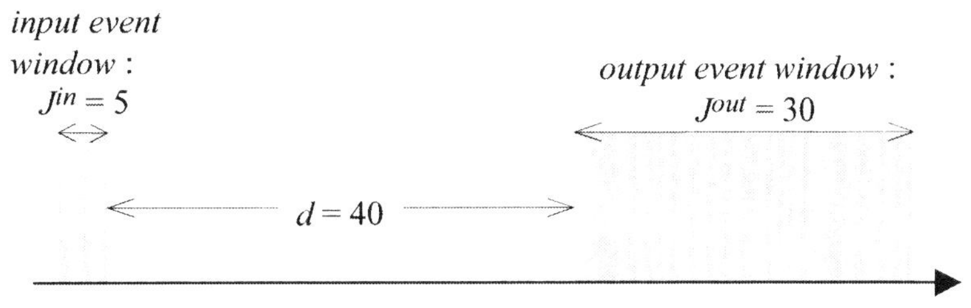

Figure 14. Example - Level 0 Model

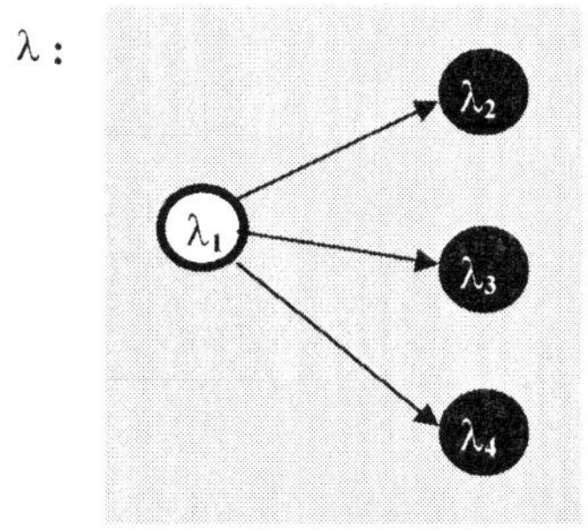

Figure 15. Example partial assignment of Level 0 attributes

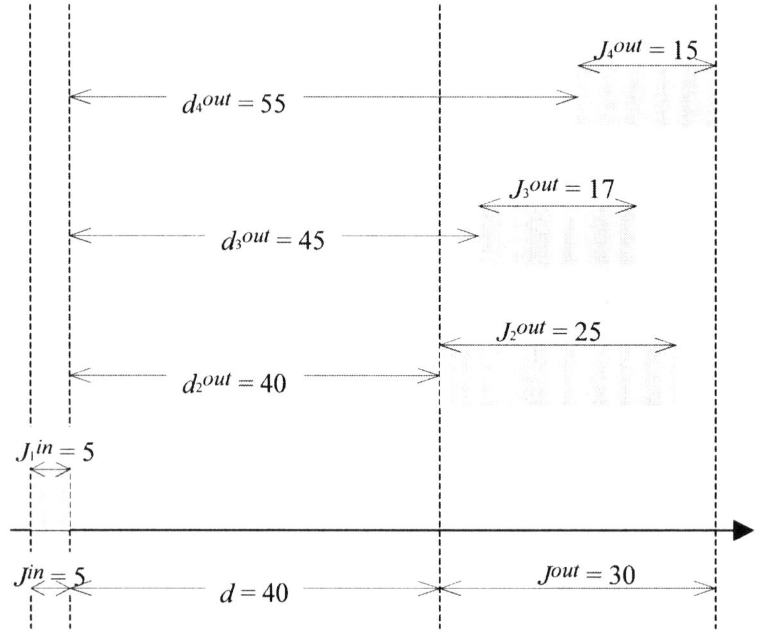

From the transaction output conditions given in Equations *(18)* and *(19)*, suitable values can be found for the output jitter and final accrued delay of λ_2, λ_3 and λ_4:

$$d_2^{out} = 40 \; d_2^{out} = 40 \; J_2^{out} = 25 \; J_2^{out} = 25$$

$$d_3^{out} = 45 \; d_3^{out} = 45 \; J_3^{out} = 17 \; J_3^{out} = 17$$

$$d_4^{out} = 55 \; d_4^{out} = 55 \; J_4^{out} = 15 \; J_4^{out} = 15$$

In this example, the parameters have been assigned such that the output event window of the transaction is exactly spanned by the set of activity level output windows. This means that the corresponding transaction level timing requirements have been met exactly, rather than leaving an element of redundancy in the transaction level requirements relative to the level 0 model timing properties. Beyond that, and the satisfaction of the boundary conditions given in Equations *(16)* to *(19)*, the actual values assigned are somewhat arbitrary and chosen purely for the purposes of illustration. Figure 15 illustrates this (partial) assignment of level 0 timing attributes.

The rest of the level 0 timing attributes can be assigned on the basis of the level 0 topology details and the appropriate means of accounting for precedence relationships as defined in Equations *(4)* to *(9)*. In practice, additional application-specific information could be taken into account here. In this example, values have been assigned as explained below.

Given the one-to-many precedence relationship between λ_1 and its successor activities λ_2, λ_3 and λ_4, Equation *(5)* implies that the parameters J_1^{out}, J_2^{in}, J_3^{in} and J_4^{in} should all be assigned the same value.

Given that jitter tends to increase in the direction of control flow along the transaction (unless specific jitter control mechanisms are introduced such as by using time-triggered releases), this value should be less than any of the output jitter values already assigned for activities λ_2, λ_3 and λ_4. For the purposes of this example, the following assignment has been made:

$$J_1^{out} = J_2^{in} = J_3^{in} = J_4^{in} = 12$$

From Equation *(4)*, the positions of the time windows whose widths are defined by the above jitter values are all fixed by the size of d_1^{out}. Hence, the parameters d_1^{out}, d_2^{in}, d_3^{in} and d_4^{in} should all be assigned the same value. Given the topology of the transaction, a reasonable assignment for illustration purposes would be:

$$d_1^{out} = d_2^{in} = d_3^{in} = d_4^{in} = 35$$

The level 0 timing attributes are now sufficiently defined to fix the position of all input and output windows in the level 0 topology. Figure 16 illustrates this (full) assignment of level 0 timing attributes.

The final stage of level 0 transaction definition is to derive the set of timing obligations that are to be inherited as constraints on the next stage of model refinement (or implementation if so desired). These obligations are in the form of a set of minimum and maximum response times and minimum I/O separation values and can be determined (uniquely[2]) for all level 0 activities from the application of Equations *(3)*, *(2)* and *(1)*, respectively:

$r_1 = 40$ $R_1 = 47$ $d_1 = 35$

$r_2 = 5$ $R_2 = 18$ $d_2 = -7$

$r_3 = 10$ $R_3 = 15$ $d_3 = -2$

$r_4 = 20$ $R_4 = 23$ $d_4 = 8$

The level 0 model is now completely defined. To illustrate how the approach supports further refinement of the timing model, a second stage of decomposition is now illustrated. The level 1 model for the nested transaction λ_1 is depicted in Figure 17.

From the statement of λ_1 timing attributes above and the set of Equations *(4)* to *(15)*, it is straight forward to assign a set of values to the corresponding level 1 timing attributes. Firstly, given the one-to-many nesting relationship (descending) between λ_1 and its child input activities $\lambda_{1,1}$ and $\lambda_{1,2}$, Equations *(6)* and *(7)* give:

$$d_{1,1}^{in} = -5 \quad d_{1,1}^{in} = -5 \quad J_{1,1}^{in} = 5 \quad J_{1,1}^{in} = 5$$

$$d_{1,2}^{in} = -5 \quad d_{1,2}^{in} = -5 \quad J_{1,2}^{in} = 5 \quad J_{1,2}^{in} = 5$$

Figure 16. Example - full assignment of Level 0 attributes

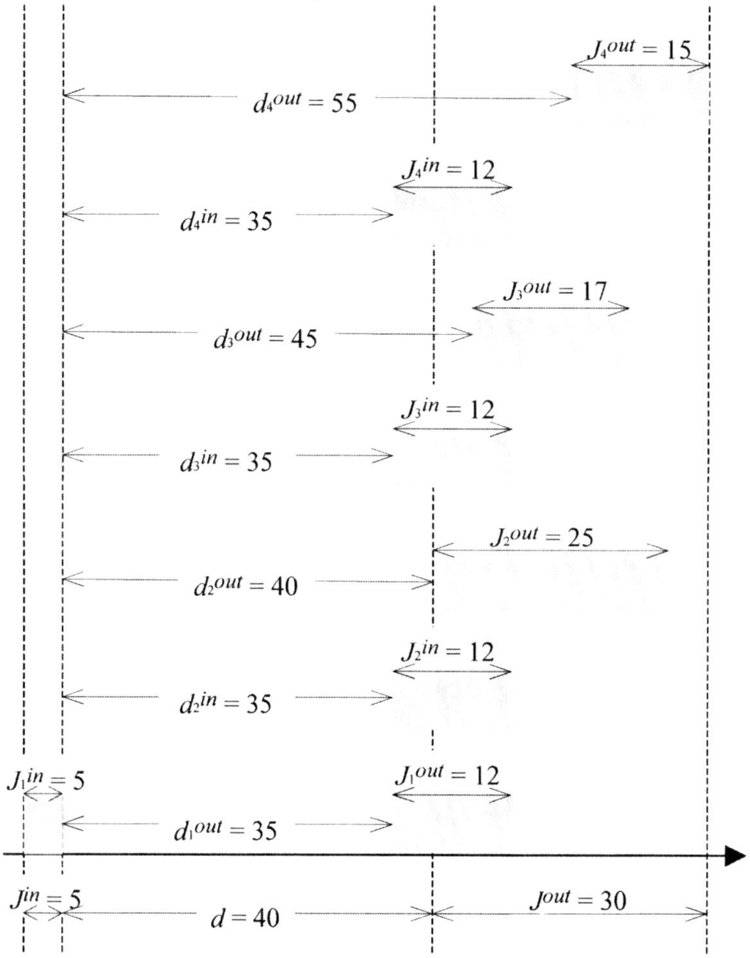

Figure 17. Example - Level 1 Model for λ_1

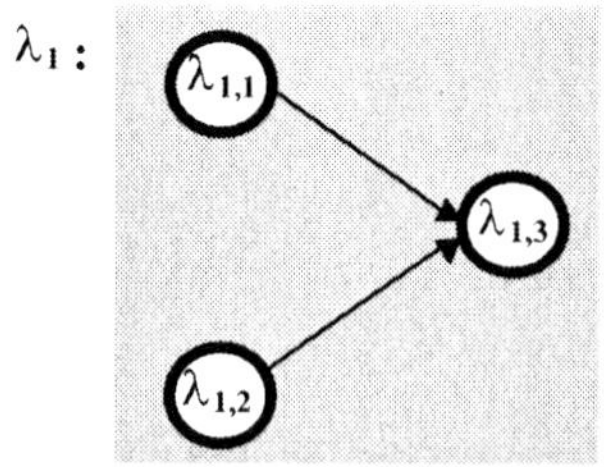

Given the one-to-one nesting relationship (ascending) between λ_1 and its child output activity $\lambda_{1,3}$, Equations *(8)* and *(9)* give:

$d^{out}_{1,3} = 35 \; d^{out}_{1,3} = 35 \; J^{out}_{1,3} = 12 \; J^{out}_{1,3} = 12$

Figure 18 illustrates this (partial) assignment of level 1 timing attributes for λ_1.

The rest of the level 1 timing attributes for λ_1 can be assigned on the basis of the level 1 topology details and the appropriate means of accounting for precedence relationships as defined in Equations *(4)* to *(9)*. Assuming $Q_{1,3}$ has been specified such that the arrival of $\lambda_{1,3}$ will be triggered only upon completion of both predecessors $\lambda_{1,1}$ and $\lambda_{1,2}$, Equations *(10b)* and *(11b)* can be applied to assign level 1 parameter values as described below.

Given that jitter tends to increase in the direction of control flow along the transaction, $J^{in}_{1,3}$ is assigned an appropriate intermediate value between the specified input and output jitter values for λ_1. $J^{out}_{1,1}$ and $J^{out}_{1,2}$ are then assigned with knowledge of $Q_{1,3}$ and the corresponding relationship with $J^{in}_{1,3}$ as expressed in Equation *(11b)*. This expression implies that larger jitter values than $J^{in}_{1,3}$ can be assigned to some (though not all) predecessors in a many-to-one precedence relationship so long as the output window terminates no later than the required successor input window. On this basis, $J^{out}_{1,1}$ has been assigned a larger value than $J^{in}_{1,3}$, which means that this must be taken into account in the assignment of $d^{out}_{1,1}$ (see below). This leads to the following assignments:

$$J^{in}_{1,3} = J^{out}_{1,2} = 9 \; J^{in}_{1,3} = J^{out}_{1,2} = 9 \; J^{out}_{1,1} = 11 \; J^{out}_{1,1} = 11$$

An appropriate intermediate value can be assigned for $d^{in}_{1,3}$ to fix the position of the input window for $\lambda_{1,3}$. The accrued minimum delay requirements can then be specified for $\lambda_{1,1}$ and $\lambda_{1,2}$ such that the latest completion time for $\lambda_{1,1}$ is less than that of $\lambda_{1,2}$.

$$d^{in}_{1,3} = d^{out}_{1,2} = 20 \; d^{in}_{1,3} = d^{out}_{1,2} = 20 \; d^{out}_{1,1} = 15 \; d^{out}_{1,1} = 15$$

Figure 19 illustrates the full assignment of level 1 timing attributes for λ_1.

Once again, a set of timing obligations can be determined for the purposes of further refinement or direct implementation. These obligations are specified in the form of a set of minimum and maximum

Figure 18. Example - partial assignment of Level 1 attributes for λ_1

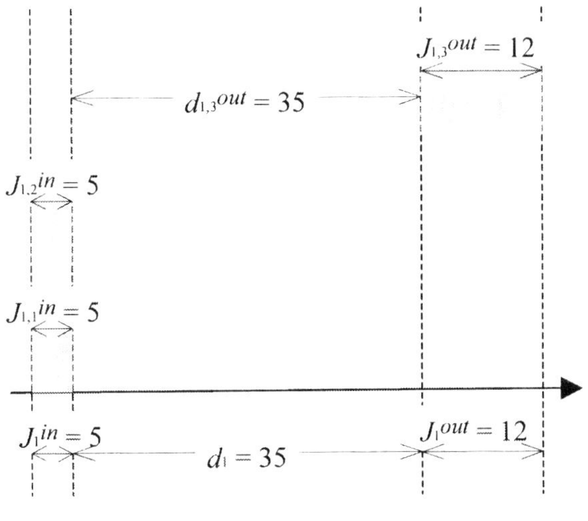

response times and minimum I/O separation values for all level 1 activities by application of Equations *(3)*, *(2)* and *(1)*, respectively:

$r_{1,1} = 20$ $R_{1,1} = 26$ $d_{1,1} = 15$

$r_{1,2} = 25$ $R_{1,2} = 29$ $d_{1,2} = 20$

$r_{1,3} = 15$ $R_{1,3} = 18$ $d_{1,3} = 6$

A final stage of decomposition for the example transaction gives the set of level 2 timing attributes for the nested transaction λ_1 as depicted in Figure 20. In practice, refinement of the transaction and its timing attributes could continue until the required level of detail is obtained. Clearly, the topological details generated at each stage of refinement and the number of refinement stages performed are dependent on the nature of the application and the software design/implementation approach. (Table 1)

The final set of timing obligations for λ_1 can now be determined via Equations *(3)*, *(2)* and *(1)*:

Assuming no further refinement of the transaction prior to its implementation, this final set of timing obligations represents a set of constraints on the implementation of the system. During the implementation stages, however, the timing model could be evolved further in the same manner as above as a means of supporting more progressive implementation (and integration) of the final system. It should be observed during any such evolution, however, that the stage at which the timing model become target-specific or integration-specific, *i.e.* appropriate to a particular scheduling or communication regime, is the stage at which it ceases to support changes to the target system without the need to restate the model.

When the final implementation and integration details of the system are stabilised, the timing model must be verified, *i.e.* the timing obligations defined in the abstract timing model must be shown to be safe. This requires some form of localised timing analysis model, *ie.* a model to determine activity

Figure 19. Example - full assignment of Level 1 attributes for λ_1

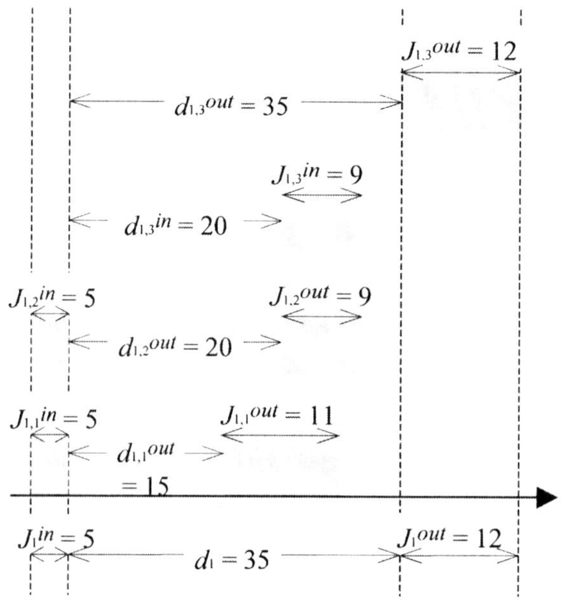

Figure 20. Example - final assignment of Level 2 attributes for λ_1

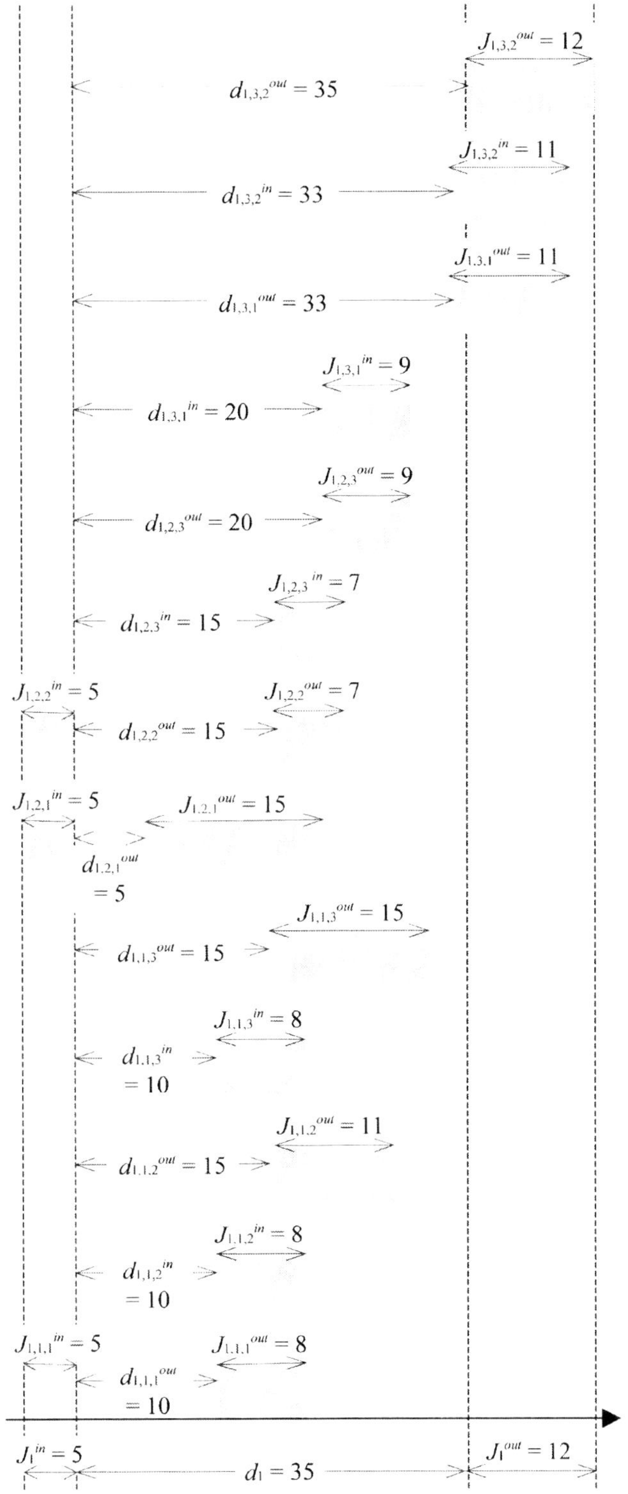

Table 1. Example transaction (localised timing attributes for λ_1)

	$r_{i,...,k}$	$d_{i,...,k}$	$R_{i,...,k}$
$\lambda_{1,1,1}$	15	10	18
$\lambda_{1,1,2}$	5	-3	8
$\lambda_{1,1,3}$	5	-3	12
$\lambda_{1,2,1}$	10	5	20
$\lambda_{1,2,2}$	20	15	22
$\lambda_{1,2,3}$	5	-2	7
$\lambda_{1,3,1}$	13	4	15
$\lambda_{1,3,2}$	2	-9	3

level delay and jitter characteristics based on some notion of what constitutes a *resource* - processor or communication medium. This is almost where the transition begins towards a target-specific model. RBA permits the transition to be deferred a little longer, however, by adopting a *rate-based execution model* – an abstract model of run-time scheduling behaviour. This abstract scheduling model can then be implemented using either cyclic or priority-based scheduling. This next stage is described below.

RATE-BASED EXECUTION MODEL

The RBA rate-based execution model is a generalised form of scheduling model that provides independence from the final target implementation and integration details of the system, including the precise form of the final run-time scheduling solution. This abstract scheduling model can be used to guide the final target scheduling solution to preserve the performance predictions of the abstract timing model. A range of compliant scheduler implementation schemes will be described later.

Let $\{\lambda_j; j=1,..,n\}$ denote the set of activities allocated to a shared system resource and denote the associated set of timing obligations by $\{(C_j, v_j, R_j); j=1,..,n\}$, where C_j is the maximum execution time (or analogous communication bandwidth requirement), v_j is the minimum required rate of execution and R_j is the worst-case response time requirement. The rate-based execution model defines the following simple linear relationship between these parameters:

$$v_j = \frac{C_j}{R_j} \quad (20)$$

An analogous set of best-case parameters is also defined by $\{(c_j, V_j, r_j); j=1,..,n\}$. The objective of any compliant implementation scheme is thus to maintain the run-time execution rate of each activity within the required range $[v_j, V_j]$, as illustrated in Figure 21.

To illustrate the application of the rate-based execution model (and subsequent implementation schemes) by example, Table 2 presents a set of timing attributes for the GAP task set (Locke, 1991).

Each GAP 'task' is modeled as a single RBA activity since there is no benefit in further decomposition in this example. All GAP tasks are periodic with period $T_j=R_j$, except for τ_{10} which is sporadic with minimum inter-arrival time a_{10}=200. Since no input jitter is specified for the periodic tasks, it is assumed that a_j=T_j for these tasks. Conversely, assigning a_{10}=T_{10} for the sporadic task (the value of 200 shown in brackets in the table) gives a total task set utilisation requirement of 83.5%.

The set of minimum execution rates are derived from Equation *(20)* but, since all GAP tasks are periodic with period=deadline (T_j=D_j), then $\{v_j=U_j; j=1,..,16\}$. The total bandwidth reservation requirement is therefore equal to the total utilisation requirement of the task set, *i.e.* 83.5%, which would be schedulable on a single processor by an 'exact' implementation of the rate-based execution model.

Basic Schedule Implementation Scheme

A form of cyclic schedule implementation scheme can be used to directly implements the RBA rate-based execution model. This allows the run-time scheduling solution for a system to be derived directly from an RBA target-independent timing analysis model for the system without compromising the original timing requirements. The simplest form of such scheme has the following attributes:

- A fixed cycle time $\Delta \leq \min_j R_j$;
- A fixed time and duration of execution δ_j for each activity λ_j within each cycle;
- The restriction $R_j \leq a_j$ for each activity λ_j.

Consequently, each activity will execute for exactly δ_j time units in *any* interval of size Δ, *ie.* not necessarily aligned to the minor cycle. The actual order of execution of activities within each cycle is arbitrary. Moreover, the execution time δ_j allocated to an activity within a cycle does not need to be contiguous.

It is necessary to assign an appropriate value for Δ and for each δ_j such that the timing obligations for each activity λ_j are met. The following scheme can be applied to achieved this but note that other valid assignments will normally exist for a given set of timing obligations. An example is developed alongside the description of the scheme by considering the activity λ_7 from the GAP task set.Firstly,

Figure 21. Valid execution space

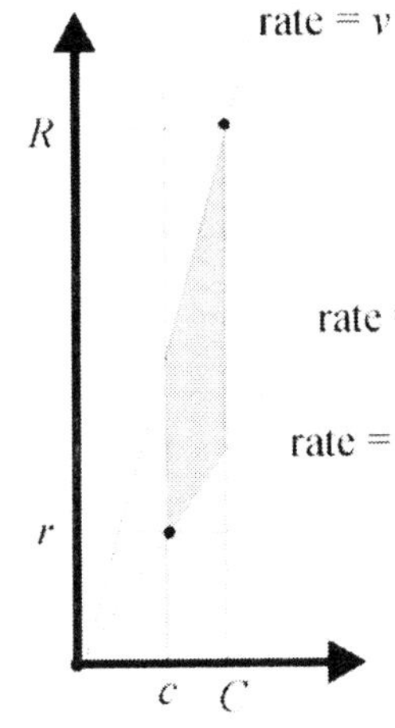

Table 2. Example task set

j	*Function*	C_j	R_j	$v_j=U_j$
1	Radar Track Filter	2	25	0.08
2	RWR Contact Mgt.	5	25	0.2
3	Data Bus Poll Device	1	40	0.025
4	Weapon Aiming	3	50	0.06
5	Radar Target Update	5	50	0.1
6	Nav. Update	8	59	0.1355
7	Display Graphic	9	80	0.1125
8	Display Hook Update	2	80	0.025
9	Target Update	5	100	0.05
10	Weapon Protocol	1	200	0.005
11	Nav. Steering Cmds.	3	200	0.015
12	Display Sores Update	1	200	0.005
13	Display Keyset	1	200	0.005
14	Display Stat. Update	3	200	0.015
15	BET E Status Update	1	1000	0.001
16	Nav. Status	1	1000	0.001

define the normalised response time value $R_j^\Delta \leq R_j$ as follows:

$$R_j^\Delta = [\frac{R_j}{\Delta}]\Delta \tag{21}$$

From Equation *(20)*, define the corresponding normalised execution rate v_j^Δ as follows:

$$v_j^\Delta = \frac{C_j}{R_j^\Delta} \tag{22}$$

It can be seen from Equation *(20)* that $v_j^\Delta \geq v_j$ since $R_j^\Delta \leq R_j$. Subsequently, assign δ_j the minimum value that will guarantee λ_j to meet its normalised response time requirement R_j^Δ:

$$\delta_j = [v_j^\Delta \Delta] \tag{23}$$

In the final schedule, each activity λ_j will consequently be executed at a guaranteed minimum rate v_j^Δ given as follows:

$$v_j^\Delta = \frac{\delta_j}{\Delta} \tag{24}$$

Hence, for the example task, a value of $\Delta = 25$ gives $R_7^\Delta = 75$, $\upsilon_7^\Delta = 0.12$, $\delta_7 = 3$ and $\upsilon_7^\delta = 0.12$.

Since each activity will be executed at a rate which is no less than that specified by its minimum rate requirement, the worst-case response time can be guaranteed for any worst-case execution time in the range $[0, C_j]$. This makes final verification for a specific target implementation very straight forward. Denoting the target-specific resource requirement of each λ_j by C_j^* gives the target-specific feasibility test:

$$C_j^* \leq C_j \tag{25}$$

This test is independent from the choice of Δ and, for any given activity, the timing and resource requirements of other activities allocated to the shared resource. The test also allows simple re-verification of λ_j following any software implementation changes that impact on the value of C_j^*.

A target-independent feasibility test (which could be applied as a resource allocation constraint) for the set of activities as a whole is as follows:

$$\sum_{j=1}^{n} \upsilon_j^\delta \leq 1 \tag{26}$$

Since the value of υ_j^δ is only dependent upon the timing obligations for activity λ_j, the test can be applied incrementally, *i.e.* to accept or reject the addition of a 'new' activity to an existing set by comparing its final rate requirement with the remaining capacity available, independent from the actual rate requirements of activities that already exist in the schedule (that are already guaranteed). Hence, denoting the new activity by λ_{n+1}, the following acceptance test can be applied:

$$\upsilon_{n+1}^\delta \leq 1 - \sum_{j=1}^{n} \upsilon_j^\delta \tag{27}$$

Neither form of the test can be applied until the value of Δ is fixed, since this determines the value of each υ_j^δ. When the value of Δ is fixed, typically at design-time, this could be taken into account in the assignment of timing obligations at the final stage of decomposition of the end-to-end transactions. For example, the value of Δ impacts on the efficiency of the final bandwidth allocation, as discussed below.

For any activity, the inefficiency of the scheme increases as the worst-case response time requirement decreases relative to the minimum inter-arrival time. This inefficiency is manifest in the final scheduling solution as an over-allocation of bandwidth compared to that which is actually required, as stipulated by the true utilisation requirement of the activity. This arises since the minimum inter-arrival time is not recognised in the construction of the cyclic schedule beyond the assumption that it is greater than the original response time requirement, *i.e.* $R_j \leq a_j$. Consequently, sufficient capacity is reserved in the schedule to execute each activity once in any time interval of duration R_j (irrespective of the minimum inter-arrival time). Any over-allocated bandwidth, however, along with any that is allocated but unused at run-time due to variation in execution times, can potentially be 'reclaimed' at run-time. Reclamation of unused bandwidth is discussed later in the paper. Alternatively, the over-allocation of bandwidth can be exploited to give a larger upper bound for the target-specific worst-case computation time for λ_j by restating the target-specific feasibility test, as previously stated in Equation *(25)*, to give:

$$C_j^* \leq C_j \tag{28}$$

where C_j^δ represents the actual maximum computation time allocated in the cyclic schedule over the time duration R_j and is given as follows:

$$C_j^\delta = \frac{R_j^\Delta}{\Delta}\delta_j \tag{29}$$

Note that the value of C_j^δ will automatically be integer since δ_j is integer and R_j^Δ is exactly divisible by Δ. This larger upper bound on the target-specific worst-case computation time can then be exploited to give a (specified) margin for error in either:

- The actual execution-time of λ_j at run-time compared to the specified value C_j such that transient over-run of the activity can be tolerated;
- The worst-case computation time of a software component procured from some third-party compared to the specified value C_j such that failure of the supplier to meet the original specification can be tolerated to a limited extent.

The final target-independent response time R_j^δ for λ_j, given the original computation time budget C_j and the final bandwidth allocation due to the cyclic scheduling solution, can be stated as follows:

$$R_j^\delta = \left[\frac{C_j}{\delta_j}\right]\Delta \tag{30}$$

Hence, the target-dependent response time R_j^* for λ_j, given an actual target-specific computation time value $C_j^* \leq C_j^\delta$ can be stated as follows:

$$R_j^* = \left[\frac{C_j^*}{\delta_j}\right]\Delta \tag{31}$$

Note that the scheme is exact, in the sense that the allocated bandwidth is both necessary and sufficient to meet true worst-case utilisation requirements, only under certain conditions. This is the case when there are nil effects from rounding in Equations *(21)* and *(23)* – the 'sufficient but not necessary' stages of the calculation. In the general case, the degree of inefficiency of the scheme is dependent upon the actual timing requirements of the activities.

Example Application of Basic Cyclic Scheme

The basic scheme can be applied to determine an RBA-compliant schedule by first selecting an appropriate value for the cycle time Δ. Then, for each activity λ_j:

- Determine the 'normalised' response time R_j^Δ;
- Determine the 'normalised' execution rate v_j^Δ;
- Determine the time δ_j for which the task must be executed in each cycle Δ;
- Derive the guaranteed response time R_j^δ;
- Derive the minimum run-time execution rate v_j^δ;
- Derive the guaranteed computation time C_j^δ.

Observing the original schedule construction constraint $\Delta \leq \min_j R_j$, assign Δ=25. This leads to the solution given in Table 3, Table 4, and Table 5.

A number of observations can be made from these results. From Table 3, the sum of the initial execution rate parameters (v_j) corresponds exactly to the total utilisation requirement of the task set (83.51%). This arises since the worst-case response time of every task is equal to its minimum inter-arrival time. After defining a cycle time of Δ=25, the sum of the rate parameters (v_j^Δ) corresponds to a total bandwidth allocation of 88.37%, a noticeable but reasonable increase compared to the true requirement. At the final stage of calculation, however, the need to provide integer values for the final rate parameters (v_j^δ) gives rise to a significant over-allocation of bandwidth due to the combination of rounding effects for the overall task set. The final bandwidth allocation is 120% and, hence, the extent of the over-allocation is sufficient to make the task set no longer schedulable on a single processor (by this scheme). The cyclic schedule has been constructed, however, to allow individual activities to be removed (or have their timing attributes changed) without affecting other activities in the schedule. Hence, it is straight forward to reduce the task set to one that is schedulable on a single processor by simply removing one or more activities (to be reallocated to another processor) until the final bandwidth allocation is less than 100%. The ability to manipulate the schedule in this manner is a considerable benefit in the context of engineering larger-scale real-time systems.

A counter effect of bandwidth over-allocation is an equivalent reduction in worst-case response times (R_j^δ) compared to the stated requirements (R_j), as can be seen in Table 4. For example, λ_{15} has a final bandwidth allocation of 4% (equivalent to its execution rate of 0.04) compared to its stated requirement of 0.1%. The corresponding reduction in its worst-case response time is apparent in the final value of 25 compared to an original requirement of 1000.

The over-allocation of bandwidth is due to the restriction that every task is executed (for a duration δ_j) in every cycle Δ, as reflected in the final computation times (C_j^δ) given in Table 5. This restriction leads to a simpler (and more readily modifiable) scheduling solution but can be lifted to allow a more flexible scheme to be defined in favour of reducing the bandwidth over-allocation. Such a scheme is described and illustrated in the next section.

Note that the basic scheme does *not* compromise the true timing requirements of the task set – there is no imposition of false iteration rates for the purposes of constructing a schedule (a criticism often levelled at cyclic scheduling solutions). Furthermore, the schedule is incrementally modifiable such that schedulability can be maintained following activities being added, removed or modified by merely ensuring that the final bandwidth allocation is less than 100% (and that the choice of Δ is still suitable).

Bandwidth Server-Based Implementation Scheme

As suggested above, it is possible to reduce the bandwidth over-allocation associated with the basic cyclic implementation scheme by relaxing the constraint that every activity must be offered the chance to execute in every cycle. This gives rise to the cyclic bandwidth server scheme.

The starting point is once again the selection of a cycle time Δ subject to the same constraint. Then define a the server activity $\lambda^S(\delta^S,N^S)$ as a notional activity that is allocated δ^S execution time units in every Δ cycle but does not actually consume that allocation itself. Instead, the server offers the resource to other activities so that these can execute with an effective cycle time of $N^S\Delta$. The total bandwidth of the server can then be used to execute a number of activities that individually have relatively low bandwidth requirements that would otherwise be allocated a disproportionate amount of bandwidth by the basic scheme. Assuming that the server executes its allocated activities in a fixed order then an activity λ_j allocated to a $\lambda^S(\delta^S,N^S)$ server will execute for a duration δ_j spread over an interval of $N^S\Delta$.

The cyclic server exploits the fact that the basic scheme, and its analysis, does not require the execution time allocated to an activity within a scheduling cycle to be contiguous. The analysis associated with the cyclic server is, therefore, exactly analogous to that for the basic cyclic scheme but with Δ replaced by $N^S\Delta$. Hence, the derivation of δ_j for an activity λ_j executed via a cyclic server $\lambda^S(\delta^S,N^S)$ is

Table 3. Example - cyclic schedule implementation (execution rate parameters)

j	U_j	v_j	υ_j^Δ	υ_j^δ
1	0.0800	0.0800	0.0800	0.0800
2	0.2000	0.2000	0.2000	0.2000
3	0.0250	0.0250	0.0400	0.0400
4	0.0600	0.0600	0.0600	0.0800
5	0.1000	0.1000	0.1000	0.1200
6	0.1356	0.1356	0.1600	0.1600
7	0.1125	0.1125	0.1200	0.1200
8	0.0250	0.0250	0.0267	0.0400
9	0.0500	0.0500	0.0500	0.0800
10	0.0050	0.0050	0.0050	0.0400
11	0.0150	0.0150	0.0150	0.0400
12	0.0050	0.0050	0.0050	0.0400
13	0.0050	0.0050	0.0050	0.0400
14	0.0150	0.0150	0.0150	0.0400
15	0.0010	0.0010	0.0010	0.0400
16	0.0010	0.0010	0.0010	0.0400
Σ	0.8351	0.8351	0.8837	1.2000

Table 4. Example - cyclic schedule implementation (response time parameters)

j	R_j	R_j^{Δ}	R_j^{δ}
1	25	25	25
2	25	25	25
3	40	25	25
4	50	50	50
5	50	50	50
6	59	50	50
7	80	75	75
8	80	75	50
9	100	100	75
10	200	200	25
11	200	200	75
12	200	200	25
13	200	200	25
14	200	200	75
15	1000	1000	25
16	1000	1000	25

Table 5. Example - cyclic schedule implementation (computation time parameters)

j	C_j	C_j^{δ}	δ_j
1	2	2	2
2	5	5	5
3	1	1	1
4	3	4	2
5	5	6	3
6	8	8	4
7	9	9	3
8	2	3	1
9	5	8	2
10	1	8	8
11	3	8	1
12	1	8	1
13	1	8	1
14	3	8	1
15	1	40	1
16	1	40	1

given by Equations *(21)* to *(23)* with Δ replaced by $N^S\Delta$. Similarly, Equations *(24)*, *(29)* and *(30)* can be applied with Δ replaced by $N^S\Delta$ to determine the final rate, computation time and response time values, respectively. For this reason, the cyclic server method is actually a generalisation of the basic cyclic scheme described previously, where multiple cycle times are supported.

For the general case of activity execution via a cyclic server $\lambda^S(\delta^S,N^S)$, the expression for determining the normalised response time for λ_j is adapted as follows:

$$R_j^{\Delta} = [\frac{R_j}{N^S\Delta}]N^S\Delta \tag{32}$$

The corresponding normalised execution rate v_j^{Δ} is then found as before by Equation *(22)*. The minimum execution time δ_j per interval $N^S\Delta$ that will guarantee λ_j to meet its normalised response time requirement R_j^{Δ} (and therefore its true requirement R_j) is given by:

$$\delta_j^{\Delta} = [v_j^{\Delta}N^S\Delta] \tag{33}$$

Allocating δ_j execution time units per interval $N^S\Delta$ in the final schedule means that each activity λ_j will be executed at a guaranteed minimum rate v_j^{δ} as follows:

$$v_j^{\Delta} = \frac{\delta_j}{N^S\Delta} \tag{34}$$

The allocated computation time C_j^{δ} over a time interval of duration R_j is as follows:

$$C_j^{\delta} = \frac{R_j^{\Delta}}{N^S\Delta}\delta_j \tag{35}$$

The final target-independent response time R_j^{δ} for λ_j, given the original computation time budget C_j and the final bandwidth allocation due to the cyclic scheduling solution, is given as follows:

$$R_j^{\delta} = [\frac{C_j}{\delta_j}]N^S\Delta \tag{36}$$

To illustrate by example, consider activity λ_{15} from the GAP case study (which was shown above to suffer a factor of 40 bandwidth over-allocation when the basic scheme is applied). For example, a cyclic server $\lambda^S(1,8)$ allocated to serve activity λ_{15} leads to the following results from successive application of Equations *(32)*, *(22)*, *(33)* and *(34)*: $R_{15}^{\Delta} = 1000$, $v_{15}^{\Delta} = 0.001$, $\delta_{15} = 1$ and $v_{15}^{\delta} = 0.005$. This represents a factor of 5 over-allocation, a significant improvement compared to the basic scheme but still quite poor, although the remaining server capacity could be used to service further activities. The use of a server $\lambda^S(1,40)$ dedicated to λ_{15} would be required to give an exact allocation for the single activity alone.

The utilisation-based feasibility test given in Equation *(26)* is no longer exact but merely a necessary condition when one or more activities are executed via servers. A sufficient test can be produced by replacing the combined execution rates of the activities executed by servers by the total capacities of the corresponding servers, where the total capacity v^S of a server $\lambda^S(\delta^S,N^S)$ is given by adaptation of Equation *(24)*:

$$v^S = \frac{\delta^S}{\Delta} \qquad (37)$$

A simple test for feasible allocation of server bandwidth is given as follows:

$$\sum_{k=1}^{m} v_k^{\delta} \leq v^S \qquad (38)$$

where v_k^{δ} denotes the final execution rate of each of m activities λ_k allocated to the server. For a server $\lambda^S(\delta^S,N^S)$ with period N^S and set of allocated activities $\{\lambda_k;\ k = 1,..,n^S\}$, the value of δ^S can be derived from the set of activity execution times $\{\delta_k \text{ in } N^S\Delta;\ k = 1,..,n^S\}$:

$$\delta^S = \left[\frac{\sum_{k=1}^{n^S} \delta_k}{N^S}\right] \qquad (39)$$

Observing that the total time required to execute non-server-based activities in the basic cyclic schedule is equivalent to that of a cyclic server $\lambda^S(\delta^S,1)$, referred to as the *base level* server, the final bandwidth requirement Ψ is given as follows:

$$\Psi = \frac{1}{\Delta}\sum_{i=1}^{nS} \delta_i^S \qquad (40)$$

given the set of servers $\{\lambda_i^S(\delta_i^S, N_i^S);\ i = 1,..,nS\}$ that includes the base level server. This expression is sufficient-but-not-necessary since, depending on the actual server periods and utilisation figures, the bandwidth requirements of a lower rate server could, in practice, be absorbed within the spare capacity of a higher rate server. In such cases, the bandwidth requirements of a lower rate server can be effectively eliminated from the total bandwidth calculation (as illustrated by example later in the paper).

Example Application of Server-Based Scheme

This example illustrates the use of the cyclic server method to improve bandwidth allocation compared to the basic cyclic implementation scheme. Assuming the same basic cycle time Δ=25, define a server $\lambda^S(2,40)$ to execute the low utilisation activities $\{\lambda_{10}, \ldots, \lambda_{16}\}$. Table 6 shows the improved results under this scheme (the values of other parameters not shown in the table are the same as before under the basic cyclic scheme).

The total capacity of the server $\lambda^S(2,40)$ is given by Equation *(37)* as: $v^S = 0.08$. Hence, 92% of the total processor capacity is available for non-server-based activities $\{\lambda_1, \ldots, \lambda_9\}$ and 8% for server-based activities $\{\lambda_{10}, \ldots, \lambda_{16}\}$. So, whilst the total bandwidth allocation is more efficient than for the basic scheme - 97.5% compared to 120%, this is not sufficient to guarantee feasibility on a single processor – it is also necessary to show separately that activities $\{\lambda_1, \ldots, \lambda_9\}$ can be executed within their 92% allocation and that activities $\{\lambda_{10}, \ldots, \lambda_{16}\}$ can be executed within their 8% allocation. From Table 6, the combined allocation for activities $\{\lambda_1, \ldots, \lambda_9\}$ turns out to be exactly 92% and the combined allocation for activities $\{\lambda_{10}, \ldots, \lambda_{16}\}$ is 5.5%. Hence, the complete set of activities *is* schedulable on a single processor under this scheme.

The improved efficiency of this scheme is also reflected in the increased number of activities that have been allocated the exact bandwidth to meet their requirements – 10 out of the 16 activities now, compared to only 4 previously.

Introducing Priorities to Improve Resource Bandwidth Allocation and System Responsiveness

It is now shown that the RBA rate-based execution model and cyclic implementation scheme can co-exist alongside a static priority-based scheduling regime to provide a flexible three-tier run-time execution model as follows:

- *High priority* activities that execute according to a static priority-based regime;
- RBA-compliant activities that execute according to the cyclic RBA implementation scheme, subject to interference from the set of high priority activities;
- *Low priority* activities that execute according to a static priority-based regime, subject to interference from the set of high priority activities and the set of RBA-compliant activities.

The motivation for this combined scheme is two-fold. Firstly, the high priority 'band' can be used to schedule activities with short response requirements compared to their minimum inter-arrival time without incurring bandwidth over-allocation. Secondly, the low priority band can be used to execute activities in the bandwidth that is over-allocated by the RBA cyclic/server scheme, plus any remaining capacity of the resource, thus reclaiming such bandwidth.

Introducing High Priority Activities for Improved Responsiveness

Activities executed in the high priority band will execute according to a static priority-based scheduling regime in accordance with their relative priorities and always in preference to activities in the RBA band. These activities can be verified by static priority-based response time analysis given in (Audsley, 1993). The rate-based execution model and cyclic implementation schemes must be extended, however, to cater for interference effects due to the execution of high priority activities.

The rate-based execution model can be adapted to recognise interference effects using an analogous approach to that for response time analysis for static priority-based scheduling. The solution is simply to add a worst-case interference time to the *actual* worst-case response time or, analogously, to subtract the interference delay from the *required* worst-case response time (deadline). The required minimum execution rate for an activity λ_j subjected to worst-case interference I_j is thus stated as follows:

Table 6. Example - cyclic server implementation (improved allocation for $\{\lambda_{10}, \ldots, \lambda_{16}\}$)

j	v_j^δ	R_j^δ	C_j^δ	δ_j
1	0.0800	25	2	2
2	0.2000	25	5	5
3	0.0400	25	1	1
4	0.0800	50	4	2
5	0.1200	50	6	3
6	0.1600	50	8	4
7	0.1200	75	9	3
8	0.0400	50	3	1
9	0.0800	75	8	2
10	0.0050	200	8	8
11	0.0150	200	8	1
12	0.0050	200	8	1
13	0.0050	200	8	1
14	0.0150	200	8	1
15	0.0050	200	40	1
16	0.0050	200	40	1
Σ	0.9750			

$$v_j = \frac{C_j}{R_j - I_j} \tag{41}$$

For an activity λ_j that shares a resource with a set of high priority activities $\{\lambda_k; k = 1,..,nH\}$, I_j equates to the interference term stated in the response time expression for static priority-based scheduling. Hence, given a set of timing attributes for the set of high priority activities, I_j can be determined as follows:

$$I_j = \sum_{k=1}^{nH} \lceil \frac{R_j + J_k^m}{T_k} \rceil C_k \tag{42}$$

Introducing high priority activities and interference into the cyclic implementation scheme has two effects (the scheme is otherwise unchanged). Firstly, the initial assignment of Δ is now subject to the constraint $\Delta \leq \min_j(R_j - I_j)$. Secondly, for the general case of activity execution via a cyclic server $\lambda^S(\delta^S, N^S)$, the expression for determining the normalised response time for λ_j, Equation *(32)*, is adapted as follows:

$$R_j^\Delta = \lfloor \frac{R_j - I_j}{N^S \Delta} \rfloor N^S \Delta \tag{43}$$

Introducing Low Priority Activities for Improved Bandwidth Allocation

The problem of bandwidth over-allocation has been highlighted in the series of examples given earlier. This problem occurs in the target-independent RBA rate-based execution model due to the calculation of activity execution rates based on response time requirements rather than minimum inter-arrival times. The problem is then compounded in the cyclic implementation scheme due to the need for a common cycle time and integer execution times within this cycle time (or some multiple of the cycle time when cyclic servers are used). This motivates the consideration of bandwidth reclamation via the execution of activities outside the RBA scheme according to a priority-based regime. This new set of priority-based activities is referred to as 'low priority' since none of these can pre-empt any RBA activity nor any high priority activity.

The RBA cyclic scheme itself does not actually require modification. The low priority activities can be guaranteed (or rejected) by adapting the response time analysis for static priority-based scheduling as shown below. Given a set of high priority activities $\{\lambda_k; k = 1,..,nH\}$, a set of RBA activities $\{\lambda_j; j = 1,..,n\}$ and a set of low priority activities $\{\lambda_i; i = 1,..,nL\}$, the following response time can be stated for a given low priority activity λ_l:

$$R_l = C_l + \sum_{k=1}^{nH}\left[\frac{R_l + J_k^m}{T_k}\right]C_k + \sum_{j=1}^{n}\left[\frac{R_l + J_j^m}{T_j}\right]C_j + \sum_{i=1}^{l-1}\left[\frac{R_l + J_i^m}{T_i}\right]C_i \quad (44)$$

Note that the difference between this expression and the response time analysis for static priority-based scheduling given in (Audsley, 1993) is merely notational - the interference term is decomposed into three 'bands' to reflect the composite nature of the scheme.

Example of Reclaiming Over-Allocated Bandwidth

Consider the GAP task set extended by the introduction of a set of low priority activities subject to deadline monotonic priority assignment: (Table 7)Equation *(44)* then gives: (Table 8)

All low priority activities are thus feasible since all response times are less than their corresponding deadline. The total bandwidth requirement for the set of low priority activities is 12.8%. This has effectively been reclaimed from the over-allocated bandwidth for the set of RBA activities, whose true requirement is 83.5% but final allocation is 97.5% (or, including spare server capacity, exactly 100%).

Table 7. Example - low priority timing attributes

i	C_i	T_i	D_i	U_i
1	3	200	150	0.015
2	8	200	180	0.04
3	25	500	400	0.05
4	4	500	450	0.008
5	15	1000	800	0.015

Table 8. Example - low priority response times

I	R_i	*Feasible?*
1	140	✓
2	148	✓
3	384	✓
4	388	✓
5	789	✓

RELATED WORK

A number of scheduling schemes that support bandwidth-based (or, analogously, rate-based) expression of timing and resource requirements have previously been proposed for multimedia applications. These schemes offer a degree of abstraction from the target platform in the way that requirements are specified but are invariably aimed at dynamic applications and generally require the use of dynamic *earliest-deadline-first* (EDF) scheduling at run-time. Examples of such schemes include *generalised processor sharing* (GPS) (Parekh, 1994), *virtual clock* (Yau, 1996), *constant utilisation server* (Deng, 1999) and *weighted fair queuing* (Demers, 1989). Due to the reliance on EDF, however, the final bandwidth allocation (or execution rate) granted to each 'task' is dependent on the actual degree of competition for resources at run-time – as the total demand on a resource increases, the bandwidth reserved for a given task will decrease in absolute terms. Such solutions are more accurately referred to as proportional share methods than bandwidth reservation methods and are not suitable for dependable applications that require *a priori* performance guarantees. See (Grigg, 2002) for a comprehensive survey of related work.

SUMMARY

RBA provides a target-independent timing analysis framework for application during the definition and decomposition stages of real-time system development, based on an abstract representation of target system processing and communication resources. Application of the abstract model provides a set of best-case and worst-case timing 'guarantees' that will be delivered subject to a set of scheduling 'obligations' being met by the target system implementation. An abstract scheduling model, known as the *rate-based execution model* then provides an implementation reference model with which compliance will ensure that the imposed set of timing obligations will be met by the target system.

The end-to-end timing properties of the system are captured, decomposed and analysed in terms of real-time *transactions*. The transaction model is hierarchical, in the form of an acyclic, directed, nested graph, capturing an evolving system definition during development. The leaf nodes of the graph capture the concurrent processing and communication elements within the transaction, termed *activities*; non-leaf nodes are referred to as nested transactions. The edges of the graph capture the precedence and nesting relationships within the transaction. The parameters via which timing behaviour is represented and observed are the same for a single activity, a group of related activities, a nested transaction and a system level transaction, thus providing a highly composable and scalable model of real-time system performance.

End-to-end delays and jitter are determined by a depth-first traversal of each transaction graph, accounting for activity level delays, precedence relationships and nesting relationships. In the earlier stages of system development, activity level delays can be specified directly in the form of budgets. Later in development, these delays can be determined via some form of localised timing analysis model. When the target platform implementation details are finally fixed, these delays can be verified.

A number of further developments of the RBA framework and implementation schemes are being investigated. This includes extending the cyclic server implementation scheme to support 'nested' or 'hierarchical' bandwidth servers as a means of further reducing the extent of bandwidth over-allocation. Other work is beginning to investigate RBA-compliant support for scheduling communication network resources, initially focusing on ATM networks for future avionics applications.

Work is also underway to develop RBA process and tool support for technology transfer into the sponsoring customer's organization. Tool support is being implemented as an extension to the customer's software design environment rather than as a separate standalone tool.

REFERENCES

Audsley, N. C., Burns, A., Richardson, M. F., Tindall, K., & Wellings, A. (1993). *Applying New Scheduling Theory to Static Priority Pre-emptive Scheduling. Software Engineering Journal*, *8*(5).

Demers, A., Keshav, S., & Shenker, S. (1989). Analysis and Simulation of a Fair Queuing Algorithm. *Proceedings of ACM SIGCOMM.*

Deng, Z., Liu, J.W.S., Zhang, L., Mouna, S., & Frei, A. (1999). An Open Environment for Real-Time Applications. *Real-Time Systems Journal, 16*(2/3).

Grigg, A. (2002). *Researvation-Based Timing Analysis – A Partitioned Timing Analysis Model for Distributed Real-Time Systems* (YCST-2002-10). York, UK: University of York, Dept. of Computer Science.

Locke, C. D., Vogel, D. R., & Mesler, T. J. (1991). Building A Predictable Avionics Platform in Ada. In *Proceedings of IEEE Real-Time Systems Symposium.*

Parekh, A.K. & Gallager, R.G. (1994). A Generalised Processor Sharing Approach to Flow Control in Integrated Services Networks. *IEEE Transactions on Networking 2*(2).

Yau, D. K. Y., & Lam, S. S. (1996). Adaptive Rate-Controlled Scheduling for Multimedia Applications. In *Proceedings of ACM Multimedia Conference.*

ENDNOTE

† The assignment can easily be shown to be unique by inspection of Equations *(3)*, *(2)* and *(1)*.

Chapter 27
Scalable Algorithms for Server Allocation in Infostations

Alan A. Bertossi
University of Bologna, Italy

M. Cristina Pinotti
University of Perugia, Italy

Romeo Rizzi
University of Udine, Italy

Phalguni Gupta
Indian Institute of Technology Kanpur, India

ABSTRACT

The server allocation problem arises in isolated infostations, where mobile users going through the coverage area require immediate high-bit rate communications such as web surfing, file transferring, voice messaging, email and fax. Given a set of service requests, each characterized by a temporal interval and a category, an integer k, and an integer h_c for each category c, the problem consists in assigning a server to each request in such a way that at most k mutually simultaneous requests are assigned to the same server at the same time, out of which at most h_c are of category c, and the minimum number of servers is used. Since this problem is computationally intractable, a scalable 2-approximation on-line algorithm is exhibited. Generalizations of the problem are considered, which contain bin-packing, multiprocessor scheduling, and interval graph coloring as special cases, and admit scalable on-line algorithms providing constant approximations.

INTRODUCTION

An infostation is an isolated pocket area with small coverage (about a hundred of meters) of high bandwidth connectivity (at least a megabit per second) that collects information requests of mobile users

DOI: 10.4018/978-1-60566-661-7.ch027

Table 1. Examples of actual time intervals to serve different kinds of requests

Category	Size (kbps)	Time (s) – low rate	Time (s) – high rate
FTP download	10000	100	10
Video stream	5000	50	5
Audio stream, E-mail attachment	512	5	0.5
E-mail, Web browsing	64	0.6	0.06

and delivers data while users are going through the coverage area. The available bandwidth usually depends on the distance between the mobile user and the center of the coverage area: increasing with decreasing distance. An infostation represents a way in the current generation of mobile communication technology for supporting at many-time many-where high-speed and high-quality services of various categories, like web surfing, file transferring, video messaging, emails and fax. It has been introduced to reduce the cost per bit on wireless communications, and hence to encourage the exchange of ever increasing volumes of information. Infostations are located along roadways, at airports, in campuses, and they provide access ports to Internet and/or access to services managed locally (Goodman, Borras, Mandayam, & Yates, 1997; Wu, Chu, Wine, Evans, & Frenkiel, 1999; Zander, 2000; Jayram, Kimbrel, Krauthgamer, Schieber, & Sviridenko, 2001).

It is desirable that the infostation be resource scalable, that is able to easily expand and contract its resource pool to accomodate a heavier or lighter load in terms of number and kind of users, and/or category of services. Indeed, the mobile user connection lasts for a temporal interval, which starts when the user first senses the infostation's presence and finishes when it leaves the coverage area. Depending on the mobility options, three kinds of users are characterized: drive-through, walk-through, and sit-through. According to the mobility options, the response time must be immediate for drive-through, slightly delayed for walk-through, and delayed for sit-through. In general, several communication paradigms are possible: communications can be either broadcast or dedicated to a single user, data can be locally provided or retrieved from a remote gateway, and the bit-rate transmission can be fixed or variable, depending on the infostation model and on the mobility kind of the user.

Each mobile user going through the infostation may require a data service out of a finite set of possible service categories available. The admission control, i.e., the task of deciding whether or not a certain request will be admitted, is essential. In fact, a user going through an infostation to obtain a (toll) service is not disposed to have its request delayed or refused. Hence, the service dropping probability must be kept as low as possible. For this purpose, many admission control and bandwidth allocation schemes for infostations maintain a pool of servers so that when a request arrives it is immediately and irrevocably assigned to a server thus clearing the service dropping probability. Precisely, once a request is admitted, the infostation assigns a temporal interval and a proper bandwidth for serving the request, depending on the service category, on the size of the data required and on the mobility kind of the user, as shown in Table 1 for a sample of requests with their actual parameters. Moreover, the infostation decides whether the request may be served locally or through a remote gateway. In both cases, a server is allocated on demand to the request during the assigned temporal interval. The request is immediately assigned to its server without knowing the future, namely with no knowledge of the next request. Requests are thus served on-line, that is in an ongoing manner as they become available.

Each server, selected out of the predefined server pool, may serve more than one request simultaneously but it is subject to some architecture constraints. For example, no more than k requests could be served simultaneously by a local server supporting k infrared channels or by a gateway server connected to k infostations. Similarly, no more than h services of the same category can be delivered simultaneously due to access constraints on the original data, such as software licenses, limited on-line subscriptions and private access.

This chapter considers the infostation equipped with a large pool of servers, and concentrates on the server allocation problem where one has to determine how many servers must be reserved to on-line satisfy the requests of drive-through users, so that the temporal, architectural and data constraints are not violated. In particular, it is assumed that the isolated infostation controls in a centralized way all the decisions regarding the server allocation. Moreover, the pool of servers of the infostation is localized in the center of the coverage area, and therefore the distance from a mobile user and any server in the pool is the same. In other words, all the servers are equivalent to serve a mobile user, independent of the user proximity.

In details, a service *request* r will be modeled by a service *category* c_r and a temporal *interval* $I_r = [s_r, e_r)$ with *starting time* s_r and *ending time* e_r. Two requests are simultaneous if their temporal intervals overlap. The input of the problem consists of a set R of service requests, a bound k on the number of mutually simultaneous requests to be served by the same server at the same time, and a set C of service categories with each category c characterized by a bound h_c. The output is a mapping from the requests in R to the servers that uses the minimum possible number of servers to assign all the requests in R subject to the constraints that the same server receives at most k mutually simultaneous requests at the same time (k-constraint), out of which at most h_c are of category c (h-constraint). In this chapter, we refer to this problem as the *Server Allocation with Bounded Simultaneous Requests* (Bertossi, Pinotti, Rizzi, & Gupta, 2004).

It is worthy to note that, equating servers with bins, and requests with items, the above problem is similar to a generalization of Bin-Packing, known as *Dynamic Bin-Packing* (Coffman, Galambos, Martello, & Vigo, 1999), where in addition to size constraints on the bins, the items are characterized by an arrival and a departure time, and repacking of already packed items is allowed each time a new item arrives. The problem considered in this chapter, in contrast, does not allow repacking and has capacity constraints also on the bin size for each category. Furthermore, equating servers with processors and requests with tasks, the above problem becomes a generalization of deterministic multiprocessor scheduling with task release times and deadlines (Lawler & Lenstra, 1993) where in addition each processor can execute more than one task at the same time, according to the k-constraints and h-constraints. Moreover, equating servers with colors and requests with intervals, our problem is a generalization of the classical interval graph coloring (Golumbic, 1980), but with the additional k-constraints and h-constraints. Another generalization of interval graph coloring has been introduced for modelling a problem involving an optical line system (Winkler & Zhang, 2003), which reduces to ours where only the k-constraint is considered. Finally, a weighted generalization of interval coloring has been introduced (Adamy & Erlebach, 2004) where there is only the k-constraint, namely, where each interval has a weight in [0,1] and the sum of the weights of the overlapping intervals which are colored the same cannot exceed 1. Further generalizations of such a weighted version were also considered (Bertossi, Pinotti, Rizzi, & Gupta, 2004).

This chapter surveys the complexity results as well as the main scalable on-line algorithms for the Server Allocation with Bounded Simultaneous Requests problem, which are published in the literature (Adamy & Erlebach, 2004; Winkler & Zhang, 2003; Bertossi, Pinotti, Rizzi, & Gupta, 2004). Briefly, the rest of this chapter is structured as follows. The first section shows that the Server Allocation with

Bounded Simultaneous Requests problem is computationally intractable and therefore a solution using the minimum number of servers cannot be found in polynomial time. The second section deals with α-approximation algorithms, that is polynomial time algorithms that provide solutions which are guaranteed to never be greater than α times the optimal solutions. In particular, a 2-approximation on-line algorithm is exhibited, which asymptotically gives a $(2 - h/k)$-approximation, where h is the minimum among all the h_c's. Finally, a generalization of the problem is considered in the third section, where each request r is also characterized by an integer *bandwidth rate* w_r, and the bounds on the number of simultaneous requests to be served by the same server are replaced by bounds on the sum of the bandwidth rates of the simultaneous requests assigned to the same server. For this problem, on-line scalable algorithms are illustrated which give a constant approximation.

COMPUTATIONAL INTRACTABILITY

The Server Allocation with Bounded Simultaneous Requests problem on a set $R = \{r_1,...,r_n\}$ of requests can be formulated as a coloring problem on the corresponding set $I = \{I_1,...,I_n\}$ of temporal intervals. Indeed, equating servers with colors, the original server allocation problem is equivalent to the following coloring problem:

Problem 1 (Interval Coloring with Bounded Overlapping). Given a set I of intervals each belonging to a category, an integer k, and an integer $h_c \leq k$ for each category c, assign a color to each interval in such a way that at most k mutually overlapping intervals receive the same color (k-constraint), at most h_c mutually overlapping intervals all having category c receive the same color (h-constraint), and the minimum number of colors is used.

To prove that Problem 1 is computationally intractable, the following simplified decisional formulation of Problem 1 was considered, where $|C| = 4$, $k = 2$, and $h_c = 1$ for each category c.

Problem 2 (Interval Coloring with Bounded Overlapping and Four Categories). Given a set I of intervals each belonging to one of four categories, and an integer b, decide whether b colors are enough to assign a color to each interval in such a way that at most two mutually overlapping intervals receive the same color and no two overlapping intervals with the same category receive the same color.

In (Bertossi, Pinotti, Rizzi, & Gupta, 2004), Problem 2 was proved to be *NP*-complete by exhibiting a polynomial time reduction from the 3-Satisfiability (3SAT) problem, a well-known *NP*-complete problem (Garey & Johnson, 1979):

Problem 3 (3SAT). Given a boolean formula B in conjunctive normal form, i.e. as a product of clauses, over a set U of boolean variables, such that each clause is the sum of exactly 3 literals, i.e. direct or negated variables, decide whether there exists a truth assignment for U which satisfies B.

Theorem 1. Interval Coloring with Bounded Overlapping and Four Categories is *NP*-complete.

By the above result, Problem 2, and hence the Server Allocation with Bounded Simultaneous Requests problem, is computationally intractable. Therefore, one is forced to abandon the search for fast algorithms that find optimal solutions. Thus, one can devise fast algorithms that provide sub-optimal solutions which are fairly close to optimal. This strategy is followed in the next section, where a scalable polynomial-time approximation algorithm is exhibited for providing sub-optimal solutions that will never differ from the optimal solution by more than a specified percentage.

Moreover, further negative results have been proved (Bertossi, Pinotti, Rizzi, & Gupta, 2004). Assume that the intervals in I arrive one by one, and are indexed by non-decreasing starting times. When an interval I_i arrives, it is immediately and irrevocably colored, and the next interval I_{i+1} becomes known only after I_i has been colored. If multiple intervals arrive at the same time, then they are colored in any order. An algorithm that works in such an ongoing manner is said *on-line* (Karp, 1992). On-line algorithms are opposed to *off-line* algorithms, where the intervals are not colored as they become available, but they are all colored only after the entire sequence I of intervals is known. While Theorem 1 shows that Problem 1 is computationally intractable even if there are only four categories, $k = 2$, and $h_c = 1$ for each category, the following result shows also that there is no optimal on-line algorithm even when the number of categories becomes three.

Theorem 2. There is no optimal on-line algorithm for the Interval Coloring with Bounded Overlapping problem even if there are only 3 categories, $k = 2$, and $h_1 = h_2 = h_3 = 1$.

ALGORITHM FOR INTERVAL COLORING WITH BOUNDED OVERLAPPING

Since there are no fast algorithms that find optimal solutions for Problem 1, on-line algorithms providing sub-optimal solutions are considered. An α-approximation algorithm for a minimization problem is a polynomial-time algorithm producing a solution of value *appr*(x) on input x such that, for all the inputs x, $appr(x) \leq \alpha_* opt(x)$, where *opt*($x$) is the value of the optimal solution on x. In other words, the approximate solution is guaranteed to never be greater than α times the optimal solution (Garey & Johnson, 1979). For the sake of simplicity, from now on, *appr*(x) and *opt*(x) will be simply denoted by *appr* and *opt*, respectively.

A simple polynomial-time on-line algorithm for the Interval Coloring with Bounded Overlapping problem can be designed based on the following greedy strategy:

AlgorithmGREEDY(I_i)

Color I_i with any already used color which does not violate the k-constraints and the h-constraints. If no color can be reused, then use a brand new color.

Theorem 3. Algorithm GREEDY provides a 2-approximation for the Interval Coloring with Bounded Overlapping problem.

Proof. Let $appr = \varphi$ be the solution given by the algorithm and assume that the colors $1, \ldots, \phi$ have been introduced in this order. Let $I_r = [s_r, e_r)$ be the first interval colored φ. Let Ω_1 be the set of intervals in I containing s_r and let Ω_2 be the set of intervals in I containing s_r whose category is c_r. Clearly, Ω_2 is contained in Ω_1. Let ω_1 and ω_2 be the cardinalities of Ω_1 and Ω_2, respectively. Clearly, $opt \geq \left\lceil \frac{\omega_1}{k} \right\rceil$ and $opt \geq \left\lceil \frac{\omega_2}{h_{c_r}} \right\rceil$. Color φ was introduced to color I_r because, for every $1 \leq \gamma \leq \varphi - 1$, at least one of the following two conditions held:

1. Exactly k intervals in Ω_1 have color γ;
2. Exactly h_{c_r} intervals in Ω_2 have color γ.

For $i = 1$ and 2, let n_i be the number of colors in $\{1, \ldots, \varphi - 1\}$ for which Condition i holds (if for a color both conditions hold, then choose one of them arbitrarily). Hence, $n_1 + n_2 = \varphi - 1$ or, equivalently,

$appr = \varphi = n_1 + n_2 + 1$. Clearly, $\Omega_1 \geq k\, n_1 + h_{c_r}\, n_2 + 1$ and $\Omega_2 \geq h_{c_r}\, n_2 + 1$. Therefore:$opt \geq max\{\left\lceil \frac{\omega_1}{k} \right\rceil$, $\left\lceil \frac{\omega_2}{h_{c_r}} \right\rceil\} \geq max\{\left\lceil \frac{kn_1 + h_{c_r} + 1}{k} \right\rceil, \left\lceil \frac{h_{c_r} n_2 + 1}{h_{c_r}} \right\rceil\} \geq max\{n_1 + \left\lceil \frac{h_{c_r} n_2 + 1}{h_{c_r}} \right\rceil, n_2 + 1\} \geq max\{n_1 + \frac{h}{k} n_2, n_2 + 1\}$ where $h = min\{h_1, \ldots, h_{|C|}\}$.

If $n_2 + 1 \geq n_1 + \frac{h}{k} n_2$, then:

$$\frac{appr}{opt} \leq \frac{n_1 + n_2 + 1}{n_2 + 1} \leq \frac{n_2(1 - \frac{h}{k}) + n_2 + 1}{n_2 + 1} = \frac{appr}{opt}\ \frac{n_1 + n_2 + 1}{n_2 + 1}\ \frac{n_2(1 - \frac{h}{k}) + n_2 + 1}{n_2 + 1}\ 2 - \frac{h}{k}\frac{n_2}{n_2 + 1}$$

$$\leq \frac{n_1 + n_2 + 1}{n_2 + 1} \leq \frac{n_2(1 - \frac{h}{k}) + n_2 + 1}{n_2 + 1} = 2 - \frac{h}{k}\frac{n_2}{n_2 + 1} \leq 2.$$

If $n_2 + 1 \leq n_1 + \frac{h}{k} n_2$, then:

$$\frac{appr}{opt} \leq \frac{n_1 + n_2 + 1}{n_1 + \frac{h}{k} n_2} \leq \frac{n_1 + n_1 + \frac{h}{k} n_2}{n_1 + \frac{h}{k} n_2} = \frac{appr}{opt}\ \frac{n_1 + n_2 + 1}{n_1 + \frac{h}{k} n_2}\ \frac{n_1 + n_1 + \frac{h}{k} n_2}{n_1 + \frac{h}{k} n_2}\ 1 + \frac{n_1}{n_1 + \frac{h}{k} n_2} \leq$$

$$\frac{n_1 + n_2 + 1}{n_1 + \frac{h}{k} n_2} \leq \frac{n_1 + n_1 + \frac{h}{k} n_2}{n_1 + \frac{h}{k} n_2} = 1 + \frac{n_1}{n_1 + \frac{h}{k} n_2} \leq 2.$$

Therefore, Algorithm Greedy gives a 2-approximation. QED

Actually, a stronger result has been proved (Bertossi, Pinotti, Rizzi, & Gupta, 2004):

Theorem 4. Algorithm Greedy asymptotically provides a $(2 - h/k)$-approximation for the Interval Coloring with Bounded Overlapping problem, where $h = min\{h_1, \ldots, h_{|C|}\}$.

Moreover, such an asymptotic bound is the best possible, even in the very special case that $h = 1$, $k = 2$, and no interval contains another interval:

Theorem 5. Algorithm Greedy admits no α-approximation with $\alpha < 2 - 1/k$ for the Interval Coloring with Bounded Categories problem, even if $min\{h_1, \ldots, h_{|C|}\} = 1$, $k = 2$, and no interval is properly contained within another interval.

Finally, the result below shows that the Greedy algorithm is optimal in some special cases.

Theorem 6. Algorithm Greedy is optimal for the Interval Coloring with Bounded Overlapping problem when either

- $\sum_{c \in C} h_c \leq k$, or
- $h_c = k$ for all $c \in C$.

Proof. Let φ be the solution given by the GREEDY algorithm and assume without loss of generality that $\varphi \geq 2$, since otherwise the solution is trivially optimal. As in the proof of Theorem 3, let $I_r = [s_r, e_r)$ be the first interval colored φ, let Ω_1 be the set of intervals in I containing s_r, let Ω_2 be the set of intervals in I containing s_r with category c_r, and let $\omega_1 = |\Omega_1|$ and $\omega_2 = |\Omega_2|$. Recall that φ was introduced to color I_r because, for every $1 \leq \gamma \leq \varphi - 1$, at least one of the following two conditions held:

1. Exactly k intervals in Ω_1 have color γ;
2. Exactly h_{c_r} intervals in Ω_2 have color γ.

When $\sum_{c \in C} h_c \leq k$, it is easy to see that if Condition 1 is true for any color γ then Condition 2 is also true. Indeed, by hypothesis, the only way to exhaust a color is to have exactly h_{c_r} intervals of category c_r all colored γ. Therefore, $\omega_2 \geq (\varphi - 1) h_{c_r} + 1$ and $opt \geq \left\lceil \frac{\omega_2}{h_{c_r}} \right\rceil = \varphi$.

When $h_c = k$ for all $c \in C$, it is easy to see that any γ cannot be used only if Condition 1 is true. Thus, $\omega_1 \geq (\varphi - 1)k + 1$ and $opt \geq \left\lceil \frac{\omega_1}{k} \right\rceil = \varphi$.

In conclusion, in both cases the GREEDY algorithm provides the optimal solution. QED

Note that, in Theorem 6, when $h_c = k$ for all $c \in C$, the h-constraint is redundant, since it is dominated by the k-constraint. When $h_c = k = 1$ for all $c \in C$, the GREEDY algorithm reduces to the well-known optimal algorithm for coloring interval graphs (Golumbic, 1980). Moreover, when $h_c = k$ for all $c \in C$ and $k > 1$, Problem 1 is the same as the Generalized Interval Graph Coloring problem (Winkler & Zhang, 2003).

As regard to the time complexity of the GREEDY algorithm, the following result holds:

Theorem 7. Algorithm GREEDY requires $O(1)$ time to color each interval I_r.

Proof. The algorithm employs $|C|$ palettes $P_1, \ldots, P_{|C|}$, one for each category. The generic palette P_c is implemented as a double linked list and stores all the colors that can be assigned to a new interval of category c. For each color γ, a record R_γ with $|C| + 1$ counters and $|C|$ pointers is maintained. For each category c, the corresponding counter $R_\gamma.count_c$ stores how many intervals of category c can be still colored γ (such a counter is initialized to h_c). Moreover, there is an additional counter $R_\gamma.kcount$ (initialized to k) storing how many intervals of any category can be still colored γ. Finally, for each category c, there is a pointer to the position of color γ in P_c.

The algorithm uses a global counter, initialized to 0, to keep track of the overall number of colors used. When a brand new color is needed, the global counter is incremented. Let γ be the new value of the global counter. Then, a new record R_γ is initialized, color γ is inserted in all the palettes, and the pointers of R_γ to the palettes are updated. This requires $O(|C|)$ time.

When a new interval I_i starts, say of category c_i, it is colored in $O(1)$ time by any color γ available in palette P_{c_i}. Then, the counters $R_\gamma.count_{c_i}$ and $R_\gamma.kcount$ are decremented. If $R_\gamma.count_{c_i}$ becomes 0, then color γ is deleted from P_{c_i}. Whereas, if $R_\gamma.kcount$ becomes 0, then color γ is deleted from all the palettes. In the worst case, $O(|C|)$ time is needed.

When interval I_i ends, the counters $R_\gamma.count_{c_i}$ and $R_\gamma.kcount$ are incremented, where γ is the color of I_i. If $R_\gamma.kcount$ becomes 1, then color γ is inserted in all the palettes P_c for which $R_\gamma.count_c$ is greater than 0. Instead, if $R_\gamma.kcount$ is larger than 1, then color γ is inserted in P_{c_i} if $R_\gamma.count_{c_i}$ becomes 1. Again, in the worst case, $O(|C|)$ time is needed.

Since $|C|$ is a constant, $O(1)$ time is required to color each single interval I_t. QED

ALGORITHM FOR WEIGHTED INTERVAL COLORING

Consider now a generalization of the Server Allocation with Bounded Simultaneous Requests problem, where each request r is also characterized by an integer *bandwidth rate* w_r, and the bounds on the number of simultaneous requests to be served by the same server are replaced by bounds on the sum of the bandwidth rates of the simultaneous requests assigned to the same server. Such a problem can be formulated as a weighted generalization of Problem 1 as follows.

Problem 4 (Weighted Interval Coloring with Bounded Overlapping). Given a set I of intervals, with each interval I_r characterized by a category c_r and an integer weight w_r, an integer k, and an integer $h_c \leq k$ for each category c, assign a color to each interval in such a way that the sum of the weights for mutually overlapping intervals receiving the same color is at most k (k-constraint), the sum of the weights for mutually overlapping intervals of category c receiving the same color is at most h_c (h-constraint), and the minimum number of colors is used.

More formally, denote by

- $I[t]$ the set of intervals which are *active* at instant t, that is, $I[t] = \{I_r \in I: s_r \leq t \leq e_r\}$;
- $I[c]$ the set of intervals belonging to the same category c, that is, $I[c] = \{I_r \in I: c_r = c\}$;
- $I(\gamma)$ the set of intervals colored γ;
- $I(\gamma)[t] = I(\gamma) \cap I[t]$, namely, the set of intervals colored γ and active at instant t; and
- $I(\gamma)[t][c] = I(\gamma)[t] \cap I[c]$, namely, the set of intervals of category c, colored γ, and active at instant t.

Then, the k-constraints and h-constraints can be stated as follows:

$$\sum_{I_r \in I(\gamma)[t]} w_r \leq k \text{ for all } \gamma \text{ and } t \text{ (}k\text{-constraints),}$$

$$\sum_{I_r \in I(\gamma)[t][c]} w_r \leq h_c \text{ for all } \gamma,\ t, \text{ and } c \text{ (}h\text{-constraints).}$$

Note that Problem 1 is a particular case of Problem 4, where $w_r = 1$ for each interval I_r. When considering only the k-constraints and normalizing each weight w_r in [0,1], Problem 4 is a generalization of that introduced in (Adamy & Erlebach, 2004) where a 195-approximate solution is provided under a particular on-line notion, namely, when the intervals are not given by their arrival time, but by some externally specified order. An approximation on-line algorithm for Problem 4, which contains Bin-Packing as a special case (Coffman, Galambos, Martello, & Vigo, 1999), is presented below.

Algorithm FIRST-COLOR(I_t)

Color interval I_t with the smallest already used color which does not violate the k-constraints and the h-constraints. If no color can be reused, then use a brand new color.

The following result has been proved in (Bertossi, Pinotti, Rizzi, & Gupta, 2004).

Theorem 8. Algorithm FIRST-COLOR asymptotically provides a constant approximation for the Weighted Interval Coloring with Bounded Overlapping problem.

The worst approximation constant proved by Theorem 8 is $5\frac{k}{h}$, when $\frac{k}{h} > \frac{8}{5}$, and 8, otherwise (by the way, an 8-approximation could be achieved even in the case that $\frac{k}{h} > \frac{8}{5}$, but by a different, off-line algorithm). It is worthy to note that in the case there are no h-constraints on the total weight of mutually overlapping intervals of the same category, the FIRST-COLOR algorithm yields a 4-approximation. As regard to the time complexity of algorithm FIRST-COLOR, an implementation similar to that described in Theorem 7 can be used, where the palettes are maintained as heaps. Then, it is easy to see that a single interval can be colored in $O(\log \varphi)$ time, where φ is the total number of colors used.

FURTHER GENERALIZATIONS

Consider now two further generalizations of the Server Allocation with Bounded Simultaneous Requests problem, where each request r is characterized by real bandwidths, normalized in [0,1] for analogy with the Bin-Packing problem (Coffman, Galambos, Martello, & Vigo, 1999).

In the first generalization, which contains Multi-Dimensional Bin-Packing as a special case, each request r is characterized by a *k-dimensional* bandwidth rate $\mathbf{w}_r = (w_r^{(1)}, \ldots, w_r^{(k)})$, where the c-th component specifies the bandwidth needed for the c-th category and k is the number of categories, i.e. $k = |C|$. The overall sum of the bandwidth rates of the simultaneous requests of the same category assigned to the same server at the same time is bounded by 1, which implies that the total sum of the bandwidth rates over all the categories is bounded by k. Such a generalized problem can be formulated as the following variant of the interval coloring problem.

Problem 5 (Multi-Dimensional Weighted Interval Coloring with Unit Overlapping). Given a set I of intervals, with each interval I_r characterized by a k-dimensional weight $\mathbf{w}_r = (w_r^{(1)}, \ldots, w_r^{(k)})$, where $w_r^{(c)} \in [0,1]$, for $1 \leq c \leq k$, assign a color to each interval in such a way that the overall sum of the weights of the same category for mutually overlapping intervals receiving the same color is bounded by 1 and the minimum number of colors is used.

More formally, according to the notations introduced in the previous section, the constraints of Problem 5 can be stated as follows:

$$\sum_{I_r \in I(\gamma)[t][c]} w_r^{(c)} \leq 1 \quad \text{for all } \gamma, t, \text{ and } c.$$

Note that the above constraints are in fact h-constraints and, when added up over all the categories in C, imply the following redundant k-constraint

$$\sum_{c=1}^{k} \sum_{I_r \in I(\gamma)[t][c]} w_r^{(c)} \leq k \quad \text{for all } \gamma \text{ and } t,$$

which is analogous to the k-constraint of Problem 4. Problem 5 can also be solved on-line by the First-Color algorithm introduced in the previous section.

Theorem 9. Algorithm First-Color provides a $4k$-approximation for the Multi-Dimensional Weighted Interval Coloring with Unit Overlapping problem.

It is worth mentioning that the above problem, when considered as an off-line problem, is *APX*-hard since it contains Multi-Dimensional Bin-Packing as a special case, which has been shown to be *APX*-hard (Woeginger, 1997) already for $k = 2$. Therefore, there is no polynomial time *approximation scheme* (*PTAS*) that solves the problem within *every* fixed constant α (that is, one different polynomial time approximation algorithm for each constant α) unless $P = NP$.

In the second generalization, instead, each request r is characterized by a *gender bandwidth rate* g_{r,c_r} associated to the category c_r and by a bandwidth rate w_r. The overall sum of the bandwidth rates of the simultaneous requests assigned to the same server at the same time is bounded by 1, as well as the overall sum of the gender bandwidth rates of the simultaneous requests of the same category assigned to the same server at the same time, which is also bounded by 1. This generalized problem can be formulated as the following variant of the interval coloring problem.

Problem 6 (Double Weighted Interval Coloring with Unit Overlapping). Given a set I of intervals, with each interval I_r characterized by a gender bandwidth $g_{r,c_r} \in (0,1]$ associated to the category c_r and by a bandwidth weight $w_r \in (0,1]$, assign a color to each interval in such a way that the overall sum of the gender weights for mutually overlapping intervals of the same category receiving the same color is bounded by 1 (h-constraint), the overall sum of the bandwidth weights for mutually overlapping intervals receiving the same color is bounded by 1 (k-constraint), and the minimum number of colors is used.

Formally, the constraints of Problem 6 are given below:

$$\sum_{I_r \in I(\gamma)[t]} w_r \leq 1 \quad \text{for all } \gamma \text{ and } t,$$

$$\sum_{I_r \in I(\gamma)[t][c]} g_{r,c} \leq 1 \quad \text{for all } \gamma,\ t, \text{ and } c.$$

Note that Problem 6 is a generalization of Bin-Packing, and hence it is *NP*-hard. However, Problem 6 can again be solved on-line by the First-Color algorithm introduced in the previous section.

Theorem 10. Algorithm First-Color provides a constant approximation and, asymptotically, an 11-approximation for the Double Weighted Interval Coloring with Unit Overlapping problem.

CONCLUSION

This chapter has considered several scalable on-line approximation algorithms for problems arising in isolated infostations, where user requests characterized by categories and temporal intervals have to be assigned to servers in such a way that a bounded number of simultaneously requests are assigned to the same server and the number of servers is minimized. However, several questions still remain open. For instance, one could lower the approximation bounds derived for the problems reviewed in this chapter. Moreover, it is still an open question to determine whether the *NP*-hardness result reported in this chapter still holds when $k = 2$, there are only 3 categories, and $h_1 = h_2 = h_3 = 1$. Finally, one could consider the scenario in which the number of servers is given in input, each request has a deadline, and the goal is to minimize the overall completion time for all the requests.

REFERENCES

Adamy, U., & Erlebach, T. (2004). *Online coloring of intervals with bandwidth* (LNCS Vol. 2909, pp. 1–12). Berlin: Springer.

Bertossi, A. A., Pinotti, M. C., Rizzi, R., & Gupta, P. (2004). Allocating servers in infostations for bounded simultaneous requests. *Journal of Parallel and Distributed Computing, 64*, 1113–1126. doi:10.1016/S0743-7315(03)00118-7

Coffman, E. G., Galambos, G., Martello, S., & Vigo, D. (1999). Bin-packing approximation algorithms: Combinatorial analysis. In D. Z. Du & P. M. Pardalos, (Ed.), *Handbook of Combinatorial Optimization*, (pp. 151–207). Dondrecht, the Netherlands: Kluwer.

Garey, M. R., & Johnson, D. S. (1979). *Computers and Intractability.* San Francisco: Freeman.

Golumbic, M. C. (1980). *Algorithmic Graph Theory and Perfect Graphs.* New York: Academic Press.

Goodman, D. J., Borras, J., Mandayam, N. B., & Yates, R. D. (1997). INFOSTATIONS: A new system model for data and messaging services. *Proceedings of the 47th IEEE Vehicular Technology Conference (VTC)*, Phoenix, AZ, (Vol. 2, pp. 969–973).

Jayram, T. S., Kimbrel, T., Krauthgamer, R., Schieber, B., & Sviridenko, M. (2001). Online server allocation in server farm via benefit task systems. *Proceedings of the ACM Symposium on Theory of Computing (STOC'01)*, Crete, Greece, (pp. 540–549).

Karp, R. M. (1992). Online algorithms versus offline algorithms: How much is it worth to know the future? In J. van Leeuwen, (Ed.), *Proceedings of the 12th IFIP World Computer Congress. Volume 1: Algorithms, Software, Architecture*, (pp. 416–429). Amsterdam: Elsevier.

Lawler, E. L., Lenstra, J. K., Rinnooy Kan, A. H. G., & Shmoys, H. (1993). *Sequencing and Scheduling: Algorithms and Complexity*. Amsterdam: North-Holland.

Winkler, P., & Zhang, L. (2003). Wavelength assignment and generalized interval graph coloring. In *Proceedings of the ACM-SIAM Symposium on Discrete Algorithms (SODA'03)*, Baltimore, MD, (pp. 830–831).

Woeginger, G. J. (1997). There is no asymptotic PTAS for two-dimensional vector packing. *Information Processing Letters, 64*, 293–297. doi:10.1016/S0020-0190(97)00179-8

Wu, G., Chu, C. W., Wine, K., Evans, J., & Frenkiel, R. (1999). WINMAC: A novel transmission protocol for infostations. *Proceedings of the 49th IEEE Vehicular Technology Conference (VTC)*, Houston, TX, (Vol. 2, pp. 1340–1344).

Zander, J. (2000). Trends and challenges in resource management future wireless networks. In *Proceedings of the IEEE Wireless Communications and Networks Conference (WCNC)*, Chicago, (Vol. 1, pp. 159–163).

KEY TERMS

α-Approximation Algorithm: An algorithm producing a solution which is guaranteed to be no worst than α times the best solution.

Bin-Packing: A combinatorial problem in which objects of different volumes must be packed into a finite number of bins of given capacity in a way that minimizes the number of bins used.

Infostation: An isolated pocket area with small coverage of high bandwidth connectivity that delivers data on demand to mobile users.

Interval Graph Coloring: A combinatorial problem in which colors have to be assigned to intervals in such a way that two overlapping intervals are colored differently and the minimum number of colors is used. Such a problem corresponds to color the vertices of an interval graph, that is, a graph representing the intersections of the set of intervals.

Multiprocessor Scheduling: A method by which tasks are assigned to processors.

On-Line Algorithm: An algorithm that processes its input data sequence in an ongoing manner, that is as they become available, without knowledge of the entire input sequence.

Scalable Algorithm: An algorithm able to maintain the same efficiency when the workload grows.

Server Allocation: An assignment of servers to the user requests.

Section 7
Web Computing

Chapter 28
Web Application Server Clustering with Distributed Java Virtual Machine[1]

King Tin Lam
The University of Hong Kong, Hong Kong

Cho-Li Wang
The University of Hong Kong, Hong Kong

ABSTRACT

Web application servers, being today's enterprise application backbone, have warranted a wealth of J2EE-based clustering technologies. Most of them however need complex configurations and excessive programming effort to retrofit applications for cluster-aware execution. This chapter proposes a clustering approach based on distributed Java virtual machine (DJVM). A DJVM is a collection of extended JVMs that enables parallel execution of a multithreaded Java application over a cluster. A DJVM achieves transparent clustering and resource virtualization, extolling the virtue of single-system-image (SSI). The authors evaluate this approach through porting Apache Tomcat to their JESSICA2 DJVM and identify scalability issues arising from fine-grain object sharing coupled with intensive synchronizations among distributed threads. By leveraging relaxed cache coherence protocols, we are able to conquer the scalability barriers and harness the power of our DJVM's global object space design to significantly outstrip existing clustering techniques for cache-centric web applications.

INTRODUCTION

Scaling applications in web server environment is a fundamental requisite for continued growth of e-business, and is also a pressing challenge to most web architects when designing large-scale enterprise systems. Following the success of the Java 2 Platform, Enterprise Edition (J2EE), the J2EE world has developed an alphabet soup of APIs (JNDI, JMS, EJB, etc) that programmers would need to slurp down if they are to cluster their web applications. However, comprehending the bunch of these APIs and the clustering technologies shipped with J2EE server products is practically daunting for even those expe-

DOI: 10.4018/978-1-60566-661-7.ch028

rienced programmers. Besides the extra configuration and setup time, intrusive application rework is usually required for the web applications to behave correctly in the cluster environment. Therefore, there is still much room for researchers to contribute improved clustering solutions for web applications.

In this chapter, we introduce a generic and easy-to-use web application server clustering approach coming out from the latest research in distributed Java virtual machines. A *Distributed Java Virtual Machine (DJVM)* fulfills the functions of a standard JVM in a distributed environment, such as clusters. It consists of a set of JVM instances spanning multiple cluster nodes that work cooperatively to support parallel execution of a multithreaded Java application. The Java threads created within one program can be distributed to different nodes and perform concurrently to exploit higher execution parallelism. The DJVM abstracts away the low-level clustering decisions and hides the physical boundaries across the cluster nodes from the application layer. All available resources in the distributed environment, such as memory, I/O and network bandwidth can be shared among distributed threads for solving more challenging problems. The design of DJVM adheres to the standard JVM specification, so ideally all applications that follow the original Java multithreaded programming model on a single machine can now be clustered across multiple servers in a virtually effortless manner.

In the past, various efforts have been conducted in extending JVM to support transparent and parallel execution of multithreaded Java programs on a cluster of computers. Among them, Hyperion (Antoniu et al., 2001) and Jackal (Veldema et al., 2001) compile multithreaded Java programs directly into distributed applications in native code, while Java/DSM (Yu & Cox, 1997), cJVM (Aridor, Factor, & Teperman, 1999), and JESSICA (Ma, Wang, & Lau, 2000) modify the underlying JVM kernel to support cluster-wide thread execution. These DJVM prototypes debut as proven parallel execution engines for high-performance scientific computing over the last few years. Nevertheless, their leverage to clustering real-life applications with commercial server workloads has not been well-studied.

We strive to bridge this gap by presenting our experience in porting the Apache Tomcat web application server on a DJVM called JESSICA2. A wide spectrum of web application benchmarks modeling stock quotes, online bookstore and SOAP-based B2B e-commerce are used to evaluate the clustering approach using DJVMs. We observe that the highly-threaded execution of Tomcat involves enormous fine-grain object accesses to Java collection classes such as hash tables all over the request handling cycles. This presents the key hurdles to scalability when the thread-safe object read/write operations and the associated synchronizations are performed in a cluster environment. To overcome this issue, we employ a home-based hybrid cache coherence protocol to support object sharing among the distributed threads. For cache-centric applications that cache hot and heavyweight web objects at the application-level, we find that by using JESSICA2, addition of nodes can grow application cache hits linearly, significantly outperforming the share-nothing approach using web server load balancing plug-in. This is attributed to our *global object space (GOS)* architecture that virtualizes network-wide memory resources for caching the application data as a unified dataset for global access by all threads. Clustering HTTP sessions over the GOS enables effortless cluster-wide session management and leads to a more balanced load distribution across servers than the traditional sticky-session request scheduling. Our coherence protocol also scales better than the session replication protocols adopted in existing Tomcat clustering. Hence, most of the benchmarked web applications show better or equivalent performance compared with the traditional clustering techniques.

Overall, the DJVM approach emerges as a more holistic, cost-effective and transparent clustering technology that disappears from the application programmer's point of view. With efficient protocol support for shared object access, such a middleware-level clustering solution is suitable for scaling most web applications in a cluster environment. Maturing of the DJVM technology would bring about stronger server resource integration and open up new vistas of clustering advances among the web community.

The rest of the chapter is organized as follows. In Section 2, we survey the existing web application clustering technologies. Section 3 presents the system architecture of our JESSICA2 DJVM. In Section 4, we describe Tomcat execution on top of the JESSICA2 DJVM. Section 5 discusses JESSICA2's global object space design and implementation. In Section 6, we evaluate the performance of Tomcat clustering using the DJVM. Section 7 reviews the related work. Section 8 concludes this chapter and suggests some possible future work.

EXISTING WEB APPLICATION CLUSTERING TECHNOLOGIES

In the web community, clustering is broadly viewed as server load balancing and failover. Here, we discuss several widely adopted clustering technologies under the hood of J2EE.

The most common and cost-effective way for load balancing is to employ a frontend web server with load balancing plug-ins such as Apache mod_jk (ASF, 2002) to dispatch incoming requests to different application servers. The plug-ins usually support *sticky-sessions* to maintain a user session entirely on one server. This solution could make the cluster resource utilization more restricted and is not robust against server failures.

More advanced solutions need to support application state sharing among servers. Large-scale J2EE server products generally ship with clustering support for HTTP sessions and stateful session beans. One traditional approach is to serialize the session contents and persist the states to a data store like a relational database or a shared file system. However, this approach is not scalable. *In-memory session replication* is an improved technique also based on Java serialization to marshal session-bound objects into byte streams for sending to peer servers by means of some group communication services such as JGroups (Ban, 1997) (based on point-to-point RMI or IP multicast). Such a technique has been implemented in common web containers such as Tomcat. However, scalability issues are still present in group-based synchronous replications, especially over the general all-to-all replication protocols which are only efficient in very small-size clusters.

Enterprise JavaBeans (EJB) is a server-side component architecture for building modular enterprise applications. Yet the EJB technology itself and its clustering are both complicated. Load balancing among EJB containers can be achieved by distributed method call, messaging or name services which correspond to the three specifications: Remote Method Invocation (RMI), Java Messaging Service (JMS) and Java Naming and Directory Interface (JNDI). In particular, JNDI is an indispensible element of EJB clustering as EJB access normally starts with a lookup of its home interface in the JNDI tree. For clients to look up clustered objects, EJB containers implement some global JNDI services (e.g. cluster-wide shared JNDI tree) and ship with special RMI compilers to generate *replica-aware stubs* for making user-defined EJBs "cluster-aware". The stub contains the list of accessible target EJB instances and codes for load balancing and failover among the instances. EJB state changes are serialized and replicated to peer servers after the related transaction commits or after each method invocation. Undoubtedly, this clustering technology is expensive, complicated and with application design restrictions.

In recent years, a growing trend in web application development has begun to adopt lightweight containers such as the Spring Framework (Johnson, 2002) to be the infrastructural backbone instead of the EJB technology. On such a paradigm, business objects are just *plain old Java objects* (POJOs) implementing data access logic and running in web containers like Tomcat. Caching POJOs in a collection object like Hashtable is also a common practice for saving long-latency access to database and file systems. To support clustering of POJOs which conform to no standard interface, it seems almost inevitable that application programmers have to rework their application code to use extra APIs to synchronize object replicas among the JVMs. Though distributed caching libraries (Perez, 2003) can facilitate POJO clustering, these solutions again rely on Java serializations and require complex configurations. The cache sizes they support are usually bounded by single-node memory capacity as a result of employing simplistic all-to-all synchronization and full replication protocols.

Although the clustering solutions surveyed so far have their own merit points, most of them share several significant shortcomings.

- **Restrictions on application design:** Many object sharing mechanisms rely on Java serializations which pose restrictions on application design and implementation. They cannot easily work in a cluster environment.
- **Possible loss of referential integrit**y: Most solutions suffer the break of referential integrity since it creates clones of the replicated object graph at deserialization and may lose the original object identity. That's why when a shared object undergoes changes, it must be put back into the container object by an explicit call like setAttribute() to reflect the new referential relation. Likewise, consistency problems occur when attributes with cross-references in HTTPSession are modified and unmarshaled separately.
- **Costly communication:** Object serialization is known to be hugely costly in performance. It performs a coarse trace and clones a lot of objects even for one field change. So there is certain limit on the number and sizes of objects that can be bound in a session.
- **No global signaling/coordination support:** Subtle consistency problems arise when some design patterns and services are migrated to clusters. For example, the *singleton pattern* sharing a single static instance among threads as well as some synchronization codes become localized to each server, losing global coordination. Event-based services like timers make no sense if they are not executed on a single platform. Only a few products (e.g. JBoss's clustered singleton facility) ship with configurable cluster-wide coordination support to ease these situations.
- **Lacking global resource sharing:** Most clustering solutions in the web domain put little focus on global integration of resources. They cannot provide a global view of the cluster resources such as memory, so each standalone server just does its own work without cooperation and may not fully exploit resources.

JESSICA2 DISTRIBUTED JVM

JESSICA2 (Zhu, Wang, & Lau, 2002) is a DJVM designed to support transparent parallel execution of multithreaded Java applications in a networked cluster environment. It was developed based on Kaffe JVM (Wilkinson, 1998). The acronym JESSICA2 spells as Java-Enabled Single-System-Image Computing Architecture version 2; this architecture promotes the *single-system image (SSI)* notion when connecting Java with clusters. Such a design concept is helpful to take away the burden of clustering by hand from application developers. The key advantage with using JESSICA2 is its provision of transparent clustering services which require no source code modification and bytecode preprocessing. It will

Figure 1. JESSICA2 DJVM System Architecture

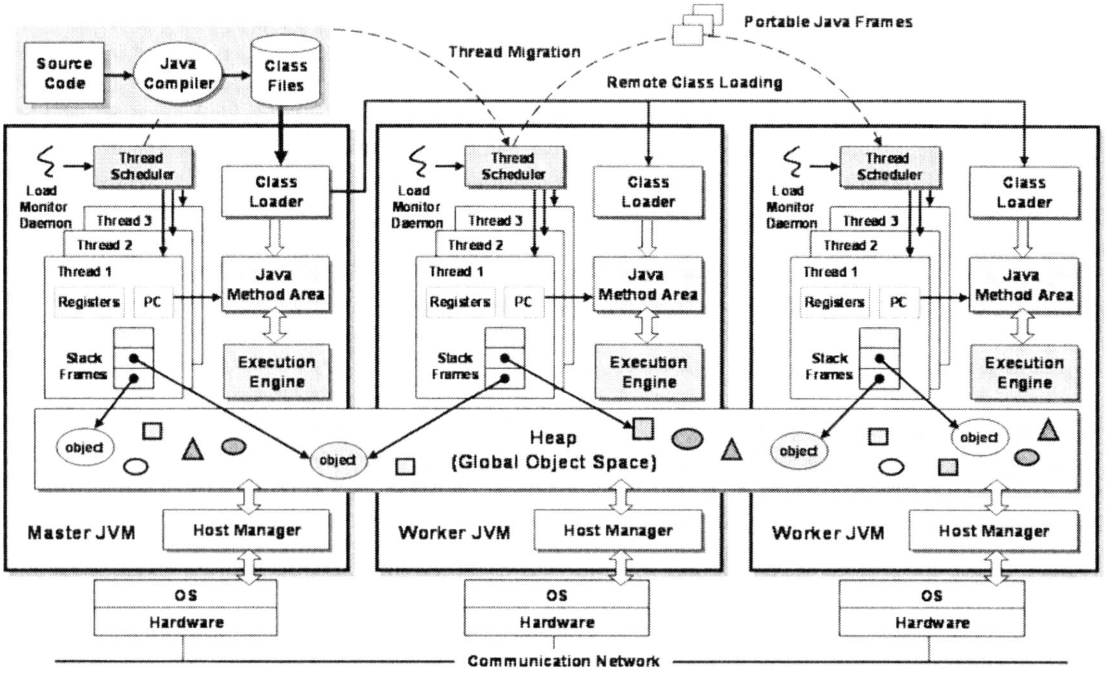

automatically take care of thread distribution, data consistency of the shared objects and I/O redirection so that the program will run under an SSI illusion with integrated computing power, memory and I/O capacity of the cluster.

Figure 1 shows the system architecture of the JESSICA2 DJVM. JESSICA2 has bundled a number of salient features extended from the standard JVM that realize the SSI services. To execute a Java application on JESSICA2, a tailored command is called to start the master JVM on the local host and the worker JVMs on remote nodes, based on the specified list of hostnames. In each JVM, a class loader is responsible for importing bytecode data (of both the basic Java class library classes and the application classes) into its method area where a Java thread can look up a specific method to invoke. The class loader of JESSICA2 is extended to support *remote class loading* which ensures when a worker JVM cannot find a class file locally, it can request the class bytecode on demand and fetch the initialized static data from the master JVM through network communication. This feature greatly simplifies cluster-wide deployment of Java applications and hence transparently provides the *web farming* support which traditionally requires application server extension to fulfill.

When the Java threads of the application are started, the thread scheduler of the JVM will put their contexts (e.g. program counter and other register values) into the execution engine in turns. The Java methods invoked by the running thread will be compiled by the Just-In-Time (JIT) compiler into native codes for high-speed execution. JESSICA2 incorporates a cluster-aware JIT compiler to support lightweight *Java thread migration* across node boundaries to assist global thread scheduling. Java threads will be assigned to each worker JVM at the startup time in a round-robin manner to strike a raw load balance. Dynamic load balancing during runtime can be done by migrating Java threads that are running into computation hotspots to the less loaded nodes. For detecting hotspots, each JVM instance has a *load monitor* daemon that periodically wakes up and sends current load status such as CPU and memory utilization to the master JVM which is then able to make thread migration decisions with a global resource view.

Java threads migrated to remote JVMs may still be carrying references to the objects under the source JVM heaps. For seamless object visibility, JESSICA2 employs a special heap-level service called the *Global Object Space (GOS)* to support location-transparent object access. Objects can be shared among distributed threads over the GOS as if they were under a single JVM heap. For this to happen, the GOS implements object packing functions to transform object graphs into byte streams for shipping to the requesting nodes. The shipped object data will be saved as a *cache copy* under the local heap of the requesting node. Caching improves data access locality but leads to cache consistency issues. To tackle the problem of stale data, the GOS employs *release-consistent* memory models stemmed from software Distributed Shared Memory (DSM) systems to preserve correct memory views on shared objects across reads/writes done by distributed threads.

JESSICA2 offers parallel I/O and location-transparent file access. We extend JESSICA2 to support *transparent I/O redirection* mechanism so that I/O requests (file and socket access) can be virtually served at any node. Our system does not rely on shared distributed file systems such as NFS, nor does it need to restrict a single IP address for all the nodes in the running cluster. Rather, we extend each JVM to run a *transparent I/O redirection* mechanism to redirect non-home I/O operations on files or sockets to their home nodes. To attain I/O parallelism atop transparency, read-only file operations and connectionless network I/O can be done at the local nodes concurrently without redirection.

Finally, all inter-node communication activities required by the subsystems at upper layers like the GOS and I/O redirections are supported by a common module called the *host manager* which wraps up the underlying TCP communication functions with connection caching and message compression optimizations.

On the whole, we can see that DJVM is a rather generic middleware system that supports parallel execution of any Java program. Since the unveiling of DJVMs, their application domains remain mostly in scientific computing over the last few years. They were used to support multithreaded Java programs that are programmed in a data-parallel manner. These applications tend to be simple, embarrassingly parallel so that DJVMs could offer good scalability. However, much more mainstream applications are business-oriented, centered at server-side platforms and run atop some Java application servers. Their object access and synchronization patterns are far more complex. In the next sections, we will elaborate on the common runtime characteristics of application servers and their impacts on the DJVM performance through a case study of Apache Tomcat running on JESSICA2.

APACHE TOMCAT ON DISTRIBUTED JVM

Apache Tomcat is a Java servlet container developed at the Apache Software Foundation (ASF). It serves as the official reference implementation of the Java Servlet and JavaServer Page (JSP) specifications. Tomcat is the world's most widely used open-source servlet engine and has been used by renowned companies like WalMart, E*Trade Securities and The Weather Channel to power their large-scale and mission-critical web applications in production systems.

As a common design in many servers, Tomcat maintains a thread pool to avoid thread creation cost for every short-lived request as well as to give an upper bound to the overall system resource usage.

Upon an incoming connection, a thread is scheduled from the pool to handle it. The web container then performs various processing such as HTTP header parsing, sessions handling, web context mapping and servlet class loading. The request eventually reaches the servlet code which implements application logics such as form data processing, database querying, HTML/XML page generation, etc. Finally, the response is sent back to the client. This request service cycle is complex, comes across many objects throughout the container hierarchy and imposes multithreading challenges to the DJVM runtime.

Being a classical and large-scale web application server, Tomcat reflects an important class of real-life object-oriented server execution patterns that are summarized as follows.

1. **I/O-intensive workload**: Most web server workloads are I/O-bound and composed of short-lived request processing. The per-request computation-communication ratio is usually small.
2. **Highly-threaded**: It is common that a server instance is configured with a large number of threads, typically a few tens to a hundred per server to hide I/O blocking latency.
3. **High read/write ratios**: Shaped by customer buying behaviors and e-business patterns, web applications usually consist of high read/write ratio, say around 90/10; the dominant reads come from browsing while only a few writes owing to ordering happen over a period.
4. **Long-running**: Typically a server application runs for an indefinitely long time, processing requests received from the client side.
5. **High utilization of collection framework**: Tomcat makes extensive use of Java collection classes like Hashtable and Vector to store information (e.g. web contexts, sessions, attributes, MIME types, status codes, etc). They are accessed frequently when checking, mapping and searching operations happen inside the container. To reduce object creation and garbage collection costs, many application servers apply the *object pooling* technique and use collection classes to implement the object pools.
6. **Fine-grain object access**: Fine-grain object access has two implications here: (1) the object size is small; (2) the interval between object accesses to the heap is short. Unlike many scientific applications which have well-structured objects with size of at least several hundred bytes, Tomcat contains an abundance of small-size objects (average about 80 bytes by our experience) throughout the container hierarchy. Object accesses are very frequent due to object-oriented design of Tomcat.
7. **Complex object graph with irregular reference locality**: Some design patterns such as facade and chain of interceptors used in Tomcat yield ramified object connectivity, cross-referencing and irregular reference locality among objects throughout the container hierarchy. By property 5, heavy use of Java Hashtable or HashMap also intensifies the irregularity of reference locality as hash entries are accessed in a shuffling pattern, contrasting with the consecutive memory access pattern in array-based scientific computations.

Figure 2 depicts the execution of the Tomcat application server on top of a 4-node cluster. When Tomcat is executed atop JESSICA2, Tomcat is exposed to an SSI view of the integrated resources of the cluster nodes as if it was in one powerful server. A customized Tomcat startup script is used to bring up the server, running atop the master JVM. The script is tailored to supply the DJVM runtime parameters (e.g. the port number for master-worker handshaking) and to read a host configuration file which defines the hostnames or IP addresses of the worker nodes the DJVM would span.

When the server spawns a pool of threads, the threads will be migrated to the worker nodes. They will load the classes of the Java library, Tomcat and the web applications deployed dynamically through

Figure 2. Execution of Tomcat on JESSICA2 DJVM

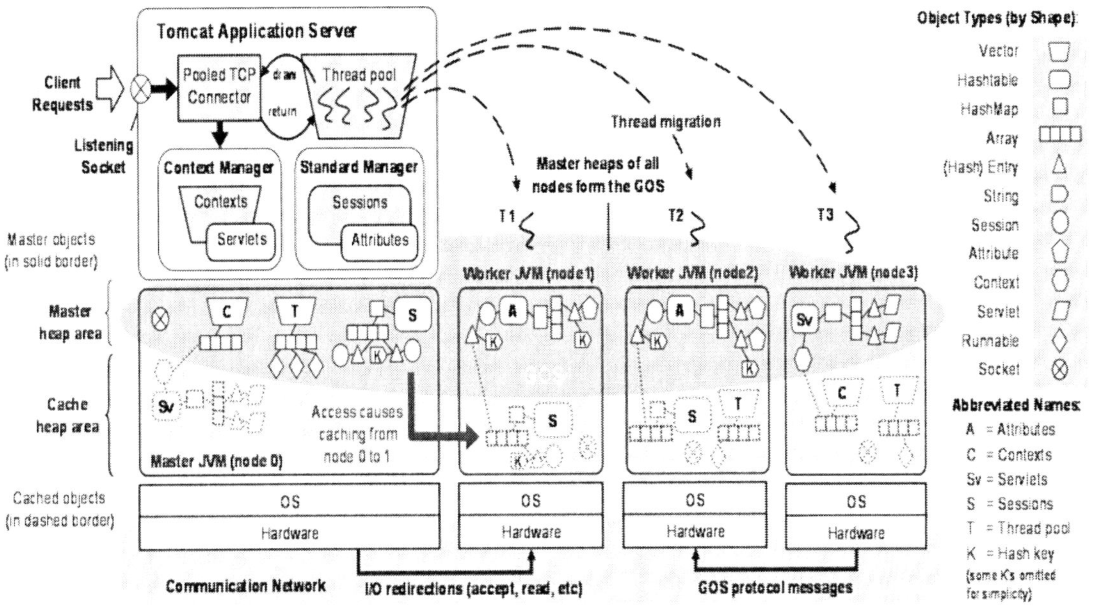

the cluster-aware class loader of JESSICA2. In this way, "virtual" web application server instances are set up on the worker nodes. The virtual server instances pull workload continuously from the master node by accepting and handling incoming connections through transparent I/O redirections. On each worker node, I/O operations (accept, read/write and close) performed on the shared server socket object (wrapped in the pooled TCP connector) will be redirected to the master node where it was bound to the outside world. Most other I/O operations can be performed on I/O objects created locally; so each cluster node can serve web page requests and database queries in parallel.

When a client request is accepted, the context manager of Tomcat will match it to the target web application context. If the request carries session state such as a cookie, the standard manager will search for the allocated session object from the sessions hash table. In essence, all Tomcat container objects including the context manager, the standard manager, the sessions hash table and web contexts allocated in the master JVM heap are transparently shared among the distributed threads by means of the underlying GOS service mentioned in section 3. When a thread gets the first access to a non-local object reference, it will encounter an *access fault* and send a fetching request to the object's home node. The home node will respond with the up-to-date object data and export the local object as the home copy of the shared object. Cluster-wide data consistency will be enforced on the home copy and all cache copies derived from it thereafter. Since each thread will be able to see the shared object updates made by others through synchronization, the global shared heap creates an *implicit cooperative caching effect* among the threads. The power of this effect can be exemplified by collection classes like hash tables.

As illustrated, all HTTP sessions stored in a Tomcat-managed hash table can be globally accessible. The responsibility of maintaining HTTP session data consistency across servers has transparently shifted to the GOS layer. In other words, every server is eligible to handle requests belonged to any client session. This leads to more freedom of choice in request scheduling policies over sticky-sessions load balancing which can run into hotspots. Another useful scenario is using the GOS to augment the effective cache size of an application-level in-memory Java cache (e.g., a hash table for looking up database query results). The fact that every thread sees the cache entries created by one another contributes to secondary (indirect) application cache hits through remote object access. The cache size can now scale linearly with additional nodes, so we can greatly take the load off the bottlenecked database tier by caching more data at the application tier.

The DJVM approach inherits most advantages of clusters. However, the aforesaid server runtime properties bring additional design challenges on the DJVM runtime. First, I/O intensive workloads are known to be more difficult to scale efficiently over a cluster. Second, the high thread count property implies higher blocking latency if contention occurs. More memory overheads would be resulted from any per-thread protocol data structures. High read/write ratio is a positive news to the GOS as it implies shared writes are limited, so our protocols can take this property as a design tradeoff. Next, for long-running applications, we need to make sure the memory overhead induced by the coherence protocol data structures scales up slowly for less frequent garbage-collection cycles. Property 5 puts up the biggest barrier to scalability. Frequent synchronizations on the globally shared thread pool and object pools produce intensive remote locking overhead. Worse still, these pools are usually built from Java collection classes which are not scalable. For example, fine-grain accesses to hash entries of a Java hash table are all bottlenecked around the single map-wide lock contention which will be much intensified by distributed locking. Finally, properties 6 and 7 together issue enormous remote access roundtrips and demand smart object prefetching techniques for aggregating fine-grain communications. These observations call for a renovation of JESSICA2's global object space (GOS) architecture.

GLOBAL OBJECT SPACE

In this section, we elaborate on the design and implementation of our enhanced GOS system. We discuss the structure of the extended JVM heap, a home-based cache coherence protocol tailored for managing locks and a cluster-wide sequential consistency protocol for handling volatile field updates.

5.1 Overview of the Extended JVM Heap

To support cluster-wide object modification propagation and consistency maintenance, the heap of the standard JVM should be extended to make it "cluster-aware". In JESSICA2, each JVM heap is logically divided into two areas: the *master heap area* and the *cache heap area*. The master heap area essentially rides on the unmodified JVM heap, storing ordinary local objects. To make it "cluster-aware", when the local objects are being shared with some remote threads, they are exported as home objects with special flags marked in their object headers. The cache heap area manages cache objects brought from the master heap of a peer node. It consists of extra data structures for maintaining cluster-wide data consistency. The original GOS follows an intuitive design in which each thread has its own cache heap area, resembling the thread-private working memory based on the *Java memory model (JMM)*. This design prevents local threads from interfering each other's cache copies (such as during invalidations) but wastes precious memory space to keep redundant per-thread cache copies on the same node. So we adopt a unified cache design in the enhanced GOS which allows all local threads running on a single node to share a common cache copy. This design not only makes better usage of available memory resources but

Figure 3. GOS internal data structures

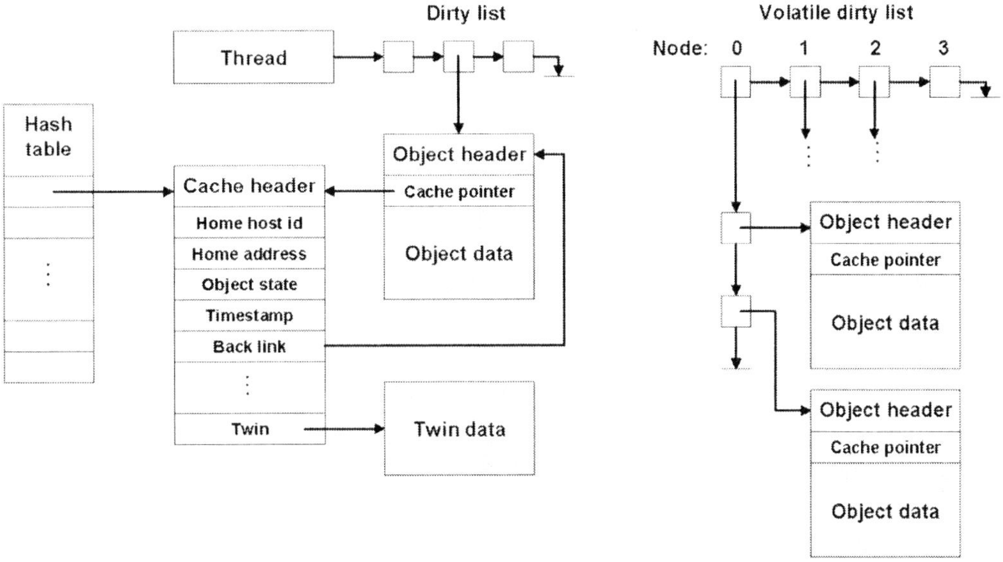

also reduce remote object fetching since when a thread faults in an object, other peer threads at the same node requesting the same object could find it in place. We also switch to a release consistency memory model in which the dominant read-only objects are never invalidated, so the interference among local threads is practically small. These modifications potentially could accommodate a high server thread count and achieve better memory utilization.

Figure 3 shows the internal data structures of the extended JVM heap. The object header of every object is augmented with special fields such as the *cache pointer*. A local or home object has a null cache pointer whereas a cache object has its cache pointer points to an internal data structure called *cache header* that contains the state and home information of the object. A node-level hash table (shared by all local threads) is used to manage and to look up cache headers during fetching events. In order to tell the home nodes of the modifications made on cache objects, each thread maintains a *dirty list* that records the ids of cache objects it has modified. At synchronization points, updates made on the dirty objects are flushed back to their home nodes. A similar per-node *volatile dirty list* is used to record updates on objects with volatile fields which are maintained by a separate single-writer protocol to be explained in section 5.3.

Object state is composed of two bits: valid/invalid and clean/dirty. The JIT compiler is tweaked to perform *inline checking* on each cache object access to see if its state is valid for read/write. Read/write on an invalid object will trigger appropriate interface functions to *fault-in* the up-to-date copy from its home. For efficiency, the software check is injected as a tiny assembly code fragment to the relevant bytecode instructions (GETFIELD, PUTFIELD, AALOAD, AASTORE, etc), testing the last two bits of the cache pointer. Valid object access passing the check will not impose any GOS interface function call overhead and is thus as fast as local object access.

Creating a single-heap illusion to distributed threads entails an advanced design of distributed cache coherence protocol as it has to be compliant to the Java memory model that defines the memory consistency semantics across multiple threads. The Java language provides two synchronization constructs for the programmers to render thread-safe code – the synchronized and volatile keywords. The synchronized keyword guarantees a code fragment or method with atomicity and memory visibility while volatile ensures that threads can see the latest values of volatile variables. We will discuss our enhancements of the GOS for handling the two types of synchronizations in Section 5.2 and 5.3 respectively.

5.2 Home-based Lazy Release Consistency Protocol

Entering and exiting a synchronized block or method correspond to acquiring and releasing the lock associated with the synchronized object. To fulfill the Java memory model, the original GOS implements an intuitive solution that works as follows. Upon a lock release, all updates to cache objects are flushed to their home nodes. Upon a lock acquire, all cache objects are invalidated, so later accesses will fault in the up-to-date copies from the home nodes. However, this would incur significant object fault-in overheads after every lock acquire. Thus, we renovate the original global object space by adopting a more relaxed *home-based lazy release consistency (HLRC)* memory model.

Contrary to the intuitive solution, upon a lock acquire, we confine invalidations to cache copies of shared objects that have been modified by other nodes only, rather than invalidating the total cache heap area. Our home-based cache coherence protocol guarantees memory visibility based on *Lazy Release Consistency (LRC)* (Keleher, Cox, & Zwaenepoel, 1992). LRC delays the propagation of modifications to a node until it performs a lock acquire. Lock acquire and release delimit the start and end of an *interval*. Specifically, LRC insures that the node can see the memory changes performed in other nodes' intervals according to the *happened-before-1* partial order (Adve & Hill, 1993), which is basically given by the local node's locking order and the shared lock transfer event. This means all memory updates preceding the release performed by a node should be made visible to the node that acquires the same lock. HLRC is similar to LRC in the sense of lock management but shapes the modification propagation into home-based patterns.

Memory updates are communicated based on a *multiple-writer* protocol implemented using the *twin-and-diff* technique that allows two or more threads to modify different parts (i.e. different fields or array portions) of the same shared object concurrently without conflict. In this technique, a *twin* copy is made as a data snapshot before the first write to a cache object in the current interval. Upon a shared lock release, for each dirty cache object, the modified part, i.e. *diff*, is differentiated from the twin. The diff is eagerly flushed to the corresponding home node, keeping the home copy always up-to-date. The thread can then safely discard the twins and diffs and close the interval. When the lock is acquired by another thread, the releaser passes *write notices* along the lock grant to the acquirer. The acquirer uses the write notices to invalidate the corresponding cached objects. It also saves the write notices so that they can be passed on to the next acquirer enforcing the happens-before partial order. A later access on an invalidated cache object will fault in the up-to-date copy from its home.

Here, we have to deal with some tricky data-race problems arising from sharing a unified cache copy among local threads. First, for systems of object-based granularity as in our case, field-level false sharing may occur since protecting different fields of one object by different locks is reckoned as well-synchronized in Java. For example, while one thread T1 holds a lock for modifying field A of a cache copy and makes it becomes in dirty state, another local thread T2 may acquire a lock for modifying field B of the same object. If another node has modified field B using the same lock, then T2 will invalidate that cache copy and fault-in the home copy, overwriting those pending modifications made by T1. Second, in systems with object prefetching, it is possible for one thread faulting in a home object A with object B prefetched to overwrite the pending modifications on the shared cache copy B made by another thread. Currently, we deal with these hazards by reconciling the timestamp field associated to each object to resolve detectable version conflicts and by incorporating techniques similar to *two-way diffing* (Stets et al., 1997).

For home objects, local read/write can be done directly without generating and applying diffs. This benefit is usually known as the *home effect* (Zhou, Iftode, & Li, 1996). Some minor overhead that home nodes still need to pay is to keep record of the local writes for the next remote acquiring thread to invalidate the relevant cache copies. Locking of home objects resembles locking of local objects if the lock ownership has not been given to any remote nodes. Otherwise, it has to wait for the lock release done by the last remote acquirer.

Compared with homeless protocols, the advantages of HLRC are: 1. the home effect for reducing high diffing overheads; 2. fewer messages since an object fault can always be satisfied by one round-trip to home instead of diff request messages to multiple writers; 3. no *diff accumulation* and so no need for garbage collection of diffs. Hence, this becomes our protocol design choice for shorter latency seen by I/O-bound workload and less garbage accruing from long-running server applications.

Nevertheless, we depart from the usual HLRC implementations in some aspects. To track and enforce the happens-before partial order, traditional HLRC implementations rely heavily on *vector timestamps* to dig out the exact minimal intervals (and write notices) that the acquirer must apply. While this ensures the most relaxed invalidation, this entails complex data structures like interval records in Treadmarks (Keleher et al., 1994) or *bins* database (Iosevich & Schuster, 2005) to keep the stacks of vectors. The storage size occupied by them scales with the number of locking on shared objects. For lock-intensive applications, these stacks can grow up quickly and consume enormous space. For long-running server applications, the problem becomes more critical and systems that rely on pre-allocation schemes such as cyclic bins buffers (Iosevich & Schuster, 2005) will ultimately run out of space and result in runtime failure. Discarding interval records is possible if they have already been applied to all nodes. But some nodes may never acquire a particular lock while some nodes intensively acquire it. This issue is not ignorable particularly in multithreaded protocols where the length of vector timestamp scales with the number of threads. For highly-threaded applications like Tomcat, this has scalability impacts on both memory and network bandwidth. Therefore, our protocol eschews the use of vector timestamps.

Rather we employ object-level scalar timestamps to assist deriving the set of write notices. The basic idea is illustrated by Figure 4. Each node maintains a data structure called *timestamp map* which is essentially a hash table recording all shared objects that have once been modified. Each map entry consists of the object id, a scalar timestamp and a n-bit binary vector (n being number of nodes) and is used to derive the corresponding write notice formatted as a couple (object id, timestamp). The n-bit binary vector is used to keep track of which node has applied the write notice (0 = not yet; 1 = applied). If all the n nodes have applied the write notice, it is considered *obsolete* and can be discarded. The size of this map scales with the number of modified shared objects rather than the number of shared locking. Repetitive locking on the same object will not generate separate interval records but go to update the same entry in the timestamp map. Due to high read/write ratios in web applications, the number of modified shared objects is limited. The timestamp map will also undergo a *periodic shrinking phase* to clean up those obsolete entries. So the map is practically small in size at most of the time.

Upon a shared lock release, modifications will be recorded into the local node's timestamp map. When a lock transfer happens, all non-obsolete map entries will be extracted as write notices and passed from the releaser to the acquirer. They will also be saved in the acquirer's map. Write notices with a

Figure 4. Timestamp map for implementing HLRC

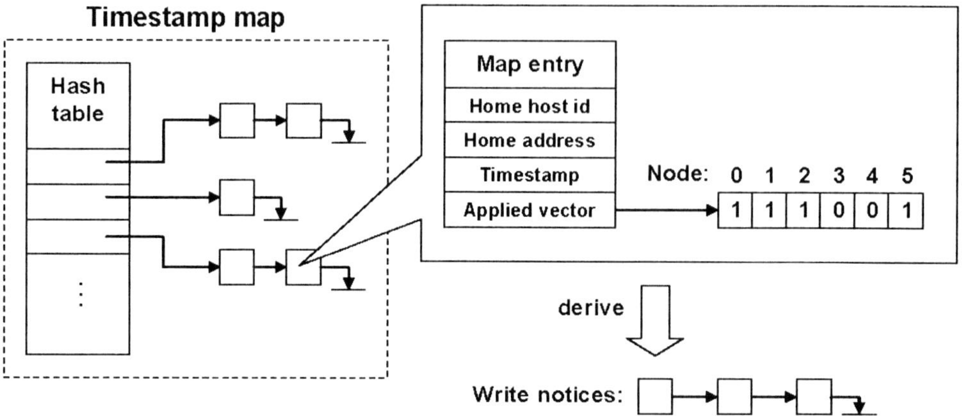

newer timestamp will overwrite an old map entry if any and reset its n-bit vector to all zeros so that future acquirers will be able to know the changes. Without tracking the exact partial order, the set of write notices sent to an acquirer may not be minimal and possibly include modifications that "happens-after" the release of the lock being acquired. The drawback is that some cache objects at the acquirer side may be invalidated earlier than necessary. However this effect is insignificant since if the thread is really going to access the invalidated cache objects, it eventually needs to see the modifications. This effect will not accrue owing to our periodic cleanup of obsolete map entries and selective invalidations based on object timestamp comparison.

5.3 Volatile Consistency Protocol

Most DJVM prototype implementations enforce cluster-wide semantics of the volatile construct in a way that is stricter than necessary. For straight-forward compatibility, the volatile construct is usually treated as if it was a lock, thus introducing unnecessary mutual exclusivity to the application. The latest Java concurrent utility package (JSR166, 2004), particularly the ConcurrentHashMap class shipped along, employs segment-based locks plus volatile count and object value fields to guard different hash bucket ranges. The advanced data structure offers much more scalable throughput than the conventional Java Hashtable. However, such a good design for concurrency will be smothered if the underlying DJVM handle the volatile fields as locks. So we decided to tailor consistency support to volatile fields.

Our new protocol for maintaining cluster-wide volatile field consistency is a *passive-based concurrent-read exclusive-write (CREW)* protocol. It enforces sequential consistency to ensure the next reader thread can see the updates made by the last writer on the same object.

To implement this model, we need to assign a manager for each object with volatile fields and it is naturally the home node where the object is created. For ease of explanation, we call an object with a volatile field as *volatile object*. The home node needs to maintain two states on the home copy of volatile object: *readable* and *exclusive*, as well as a list called *copyset* of the nodes that currently have a valid cache copy of this object. When the home node receives a fetch request from a node on a readable volatile object, the node's id will be added to the copyset list of the home copy. The consistency of a volatile object relies on the active writer to tell the readers of such an update. When a thread wants to write the object, no matter the home or cache copy, it must first gain the exclusive right on it from its home node. Before the exclusive right is granted to the candidate writer, the home will broadcast invalidations to all members of the copyset and clean up the copyset. The writer will record its modified objects into the per-node volatile dirty list. The exclusive right will be returned to the home along when the modification (diff) is flushed. Read/write on home objects similarly need to go through the state check except that they are done directly on the object data without diff generation and flushing. There is no need to generate any write notices because volatile cache copies are *passively* invalidated by the home when a writer exists.

Upon read on an invalid volatile object, it will need to contact the home for the latest copy and join the copyset again. If the state of the home copy is exclusive, then the fetch request will be put into a queue pointed by volatile object header. When the writer returns the diff and exclusive right to the home, the home will turn the object state back to readable and reply all queued readers with the updated object data. As long as the state of a cache volatile object stays valid, its consistency has been guaranteed and the thread can directly trust it until invalidation is received when some writer exists. This leads to the beauty of this protocol that results in much better concurrency. Reads on a valid volatile object are pure local operations without remote locks and any communications. For high application read/write ratio, our design tradeoff shifts the communication overhead of the dominant reads to writes.

PERFORMANCE ANALYSIS

In this section, we present the performance results obtained by running Tomcat on JESSICA2.

6.1 Experimental Setup

Our experimental platform consists of three tiers: 1. *web tier*: a 2-way Xeon SMP server with 4GB RAM for running the master JVM of JESSICA2 with Apache Tomcat 3.2.4 started up on it. 2. *application tier*: a cluster of eight x86-based PCs with 512 MB RAM serving as the DJVM worker nodes. 3. *data tier*: a cluster of four x86-based PCs with 2GB RAM supporting MySQL Database Server 5.0.45. All nodes run under Fedora Core 1 (kernel 2.4.22). A Gigabit Ethernet switch is used to link up the three tiers, while nodes within the same tier are connected by Fast Ethernet networks.

The initial and maximum heap sizes of each worker JVM are set to 128MB and 256MB respectively. Each database node has the same dataset replica with MySQL replication enabled to synchronize data updates across database servers at nearly real time. Jakarta JMeter 2.2 is used to synthesize varying workloads to stress the testing platform.

Table 1 shows the application benchmark suite that we use to evaluate our clustering approach using the DJVM. They are designed to model real-life web application patterns.

1. *Bible-quote* characterizes applications like text search engines, news archives and company catalogs. The servlet application is I/O intensive, serving document retrievals and search requests over a set of text files of books.
2. *Stock-quote* models stock market data providers. We follow the trend of web services that deliver price data by XML messages. The application reads stock price data matching the input date range from the database and formats the query result into an XML response.

Table 1. Application Benchmark Suite

Application	Object Sharing	Workload Nature	I/O
Bible-quote	No sharing	I/O-intensive	Text files
Stock-quote		Relatively compute-intensive	Database
Stock-quote/RSA			
SOAP-order	HTTP session	I/O-intensive	
TPC-W			Database and image files
Bulletin-search	Cached database records	Memory-intensive	Database

3. *Stock-quote/RSA* is secure version of Stock-quote involving compute-intensive operations of 1024-bit RSA encryption on the price data.
4. *SOAP-order* models a B2B e-commerce web service. A SOAP engine is needed to support the service. We choose Apache SOAP 2.3.1 and deploy it to Tomcat. The application logic is to parse a SOAP message enclosing securities order placements, validate the user account and order details and then put the successful transactions into the database.
5. *TPC-W* is a standard transactional web benchmark specification. It models an online bookstore with session-based workloads and a mix of static and dynamic web interactions. We adopt the Java servlet implementation developed by (ObjectWeb, 2005) but tailor the utility class for data access by disabling the default database connection pooling and utilizing thread-local storage to cache connections instead.
6. *Bulletin-search* emulates a search engine in a bulletin board or web forum system. We take the data dump from the RUBBoS benchmark (ObjectWeb, 2004) to populate the database. The application maintains a hash-based LRU-cache map of the results of the costly database searches, and is thus memory-intensive. In order not to lift up garbage collection frequency too much, we impose a capacity limit on the cache map, taking up about one-forth of the local JVM heap.

The original Tomcat is ported to JESSICA2 with a few customizations as follows: 1. the shared thread pool is disbanded. We replace the original thread pool by a simpler implementation which spawns a static count of non-pooled threads based on the server configuration file. 2. several shared object pools (e.g. static mapping tables for MIME types and status codes) are disintegrated into thread-local caches. The total lines of modified code including the new thread pool source file we introduce are less than 370 (about 0.76% of the Tomcat source base).

6.2 Scalability Study

In this experiment, we measure the maximum throughputs and average response times obtained by scaling the number of worker nodes from two to eight. The speedup is calculated by dividing the baseline runtime of Tomcat on Kaffe JVM 1.0.7 by the parallel runtime of Tomcat on JESSICA2. Figure 5 shows the results obtained for each benchmark. We can see that most of the applications scale well and achieve efficiency ranging from 66% (SOAP-order) to 96.7% (Stock-quote). Bible-quote, Stock-quote and Stock-quote/RSA show almost linear speedup because they belong to the class of stateless applications, undergoing true parallelism without any GOS communications between the JVMs. In particular, Stock-quote

Figure 5. Scalability and average response time obtain by Tomcat on JESSICA2

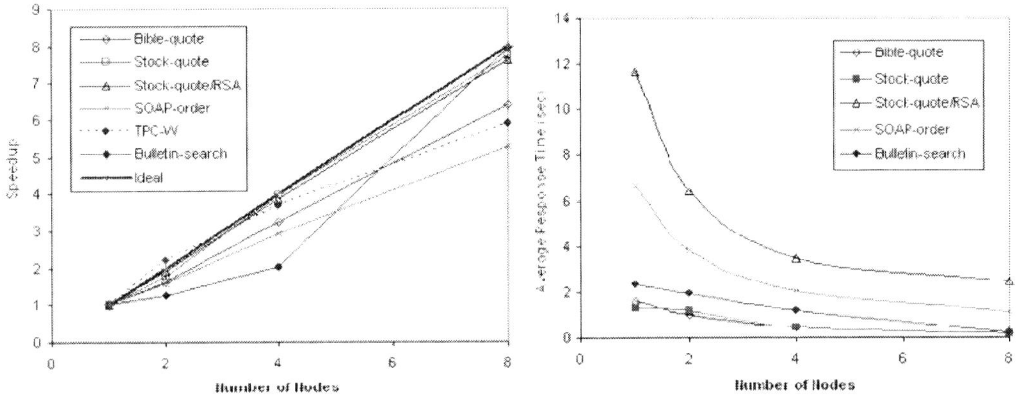

and Stock-quote/RSA involve operations of coarser work granularity, such as string manipulations and RSA encryptions, and are hence more readily to attain nearly perfect scalability. The relatively poorer speedups seen by SOAP-order and TPC-W are expected as they are stateful applications and involve GOS overheads when sharing HTTP session objects among JVM heaps. We will further discuss the limited speedup obtained by SOAP-order in section 6.4.

Bulletin-search shows a nonlinear but steepening curve in speedup when the number of worker nodes scales out due to the implicit cooperative cache effect given by the GOS that we described in section 4. Along the scaling of nodes, when the cluster-wide aggregated available memory becomes large enough to accommodate most of the data objects cached in the application, the cache benefit will contribute an impulsive rise in speedup. Further study on this effect will be given in section 6.3.

Table 2 shows the cluster-wide thread count used in each application and the overall protocol messaging overheads inside JESSICA2 in the 8-node configuration. The count of I/O redirections is proportional to the request throughput and generally does not have impact on the scalability. The higher number of GOS protocol messages explains the poorer scalability obtained by the application if we reconcile with Figure 5. Bulletin-search is regarded as an exceptional case for its performance is more determined by its cooperative caching benefits which could supersede the cost of GOS communications.

6.3 Comparison with Existing Tomcat Clustering

A control experiment is conducted on the same platform to compare the DJVM approach with an existing clustering method for Tomcat using web load balancing plug-ins. We run an instance of Apache web server 2.0.53 on the web tier and eight standalone Tomcat servers on the application tier of our platform. The web server is connected to the Tomcat servers via the mod_jk connector 1.2.18 with sticky-session enabled (in-memory session replication is not supported in this comparison). The cluster-wide total number of threads and heap size configurations in this experiment are equal to the previous ones used in the DJVM approach.

Figure 6 shows the throughputs obtained by the two clustering approaches on eight nodes. We can see that both solutions achieve similar performance (within ±8%) for those stateless web applications (Bible-quote, Stock-quote and Stock-quote/RSA). These applications exhibit embarrassing parallelism

Table 2. Protocol message overheads of JESSICA2 DJVM

Application	# Threads	# GOS Messages / Sec	# I/O Redirections / Sec
Bible-quote	80	0	2006
Stock-quote	80	0	1791
Stock-quote/RSA	80	0	275
SOAP-order	16	979	146
TPC-W	40	351	1413
Bulletin-search	16	483	297

and will not gain much advantage from the GOS. So putting the GOS aside, we can expect both solutions should perform more or less the same because both our transparent I/O redirection and mod_jk's socket forwarding are functionally alike for dispatching requests and collecting responses. Yet, extra overheads could be incurred in our solution when transferring big trunks of data via fine-grain I/O redirections and during object state checks.

TPC-W performs about 11% better on the DJVM than with mod_jk. One reason is that servers sharing sessions over the GOS are no longer restricted to handle requests bounded to their sticky sessions while load hotspots could happen intermittently when using mod_jk. On the other hand, SOAP-order performs 26% poorer on JESSICA2 than with mod_jk. The main factor that pulls down the performance is that the SOAP library has some code performing fairly intensive synchronizations in every request processing cycle. We will see later that the overhead breakdown presented in Section 6.5 echoes this factor. Bulletin-search performs 8.5 times better on the DJVM due to application cache hits augmented by the GOS. We will explain why the DJVM approach has significantly outplayed the existing solution in the next section.

Figure 6. Comparison of Tomcat on DJVM and existing Tomcat clustering

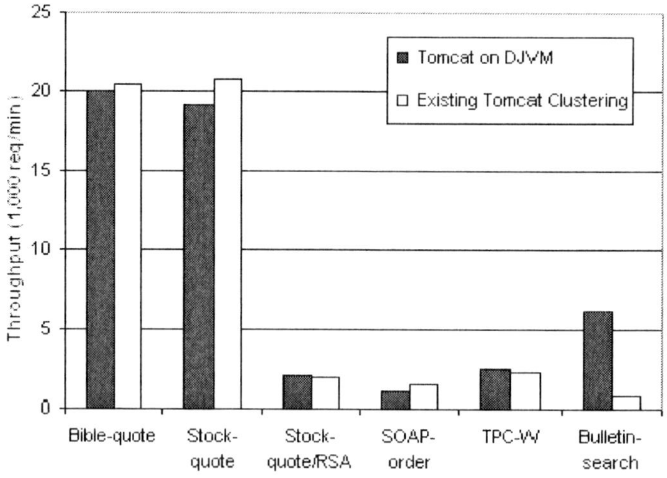

Table 3. Bulletin-search's cache size setting and hit rates augmented by GOS

No. of Nodes	Cache Size (#Cache Entries)	Relative Cache Size	Total Hit Rate	Indirect Hit Latency (ms)	Cost Ratio of Miss: Indirect Hit	Throughput Speedup
1	512	12.5%	18.6%	N/A	N/A	N/A
2	931	22.7%	33.9%	9.07	40.79	1.26
4	1862	45.5%	59.3%	8.18	45.23	2.02
8	3724	90.9%	90.7%	11.74	31.52	7.96

6.4 Effect of Implicit Cooperative Caching

Bulletin-search exemplifies the class of web applications that can exploit the GOS to virtualize a large heap for caching application data. Table 3 shows the application cache hits obtained by Bulletin-search when the number of cluster nodes scales from one to eight. With the GOS, the capacity setting of the cache map can be increased proportional to the node count beyond the single-node limit for different portions of the map are stored under different heaps. This is not possible without the GOS. Upon the creation of a new cache entry, its object reference built to the map is brought visible to all threads across synchronization points. So redundant caching is eliminated. Threads can exploit *indirect (or global) cache hits* in case the desired object is not in the local heap, easing the database bottleneck.

We can see from Figure 7 that the overall hit rate keeps rising along with the scaling of worker nodes of the DJVM and most of the cache hits are contributed by the indirect hits when the single-node capacity has been exceeded. This is the reason why our approach achieves a multifold throughput than the existing clustering approach in which there are only direct (local) hits that would level off or even drop slightly no matter how many nodes are added.

Here we define a term called *relative cache size (RCS)* that refers to the percentage of the aggregated cache size (combining all nodes) relative to the total size of the data set. When the RCS is below 50% in the 4-node case, the achievable cache hit rate is only around 60% and the 40% misses get no improvement

Figure 7. Composition of application cache hits in Bulletin-search with GOS

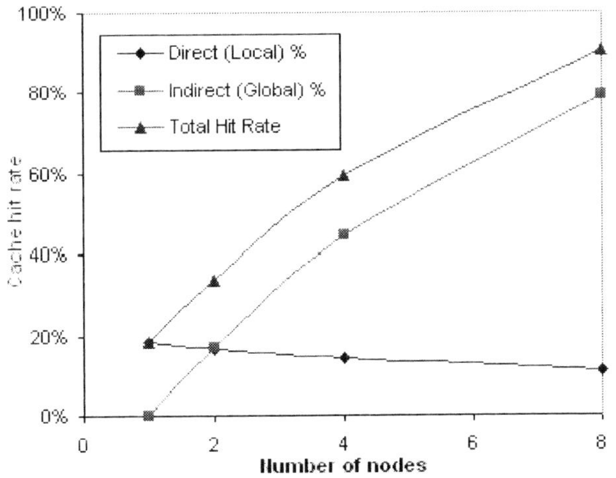

Table 4. GOS overhead breakdown

GOS Message Type	# Messages / Sec		
	SOAP-order	TPC-W	Bulletin-search
Lock acquire	198	48	61
Lock release	198	48	61
Flush	217	70	92
Static data fetch	18	10	0
Object fault-in	197	99	160
Array fault-in	79	50	105

such that the application obtains a speedup of merely two. But when the RCS exceeds certain level (e.g. 90% in the 8-node case), most of the requests are fulfilled by the global cache instead of going through the database tier. This explains the non-uniform scalability curve of this application in Figure 5.

6.5 GOS Overhead Breakdowns

Table 4 shows the GOS overhead breakdowns in terms of message count per second for the three stateful applications. Figure 8 supplements with percentage breakdown of the message count as well as message latency. Lock acquire and release messages are issued when locking a remote object. Flush messages are sent upon lock releases but the flush message count is a bit more than lock release messages because in some cases updates are flushed to more than one homes. Other overheads are related to access faults which translate to communications with the corresponding home nodes. It is obvious that SOAP-order involves much more remote locking overhead than the other applications.

Our further investigation finds that one utility class of the deployed SOAP library would induce for each request about five to six remote locks on several shared hash tables and four remote locks on

Figure 8. GOS percentage overhead

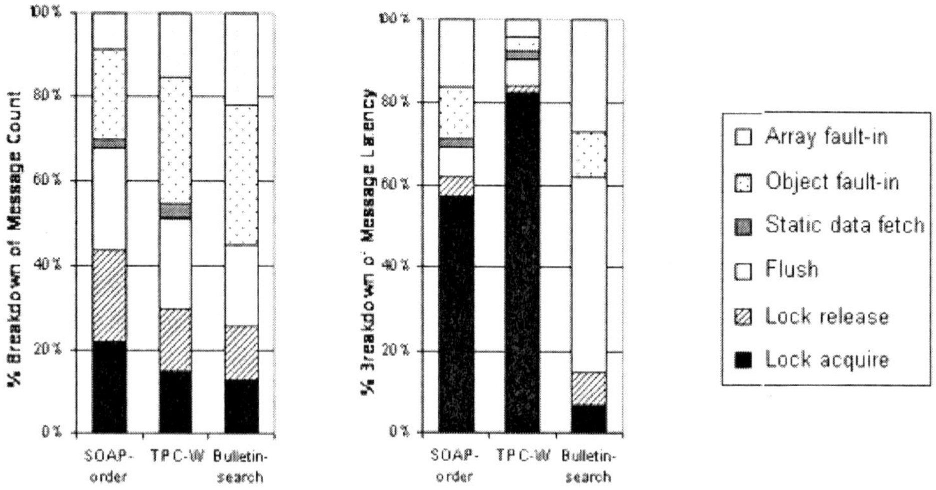

Table 5. Cluster-wide locking overheads

Application	# Local Locks / Sec	# Remote Locks / Sec	% Remote Locks Under Contention	Ratio of Local: Remote Locks
SOAP-order	232631	198	35%	1175:1
TPC-W	240470	48	45%	5010:1
Bulletin-search	27380	61	6.5%	449:1

ServletContextFacade coming from the facade design pattern of Tomcat. Such heavy cluster-wide synchronization overheads justify the relatively poorer scalability given by this application.

Table 5 presents the local and remote locking rates for each application. We can see that local locks are much more than remote locks. The main reason behind this is that in Java-based servers, thread-safe reads/writes on I/O stream objects are exceptionally frequent, producing tremendous local locks. While local lock latency is very short (benchmarks shows an average of 0.2us), remote lock latency is however at least several thousand times longer in commodity clusters; yet remote locks are practically much fewer in most web applications. Another piece of information given by Table 5 is that SOAP-order and TPC-W have about 35% to 45% remote locks under cluster-wide contention, thus prolonging the wait time before locks are granted. This is why lock acquire has been the dominant part in the message latency for these two applications in Figure 8.

RELATED WORK

Despite the boom of software DSM and the later DJVM research, it seems there have been only a few attempts at transparently supporting real-life server applications by means of shared virtual memory systems. Even fewer have been successful cases demonstrating good scalability though some of them had relied on non-commodity hardware to support their systems.

Shasta (Scales & Gharachorloo, 1997) is a fine-grained software DSM system that uses binary code instrumentation techniques extensively to transparently extend memory accesses to have cluster-wide semantics. Oracle 7.3 database server was ported to Shasta running on SMP clusters, albeit without success in achieving good scalability. They used TPC-B and TPC-D database benchmarks which model online transaction processing and decision support queries respectively. TPC-B failed to scale at all due to too frequent updates while TPC-D strived to achieve a speedup of one point something on three servers connected by non-commodity Memory Channel Network. To some extent, their experience and result exhibit many limitations of implementing a single system image at operating system level, compared to our approach of clustering at middleware level. For example, relaxed memory consistency model cannot be adopted at operating system level in usual cases, since correctness of binary applications often relies on consistency model imposed by hardware, which is generally much stricter than Java memory model. Being able to adopt relaxed memory model such as HLRC in our case is very important to server applications which may be intensive in synchronization.

cJVM (Aridor et al., 1999) is one of the earliest DJVM designed with intent to enable large multi-threaded server applications such as Jigsaw to run transparently on a cluster. cJVM operates in interpreter-mode; it employs a *master-proxy model* and a *method shipping* approach to support object sharing among distributed threads. The system relies on proxy objects to redirect field access and method invocation to the node where the object's master copy resides. This model basically conforms to sequential consistency and is not efficient since every object access and method invocation may require communication although some optimization techniques were developed to avoid needless shipping. In contrast, our DJVM runs in JIT-compilation mode and conforms to release consistency, both propelling faster execution. In (Aridor et al., 2000), cJVM was evaluated by running pBOB (Portable Business Object Benchmark), a multithreaded business benchmark inspired by TPC-C, on a 4-node cluster connected by non-commodity Myrinet. They obtained an efficiency of around 80%. However, it is unclear that whether cJVM will perform such well if JIT gets enabled and commodity Ethernet is used as in our case.

Terracotta (Zilka, 2006) is a JVM-level clustering product emerged on the market for a couple of years. It applies *bytecode instrumentation* techniques similar to JavaSplit (Factor, Schuster, & Shagin, 2003) to a predefined list of common products and to user-defined classes for clustering among multiple Java application instances. Users need to manually specify shared classes as *distributed shared objects (DSOs)* and their cluster-aware concurrency semantics. Contrasting with our SSI-oriented approach, this configuration-driven approach may impair user transparency and create subtle semantic violation. Terracotta uses a hub and spoke architecture that requires setting up a central server, namely the "*L2 server*", to store all DSOs and to coordinate heap changes (field-level diffs) across JVMs. At synchronization points, changes on a DSO have to be sent to the L2 server that forwards the changes to all other clustered JVMs under the DSO's copyset to keep all replicas consistent. Our home-based protocol needs to keep only the home copy up-to-date by flushing diffs, then the next acquirer can see the changes by faulting in the whole object. Terracotta's centralized architecture may make the cluster susceptible to a global bottleneck when scaling out. Tailoring the bottleneck requires forklift upgrades on the L2 server (i.e. vertical scaling) that spoil the virtue of horizontal scaling using commodity hardware. We believe a home-based peer-to-peer protocol is a more scalable architecture for distributed object sharing.

CONCLUSION AND FUTURE WORK

In this chapter, we introduce a new transparent clustering approach using distributed JVMs (DJVMs) for web application servers like Apache Tomcat. A DJVM couples a group of extended JVMs for distributing a multithreaded Java application on a cluster. It realizes transparent clustering without the need for introducing new APIs and incorporates most of the advantages of a SSI-centric system such as global resource integration and coordination. Using DJVMs to cluster web application servers can enhance the ease of web application clustering and global resource utilization – both have been poorly met in most existing clustering solutions among the web community.

We port Tomcat to the JESSICA2 DJVM to testify this clustering approach. Our study addresses new challenges of supporting web application servers that characterize unique runtime properties of today's object-oriented servers over the classical scientific applications evaluated in the previous DJVM projects. The key challenge lies in making the system scalable with a large number of threads and offering efficient shared memory support for fine-grain object sharing among the JVMs. We enhance the cache coherence protocol design accordingly in several aspects: 1. adopt a unified cache among local threads to make better memory utilization; 2. implement a timestamp-assisted HLRC protocol to ensure release consistency of shared objects; 3. enforce sequential consistency among cluster-wide volatile fields via a concurrent-read exclusive-write (CREW) protocol. These improvements result in more relaxed coherence maintenance and higher concurrency. Our experimental result has illustrated significant cache hits obtained by using the global object space (GOS) to cache a large application dataset with automatic consistency guarantee.

Several trends have put forward the advent of the DJVM clustering technology. Today's web applications are becoming increasingly resource-intensive due to security enhancement, more complicated business logics and XML-based standards. Collaborative computing paradigm provisioned by DJVMs becomes vital to generate helpful cache effect across cluster nodes for efficient resource usage. Second, application logics tend to increase in complexity and now more and more application frameworks are POJO-based. Clustering at application level and adoption of proprietary clustering mechanisms shipped with particular application server products will tend to be laborious and error-prone, if not unfeasible. We foresee DJVMs, typifying the kind of generic clustering middleware systems, will be gaining more user acceptance. Third, design and development for user applications, server programs and library support nowadays have put more emphasis on scalability than ever. When scalability or performance portability is not a problem and meanwhile DJVMs are supreme in cost-effectiveness, this would have a catalytic effect that more applications readily go for the DJVM technology.

In future, we will investigate solutions to enhance fine-grain object sharing efficiency in the DJVM environment. In our research plans, we would consider incorporating transactional consistency (Hammond et al., 2004) into the cluster-wide memory coherence protocol.

REFERENCES

Adve, S. V., & Hill, M. D. (1993). A Unified Formalization of Four Shared-Memory Models. *IEEE Transactions on Parallel and Distributed Systems*, *4*(6), 613–624. doi:10.1109/71.242161

Antoniu, G., Bougé, L., Hatcher, P., MacBeth, M., McGuigan, K., & Namyst, R. (2001). The Hyperion system: Compiling multithreaded Java bytecode for distributed execution. *Parallel Computing*, *27*(10), 1279–1297. doi:10.1016/S0167-8191(01)00093-X

Aridor, Y., Factor, M., & Teperman, A. (1999). *cJVM: A Single System Image of a JVM on a Cluster*. Paper presented at the Proceedings of the 1999 International Conference on Parallel Processing.

Aridor, Y., Factor, M., Teperman, A., Eilam, T., & Schuster, A. (2000). Transparently obtaining scalability for Java applications on a cluster. *Journal of Parallel and Distributed Computing*, *60*(10), 1159–1193. doi:10.1006/jpdc.2000.1649

ASF. (2002). *The Apache Tomcat Connector*. Retrieved June 18, 2008, from http://tomcat.apache.org/connectors-doc/

Ban, B. (1997). *JGroups - A Toolkit for Reliable Multicast Communication*. Retrieved June 18, 2008, from http://www.jgroups.org/javagroupsnew/docs/index.html

Factor, M., Schuster, A., & Shagin, K. (2003). *JavaSplit: a runtime for execution of monolithic Java programs on heterogenous collections of commodity workstations*. Paper presented at the Proceedings of the IEEE International Conference on Cluster Computing.

Hammond, L., Wong, V., Chen, M., Carlstrom, B. D., Davis, J. D., & Hertzberg, B. (2004). Transactional Memory Coherence and Consistency. *SIGARCH Comput. Archit. News*, *32*(2), 102. doi:10.1145/1028176.1006711

Iosevich, V., & Schuster, A. (2005). Software Distributed Shared Memory: a VIA-based implementation and comparison of sequential consistency with home-based lazy release consistency: Research Articles. *Software, Practice & Experience*, *35*(8), 755–786. doi:10.1002/spe.656

Johnson, R. (2002). *Spring Framework - a full-stack Java/JEE application framework*. Retrieved June 18, 2008, from http://www.springframework.org/

JSR166. (2004). *Java concurrent utility package in J2SE 5.0* (JDK1.5). Retrieved June 24, 2008, from http://java.sun.com/j2se/1.5.0/docs/api/java/util/concurrent/package-summary.html

Keleher, P., Cox, A. L., Dwarkadas, S., & Zwaenepoel, W. (1994). *TreadMarks: Distributed Shared Memory on Standard Workstations and Operating Systems*. Paper presented at the Proceedings of Winter 1995 USENIX Conference.

Keleher, P., Cox, A. L., & Zwaenepoel, W. (1992). *Lazy release consistency for software distributed shared memory*. Paper presented at the Proceedings of the 19th annual international symposium on Computer architecture.

Ma, M. J. M., Wang, C. L., & Lau, F. C. M. (2000). JESSICA: Java-enabled single-system-image computing architecture. *Journal of Parallel and Distributed Computing*, *60*(10), 1194–1222. doi:10.1006/jpdc.2000.1650

ObjectWeb. (2004). *RUBBoS: Bulletin Board Benchmark*. Retrieved June 19, 2008, from http://jmob.objectweb.org/rubbos.html

ObjectWeb. (2005). *TPC-W Benchmark* (Java Servlets version). Retrieved June 19, 2008, from http://jmob.objectweb.org/tpcw.html

Perez, C. E. (2003). *Open Source Distributed Cache Solutions Written in Java*. Retrieved June 24, 2008, from http://www.manageability.org/blog/stuff/distributed-cache-java

Scales, D. J., & Gharachorloo, K. (1997). *Towards transparent and efficient software distributed shared memory*. Paper presented at the Proceedings of the sixteenth ACM symposium on Operating systems principles.

Stets, R., Dwarkadas, S., Hardavellas, N., Hunt, G., Kontothanassis, L., & Parthasarathy, S. (1997). Cashmere-2L: software coherent shared memory on a clustered remote-write network. *SIGOPS Oper. Syst. Rev.*, *31*(5), 170–183. doi:10.1145/269005.266675

Veldema, R., Hofman, R. F. H., Bhoedjang, R., & Bal, H. E. (2001). *Runtime optimizations for a Java DSM implementation*. Paper presented at the Proceedings of the 2001 joint ACM-ISCOPE conference on Java Grande.

Wilkinson, T. (1998). Kaffe - a clean room implementation of the Java virtual machine. Retrieved 2002, from http://www.kaffe.org/

Yu, W., & Cox, A. (1997). Java/DSM: A Platform for Heterogeneous Computing. *Concurrency (Chichester, England), 9*(11), 1213–1224. doi:10.1002/(SICI)1096-9128(199711)9:11<1213::AID-CPE333>3.0.CO;2-J

Zhou, Y., Iftode, L., & Li, K. (1996). Performance evaluation of two home-based lazy release consistency protocols for shared virtual memory systems. *SIGOPS Oper. Syst. Rev., 30*(SI), 75-88.

Zhu, W., Wang, C. L., & Lau, F. C. M. (2002). *JESSICA2: A Distributed Java Virtual Machine with Transparent Thread Migration Support*. Paper presented at the Proceedings of the IEEE International Conference on Cluster Computing.

Zilka, A. (2006). *Terracotta - JVM Clustering, Scalability and Reliability for Java*. Retrieved June 19, 2008, from http://www.terracotta.org

KEY TERMS AND DEFINITIONS

Copyset: The current set of nodes or threads that hold a valid cache copy of an object. This data structure is kept at the home node of the object and is helpful for sending invalidations in a single-writer-multiple-reader cache coherence protocol.

Distributed Java Virtual Machine (DJVM): A parallel execution environment composed of a collaborative set of extended Java virtual machines spanning multiple cluster nodes for running a multithreaded Java application.

Global Object Space (GOS): A virtualized memory address space for location-transparent object access and sharing across distributed threads. The GOS for distributed Java virtual machines is built upon a distributed shared heap architecture.

Java Memory Model (JMM): A memory (consistency) model that defines legal behaviors in a multi-threaded Java code with respect to the shared memory. The JMM serves as a contract between programmers and the JVM.

Lazy Release Consistency (LRC): The most widely adopted memory consistency model in software distributed shared memory (DSM) in which the propagation of shared page/object modifications (in forms of invalidation/update) is delayed to lock-acquire time.

Implicit Cooperative Caching (ICC): – A helpful cache effect created by distributed threads through cluster-wide accesses to a collection of shared object references.

ENDNOTE

[1] This research was supported by Hong Kong RGC grant (HKU7176/06E) and China 863 grant (2006AA01A111).

Chapter 29
Middleware for Community Coordinated Multimedia

Jiehan Zhou
University of Oulu, Finland

Zhonghong Ou
University of Oulu, Finland

Junzhao Sun
University of Oulu, Finland

Mika Rautiainen
University of Oulu, Finland

Mika Ylianttila
University of Oulu, Finland

ABSTRACT

Community Coordinated Multimedia (CCM) envisions a novel paradigm that enables the user to consume multiple media through requesting multimedia-intensive Web services via diverse display devices, converged networks, and heterogeneous platforms within a virtual, open and collaborative community. These trends yield new requirements for CCM middleware. This chapter aims to systematically and extensively describe middleware challenges and opportunities to realize the CCM paradigm by reviewing the activities of middleware with respect to four viewpoints, namely mobility-aware, multimedia-driven, service-oriented, and community-coordinated.

INTRODUCTION

With the popularity of mobile devices (e.g. mobile phone, camera phone, PDA), the advances of mobile ad hoc networks (e.g. enterprise networks, home networks, sensor networks), and the rapidly increasing amount of end user-generated multimedia content (e.g. audio, video, animation, text, image), human experience is being enhanced and extended by the consumption of multimedia content and multimedia

DOI: 10.4018/978-1-60566-661-7.ch029

services over mobile devices.

This enhanced human experience paradigm is generalized with the term of Community Coordinated Multimedia, abbreviated as CCM, in this chapter. The emerging CCM communication takes on the feature of pervasively or wirelessly accessing multimedia-intensive Web services for aggregating, sharing, viewing TV broadcasting/multicasting services, or on-demand audiovisual content over mobile devices collaboratively. Thus the end user's experience is enhanced and extended by mobile multimedia communication with the transparencies in networking, location, synchronization, group communication, coordination, collaboration, etc.(Zhou et al, 2008a).

Middleware plays a key role in offering the transparent networking, location, synchronization, group communication, coordination, collaboration, etc. In this chapter, middleware is perceived as a software layer that sits above the network operating system and below the application layer. It encapsulates the knowledge from presentation layer and session layer in OSI model that provides controls on the dialogues/connections (sessions) and the understanding of syntax and semantics between distributed applications, and abstracts the heterogeneity of the underlying environment between distributed applications.

This chapter presents a survey and initial design of P2P service-oriented community coordinated multimedia middleware. This work is a part of EUREKA ITEA2 project CAM4Home[1] metadata-enabled content delivery and service framework. The chapter investigates technological CCM middleware challenges and opportunities from four viewpoints that describe the CCM: mobility-aware, multimedia-driven, service-oriented, and community-coordinated. These are the most highlighted characteristics for CCM applications. The following lists identified middleware categories for addressing challenges and opportunities in the CCM paradigm:

- Middleware for mobility management. The middleware for mobility management aims to provide mobile access to distributed multimedia applications and services, and addresses the limitations caused by terminal heterogeneity, network resource limitation, and node mobility.
- Middleware for multimedia computing and communication. The middleware for multimedia computing and communication aims to provide standard formats, specification and techniques for representing all multimedia types in a digital form, handling compressed digital video and audio data, and delivery streams.
- Middleware for service computing and communication. The middleware for service computing and communication aims to provide specifications and standards in the context of Web services to achieve the service-oriented multimedia computing paradigm covering service description, interaction, discovery, and composition.
- Middleware for community computing and communication. The middleware for community computing and communication aims to provide standards and principles which govern the participation of peers into the community and messaging models.

The remainder of the chapter is organized as follows: Section 2 defines concepts relevant to CCM and middleware. Section 3 illustrates a generic CCM scenario. Section 4 analyzes the requirements of middleware for CCM. Section 5 designs a middleware architecture for CCM. Section 6 surveys middleware technology for CCM with respect to mobility-aware, multimedia-driven, service-oriented, and community coordinated viewpoints. Section 7 discusses the future trends towards the evolution of CCM. Finally, Section 8 draws a conclusion for the chapter.

Figure 1. Middleware ontology in the context of CCM

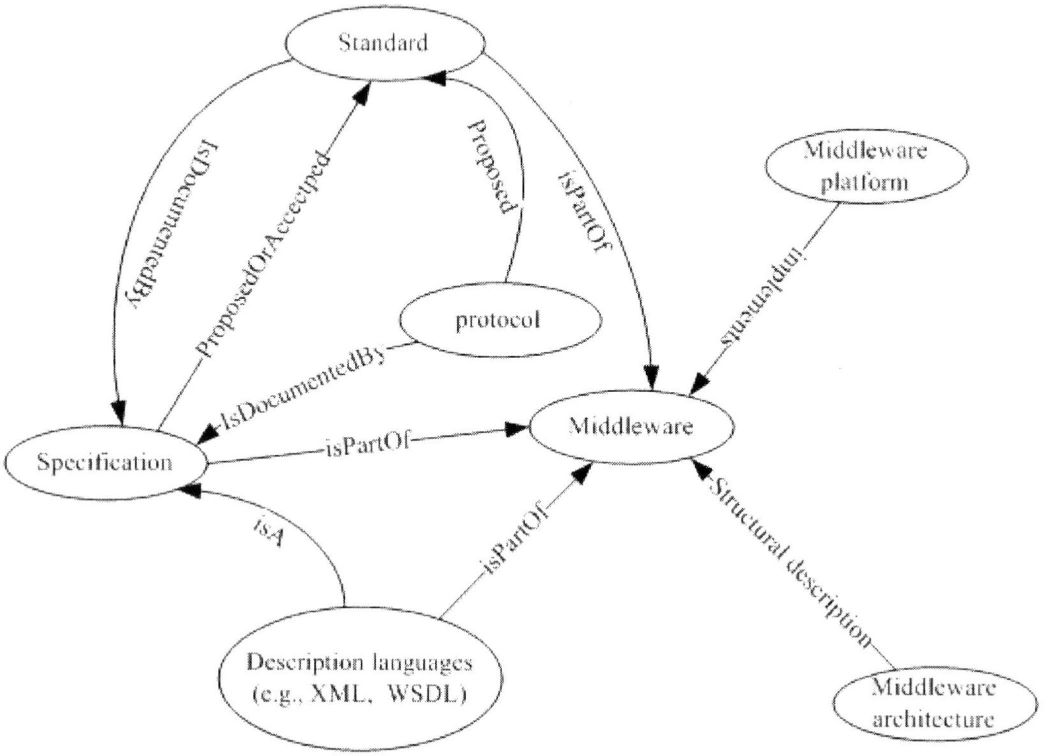

DEFINITIONS

This section specifies a few concepts relevant to the CCM paradigm and CCM middleware as follows:**Multimedia:** Represents a synchronized presentation of bundled media types, such as text, graphic, image, audio, video, and animation.**Community:** Is generally defined as groups of limited number of people held together by common interests and understandings, a sense of obligation and possibly trust (Bender, 1982).**Community Coordinated Multimedia:** (CCM) system maintains a virtual community for the consumption of CCM multimedia elements, i.e. both content generated by end users and content from professional multimedia provider (e.g., Video on Demand). The consumption involves a series of interrelated multimedia intensive processes such as content creation, aggregation, annotation, etc. In the context of CCM, these interrelated multimedia intensive processes are encapsulated into Web services, instead of multimedia applications, namely multimedia intensive services, briefly multimedia services.**Standard:** Refers to an accepted industry standard. Protocol refers to a set of governing rules in communication between computing endpoints. A specification is a document that proposes a standard. **Middleware:** is the key technology which integrates two or more distributed software units and allows them to exchange data via heterogeneous computing and communication devices (Quasy, 2004). In this chapter, middleware is perceived as an additional software layer in OSI model encapsulating knowledge from presentation and session layers, consisting of standards, specifications, forms, and protocols for multimedia, service, mobility and community computing and communication. Figure 1 illustrates the middleware ontology with relationship to other defined concepts.

Figure 2. An example scenario for CCM as presented in (Zhou et al, 2008b)

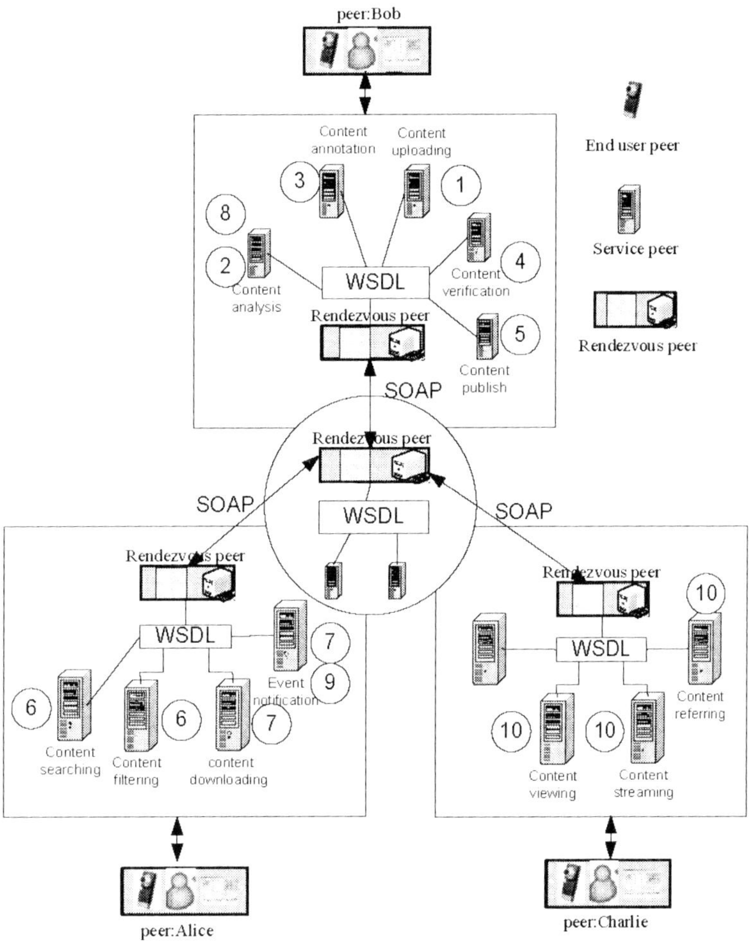

USAGE SCENARIO

CCM envisions that user experiences are enriched and extended by the collaborative consumption of multimedia services with the interplay of two key enabling technologies of web services and P2P technology. Figure 2 illustrates the CCM paradigm. The use sequence about the CCM paradigm is given in (Zhou et al, 2008b).

CCM MIDDLEWARE REQUIREMENTS

Figure 3 illustrates the four major viewpoints which provide a cooperating outline for the specification of CCM middleware which supports the emerging CCM application solutions (e.g. mobile content creation, online learning, collaborative multimedia creation, etc.). These four viewpoints are mobility-aware, multimedia-driven, service-oriented, and community-coordinated perspectives. The requirements associ-

Figure 3. CCM middleware viewpoints

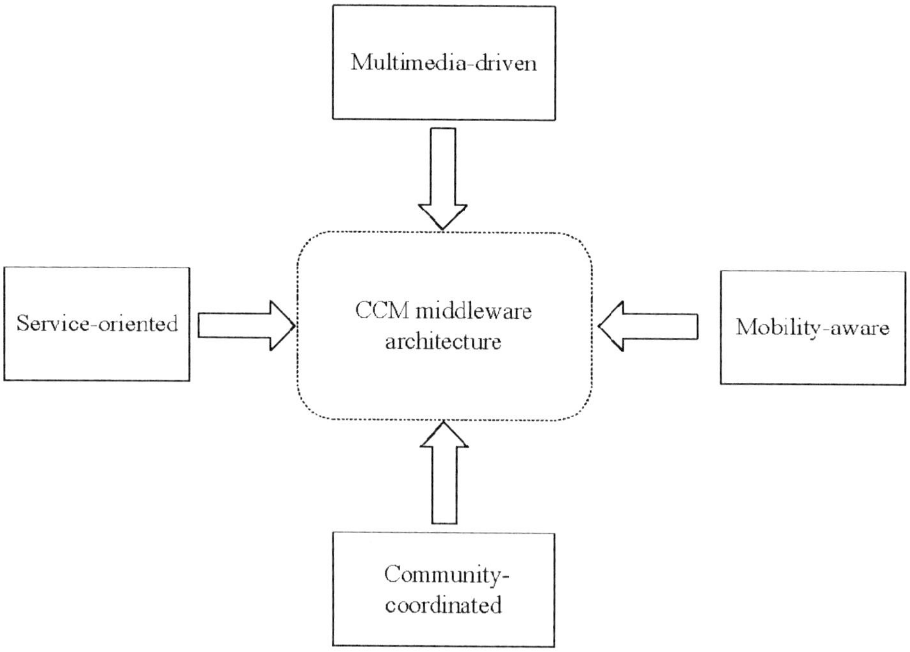

ated with each viewpoint comprises the complete requirements for CCM middleware specifications.

Mobility-aware CCM. Ubiquitous computing is becoming prominent as small portable devices, and the wireless networks to support them, have become more and more pervasive. In the CCM system, content can be consumed, created, analyzed, aggregated, and transmitted over mobile devices. Also services can be requested, discovered, invoked and interacted over mobile devices. Examples of such mobile devices are portable computers, PDAs, and mobile phones. Mobile communication is the key technical enabler allowing mobile service computing to deliver services, including conventional voice and video on demand over broadband 3G connection. In the last decade, the mobile communication industry has been one of the most flourishing sectors within the ICT industry. Mobile communication is a solution that enables flexible integration of smart mobile phones, such as camera phones, to other computer systems. Smart phones make it possible to access services anywhere and anytime. In the context of mobility-aware CCM, mobile communication systems and infrastructures play an important role in delivering services cost-efficiently and high QoS-guaranteed to support the users' activities on the air. Therefore, the CCM middleware systems must provide context management, dynamic configuration, connection management, etc. to facilitate anytime, anywhere service access.

Multimedia-driven CCM. Digital convergence between audiovisual media, high-speed networks and smart devices becomes a reality and helps make media content more directly manageable by computers (ERCIM, 2005). It presents new opportunities for CCM applications to enhance, enrich and extend user daily experiences. The CCM applications are multimedia intensive. These applications include multimedia content creation, annotation, aggregation, and sharing. The CCM is expected to facilitate multimedia content management through multimedia-intensive automatic or semi-automatic applications (e.g. automatic content classification and annotation), or services. The nature of multimedia-driven CCM yields the requirements for multimedia representation, compression, and streaming delivery.

Service-driven CCM. The CCM system is expected to employ service-oriented computing (Krafzig et al, 2005, Erl, 2005) and content delivery networking (Vakali et al, 2003, Dixit et al, 2004) technologies for delivering content by broadcasting (e.g. music, TV, radio). By providing Web sites and tool suites, the CCM system enables all end users to access to content and services with desired quality and functionality. This vision takes advantages of the nature of registration, discoverability, composibility, open standards, etc. in service orientation approach. Service-orientation perceives functions as distinct service units, which can be registered, discovered, and invoked over a network. Technically, a service consists of a contract, one or more interfaces, and an implementation (Krafzig et al, 2005). The service orientation principles for modern software system design are gained and promoted through contemporary service-oriented architecture (SOA) by introducing standardizations to service registration, semantic messaging platforms, and Web services technology. Therefore the CCM middleware system must provide description, discovery, and interaction mechanisms in the context of multimedia services. Multimedia services dealing with multimedia computing such as content annotation are networked and made available by service discovery.

Community-coordinated CCM. The CCM attempts to build an online community for end users and service providers by providing the means of managing community memberships and member's contacts. As illustrated in the scenario, end user Bob aggregates content with information that is relevant within a common subject and sends it to his friend Alice in the community who are also interested in it. Moreover, the CCM attempts to provide the end user with individual and customized content and service by managing CCM users' preferences and profiles. The CCM usually has a large user base for sharing multimedia. The user base is usually organized in terms of specific interest ties and membership management. In order to succeed community coordination in multimedia sharing, the CCM middleware system must provide standards and principles which govern the participation of peers into the community (peer management), preference management, and various messaging models.

MIDDLEWARE ARCHITECTURE FOR CCM

Based on the analysis of the middleware requirements from the four viewpoints, a middleware architecture for CCM is introduced in Figure 4. It comprises of four layered categories which abstract the components for computing and communication into multimedia, service, mobility, and community management perspectives. From top to bottom, the CCM middleware architecture consists of the Community-coordinated, Service-oriented, Multimedia-driven, and Mobility-aware layers. Each layer is a collection of related standards and specifications that provides services to manage multimedia data representations, sessions, and end-to-end collaboration in a heterogeneous computer environment (Table 1).

The lowest layer is the mobility-aware middleware, which aims to provide multimedia service access to the multimedia user equipped with a portable device anytime and anywhere. Due to the limitations on the terminal heterogeneity, network resource, and node mobility, this mobility-aware middleware layer meets various requirements such as management of context, resource, and connections.

The second layer is multimedia-driven middleware, which establishes the context of video and audio representation, encoding standards, and communications protocol for audio, video, and data. In this sense, the multimedia-driven middleware layer contains specifications and standards for multimedia representation and multimedia communication.

Figure 4. The middleware architecture for CCM

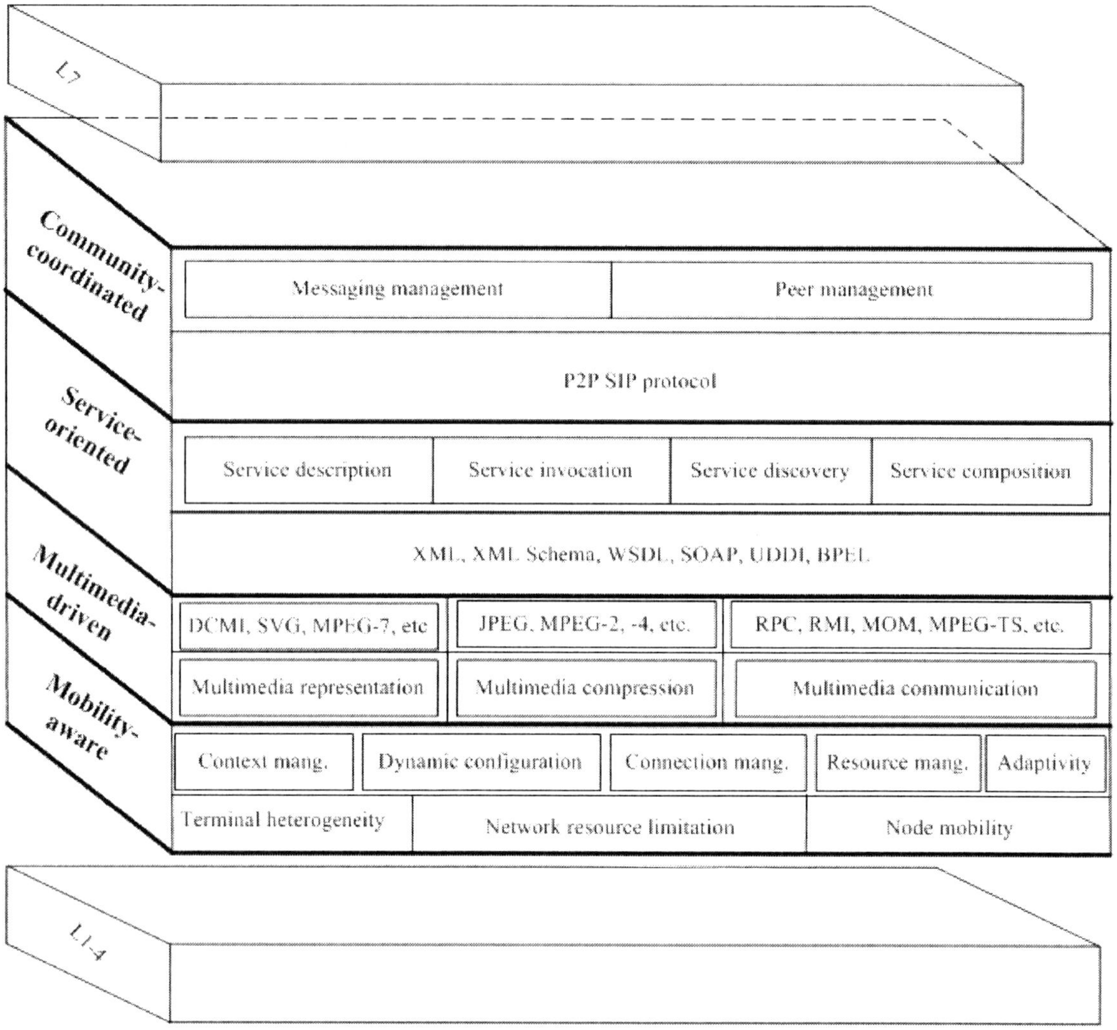

Table 1. Overview of the middleware architecture for CCM

Middleware layer	Specification	Keywords	Related CCM viewpoints
Mobility-aware	Context management, connection management, dynamic configuration, and adaptivity	Context-awareness, network connection, mobile nodes	Mobility and pervasiveness-aware CCM
Multimedia-driven	Multimedia representation, compression, and communication	Multimedia description language, audio, image, video codec, and multimedia streaming	Multimedia-driven CCM
Service-oriented	Service description languages, messaging formats, discovery mechanisms	Service description, service discovery, service composition	Service-oriented CCM
Community-coordinated	Principles and rules for grouping and messaging management	Peer, group, messaging modes, etc.	Community-coordinated CCM

The third layer is service-oriented middleware, which comprises of specifications and standards which allow traditional software applications to exchange data with one another as they participate in multimedia business processes. These specifications include XML, SOAP, WSDL, UDDI, etc. By using service-oriented middleware, the traditional multimedia applications are transformed into multimedia services which are made accessible over a network and can be combined and reused in the development of multimedia applications.

The top layer is community-coordinated middleware, which establishes the technical context that allows any peer connected to a network to exchange messages and collaborate independently of the underlying network topology. This ultimately leads to the idea of creating a community-coordinated multimedia communication environment for social, professional, educational, or other purposes.

SURVEY IN MIDDLEWARE FOR CCM

This section aims to elaborate the middleware layers identified above. On the one hand, this section describes the state of the art of middleware with respect to four major viewpoints, i.e. multimedia-driven, mobility-aware, service-oriented, and community-coordinated CCM. On the other hand, this section presents a feasible and integrated middleware solution to meet the generic CCM requirements specified in Section 4.

MIDDLEWARE FOR MOBILITY-AWARE CCM

Limitations and Requirements

The rapid growth of wireless technologies and the development of smaller and smaller portable devices have led to the widespread use of mobile computing. Any user, equipped with a portable device, is able to access any service at anytime and anywhere. Mobile access to distributed applications and services brings with it a great number of new issues. The limitations caused by the inherent characteristics of mobility are as follows:

- Terminal heterogeneity (Gaddah et al, 2008). Mobile devices usually have diverse physical capabilities, e.g. CPU processing, storage capacity, power consumption, etc. For example, laptops own much more storage capacity and provide faster CPU processing capability, etc., while pocket PCs and mobile phones usually have much less available resources. Though the mobile terminal technology has been progressed promptly in the recent years, it is still impossible to make mobile devices as competitive as fixed terminals. Hence, middleware should be designed to achieve optimal resource utilization.
- Network resource limitation. Compared with fixed networks, the performance of wireless networks (GPRS, UMTS, Beyond 3G networks, Wi-Fi/WiMAX, HiperLAN, Bluetooth, etc.) vary significantly depending on various protocols and technologies. Meanwhile, mobile devices may encounter sharp drop in network bandwidth, high interference, or temporary disconnection when moving around different areas. Therefore, the middleware should be designed in a way that takes into account intrinsically the optimization of the limited network resource.

- Mobility. According to the node mobility, when mobile devices move from one place to another, they will have to deal with different types of networks, services, and security policies. In turn, this requires applications to behave accordingly to handle various dynamic changes of the environment parameters. Henceforth, the design of middleware should take into consideration the mobility of nodes as well.

Various requirements of middleware for mobility-aware CCM are as follows:

- Context management. The characteristics of mobile networks in the CCM environment are the intermittent network connection and limited network bandwidth. Disconnection can happen frequently, either by active reason, i.e. saving power, or passive reason, temporary uncoverage or high interference. In order to deal with the disconnection effectively and efficiently, the context of middleware should be disclosed to the upper application layer instead of being hidden from it to make the application development much easier. Bellavista (Bellavista et al, 2007) summarized the context in a mobile computing environment as three different categories: network context, device context, and user context. The network context consists of the adopted wireless technology, available bandwidth, addressing protocol, etc. The device context includes details on the status of the available resources, such as CPU, batteries, memory, etc. The user context, in its turn, is composed of information related to the location, preferences and QoS requirement of the user.
- Dynamic reconfiguration (Gaddah et al, 2008). During the CCM application lifetime, dynamic changes in infrastructure facilities, e.g. the availability of certain services, will require the application behavior to be altered accordingly. Therefore, dynamic reconfiguration is needed in such environment. It can be achieved by adding a new functionality or changing an existing one at the CCM application runtime. For the purpose of supporting dynamic reconfiguration, middleware should be able to detect changes happening in the available resources and adopt corresponding approaches to deal with it. Reflective middleware is the widespread solution adopted to solve this problem.
- Connection management. User mobility and intermittent wireless signals result in the frequent disconnection and reconnection of mobile devices, which is exceptional in fixed distributed systems. Therefore, middleware for mobility-aware CCM should adopt different connection management mechanism from fixed distributed systems. Asynchronous communication mechanism is usually used to decouple the client from the server, with which tuple space system is one of the typical solutions. Another issue related to connection management is the provision of services based on the concept of session. In this case, the proxy can be adopted to hide the disconnection from the service layer.
- Resource management. Mobile devices are characterized by their limited resources, such as battery, CPU, memory, etc. Henceforth, mobile middleware for CCM should be lightweight enough to avoid overloading the mobile devices. Currently, middleware platforms designed for fixed distributed systems, e.g. CORBA, are too heavy to run on mobile devices as they usually have a number of functionalities which are not necessarily needed in resource-limited devices. Modular middleware design is adopted widely to make the middleware more lightweight.
- Adaptability. In mobile CCM, adaptability mainly refers to the ability to adapt to context changes dynamically. According to the currently available resources, adaptability allows middleware to

optimize the system behavior by choosing the corresponding protocol suite that better suits the current environment, integrating new functionalities and behaviors into the system, and so on.

STATE OF THE ART IN MIDDLEWARE FOR MOBILITY-AWARE CCM

Traditional middleware for fixed distributed systems are too heavy to be used in mobile computing environments. In order to provide new solutions, the research work has been progressed along two distinct directions in the last decade (Cotroneo et al, 2008): (1) extending traditional middleware implementations with primitive mobile-enabled capabilities (e.g. Wireless-CORBA (Kangasarju, 2008)), and (2) proposing middleware that adopts mobile-enabled computing models (e.g. Lime (Murphy et al, 2001)). The former adopts a more effective computing model, but does not effectively overcome the intrinsic limitation of the synchronous remote procedure call; the latter adopts decoupled interaction mechanisms, but fails in providing a high level and well understood computing model abstraction (Migliaccio, 2006, Quasy, 2004). Following the similar categories, we divide middleware for mobility-aware CCM into four categories: extended traditional middleware, reflective middleware, tuple space middleware, and context-aware middleware.

Extending traditional middleware. To be able to operate within existing fixed networks, object-oriented middleware has been proposed to mobile environments. Wireless CORBA is a CORBA specification in Wireless Access and Terminal Mobility (OMG, 2008). The overall system architecture is divided into three separate domains: home domain, terminal domain, and visited domain. In ALICE (Haahr et al, 1999), in order to support client/server architecture in nomadic environments, mobile devices with Windows CE operating system and GSM sensors have been adopted. The main focus of the existing examples of extending traditional middleware is on the provision of services from a back-bone network to the network-edge, i.e. mobile devices. Therefore, the main concerns are how to deal with connectivity and exchange messages. However, in cases where the networks are unstructured and the services have to be provided by the mobile devices, traditional middleware does not work well and new paradigms have to be put forward. This has motivated the birth of e.g. reflective middleware, tuple space middleware, and context-aware middleware.

Reflective middleware. The primary motivation of reflective middleware is to increase its adaptability to the changing environment. A reflective system consists of two levels referred to as meta-level and base-level. The former performs computation on the objects residing in the lower levels, the latter performs computation on the application domain entities (Gaddah et al, 2008). Open-ORB (Blair et al, 2002) and Globe (Steen et al, 1999) are two examples of middleware which utilized the concept of reflection.

Tuple space middleware. The characteristics of wireless propagation environment make the synchronous communication mechanism, typical in most of the traditional distributed systems, not suitable for mobile applications. One solution for this is the so-called tuple space. A Tuple space is a globally shared, associatively addressed memory space that is organized as a bag of tuples (Ciancarini, 1996). Client processes can create the tuples by utilizing write operation and then retrive the tuples by read operation. LIME (Murphy et al, 2001), TSpaces (Wyckoff et al, 1998), JavaSpace (Bishop et al, 2002) are examples of the tuple space based systems.

Context-aware middleware. Mobile systems are characterized by the dynamic execution context due to the mobility of the mobile devices. The context information has to be exposed to the application layer to make it adaptable to the corresponding changes which happen in the lower-levels. Context-aware computing was first proposed by (Schilit et al, 1994, Haahr et al, 1999). After that, lots of research inter-

Table 2. Overview of standards and specifications for multimedia representation

Specification	Key notes	Role in CCM
DCMI	Element, qualifier, application, profile	Document description
DICOM	Image specific	Image specific
SMDL	Music data, SGML-based	Music data
MULL	Course, XML-based	Multimedia course preparation
MRML	Multimedia, XML-based	Multimedia
EDL	Sessions, XML-based	Session description
SMIL	Audiovisual, XML-based	AV data
SMEF	Media, SMEF-DM	Media description
P/Meta	Metadata, XML-based, P/Meta scheme	Metadata framework
SMPTE	Metadata, XML-based	Metadata framework
MXF	Audio-visual, SMPTE-based	AV data description
SVG	Describing 2D graphics, XML-based	Describing 2D graphics
TV-Anytime	Audio-visual, descriptor, preferences	AV data description
MPEG-7	Multimedia content data, interactive, integrated audio-visual	Multimedia description
MPEG-21	Common framework, multimedia delivery chain, digital item	Common multimedia description framework

ests are plunged into this field, but most of them focus on the location awareness, e.g. Nexus (Fritsch et al, 2000) was designed to provide various kinds of location-aware applications. Some other approaches investigated the feasibility of utilizing reflection in the context of mobile systems to offer dynamic context-awareness and adaptation mechanisms (Roman et al, 2001).

MIDDLEWARE FOR MULTIMEDIA-DRIVEN CCM

In order to support multimedia content transmission via various networks, the issues of semantic multimedia representation, multimedia storage capacity, and the delivery time delay must be taken into consideration. Middleware for multimedia-driven CCM aims to abstract the knowledge about multimedia representation and communication, which comprises of specifications and standards for multimedia representation, compression, and communication.

STANDARDS FOR MULTIMEDIA REPRESENTATION AND COMPRESSION

Table 2 presents an overview of standards and specifications for multimedia representation. A brief description about these specifications is given as follows and detailed in corresponding references.

Dublin Core Metadata Initiative (DCMI). In the Dublin Core (DC) (Stuart et al, 2008), the description of the information resources is created using Dublin Core elements, and may be refined or further explained by a qualifier. Qualification schemes are used for ensuring a minimum level of metadata interoperability. No formal syntax rules are defined. DCMI evolution involves in extending the element

Table 3. Some compression standards for multimedia

Specification	Key notes	Role in CCM
JPEG	Image, discrete cosine transform-based, codec specification, ISO standard	Compression for single images
JPEG-2000	Image, wavelet-based, greater decompression time than JPEG	Compression for single images
MPEG-1	Lossy video and audio compression, MP3, ISO standard	Compression for video and audio
MPEG-2	Lossy video and audio compression, popular DTV format, ISO standard	Compression for video and audio
MPEG-4	AV compression for web, CD distribution, voice and TV applications.	Compression for video and audio

set, description of images, standardization, special interests, and metadata scheme. The Digital Imaging and Communications in Medicine (DICOM) standard (ACR, 2008) is used for the exchange of images and related information. The DICOM standard has several supports, including the support for image exchange between senders and receivers, support for retrieving image information, and image management. Standard Music Description Language (SMDL) (ISO/IEC, 2008) defines an architecture for the representation of music information, either alone or in conjunction with text, graphics, or other information needed for publishing or business purposes. MUltimedia Lecture description Language (MULL) (Polak et al, 2001) enables to modify a remote presentation and control this presentation. Multimedia Retrieval Markup Language (MRML) (MRML, 2008) aims to unify access to multimedia retrieval and manage software component in order to extend their capabilities. Event Description Language (EDL) (Rodriguez, 2002) describes advanced multimedia sessions for supporting multimedia services management, provision and operation. The Synchronized Multimedia Integration Language (SMIL) (SMIL, 2005) enables simple authoring of interactive audiovisual presentations, which integrate streaming audio and video with images, text, or any other media type. Standard Media Exchange Framework (SMEF) (BBC, 2005) is defined by BBC to support and enable media asset production, management, and delivery. P/Meta (Hopper, 2002) is developed for content exchange by providing the P/Meta Scheme which consists of common attributes and transaction sets for P/Meta members such as content creators and distributors. Metadata Dictionary & Sets Registry (SMPTE) (SMPTE, 2004) creates the Metadata Dictionary (MDD) and a sets registry. The MDD dynamic document encompasses all the data elements considered relevant by the industry. The sets registry describes the business purpose and the structure of the sets. The Material eXchange Format (MXF) (Pro-MPEG, 2005) targets at supporting the interchange of audio-visual material with associated data and metadata. Scalable Vector Graphics (SVG) (Watt et al, 2003) describes 2D graphics and graphical applications in XML. It contains two parts: (1) an XML-based file format and (2) a programming API for graphical applications. TV-Anytime metadata (TV-Anytime, 2005) consists of the attractors/descriptors used, e.g. in Electronic Program Guides (EPG), or in Web pages to describe content. Multimedia Content Description Interface (MPEG-7) (ISO/IEC, 2003) describes the multimedia content data that supports some degree of interpretation of the information meaning, which can be passed onto, or accessed by a device or a computer code. The MPEG-21 multimedia framework (Burnett, 2006) identifies and defines the key elements needed to support the multimedia delivery chain.

Table 3 presents widely used compression techniques that are in part competitive and in part complementary. The details about the standards and specifications are given as follows.

Table 4. Protocols and specifications for multimedia communication

Middleware	Specification
Remote Procedure Call (RPC)	Procedure-oriented call, synchronous interaction model
Remote Method Invocation (RMI)	Object-oriented RPC, object-oriented references
Message Oriented Middleware	Message oriented communication, asynchronous interaction model
Stream-oriented communication	Continuous asynchronous, synchronous, isochronous, and QoS-specified multimedia transmission

ISO JPEG standard (William et al, 1992) defines how an image is compressed into a stream of bytes using discrete cosine transform and decompressed back into an image. It also defines the file format used to contain that stream. JPEG 2000 (Taubman et al, 2001) is an image compression standard advanced from JPEG. It is based on wavelet-based compression, which requires longer decompression time than JPEG and allows more sophisticated progressive downloads. MPEG-1 (Harte et al, 2006) is a standard for lossy compression of video and audio. It has been used for example as the standard for video CDs, but later video disc formats adopt newer codecs. It also contains the well-known MP3 audio compression. MPEG-2 (Harte et al, 2006) describes several lossy video and audio compression methods for various purposes. It is widely used in the terrestrial, cable, and satellite digital television formats. MPEG-4 (Harte et al, 2006) defines newer compression techniques for audio and video data. H.264/AVC (Richardson et al, 2003) is also known as MPEG-4 Part 10 for video compression, which is widely utilized in modern mobile TV standards and specifications. Audio counterpart is AAC, defined in MPEG-4 Part 3.

MIDDLEWARE FOR MULTIMEDIA COMMUNICATION

The CCM multimedia applications support the view that local multimedia systems expand towards distributed solutions. Applications such as multimedia creation, aggregation, consumption, and others require high speed networks with a high transfer rate. Multimedia communication sets several requirements on services and protocols, e.g. processing of AV data needs to be bounded by deadlines or by a time interval. Multimedia communication standards and protocols can be categorized into Remote Procedure Call (RPC) based (Nelson, 1981, Tanenbaum et al, 2008), Message Oriented Middleware (MOM) based (Tanenbaum et al, 2008, Quasy, 2004), Remote Method Invocation (RMI) based (Tanenbaum et al, 2008), and Stream based (Tanenbaum et al, 2008, Halsall, 2000). They define the middleware alternatives for multimedia communication (Table 4). Details about the protocols and specifications are given below with relevant references.

Remote procedure call (RPC) (Nelson, 1981, Tanenbaum et al, 2008) allows a software program to invoke a subroutine or procedure to execute in another computer. In the remote procedure call, the programmer writes the subroutine call code whether it is local or remote. Remote Method Invocation (RMI) (Nelson, 1981, Tanenbaum et al, 2008) is another RPC paradigm based on distributed objects. In the case of Java RMI, the programmer can create applications consisting of Java objects from different host computers. Message-oriented middleware (MOM) (Tanenbaum et al, 2008, Quasy, 2004) typically supports asynchronous calls between the client and server. With the message queue mechanism, MOM reduces the involvement of application developers. For example, applications send a subjective mes-

Figure 5. The relationship between Web service technologies

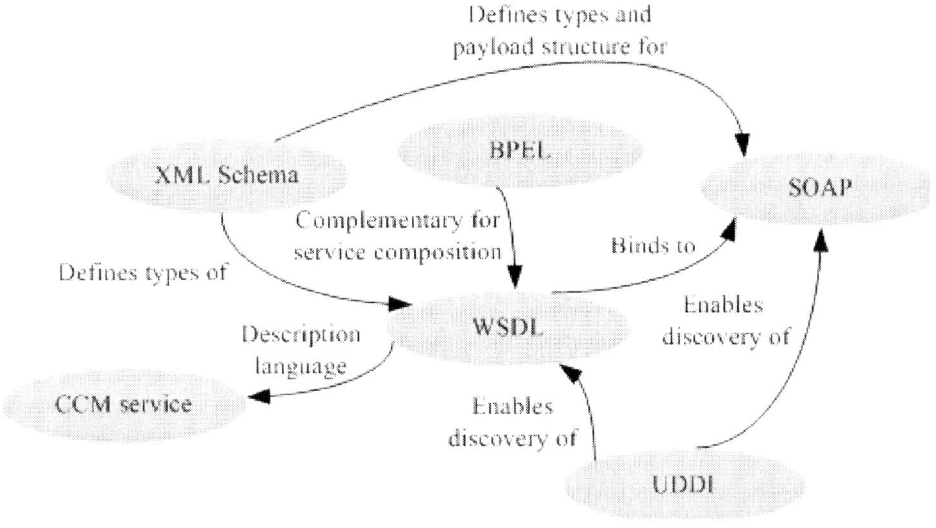

sage to logical contact points or indicate theirs interest for a specific type of message. As examined in CCM scenario, CCM multimedia communication involves multiple media types of audio and video. It becomes necessary for CCM to use stream-oriented middleware for streaming multimedia which purposes to support for continuous asynchronous, synchronous, isochronous, and QoS-specified media transmission. Stream-oriented middleware (Tanenbaum et al, 2008) examples are MPEG-TS (Harte, 2006), Resource ReSerVation Protocol (RSVP) (Liu et al, 2006), and Real-time Transport Protocol (RTP) (Perkins, 2003), etc. The MPEG-TS (Harte, 2006) is designed to allow multiplexing of digital video and audio and to synchronize the output. The RSVP (Liu et al, 2006) is a transport layer protocol designed to reserve resources across a network for an integrated services Internet. The RTP (Ray, 2003) defines a standardized packet format for delivering audio and video over the Internet.

MIDDLEWARE FOR SERVICE-ORIENTED CCM

This section discusses middleware for service-oriented CCM, which consists of standards and specifications which govern the conversion of conventional multimedia applications into a service-oriented computing environment. These standards and specification are based on several notable Web service technologies, i.e. XML (Ray, 2003), WSDL (WSDL, 2005, Erl, 2005), UDDI (UDDI, 2004), SOAP (SOAP, 2003), and BPEL (Thatte, 2003). See Figure 5.

As a successor to HTML, the eXtensible Markup Language (XML) (Ray, 2003) is used to represent information objects consisting of elements (e.g. tags and attributes). XML defines the syntax for markup languages. XML Schema allows definition of languages in a machine readable format. Web Services Description Language (WSDL) (WSDL, 2005) is an XML-based language for describing Web services in a machine understandable form. WSDL describes and exposes a web service using major elements of portType, message, types, and binding. The portType element describes the operations performed by a web service. The message element defines the data elements of an operation. The types element defines the data type used by the web service. The binding element defines the message format and protocol details for each port. Universal Description Discovery and Integration (UDDI) (UDDI, 2004) is regarded as a specification of the service, service definition, and metadata "hub' for service-oriented architecture. Various structural templates are provided by UDDI for representing data about business entities, their services, and the mechanisms for governing them. The UDDI upper service model consists of a BusinessEntity (who), a BusinessService (what), a BindingTemplate (how and where) and a tModel (service interoperability). XML Schema Language is used in UDDI to formalize its data structures. Simple Object Access Protocol (SOAP) (SOAP, 2003) is regarded as a protocol for exchanging XML-based messages over computer networks. One of the most common SOAP messaging patterns is the Remote Procedure Call (RPC) pattern, in which the client communicates with the server by sending a request/response message. Business Process Execution Language for Web Services (BPEL, also WS-BPEL or BPEL4WS) (Thatte, 2003) provides a flexible way to define business processes comprised of services. BPEL supports executable processes and abstract processes. Executable processes allow specifying the exact details of business processes and can be executed by an orchestration engine. The process descriptions for business protocols are called abstract processes, which allow to specifying the public message exchange between parties. With BPEL, complex business processes can be defined in an algorithmic manner (Thatte, 2003).

MIDDLEWARE FOR COMMUNITY-COORDINATED CCM

In the CCM scenario, end users' experience is enriched and extended by community-coordinated multimedia. In the case of community-coordinated TV channel, TV viewers can watch video clips which are uploaded by themselves, add comments and even vote for them. The user preference profile is maintained in the community coordinator. The moderator moderates the incoming videos and compiles a playlist for the TV program. The moderator also filters the incoming comments and chooses which can be shown on the program. This section discusses standards and principles that govern the participation of peers into the community (peer management); messaging models, e.g. point-to-point, publish/subscribe, multicast and broadcast, and profile management, P2P SIP new features, and coordination, etc.

CLASSIFICATION OF COMMUNITIES

From the technical point of view, user communities can be classified into private and public communities, as done in the project JXTA (Oaks et al, 2002). When taking the purpose of communities into account, these two fundamental classes could be further divided at least into social, commercial, and professional communities (Koskela et al, 2008) that are somewhat paid attention to in an attribute-based system.

In practice, there will probably be situations where the members of a public community do not want to reveal their memberships to nodes outside of their sub-community. These kinds of communities, where a part of the members do not publish their membership to the main overlay, are called partially private communities. However, to maintain the community, at least one of the peer members must publish their membership to the main overlay (Koskela, 2008).

REQUIREMENTS FOR COMMUNITY MIDDLEWARE

The requirements of middleware for community are initially specified as messaging management and peer management.

Messaging management. Messaging management is crucial for the middleware for community, as it provides the basic communication methods based on the messaging models.

Peer management. Peer management functionality manages the formation of the peer group, the scale of the community, the joining and leaving of the peers.

SURVEY ON MIDDLEWARE TECHNOLOGY FOR COMMUNITY-COORDINATED CCM

Messaging models. A solid understanding of the available messaging models is crucial to understand the unique capabilities it provides. Four main message models are commonly available, unicast, broadcast, multicast, anycast. The unicast model, also known as point-to-point messaging model, provides a straightforward exchanging of messages between software entities. Broadcast is a very powerful mechanism used to disseminate information between anonymous message consumers and producers. It provides a one-to-many distribution mechanism where the number of receivers is not limited. The multicast model (Pairot et al, 2005) is a variation of the broadcast. It works by sending a multicast message to a specific group of members. The main difference between broadcast and multicast is that multicast just sends messages to the members of a subscribed group, while the broadcast sends messages to everyone without any membership limitation. The broadcast model can also be implemented as a publish/subscribe messaging model so that it resembles multicast. The anycast model means sending anycast notification to a group, which will make the sender's closest member in the network answer, as long as it satisfies a condition (Pairot et al, 2005). This feature is very useful for retrieving object replicas from the service network.

Peer management protocols. For the purpose of interoperability and other peer management functionalities, Internet Engineering Task Force (IETF) founded a Peer-to-Peer Session Initiation Protocol (P2PSIP) working group recently. The P2PSIP working group is chartered to develop protocols and mechanisms for the use of the Session Initiation Protocol (SIP) in settings where the service of establishing and managing sessions is principally handled by a collection of intelligent endpoints, rather than centralized servers, as in SIP as currently deployed (P2PSIP, 2008). There are two different kinds of nodes in P2PSIP networks: 'P2PSIP peers' and 'P2PSIP clients'. P2PSIP peers participate the P2PSIP overlay networks, provides routing information to other peers, etc. P2PSIP clients do not participate the P2PSIP overlay networks, but instead utilize the service provided by the peers to locate users and resources. In this way, P2PSIP can determine the correct destination of SIP requests by this distributed mechanism. The other functionalities, e.g. session management, messaging, and presence functions are performed using conventional SIP. The work on the P2PSIP working group is still work-in-progress, but it has put forward some peer protocols, such as RELOAD (Jennings et al, 2008), SEP (Jiang et al, 2008), etc. for the management of peers, and two client protocols (Pascual et al, 2008, Song, 2008) to manage the clients. Furthermore, JXTA also supports community concept which it calls as 'group'. It provides a dedicated Membership Service to manage the group related issues.

FUTURE TRENDS

The trend of CCM is towards delivering multimedia services in a customized quality over heterogeneous network, which enables multimedia services to be adapted to any IP-based mobile and P2P content delivery networks. The future work of middleware on CCM is identified as the follows:

- Context-aware middleware. Context-aware middleware provides mobile applications with necessary knowledge about the execution context in order to make them adapt to dynamic changes in mobile condition. But most of the current systems just focus on the location awareness. Thus, there is no middleware which can fully support all the requirements of mobile applications. Further research is still needed.
- QoS-aware middleware. The strong motivation to QoS-aware middleware is initiated by meeting stringent QoS requirements such as predictability, latency, efficiency, scalability, dependability, and security. The goal is to help accelerate the software process by making it easier to integrate parts together and shielding developers from many inherent and accidental complexities, such as platform and language heterogeneity, resource management, and fault tolerance (Quasy, 2004). The extension of Web service specification, i.e. WS-* specifications (Erl, 2005), provide a means to assert control over QoS management.
- Middleware for multimedia service delivery over 4G networks. The motivation to 4G network operators is initiated by providing multimedia service for mobile devices. Incorporating IMS (Camarillo, 2006) into mobile multimedia services is part of the vision for evolving mobile networks beyond GSM.
- Middleware for multimedia service delivery over P2P SIP. P2P technologies have been widely used on the Internet in file sharing and other applications including VoIP, Instant Message, and presence. This research continues the study of community middleware and extends capabilities of delivering multimedia services to mobile devices over P2P network, especially, by employing SIP session management.

CONCLUSION

Community Coordinated Multimedia presents a novel use paradigm for consuming multimedia through requesting multimedia-intensive Web services via diverse terminal devices, converged networks, and heterogeneous platforms within a virtual, open and collaborative community. In order to reach the paradigm, this chapter focused on addressing the key enabling technology of middleware for CCM. It started with the concept definition relevant with CCM and the specification of middleware ontology in the context of CCM. Then a generic CCM scenario was described and the requirements for CCM middleware were analyzed with respect to the characteristics of mobility-aware, multimedia-driven, service-oriented, and community-coordinated CCM. A middleware architecture for CCM was introduced to address the requirements from four viewpoints. Each part of the middleware architecture for CCM was surveyed. Finally, the future trends in the evolution of CCM middleware were discussed.

ACKNOWLEDGMENT

This work is being carried out in the EUREKA ITEA2 CAM4Home project funded by the Finnish Funding Agency for Technology and Innovation (Tekes).

REFERENCES

p2psip working group. (2008). *Peer-to-Peer Session Initiation Protocol Specification*. Retrieved June 15th, 2008, from http://www.ietf.org/html.charters/p2psip-charter.html

ACR-NEMA. (2005). *DICOM (Digital Image and Communications in Medicine)*. Retrieved June 15th, 2008, from http://medical.nema.org/

BBC. (2005). *SMEF- Standard Media Exchange Framework*. Retrieved June 15th, 2008, from http://www.bbc.co.uk/guidelines/smef/. 15th June, 2008.

Bellavista, P., & Corradi, A. (2007). *The Handbook of Mobile Middleware*. New York: Auerbach publications.

Bender, T. (1982). *Community and Social Change in America*. Baltimore, MD: The Johns Hopkins University Press.

Bishop, P., & Warren, N. (2002). *JavaSpaces in Practice*. New York: Addison Wesley.

Blair, G. S., Coulson, G., & Blair, L. DuranLimon, H., Grace, P., Moreira, R., & Parlavantzas, N. (2002). Reflection, self-awareness and self-healing in OpenORB. In *WOSS '02 Proceedings of the First Workshop on Self-Healing Systems*, (pp. 9-14).

Burnett, I. (2006). *MPEG-21: Digital Item Adaptation - Coding Format Independence*, Chichester, UK. Retrieved 15th June, 2008, from http://www.ipsi.fraunhofer.de/delite/projects/mpeg7/Documents/mpeg21-Overview4318.htm#_Toc523031446.

Ciancarini, P. (1996). Coordination Models and Languages as Software Integrators. *SCM Comput. Surv.*, *28*(2), 300–302. doi:10.1145/234528.234732

Cotroneo, D., Migliaccio, A., & Russo, S. (2007). The Esperanto Broker: a communication platform for nomadic computing systems. *Software, Practice & Experience*, *37*(10), 1017–1046. doi:10.1002/spe.794

Dixit, S., & Wu, T. (2004). *Content Networking in the Mobile Internet*. New York: John Wiley & Sons.

ERCIM. (2005). Multimedia Informatics. *ERCIM News, 62*.

Erl, T. (2005). *Service-Oriented Architecture (SOA): Concepts, Technology, and Design*. Upper Saddle River, NJ: Prentice Hall.

Fritsch, D., Klinec, D., & Volz, S. (2000). NEXUS positioning and data management concepts for location aware applications. In the *2nd International Symposium on Telegeoprocessing* (Nice-Sophia-Antipolis, France), (pp. 171-184).

Gaddah, A., & Kunz, T. (2003). *A survey of middleware paradigms for mobile computing. Carleton University and Computing Engineering* [Research Report]. Retrieved June 15th, 2008, from http://www.sce.carleton.ca/wmc/middleware/middleware.pdf

Gonzalo, C., & García-Martín, M.-A. (2006). *The 3G IP Multimedia Subsystem (IMS): Merging the Internet and the Cellular Worlds.* New York: Wiley.

Haahr, M., Cunningham, R., & Cahill, V. (1999). Supporting CORBA applications in a mobile environment. In *MobiCom '99: Proceedings of the 5th Annual ACM/IEEE International Conference on Mobile Computing and Networking,* (pp. 36-47).

Halsall, F. (2000). *Multimedia Communications: Applications, Networks, Protocols and Standards (Hardcover).* New York: Addison Wesley.

Harte, L., Wiblitzhouser, A., & Pazderka, T. (2006). *Introduction to MPEG; MPEG-1, MPEG-2 and MPEG-4.* Fuquay Varina, NC: Althos Publishing.

Hopper, R. (2002). *P/Meta - metadata exchange scheme.* Retrieved June 15th, 2008, from http://www.ebu.ch/trev_290-hopper.pdf

ISO/IEC. (1995). *SMDL (Standard Music Description Language) Overview.* Retrieved June 15th, 2008, from http://xml.coverpages.org/gen-apps.html#smdl

ISO/IEC. (2003). *MPEG-7 Overview.* Retrieved June 15th, 2008, from http://www.chiariglione.org/mpeg/standards/mpeg-7/mpeg-7.htm.

Jennings, C., Lowekamp, B., Rescorla, E., Baset, S., & Schulzrinne, H. (2008). *REsource LOcation And Discovery (RELOAD).* Retrieved June 15th, 2008, from http://tools.ietf.org/id/draft-bryan-p2psip-reload-04.txt.

Jiang, X.-F., Zheng, H.-W., Macian, C., & Pascual, V. (2008). *Service Extensible P2P Peer Protocol.* Retrieved June 15th, 2008, from http://tools.ietf.org/id/draft-jiang-p2psip-sep-01.txt

Kangasharju, J. (2002). *Implementing the Wireless CORBA Specification.* PhD Disertation, Computer Science Department, University of Helsinki, Helsinki, Finland. Retrieved June 15th, 2008, from http://www.cs.helsinki.fi/u/jkangash/laudatur-jjk.pdf

Koskela, T., Kassinen, O., Korhonen, J., Ou, Z., & Ylianttila, M. (2008). Peer-to-Peer Community Management using Structured Overlay Networks. In *the Proc. of International Conference on Mobile Technology, Applications and Systems*, September 10-12, Yilan, Taiwan.

Krafzig, D., Banke, K., & Slama, D. (2005). *Enterprise SOA: Service-Oriented Architecture Best Practices.* Upper Saddle River, NJ: Prentice Hall.

Liu, C., Qian, D., Liu, Y., Li, Y., & Wang, C. (2006). RSVP Context Extraction in IP Mobility Environments. *Vehicular Technology Conference, 2006, VTC 2006-Spring, IEEE 63rd,* (Vol. 2, pp. 756-760).

Matjaz, B. J. (2008). *BPEL and Java*. Retrieved June 15th, 2008, from http://www.theserverside.com/tt/articles/article.tss?l=BPELJava

Migliaccio, A. (2006). *The Design and Development of a Nomadic Computing Middleware: the Esperanto Broker*. PhD Dissertation, Department of Computer and System Engineering, Federico II, University of Naples, Naples, Italy.

MRML. (2003). *MRML- Multimedia Retrieval Markup Language*. Retrieved June 15th, 2008, from http://www.mrml.net/

Murphy, A. L., Picco, G. P., & Roman, G. (2001). LIME: a middleware for physical and logical mobility. *21st International Conference on Distributed Computing Systems,* (pp. 524-533).

Nelson, B. J. (1981). *Remote Procedure Call.* Palo Alto, CA: Xerox - Palo Alto Research Center.

Oaks, S., Traversat, B., & Gong, L. (2002). *JXTA in a Nutshell.* Sebastopol, CA: O'Reilly Media, Inc.

OMG. (2002). *Wireless Access and Terminal Mobility in CORBA Specification*. Retrieved June 15th, 2008, from http://www.info.fundp.ac.be/~ven/CIS/OMG/new%20documents%20from%20OMG%20on%20CORBA/corba%20wireless.pdf

Pairot, C., Garcia, P., Rallo, R., Blat, J., & Gomez Skarmeta, A. F. (2005). The Planet Project: collaborative educational content repositories on structured peer-to-peer grids. *CCGrid 2005, IEEE International Symposium on Cluster Computing and the Grid,* (Vol. 1, pp. 35-42).

Pascual, V., Matuszewski, M., Shim, E., Zheng, H., & Song, Y. (2008). *P2PSIP Clients.* Retrieved June 15th, 2008, from http://tools.ietf.org/id/draft-pascual-p2psip-clients-01.txt

Pennebaker, W. B., & Mitchell, J. L. (1992). *JPEG: Still Image Data Compression Standard (Digital Multimedia Standards).* Berlin: Springer.

Perkins, C. (2003). *RTP: Audio and Video for the Internet.* New York: Addison-Wesley.

Polak, S., Slota, R., Kitowski, J., & Otfinowski, J. (2001). XML-based Tools for Multimedia Course Preparation. *Archiwum Informatyki Teoretycznej i Stosowanej, 13,* 3–21.

Pro-MPEG. (2005). *Material eXchange Format (MXF).* Retrieved 15th June, 2008, from http://www.pro-mpeg.org.

Quasy, H. M. (2004). *Middleware for Communications.* Chichester, UK: John Wiley Sons ltd.

Ray, E. (2003). *Learning XML.* Sebastopol, CA: O'Reilly Media, Inc.

Richardson, I., & Richardson, I. E. G. (2003). *H.264 and MPEG-4 Video Compression: Video Coding for Next Generation Multimedia.* Chichester, UK: Wiley.

Rodriguez, B. (2002). *EDLXML serialization*. Retrieved 15th June, 2008, from download.sybase.com/pdfdocs/prg0390e/prsver39edl.pdf

Roman, M., Kon, F., & Campbell, R. (2001). Reflective Middleware: From your Desk to your Hand. *IEEE Communications Surveys, 2*(5).

Schilit, B., Adams, N., & Want, R. (1994). Context-aware computing applications. In *Proceedings of Mobile Computing Systems and Applications,* (pp. 85-90).

SMIL/ W3C. (2005). *SMIL- Synchronized Multimedia Integration Language.* Retrieved June 15th, 2008 from http://www.w3.org/AudioVideo/

SMPTE. (2004). *Metadata dictionary registry of metadata element descriptions.* Retrieved June 15th, 2008, from http://www.smpte-ra.org/mdd/rp210-8.pdf

SOAP/W3C. (2003). *SOAP Version 1.2 Part 1: Messaging Framework.* Retrieved June 15th, 2008, from Http://www.w3.org/TR/2003/REC-soap12-part1-20030624/

Song, Y., Jiang, X., Zheng, H., & Deng, H. (2008). *P2PSIP Client Protocol.* Retrieved June 15th, 2008, from http://tools.ietf.org/id/draft-jiang-p2psip-sep-01.txt.

Steen, van M., Homburg, P., & Tanenbaum, A. S. (1999). Globe: a wide area distributed system. *Concurrency, IEEE [See also IEEE Parallel & Distributed Technology], 7*, 70-78.

Stuart, W., & Koch, T. (2000). *The Dublin Core Metadata Initiative: Mission, Current Activities, and Future Directions,* (Vol. 6). Retrieved June 15th, 2008, from http:/www/dlib.org/dlib/december00/weibel/12weibel.html

Tanenbaum, A. S., & Steen, M. V. (2008). *Distributed Systems: Principles and Paradigms.* Upper Saddle River, NJ: Prentice Hall.

Taubman, D., & Marcellin, M. (2001). *JPEG2000: Image Compression Fundamentals, Standards and Practice.* Berlin: Springer.

Thatte, S. (2003). *BPEL4WS, business process execution language for web services.* Retrieved June 15th, 2008, from http://xml.coverpages.org/ni2003-04-16-a.html

TV-Anytime. (2005). *TV-Anytime.* Retrieved June 15th, 2008, from http://www.tv-anytime.org

UDDI. (2004). *UDDI Version 3.0.2.* Retrieved June 15th, 2008, from http://www.Oasis-Open.org/committees/uddi-spec/doc/spec/v3/uddi-v3.0.2-20041019.Htm

Vakali, A., & Pallis, G. (2003). Content Delivery Networks: Status and Trends. *IEEE Internet Computing*, (November 6): 68–74. doi:10.1109/MIC.2003.1250586

Watt, A. Lilley Chris, & J., Daniel. (2003). *SVG Unleashed.* Indianapolis, IN: SAMS.

WSDL/W3C. (2005). *WSDL: Web Services Description Language (WSDL) 1.1.* Retrieved June 15th, 2008, from http://www.w3.org/TR/wsdl.

Wyckoff, P., McLaughry, S. W., Lehman, T. J., & Ford, D. A. (1998). T Spaces. *IBM Systems Journal, 37*, 454–474.

Zhou, J., Ou, Z., Rautiainen, M., & Ylianttila, M. (2008b). P2P SCCM: Service-oriented Community Coordinated Multimedia over P2P. In *Proceedings of 2008 IEEE International Conference on Web Services,* Beijing, China, September 23-26, (pp. 34-40).

Zhou, J., Rautiainen, M., & Ylianttila, M. (2008a). Community coordinated multimedia: Converging content-driven and service-driven models. In *proceedings of 2008 IEEE International Conference on Multimedia & Expo,* June 23-26, 2008, Hannover, Germany.

KEY TERMS AND DEFINITIONS

Community: is generally defined as groups of limited number of people held together by common interests and understandings, a sense of obligation and possibly trust.

Community Coordinated Multimedia (CCM): system maintains a virtual community for the consumption of CCM multimedia elements, i.e. both content generated by end users and content from professional multimedia provider (e.g., Video on Demand). The consumption involves a series of interrelated multimedia intensive processes such as content creation, aggregation, annotation, etc. In the context of CCM, these interrelated multimedia intensive processes are encapsulated into Web services, instead of multimedia applications, namely multimedia intensive services, briefly multimedia services.

Middleware: is the key technology which integrates two or more distributed software units and allows them to exchange data via heterogeneous computing and communication devices. In this chapter, middleware is perceived as an additional software layer in OSI model encapsulating knowledge from presentation and session layers, consisting of standards, specifications, forms, and protocols for multimedia, service, mobility and community computing and communication.

Multimedia: represents a synchronized presentation of bundled media types, such as text, graphic, image, audio, video, and animation.

Standard: refers to an accepted industry standard. Protocol refers to a set of governing rules in communication between computing endpoints. A specification is a document that proposes a standard.

ENDNOTE

1 http://www.cam4home-itea.org/

Section 8
Mobile Computing and Ad Hoc Networks

Chapter 30
Scalability of Mobile Ad Hoc Networks

Dan Grigoras
University College Cork, Ireland

Daniel C. Doolan
Robert Gordon University, UK

Sabin Tabirca
University College Cork, Ireland

ABSTRACT

This chapter addresses scalability aspects of mobile ad hoc networks management and clusters built on top of them. Mobile ad hoc networks are created by mobile devices without the help of any infrastructure for the purpose of communication and service sharing. As a key supporting service, the management of mobile ad hoc networks is identified as an important aspect of their exploitation. Obviously, management must be simple, effective, consume least of resources, reliable and scalable. The first section of this chapter discusses different incarnations of the management service of mobile ad hoc networks considering the above mentioned characteristics. Cluster computing is an interesting computing paradigm that, by aggregation of network hosts, provides more resources than available on each of them. Clustering mobile and heterogeneous devices is not an easy task as it is proven in the second part of the chapter. Both sections include innovative solutions for the management and clustering of mobile ad hoc networks, proposed by the authors.

INTRODUCTION

In this chapter, we discuss the concept of scalability applied to Mobile Ad hoc NETworks (**MANET**). MANETs are temporarily formed networks of mobile devices without the support of any infrastructure. One of the most important characteristics of MANETs is the unpredictable evolution of their configuration. The number of member nodes within a MANET can vary immensely over a short time interval, from tens to thousands and vice-versa. Therefore, the scalability of network formation and management,

DOI: 10.4018/978-1-60566-661-7.ch030

mobile middleware and applications is a key factor in evaluating the overall MANET effectiveness.

The large diversity and high penetration of mobile wireless devices make their networking a very important aspect of their use. By self-organizing in mobile ad hoc networks, heterogeneous devices can communicate, share their resources and services and run new and more complex distributed applications. Mobile applications such as multiplayer games, personal health monitoring, emergency and rescue, vehicular nets and control of home/office networks illustrate the potential of mobile ad hoc networks. However, the complexity of these networks brings new challenges regarding the management of heterogeneity, mobility, communication and scarcity of resources that all have an impact on scalability.

The scalability property of complex distributed systems does not have a general definition and evaluation strategy. Within the realm of MANET, scalability can refer to several aspects, from performance at the application layer to the way scarce resources are consumed. One example is the case where the mobile system is not scalable if batteries' energy is exhausted by demanding management operations. A mobile middleware service is not scalable if it does not meet the mobile clients' requirements with similar performance, irrespective of their number or mobility patterns.

All current MANET deployments or experiments involve a small number of devices, at most of the order of few tens, but, in the future, hundreds, thousands or even more devices will congregate and run the same application(s). Therefore it is essential to consider the strategies by which scalability will be provided to the network and application layers such that any number of devices and clients will be accommodated with the same performance. When used, **mobile middleware** systems will also be required to be scalable.

Following, the most important aspects of scalability with regard to mobile ad hoc networks will be reviewed considering how MANET can be managed cost-effectively and how an important application of large distributed systems, clustering, can be implemented in a scalable manner on MANET.

This chapter is organized as follows. The first Section discusses the management service of mobile ad hoc networks and innovative means for making it a scalable service. The rapid change of MANET membership impacts on the node address management. Additionally, frequent operations as split and merge require address management as well. Therefore, MANET management is mostly the management of node addresses.

As potentially large networks, MANET can be used as the infrastructure that supports mobile cluster computing. Consequently, the second section is dedicated to cluster computing on MANET and its related scalability issues.

MANAGEMENT OF MANET

The Set of Management Operations for MANET

An ad hoc network is a dynamic system whose topology and number of member nodes can change at any time. The MANET scenario assumes that there will always be one node which will set up the network followed up by other nodes which will join the network by the acquisition of unique addresses. This is, for example, the strategy of **Bluetooth**, where the initial node, also known as the master, creates the network identity and allocates individual addresses to up to seven new members of the network as they join it.

During its lifetime, any MANET can be characterized by the following set of management operations:

- *Network setup*, usually executed by one (initial) node that also creates the MANET identity;
- *Join/leave*, when a node joins or leaves an existing MANET;
- *Merge* of two or more MANETs and the result is one larger MANET;
- *Split* of MANET into two or more sub-MANETs;
- *Termination* when nodes leave the network and the MANET ceases to exist.

As, due to nodes' mobility, these operations can be quite frequent, the MANET management becomes complex and resource-consuming, especially in terms of node addresses, battery energy and bandwidth. Therefore it is important to study strategies proposed for MANET organization in respect to the way these critical resources are managed. Although one of the main goals of mobile platforms is to minimize energy consumption, by introducing more sleep states for the CPU and the idle thread in the operating system for example, less attention is paid to MANET management operations cost in terms of resources. For example if lots of messages are used for a basic join operation, there will be high energy and bandwidth costs for each joining node and for the entire system. A good strategy would use a minimum number of short messages and be scalable while a poor strategy fails to manage a large number of devices.

Currently, there are two main technologies, Bluetooth (Bluetooth, 2008) and **IEEE 802.11x** (WiFi, 2008), used to create MANET. Almost all new mobile phones, PDAs and laptops are Bluetooth-enabled making them potentially members of Bluetooth MANET. However, Bluetooth accepts only eight devices in a piconet (this is the name of the Bluetooth MANET) as the standard adopted only three bits for addressing a node. The first node, setting up the piconet, becomes its master. It creates the piconet identity and allocates addresses to nodes that join the network. Regarding the merge operation, Bluetooth does not have any specific procedure for it. However, a node that is within the range of two piconets can switch from one to the other. Alternative membership to the two piconets creates the potential for the node of acting like a gateway – the larger network is called scatternet.

There is no provision for split as this was probably not considered as a likely event for such a small network. There is no clear protocol for piconet termination, this operation being left to user's intervention. The lack of provision for MANET management in the case of Bluetooth is explained by its primary goal of eliminating cables and not to create P2P mobile networks. However the increasing popularity of Bluetooth may lead to the necessity to manage large scatternets (collections of interconnected piconets) and a rethink of this technology.

The 802.11x standards cover only the physical and link layer. A WiFi MANET is generally an **IP-based** network.

Solutions for the Management of IP-based MANET

The management of an IP-based MANET is the management of the IP addresses. Considering the role of IP addresses as a pointer to a unique computer/node in a certain network, it is easy to understand the difficulty of porting this concept to the mobile area, where nodes can change network membership often.

Several solutions were proposed for IP address allocation to mobile nodes. The simplest use the current features of the protocol. Either, there is a **DHCP server** that has a pool of IP addresses, or mobile nodes are self-configuring. In the former situation, it is assumed that one node runs the DHCP server, the pool has enough IP addresses for all potential candidates to membership, and the DHCP host will belong to MANET for its entire lifetime. Obviously, all these assumptions are difficult to guarantee. In the latter situation, each node picks an IP address from the link-local range or from a private range of addresses and then checks for duplicates. From time to time, nodes will search for a DHCP server and if this is present, will ask for an IP address. Although much simpler, this strategy assumes that nodes share the same link and the size of the network is not too large. Otherwise, duplicate checks would dominate the network communication. Moreover, join and merge can be committed only after duplicate check confirms the lack of duplicates. If these operations are frequent, the management of IP addresses will consume a lot of the most important resources of mobile nodes, battery energy and bandwidth.

IP-based MANET termination is either triggered by the return of all IP addresses to the pool, or by a user defined protocol.

MANETconf

One of the earliest projects that offered a full solution to IP-based MANET management is MANETconf (Nesargi, 2002). This protocol assumes that all nodes use the same private address block, e.g., 10.0.0.0 to 10.255.255.255, and each node that requests to join a network will benefit of the services of an existing member of the network. This node, acting as a proxy, will allocate an IP address to the newly arrived node after checking with all the other nodes that that IP address is idle. Conflicts among multiple proxies trying to allocate IP addresses in the same time are solved by introducing priorities. The proxy with the lower IP address has priority over the other(s). Split and merge were considered as well. While split is managed by simply cleaning up the IP addresses of departed nodes, belonging to all the other partitions, merge requires a more elaborated algorithm. The authors associate with each partition an identity represented by a 2-tuple. The first element of the tuple is the lowest IP address in use in the partition. The second element is a universally unique identifier (UUID) proposed by the node with this lowest IP address. Each node in the partition stores the tuple. When two nodes come into each other's radio range, they exchange their partitions identities. If they are different, a potential merge is detected. This operation will proceed by exchanging the sets of idle IP addresses and then broadcasting them to all the other members of each partition. If by merging there are conflicting addresses (duplicates) the node(s) with the lower number of active TCP connections will request a new IP address.

MANETconf as a complete solution requires a lot of communication that increases with the size of the network. Therefore, we cannot consider this protocol a scalable solution to MANET management.

IP addressing and the associated protocol are effective for wired networks and to a certain extent to Access Point-based mobile networks (Mobile IPv4, or IPv6), but difficult to manage in a MANET (Ramjee, 2005) (Tseng, 2003). The main difficulty arises from the fact that an IP address has no relevance for a mobile node that can change network membership frequently. Any such change may result in a new address allocated to that node, each time, followed by duplicate checks. More important than a numeric address is the set of services and resources made available to other peers by the node. In this respect, there are initiatives to introduce new ways of addressing mobile nodes of MANET (Adjie-Winoto, 1999), (Balazinska, 2002). One particular project deals with a service oriented strategy which builds on the assumption that MANET are mainly created for the purpose of sharing services and, in this context, IP addresses as an indication of location have no relevance (Grigoras, 2005). Then, service discovery, remote execution and service composition are the most important operations related to service sharing.

If the Internet Protocol is not used anymore, new transport protocols, probably simpler but still reliable if replacing TCP, have to be designed.

To define the scope of MANET, a new concept of soft network identity was proposed in (Grigoras, 2007a). As this concept provides a totally new approach in the way MANET are managed and moreover assures scalability, we will explain it in the following section.

The Management of Non-IP MANET

The difficulties and high cost of managing IP addresses led to the idea that we might find better ways to manage MANET, preserving the requirements of communication and service provisioning among all nodes. Because MANET is a system with a limited lifetime, it makes sense to allocate it an identity that is valid only as long as MANET is active/alive. This identity is then used for all the management operations.

The first node that organizes MANET computes a network identity, **net_id** for short, based on its MAC address, date and time. It then attaches to it a time-to-live (TTL), an expectation of how long that network will be alive:{net_id, TTL}

This pair represents the soft identity state of the new network. For example, {112233, 200} corresponds to network 112233 with a living expectation of 200 seconds. A node joins the network after requesting, receiving and storing, from any one-hop neighbour already in the network, the net_id and updated TTL, for example {112233, 150}. TTL is counted down by each node. When it times out, the associated net_id is cancelled, meaning that the node is no more a member of the network, 112233 in our example. On the other hand, TTL is prolonged when a message carrying the net_id in the header is received by the node. The significance is that messages mean activity and therefore the network should be kept alive (i.e. the node is or can be on an active path).

For increasing the chance to find services of interest, a node may join as many MANET as it wants – using the **Greedy join algorithm** (Grigoras, 2007a). All {net_id, TTL} records are cached and each of them managed separately. If a node leaves a network, it may still be active in other network(s).

Within MANET, a node is uniquely addressed by the MAC address and its set of public and private services.

The MANET Management Operations

MANET setup and join are executed by the same algorithm: initially, the host broadcasts a message to join an existing network; if there is a reply, carrying the net_id and TTL, the host caches them and becomes a member of the network; if there is no reply within a join time interval, it will still wait for a delay interval for possible late replies and, then, if no reply was received, it will compute its own net_id and attach an TTL. The expectation is that other hosts will join this network and activity will start. Otherwise, the TTL counter will time out and the net_id will be cancelled. The host is free to start the procedure again. For example, this can be a background process that will assist a distributed application by providing the network infrastructure.

The join and delay time intervals are two parameters whose initial values, picked by the user, can be updated depending on the environment (number of failures, mobility pattern etc).

Merge is triggered by a host that receives messages carrying in the header a new net_id. This operation can be executed on demand or implicitly – two or more overlapping networks merge. In both cases, the contact host will forward the new {net_id, TTL} pair to all peers. The merge can be mandatory or not.

Obviously, islands of nodes may lose the membership by time out if they don't receive/route messages. This behaviour was indeed noticed during simulation (Grigoras, 2007a).

Split is simpler: all sub-networks preserve the net_id; if there is activity, TTL will be prolonged, otherwise it will time out. If split networks from the same network will come together again, the net_id is still the same.

Termination is signalled by time out. Indeed, when there is no activity, the counter will time out and hosts will gracefully leave.

The MANET management based on the soft net_id concept, presented here, is simple, uses the minimum number of messages (2), is scalable and offers a full solution.

Experimental results (Grigoras, 2007b) showed not only that the net_id strategy uses the minimum number of messages for carrying out the management operations but also is scalable. Scalability is provided by the use of local operations. Indeed, when a node plans to join one or more networks, it simply broadcast its join request and then listens for offers. By storing the net_id, the node becomes a de facto member of the network and can now communicate with other nodes. No management operation requires global communication and this is a key rule for scalable distributed systems.

As MANET is still a new networking model, there will be more and potentially better strategies for their management that will also be scalable - accept any number of new nodes with minimum consumption of resources.

CLUSTER COMPUTING ON MANET

Global High Performance Mobile Computing

The world of **High Performance Computing** (HPC) utilises the combined processing power of several inter-connected nodes to compute the solution of a complex problem within a reasonable timeframe. Presently the top rated HPC machine is IBM's Blue Gene/L (IBM, 2007) comprising of 131,072 processors providing a peak performance of 596 Teraflops. According to performance projections it is expected that a Petaflop capable machine should be in place before 2009 (TOP500, 2007) and a ten Petaflop machine by 2012.

The SETI@Home project is the most well know distributed Internet computing project in the world. It is just one of several projects (BOINC, 2008) that are part of the Berkeley Open Infrastructure for Network Computing (BOINC). The recent upgrade of the world's largest radio telescope in Arecibo, Puerto Rico from where SETI@Home receives its data stream means a five hundred fold increase in the amount of data that needs to be processed (Sanders, 2008). This amounts to 300 gigabytes of data per day. The Seti@Home project uses a divide and conquer strategy implemented as a Client/Server architecture whereby client applications running on personal computers throughout the world carry out the task of processing the data and returning the results to the servers at Berkeley. The project has over five million registered volunteers, with over 201,147 users processing data blocks on a regular basis across 348,819 hosts. The project was running at 445.4 teraflops (SETIstats, 2008), the combined speed of all the BOINC projects was rated at 948.7 teraflops comprising 2,781,014 hosts (BOINCstats, 2008) as of 10th March 2008. The Folding@home project is similar to SETI@home using the processing power of volunteers from around the globe. The client statistics for Folding@home (as of 9th March 2008) had

Table 1. Comparison of mobile phone CPU speeds

Phone	Announced	OS	CPU	JBenchmark ACE
Nokia N96	11/02/2008	Symbian OS v9.3	400Mhz	Unknown
Nokia N93	25/04/2006	Symbian OS v9.1	330Mhz	329Mhz
Nokia N70	27/04/2005	Symbian OS v8.1a	220Mhz	220Mhz
Nokia N73	25/04/2006	Symbian OS v9.1	206Mhz	221Mhz
Nokia 6680	14/02/2005	Symbian OS v8.0a	220Mhz	224Mhz
Nokia 6630	14/06/2004	Symbian OS v8.0a	220Mhz	227Mhz
Nokia 7610	18/03/2004	Symbian OS v7.0s	123Mhz	126Mhz

264,392 active nodes operating at 1,327 Teraflops (Folding@home, 2008), well over twice that of the world's most powerful supercomputer. The bulk of this processing came from Playstation 3 gaming machines giving 1,048 Teraflops from 34,715 active nodes.

Clearly for applications that require a high degree of processing, the architecture of distributing the work out to numerous clients can achieve processing speeds far in excess of the world's top HPC machines. Scalability still poses many questions within the realm of HPC such as what type of architecture should a million-node system have, or how should an application be scheduled on a 1,024 core processor. Could the principle of client applications carrying out CPU intensive operations be feasible within the world of mobile computing? If so what possibilities may lie in store for the future of mobile distributed computation?

The rate at which mobile phone technology is being adopted is astonishing, the first billion subscribers took 20 years, the next billion required just 40 months, while the third required a mere 24 months. It would appear that the world has an ever growing and insatiable hunger for mobile technology. November 29, 2007 saw a significant milestone in global mobile phone ownership when it was announced that mobile telephone subscriptions reached 50%, this amounts to over 3.3 billion subscribers (Reuters, 2007). Reports predict that subscriptions may be as high as five billion by 2012 (PortoResearch, 2008). Could the computing power of these billions and billions of mobile phones be harnessed? If so what would the combined computing power of all these devices be? The present number of phones outstrips the total number of processors of the world's largest supercomputer by over 25,000 times. Mobile devices may have far less computing power than high-end server machines, but their sheer and ever growing number more that counteracts this, as well as their rapidly increasing processing capabilities. In January 2008, ARM announced that it achieved the ten billion processor milestone. The current rate at which these chips are being created is staggering with the annual run rate now estimated at three billion units per year (ARM, 2008).

What level of computing power could the mobiles of today provide? In 1999 a 500 Mhz Pentium III machine had a capacity of about 1,354MIPS. In October 2005 ARM announced the 1 Ghz Cortex A8 processor capable of a whopping 2,000MIPS. Even the processors of a phone of five years ago are rated at 200MIPS. Table 1 gives a cross section overview of a selection of mobile phone types and their associated processor speeds. The table was compiled using information from the Nokia developer forum, the reviews section of the my-symbian.com website and was cross referenced with yet another site that provides detailed and up-to-date comparisons of mobile phone specifications (Litchfield S, 2008). The phones presented were also evaluated against JBenchmark's ARM CPU Estimator (ACE) which provides an accurate estimate the processors CPU speed. It is generally very difficult to obtain concrete and detailed information about a phones specification. Most manufacturers neglect to provide detailed specifications so that mobile phones are not weighed up by the common factors such as system memory, processor speed and persistent storage, by which desktop/laptop machines are examined by consumers. This may change in time as phones are gaining more and more computing capabilities. A testament to the increasing power of the mobile device is Sun Microsystems (Shankland, 2007) discontinuation of the use of Java Micro Edition in favour of a full blown virtual machine the likes of which run on the desktop systems of today.

An article in late 2007 (Davis, 2007) considered the notion of cell-phone grid computing, and proposed the question of whether Android, the new open-source mobile platform, could provide a foundation for the same. It is therefore becoming evident that people are now becoming aware of the huge potential computing capabilities that the billions of mobile phones could provide. In summary, the combined might of all the worlds' mobile phones could be the most powerful supercomputer in the world if we could just harness their processing capabilities in a manner similar to the BOINC projects. One of course may say that processor intensive computation would quickly drain the limited battery. Even if processing was carried out only while the phone was connected to mains power it would still allow for probably two hours of solid processing per week. Given this, then at any one time one would still have upwards of 40 million devices contributing their processing power at any instant given the 3.3 billion mobile phone population at the end of 2007.

Such extreme mobile parallel computing systems would of course be suitable only for hyper-parallel tasks that can be easily divided into million/billions of distinct jobs. Third generation phones allows for relatively fast internet connectivity with rates of several hundred kbit/s. The main prohibiting factors in the creation of a hyper parallel mobile grid are the interconnectivity costs and people's willingness to participate. Costs are continually reducing, and as more and more people join BOINC like projects they are realising that they can contribute to the solving of complex and processor intensive problems. Moving in to the future Science will tackle larger and larger problems that will require all the potential processing power we can muster to solve within a reasonable timeframe.

It may take some time before we see a hyper-parallel globalised mobile grid, but on a smaller scale the alternative is to use the processing power of the phones within our local vicinity. This is where technologies such as Bluetooth and message passing come into their own.

Localised Mobile Parallel Computing

The majority of today's phones are Bluetooth-enabled as standard; they also have the ability of executing java based applications in the form of MIDlets. Most of these Bluetooth enabled devices allow for data transmission rates of up to 723kbit/s (Bluetooth 1.2) and have an effective range of 10 meters. These mobile phones are therefore perfect platforms for parallel computing tasks on a small scale. The standard Bluetooth **Piconet** allows for up to eight devices to be interconnected together. This functions in a star network topology using a Client/Server architecture. A star network is of limited use when one Client device wishes to communicate with another client device. In this case, all traffic will have to be routed through the Master device. The solution lies within the bedrock that is parallel computing today, the message passing interface, whereby any node is capable of communicating with any other node. In the mobile world this is achieved by firstly creating the standard star network topology after the process of device and service discovery have been carried out. With connections established to a central node

Figure 1. MMPI network structure for Piconet and Scatternet sized networks

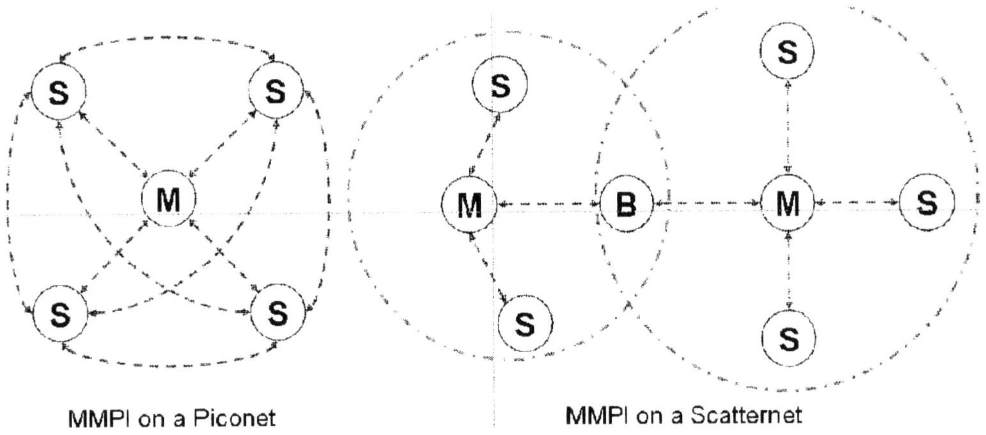

the process of creating the inter-client connections can take place allowing for the building up of a fully interconnected mesh network (Figure 1). A system called the **Mobile Message Passing Interface** (MMPI) allows for such an infrastructure to be created and provides methods for both point to point and global communications (Doolan, 2006).

Bluetooth itself is inherently Client/Server based, therefore when establishing a parallel world using the MMPI system it is necessary for the user to indicate if the application should be started in Client or Server mode. In the case of a node started with a Client setting, its primary task is to create a Server object to advertise itself as being available. With all the Client nodes up and running, the remaining node can be started as a Master node, which will carry out the discovery process and coordinate the creation of the inter-client links. Bluetooth programming in itself changes the form of how a typical Client/Server system works, as the Client devices are required to establish server connections to allow the Server device to carry out the discovery process and establish Client connections to same. In standard Client/Server systems it is the Server application that is started first and left running, and remains in a constant loop awaiting of incoming Client applications to connect to it, a web server being a typical example.

To ensure correct inter-node communication each node maintains an array of connections to every other device within the world. This takes the form of a set of DataInputStreams and DataOutputStreams. Communication is achieved between nodes through a set of methods that abstracts the developer from dealing with streams, communication errors and so forth. In the case of point to point communication one needs to simply call a method such as send(…) to transmit a message to another node. The parameters that are passed are firstly the data to be transmitted (an array of data), an offset, the amount of data to send the data type, and most importantly the id (rank) of the receiving device. Correspondingly the receiving device must have a matching recv(…) method call, to correctly receive the message from the source node.

Can the MMPI system scale to a world larger than eight nodes? The Bluetooth Piconet allows for a maximum of eight interconnected devices; however one may use the **Scatternet** architecture to build larger systems, by interconnecting two or more Piconets together by way of a bridging node common to both Piconets. Using a Scatternet framework, the MMPI system can be scaled to allow for larger networks, for example one could have a network of twelve, fifteen or even twenty devices that allows for inter-node communications between all nodes. This is achieved by the creation of a java class called

CommsCenter which forms the heart of the Scatternet MMPI system (Donegan, 2008). The CommsCenter receives raw data from the network and translates it into MMPI messages. These messages are passed on to the MMPI interface that is exposed to the developer by means of an additional intermediary class called the MMPINode. The purpose of this is to interface between the high level MMPI methods and the lower level communications; it also helps to take care of the discovery process. Messages that are sent out on to the Bluetooth network are fed up and down through this chain of classes that allows for the abstraction of lower level operations.

Messages that are received by the CommsCenter are identified by the header and may take one of five forms: Bridge, Master, Slave, Confirm and Data. The first three are used for the establishment of the network structure to inform what role a specific device should take. The Confirm message is initiated on completion of the network formation process. The Data header is used for the transportation of inter-node messages.

In the case that the number of devices that are discovered exceeds the limit of seven, then one of these devices will be chosen to act as a bridging node, therefore forming essentially two distinctive Piconets. The root node will carry out this selection process as it is aware of the number of active nodes that are advertising themselves of inclusion within the parallel world. The root node will build up a list of what devices are to be in each network, and in the case of devices that will appear in a network connected to a bridging node, a Bridging message will be sent to the bridge in question with a list of the node addresses to which it should establish connections to.

A routing table is also established as many nodes may not have a direct connection to several of the other nodes in the world. A routing table is maintained by each node, which maintains an entry for every other node except itself. The entries in the table are an index to which node a message should be routed through in order to get to its destination. In the case of a slave node on one Piconet wishing to communicate to a slave node on another Piconet, the message is firstly transmitted to the Master node of the first Piconet (Figure 1). The Master will then forward the message on to the bridging node that interconnects the two networks, and is again forwarded to the Master node of the second Piconet. The message can then be finally sent on to its final destination (a slave node on the second Piconet).

Figure 1 clearly shows the interconnections for MMPI running on Piconet sized (limited to eight or less) and Scatternet sized network. In the case of the Piconet sized worlds every node maintains direct connections with every other node. This differs greatly in the case of larger MMPI worlds where the network structure reverts back to a Scatternet structure, comprising of star network topologies interconnected by bridges. The Master node for each sub-network in this case must deal with the routing of messages between Slave nodes, therefore this node can easily become a communications bottleneck when there is a high amount of data transmissions. The larger incarnation of the MMPI architecture was developed in a Scatternet manner to keep the routing tables as simple as possible. This however, could be improved by creating inter-slave/bridge connections between each of the nodes in each sub-network. The process of network formation and routing would be more complex for the initial creation of the world, but it would have the effect of reducing the bottleneck effect on the sub-network Master nodes in the case of inter-slave communications.

The MMPI system can be used for a myriad of applications, from parallel processing and graphics to mLearning and multiplayer gaming. Due to the high level of abstraction it liberates the developer from java Bluetooth development, network formation, and the handling of data streams. One can develop a multi-node application very rapidly in comparison to a multi-node application developed from scratch. Instead of writing hundreds of lines to carry out discovery and establish connections, one needs only to call the constructor of the MMPI system. Therefore one single line replaces hundreds, when carrying out communications between nodes one simply just needs to call and appropriate method be it for point to point or global communications. In the space of less than a dozen lines one can develop the necessary code to build a fully functional Bluetooth network, and achieve communications between the nodes. This has several advantages such as the speeding up of application development, allowing the developer to focus on the domain specific task at hand, and not having to worry about handling detailed communications issues. In the area of games development a well built single user game can be transformed into a multiplayer game in a matter of hours requiring minimal code changes. Many people enjoy playing computer games, but playing against another human player rather than an AI algorithm adds far more unpredictably to the game. The number of multiplayer Bluetooth-enabled games for mobile phones is quite limited; one reason is so that a game is compatible with as many devices as possible. The process of transforming a single player game in to a multiplayer game can also be time consuming and require significant development resources, but this however is no longer the case. Perhaps as more and more people invest in Bluetooth enabled phones we will see a change in the market, with more multiplayer games being developed, as such the MMPI system may prove to be of significant advantage to these developers, both in reducing development time and costs, and reducing code complexity.

CONCLUSION

In this chapter, we addressed aspects of scalability of MANET management and MANET clusters. Regarding the MANET management, the prevalent strategy is to use IP. However, managing IP addresses is resource-consuming and for large MANET can become a nightmare. Our conclusion is that IP-based MANET can not be scalable. New approaches such as the net_id are simpler, use less resources and, more important, provide scalability.

Clustering is an interesting solution for creating more powerful systems out of many basic devices. For example, mobile phones can generally be classed as having very limited resources, be it a combination of electrical power, processor and system memory. The use of parallel computing techniques can allows for these small devices to divide up large tasks among themselves and carryout jobs that would otherwise be impossible for a single device. Such examples of this would be a job may have higher memory requirements than what is available on a single device. Another and more imperative restriction is electrical power, where by a task may take too long to process, given a limited battery. The division of work among multiple nodes can spread the resource cost among a number of devices allowing for tasks impossible for one single device to solve to be completed and the results from same obtained at a far reduced wall clock time. The amalgamation of Bluetooth and message passing paradigms to form Java based mobile parallel applications is one solution to this problem, allowing for mobile parallel computing to take place between a limited number of mobile devices. Perhaps in the not too distant future we will see the rise of the hyper-parallel globalised mobile grid as the information processing needs of research projects escalate. Supercomputing may no longer be the realm of high end server farms, but ubiquitous throughout the world with devices such as our phones, set top boxes, desktop computers, and even our cars providing their free clock cycles to solve the data processing requirements of tomorrow.

REFERENCES

Adjie-Winoto, W., Schwartz, E., Blakrishnan, H., & Lilley, J. (1999). The design and implementation of an intentional naming system. *Operating Systems Review, 34*(5), 186–201. doi:10.1145/319344.319164

ARM. (2008). *ARM Achieves 10 Billion Processor Milestone*. Retrieved March 10, 2008, from http://www.arm.com/news/19720.html

Balazinska, M., Blakrishnan, H., & Karger, D. (2002). INS/Twine: a scalable peer-to-peer architecture for intentional resource discovery. In *Pervasive 2002*, Zurich, Switzerland, August. Berlin: Springer Verlag.

Bluetooth (2008). Retrieved November 2008 from www.bluetooth.com

BOINC. (2008). *Berkeley Open Infrastructure for Network Computing*. Retrieved March 10, 2008 from http://boinc.berkeley.edu

BOINCstats. (2008). *Seti@home Project Statistics*. Retrieved March 10, 2008, from http://boincstats.com/stats/project_graph.php?pr=sah

Davis, C. (2007). *Could Android open door for cellphone Grid computing?* Retrieved March 10, 2008, from http://www.google-phone.com/could-android-open-door-for-cellphone-grid-computing-12217.php

Donegan, B., Doolan, D. C., & Tabirca, S. (2008). Mobile Message Passing using a Scatternet Framework. *International Journal of Computers, Communications & Control, 3*(1), 51–59.

Doolan, D. C., Tabirca, S., & Yang, L. T. (2006). Mobile Parallel Computing. *In Proceedings of the Fifth International Symposium on Parallel and Distributed Computing (ISPDC 06)*, (pp. 161-167).

Folding@home, (2008). *Client statistics by OS*. Retrieved March 10, 2008, from http://fah-web.stanford.edu/cgi-bin/main.py?qtype=osstats

Grigoras, D. (2005). Service-oriented Naming Scheme for Wireless Ad Hoc Networks. In the *Proceedings of the NATO ARW "Concurrent Information Processing and Computing"*, July 3-10 2003, Sinaia, Romania, 2005, (pp. 60-73). Amsterdam: IOS Press

Grigoras, D., & Riordan, M. (2007a). Cost-effective mobile ad hoc networks management. *Future Generation Computer Systems, 23*(8), 990–996. doi:10.1016/j.future.2007.04.001

Grigoras, D., & Zhao, Y. (2007b). *Simple Self-management of Mobile Ad Hoc Networks*. Proc of the 9th IFIP/IEEEInternational Conference on Mobile and Wireless Communication Networks, 19-21 September 2007, Cork, Ireland.

IBM. (2007). *Blue Gene*. Retrieved March 10, 2008, from http://domino.research.ibm.com/comm/research_projects.nsf/pages/bluegene.index.html

Litchfield, S. (2008). *A detailed comparison of Seires 60 (S60) Symbian smartphones*. Retrieved March 10, 2008, from http://3lib.ukonline.co.uk/s60history.htm

Nesargi, S., & Prakash, R. (2002). *MANETconf: Configuration of Hosts in a Mobile Ad Hoc Network.* In Proceedings of the IEEE Infocom 2002, New York, June 2002.

PortoResearch. (2008). *Slicing Up the Mobile Services Revenue Pie*. Retrieved March 10, 2008, from http://www.portioresearch.com/slicing_pie_press.html

Ramjee, R., Li, L., La Porta, T., & Kasera, S. (2002). IP paging service for mobile hosts. *Wireless Networks*, *8*, 427–441. doi:10.1023/A:1016534027402

Reuters (2007). *Global cellphone penetration reaches 50 pct.* Retrieved March 10, 2008, from http://investing.reuters.co.uk/news/articleinvesting.aspx?type=media&storyID=nL29172095

Sanders, R. (2008). *SETI@home looking for more volunteers*. Retrieved 10 March, 2008, from http://www.berkeley.edu/news/media/releases/2008/01/02_setiahome.shtml

SETIstats. (2008). *Seti@home Project Statistics*. Retrieved March 10, 2008, from http://boincstats.com/stats/project_graph.php?pr=bo

Shankland, S. (2007). *Sun starts bidding adieu to mobile-specific Java*. Retrieved March 10, 2008, from http://www.news.com/8301-13580_3-9800679-39.html?part=rss&subj=news&tag=2547-1_3-0-20

TOP500. (2007). *TOP 500 Supercomputer Sites, Performance Development, November 2007*. Retrieved March 10, 2008 from http://www.top500.org/lists/2007/11/performance_development

Tseng, Y-C., Shen, C-C. & Chen, W-T. (2003). Integrating Mobile IP with ad hoc networks. *IEEE Computer*, May, 48-55.

WiFi (2008). Retrieved November 2008 from http://www.ieee802.org/11/

KEY TERMS AND DEFINITIONS

Bluetooth: An RF based, wireless communications technology that has very low power requirements making it a suitable system for energy conscious mobile devices. The JSR-82 Bluetooth API facilitates the development of Java based Bluetooth applications.

IEEE 802.11x (WiFi): A set of standards defined by IEEE for wireless local area networks.

IP: The Internet Protocol is a data communication protocol used on packet-switched networks.

MANET: Mobile ad hoc network, a temporarily created network by mobile devices without any infrastructure support.

MMPI: The Mobile Message Passing Interface is a library designed to run on a Bluetooth piconet network. It facilitates application development of parallel programs, parallel graphics applications, multiplayer games and handheld multi-user mLearning applications.

Net_id: The mobile ad hoc network identity created by the mobile host which organizes it. It is soft variable that is valid only as long as the network is active.

Chapter 31
Network Selection Strategies and Resource Management Schemes in Integrated Heterogeneous Wireless and Mobile Networks

Wei Shen
University of Cincinnati, USA

Qing-An Zeng
University of Cincinnati, USA

ABSTRACT

Integrated heterogeneous wireless and mobile network (IHWMN) is introduced by combing different types of wireless and mobile networks (WMNs) in order to provide more comprehensive service such as high bandwidth with wide coverage. In an IHWMN, a mobile terminal equipped with multiple network interfaces can connect to any available network, even multiple networks at the same time. The terminal also can change its connection from one network to other networks while still keeping its communication alive. Although IHWMN is very promising and a strong candidate for future WMNs, it brings a lot of issues because different types of networks or systems need to be integrated to provide seamless service to mobile users. In this chapter, the authors focus on some major issues in IHWMN. Several noel network selection strategies and resource management schemes are also introduced for IHWMN to provide better resource allocation for this new network architecture.

INTRODUCTION

Wireless and mobile networks (WMNs) attract a lot of attention in both academic and industrial fields. They are also witnessing a great success in recent years. Generally, WMN can be classified into two types, centralized (or infrastructure-based) and distributed (or infrastructure-less) WMNs. Cellular net-

DOI: 10.4018/978-1-60566-661-7.ch031

works are the most widely deployed centralized WMNs and have evolved from the earliest 1G cellular network to current 2G/3G cellular networks. Generally, the service area of a cellular network is divided into multiple small areas that are called cells. Each cell has a central control unit that is referred to as base station (BS). All the communications in the cellular network take place via the BSs. That is, the communication in a cellular must be relayed through a BS. The IEEE 802.11 WLAN (Wireless Local Area Network) is another type of centralized WMNs, which has much smaller coverage compared to cellular networks. Because WLANs are easy to deploy and can provide high bandwidth service, they have experienced rapid growth and wide deployment since they were launched to the market. In a WLAN, the central control unit is called access point (AP). Similar to cellular networks, the communications in a WLAN must be via the APs. The BSs or APs are connected to the backbone networks and provide connections with other external networks, such as Public Switched Telephone Network (PSTN) and Internet. Besides the cellular network and WLANs, there are also many other types of centralized WMNS such as satellite network, WiMax, HiperLan etc.

Unlike centralized WMNs, there is no fixed network structure in a decentralized (or distributed) WMN. Wireless and mobile ad hoc network is a typical distributed WMN that attracts a lot of research interests recently (Agrawal, 2006). The wireless and mobile ad hoc network is dynamically created and maintained by the nodes. The nodes forward packets to/from each other via a common wireless channel without the help of any wired infrastructure. When a node needs to communicate with other nodes, it needs a routing discovery procedure to find a potential routing path to the destination node. Due to frequent movement of communication nodes, the routing path between two communication nodes is not fixed. When a relay node moves out of transmission range of other communication nodes, the current routing path is broken. As a result, another routing path has to be found in order to keep the communication alive. Wireless and mobile ad hoc networks are very useful in some areas that a centralized WMN is not possible or inefficient, such as disaster recovery and battle field.

Although there are a lot of wireless and mobile networks and they are witnessing a great success in recent years, different types of WMNs have different design goals and restriction in the wireless signal transmission which results in the limitation of the services. Therefore, they cannot satisfy all the communication needs for the mobile users. For example, any single type of existing WMN is not able to provide a comprehensive service such as high bandwidth with wide coverage. In order to provide more comprehensive services, a concept of *integrated heterogeneous wireless and mobile network* (IHWMN) is introduced by combing different types of WMNs.

On the other hand, any traditional mobile terminal only supports one network interface, which can only connect to one type of network. With the advance of the software defined radio technology, it is possible to integrate multiple WMN interfaces (multi-mode interfaces) into a single mobile terminal now. Such multi-mode terminal is able to access multiple WMNs if it is under the coverage of multiple WMNs. For example, a mobile terminal equipped with cellular network interfaces and WLAN can connect cellular network or WLAN if both networks are available. It can further connect to both networks at the same time. However, it is a big challenge since effective and efficient schemes are required to manage the connection.

It is obvious that the introduction of IHWMN as well as multi-mode terminal brings more flexible and plentiful access options for mobile users. The mobile users can connect the more suitable network for different communication purpose. One example is that the mobile user may connect to cellular network for the voice communication and connect to the WLANs to receive email and surf the Internet. However, there is a lot of challenge, such as the architecture of network integration, network selection strategies,

Figure 1. An example of integrated heterogeneous wireless and mobile network

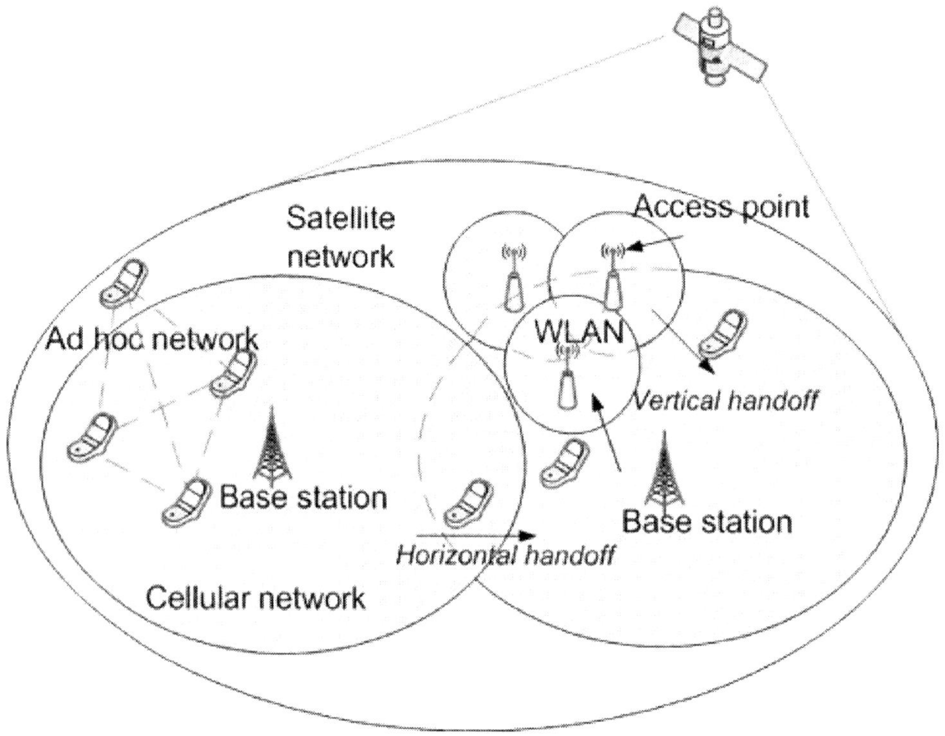

handoff scheme, resource allocation, etc. These problems have to be solved before launching IHWMN to the commercial market and enjoying its benefit. The major challenges for IHWMN are:

- *How to integrate different types of wireless and mobile networks?* In the same geographic area, it is possible to have more than one network as shown in Figure 1. If these networks belong to the same operator, it is obvious that the network operator can allocate the network resource in a centralized way. However, these networks may belong to different operators in most cases. These different networks may manage resources individually based on different policies, which is possible to cause low resource utilization for the whole IHWMN. Therefore, how to integrate these different types of WMNs from different operators directly affects the performance of the whole systems.

- *How to manage radio resource in IHWMNs?* The resource management becomes more complex in IHWMN due to the diversity of the services (or traffic) provided by heterogeneous WMNs. Another challenging issue has to be handled in multiple traffic system is the fairness among different types of traffic and different types of networks. That is, some low priority traffic obtains poor performance while some high priority traffic obtains over-qualified services. From the point of view of network, the throughput of some networks may saturate due to high volume traffic while other networks have much less traffic to handle.
- *How to select a network in the IHWMN?* When a mobile user having a multi-mode terminal generates a new (or originating) call in an IHWMN, it needs a network selection strategy to determine

which network should be accessed.

- *How to manage the vertical handoff?* When a mobile user roams in an IHWMN, the multi-mode terminal may change the connection from one network to another network. Such process is called vertical handoff which will be disused in the following section. A great challenge for IHWMN is how to manage the vertical handoff since frequent vertical handoff causes a lot of signaling burden and fluctuation of the service quality.
- *How to efficiently manage multi-mode interfaces?* Since the power consumption of each wireless network interface cannot be neglected even in the idle or power saving mode, the terminal cannot activate all the interfaces all the times. Therefore, some algorithms are required to find the preferred networks promptly. Another problem of managing multi-mode interface is how to use multiple interfaces at the same time. Such kind of technology is very useful to support services that require very high bandwidth. However, it brings a lot of issues such as bandwidth allocation among different types of networks, synchronization etc.

In the chapter, we focus on several issues in IHWMN. The existing strategies and schemes are reviewed and compared. Several novel schemes are proposed to improve the performance of the IHWMN, which can be categorized as network selection strategies and resource management schemes. The issues addressed in this chapter provide many insights into characterizing the emerging problems in IHWMNs.

The remainder of this chapter is organized as followings. We first introduce some basic definition for IHWMN and review the existing work in the next section. Then, we tackle the network selection and resource management problems in IHWMNs and provide several novel solutions for these problems. After that, we analyze the potential direction in the next step for IHWMNs.

BACKGROUND

Figure 1 is an example of integrated heterogeneous wireless and mobile networks. The entire service area in Figure 1 is covered by satellite network. There are two cells of cellular network which has smaller cell size than satellite network. Each cell of cellular network has a BS which manages the communication in the cell. Several WLAN cells are overlapped with the cells of cellular networks, where some areas are covered by both networks. All these networks can be integrated as a whole, which is an IHWMN. The mobile user having multi-mode terminal can enjoy multiple communication modes in the IHWMN. In the following, we give some basic definitions for the IHWMN.

In a traditional WMN such as cellular or WLAN network, an active mobile user (in communication) may move from one cell to another cell. In order to keep the communication alive, the connection has to be changed from one BS (or AP) to another BS (or AP). Such process of changing the connection within the same network is called *handoff* (Wang, 2003). In this chapter, we define such handoff as *horizontal handoff*. For example, the handoff between two adjacent cellular network cells in Figure 1 is a horizontal handoff. In an IHWMN, however, the connection may be changed from one network to another network for better service besides the horizontal handoff. Such process of changing the connection between two different types of networks is called *vertical handoff* (Chen, 2004). For example, the handoff between cellular network and WLAN in Figure 1 is a vertical handoff. Since the vertical handoff happens between two different types of networks (or systems), it is also known as *inter-network handoff or inter-system handoff*. Therefore, the horizontal handoff can be called *intra-network or intra-*

system handoff. Compared to horizontal handoff, vertical handoff is more complex and brings a lot of issues such as vertical handoff decision and vertical handoff execution, need to be handled carefully. The horizontal handoff usually has to be made in order to keep the communication alive in the traditional cellular networks or WLANs. Therefore, it is mandatory. Vertical handoff is more complicated than horizontal handoff, which can be divided into two categories. If an active mobile user roams into a new network which provides better service than the current serving network, it may request a vertical handoff and change the connection to the better network. Unlike the horizontal handoff, this type of vertical handoff is optional and is called *downward vertical handoff* (DVH) (Chen, 2004). Furthermore, the mobile user may still keep the communication with the current serving network. On the other hand, when an active mobile user moves out the coverage of the current serving network, it has to make a vertical handoff to other available networks. Such type of vertical handoff is called *upward vertical handoff* (UVH) (Chen, 2004). Similar to the horizontal handoff, the UVH is mandatory since a failed vertical handoff terminates the communication. In the following, we review the related work that has been done in the field of IHWMN.

Some research has been done to integrate different types of wireless and mobile networks. In (Salkintzis, 2002; Salkintzis, 2004), two different mechanisms, *tight coupling* and *loose coupling*, have been introduced to interconnect WLANs and cellular networks (GPRS and 3G networks). In the tight coupling mechanism, WLAN connects to the GPRS core network like other Radio Access Networks (RAN). In other words, the traffic between WLAN and other external communication networks goes through the core network of cellular network. Therefore, the traffic of WLAN incurs a burden to the core network of cellular network. In the loose coupling mechanism, however, WLAN is deployed as a complementary network for the cellular network. The traffic of WLAN does not go through the core network of cellular network. The tight coupling mechanism requires that WLAN and cellular networks belong to the same operator. By using loose coupling mechanism, WLAN and cellular networks can be deployed individually. Both WLANs and cellular networks need not belong to the same operator, which is more flexible than the tight coupling mechanism. Additionally, 3GPP (the 3rd Generation Partnership Project) (3GPP, 2007) working group also has discussed the requirements, principles, architectures, and protocols to interwork the 3G networks and WLANs. In (Akyildiz, 2005), the authors proposed to use a third party to integrate different types of wireless and mobile networks. The third party, called as Network Inter-operating Agent, resides in the Internet and manages the vertical handoff between different types of networks.

When a multi-mode terminal generates a call in an IHWMN, it requires a strategy to determine which network should be accessed. In (Stemm, 1998), since a mobile user always selects the network with the highest available bandwidth among all the available networks during its communication, the only concern of the network selection for the mobile user is bandwidth. From the user's point of view, this is good for the service quality. In (Nam, 2004), a network selection strategy that only considers the power consumption mobile users has been introduced. In order to maximize the battery life, the mobile user selects the uplink and downlink from 3G network or WLAN that have the lowest power consumption. Consider the scenario that the power consumption of the uplink in the 3G network is less than the uplink in WLAN and the power consumption of the downlink in the 3G network is larger than the downlink in WLAN. In (Wang, 1999), the authors have proposed a policy-enabled network selection strategy which combines several factors such as bandwidth provision, price, and power consumption. A mobile user defines the "best" network based on his preferences. By setting different weights over different factors, a mobile user can calculate the total preference of each available network. The mobile user connects to the network with the highest preference, which is its most desired network. In order to reduce the computation complexity of the cost function in (Wang, 1999), an optimization algorithm has been proposed in (Zhu, 2004). The authors have proposed another network selection algorithm in (Song, 2005) by using two mathematic methods: analytical hierarchy process (AHP) and grey relational analysis (GRA). The AHP algorithm divides the complex network selection problem into a number of decision factors and the optimal solution can be found by integrating the relative dominance among these factors. The GRA [17] has also been proposed for selecting the best network for a mobile user. Although the above network selection strategies have their own advantages, they are all designed to meet individual mobile user's needs. That is, they are user-centric. Furthermore, they do not put much attention on the system performances, such as the blocking probability of originating calls and the forced termination probabilities of horizontal and vertical handoff calls.

Generally, the vertical handoff can be divided into three phases: system discovery, vertical handoff decision, and vertical handoff execution (McNair, 2004). In the first phase, the multi-mode mobile terminal keeps searching for another network that can provide better service. Once such network is found, vertical handoff decision is made. The vertical handoff decision is a multiple criteria process which involves many factors like bandwidth usage, money cost, QoS parameters etc. The decision results also affect both the degree of user's satisfaction and system performance. If the vertical handoff decision has been made to change the connection to the new network, the context has to be switched to make the change smoothly and user-transparent. Since the vertical handoff may not be mandatory and it incurs significant signaling messages, the decision algorithm is critical to the IHWMN. The vertical handoff decision is also seen as network selection problem in some literature (Wang, 1999; Song, 2005). The number of users in a WMN after a successful vertical handoff is considered to affect the QoS of the IHWMN. A modiffed Elman neural network is used to predict such number. The predicted number of mobile users is fed into a fuzzy interference system to make a vertical handoff decision.

With the rapid emergence of multimedia applications such as voice, video, and data, these different types of traffic should be supported in wireless and mobile networks. Generally, multiple traffic can be classified into real-time and non-real-time traffic based on their sensitivity to the delay. The major challenge to support such multiple traffic is that different types of traffic are incorporated into one system and each traffic has its distinct QoS requirements. For example, real-time traffic (such as voice and video) is delay-sensitive, while non-real-time traffic (such as data) is delay-tolerant. Therefore, an efficient resource management scheme to support multiple traffic has to treat them differently and satisfy their individual QoS requirements. In an integrated wireless and mobile network, resource management faces more challenges due to the diversity of the services provided by different types of wireless and mobile networks. Unfairness may happen among different types of traffic when handling multiple traffic. That is, the performance of lower priority traffic should be improved when the higher priority traffic has been provided satisfied services.

In (Pavlidou, 1994), the authors have presented different call admission control polices for voice and data traffic. Since data traffic is delay-insensitive and voice traffic is stringent to access delay, they have proposed to allow voice traffic to preempt data traffic. A priority queue is introduced to hold the preempted data calls. When a data call arrives, it is also put into the queue if there is no enough resource. Although their scheme improves the blocking probability of originating voice calls, it treats the originating calls and the handoff calls equally. Since terminating an ongoing call is more frustrating than blocking an originating call from a user's point of view, higher priority should be provided to the ongoing calls (handoff calls). In (Wang, 2003), the authors have proposed an analytical model that supports preemptive and priority reservation for handoff calls. Detailed performance analysis is also provided to give guidelines on how to configure system parameters to balance the blocking probability of originating calls and the forced termination probability of handoff calls. Multiple traffic with different QoS requirements have been discussed in (Xu, 2005). In order to support different types of traffic, a model that gives different priorities to different types of traffic has been designed. Their model allows the traffic with lower priority to be preempted by the traffic with higher priority, which can support DiffServ (Differentiate Service) in WMNs. Although all of the above resource management schemes achieve significant improvements on the system performances, they focus on a single WMN, which may not efficiently support multiple traffic in an IHWMN.

Compared to a single type of WMN, the resource management in an IHWMN has to face more challenges due to the heterogeneity of different types of WMNs. That is, different types of WMNs may have different resource management policies for the same type of traffic. The resource management scheme in (Park, 2003) treats the real-time and non-real-time traffic differently in an integrated CDMA-WLAN network. For real-time traffic, vertical handoff is made as soon as possible to minimize the handoff delay. For non-real-time traffic, they considered that the amount of data being transmitted is more important than the delay. Therefore, the connection to the higher bandwidth network is kept as long as possible to maximize the throughput. In (Zhang, 2003), the authors have also proposed different vertical handoff policies for real-time and non-real-time traffic. Although all of the above schemes improve the system performances in certain perspectives, call-level performances such as the blocking probability of originating calls and the forced termination probability of handoff calls are not examined. Furthermore, in all of above schemes, any type of traffic is switched to a higher bandwidth network when a higher bandwidth network becomes available. However, this policy may not be suitable for some delay-sensitive traffic because frequent handoffs may interrupt the ongoing communications. The goal of the proposed resource management scheme in (Liu, 2006) is to increase user's data rate and decrease the blocking probability and the forced termination probability. A switch profit is used to encourage the vertical handoff to the network that can offer better bandwidth. On the other hand, a handoff cost is used to prevent excessive vertical handoff. The switch profit depends on the bandwidth gain obtained from the vertical handoff, while the handoff cost depends on the delay incurred by the vertical handoff. The simulation results show that their scheme can reduce the blocking probability and the forced termination probability. It also achieves better throughput and grade of service. Although the above schemes focus on the resource management scheme in IHWMNs, they only consider a single type of traffic. Therefore, they may not efficiently support multiple traffic in IHWMNs.

NETWORK SELECTION STRATEGIES AND RESOURCE MANAGEMENT SCHEMES

Cost-Function-Based Network Selection Strategies

System Model

As we mentioned before, most existing network selection strategies are user-centric and focus on the individual user's needs. Our motivation is to design a network selection strategy from system's perspective and the network selection strategy can also meet certain individual user's needs. Before we discuss how our proposed cost-function-based network selection strategy (CFNS) works, we briefly describe our system model.

We consider an integrated heterogeneous wireless and mobile system having M different types of networks. We assume that the entire service area of the system is covered by network N_1 that consists of many homogeneous cells and provides a low bandwidth service. Assume that network $N_i (2 \leq i \leq M)$ is randomly distributed in the service area covered by network N_1 and provides a higher bandwidth service than network N_1. Network $N_i (2 \leq i \leq M)$ has limited coverage, which only covers some portion of the entire service area. For example, a cellular network N_1 covers several WLANs (N_1, N_2,...,N_M). For the purpose of simplicity, we focus on one cell of network N_1, which is called marked cell, where some area is covered by several high bandwidth networks. Each cell of a higher bandwidth network $N_i (2 \leq i \leq M)$ has an AP (access point), and each cell of network N_1 has a BS (base station).

We assume that each cell of network $N_i (1 \leq i \leq M)$ has a circular cell shape with radius R_i. We denote the area covered by network $N_i (2 \leq i \leq M)$ as area $A_i (2 \leq i \leq M)$. In the overlapped areas, mobile users may have more than one connection option. We assume that each cell of network $N_i (2 \leq i \leq M)$ has B_i bandwidth units. It is necessary to clarify that each bandwidth unit is a logic channel which can be allocated to a mobile user. We assume that mobile users are uniformly distributed in the service area. They move in all the directions with equal probability. The moving speed V (random variable) of mobile user follows an arbitrary distribution with a mean value of $E[V]$. In the system, we assume that there are three types of calls, namely originating calls, horizontal handoff calls, and vertical handoff calls. An originating call is an initial call in the system, and a handoff call, either horizontal or vertical handoff call, is an ongoing call. When an active mobile user changes its connection from its current serving network N_i to network N_j (for all i, j), a handoff call (request) is generated in network N_j. If $i = j$, the handoff call is a horizontal handoff call. If $i \neq j$, it is a vertical handoff call .

Cost-Function-Based Network Selection Strategy

When an originating call is generated, the proposed network selection strategy works as follows.

- If there is no free bandwidth unit, the originating call is blocked;
- If only one available network has free bandwidth units, the originating call is accepted by that network;
- If there are more than one available network having free bandwidth units, all these candidate networks are compared based on network selection strategy and the originating call is accepted by the most desired network.

Since we focus on network selection strategy in this chapter, horizontal handoff is handled in a traditional way like (Wang, 2003) and vertical handoff is handled in the following ways: when an active mobile user moves from area covered by network N_i into adjacent area covered by network N_j, it changes its connection from network N_i to network N_j if network N_j has a higher bandwidth than N_i and there are free bandwidth units in N_j. If the target area is not covered by network N_i, the mobile user has to change its connection to other available networks. If there is no free bandwidth unit in other available networks, the vertical handoff call will be forcedly terminated. If there are more than one available network having free bandwidth units, the vertical handoff call is randomly accepted by any one of these networks.

Our proposed network selection strategy prefers an originating call to be accepted by a network with a low traffic load and stronger received signal strength, which can achieve better traffic balance among different types of networks and a good service quality. Consequently, we define a cost function to combine these two factors, traffic load and received signal strength. Therefore, the cost to use network N_i for an originating call is defined as

$$C_i = w_g \cdot G_i + w_s \cdot S_i, \text{ for i=1,2,...,M.} \quad (1)$$

where G_i is the complementary of normalized utilization of network N_i, S_i is the relative received signal strength from network N_i. w_g and w_s are the weights that provide preferences to G_i and S_i, where $0 \leq w_{g,s} \leq 1$. The constraint between w_g and w_s is given by

$$w_g + w_s = 1 \quad (2)$$

The complementary of normalized utilization G_i is defined by

$$G_i = \frac{B_{if}}{B_i}, \text{ for i=1,2,...,M,} \quad (3)$$

where B_{if} is the available bandwidth units of network N_i and B_i is the total bandwidth units of network N_i. In general, stronger received signal strength indicates better signal quality. Therefore, an originating call prefers to be accepted by a network with a higher received signal strength. However, it is difficult to compare received signal strengths among different types of networks because they have different maximum transmission powers and receiver threshold. As a result, we propose to use a relative received signal strength to compare different types of WMNs. Therefore, S_i in Equation (1) is defined by

$$S_i = \frac{P_i^c - P_i^{th}}{P_i^{\max} - P_i^{th}} \text{ for i=1,2,...,M,} \quad (4)$$

where P_i^c is the current received signal strength from network N_i. P_i^{th} is the receiver threshold from network N_i. $P_i^{\max}$ is the maximum transmitted signal strength from network N_i. Note that we only consider path loss in the propagation model. Consequently, the received signal strength (in decibel) from network N_i is given by

$$P_i^c = P_i^{\max} - 10\gamma \log(r_i) \quad (5)$$

where r_i is the distance between the mobile user and the BS (or AP) of network N_i, and γ is the fading factor that is generally in the range of [2, 6]. Therefore, the receiver threshold from network N_i is given by

$$P_i^{th} = P_i^{\max} - 10\gamma \log(R_i) \quad (6)$$

The relative received signal strength from network N_i is rewritten as

$$S_i = 1 - \frac{\log(r_i)}{\log(R_i)}, \text{ for i=1,2,...,M.} \tag{7}$$

If an originating call has more than one connection option, the costs for all candidate networks are calculated by using cost function of Equation (1). The originating call is accepted by a network that has the largest cost, which indicates the "best" network. If there are more than one "best" network, the originating call is randomly accepted by any one of these "best" networks.

In the following, we discuss two special cases of the proposed CFNS strategy, i.e., $w_g = 1$ and $w_g = 0$. When $w_g = 1$, the cost function of Equation (1) only considers G_i. It gives rise to another network selection strategy and we call it traffic balanced-based network selection (TBNS) strategy. This network selection strategy tries to achieve the best traffic balance among different types of networks. In this case, when an originating call is generated and there are more than one network having free bandwidth units, the originating call is accepted by a network that has the largest G_i. That is, the call is accepted by a network which has more free bandwidth units. In the second case, when $w_g = 0$, the proposed CFNS strategy gives rise to another network selection strategy, i.e., received signal strength-based network selection (RSNS) strategy. It is obvious that the only concern of selecting a desired network is based on received signal quality. In this case, when an originating call is generated in an area covered by more than one network, the call is accepted by the network that has the largest S_i.

In this chapter, although our cost function only consists of two factors, traffic load and received signal strength, it is easy to extend to involve more factors like access fee of using network N_i, which can be rewritten as

$$C_i = w_g \cdot G_i + w_s \cdot S_i + w_\varphi \cdot \Phi_i, \tag{8}$$

and access fee Φ_i is given by

$$\Phi_i = 1 - \frac{\Phi_i}{\Phi_{max}} \tag{9}$$

where φ_{max} is the highest access fee that the mobile user likes to pay and φ_i is the actual access fee to use network N_i. The mobile user does not connect to a network which charges more than φ_{max} even if the network has free bandwidth units. w_φ $(0 \le \varphi_i \le 1)$ is the weight for the access fee with the constraint:

$$w_g + w_s + w_\varphi = 1 \tag{10}$$

Therefore, a network with a cheaper price has a larger cost, and the mobile user is more likely to be accepted by that network. Using the similar way, other factors also can be included into the cost function after properly normalization.

Numerical Results

We also apply Markov model method to analyze the system performance of the proposed CFNS strategy. Due to space limitations, we do not provide the details of the performance analysis and results, which can be found in (Shen, 2007; Shen, 2008). In the following, we give some numerical results for the system performance of the proposed CFNS strategy. By comparing major system performance, CFNS strategy can achieve a tradeoff between the blocking probability of originating calls and the average received signal strength, which are very important for both systems and users. This is the major difference of our strategies compared to most existing strategies, which considers both system performance and users' needs.

RESOURCE MANAGEMENT SCHEMES FOR MULTIPLE TRAFFIC

System Model

Since the IHWMN is a new concept, there is not much research to discuss about the resource management schemes to support multiple traffic in IHWMN. In this section, we propose a novel resource management scheme to support real-time and non-real-time traffic in IHWMN. The fairness issue between real-time and non-real-time traffic is also addressed to avoid the unbalanced QoS provision to non-real-time traffic.

The system model used in this section is similar to the last section, except we consider two types of traffic: real-time and non-real-time traffic. In this chapter, voice traffic is used as a real-time traffic and data traffic is used as non-real-time traffic. Each bandwidth unit in different networks has different bandwidth provision, while bandwidth provision in network N_2 is much larger than that in network N_1. In the following, we describe our schemes from handling the voice traffic.

Preemption-Based Resource Management Scheme

An ongoing voice call is forcedly terminated due to a failure handoff since voice traffic is delay-sensitive. Therefore, a resource management scheme needs to reduce the number of handoff. On the other hand, a voice call only needs a low bandwidth. The call holding time of a voice call does not change even if a higher bandwidth channel is allocated. In other words, the resource utilization is not efficient if a higher bandwidth channel is allocated to a voice call. Therefore, we assume that a voice call is accepted only by network N_1 to prevent vertical handoff and occupation of a higher bandwidth channel. As a result, there are only two types of voice calls arrival in our system, i.e., originating voice calls and horizontal handoff voice calls. A horizontal handoff voice request is generated in the marked cell when an active voice call user moves into the marked cell from neighboring cells of network N_1. When an originating voice request or horizontal handoff voice request is generated in the marked cell of network N_1, it is accepted if there are free channels in the marked cell of network N_1. We assume that voice traffic has a higher priority than data traffic since voice traffic is delay-sensitive. Therefore, an incoming voice call, either originating or horizontal handoff voice call, can preempt ongoing data call in the marked cell of network N_1 if there is no free bandwidth unit upon its arrival. We adopt a queue to hold those preempted data calls in the marked cell of network N_1. Two concerns may arise in such preemption-based resource management scheme. First of all, excessive preemption easily results in unfairness between voice traffic and data traffic, which must be avoided. The other concern is the priority of horizontal handoff voice calls over originating voice calls. From a user's point of view, terminating a horizontal handoff voice call is more frustrating than blocking an originating voice call. Therefore, higher priority should be provided to horizontal handoff voice calls. In some channel reservation schemes, certain logic channels are exclusively reserved for handoff calls to provide such priority. However, the originating and horizontal handoff voice calls completely share the resources in our scheme unlike the reservation scheme. Therefore, we have to treat them differently during the preemptions in order to provide higher priority to horizontal handoff voice calls. In the following, we describe how the preemption works to differentiate the originating and horizontal handoff voice calls.

Firstly, we do not want to terminate an ongoing data call for accepting an incoming voice call. Therefore, the preemption fails if the queue of the marked cell of network N_1 is full. We further propose two thresholds, V_H^{max} and V_O^{max}, to prevent excessive preemption. Both thresholds are defined as the maximum capacities of ongoing voice calls when an incoming voice call tries to make a preemption. V_H^{max} is used for the preemption of horizontal handoff voice calls, and V_O^{max} is used for the preemption of originating voice calls. In the following, we introduce how the preemption works with V_H^{max} and V_O^{max}.

V_H^{max} is a real value and can be presented as

$$V_H^{max} = \left\lfloor V_H^{max} \right\rfloor + V_H^{max} \left\lfloor V_H^{max} \right\rfloor \alpha_H = \left\lfloor V_H^{max} \right\rfloor + \alpha_H \tag{11}$$

where $\left\lfloor V_H^{max} \right\rfloor$ is the integral part of $\left\lfloor V_H^{max} \right\rfloor$, and α_H is the decimal part of V_H^{max}.

When an incoming horizontal handoff voice call tries to make a preemption, the result of the preemption depends on the value of V_H^{max} and the state of the marked cell, which is given by

- If the number of current ongoing voice calls is less than $\left\lfloor V_H^{max} \right\rfloor$, the incoming horizontal handoff call can successfully preempt ongoing data calls if there are ongoing data calls and the queue is not full;
- If the number of current ongoing voice calls is equal to $\left\lfloor V_H^{max} \right\rfloor$, the incoming horizontal handoff call can successfully preempt ongoing data calls only with probability α_H if there are ongoing data calls and the queue is not full. In other words, the preemption fails with probability α_H;
- If the number of current ongoing voice calls is larger than $\left\lfloor V_H^{max} \right\rfloor$, the preemption fails even if there are ongoing data calls and the queue is not full in the marked cell of network N_1.

When implementing the above preemption scheme, the preemption succeeds (or fails) if the number of current ongoing voice calls is less (or larger) than $\left\lfloor V_H^{max} \right\rfloor$. If the number of current ongoing voice calls is equal to $\left\lfloor V_H^{max} \right\rfloor$, a random number is generated uniformly in the range of [0; 1). If the generated random number is less than α_H, the preemption succeeds. Otherwise, the preemption fails and the incoming horizontal handoff voice call is forcedly terminated.

Similar to Equation (11), V_O^{max} can be presented as

$$V_O^{\max} = \left\lfloor V_O^{\max} \right\rfloor + V_O^{\max} \left\lfloor V_O^{\max} \right\rfloor \alpha_O = \left\lfloor V_O^{\max} \right\rfloor + \alpha_O \tag{12}$$

where $\left\lfloor V_O^{\max} \right\rfloor$ is the integral part of $\left\lfloor V_O^{\max} \right\rfloor$, and α_O is the decimal part of $V_O^{\max}$. The preemption of originating voice calls is the same as the preemption of horizontal handoff voice calls except using $V_O^{\max}$ instead of $V_H^{\max}$. If the preemption fails, the incoming originating voice call is blocked. It is obvious that thresholds, $V_O^{\max}$ and $V_H^{\max}$, provide certain limitation to the preemption.

Unlike voice traffic, data traffic is delay-tolerant and benefits from a higher bandwidth channel. That is, a higher bandwidth channel can improve the throughput of a data call and reduce its holding time. Therefore, we assume that an originating data call always tries the highest bandwidth network first if there are more than one network available. When an originating data call is generated in an overlapped area, it tries network $N_i(2 < i \leq M)$ first. If there is no free channel in network N_i, the originating data call is put into the queue of network $N_i(2 < i \leq M)$. When an originating data call is generated in the area that is only covered by network N_1, it is accepted by network N_1 if there are free channels in the marked cell of network N_1. Otherwise, it is put into the queue of network N_1 if the queue is not full or terminated if the queue is full.

If an active data call mobile user moves into the marked cell from neighboring cells of network N_1, a horizontal handoff data request is generated if only network N_1 is available. The horizontal handoff data call is accepted if there are free channels in the marked cell of network N_1. Otherwise, it is put into the queue of the marked cell if the queue is not full or terminated if the queue is full. For a data call waiting in the queue of neighboring cells of network N_1, it also generates a horizontal handoff data request in the marked cell of network N_1 when its mobile user moves into the marked cell. If an active data call mobile user in singly covered area moves into area covered by more than one network, a DVH (downward vertical handoff) request is generated in the higher bandwidth network N_i. A data call in the queue of network N_1 also generates a DVH request in network $N_i(2 < i \leq M)$ when its mobile user moves into doubly covered area. If an active data call mobile user in a higher bandwidth network $N_i(2 < i \leq M)$. moves out of its coverage before call completion, it generates a UVH (upward vertical handoff) request in an available network $N_j(i \neq j)$. A data call in the queue of network $N_i(2 < i \leq M)$. also generates a UVH request in an available network N_j when the mobile user moves out of coverage of N_i.

In the following, we define λ_{ODA} as the average arrival rate of originating data call in different areas, λ_{OV} is the average arrival rate of originating voice calls in the marked cell, λ_{HHV} and λ_{HHD} is the average arrival rate of horizontal handoff voice and data call, respectively. Λ_{DVH} (λ_{UVH}) is the average arrival rate of downward (upward) vertical handoff data calls.

Fairness Between Voice and Data Traffic

The aim of WMNs is to provide desired services to mobile users, which can be measured using QoS requirements. Two main QoS requirements of voice traffic are the blocking probability B_{OV} of originating calls and the forced termination probability B_{HHV} of handoff calls. For data traffic, main QoS requirements include the blocking probability of originating data calls and the average delay. In our system, the QoS requirements of voice traffic are our main concern. We also do not want to ignore the performances of data traffic. That is, the system provides the guaranteed B_{OV} and B_{HHV} to voice traffic and the best effort service to data traffic. In other words, B_{OV} and B_{HHV} must be less than certain thresholds. Therefore, we

Figure 2. Performances of voice traffic with different V_O^{max}

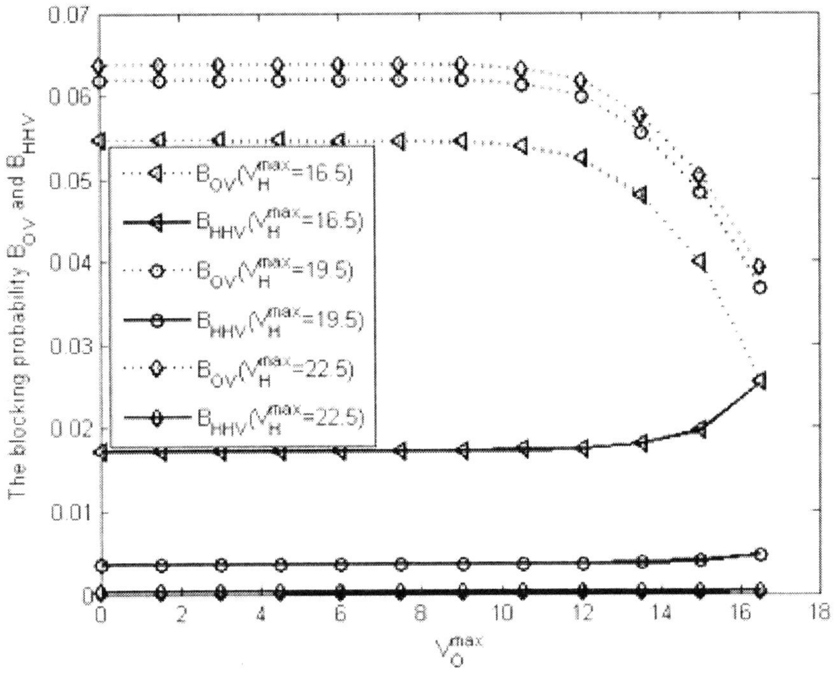

define two probability thresholds, B_{OV}^{th} and B_{HHV}^{th}, where the blocking probability of originating voice calls must not be larger than B_{OV}^{th} and the forced termination probability of handoff voice calls must not be larger than B_{HHV}^{th}.

Intuitively, by increasing the values of V_O^{max} and V_H^{max}, B_{OV} and B_{HHV} decrease since the originating voice calls and the horizontal handoff voice calls obtain more priority. Since resources are completely shared by voice and data traffic, the performances of data traffic deteriorate simultaneously when the performances of voice traffic improve. If the QoS requirements of voice traffic have been met, the further increase of V_O^{max} and V_H^{max} imposes the unfairness to data traffic. In order to provide the best effort service to data traffic and guaranteed QoS to voice traffic, we have to find the minimum values of V_O^{max} and V_H^{max} that satisfy the QoS requirements of voice traffic. It is obvious that these minimum values of V_O^{max} and V_H^{max} result in the best performances for data traffic. Bisection algorithm is used to find the minimum values of V_O^{max} and V_H^{max}.

Numerical Results

Due to space limitation, we do not provide the details on how to obtain the performance metric through Markov methods. Figure 2, Figure 3, Figure 4, and Figure 5 gives the numerical results to show the performance of our proposed schemes.

Figure 2 shows the blocking probability of originating voice calls and the forced termination prob-

Figure 3. Average delay of data calls with different V_O^{max}

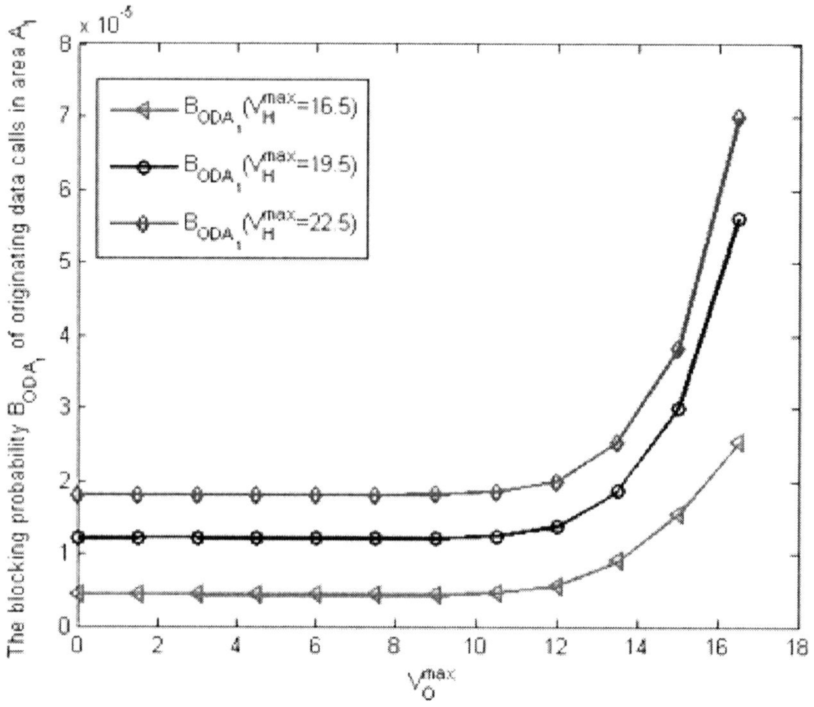

ability of horizontal handoff voice calls with different V_O^{max} and V_H^{max}. The offered voice traffic load is fixed. With the increase of V_O^{max}, the blocking probability of originating voice calls becomes less. For fixed V_H^{max}, the forced termination probability of horizontal handoff voice calls improves significantly when V_H^{max} increases. It is obvious that larger V_O^{max} and V_H^{max} can provide better performances for voice traffic. However, larger V_O^{max} and V_H^{max} result in deterioration of data traffic. Figure 3 shows that the average delay becomes longer when V_O^{max} and V_H^{max} increase. Therefore, we have to find the suitable V_O^{max} and V_H^{max} to provide the best service for data traffic.

In the following, we examine the system performances under our optimum V_O^{max} and V_H^{max}. The total offered traffic load is fixed while the ratio between voice and data traffic changes. The QoS requirements of voice traffic are set to $B_{OV}^{th} = 5\%$ and $B_{HHV}^{th} = 2\%$. In order to compare the performances of voice traffic using optimum set of V_O^{max} and V_H^{max} with other sets, we define three sets of V_O^{max} and V_H^{max}, set 1 = {12.6, 14.6}, set 2={16.5, 19.1}, and set 3={20.2, 21.2}. Figure 4 shows the performances of voice traffic using different sets of V_O^{max} and V_H^{max}. Only Set 3 and the optimum set can provide the guaranteed B_{OV}^{th} and B_{HHV}^{th} under any offered voice traffic load. When using optimum set, the blocking probability of originating voice calls and the forced termination probability of horizontal handoff calls are not larger than the guaranteed values, i.e., B_{OV}^{th} and B_{HHV}^{th}. In low traffic load, Set 2 can only provide guaranteed B_{OV}^{th} and B_{HHV}^{th}. QoS requirements of voice traffic cannot be met by Set 1 since the forced termination probability of horizontal handoff voice calls is larger than B_{HHV}^{th} under any offered voice traffic load. Figure 5 show the average delay of data traffic. Although Set 3 can provide better service

Figure 4. Performances of voice traffic with different offered voice traffic load

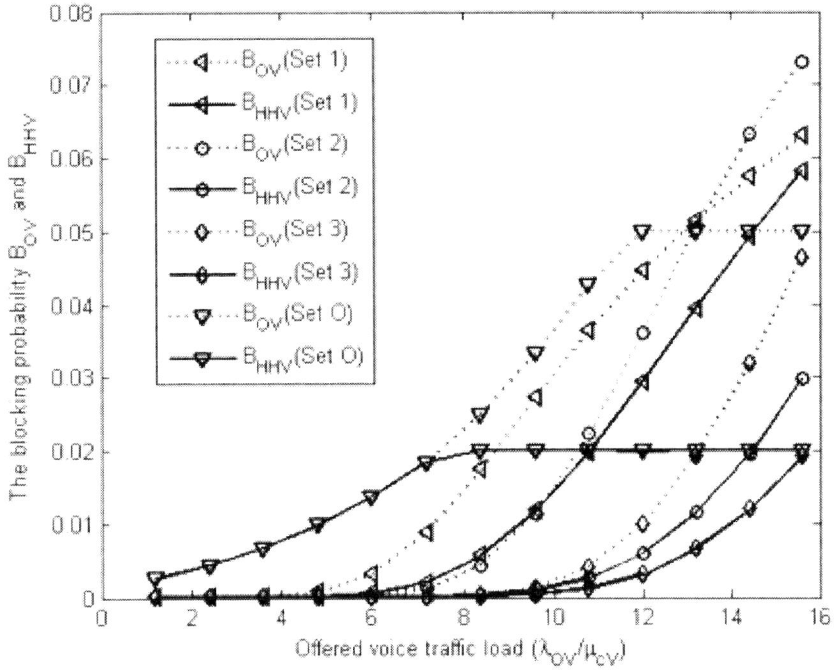

Figure 5. Average delay of data calls with different offered voice traffic load

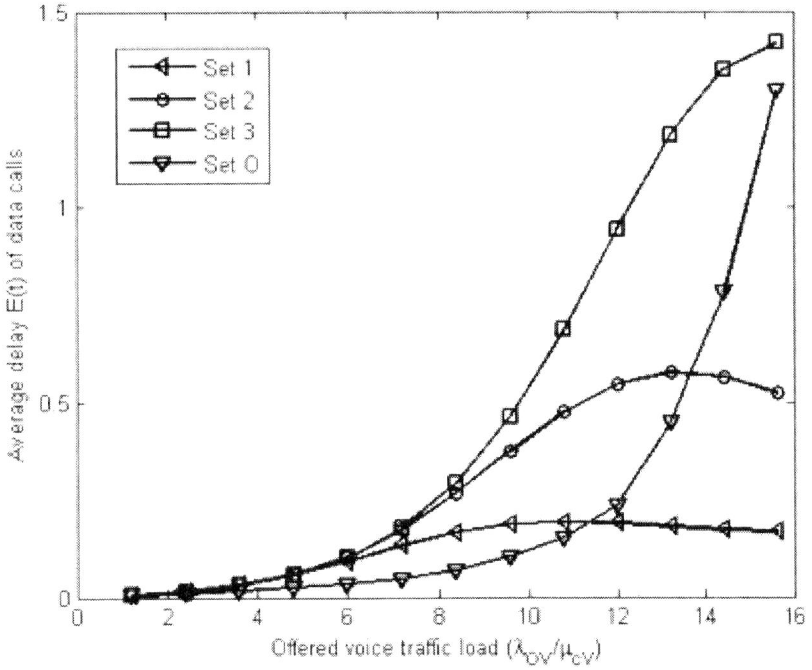

for voice traffic than other sets, it achieves the worst average delay of data traffic. Set 1 provides the best service for data traffic as shown in Figures 5. However, it cannot provide satisfied service for voice traffic. Compared to Set 2, the optimum set achieves better performances of data traffic when both of them satisfy the QoS requirements of voice traffic. Therefore, the optimum set can provide the best service for data traffic while satisfying the QoS requirements for voice traffic.

FUTURE TRENDS

In the next generation wireless and mobile networks (Beyond 3G or 4G), cellular networks still play a major role due to their dominant market share and good service quality. Other types of networks, such as WiMax and WLAN, are also witnessing fast deployment. However, any single type of WMN cannot always provide the ``best'' service for every mobile user everywhere. Network integration is a promising choice to offer the "best" service. Based on the type of user's service request and network availability, the mobile user can obtain the "best" service from IHWMNs. However, such integration still faces a lot of challenges as follows:

- Adjustment of bandwidth allocation in IHWMNs: In the IHWMN, different types of WMN have different bandwidth provision. On the other hand, different types of traffic have different bandwidth requirements. Therefore, the users may experience unstable QoS when the vertical handoff happens frequently. Some bandwidth adjustment or smoothing algorithms are required to make the transition smooth and achieve more stable QoS.
- Application of bandwidth splitting in IHWMNs: Some applications have very high bandwidth requirement, like Internet TV. As a result, any single type of WMN may not support such high bandwidth application very well. Bandwidth splitting is an approach to solve this problem, where the whole bandwidth requirement is divided into several parts and different parts are serviced by different types of WMNs. However, such splitting approach brings a lot of issues, such as bandwidth splitting strategies and synchronization among different networks. Efficient algorithms are required to provide satisfying services through multiple networks at the same time.
- Adaptive bandwidth allocation in IHWMNs: In modern wireless and mobile systems, adaptive bandwidth allocation can be applied to accept more mobile users when the incoming traffic becomes heavy. However, it becomes more difficult when it is applied to support multiple services in IHWMNs. It needs to decide to make a vertical handoff that may cause adaptive bandwidth reallocation, or stay within the current serving networks.
- Charging model and its effect: Different types of WMNs have different charging models. For example, some networks charge the access fee based on the amount of traffic, while other networks have the monthly charging plan. Therefore, such diversity of charging models will affect the user's preference. An approach to combine charging models and resource management schemes is emergently required.

CONCLUSION

In this chapter, we have reviewed the current research in integrated heterogeneous wireless and mobile networks. We also proposed network selection strategies and resource management schemes in IHWMNs and analyzed their system performance. Unlike most existing network selection strategies which are user-centric, our proposed CFNS (cost-function-based network selection) strategy is designed based on system's perspective and also considers user's needs. The numerical results showed that the proposed CFNS strategy can achieve a tradeoff between the blocking probability of originating calls and the average received signal strength. We also proposed preemption-based resource management schemes to support voice and data traffic in IHWMNs, which takes advantages of heterogeneities of traffic and networks, and the moving nature of mobile users. In the proposed preemption scheme, two thresholds were set to differentiate the originating and horizontal handoff voice calls. In order to provide the best service for data traffic and the guaranteed QoS for voice traffic, a bisection algorithm was used to find the suitable thresholds. The numerical results showed that the proposed scheme can provide the best effort service to data traffic while satisfying the QoS requirement of voice traffic. Finally, we discuss the open issues for the IHWMNs. We believe that the research topics and analytic methods presented in our work will contribute to the research and development of the future IHWMNs.

REFERENCES

Agrawal, D. P., & Zeng, Q.-A. (2006). *Introduction to wireless and mobile systems* (2nd Ed.). Florence, KY: Thomson.

Akyildiz, I., Mohanty, S., & Xie, J. (2005). A ubiquitous mobile communication architecture for next-generation heterogeneous wireless systems. *IEEE Radio Communications*, *43*(6), 29–36. doi:10.1109/MCOM.2005.1452832

Chen, W., Liu, J., & Huang, H. (2004). An adaptive scheme for vertical handoff in wireless overlay networks. *IEEE International Conference on Parallel and Distributed Systems* (ICPADS) (pp. 541-548). Washington, DC: IEEE.

3GPP TS 23.234 V7.5.0 (2007). *3GPP system to WLAN interworking, 3GPP Specification*. Retrieved May 1, 2008, from http://www.3gpp.org, 2007.

Liu, X., Li, V., & Zhang, P. (2006). *Joint radio resource management through vertical handoffs in 4G networks IEEE GLOBECOM* (pp. 1-5). Washington, DC: IEEE.

McNair, J., & Fang, Z. (2004). Vertical handoffs in fourth-generation multinetwork environments. *IEEE Wireless Communications.*, *11*(3), 8–15. doi:10.1109/MWC.2004.1308935

Nam, M., Choi, N., Seok, Y., & Choi, Y. (2004). WISE: Energy-efficient interface selection on vertical handoff between 3G networks and WLANs. *IEEE PIMRC 2004, 1*, (pp. 692-698). Washington, DC: IEEE.

Park, H.-S., Yoon, S.-H., Kim, T.-Y., Park, J.-S., Do, M., & Lee, J.-Y. (2003). *Vertical handoff procedure and algorithm between IEEE 802.11 WLAN and CDMA cellular network* (LNCS, pp.103-112). Berlin: Springer.

Pavlidou, F. N. (1994). Two-dimensional traffic models for cellular mobile systems. *IEEE Transactions on Communications, 42*(234), 1505–1511. doi:10.1109/TCOMM.1994.582831

Salkintzis, A. K. (2004). Interworking techniques and architectures for WLAN-3G integration toward 4G mobile data networks. *IEEE Wireless Communications, 11*(3), 50–61. doi:10.1109/MWC.2004.1308950

Salkintzis, A. K., Fords, C., & Pazhyannur, R. (2002). WLAN-GPRS integration for next generation mobile data networks. *IEEE Wireless Communications, 9*(5), 112–124. doi:10.1109/MWC.2002.1043861

Shen, W., & Zeng, Q.-A. (2007). Cost-function-based network selection strategy in heterogeneous wireless networks. *IEEE International Symposium on Symposium on Ubiquitous Computing and Intelligence (UCI-07).* Washington, DC: IEEE.

Shen, W., & Zeng, Q.-A. (2008). Cost-function-based network selection strategy in integrated heterogeneous wireless and mobile networks. To appear in *IEEE Transactions on Vehicle Technology.*

Song, Q., & Jamalipour, A. (2005). Network selection in an integrated wireless LAN and UMTS environment using mathematical modeling and computing techniques. *IEEE Wireless Communications, 12*(3), 42–48. doi:10.1109/MWC.2005.1452853

Stemm, M., & Katz, R. H. (1998). Vertical handoffs in wireless overlay networks. *ACM Mobile Networking (MONET)* [New York: ACM.]. *Special Issue on Mobile Networking in the Internet, 3*(4), 335–350.

Wang, H., Katz, R., & Giese, J. (1999). Policy-enabled handoffs across heterogeneous wireless networks. *Mobile Computing Systems and Applications (PWMCSA),* (pp. 51-60).

Wang, J., Zeng, Q.-A., & Agrawal, D. P. (2003). Performance analysis of a preemptive and priority reservation handoff scheme for integrated service-based wireless mobile networks. *IEEE Transactions on Mobile Computing, 2*(1), 65–75. doi:10.1109/TMC.2003.1195152

Xu, Y., Liu, H., & Zeng, Q.-A. (2005). Resource management and Qos control in multiple traffic wireless and mobile Internet systems. [WCMC]. *Wiley's Journal of Wireless Communications and Mobile Computing, 2*(1), 971–982. doi:10.1002/wcm.360

Zhang, Q., Guo, C., Guo, Z., & Zhu, W. (2003). Efficient mobility management for vertical handoff between WWAN and WLAN. *IEEE Communications Magazine, 41*(11), 102–108. doi:10.1109/MCOM.2003.1244929

Zhu, F., & McNair, J. (2004). Optimizations for vertical handoff decision algorithms. *IEEE Wireless Communications and Network Conference (WCNC)*, (pp. 867-872).

KEY TERMS AND DEFINITIONS

Fairness Among Different Types of Traffic: Due to the limitation of some resource management schemes, some traffic may be allocated too much resource while other traffic may achieve very bad performance

Integrated Heterogeneous Wireless and Mobile Networks: A new network architecture that combines different types of wireless and mobile networks and provide comprehensive services

Multi-Mode Terminal: A terminal equipped with multiple network interfaces

Multiple Traffic: The combination of different types of traffic, e.g., voice and data traffic in this chapter

Network Selection Strategy: A strategy to determine which network should be connected in an IHWMN

Preemption: a resource allocation scheme that preempt ongoing lower priority traffic when higher priority traffic is coming and there is no enough resource in the system

Resource Management: The allocation of radio resource like channel, bandwidth to different types of traffic. Optimization of resource management can achieve better system performance.

Vertical Handoff: A switch process that changes the connection from one network to another different type of network in integrated heterogeneous wireless and mobile networks

Section 9

Fault Tolerance and QoS

Chapter 32
Scalable Internet Architecture Supporting Quality of Service (QoS)

Priyadarsi Nanda
University of Technology, Sydney (UTS), Australia

Xiangjian He
University of Technology, Sydney (UTS), Australia

ABSTRACT

The evolution of Internet and its successful technologies has brought a tremendous growth in business, education, research etc. over the last four decades. With the dramatic advances in multimedia technologies and the increasing popularity of real-time applications, recently Quality of Service (QoS) support in the Internet has been in great demand. Deployment of such applications over the Internet in recent years, and the trend to manage them efficiently with a desired QoS in mind, researchers have been trying for a major shift from its Best Effort (BE) model to a service oriented model. Such efforts have resulted in Integrated Services (Intserv), Differentiated Services (Diffserv), Multi Protocol Label Switching (MPLS), Policy Based Networking (PBN) and many more technologies. But the reality is that such models have been implemented only in certain areas in the Internet not everywhere and many of them also faces scalability problem while dealing with huge number of traffic flows with varied priority levels in the Internet. As a result, an architecture addressing scalability problem and satisfying end-to-end QoS still remains a big issue in the Internet. In this chapter the authors propose a policy based architecture which they believe can achieve scalability while offering end to end QoS in the Internet.

INTRODUCTION

The concept of Policy Based Networking has long been in use by networks for controlling traffic flows and allocating network resources to various applications. A network policy defines how traffic, user and/or applications should be treated differently within the network based on QoS parameters, and may include policy statements. In most cases, such statements are defined and managed manually by the

DOI: 10.4018/978-1-60566-661-7.ch032

network administrator based upon the Service Level Agreements (SLA) between the network and its customers. Management of network devices for policy conditions to be satisfied is usually performed by a set of actions performed on various devices. For example, Internet Service Providers (ISPs) rely on network operators to monitor their networks and reconfigure the routers when necessary. Such actions may work well within the ISPs own network, but when considered across the Internet, may have serious effect in balancing traffic across many ISPs on an end-to-end basis. Hence, managing traffic over multiple Autonomous System (AS) domains requires an obvious need for change in the architecture for the current Internet and the way they function.

Traffic control and policy management between these AS domains also encounter an additional set of challenges that are not present in the intra-domain case, including trust relationship between different competing ISPs. We demonstrated the architecture based on these heterogeneous policy issues and identified various architectural components which may contribute significantly towards simplification of traffic management over the Internet. Validity of the architecture and its deployment in the Internet heavily depends on the following factors:

1. Service Level Agreements (SLAs)
2. Autonomous Systems (ASs) relationship
3. Traffic engineering and Internet QoS routing
4. Internet wide resource and flow management
5. Device configuration in support for QoS

The architecture takes into account above-mentioned factors in an integrated approach in order to support end-to-end QoS over the Internet. These factors are discussed and the design objectives of our architecture are presented throughout this chapter. We first discuss the design objectives of the architecture. In section two, we introduce background knowledge about the Internet topology and hierarchy, and identify various relationships which exist between those hierarchies. We also discuss how this knowledge of relationship between Autonomous Systems affects key design decisions. Section three provides an overview of our architecture with a brief description on various components involved within them. Section four summarizes the key features of the architecture and concludes this chapter.

DESIGN OBJECTIVES

Service Level Agreement (SLA) is one of the first requirements towards implementing policy based network architecture in the Internet. With a growing demand for better QoS, AS domains and network operators need to enforce strong SLA at various service boundaries by having some additional mechanisms for such support. Hence, in order to achieve end-to-end QoS over the Internet, the SLAs must be extended beyond the standard customer and provider relationships as used in the past and the architecture should incorporate necessary components to build such SLAs dynamically spanning different ASs in the end-to-end path.

Current Internet is a connection of ASs where the connection between the ASs are very much influenced by the relationship based on which such connectivity are formed. Fundamentally, the relationships between those ASs may be categorized as peer-to-peer, client-server and sibling (Gao, 2001), and are the driving forces behind economic benefits of individual domains. Most of the ASs try to perform load balancing through certain links connected to their neighbors and peers by using either traffic engineering approaches, such as MPLS and ATM, or policy routing decisions supported by Border Gateway Protocol (BGP) or/and a combination of traffic engineering and Internet routing. But there is no standard mechanism which may be applied universally by individual networks.

One of the alternatives to support better QoS on an end-to-end basis over the Internet may be considered by deploying overlay networks. Such approaches are also being deployed by various network service providers to support many new applications and protocols without any changes to its underlying network layer (Li & Mohapatra, 2004). Because overlay traffic use application layer profiles, they can effectively use the Internet as a low level infrastructure to provide high level services to end users of various applications provided that the lower layers support adequate QoS mechanisms.

Traffic engineering (Awduche, Chiu, Elqualid, Widjaja & Xiao, 2002) is crucial for any operational network and such thoughts have been put into the architecture by using BGP based parameter tuning in support for end-to-end QoS. We discuss various aspects of traffic engineering and its impact on the architecture in this chapter.

Managing resources for QoS flows play an important role in supporting multiple users with multiple service requirements and can be directly seen as a result of traffic engineering in the Internet. Because ASs act upon their own policy rules defined by their network administrators, achieving network wide traffic engineering and resource management is quite difficult though not impossible. Our proposed architecture is based upon a hierarchical resource management scheme (Simmonds & Nanda, 2002) which distributes the control of network functions at three different levels.

Policy Based Networking has been seen as a major area of research in the past few years and continues to draw attention from various researchers, network vendors and service providers due to increased number of network services over the Internet. Also the need for policy based network architecture should be considered more actively for the current as well as future demands for Internet use.

Earlier works on policy based network management within the IETF have resulted in two standard working groups: Resource Allocation Protocol (RAP), and the policy framework working groups (Yavatkar, Pendarakis & Guerin, 2000), (Salsano, 2001). These standard architectures describe standard policy mechanisms (mainly policy core schemas and QoS schemas that are currently being used in policy servers and specifically to manage intra-domain traffic) but do not include how and where they should be applied within the current structure of the Internet. Following key components are addressed within the architecture using a bottom up approach:

1. Service differentiation mechanism
2. Network wide traffic engineering
3. Resource availability to support QoS
4. Routing architecture to dynamically reflect any policy changes
5. Inter, intra and device level policy co-ordination mechanisms

The bottom up approach emphasizes that the network can be ready for policy compliance considering device level policy being configured first and stored in a database. Then looking at the high level policies based on business relationship, a mapping function would be able to pick up right devices, traffic routes and other associated resources in order to satisfy the QoS for various services. Based on this, the architecture is broadly divided into a three layer model and is presented later in this chapter.

The architecture would be able to control various network devices with policy rules both within and between the AS domains dynamically, as opposed to current static procedures deployed in the Internet. The architecture would then work collaboratively with the underlying technologies such as Diffserv, Intserv, and other lower layer support for achieving performance enhancements over the Internet. Scalability is considered one of the important features of the architecture and in order to address the scalability issue within such architecture, we emphasized that each domain may manage its so called policy devices in a hierarchical way in three groups:

1. Service support provided within the network with their related traffic characteristics such as bandwidth, delay, loss, jitter etc. for any traffic belonging to that specific service class
2. Devices (such as routers, switches, servers etc.) falling within each of the service class in support for QoS
3. The third group deals with management of all these devices in the second group by fine tuning traffic engineering through proper selection of protocols, and their related parameters

Currently most networks involving policy based management activities support intra-domain QoS guaranteed services for their networks only. However in this architecture we considered support for inter-domain QoS (Quoitin & Bonaventure, 2005),(Agarwal, Chuah & Katz, 2003) with an assumption that QoS inside the network will still be met.

Hence, our effort is to present design a network architecture based on the policies negotiated between the customer and the service provider on a direct SLA agreement, and define a policy negotiation/co-ordination mechanism between the ASs because, without such negotiation an end-to-end QoS model is difficult, particularly at a service level. By doing so, the architecture can allow network administrators to automate many key labor intensive tasks and hence increase overall performance related to QoS for various services. The network architecture is described to achieve the following objectives when deployed across the Internet:

- **Scalability:** Considering the intrinsic characteristics of various traffic and their requirements for QoS in the Internet, the architecture can incrementally scale to support large number of users with heavy traffic volumes and real-time performance requirements. It is also intended to manage control plane activities by easily adapting to a three layer hierarchy and with a clear understanding of communication between each layer.
- **Efficient use of network resources:** The architecture attempts to allocate resources at three different levels: Device level, Network level and Application level. Interactions between these three levels are controlled through dedicated resource managers and their associated protocols. One of the key components for such resource management strategy is based upon resource availability mechanism through the use of BGP based community attribute announcement carrying specific values for resources available within an AS domain.
- **Provisioning QoS parameters between end nodes:** The architecture does not restrict itself to technology specifics such as: Intserv, Diffserv, MPLS etc. However, it does recommend using aggregated resource allocation strategies along the source and destination networks in the Internet. Such an approach would simplify overall network management; achieve scalability in the face of increased user base and better co-ordination between the control and data planes.
- **Support for standard architectural components:** In order to support optimal QoS performance involving various applications in the Internet, the architecture is built upon various key functions

such as: Traffic engineering, Inter-domain routing, Resource management and Service Level Agreements. Hence an Integrated frame-work is presented without which end-to-end QoS would be difficult to achieve in the Internet.

The resource management mechanism is implemented through proper co-ordination of service parameters both within an AS and between the neighboring ASs in a hierarchical manner. The architecture also ensures that there are sufficient available resources on both intra and inter-domain links to carry any QoS aware applications before admitting the flow into the network. Such strategy would then control various factors such as maximum loss rate, delay and jitter contributing to performance improvement before deciding which QoS flows to allow and which to deny for a better QoS model in the Internet.

We define the policy and trust issues between various AS domains based on their connectivity in the Internet. We also investigate the effect of such policies on various other components of the architecture. Policies are central to two or more entities where various levels of services are offered, based upon the Service Level Agreements (SLAs) between them. Current Internet is comprised of groups of ASs (ISPs) placed into different tiers and the connectivity between these tiers are performed through Internet Exchange Points (IXPs) (Huston, n.d.). One of the key concerns about connectivity among various tiers is based on the kind of relationship each AS holds with their neighbors and peers. Hence the architecture considers those relationships between ASs and investigate further to identify their effect on various components of the architecture. Following section of this chapter presents AS relationships along with the AS hierarchy in the Internet.

AUTONOMOUS SYSTEM (AS) RELATIONSHIPS AND NETWORK POLICIES

Current Internet with more than 16,000 Autonomous Systems (ASs) reflects tremendous growth both in its size and complexity since its commercialization. These ASs may be classified into different types such as Internet Service Providers (ISPs), Universities or other enterprises having their own administrative domains. Sometimes, each administrative domain may have several ASs. Based upon the property of each AS and their connections between each other, it is important to develop intelligent routing policies for transportation of Internet traffic and achieve desired performance objectives for various applications. We first describe those properties related to individual AS and then work further to reflect our principles within the scope of the proposed architecture. In (Rekhter & Li, 2002) Gao et al, classified the types of routes that could appear in BGP routing tables on the basis of relationships between the ASs and presented a heuristic algorithm based on the degree of connectivity, inferring AS relationships from BGP routing tables.

Internet Connectivity

Based on network property, type of connectivity and traffic transportation principles, ASs may be classified under the following three categories. While most of the Stub networks are very much generic in nature and mainly limited to customer networks only, multi-homed and transit ASs are widely used within the Internet hierarchy because of their working relationship through which traffics are transported through them.

1. *Stub AS*: A stub AS is usually referred to an end user customer's internal network, typically a LAN (Local Area Network). One of the most important properties of stub network is that hosts in a stub network do not carry traffic for other networks (i.e. no transit service).
2. *Multi-homed AS*: Many organizations having their own AS depend upon Internet connectivity to support critical applications. One popular approach for improving Internet connectivity is to use a technique called multi-homing to connect to more than one Internet service provider (ISP). Multi-homing can be very effective ensuring continuous connectivity, eliminating the ISP as a single point of failure, and it can be cost effective as well. However, ASs must plan their multi-homing strategy carefully to ensure that such a scheme actually improves connectivity instead of degrading the service availability. Also the number of providers an AS can subscribe to is always limited because of economic considerations. In most cases, an AS uses only one of its ISP connectivity for normal traffic, whilst the second one is reserved as a back-up link in case of failure. From traffic engineering point of view such scheme improves the performance of traffic throughput between multiple links.
3. *Transit AS:* Transit ASs are described as multi-homed due to multiple connections with other service providers and carry both local and transit traffic. Such networks are generally the ISPs located within the Internet hierarchy (tier-1, tier-2,..., Customer network) as shown and described below. The figure does not show tiers 3 to 1. However connectivity between tiers is through exchange points in the Internet. Such exchange points then carry the transit traffic between each tier connected to them. (Figure 1)

Connectivity among different ISPs in the Internet is always subjected to the tier, in which they are placed in, the size of each ISP and the number of subscribers. There are mainly four ISP tier levels:

- **Tier-1:** These ISPs are called Transit providers in each country which carries core traffic in the Internet.

Figure 1. Transit AS: Multiple connections in the Internet hierarchy

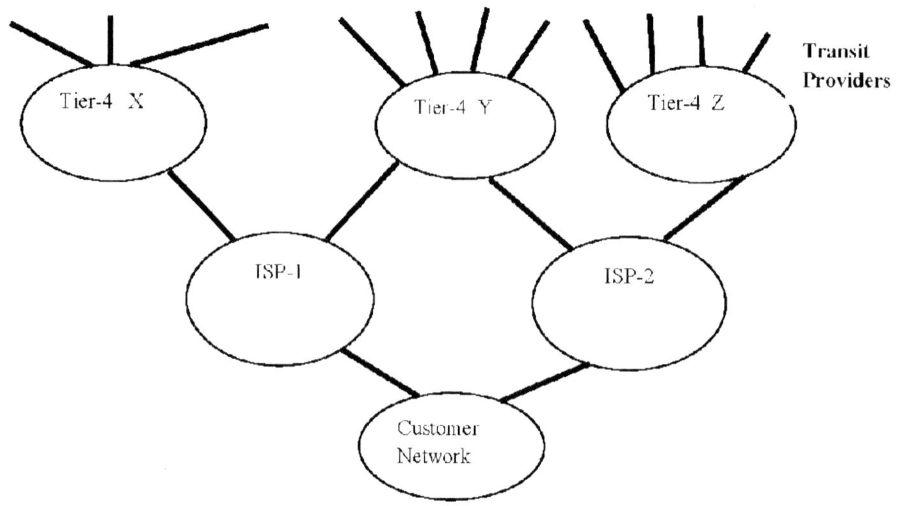

- **Tier-2:** These are nationwide backbone networks with over a million subscribers. Such networks are connected to transit ISPs in each country.
- **Tier-3:** Tier-3 ISPs are regional backbone networks which may have over 50,000 subscribers and connect to Tier-1 ISPs through peering relationship.
- **Tier-4:** These ISPs belong to local service providers and consist of major small ISPs in each country. Tier-4 ISPs support less than 50,000 users offering local services to their customers.

Apart from the above mentioned properties of ASs, they can be categorized based upon contractual relationship and agreements between them. These agreements between the ASs play an important role in representing the structure of the Internet as well end-to-end performance characteristics. Such relationships between the ASs are fundamental to the architecture and are discussed in the following:

1. *Customer-Provider relationship:* In a customer-provider relationship scenario, a customer buys services (network connectivity and service support) from its provider which is typically an ISP. Similarly, the ISPs buy the services they offer to their customers from their upstream service providers such as tier-4. In other words, a provider does transit traffic for its own customers, whereas a customer does not transit traffic between any two of its providers even if multi-homed. Network architecture supporting customer-provider relationship need to address issues in relation with Service Level Agreements (SLA) enforced between the customer and its providers.
2. *Peer-to-Peer relationship:* Two ASs offering connectivity between their respective customers without exchange of any payments are said to have peer-to-peer relationship. Hence these two ASs agree to exchange traffic between their respective customers free of charge. Such relationship is enforced through routing policies between the ASs at the same level within the Internet hierarchy. For example, a tier-4 service provider must peer with another service provider at the same level, i.e. another tier-4 only. Such a relationship and agreement between two ASs would mutually benefit both, perhaps because roughly equal amounts of traffic flow between them.
3. *Sibling relationship:* Sibling relationship may be established between two or more ASs if they are closely placed to each other. In this situation, the relationship allows the individual domains to provide connectivity to the rest of the Internet for each other. Also sometimes called mutual transit relationship, they may be used to provide backup connectivity to the Internet for each other when connection for one of the AS fails. Sibling relationship between ASs may also be used for load balancing and using bandwidth efficiently among various services in the Internet provided the ASs involved agree to such an arrangement.

In order to design a new Internet architecture based on the AS properties and their relationship (stub, multi-homed, transit and customer-provider, peer, or sibling), it is important that the architecture must first of all support them and then derive related policies to enforce them across the Internet. Such architecture will then be able to answer the following issues when deployed across the Internet:

- Resource management with multiple service support
- End-to-End QoS for individual service
- Load Balancing
- Fault management
- Facilitate Overlay routing

- Security related to information sharing between ASs

One such mechanism which has potential to address above issues is the BGP that is dynamic and also support network policies. Next section of this chapter provides details about how BGP can be used to support network policies in our proposed architecture.

Border Gateway Protocol (BGP) and AS Relationships

Currently, Border Gateway Protocol (BGP) is being deployed across the Internet as a standard routing protocol between AS domains, where AS relationships are enforced by configuring certain BGP parameters. Routing traffic containing BGP carry nearly 90% of Internet route announcements due to its rich feature supporting network policies and contributing significantly towards Internet load balancing, traffic engineering and support for fall-back procedures in the event of network bottlenecks. BGP as part of the Inter-domain routing protocol standard for the current Internet allows each AS domain to select its own administrative policy by choosing the best route and announcing and accepting routes to and from other AS domains connected as neighbors. Though such an approach works reasonably well for most of the ASs individually to satisfy their personal objectives and maximizing their profits, it does not address the impact of such an approach on a global scale.

Before presenting the architecture in detail, in the following, we present a few of the BGP approaches for policy enforcement between ASs. We try to present those policy issues and how BGP is currently configured related to AS relationships mentioned above.

Border Gateway Protocol (BGP-4) (Rekhter & Li, 2002) was a simple path vector protocol when first developed and the main purpose of BGP was to communicate and control path level information between ASs so as to control route selection process between them. Using path level announcements by neighbors, an AS decides which path to use in order to reach specific prefixes. One of the main reasons

Figure 2. Connectivity among autonomous systems

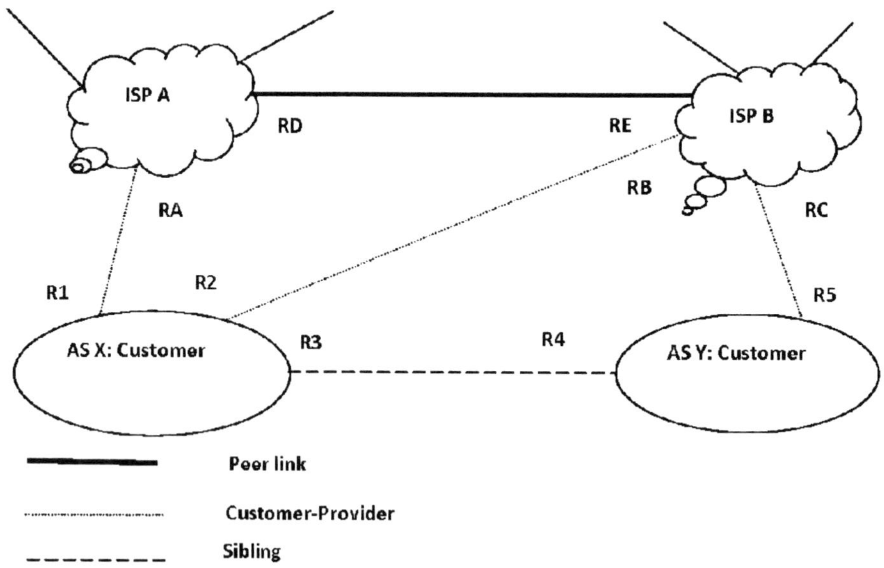

Table 1. BGP routing decision process

1. Find the path with highest Local-Preference
2. Compare AS-Path length and choose the one with least length
3. Look for the path with Lowest MED attribute
4. Prefer e-BGP learned routes over i-BGP routes
5. Choose the path with lowest IGP metric to next hop

ASs use BGP for Inter-domain routing is for their own policies to be communicated to their neighbors and subsequently across the whole Internet.

Many modifications to the original BGP have happened over time, and today we see BGP as a protocol weighed down with a huge number of enhancements overlapping and conflicting in various unpredictable ways. In this chapter we do not try to analyze those complex issues with BGP, instead our aim is to use BGP as a transport vehicle across ASs and implement network wide policies between them. It is sensible at this point of time to consider the ASs as ISPs and then we can be more specific in terms of exploring policies related to those ISPs and work for a better management of Internet wide traffic mapping to the relationships we have mentioned before. Henceforth, this chapter will use the terms AS and ISP interchangeably. Figure 2, shows a scenario connecting different ASs and representing their relationships with each other.

One of the key features of BGP is the decision process through which each BGP router determines the path to destination prefixes. The rules are given in Table 1 below:

As shown in Table 1, the relationships between individual ASs are realized by BGP attributes and in order to determine the actions to be performed for the purpose of traffic engineering between them, the following must be considered:

- *Use of Local Preference to influence Path announcement:* In a customer-provider relationship, providers prefer routes learned from their customers over routes learned from peers and providers, when all those routes to the same prefix are available. Hence in the above figure, ISP A would certainly prefer routes to all those prefixes within customer Y from customer X instead from ISP B. By doing so, ISP A can generate revenue by sending traffic through its own customer. Instead, if ISPA sends traffic through its own provider (not shown), it costs money for ISP A and through ISP B (peer), the credit rating of ISP A will be down graded. In order to implement such a policy (prefer customer route advertisements) using the local preference attribute, ISPs in general must assign higher local preference value to the path for a given prefix learned from their customer. In (Caesar & Rexford, 2002), Caesar et al described the use of assigning a non-overlapping range of Local Preference values to each type of peering relationships between AS domains and mentioned that Local Preference be varied within each range to perform traffic engineering between them. Hence Local Preference attribute in BGP can be used to perform the job of traffic engineering especially controlling outgoing traffic between ASs as well holding the policy relationships between them.
- *Use of AS path pre-pending and Multi-Exit Discriminator (MED) attributes to influence transit and peering relationships:* ISPs may influence the load balance of incoming traffic on different links connected to their neighbors. Such a scheme can be implemented by selectively exporting

the routes to their neighbors. For example, an ISP may selectively announce its learned paths to its peer thereby forcing the peer to only get information on specific routes. Transit ISPs can control their incoming traffic by selectively announcing their learned routes to their peers. Apart from this, BGP makes use of AS path pre-pending technique where an ISP can apply its own AS number to multiple times and announce the path to its neighbor.

Because BGP decision process selects lowest AS path length (rule-2 in Table1) such a technique will force the neighbor to choose another path if available, instead of a pre-pended AS path announced by the neighbor. To investigate further into the policy mechanisms associated with AS path pre pending and load balancing between peers, consider Figure 2 again. In this, ISP A decides to pre-pend its AS number in the path announcement to ISP B 3 times, ISP A will announce the path: ISP A, ISP A, ISP A, Customer A to ISP B. Hence ISP B will instead choose a different path to reach the prefixes with Customer A. But such a scheme is often selected manually on a trial and error basis simply to avoid more traffic from other domains. In the architecture we discuss to use AS path pre-pending only when the relationship between peers is based upon strict exchange of traffic without monetary involvement.

Another scheme in which ISPs use the Multi Exit Discriminator (MED) attribute to control incoming traffic from its neighbors. ISPs having multiple links to other ISPs can use MED attribute in order to influence the link that should be used by the other ISP to send its traffic towards a specific destination. However, use of MED attribute must be negotiated beforehand between two peering ISPs. In the architecture, MED attribute is only used between transit ISPs having multiple links to other ISPs.

- *Use of community attribute for route export to neighbors:* ISPs have been using the BGP community attributes for traffic engineering and providing their customers a finer control on the redistribution of their routes (Quoitin, Uhlig, Pelsser, Swinnen & Bonaventure, 2003).

Internet Assigned Numbers Authority (IANA) typically assigns a block of 65536 community values to each AS, though only a few of them are used to perform community based traffic engineering. Using these attributes, by tagging them into the AS path announcement, an ISP may ask its neighbor or customer to perform a set of actions on the AS path when distributing that path to its neighbor (Li & Mohapatra, 2004),(Uhlig, Bonaventure, & Quoitin, 2003). For example in Figure 2, ISP A may want its customer (customer X) to pre-pend customer Xs AS path information 3 times before announcing further up stream. Similarly, ISP B may ask ISP A not to announce any path to customer X (e.g. NO_EXPORT). By doing so, ISPs are able to better control their incoming traffic. However, because community based attributes are yet to be standardized, there is a need for uniform structure in these attributes in order to apply them in the Internet. Also because each community attribute value requires defining a filter for each supported community in the BGP router, such a process will add more complexity into already fragile BGP and hence increase the processing time of the BGP message (Yavatkar, Pendarakis & Guerin, 2000).

In summary, AS relationships play important role in Internet connectivity between various ISPs and contribute significantly towards designing a new architecture for the Internet. BGP based traffic engineering can be made more scalable by carefully selecting and configuring the attributes based on business relationships between various ISPs. The architecture is presented in next section which is based upon the analysis we have presented before on the use of ISP relationships and their corresponding traffic engineering attributes supported by many features of BGP.

THREE-LAYER POLICY ARCHITECTURE FOR THE INTERNET

We present the architecture supporting scalability and end-to-end performance in this section while accomplishing the following major tasks:

- **Traffic flow management and resource monitoring:** Flows are usually aggregated based on desired characteristics such as delay, loss, jitter, bandwidth requirements and assigned priority levels which determine end-to-end performance for various applications. Based on such aggregated flow characteristics Bandwidth Brokers in each AS domain then decide whether to accept the flow or reject them. Such flow management activities are performed at layer-2 of the architecture delivering network layer QoS across multiple domains in the end-to-end path.
- **QoS Area identification:** Each domain in the Internet is engineered and provisioned to support a variety of services to their customers. In the worst case an AS having connectivity to the Internet at least supports Best Effort service as a default service. In addition many of these ASs are also engineered to support VoIP, Video Conferencing and other time critical applications. Identifying these AS domains in the Internet and routing traffics through them improves overall QoS for various applications. This function is supported at layer-3 of the architecture which essentially performs Inter-domain QoS routing by identifying QoS areas in support for a specified service. This layer is different from TCP based session establishment because, in our architecture it is assumed that, there exist multiple AS domains with multiple QoS. Hence using QoS routing the architecture then supports selection of different QoS networks based on AS relationships for QoS sensitive applications.
- **Traffic engineering and load balancing:** Since traffic engineering is important to improve end-to-end QoS, the architecture tries to balance traffic flows between various domains through policy co-ordination mechanism. The mechanism uses an approximation technique to balance any traffic parameter conflict between neighboring domains and improve overall QoS for services.
- **Policy based routing:** Applications requiring strict QoS must adhere to certain policies and our architecture uses BGP based policy decisions and applies various attributes of BGP to compute optimized routing paths. A route server in each domain relieves the routers from such complex policy decisions and processes information in fast mode.

The above mentioned functions are integrated and operate at different levels within our proposed architecture. Resource management within and between AS domains are clearly supported through the hierarchical grouping of various architectural components and are described below:

1. The architecture is hierarchical and operates at different levels to support both high level (business focused) and low level (device focused) resource availability for maintaining end-to-end QoS.
2. The control plane of the architecture is separated from the data plane in order to maintain scalability across the Internet with wide variety of service classes.
3. Each level in the hierarchy is controlled by a manager which receives resource availability information from components within that level only and the output is informed to a higher level in the hierarchy. Hence the approach is bottom up.
4. Communication between same levels is allowed through peer-to-peer session establishment without additional overhead to manage the Internet. Any conflict for end-to-end QoS is resolved through

proper policy co-ordination mechanisms.

5. Apart from resource management, the architecture also includes routing and traffic engineering and hence is an integrated approach to manage various services in the Internet.

The logical view of the architecture is presented in Figure 3. Each level in the hierarchy is associated with number of functions independent of any technology choice.

One of the key components of the architecture is to separate out the control plane from the data forwarding plane by hierarchically grouping network management functions. Also important to note that, both layer-2 and layer-3 can be combined to form the Inter-network layer of TCP/IP network architecture. Essentially, layer-3 of the architecture determines the AS domains in support for a specified QoS through which a flow can be set-up but does not go beyond that to address the issue of resource and flow management which are performed by layer-2 only. The architecture also considers both flow and resource management functions between domains only as individual domains need to guarantee QoS based on device capabilities within their own domain. A detailed description on individual layers of the architecture is presented below.

Layer-1: Device Layer QoS

Network devices including routers, switches, servers etc. are the key components to maintain and manage traffic flows across networks in an AS domain. These devices can be configured with low-level policy information managed by a single or multiple device managers depending on the size of the network. Support for QoS to various applications heavily depends on identifying, configuring, maintaining and accounting for these QoS aware devices within an AS. In order to support device level QoS in our architecture, following policies may be applied:

Figure 3. Scalable QoS architecture, logical view

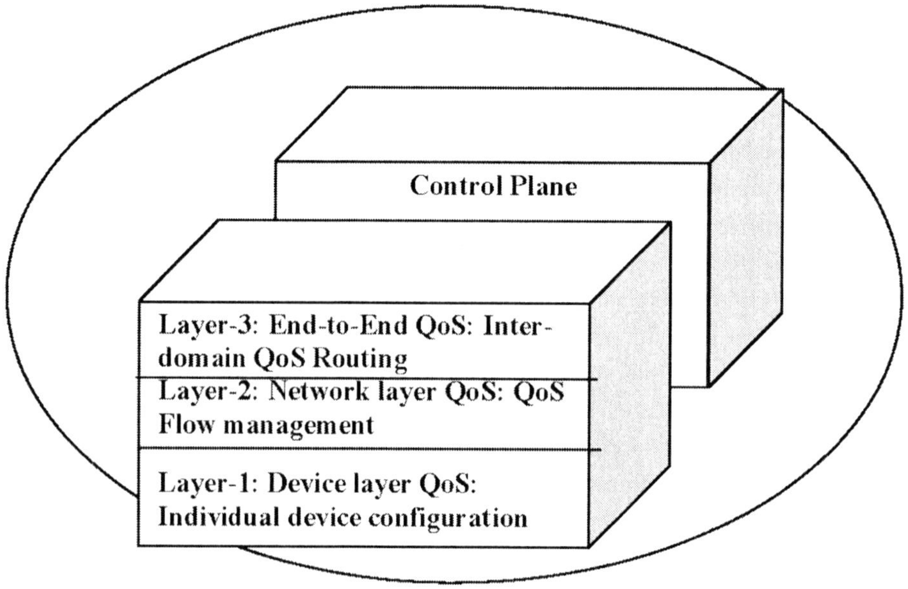

1. Each device registers their device functionalities through a policy repository indicating the kind of service support to different applications
2. The repository has a direct interface with network management tool such as SNMPv3 which monitors the devices on a time scale to determine fairly accurate assessment of the physical connectivity of various devices in the network.
3. Information supporting various queuing strategies, scheduling mechanisms and prioritized traffic handling for different devices may also be obtained from the repository. Such information is useful to determine the kind of QoS architecture supported (Intserv, Diffserv, MPLS) within a network domain.
4. Decision on admitting a traffic flow and offering particular level of QoS to the flow depends on the ability of those devices falling on the path of the flow. However such decision on admission control is managed at the next level of the architecture by inspecting the policy repository along with any routing decisions.
5. The overall management of network devices within an AS is performed by a Device manager. The device manager will then need a direct interface with the management tool and the policy repository. Use of separate management component reduces the load of SNMP tool and carries out next level communication within the architecture. Hence the device manager handles device configuration decisions and communicates with higher level managers to indicate various device level QoS support in the network. One thing to note in the architecture is that the device level QoS is only responsible for obtaining different device resources and help in preparing network topology for QoS support to various flows within the AS domain only.

The logical view of device level QoS is shown in Figure 4. It is assumed that resources within an AS are computed based on aggregated bandwidth requirements by different service classes. For scalability reasons, the architecture handles aggregated reservation for resources within each device in the path of

Figure 4. Device layer QoS components

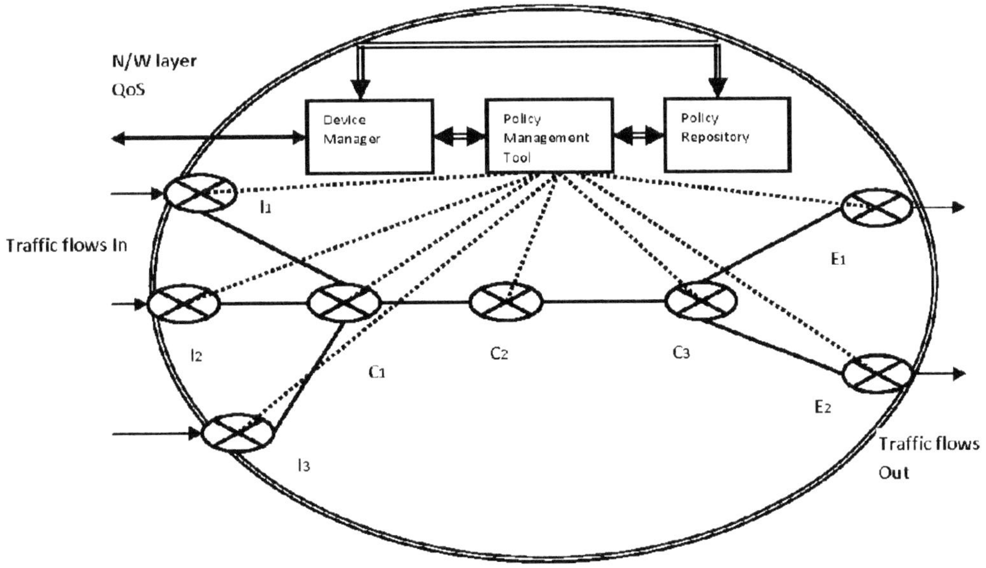

the flow sharing same link and request for the same traffic class.

If any one of the devices cannot support the required resources and QoS parameters, either of the following actions may be performed which is based on service priority and any further economic incentives:

- The request for the flow may be denied
- Alternative devices may be selected and informed to the next layer, the network layer, where a separate path may be created by applying network QoS flow management using BB resource management strategy
- The device manager may negotiate with network layer and further up the line in the hierarchy, and the final decision to offer a lower QoS level may be communicated between different entities involved in this process

However network layer decision on QoS flow management across various AS domains is important within the architecture in order to determine how traffic can best be handled with the desired QoS support from the devices below. The architectural support at next level in the hierarchy (network layer QoS) is based on admission control policy, inter-domain flow management and signaling for various flows. The layer-2 functions of the architecture are presented below.

Layer-2: Network Layer QoS

Network layer service guarantees for QoS sensitive applications are supported through the information from device managers and their associated management tools which are located in the bottom most layer of the architecture. Once this information is obtained, the network layer QoS determines and supports QoS guarantees between network boundaries within an AS domain. Hence this layer performs flow and resource management functions for both intra-domain and inter-domain in the Internet. The intra-domain functions are presented below, followed by inter-domain functions which are important. However for intra-domain following procedures may be noted:

1. Identifying paths between edge routers applying intra-domain routing and ranking them (high-to-low) according to QoS service support based on parameters such as: bandwidth, delay, jitter, loss and cost.
2. Resource allocation for each device, in every edge-to-edge path based on aggregated reservation strategy, and is classified under the intra-domain resource management framework. Such aggregated reservation is made for a group of flows sharing same link and request for the same traffic class.
3. Once allocations of resources are completed, such information is stored in a repository which is updated at regular intervals.
4. Admission control for individual flows at the edge (ingress) routers by checking SLAs and any policy related information.
5. A QoS manager within each AS ensures support for network layer QoS to various applications as well as communicating with the device manager and other higher level components in the architecture.

The network layer QoS is also responsible for topology discovery within an AS where connectivity information between various devices is obtained in order to know the exact path between end points within an AS domain. Such topology discovery information is required for two different cases. The first one is the information related to physical topology of the network, describing physical connectivity between different devices which in most cases is static unless physical changes happen within the network. The second one is based on routing topology, which changes frequently as the routes taken between any pair of devices within the network are likely to change relatively more frequently e.g. effect of traffic engineering to load balance traffic among different links.

Physical topology information is obtained by interacting with the device manager while the routing topology information is based on factors such as the type of routing protocol, various routing schemes (overlay routing vs. standard next-hop routing) and any routing policies applied in order to support service guarantees for different traffic flows within the AS domain. However, we only describe the architecture and its associated components without further details on any specific mechanisms for deployment in the Internet. For the sake of an example we consider Diffserv, but it is entirely up to the network managers/designers to decide the kind of technology to be used with their relevant QoS support for various applications in the Internet. The logical view of the network layer QoS for intra-domain flow management is shown in Figure 5.

The QoS manager plays a central role in managing network wide QoS delivery by interacting with other components of the architecture. As device managers manage various devices and interact with device repository and management tool to monitor, configure, and record any device level statistics in support for QoS in the network, such information are crucial for QoS manager at the network layer to apply between network edges for intra-domain QoS guarantee. Hence an accurate view of both device support at lower layers and resource management contributes significantly towards building good architecture for the Internet.

One of the important tasks at the network layer is to make sure sufficient resources are available for different QoS sensitive flows originating from both within the network and outside the network. While flows originating within the network are guaranteed resources for specific QoS based on SLAs and poli-

Figure 5. Network level QoS (intra-domain): logical view

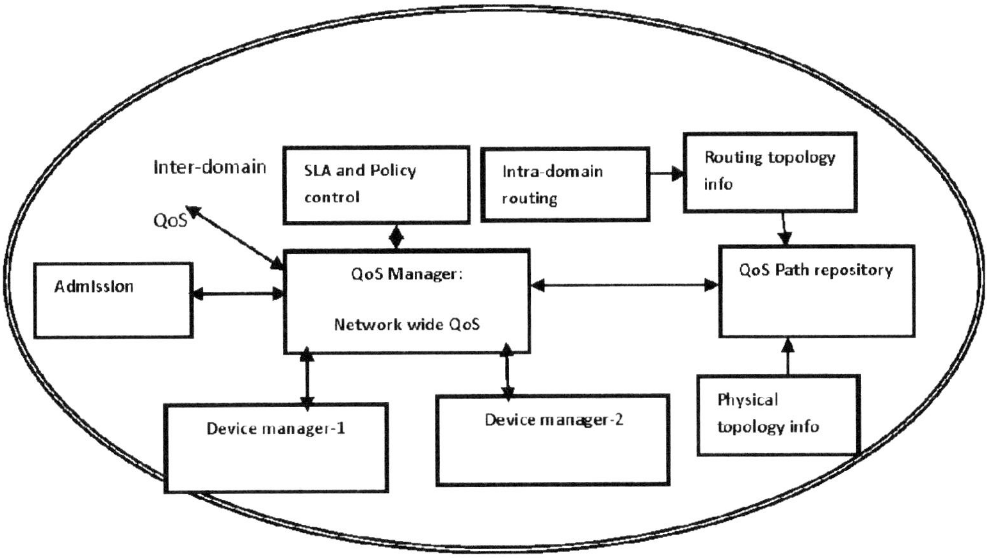

cies between the network and its customers, flows entering from outside the network are permitted if prior contract and relationships are established between other network domains. Otherwise, the network treats the flows as BE specific without further guarantees on QoS.

Another interesting point to note within the architecture is the interaction between routing topology and physical topology information. While intra-domain routing protocols are used to determine the network level path within an AS, such path may not give an optimized solution to support QoS for the application. Hence, the QoS manager communicates with the QoS path repository to determine any better path availability with the desired resources for that application at that instant. If an alternative path is discovered between the same edge points, actions may be taken by the QoS manager to inform the device manager to configure those devices falling on the path. Physical topology of a network describing connectivity between devices may be used as a choice for forwarding the traffic in situations where routing protocols may not be useful in support for QoS within an AS. Such considerations are taken within the architecture in order to support "better than best-effort" QoS particularly involving control load services defined in Diffserv.

QoS manager is responsible for providing service level guarantees within an AS only. However end-to-end QoS guarantee in the Internet needs to be supported by multiple domains through which Internet wide connectivity is established. Various factors apart from individual network level QoS are important to consider in this regard. Within the architecture, third layer in the hierarchy, the Inter-domain QoS, is designed to further manage end-to-end QoS for various applications. Issues in relation to trust management, policy co-ordination, inter-domain routing, traffic engineering and competitive pricing structures are some of the key factors which are considered at the next level in the architecture and are described below.

Layer-3: End-to-End QoS

The End-to-End QoS layer in the architecture is responsible for managing higher level policies in the networks in order to guarantee end-to-end QoS across the Internet. One of the most important functions performed by this layer is selecting QoS areas between end nodes and routing traffic flows based on their QoS parameters. Inter-domain policy routing, traffic engineering for load balancing and supporting various user QoS requirements using SLAs are the key functions of this layer. Hence this layer extends single AS level QoS (offered at layer-2 of the architecture) to multiple AS level QoS by adding following functions into the architecture.

1. Application level QoS are supported through SLAs between the network service provider and customers. Hence identifying various parameters from the SLAs such as customer identification, service category, resource support, service schedule, traffic descriptor, QoS parameters and out-of-profile traffic treatments are important to consider at this layer of the architecture.
2. Admission control policies determine user authentication through a central repository within each AS and find out the level of QoS support for the flows.
3. Administrative and pricing policies are considered part of admission control process and resource allocation strategy to various applications. However the architecture does not include pricing issues.
4. AS relationships and trust issues are central to determine existence of any QoS paths between end nodes spanning multiple domains in the Internet. Such approach investigates a number of QoS paths

rather than simply choosing the lowest metric routing path between end points in the Internet. AS relationships are determined by inferring various Internet characteristics as well as using policy based routing information between different domains.

5. Inter domain routing decisions based on various policies are given preferences, allowing the set of service requirements to be optimally supported within the network's aggregate resource capability.
6. A central domain coordinator within each AS is responsible for the above mentioned activities by interacting with domain coordinators from other domains in the Internet. Hence, identifying QoS domains and investigating their service offerings are keys to such architecture.
7. Any conflict in resource and traffic management including simple pricing parameters is resolved by applying resource co-ordination or similar algorithm between various domains in the QoS path.
8. Once QoS discovery process is completed, the extracted technical parameters from the SLAs, which are referred to as service level specifications (Goderis, et al., 2001), are mapped across network layer QoS components and finally through the device managers in individual ASs.

The architectural support at the End-to-End QoS layer which does the above mentioned functions are achieved largely through a series of negotiation and policy co-ordination activities before the exact QoS parameters are determined by the domain coordinator and applied across various domains in the QoS path. Such approach would then guarantee the SLAs between the service provider and its customers supporting end-to-end QoS objectives for various applications. The logical view of End-to-End QoS layer is presented in Figure 6 with various interactions among the components present within them.

The function of the domain coordinator can be compared with a Bandwidth Broker (Terzis, Wang, Ogawa & Zhang, 1999), (Li, Zhang, Duan, Gao & Hou, 2000) or a Policy Server (Yavatkar, Pendarakis & Guerin, 2000) which does the job of policy based admission control by comparing SLSs with user

Figure 6. End-to-End QoS: Logical view

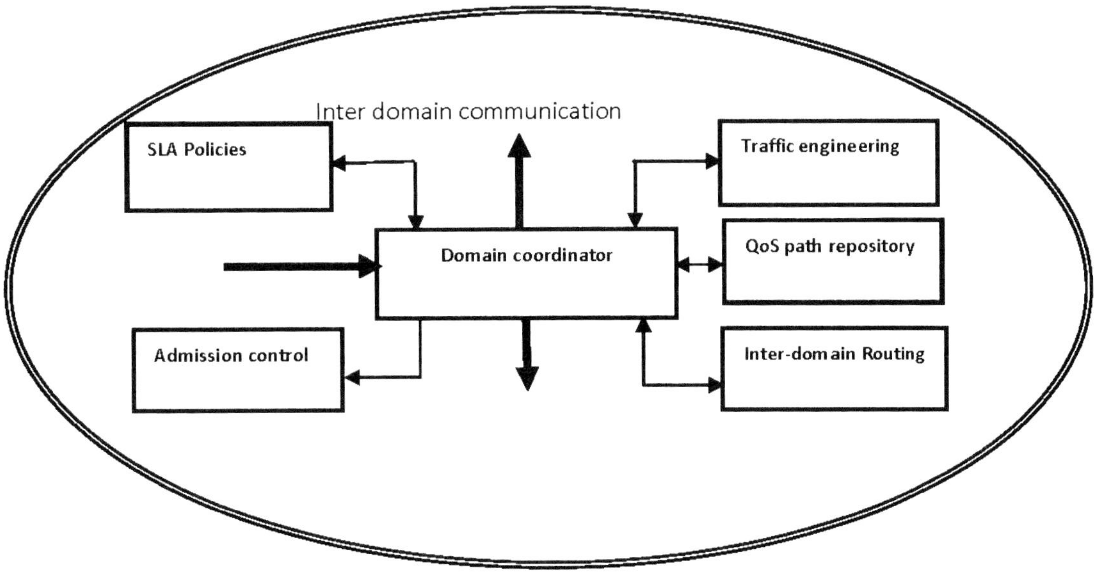

flow parameters. Resource control similar to the work stated in both (Yavatkar, Pendarakis & Guerin, 2000), (Terzis, Wang, Ogawa & Zhang, 1999) is also performed by the domain coordinator. The domain coordinator primarily manages two different sets of policies as specified in the logical diagram and exchanges with other domains.

The customer specific policy controls access to available services within a service provider's domain by comparing parameters such as: priorities, usable services, resource availability, valid time against SLA rules as specified between the service provider and its customer. A decision on whether to accept the customer's flow or to deny it is finally conveyed through the admission control module. The right side of the domain coordinator as shown in Figure 6 is responsible for service and resource specific policies. Service parameters related to QoS values, valid time and cost are compared against any policy rules found in their respective SLAs. In order to determine optimized values for these service parameters, the domain coordinator needs to consider various traffic engineering policies as well as routing policies involving peering domains. Finally the architecture deals with resource specific policies such as: bandwidth, delay and jitter available at the network level by communicating with the QoS manager.

In case of policy conflicts (e.g. available resources are not sufficient), the domain coordinator initiates a policy coordination algorithm between domains present in the end-to-end QoS path. In order to understand the overall architecture on an end-to-end basis, the flow diagram in Figure 7 demonstrates various activities and their sequence of operations between end systems in the Internet. In the functional description of the architecture, while the objective is to support QoS between various domains under different AS administrative control, individual domains should support both network level and device level QoS throughout the life of the flow.

Figure 7. Functional descriptions and interactions among different layers

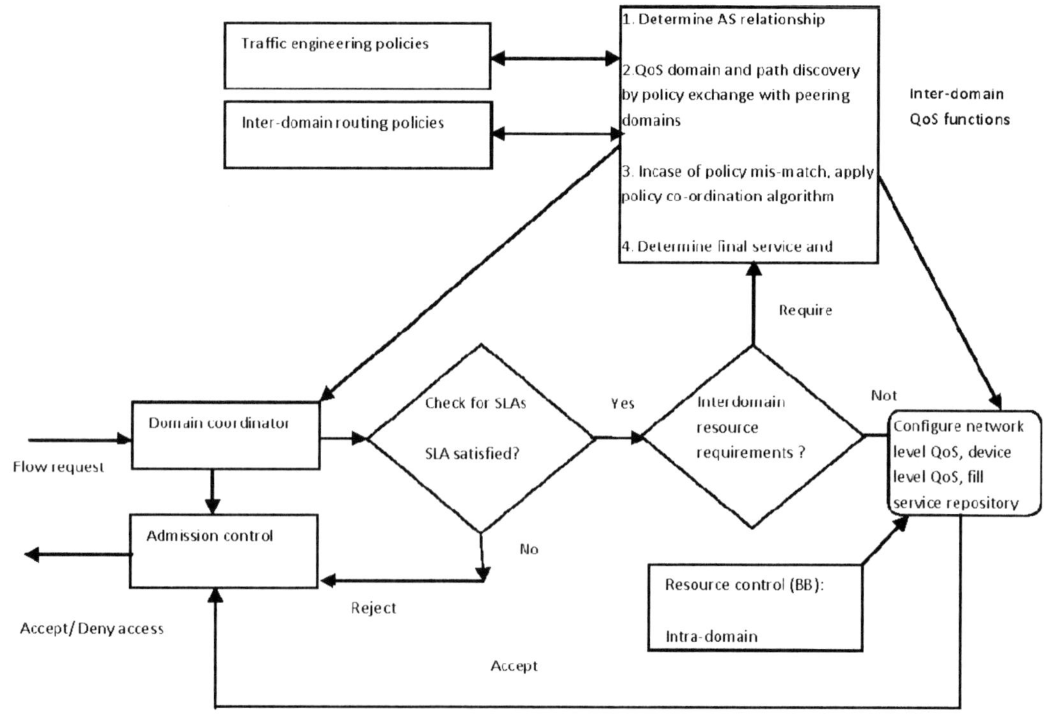

CONCLUSION

We discussed a Policy architecture that handles resource management for both intra and inter domain resources for QoS specific (high-priority) applications. One of the strengths of the architecture is its separation of control and management plane from the data plane in order to facilitate better end-to-end QoS control. The architecture is also hierarchical and operates at different levels to support both high level (business focused) and low level (device focused) resource availability for maintaining end-to-end QoS. Various levels in the hierarchy are controlled by a manager that receives resource availability information from components within that level only, and the output is informed to a higher level in the hierarchy. Hence the approach is also bottom up.

Communication between same levels is allowed through peer-to-peer session establishment and making use of necessary signaling protocols. Any conflict for end-to-end QoS is resolved through proper policy co-ordination mechanism. Apart from resource management, the architecture also includes policy based routing and traffic engineering through fine tuning of BGP routing policy structures. Hence the architecture is scalable, integrated and is aimed at improving end-to-end QoS for various services in the Internet.

Validation of the architecture presenting functionalities of the three different layers is performed using three different environments. Layer-1 functionalities of the architecture demonstrating Diffserv network is presented by creating a test bed scenario with Diffserv capable domain and measuring end-to-end QoS parameters for VoIP application in the presence of other background traffic. Such experiments then motivate to consider various QoS parameters and use resource management strategy between AS domains. However, layer-2 of our architecture mainly deals with resource management between neighboring AS domains on an end-to-end basis. For this we designed a prototype based on Bandwidth Broker and using our own signaling scheme to properly manage traffic flows with different QoS classes. Finally layer-3 of our architecture is designed to select QoS domains and forwarding traffic based on Inter domain routing protocol such as BGP to enforce routing policies in a dynamic way. In order to demonstrate such functions of our architecture we used several simulation experiments based on OPNET simulator. The simulation environment also considered parameters used by the real routers and demonstrated the efficiency of using community based attribute and policy co-ordination algorithm in case of policy conflict. A series of experiments are conducted to investigate the effect of BGP based policy enforcement, load balancing between AS domains and traffic engineering for scalability and better management of QoS in the Internet.

We presented a Policy based architecture which is designed to support end-to-end QoS for multiple service classes in an integrated way. With the integrated approach, our design and performance evaluation results presented in (Nanda, 2008) indicated such end-to-end QoS can be achieved with the help of service mapping, policy based routing and traffic engineering, resource management using BB functionalities, and device level QoS support across the Internet. The main strengths of our design are scalability, ability to handle heterogeneous policies, and distributed resource management support. This chapter also established a foundation for further research on policy routing involving security, policy based billing and charging in the Internet, and application level resource management in the Internet.

REFERENCES

Agarwal, S., Chuah. C. N., & Katz, R. H. (2003). *OPCA: Robust Inter-domain Policy Routing and Traffic Control,* OPENARCH.

Awduche, D.O., Chiu, A., Elqalid, A., Widjaja, I., & Xiao, X. (2002). *A Framework for Internet Traffic Engineering* [draft 2]. Retrieved from IETF draft database.

Caesar, M., & Rexford, J. (2005, March). *BGP routing policies in ISP networks*, (Tech. Rep. UCB/CSD-05-1377). U. C. Berkeley, Berkeley, CA.

Gao, L. (2001). On inferring autonomous system relationships in the Internet. *IEEE/ACM Transactions on networking, 9*(6), December.

Goderis, D. et al. (2001, July). *Service Level Specification Semantics and parameters*: *draft-tequila-sls-01.txt* [Internet Draft].

Huston, G. (n.d.). Peering and settlements Part-1. *The Internet protocol journal.* San Jose, CA: CISCO Systems.

Li, Z. Zhang, Duan, Z., Gao, L.& Hou, Y.T.(2000). Decoupling QoS control from Core routers: A Novel bandwidth broker architecture for scalable support of guaranteed services. *Proc. Of SIGCOMM'00*, Stockholm, Sweden, (pp. 71-83).

Li, Z., & Mohapatra, P. (2004, January). QoS Aware routing in Overlay networks (QRON). *IEEE Journal on Selected Areas in Communications, 22*(1).

Nanda, P. (2008, January). *A three layer policy based architecture supporting Internet QoS*. Ph.D. thesis, University of Technology, Sydney, Australia.

Quoitin, B., & Bonaventure, O. (2005). A Co-operative approach to Inter-domain traffic engineering. *1st Conference on Next Generation Internet Networks Traffic Engineering* (NGI 2005), Rome, Italy, April 18-20th.

Quoitin, B., Uhlig, S., Pelsser, C., Swinnen, L., & Bonaventure, O. (2003). *Internet traffic engineering with BGP: Quality of Future Internet Services*. Berlin: Springer

Rekhter, Y. & Li, T. (2002, January). *A border gateway protocol 4 (BGP-4)*: *draft-ietf-idr-bgp4-17.txt* [Internet draft, work in progress].

Salsano, S. (2001 October). *COPS usage for Diffserv resource allocation (COPS-DRA)* [Internet Draft].

Simmonds, A., & Nanda, P. (2002). Resource Management in Differentiated Services Networks. In C McDonald (Ed.), *Proceedings of 'Converged Networking: Data and Real-time Communications over IP,' IFIP Interworking 2002*, Perth, Australia, October 14 - 16, (pp. 313 – 323). Amsterdam: Kluwer Academic Publishers.

Terzis, A., Wang, L., Ogawa, J. & Zhang, L. (1999, December). *A two tier resource management model for the Internet, Global Internet*, (pp. 1808 – 1817).

Uhlig, S., Bonaventure, O., & Quoitin, B. (2003). Internet traffic engineering with minimal BGP configuration. *18th International Teletraffic Congress*.

Yavatkar, R., Pendarakis, D., & Guerin, R. (2000, January). *A framework for policy based admission control*, (RFC 2753).

KEY TERMS AND DEFINITIONS

Autonomous System (AS): An autonomous system is an independent routing domain connecting multiple networks under the control of one or more network operators that presents a common, clearly defined routing policy to the Internet and has been assigned an Autonomous System Number (ASN).

Bandwidth Broker(BB): Bandwidth Broker (BB) is a logical entity used to act as a resource manager both within a network and between networks so as to guarantee performance.

Border Gateway Protocol (BGP): BGP is a routing protocol which allows networks to tell other networks about destinations that they are "responsible" by exchanging routing information in different autonomous systems.

Differentiated Services (Diffserv): Diffserv supports QoS guarantee by aggregating traffic flows on a per class basis.

Integrated services (Intserv): Intserv supports end-to-end QoS guarantee on a per flow basis.

Policy Based Networking (PBN): Policy based networking is defined as the management of a network so that various kinds of traffic get certain priority of availability and bandwidth needed to serve the network's users effectively.

Quality of Service (QoS): Quality of Service (QoS) is defined as supporting and guaranteeing network resources to various users, applications and services in the Internet.

Traffic Engineering (TE): Traffic Engineering (TE) is concerned with performance optimization of operational IP networks and can be used to reduce congestion and improve resource utilization by careful distribution of traffic in the network.

Chapter 33
Scalable Fault Tolerance for Large-Scale Parallel and Distributed Computing

Zizhong Chen
Colorado School of Mines, USA

ABSTRACT

Today's long running scientific applications typically tolerate failures by checkpoint/restart in which all process states of an application are saved into stable storage periodically. However, as the number of processors in a system increases, the amount of data that need to be saved into stable storage also increases linearly. Therefore, the classical checkpoint/restart approach has a potential scalability problem for large parallel systems. In this chapter, we introduce some scalable techniques to tolerate a small number of process failures in large parallel and distributed computing. We present several encoding strategies for diskless checkpointing to improve the scalability of the technique. We introduce the algorithm-based checkpoint-free fault tolerance technique to tolerate fail-stop failures without checkpoint or rollback recovery. Coding approaches and floating-point erasure correcting codes are also introduced to help applications to survive multiple simultaneous process failures. The introduced techniques are scalable in the sense that the overhead to survive k failures in p processes does not increase as the number of processes p increases. Experimental results demonstrate that the introduced techniques are highly scalable.

INTRODUCTION

The unquenchable desire of scientists to run ever larger simulations and analyze ever larger data sets is fueling a relentless escalation in the size of supercomputing clusters from hundreds, to thousands, and even tens of thousands of processors (Dongarra, Meuer & Strohmaier, 2004). Unfortunately, the struggle to design systems that can scale up in this way also exposes the current limits of our understanding

DOI: 10.4018/978-1-60566-661-7.ch033

of how to efficiently translate such increases in computing resources into corresponding increases in scientific productivity. One increasingly urgent part of this knowledge gap lies in the critical area of reliability and fault tolerance.

Even making generous assumptions on the reliability of a single processor, it is clear that as the processor count in high end clusters grows into the tens of thousands, the mean time to failure (MTTF) will drop from hundreds of days to a few hours, or less. The type of 100,000-processor (Adiga, et al., 2002) machines projected in the next few years can expect to experience a processor failure almost daily, perhaps hourly. Although today's architectures are robust to enough incur process failures without suffering complete system failure, at this scale and failure rate, the only technique available to application developers for providing fault tolerance within the current parallel programming model checkpoint/restart has performance and conceptual limitations that make it inadequate to the future needs of the communities that will use these systems. Alternative fault tolerance techniques need to be investigated.

In this chapter, we present some scalable techniques to tolerate a small number of process failures in large scale parallel and distributed computing. The introduced techniques are scalable in the sense that the overhead to survive k failures in p processes does not increase as the total number of application processes p increases. We introduced several encoding strategies into diskless checkpointing to improve the scalability of the technique. We present an algorithm-based checkpoint-free fault tolerance approach, in which, instead of taking checkpoint periodically, a coded global consistent state of the critical application data is maintained in memory by modifying applications to operate on encoded data. Because no periodical checkpoint or rollback-recovery is involved in this approach, process failures can often be tolerated with a surprisingly low overhead. We explore a class of numerically stable floating-point number erasure codes based on random matrices which can be used in the algorithm-based checkpoint-free fault tolerance technique to tolerate multiple simultaneous process failures. Experimental results demonstrate that the introduced fault tolerance techniques can survive a small number of simultaneous processor failures with a very low performance overhead.

BACKGROUND

Current parallel programming paradigms for high-performance distributed computing systems are typically based on the Message-Passing Interface (MPI) specification (Message Passing Interface Forum,1994). However, the current MPI specification does not specify the behavior of an MPI implementation when one or more process failures occur during runtime. MPI gives the user the choice between two possibilities on how to handle failures. The first one, which is the default mode of MPI, is to immediately abort all survival processes of the application. The second possibility is just slightly more flexible, handing control back to the user application without guaranteeing that any further communication can occur.

FT-MPI Overview

FT-MPI (Fagg, Gabriel, Losilca, Angskun, Chen, Pjesivac-Grbovic, et al., 2004) is a fault tolerant version of MPI that is able to provide basic system services to support fault survivable applications. FT-MPI implements the complete MPI-1.2 specification and parts of the MPI-2 functionality, and extends some of the semantics of MPI to support self-healing applications. FT-MPI is able to survive the failure of $n - 1$ processes in an n-process job, and, if required, can re-spawn the failed processes. However, fault tolerant applications have to be implemented in a self-healing way so that they can survive failures. Although FT-MPI provides basic system services to support self-healing applications, prevailing benchmarks show that the performance of FT-MPI is comparable (Fagg, Gabriel, Bosilca, Angskun, Chen, Pjesivac-Grbovic, et al., 2005) to the current state-of-the-art non-fault-tolerant MPI implementations.

FT-MPI Semantics

FT-MPI provides semantics that answer the following questions:

1. What is the status of an MPI communicator after recovery?
2. What is the status of the ongoing communication and messages during and after recovery?

When running an FT-MPI application, there are two parameters used to specify which modes the application is running. The first parameter is *communicator mode* which indicates the status of an MPI object after recovery. FT-MPI provides four different communicator modes, which can be specified when starting the application:

- ABORT: like any other MPI implementation, in this FT-MPI mode, application aborts itself after failure.
- BLANK: failed processes are not replaced; all survival processes have the same rank as before the crash and MPI COMM WORLD has the same size as before.
- SHRINK: failed processes are not replaced; however the new communicator after the crash has no 'holes' in its list of processes. Thus, processes might have a new rank after recovery and the size of MPI COMM WORLD will change.
- REBUILD: failed processes are re-spawned; survival processes have the same rank as before. The REBUILD mode is the default, and the most used mode of FT-MPI.

The second parameter, the *communication mode*, indicates how messages, which are sent but not received while a failure occurs, are treated. FT-MPI provides two different communication modes, which can be specified while starting the application:

- CONT/CONTINUE: all operations which returned the error code MPI SUCCESS will finish properly, even if a process failure occurs during the operation (unless the communication partner has failed).
- NOOP/RESET: all pending messages are dropped. The assumption behind this mode is that on error the application returns to its last consistent state, and all currently pending operations are not of any further interest.

FT-MPI Usage

It usually takes three steps to tolerate a failure: 1) failure detection, 2) failure notification, and 3) recovery. The only assumption the FT-MPI specification makes about the first two points is that the run-time environment discovers failures and all remaining processes in the parallel job are notified about these events. The recovery procedure consists of two steps: recovering the MPI run-time environment, and recovering the application data. The latter one is considered to be the responsibility of the application developer.

In the FT-MPI specification, the communicator-mode discovers the status of MPI objects after recovery, and the message-mode ascertains the status of ongoing messages during and after recovery. FT-MPI offers for each of these modes several possibilities. This allows application developers to take the specific characteristics of their application into account and use the best-suited method to tolerate failures.

SCALABLE DISKLESS CHECKPOINTING FOR LARGE SCALE SCIENTIFIC COMPUTING

In this section, we introduce some techniques to improve the scalability of classical diskless checkpointing technique.

Diskless Checkpointing: From an Application Point of View

Diskless checkpointing (Plank, Li & Puening, 1998) is a technique to save the state of a long running computation on a distributed system without relying on stable storage. With diskless checkpointing, each processor involved in the computation stores a copy of its state locally, either in memory or on local disk. Additionally, encodings of these checkpoints are stored in local memory or on local disk of some processors which may or may not be involved in the computation. When a failure occurs, each live processor may roll its state back to its last local checkpoint, and the failed processor's state may be calculated from the local checkpoints of the surviving processors and the checkpoint encodings. By eliminating stable storage from checkpointing and replacing it with memory and processor redundancy, diskless checkpointing removes the main source of overhead in checkpointing on distributed systems (Plank, Li & Puening, 1998). Figure 1 is an example of how diskless checkpoint works.

To make diskless checkpointing as efficient as possible, it can be implemented at the application level rather than at the system level (Plank, Kim & Dongarra, 1997). In typical long running scientific applications, when diskless checkpointing is taken from application level, what needs to be checkpointed is often some numerical data (Kim, 1996). These numerical data can either be treated as bit-streams or as floating-point numbers. If the data are treated as bitstreams, then bit-stream operations such as parity

Figure 1. Fault tolerance by diskless checkpointing

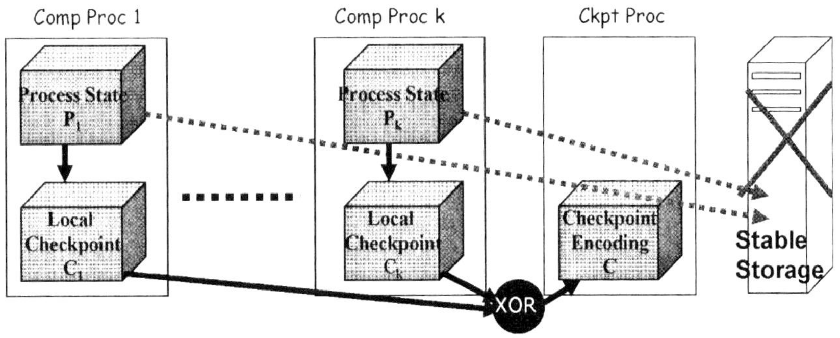

can be used to encode the checkpoint. Otherwise, floating-point arithmetic such as addition can be used to encode the data. In this research, we treat the checkpoint data as floating-point numbers rather than bit-streams. However, the corresponding bit-stream version schemes could also be used if the the application programmer thinks they are more appropriate. In the rest of this chapter, we discuss how local checkpoints can be encoded efficiently so that applications can survive process failures.

Checksum-Based Checkpointing

The checksum-based checkpointing is a floating-point version of the parity-based checkpointing scheme proposed in (Plank, Li, & Puening, 1998). In the checksum-based checkpointing, instead of using parity, floating-point number addition is used to encode the local checkpoint data. By encoding the local checkpoint data of the computation processors and sending the encoding to some dedicated checkpoint processors, the checksum-based checkpointing introduces a much lower memory overhead into the checkpoint system than neighborbased checkpoint. However, due to the calculating and sending of the encoding, the performance overhead of the checksum-based checkpointing is usually higher than neighbor-based checkpoint schemes. The basic checksum scheme works as follow. If the program is executing on N processors, then there is an $N + 1$-st processor called the checksum processor. At all points in time a consistent checkpoint is held in the N processors in memory. Moreover a checksum of the N local checkpoints is held in the checksum processor. Assume P_i is the local checkpoint data in the memory of the *i-th* computation processor. C is the checksum of the local checkpoints in the checkpoint processor. If we look at the checkpoint data as an array of real numbers, then the checkpoint encoding actually establishes an identity (1) between the checkpoint data P_i on computation processors and the checksum data C on the checksum processor. If any processor fails, then the identity (1) becomes an equation with one unknown. Therefore, the data in the failed processor can be reconstructed through solving this equation. $P_1 + \ldots + P_n = C$ (1)

Due to the floating-point arithmetic used in the checkpoint and recovery, there will be round-off errors in the checkpoint and recovery. However, the checkpoint involves only additions and the recovery involves additions and only one subtraction. In practice, the increased possibility of overflows, underflows, and cancellations due to round-off errors in the checkpoint and recovery algorithm is negligible.

Overhead and Scalability Analysis

Assume diskless checkpointing is performed in a parallel system with p processors and the size of checkpoint on each processor is m bytes. It takes $\alpha + \beta x$ to transfer a message of size x bytes between two processors regardless of which two processors are involved. α is often called latency of the network, $1/\beta$ is called the bandwidth of the network. Assume the rate to calculate the sum of two arrays is γ seconds per byte. We also assume that it takes $\alpha + \beta x$ to write x bytes of data into the stable storage. Our default network model is the duplex model where a processor is able to concurrently send a message to one partner and receive a message from a possibly different partner. The more restrictive simplex model permits only one communication direction per processor. We also assume that disjoint pairs of processors can communicate each other without interference each other.

In classical diskless checkpointing, binary-tree based encoding algorithm is often used to perform the checkpoint encoding (Chiueh & Deng, n.d.), (Kim, 1996), (Plank, 1997), (Plank, Li & Puening, 1998), (Silva & Silva, 1998). By organizing all processors as a binary tree and sending local checkpoints along the tree to the checkpoint processor (see Figure 2 (Plank, Li & Puening, 1998)), the time to perform one checkpoint for a binary-tree based encoding algorithm, $T_{diskless-binary}$, can be represented as

$$T_{diskless-binary} = 2\lceil \log p \rceil (\alpha + (\beta + \gamma)m).$$

In high performance scientific computing, the local checkpoint is often a relatively large message (megabyte level), so $(\beta + \gamma)m$ is usually much larger than $T_{diskless-binary} \approx 2\lceil \log p \rceil (\beta + \gamma)m$. Therefore,

$$\begin{aligned}
T_{total}(s) &= (t + p - 2)(\alpha + \beta s + \gamma s) \\
&= (m/s + p - 2)(\alpha + \beta s + \gamma s) \\
&= \alpha m/s + (p-2)(\beta + \lambda)s + (p-2)\alpha + (\beta + \gamma)m \\
&\leq 2\sqrt{(p-2)\alpha(\beta+\gamma)m} + (p-2)\alpha + (\beta+\gamma)m \\
&= (\beta + \gamma)m \cdot (1 + O(p/\sqrt{m})
\end{aligned}$$

Note that, in a typical checkpoint/restart approach where βm is usually also much larger than α, the time to perform one checkpoint, $T_{checkpoint\ restart}$, is $T_{checkpoint\ restart} = p(\alpha + \beta m) \approx p\alpha$

Therefore, by eliminating stable storage from checkpointing and replacing it with memory and processor redundancy, diskless checkpointing improves the scalability of checkpointing greatly on parallel and distributed systems.

A Scalable Checkpoint Encoding Algorithm for Diskless Checkpointing

Although the classical diskless checkpointing technique improves the scalability of checkpointing dramatically on parallel and distributed systems, the overhead to perform one checkpoint still increases logarithmicly as the number of processors increases. In this section, we propose a new style of encoding algorithm which improves the scalability of diskless checkpointing significantly. The new encoding algorithm is based on the pipeline idea. When the number of processors is one or two, there is not much that we can improve. Therefore, in what follows, we assume the number of processors is at least three.

Figure 2. Encoding local checkpoints using the binary tree algorithm

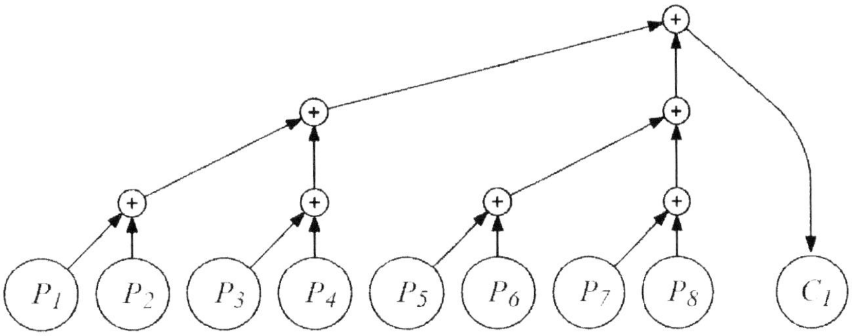

Pipelining

The key idea of pipelining is (1) the segmenting of messages and (2) the simultaneous non-blocking transmission and receipt of data. By breaking up a large message into smaller segments and sending these smaller messages through the network, pipelining allows the receiver to begin forwarding a segment while receiving another segment. Data pipelining can produce several significant improvements in the process of checkpoint encoding. First, pipelining masks the processor and network latencies that are known to be an important factor in high-bandwidth local area networks. Second, it allows the simultaneous sending and receiving of data, and hence exploits the full duplex nature of the interconnect links in the parallel system. Third, it allows different segments of a large message being transmitted in different interconnect links in parallel after a pipeline is established, hence fully utilize the multiple interconnects of a parallel and distributed ststem.

Chain-Pipelined Encoding for Diskless Checkpointing

Let $m[i]$ denote the data on the ith processor. The task of checkpoint encoding is to calculate the encoding which is $m[0] + m[1] + \ldots + m[p-1]$ and deliver the encoding to the checkpoint processor. The chain-pipelined encoding algorithm works as follows. First, organize all computational processors and the checkpoint processor as a chain. Second, segment the data on each processor into small pieces. Assume the data on each processor are segmented into t segment of size s. The jth segment of $m[i]$ is denoted as $m[i][j]$. Third, $m[0]+m[1]+\ldots+m[p-1]$ are calculated by calculating $m[0][j]+m[1][j]+\ldots+m[p-1][j]$ for each $0 \leq j \leq t-1$ in a pipelined way. Fourth, when the jth segment of encoding $m[0][j]+m[1][j]+\ldots+m[p-1][j]$ is available, start to send it to the checkpoint processor.

Figure 3 demonstrates an example of calculating a chain-pipelined checkpoint encoding for three processors (processor 0, processor 1, and processor 2) and deliver it to the checkpoint processor (processor 3). In step 0, processor 0 sends its $m[0][0]$ to processor 1. Processor 1 receives $m[0][0]$ from processor 0 and calculates $m[0][0]+m[1][0]$. In step 1, processor 0 sends its $m[0][1]$ to processor 1. Processor 1 first concurrently receives $m[0][1]$ from processor 0 and sends $m[0][0] + m[1][0]$ to processor 2 and then calculates $m[0][1] + m[1][1]$. Processor 2 first receives $m[0][0] + m[1][0]$ from processor 1 and then calculate $m[0][0] + m[1][0] + m[2][0]$. As the procedure continues, at the end of step 2, the checkpoint processor will be able to get its first segment of encoding $m[0][0] + m[1][0]+m[2][0]+m[3][0]$. From now on, the checkpoint processor will be able to receive a segment of the encoding at the end of each step. After the checkpoint processor receives the last checkpoint encoding, the checkpoint is finished.

Overhead and Scalability Analysis

In the chain-pipelined checkpoint encoding, the time for each step is $T_{each\text{-}step} = \alpha + \beta s + \gamma s$, where s is the size of the segment. The number of steps to encode and deliver t segments in a p processor system is $t + p - 2$. If we assume the size of data on each processor is m ($= ts$), then the total time for encoding and delivery is

$$s = \sqrt{\frac{\alpha m}{(p-2)(\beta + \gamma)}}$$

The minimum is achieved when

$$2\lceil \log p \rceil((\beta + \gamma)m + \alpha) \quad (2)$$

Therefore, by choosing an optimal segment size, the chain-pipelined encoding algorithm is able to reduce the checkpoint overhead to tolerate single failure from $(\beta + \gamma)m \cdot (1 + O(p / \sqrt{m})$ to

$$\begin{cases} a_{11}P_1 + \ldots + a_{1n}P_n & = & C_1 \\ & \vdots & \\ a_{M1}P_1 + \ldots + a_{Mn}P_n & = & C_M \end{cases}$$

In diskless checkpointing, the size of checkpoint m is often large (megabytes level). The latency α is often a very small number compared with the time to send a large message. If p is not too large, then $T_{total} \approx (\beta + \gamma)m$. Therefore, in practice, the number of processors often has very little impact on the time to perform one checkpoint unless p is very large. If p does become very large, strategies in one dimensional weighted checksum scheme can be used to guarantee small latency related terms.

Coding to Tolerate Multiple Simultaneous Process Failures

To tolerate multiple simultaneous process failures of arbitrary patterns with minimum process redundancy, a weighted checksum scheme can be used. A weighted checksum scheme can be viewed as a version of the Reed-Solomon erasure coding scheme (Plank, 1997) in the real number field. The basic idea of this scheme works as follow: Each processor takes a local in-memory checkpoint, and M equalities are established by saving weighted checksums of the local checkpoint into M checksum processors. When f failures happen, where $f \leq M$, the M equalities becomes M equations with f unknowns. By appropriately choosing the weights of the weighted checksums, the lost data on the f failed processors can be recovered by solving these M equations.

Figure 3. Chain-pipelined encoding for diskless checkpointing

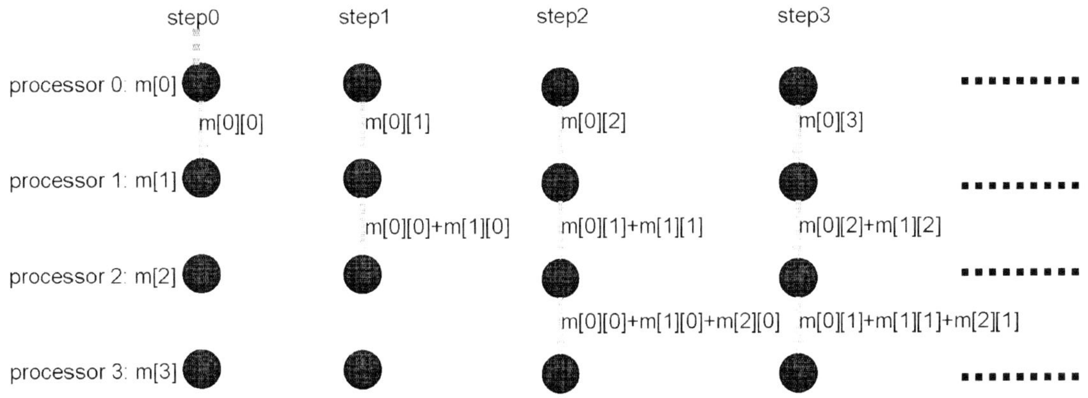

The Basic Weighted Checksum Scheme

Suppose there are n processors used for computation. Assume the checkpoint data on the ith computation processor is P_i. In order to be able to reconstruct the lost data on failed processors, another M processors are dedicated to hold M encodings (weighted checksums) of the checkpoint data (see Figure 4).

The weighted checksum C_j on the jth checksum processor can be calculated from

$$2\lceil \log p \rceil((\beta + 2\gamma)m + \alpha) \qquad (3)$$

where a_{ij}, $i = 1, 2, ..., M$, $j = 1, 2, ..., n$, is the weight we need to choose. Let $A = (a_{ij})_{Mn}$. We call A the checkpoint matrix for the weighted checksum scheme. Suppose that k computation processors and $M - h$ checkpoint processors have failed. Then there are $n - k$ computation processors and h checkpoint processors that have survived. If we look at the data on the failed processors as unknowns, then (3) becomes M equations with $M - (h - k)$ unknowns.

If $k > h$, then there are fewer equations than unknowns. There is no unique solution for (3), and the lost data on the failed processors can not be recovered. However, if $k < h$, then there are more equations than unknowns. By appropriately choosing A, a unique solution for (3) can be guaranteed, and the lost data on the failed processors can be recovered by solving (3).

Let A_r denote the coefficient matrix of the linear system that need to be solved to recover the lost data. Whether we can recover the lost data on the failed processes or not directly depends on whether A_r has a full column rank or not. However, A_r can be any sub-matrix (including minor) of A depending on the distribution of the failed processors. If any square sub-matrix (including minor) of A is non-singular and there are no more than M process failed, then A_r can be guaranteed to have full column rank. Therefore, to be able to recover from no more than any M failures, the checkpoint matrix A has to satisfy the condition that *any square sub-matrix (including minor) of A is non-singular*. How can we find such kind of matrices? It is well known that some structured matrices such as Vandermonde matrix and Cauchy matrix satisfy this condition (Golub & Van Loan, 1989).

Let $T_{diskless\ pipeline}(k, p)$ denotes the encoding time to tolerate k simultaneous failures in a p-processor system using the chain-pipelined encoding algorithm and $T_{diskless\ binary}(k, p)$ denotes the corresponding encoding time using the binary-tree encoding algorithm.

Figure 4. Basic weighted checksum scheme for diskless checkpointing

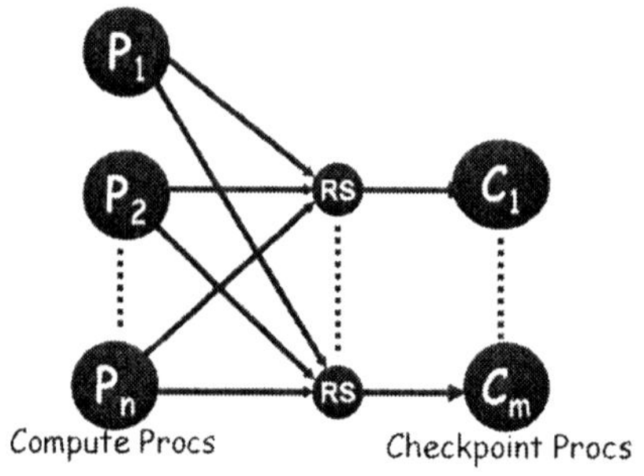

When tolerating *k* simultaneous failures, *k* basic encodings have to be performed. Note that, in addition to the summation operation, there is an additional multiplication operation involved in (3). Therefore, the computation time for each number will increase from γ to 2γ. Hence, when the binary-tree encoding algorithm is used to perform the weighted checksum encoding, the time for one basic encoding is $2\lceil \log p \rceil ((\beta + 2\gamma)m + \alpha)$. Therefore, the time for *k* basic encodings is

$$T_{diskless-binary}(k,p) = k \cdot 2\lceil \log p \rceil (\alpha + (\beta + 2\gamma)m) \approx 2\lceil \log p \rceil \cdot k(\beta + 2\gamma)m.$$

When the chain-pipelined encoding algorithm is used to perform the checkpoint encoding, the overhead to tolerate *k* simultaneous failures becomes

$$T_{diskless-pipeline}(k,p) = k \cdot \left(1 + O\left(\frac{p}{\sqrt{m}}\right)\right) \cdot (\beta + 2\gamma)m = \left(1 + O\left(\frac{p}{\sqrt{m}}\right)\right) \cdot k(\beta + 2\gamma)m.$$

When the number of processors p is not too large, the overhead for the basic weighted checksum scheme $T_{diskless\text{-}pipeline}(k, p) \approx k(\beta + 2\gamma)m$.

However, in today's large computing systems, the number of processors p may become very large. If we do have a large number of processors in the computing systems, either the one dimensional weighted checksum scheme or the localized weighted checksum scheme discussed in the following can be used.

One Dimensional Weighted Checksum Scheme

The one dimensional weighted checksum scheme works as follows. Assume the program is running on $p = g \times s$ processors. Partition the $g \times s$ processors into s groups with g processors in each group. Dedicate another M checksum processors for each group. In each group, the checkpoint are done using the basic weighted checksum scheme (see Figure 5). This scheme can survive M processor failures in each group. The advantage of this scheme is that the checkpoints are localized to a subgroup of processors, so the checkpoint encoding in each sub-group can be performed in parallel. Therefore, compared with the basic weighted checksum scheme, the performance of the one dimensional weighted checksum scheme is usually better.

By using a pipelined encoding algorithm in each subgroup, the time to tolerate *k* simultaneous failures in a p-processor system is now reduced to

$$T_{diskless-pipeline}(k,p) = T_{diskless-pipeline}(k,g) = \left(1 + O\left(\frac{g}{\sqrt{m}}\right)\right) \cdot k(\beta + 2\gamma)m.$$

which is independent of the total number of processors p in the computing system. Therefore, in this fault tolerance scheme, the overhead to survive *k* failures in a p-processor system does not increase as the total number of processors p increases. It is in this sense that the sub-group based chain-pipelined checkpoint encoding algorithm is a scalable recovery algorithm.

CHECKPOINT-FREE FAULT TOLERANCE FOR MATRIX MULTIPLICATION

It has been proved in previous research (Huang & Abraham, 1984) that, for some matrix operations, the checksum relationship in input checksum matrices is preserved *in the final computation results at the end of the operation*. Based on this checksum relationship in the final computation results, Huang and Abraham have developed the famous algorithm-based fault tolerance (ABFT) (Huang & Abraham, 1984) technique to detect, locate, and correct certain processor miscalculations in matrix computations with low overhead. The algorithm-based fault tolerance proposed in (Huang & Abraham, 1984) was later extended by many researches (Afinson & Luk, 1988), (Banerjee, Rahmeh, Stunkel, Nair, Roy, Balasubramanian & Abraham, 1990), (Balasubramanian & Banarjee, 1990), (Boley, Brent, Golub & Luk, 1992), (Luk & Park, 1986).

In order to be able to recover from a fail-stop process failure in the middle of the computation, a global consistent state of the application is often required when a process failure occurs. Checkpointing and message logging are typical approaches to maintain or construct such global consistent state in a distributed environment. But if there exists a checksum relationship between application data on different processes, such checksum relationship can actually be treated as a global consistent state. However, it is still an open problem that whether the checksum relationship in input checksum matrices in ABFT can be maintained during computation or not. Therefore, whether ABFT can be extended to tolerate fail-stop process failures in a distributed environment or not remains open.

In this section, we first demonstrate that, for many matrix matrix multiplication algorithms, the checksum relationship in the input checksum matrices does not preserve during computation. We then prove that, however, for the outer product version matrix matrix multiplication algorithm, it is possible to maintain the checksum relationship in the input checksum matrices during computation. Based on this checksum relationship maintained during computation, we demonstrate that it is possible to tolerate fail-stop process failures (which are typically tolerated by checkpoting or message logging) in distributed outer product version matrix multiplication without checkpointing. Because no periodical checkpoint or rollback-recovery is involved in this approach, process failures can often be tolerated with a surprisingly low overhead.

Figure 5. One dimensional weighted checksum scheme for diskless checkpointing

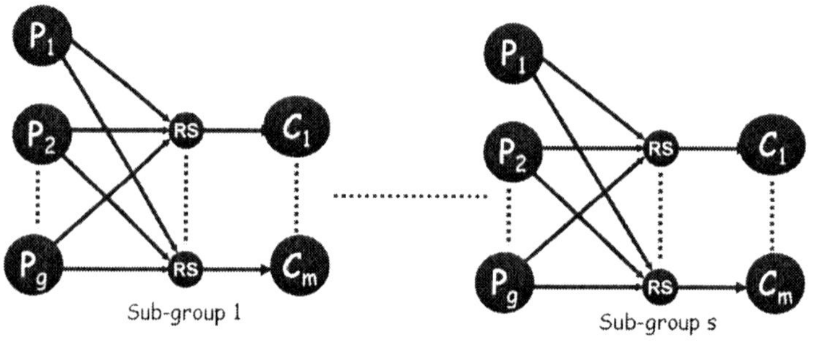

Maintaining Checksum at the End of Computation

For any general m-by-n matrix A defined by

$$A = \begin{pmatrix} a_{00} & \cdots & a_{0\,n-1} \\ \vdots & \cdots & \vdots \\ a_{m-1\,0} & \cdots & a_{m-1\,n-1} \end{pmatrix}$$

The *column checksum* matrix A^c of the matrix A is defined by

$$A^c = \begin{pmatrix} a_{00} & \cdots & a_{0\,n-1} \\ \vdots & \cdots & \vdots \\ a_{m-1\,0} & \cdots & a_{m-1\,n-1} \\ \sum_{i=0}^{i=m-1} a_{i\,0} & \cdots & \sum_{i=0}^{i=m-1} a_{i\,n-1} \end{pmatrix}$$

The *row checksum* matrix A^r of the matrix A is defined by

$$A^r = \begin{pmatrix} a_{00} & \cdots & a_{0\,n-1} & \sum_{j=0}^{j=n-1} a_{0\,j} \\ \vdots & \cdots & \vdots & \vdots \\ a_{m-1\,0} & \cdots & a_{m-1\,n-1} & \sum_{j=0}^{j=n-1} a_{m-1\,j} \end{pmatrix}$$

The *full checksum* matrix A^f of the matrix A is defined by

$$A^f = \begin{pmatrix} a_{00} & \cdots & a_{0\,n-1} & \sum_{j=0}^{j=n-1} a_{0\,j} \\ \vdots & \cdots & \vdots & \vdots \\ a_{m-1\,0} & \cdots & a_{m-1\,n-1} & \sum_{j=0}^{j=n-1} a_{m-1\,j} \\ \sum_{i=0}^{i=m-1} a_{i\,0} & \cdots & \sum_{i=0}^{i=m-1} a_{i\,n-1} & \sum_{i=0}^{i=m-1} \sum_{j=0}^{j=n-1} a_{i\,j} \end{pmatrix}$$

Theorem 1: Assume A, B, and C are three matrices. If $A\,B = C$, then $A^c\,B^r = C^f$.

Proof: Assume A is m-by-n, B is n-by-k, then C is m-by-k. Let e^T denote a 1-by-m vector [1, 1, . . ., 1], then

$$A^c = \begin{pmatrix} A \\ e^T A \end{pmatrix};$$
$$B^R = \begin{pmatrix} B & B\,e \end{pmatrix};$$
$$C^f = \begin{pmatrix} C & C\,e \\ e^T C & e^T C\,E \end{pmatrix}.$$

$$\begin{aligned} A^c B^r &= \begin{pmatrix} A \\ e^T A \end{pmatrix} \begin{pmatrix} B & B\,e \end{pmatrix} \\ &= \begin{matrix} AB & ABe \\ e^T AB & e^T ABe \end{matrix} \\ &= \begin{matrix} C & Ce \\ e^T C & e^T Ce \end{matrix} \\ &= C^f. \end{aligned}$$

Theorem 1 was first proved by Huang and Abraham in (Huang & Abraham, 1984). The reason that we repeat the proof here again is that we want to point out the fact that the proof of Theorem 1 is independent of the algorithms used for the matrix matrix multiplication operation. Therefore no mater which algorithm is used to perform the matrix matrix multiplication, the checksum relationship of the input matrices will always be preserved in the final computation results at the end of the computation.

Based on this checksum relationship in the final computation results, the low-overhead algorithm-based fault tolerance technique has been developed in (Huang & Abraham, 1984) to detect, locate, and correct certain processor miscalculations in matrix computations.

Is the Checksum Maintained During Computation?

Algorithm-based fault tolerance usually detects, locates, and corrects errors at the end of the computation. But in today's high performance computing environment such as MPI, after a fail-stop process failure occurs in the middle of the computation, it is often required to recover from the failure first before the continuation of the rest of the computation.

In order to be able recover from fail-stop failures occurred in the middle of the computation, a global consistent state of an application is often required in the middle of the computation. The checksum relationship, if exists, can actually be treated as a global consistent state. However, from Theorem 1, it is still uncertain whether the checksum relationship is preserved in the middle of the computation or not.

In what follows, we demonstrate, for both cannon's algorithm and fox's algorithm for matrix matrix multiplication, this checksum relationship in the input checksum matrices is generally not preserved in the middle of the computation.

Assume A is an $(n-1)$-by-n matrix, B is an n-by-$(n-1)$ matrix. Then $A^c = (a_{ij})_{n\times n}$, $B^r = (b_{ij})_{n\times n}$, and $C^f = A^c * B^r$ are all n-by-n matrices. For convenience of description, but without loss of generality, assume there are n^2 processors with each processor stores one element from A^c, B^r,and C^f respectively. The n^2 processors are organized into an n-by-n processor grid.

Consider using the cannon's algorithm (Cannon, 1969) in Figure 6 to perform $A^c * B^r$ in parallel on an n-by-n processor grid. We can prove the following Theorem 2.

Theorem 2: If the cannon's algorithm in Figure 6 is used to perform parallel matrix matrix multiplication, then there exist matrices A and B such that, at the end of each step s, where $s = 0, 1, 2, \cdots, n-2$, the matrix $C = (c_{ij})$ is not a full checksum matrix.

When the cannon's algorithm in Figure 6 is used to perform $A^c * B^r$ in parallel for general matrix A and B, it can be proved that at the end of the sth step

$$c_{ij} = \sum_{k=0}^{s} a_{i,(i+j+k) \bmod n} * b_{(i+j+k) \bmod n, j}$$

It can be verified that $C = (c_{ij})_{n \times n}$ is not a full checksum matrix unless $s = n - 1$ which is the end of the computation. Therefore the checksum relationship in the matrix C is generally not preserved during computation in the cannon's algorithm for matrix multiplication.

It can also be demonstrated that the checksum relationship in the input matrix C is not preserved during computation in many other parallel algorithms for matrix matrix multiplication algorithms such as Fox's algorithm.

Figure 6. Matrix matrix multiplication by Cannon's algorithm with checksum matrices

```
/* Calculate A^c * B^r by cannon's algorithm. */
initialize C = (c_ij) = 0;
for i = 0 to n - 1
    left-circular-shift row i of A^c by i
        so that a_i,j is overwritten by a_i,(j+i) mod n;
end
for i = 0 to n - 1
    up-circular-shift column i of B^r by i
        so that b_i,j is overwritten by b_(i+j) mod n, j;
end
for s = 0 to n - 1
    every processor (i, j) performs c_ij = c_ij + a_ij * b_ij
        locally in parallel;
    left-circular-shift each row of A^c by 1;
    up-circular-shift each column of B^r by 1;
    /* Here is the end of the s^th step. */
end
```

Figure 7. Matrix-matrix multiplication by outer product algorithm with input checksum matrices

```
/* Calculate A_r * B_c by outer product algorithm.*/
initialize C = (c_ij) = 0;
for s = 0 to n - 1
    row broadcast the s^th row of A_c;
    column broadcast the s^th column of B_r;
    every processor (i,j) performs c_ij = c_ij + a_is * b_sj
       locally in parallel;
    /* Here is the end of the s^th step. */
end
```

An Algorithm That Maintains the Checksum during Computation

Despite the checksum relationship of the input matrices is preserved in final results at the end of computation no matter which algorithm is used, from last subsection, we know that the checksum relationship is not necessarily preserved during computation. However, it is interesting to ask: is there any algorithm that preserves the checksum relationship during computation?

Consider using the outer product version algorithm (Golub & Van Loan, 1989) in Figure 7 to perform A^c * B^r in parallel. Assume the matrices A^c, B^r, and C^f have the same data distribution scheme as before.

Theorem 3: If the algorithm in Figure 7 is used to perform the parallel matrix matrix multiplication, then the matrix $C = (c_{ij})_{n \times n}$ is a full checksum matrix at the end of each step s, where $s = 0, 2, \cdots, n - 1$.

Proof: It is trivial to show that, at the end of the sth step in Figure 7, the c_{ij} in the algorithm satisfies

$$c_{ij} = \sum_{k=0}^{s} a_{ik} * b_{kj},$$

where $i, j = 0, 2, \cdots, n - 1$.

Note that A_c is a column checksum matrix, therefore

$$\sum_{t=0}^{n-2} a_{t\,j} = a_{n-1\;\;j}$$

where $j = 0, 2, \cdots, n - 1$.

Since B^r is a column checksum matrix, we have

$$\sum_{t=0}^{n-2} b_{i\,t} = b_{i\;n-1}$$

where $i = 0, 2, \cdots, n-1$.

Therefore, for all $j = 0, 2, \cdots, n-1$, we have

$$\sum_{t=0}^{n-2} c_{tj} = \sum_{t=0}^{n-2}\sum_{k=0}^{s} a_{tk} * b_{kj}$$
$$= \sum_{k=0}^{s}\left(\sum_{t=0}^{n-2} a_{tk}\right) * b_{kj}$$
$$= \sum_{k=0}^{s} a_{n-1k} * b_{kj}$$
$$= c_{n-1j}$$

Similarly, for all $i = 0, 2, \cdots, n-1$, we have

$$\sum_{t=0}^{n-2} c_{it} = \sum_{t=0}^{n-2}\sum_{k=0}^{s} a_{ik} * b_{kt}$$
$$= \sum_{k=0}^{s} a_{ik} * \left(\sum_{t=0}^{n-2} b_{kt}\right)$$
$$= \sum_{k=0}^{s} a_{ik} * b_{kn-1}$$
$$= c_{in-1}$$

Therefore, we can conclude that C is a full checksum matrix. Hence, at the end of each step s, where $s = 0, 2, \cdots, n-1$, $C = (c_{ij})_{n\times n}$ is a full checksum matrix.

Theorem 3 implies that a coded global consistent state of the critical application data (i.e. the checksum relationship in A^c, B^r, and C^f) can be maintained in memory at the end of each iteration in the outer product version matrix matrix multiplication if we perform the computation with the checksum input matrices.

However, in a high performance distributed environment, different processes may update their data in local memory asynchronously. Therefore, if a failure happens at a time when some processes have updated their local matrix in memory and other processes are still in the communication stage, then the checksum relationship in the distributed matrix will be damaged and the data on all processes will not form a global consistent state.

But this problem can be solved by simply performing a synchronization before performing local memory update. Therefore, it is possible to maintain a coded global consistent state (i.e. the checksum relationship) of the matrix Ac, Br and Cf in the distributed memory at any time during computation. Hence, a single fail-stop process failure in the middle of the computation can be recovered from the checksum relationship.

Note that it is also the outer product version algorithm that is ofen used in today's high performance computing practice. The outer product version algorithm is more popular due to both its simplicity and its efficiency in modern high performance computer architecture. In the widely used parallel numerical linear algebra library ScaLAPACK (Blackford, Choi, Cleary, Petitet, Whaley, Demmel, et al. 1996), it is also the outer product version algorithm that is chosen to perform the matrix matrix mulitiplication. More importantly, it can also be proved that similar checksum relationship exists for the outer product version of many other matrix operations (such as Cholesky and LU factorization).

PRACTICAL NUMERICAL ISSUES

Both the encoding schemes introduced in the scalable checkpointing and the algorithm-based fault tolerance presented before involve solving system of linear equations to recover multiple simultaneous process failures. Therefore, the practical numerical issues involved in recovering multiple simultaneous process failures have to be addressed.

Numerical Stability of Real Number Codes

From previous section, it has been derived that, to be able to recover from any no more than m failures, the encoding matrix A has to satisfy: any square sub-matrix (including minor) of

A is non-singular. This requirement for the encoding matrix coincides with the properties for the generator matrices of real number Reed-Solomon style erasure correcting codes. In fact, our weighted checksum encoding discussed before can be viewed as a version of the Reed-Solomon erasure coding scheme (Plank, 1997) in real number field. Therefore any generator matrix from real number Reed-Solomon style erasure codes can actually be used as the encoding matrix of algorithm-based checkpoint-free fault tolerance In the existing real number or complex-number Reed-Solomon style erasure codes in literature, the generator matrices mainly include: Vandermonde matrix (Vander), Vandermonde-like matrix for the Chebyshev polynomials (Chebvand), Cauchy matrix (Cauchy), Discrete Cosine Transform matrix (DCT), Discrete Fourier Transform matrix (DFT). Theoretically, these generator matrices can all be used as the encoding matrix of the algorithm-based checkpoint-free fault tolerance scheme. However, in computer floating point arithmetic where no computation is exact due to round-off errors, it is well known (Golub & Van Loan, 1989) that, in solving a linear system of equations, a condition number of 10^k for the coefficient matrix leads to a loss of accuracy of about k decimal digits in the solution. Therefore, in order to get a reasonably accurate recovery, the encoding matrix A actually has to satisfy *any square sub-matrix (including minor) of A is well-conditioned.*

The generator matrices from above real number or complex-number Reed-Solomon style erasure codes all contain ill-conditioned sub-matrices. Therefore, in these codes, when certain error patterns occur, an ill-conditioned linear system has to be solved to reconstruct an approximation of the original information, which can cause the loss of precision of possibly all digits in the recovered numbers.

Numerically Good Real Number Codes Based on Random Matrices

In this section, we will introduce a class of new codes that are able to reconstruct a very good approximation of the lost data with high probability regardless of the failure patterns processes. Our new codes are based on random matrices over real number field. It is well-known (Edelmann, 1988) that Gaussian random matrices are well-conditioned. To estimate how well conditioned Gaussian random matrices are, we have proved the following theorem:

Theorem 4: Let $G_{m\times n}$ be an $m\times n$ real random matrix whose elements are independent and identically distributed standard normal random variables, and let $\kappa_2(G_{m\times n})$ be the 2-norm condition number of $G_{m\times n}$. Then, for any $m\geq 2$, $n\geq 2$ and $x\geq|n-m|+1$, $\kappa_2(G_{m\times n})$ satisfies

$$\frac{\left(\frac{c}{x}\right)^{|n-m|+1}}{\sqrt{2\pi}} < P\left(\frac{k_2(G_{m\times n})}{n/(|n-m|+1)} > x\right) < \frac{\left(\frac{C}{x}\right)^{|n-m|+1}}{\sqrt{2\pi}},$$

and

$$E(\ln k_2(G_{m\times n})) < \ln\frac{n}{|n-m|+1} + 2.258,$$

where $0.245 \leq c \leq 2.000$ and $5.013 \leq C \leq 6.414$ are universal positive constants independent of m, n and x.

Due to the length of the proof for Theorem 4, we omit the proof here and refer interested readers to (Chen & Dongarra, n.d.) for complete proof.

Note that any sub-matrix of a Gaussian random matrix is still a Gaussian random matrix. Therefore, a Gaussian random matrix would satisfy any sub-matrix of the matrix is well-conditioned with high probability.

Theorem 4 can be used to estimate the accuracy of recovery in the weighted checksum scheme. For example, if an application uses 100,000 processes to perform computation and 20 processes to hold encodings, then the encoding matrix is a 20 by 100,000 Gaussian random matrix. If 10 processors fail concurrently, then the coefficient matrix in the recovery algorithm is a 20 by 10 Gaussian random matrix. From Theorem 4, we can get$E(\log 10\ \kappa_2(A_r) < 1.25andP\{\kappa_2(A_r) > 100\} < 3.1 \times 10^{-11}$.

Therefore, on average, we will loss about one decimal digit in the recovered data and the probability to loss 2 digits is less than 3.1×10^{-11}.

EXPERIMENTAL EVALUATION

In this section, we evaluate the performance of the introduced fault tolerance schemes experimental.

Performance of the Chain-Pipelined Checkpoint Encoding

In this section, we evaluate the scalability of the proposed chain-pipelined checkpoint encoding algorithm using a preconditioned conjugate gradient (PCG) equation solver (Barrett, Berry, Chan, Demmel, Donato, Dongarra, Eijkhout, et al., 1994). The basic weighted checksum scheme is incorporates into our PCG code. The checkpoint encoding matrix we used is a pseudo random matrix. The programming environment we used is FT-MPI (Fagg & Dongarra, 2000), (Fagg, et al., 2004), (Fagg, et al., 2005). A process failure is simulated by killing one process in the middle of the computation. The lost data on the failed process is recovered by solving the checksum equation.

We fix the number of simultaneous processor failures and increase the total number of processors for computing. But the problems to solve are chosen very carefully such that the size of checkpoint on each processor is always the same (about 25 Megabytes) in every experiment. By keeping the size of checkpoint per processor fixed, we are able to observe the impact of the total number of computing processors on the performance of the checkpointing.

In all experiments, we performed checkpoint every 100 iterations and run PCG for 2000 iterations; In practice, there is an optimal checkpoint interval which depends on the failure rate, the time cost of each checkpoint and the time cost of each recovery. Much literature about the optimal checkpoint interval (Gelenebe, 1979), (Plank & Thomason, 2001), (Young, 1998) is available. We will not address this issue further here.

Figure 8 reports both the checkpoint overhead (for one checkpoint) and the recovery overhead (for one recovery) for tolerating 4 simultaneous process failures on a IBM RS/6000 with 176 Winterhawk II thin nodes (each with 4 375 MHz Power3-II processors). The number of checkpoint processors in the experiment is four. We simulate a failure of four simultaneous processors by killing four processes during the execution.

Figure 8 demonstrates that both the checkpoint overhead and the recovery overhead are very stable as the total number of computing processes increases from 60 to 480. This is consistent with our theoretical result in previous section.

Performance of the Algorithm-Based Checkpoint-Free Fault Tolerance

In this section, we experimentally evaluate the performance overhead of applying this checkpoint-free fault tolerance technique to tolerate single fail-stop process failure in the widely used ScaLAPACK matrix-matrix multiplication kernel. The size of the problems and the number of computation processes used in our experiments are listed in Figure 9.

All experiments were performed on a cluster of 64 dual-processor nodes with AMD Opteron(tm) Processor 240. Each node of the cluster has 2 GB of memory and runs a Linux operating system. The nodes are connected with Myrinet. The timer we used in all measurements is MPI Wtime. The programming environment we used is FT-MPI (Fagg, et al., 2005).

When there is no failure occurs, the total overhead equals to the overhead for calculating encoding

Figure 8. Scalability of the checkpoint encoding and recovery decoding

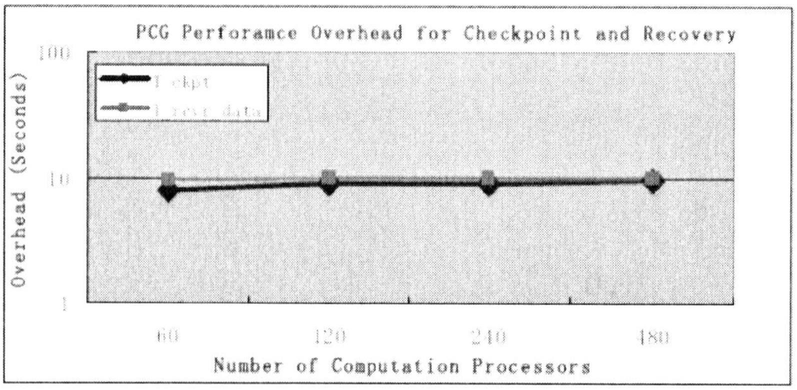

Figure 9. Experiment configurations

Process grid w/out FT	Process grid w/ FT	Size of orig mat.	Size of chk mat.
2 by 2	3 by 3	12,800	19,200
3 by 3	4 by 4	19,200	25,600
4 by 4	5 by 5	25,600	32,000
5 by 5	6 by 6	32,000	38,400
6 by 6	7 by 7	38,400	44,800
7 by 7	8 by 8	44,800	51,200
8 by 8	9 by 9	51,200	57,600
9 by 9	10 by 10	57,600	64,000
10 by 10	11 by 11	64,000	70,400

Figure 10. The total overhead (time) for fault tolerance

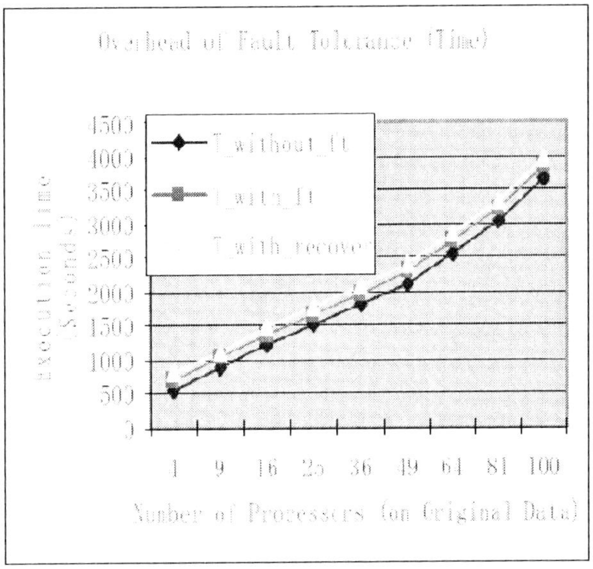

at the beginning plus the overhead of performing computation with larger (checksum) matrices. If there are failures occur, then the total performance overhead equals the overhead without failures plus the overhead for recovering FT-MPI Environment and the overhead for recovering the application data from the checksum relationship.

Figure 10 reports the execution times of the original matrix-matrix multiplication, the fault tolerant version matrix-matrix multiplication without failures, and the fault tolerant version matrix-matrix multiplication with a single fail-stop process failure. Figure 11 reports the total fault tolerance overhead (%).

Figure 11 demonstrates that, as the number of processors increases, the total overhead (%) decreases. This is because, as the number of processors increases, the time overhead is pretty stable but the total amount of time to solve a problem increases. The percentage overhead equals to the time overhead divided by the total amount of time to solve the problem.

CONCLUSION AND FUTURE WORK

In this chapter, we presented two scalable fault tolerance techniques for large-scale high performance computing. The introduced techniques are scalable in the sense that the overhead to survive k failures in p processes does not increase as the number of processes p increases. Experimental results demonstrate that the introduced techniques scale well as the total number of processors increases.

REFERENCES

Adiga, N. R., et al. (2002). An overview of the BlueGene/L supercomputer. In *Proceedings of the Supercomputing Conference (SC'2002), Baltimore MD, USA*, (pp. 1–22).

Anfinson, J., & Luk, F. T. (1988, December). A Linear Algebraic Model of Algorithm-Based Fault Tolerance. *IEEE Transactions on Computers*, *37*(12), 1599–1604. doi:10.1109/12.9736

Balasubramanian, V., & Banerjee, P. (1990). Compiler-Assisted Synthesis of Algorithm-Based Checking in Multiprocessors. *IEEE Transactions on Computers*, *C-39*, 436–446. doi:10.1109/12.54837

Figure 11. The total overhead (%) for fault tolerance

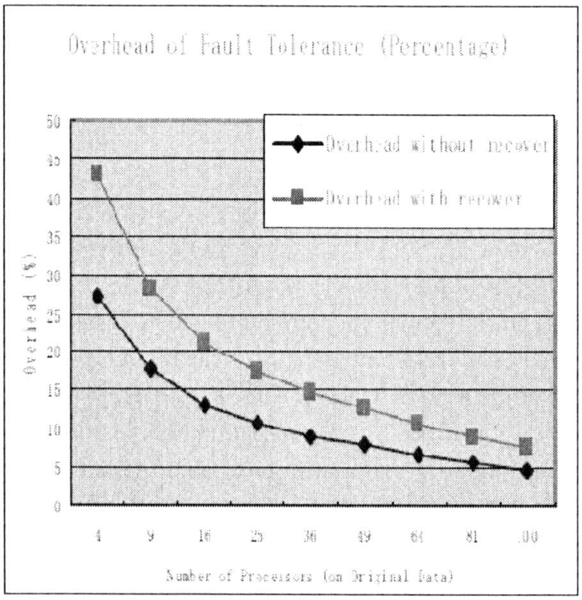

Banerjee, P., Rahmeh, J. T., Stunkel, C. B., Nair, V. S. S., Roy, K., & Balasubramanian, V. (1990). Algorithmbased fault tolerance on a hypercube multiprocessor. *IEEE Transactions on Computers*, *C-39*, 1132–1145. doi:10.1109/12.57055

Barrett, R., Berry, M., Chan, T. F., Demmel, J., Donato, J., Dongarra, J., et al. (1994). *Templates for the Solution of Linear Systems: Building Blocks for Iterative Methods, 2nd Edition*., Philadelphia, PA: SIAM.

Blackford, L. S., Choi, J., Cleary, A., Petitet, A., & Whaley, R. C. Demmel, et al. (1996). ScaLAPACK: a portable linear algebra library for distributed memory computers - design issues and performance. In *Supercomputing '96: Proceedings of the 1996 ACM/IEEE conference on Supercomputing (CDROM)*, (p. 5).

Boley, D. L., Brent, R. P., Golub, G. H., & Luk, F. T. (1992). Algorithmic fault tolerance using the lanczos method. *SIAM Journal on Matrix Analysis and Applications*, *13*, 312–332. doi:10.1137/0613023

Cannon, L. E. (1969). *A cellular computer to implement the kalman filter algorithm*. Ph.D. thesis, Montana State University, Bozeman, MT.

Chen, Z., & Dongarra, J. (2005). Condition numbers of gaussian random matrices. *SIAM Journal on Matrix Analysis and Applications*, *27*(3), 603–620. doi:10.1137/040616413

Chiueh, T., & Deng, P. (1996). Evaluation of checkpoint mechanisms for massively parallel machines. In *FTCS*, (pp. 370–379).

Dongarra, J., Meuer, H., & Strohmaier, E. (2004). TOP500 Supercomputer Sites, 24th edition. In *Proceedings of the Supercomputing Conference (SC'2004), Pittsburgh PA*. New York: ACM.

Edelman, A. (1988). Eigenvalues and condition numbers of random matrices. *SIAM Journal on Matrix Analysis and Applications*, *9*(4), 543–560. doi:10.1137/0609045

Fagg, G. E., & Dongarra, J. (2000). FT-MPI: Fault tolerant MPI, supporting dynamic applications in a dynamic world. In *PVM/MPI 2000*, (pp. 346–353).

Fagg, G. E., Gabriel, E., Bosilca, G., Angskun, T., Chen, Z., Pjesivac-Grbovic, J., et al. (2004). Extending the MPI specification for process fault tolerance on high performance computing systems. In *Proceedings of the International Supercomputer Conference*, Heidelberg, Germany.

Fagg, G. E., Gabriel, E., Chen, Z., Angskun, T., Bosilca, G., & Pjesivac-Grbovic, J. (2005). Process faulttolerance: Semantics, design and applications for high performance computing. [Winter.]. *International Journal of High Performance Computing Applications*, *19*(4), 465–477. doi:10.1177/1094342005056137

Fox, G. C., Johnson, M., Lyzenga, G., Otto, S. W., Salmon, J., & Walker, D. (1988). *Solving Problems on Concurrent Processors: Vol. 1*. Englewood Cliffs, NJ: Prentice-Hall.

Gelenbe, E. (1979). On the optimum checkpoint interval. *Journal of the ACM*, *26*(2), 259–270. doi:10.1145/322123.322131

Golub, G. H., & Van Loan, C. F. (1989). *Matrix Computations*. Baltimore, MD: The John Hopkins University Press.

Huang, K.-H., & Abraham, J. A. (1984). Algorithm-based fault tolerance for matrix operations. *EEE Transactions on Computers*, *C-33*, 518–528. doi:10.1109/TC.1984.1676475

Kim, Y. (1996, June). *Fault Tolerant Matrix Operations for Parallel and Distributed Systems.* Ph.D. dissertation, University of Tennessee, Knoxville.

Luk, F. T., & Park, H. (1986). An analysis of algorithm-based fault tolerance techniques. *SPIE Adv. Alg. and Arch. for Signal Proc.*, *696*, 222–228.

Message Passing Interface Forum. (1994). MPI: A Message Passing Interface Standard. (Technical Report ut-cs-94-230), University of Tennessee, Knoxville, TN.

Plank, J. S. (1997, September). A tutorial on Reed-Solomon coding for fault-tolerance in RAID-like systems. *Software, Practice & Experience*, *27*(9), 995–1012. doi:10.1002/(SICI)1097-024X(199709)27:9<995::AID-SPE111>3.0.CO;2-6

Plank, J. S., Kim, Y., & Dongarra, J. (1997). Fault-tolerant matrix operations for networks of workstations using diskless checkpointing. *Journal of Parallel and Distributed Computing*, *43*(2), 125–138. doi:10.1006/jpdc.1997.1336

Plank, J. S., & Li, K. (1994). Faster checkpointing with *n*+1 parity. In *FTCS*, (pp. 288–297).

Plank, J. S., Li, K., & Puening, M. A. (1998). Diskless checkpointing. *IEEE Transactions on Parallel and Distributed Systems*, *9*(10), 972–986. doi:10.1109/71.730527

Plank, J. S., & Thomason, M. G. (2001, November). Processor allocation and checkpoint interval selection in cluster computing systems. *Journal of Parallel and Distributed Computing*, *61*(11), 1570–1590. doi:10.1006/jpdc.2001.1757

Silva, L. M., & Silva, J. G. (1998). An experimental study about diskless checkpointing. In *EUROMICRO'98*, (pp. 395–402).

Young, J. W. (1974). A first order approximation to the optimal checkpoint interval. *Communications of the ACM*, *17*(9), 530–531. doi:10.1145/361147.361115

KEY TERMS AND DEFINITIONS

Checkpointing: Checkpointing is a type of techniques to incorporate fault tolerance into a system.

Erasure Correction Codes: An erasure correction code transforms a message of *n* blocks into a message with more than *n* blocks, such that the original message can be recovered from a subset of those blocks.

Fail-Stop Failure: Fail-stop failure is a type of failures that cause the component of a system experiencing this type of failure stops operating.

Fault Tolerance: Fault tolerance is the property of a system that enables it to continue operating properly after a failure occurred in the system.

Message Passing Interface: Message Passing Interface is a specification for an API that allows different processes to communicate with one another.

Parallel and Distributed Computing: Parallel and distributed computing is a sub-field of computer science that handles computing involving more than one processing unit.

Pipeline: A pipeline is a set of data processing elements connected in series so that the output of one element is the input of the next one.

Section 10
Applications

Chapter 34
Efficient Update Control of Bloom Filter Replicas in Large Scale Distributed Systems

Yifeng Zhu
University of Maine, USA

Hong Jiang
University of Nebraska – Lincoln, USA

ABSTRACT

This chapter discusses the false rates of Bloom filters in a distributed environment. A Bloom filter (BF) is a space-efficient data structure to support probabilistic membership query. In distributed systems, a Bloom filter is often used to summarize local services or objects and this Bloom filter is replicated to remote hosts. This allows remote hosts to perform fast membership query without contacting the original host. However, when the services or objects are changed, the remote Bloom replica may become stale. This chapter analyzes the impact of staleness on the false positive and false negative for membership queries on a Bloom filter replica. An efficient update control mechanism is then proposed based on the analytical results to minimize the updating overhead. This chapter validates the analytical models and the update control mechanism through simulation experiments.

INTRODUCTION TO BLOOM FILTERS

A standard Bloom filter (BF) (Bloom, 1970) is a lossy but space-efficient data structure to support membership queries within a constant delay. As shown in Figure 1, a BF includes k independent random hash functions and a vector B of a length of m bits. It is assumed that the BF represents a finite set $S = \{x_1, x_2,\ldots,x_n\}$ of n elements from a universe U . The hash functions $h_i(x)$, $1 \leq i \leq k$, map the universe U to the bit address space $[1,m]$, shown as follows,

$$H(x) = \{h_i(x) \mid 1 \leq h_i(x) \leq m \text{ for } 1 \leq i \leq k\} \tag{1}$$

DOI: 10.4018/978-1-60566-661-7.ch034

Figure 1. A Bloom filter with a bit vector of m bits, and k independent hash functions. When an element x is added into the set represented, all bits indexed by those hash functions are set to 1.

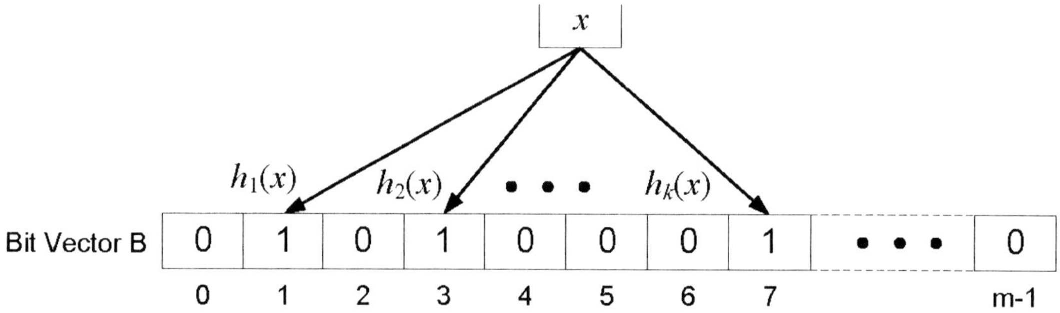

Definition 1. For all $x \in U$, $B[H(x)] \equiv \{B[h_i(x)] \mid 1 \le i \le k\}$.

This notation facilitates the description of operations on the subset of B addressed by the hash functions. For example, $B[H(x)] = 1$ represents the condition in which all the bits in B at the positions of $h_1(x)$,..., and $h_k(x)$ are 1. "Setting $B[H(x)]$" means that the bits at these positions in B are set to 1.

Representing the set S using a BF B is fast and simple. Initially, all the bits in B are set to 0. Then for each $x \in S$, an operation of setting $B[H(x)]$ is performed. Given an element x, to check whether x is in S, one only needs to test whether $B[H(x)] = 1$. If no, then x is not a member of S; If yes, x is *conjectured* to be in S. Figure 1 shows the results after the element x is inserted into the Bloom filter.

A standard BF has two well-known properties that are described by the following two theorems.

Theorem 1. *Zero false negative*

For $\forall x \in U$, if $\exists i$, $B[h_i(x)] \ne 1$, then $x \notin S$.

For a static set S whose elements are not dynamically deleted, the bit vector indexed by those hash functions always never returns a false negative. The proof is easy and is not given in this chapter.

Theorem 2. *Possible false positive*

For $\forall x \in U$, if $B[H(x)] = 1$, then there is a small probability f^+ that $x \notin S$. This probability is called the *false positive rate* and $f^+ \approx (1 - e^{-kn/m})^k$. Given a specific ratio of m/n, f^+ is minimized when $k = (m/n)ln2$ and $f^+_{min} \approx (0.6185)^{m/n}$.

Proof: The proof is based on the mathematical model proposed in (James, 1983; McIlroy, 1982). Detailed proof can be found in (Li et al., 2000; Michael, 2002). For the convenience of the reader, the proof is briefly presented here.

After inserting n elements into a BF, the probability that a bit is zero is given by:

Figure 2. Expected false positive rate in a standard Bloom filter. A false positive is due to the collision of hash functions, where all indexed bits happen to be set by other elements.

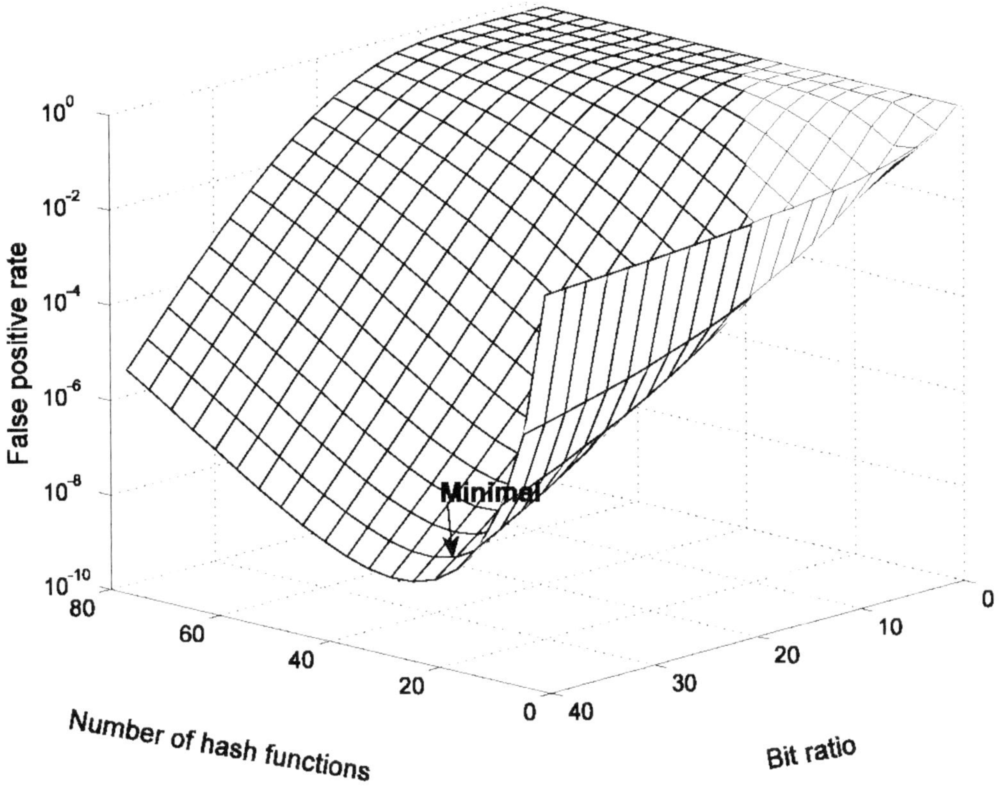

$$P_0(n) = \left(1 - \frac{1}{m}\right)^{kn} \approx e^{-kn/m}. \tag{2}$$

Thus the probability that k bits are set to 1 is

$$P(k \text{ bits set}) = \left(1 - \left(1 - \frac{1}{m}\right)^{kn}\right)^{k} \approx (1 - e^{-kn/m})^{k}. \tag{3}$$

Assuming each element is equally likely to be accessed and $|S| \| U|$, then the false positive rate is

$$f^{+} = \left(1 - \frac{|S|}{|U|}\right) P(k \text{ bits set}) \approx (1 - e^{-kn/m})^{k}. \tag{4}$$

Given a specific ratio of $\frac{m}{n}$, i.e., the number of bits per element, it can be proved that the false positive rate $f^{\dagger}$ is minimized when $k = \frac{m}{n} ln2$ and the minimal false positive rate is, as has been shown (Michael, 2002)

$$f^{\dagger} \approx 0.5^k = (0.6185)^{m/n} \quad (5)$$

The key advantage of a Bloom filter is that its storage requirement falls several orders of magnitude below the lower bounds of error-free encoding structures. This space efficiency is achieved at the cost of allowing a certain (typically none-zero) probability of *false positives*, that is, it may incorrectly return an "yes" although x is actually not in S. Appropriately adjusting m and k can minimize this probability of false-positive to a sufficiently small value so that benefits from the space and time efficiency far outweigh the penalty incurred by false positives in many applications. For example, when the bit-element ratio is 8 and the number of hash functions is 6, the expected false positive rate is only 0.0216. Figure 2 shows the false positive rate under different configurations.

In order to represent a dynamic set that is changing over time, (Li et al., 2000) proposes a variant named counting BF. A counting BF includes an array in which each entry is not a bit but rather a counter consisted of several bits. Counting Bloom filters can support element deletion operations. Let $C = \{c_j \mid 1 \leq j \leq m\}$ denote the counter vector and the counter c_j represents the difference between the number of settings and the number of unsetting operations made to the bit $B[j]$. All counters c_j for $1 \leq j \leq m$ are initialized to zero. When an element x is inserted or deleted, the counters $C[H(x)]$ are incremented or decreased by one, respectively. If c_j changes its value from one to zero, $B[j]$ is reset to zero. While this counter array consumes some memory space, (Li *et al.*, 2000) shows that 4 bits per counter will guarantee the probability of overflow minuscule even with several hundred million elements in a BF.

APPLICATIONS OF BLOOM FILTERS IN DISTRIBUTED SYSTEMS

Bloom filters have been extensively used in many distributed systems where information dispersed across the entire system needs to be shared. For example, to reduce the message traffic, (Li et al, 2000) propose a web cache sharing protocol that employs a BF to represent the content of a web proxy cache and then periodically propagates that filter to other proxies. If a cache miss occurs on a proxy, that proxy checks the BFs replicated from other proxies to see whether they have the desired web objects in their caches. (Hong & Tao, 2003; Hua et al., 2008; Ledlie et al., 2002; Matei & Ian, 2002; Zhu et al., 2004; Zhu et al., 2008) use BFs to implement the function of mapping logical data identities to their physical locations in distributed storage systems. In these schemes, each storage node constructs a Bloom filter that summarizes the identities of data stored locally and broadcasts the Bloom filter to other nodes. By checking all filters collected locally, a node can locate the requested data without sending massive query messages to other nodes. Similar deployments of BFs have been found in geographic routing in wireless mobile systems (Pai-Hsiang, 2001), peer-to-peer systems (Hailong & Jun, 2004; John et al., 2000; Mohan & Kalogeraki, 2003; Rhea & Kubiatowicz, 2002), naming services (Little et al., 2002), and wireless sensor networks (Ghose et al. 2003; Luk et al. 2007).

A common characteristic of distributed applications of BFs, including all those described above, is that *a BF at a local host is replicated to other remote hosts to efficiently support distributed queries*. In such dynamical distributed applications, the information that a BF represents evolves over time. However, the updating processes are usually delayed due to the network latency or the delay necessary in aggregating small changes into single updating message in order to reduce the updating overhead. Accordingly the contents of the remote replicas may become partially outdated. This possible staleness in the remote replicas not only changes the probability of false positive answers to membership queries on the remote hosts, but also brings forth the possibility of *false negatives*. A false negative occurs when a BF replica answers "no" to the membership query for an element while that element actually exists in its host. It is generated when a new element is added to a host while the changes of the BF of this host, including the addition of this new element, have not been propagated to its replicas on other hosts. In addition, this staleness also changes the probability of *false positives*, an event in which an element is incorrectly identified as a member. Throughout the rest of this chapter, the probabilities of false negatives and false positives are referred to as the false negative rate and false positive rate, respectively.

While the false negative and false positive rates for a BF at a local host have been well studied in the context of non-replicated BF (Bloom, 1970; Broder & Mitzenmacher, 2003; James, 1983; Li et al., 2000; Michael, 2002), very little attention has been paid to the false rates in the Bloom filter replicas in a distributed environment. In the distributed systems considered in this chapter, the false rates of the replicas are more important since most membership queries are performed on these replicas. A good understanding of the impact of the false negatives and false positives can provide the system designers with important and useful insights into the development and deployment of distributed BFs in such important applications as distributed file, database, and web server management systems in super-scales. Therefore, the first objective of this chapter is to analyze the false rates by developing analytical models and considering the staleness.

Since different application may desire a different tradeoff between false rate (e.g, miss/fault penalty) and update overhead (e.g., network traffic and processing due to broadcasting of updates), it is very important and significant for the systems overall performance to be able to control such a tradeoff for a given application adaptively and efficiently. The second objective is to develop an adaptive control algorithm that can accurately and efficiently maintain a desirable level of false rate for any given application by dynamically and judiciously adjusting the update frequency.

The primary contribution of this chapter is its developments of accurate closed-form expressions for the false negative and false positive rates in BF replicas, and the development of an adaptive replica-update control, based on our analytical model, that accurately and efficiently maintains a desirable level of false rate for any given application. To the best of our knowledge, this study is the first of its kind that has considered the impact of staleness of replicated BF contents in a distributed environment, and developed a mechanism to adaptively minimize such an impact so as to optimize systems performance.

The rest of the chapter is organized as follows. Section 3 presents our analytical models that theoretically derive false negative and false positive rates of a BF replica, as well as the overall false rates in distributed systems. Section 4 validates our theoretical results by comparing them against results obtained from extensive experiments. The adaptive updating protocols based on our theoretical analysis models are presented in Section 5. Section 6 gives related work and Section 7 concludes the chapter. The chapter is extended from our previous publication (Zhu & Jiang, 2006).

FALSE RATES IN THEORY

In many distributed systems, the information about what data objects can be accessed through a host or where data objects are located usually needs to be shared to facilitate the lookup. To provide high scal-

Figure 3. An example application of Bloom filters in a distributed system with 3 hosts.

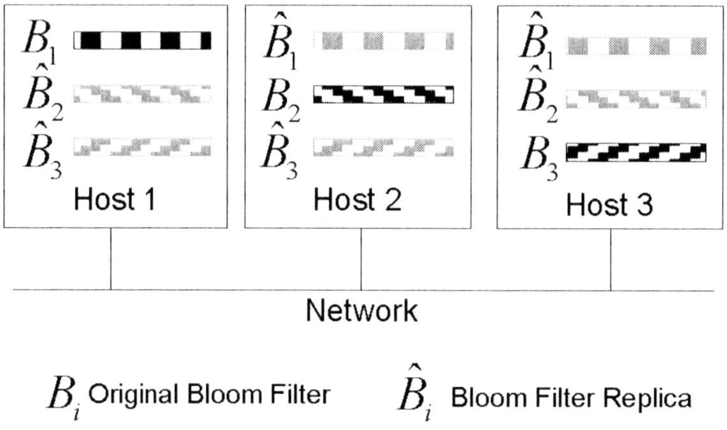

ability, this information sharing usually takes a decentralized approach, to avoid potential performance bottleneck and vulnerability of a centralized architecture such as a dedicated server. While BFs were initially used in non-distributed systems to save the memory space in the 1980's when memory was considered a precious resource (Lee, 1982; McIlroy, 1982), they have recently been extensively used in many distributed systems as a scalable and efficient scheme for information sharing, due to their low network traffic overhead.

The inherent nature of such information sharing in almost all these distributed systems, if not all, can be abstracted as a location identification, or mapping problem, which is described next. Without loss of generality, the distributed system considered throughout this chapter is assumed to consist of a collection of γ autonomous data-storing host computers dispersed across a communication network. These hosts partition a universe U of data objects into γ subsets $S_1, S_2, \ldots, S_\gamma$, with each subset stored on one of these hosts. Given an arbitrary object x in U, the problem is how to efficiently identify the host that stores x from any one of the hosts.

BFs are useful to solve this kind of problems. In a typical approach, each host constructs a BF representing the subset of objects stored in it, and then broadcasts that filter to all the other hosts. Thus each host keeps $\gamma - 1$ additional BFs, one for every other host. Figure 3 shows an example of a system with three hosts. Note that a filter $\hat{B}_i$ is a replica of B_i from Host i and $\hat{B}_i$ may become outdated if the changes to B_i are not propagated instantaneously. While the solution to the above information sharing problem can implemented somewhat differently giving rise to a number of solution variants (Hua et al., 2008; Ledlie et al., 2002; Zhu et al., 2004), the analysis of false rates presented in this chapter can be easily applied to these variants.

The detailed procedures of the operations of insertion, deletion and query of data objects are shown in Figure 4. When an object x is deleted from or inserted into Host i, the values of the counting filters $C_i[H(x)]$ and bits $B_i[H(x)]$ are adjusted accordingly. When the fraction of modified bits in B_i exceeds some threshold, B_i is broadcast to all the other hosts to update $\hat{B}_i$. To look up x, Host i performs the membership tests on all the BFs kept locally. If a test on B_i is positive, then x can potentially be accessed locally. If a test in the filter $\hat{B}_j$ for any $j \neq i$ is positive, then x is conjectured to be on Host j with high probability. Finally, if none of the tests is positive, x is considered nonexistent in the system.

Figure 4. Procedures of adding, deleting and querying object x at host i

AddObject(Object x, Host i)

Set ($B_i[H(x)]$) to 1;
Increase $C_i[H(x)]$ by 1;
if(the changed portion of B_i is larger than some threshold)
    Multicast B_i to the other hosts;

DeleteObject(Object x, Host i)

Decrease $C_i[H(x)]$ by 1;
for($j = 1$; $j \le k$; $j{+}{+}$)
    if($C_i[h_j(x)] = 0$)
        Unset bit $B_i[h_j(x)]$ to 0;

QueryObject(Object x, Host i)

$\psi = \varnothing$;
/* check the BF of the local host */
if($B_i[H(x)] = 1$)
    $\psi = \{i\}$;
/* check all BF replicas */
for($j = 1$; $j \le \gamma$; $j{+}{+}$)
    if($j \ne i$ and $\hat{B}_i[H(x)] = 1$)
        $\psi = \psi \cup \{j\}$
return ψ;

In the following, we begin the analysis by examining the false negative and false positive rate of a single BF replica and then present the analysis of the overall false rates of all BFs kept locally on a host. The experimental validations of the analytical models are presented in the next section.

False Rates of Bloom Filter Replicas

Let B be a BF with m bits and $\hat{B}$ a replica of B. Let n and $\hat{n}$ be the number of objects in the set represented by B and by $\hat{B}$, respectively. We denote Δ_1 (Δ_0) as the set of all one (zero) bits in B that are different than (i.e., complement of) the corresponding bits in $\hat{B}$. More specifically,

$$\Delta_1 = \{B[i] \mid B[i] = 1, \hat{B}[i] = 0, \forall i \in [1, m]\}$$

Figure 5. An example of a BF B and its replica $\hat{B}$ where bits are reordered such that bits in Δ_1 and Δ_0 are placed together.

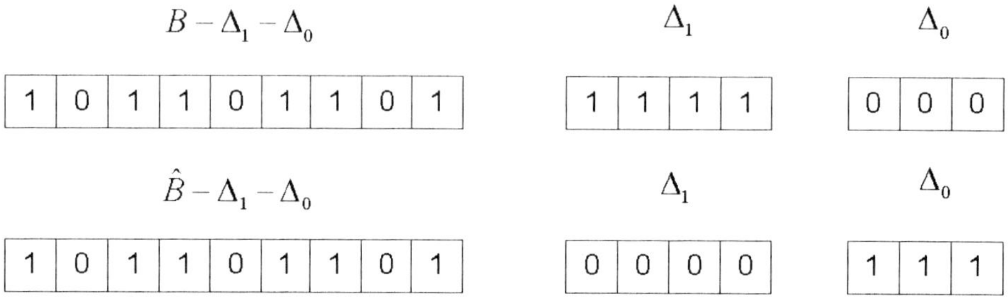

$$\Delta_0 = \{B[i] \mid B[i] = 0, \hat{B}[i] = 1, \forall i \in [1, m]\}.$$

Thus, $\Delta_0 + \Delta_1$ represent the set of changed bits in B that have not been propagated to $\hat{B}$. The number of bits in this set is affected by the update threshold and update latency. Furthermore, if a nonempty Δ_1 is hit by least one hash function of a membership test on $\hat{B}$ while all other hash functions of the same test hit bits in $\hat{B} - \Delta_1 - \Delta_0$ with a value of one, then a false negative occurs in $\hat{B}$. Similarly, a false positive occurs if the nonempty Δ_1 is replaced by a nonempty Δ_0 in the exact membership test scenario on a $\hat{B}$ described above.

Lemma 1. Suppose that the numbers of bits in Δ_1 and in Δ_0 are $m\delta_1$ and $m\delta_0$, respectively. Then $\hat{n}$ is a random variable following a normal distribution with an extremely small variance (i.e., extremely highly concentrated around its mean), that is,

$$E(\hat{n}) = -\frac{m}{k}\ln(e^{-kn/m} + \delta_1 - \delta_0). \tag{6}$$

Proof: In a given BF representing a set of n objects, each bit is zero with probability $P_0(n)$, given in Equation 2, or one with probability $P_1(n) = 1 - P_0(n)$. Thus the average fractions of zero and one bits are $P_0(n)$ and $P_1(n)$, respectively. Ref. (Michael, 2002) shows formally that the fractions of zero and one bits are random variables that are highly concentrated on $P_0(n)$ and $P_1(n)$ respectively.

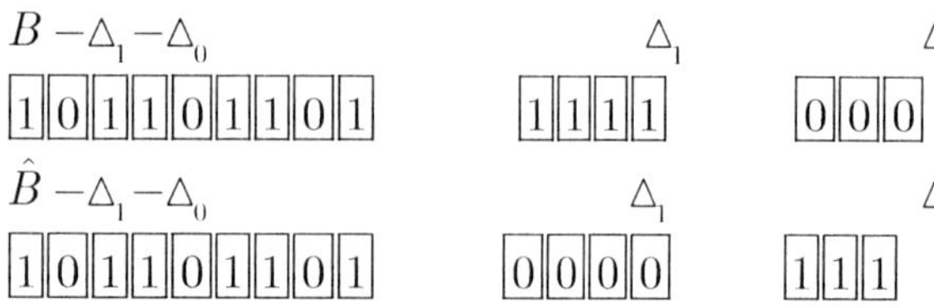

Figure 5 shows an example of B and $\hat{B}$ where bits in Δ_1 and Δ_0 are extracted out and placed together. The expected numbers of zero bits in $B - \Delta_1 - \Delta_0$ and in $\hat{B} - \Delta_1 - \Delta_0$ should be equal since the bits in them are always identical for any given B and $\hat{B}$. Thus for any given n, δ_1 and δ_0, we have

Figure 6. Expected false negative rate of a Bloom filter replica when the configuration of its original Bloom filter is optimal.

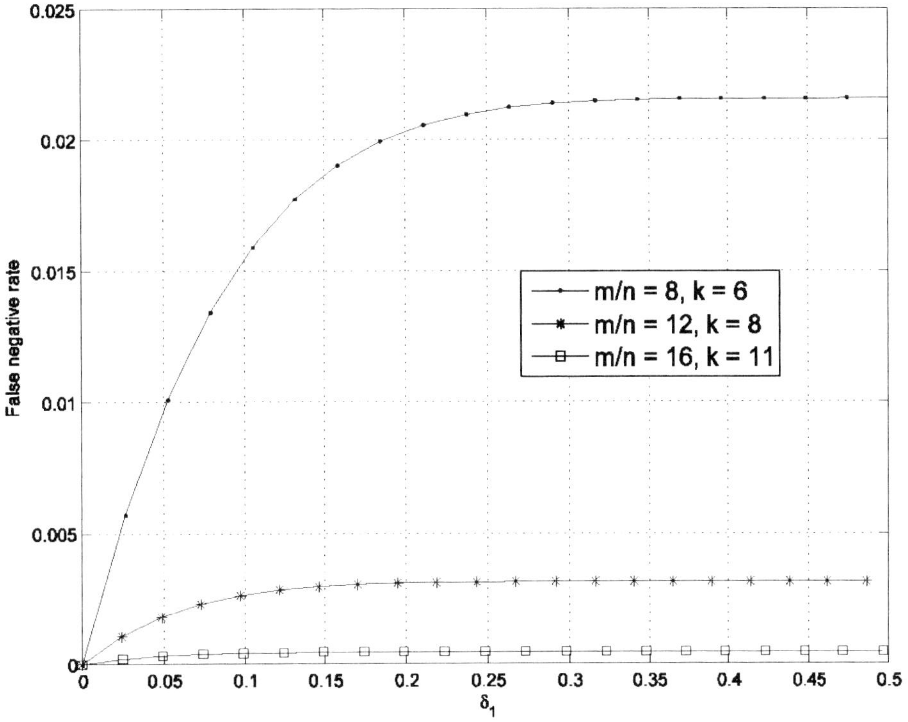

$$P_0(n) - \delta_0 = E(P_0(\hat{n})) - \delta_1 \tag{7}$$

Substituting Equation 2 into the above equation, we have

$$e^{-kn/m} - \delta_0 = e^{-kE(\hat{n})/m} - \delta_1 \tag{8}$$

After solving Equation 8, we obtain Equation 6.

Pragmatically, in any given BF with n objects, the values of δ_1 and δ_0, which represent the probabilities of a bit falling in Δ_1 and Δ_0 respectively, are relatively small. Theoretically, the number of bits in Δ_1 is less than the total number of one bits in B, thus we have $\delta_1 \leq 1 - e^{-kn/m}$. In a similar way, we can conclude that $\delta_0 \leq e^{-kn/m}$.

Theorem 3. *False Negative Rate*

The expected false negative rate $\hat{f}^-$ in the BF replica $\hat{B}$ is $P_1(n)^k - (P_1(n) - \delta_1)^k$, where $P_1(n) = 1 - e^{-kn/m}$.

Proof: As mentioned earlier, a false negative in $\hat{B}$ occurs when at least one hash function hits the bits in Δ_1 in $\hat{B}$ while the others hit the bits in $\hat{B} - \Delta_1 - \Delta_0$ with a value of one. Hence, the false nega-

Figure 7. Expected false positive rate of a Bloom filter replica when the configuration of its original Bloom filter is optimal.

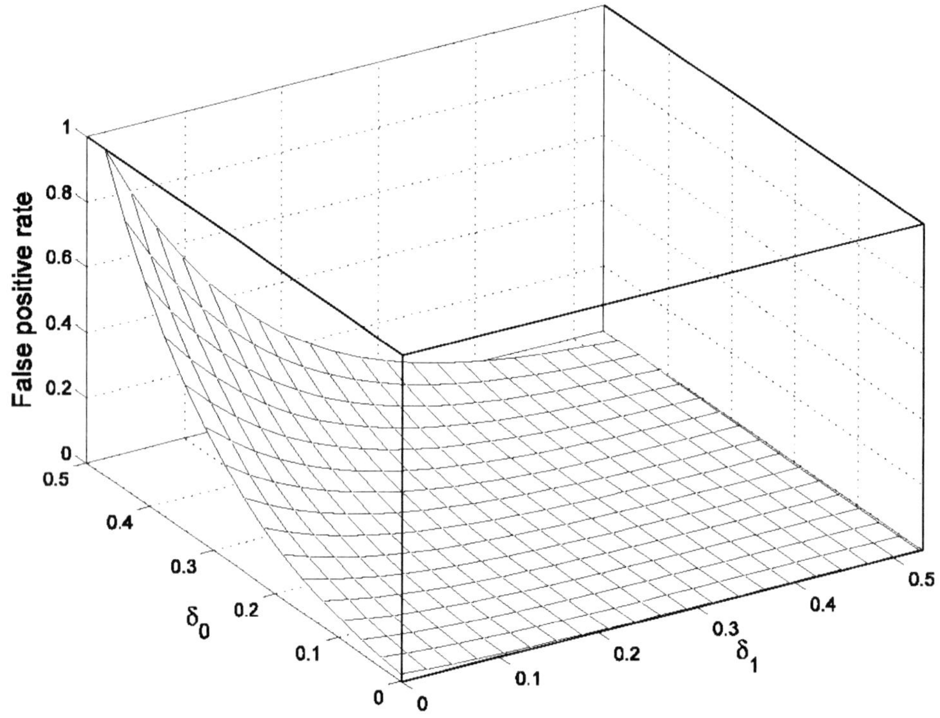

tive rate is

$$\hat{f}^- = \sum_{i=1}^{k} \binom{k}{i} \delta_1^i \left(P_1(\hat{n}) - \delta_0\right)^{k-i} = \left(P_1(\hat{n}) - \delta_0 + \delta_1\right)^k - \left(P_1(\hat{n}) - \delta_0\right)^k$$

Since $P_0(n) = 1 - P_1(n)$ and $P_0(\hat{n}) = 1 - P_1(\hat{n})$, Equation 7 can be rewritten as:

$$E(P_1(\hat{n})) = P_1(n) + \delta_0 - \delta_1 \quad (9)$$

Hence

$$E(\hat{f}^-) = \left(E(P_1(\hat{n})) - \delta_0 + \delta_1\right)^k - \left(E(P_1(\hat{n})) - \delta_0\right)^k$$

$$= P_1(n)^k - \left(P_1(n) - \delta_1\right)^k \quad (10)$$

Figure 6 shows the expected false negative rate when the false positive of the original BF is minimized. The minimal false positive rate is 0.0214, 0.0031 and 0.00046 when the bit-element ratio is 8, 12 and 16 respectively. Figure 6 shows that the false negative rates of a BF replica are more than 50% of the false positive rates of the original BF when δ_1 is 5%, and more than 75% when δ_1 is 10%. This proves that the false negative may be significant and should not be neglected in distributed applications.

Theorem 4. *False Positive Rate*

The expected false positive rate $\hat{f}^+$ for the Bloom filter replica $\hat{B}$ is $(P_1(n) + \delta_0 - \delta_1)^k$, where $P_1(n) = 1 - e^{-kn/m}$.

Proof: If $\hat{B}$ confirms positively the membership of an object while this object actually does not belong to B, then a false positive occurs. More specifically, a false positive occurs in $\hat{B}$ if for any $x \notin B$, all hit bits by hash functions of the membership test for x are ones in $\hat{B} - \Delta_1 - \Delta_0$, or for any $x \in U$, all hit bits are ones in $\hat{B}$ but at least one hit bit is in Δ_0. Thus, we find that

$$\hat{f}^+ = \left(1 - \frac{n}{|U|}\right)\left(P_1(\hat{n}) - \delta_0\right)^k + \sum_{i=1}^{k}\binom{k}{i}\delta_0^i(P_1(\hat{n}) - \delta_0)^{k-i}$$
$$= P_1(\hat{n})^k - \frac{n}{|U|}(P_1(\hat{n}) - \delta_0)^k \tag{11}$$

Considering $n \ll |U|$ and Equation 9, we have

$$E(\hat{f}^+) = (E(P_1(\hat{n})))^k - \frac{n}{|U|}(E(P_1(\hat{n})) - \delta_0)^k$$
$$= \left(P_1(n) + \delta_0 - \delta_1\right)^k - \frac{n}{|U|}(P_1(n) - \delta_1)^k$$
$$\approx \left(P_1(n) + \delta_0 - \delta_1\right)^k \tag{12}$$

Overall False Rates

In the distributed system considered in this study, there are a total of γ hosts and each host has γ BFs, with $\gamma-1$ of them replicated from the other hosts. To look up an object, a host performs the membership tests in all the BFs kept locally. This section analyzes the overall false rates on each BF replica and each host.

Give any BF replica $\hat{B}$, the events of a false positive and a false negative are exclusive. Thus it is easy to find that the overall false rate of $\hat{B}$ is

$$E(f_{overall}) = E(f^-) + E(f^+) \tag{13}$$

where $E(f^-)$ and $E(f^+)$ are given in Equation 10 and 12 respectively.

Figure 8. Comparisons of estimated and experimental $\hat{f}^-$ of $\hat{B}$ when k is 6, 8 and 11 respectively. The initial object number in both B and $\hat{B}$ is 25, 75, 150 and 300 (m = 1200).

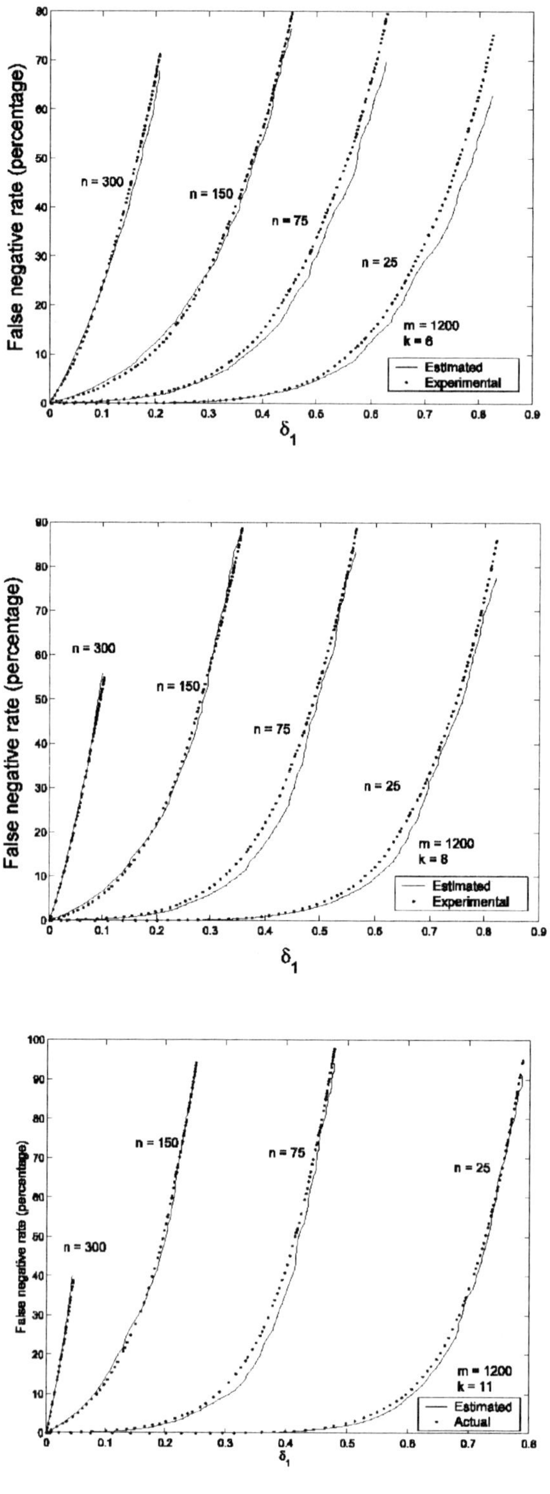

Table 1. False positive rates comparisons when k is 6 and 8 respectively (m = 1200).

				$\hat{f}^+$ (percentage)	
k	$\hat{n}$	δ_0	δ_1	Estimated	Experimental
6	25	0.0942	0.2042	0.0002	0
6	25	0.0800	0.3650	0.0002	0
6	25	0.0600	0.4875	0.0001	0
6	75	0.0800	0.1608	0.0934	0.1090
6	75	0.0600	0.2833	0.0794	0.1090
6	75	0.0483	0.3758	0.0799	0.1090
6	150	0.0533	0.1042	2.2749	2.6510
6	150	0.0400	0.1800	2.3540	2.6510
6	150	0.0325	0.2508	2.1872	2.6530
6	300	0.0250	0.0417	23.6555	25.4790
6	300	0.0183	0.0692	25.4016	25.4710
6	300	0.0117	0.1000	24.7241	25.4750
8	25	0.1083	0.2425	0.00002	0
8	25	0.0792	0.4192	0.00002	0
8	25	0.0550	0.5425	0.00002	0
8	75	0.0792	0.1767	0.0525	0.0540
8	75	0.0550	0.3000	0.0504	0.0540
8	75	0.0425	0.3917	0.0506	0.0540
8	150	0.0475	0.1050	2.5163	2.5770
8	150	0.0350	0.1758	2.6783	2.5780
8	150	0.0283	0.2367	2.5384	2.5790
8	300	0.0192	0.0333	33.2078	33.2580
8	300	0.0133	0.0558	34.4915	33.2550
8	300	0.0083	0.0817	32.1779	33.2550

On Host i, BF B_i represents all the objects stored locally. While only false positives occur in B_i, both false positives and false negatives can occur in the replicas $\hat{B}_j$ for any $j \neq i$. Since the failed membership test in any BF leads to a lookup failure, the overall false positive and false negative rates on Host i are therefore

$$E(f^+_{host}) = 1 - (1 - f^+_i) \prod_{j=1, j\neq i}^{?} (1 - \hat{f}^+_j) \tag{14}$$

and

Figure 9. Comparisons of estimated and experimental $f_{overall}$ in a distributed system with 5 hosts when k is 6, 8, and 11 respectively. The initial object number n on each host is 25, 75, 150 and 300 respectively. Then each host adds a set of new objects. The number of new objects on each host increases from 50 to 300 with a step size of 50. (m = 1200)

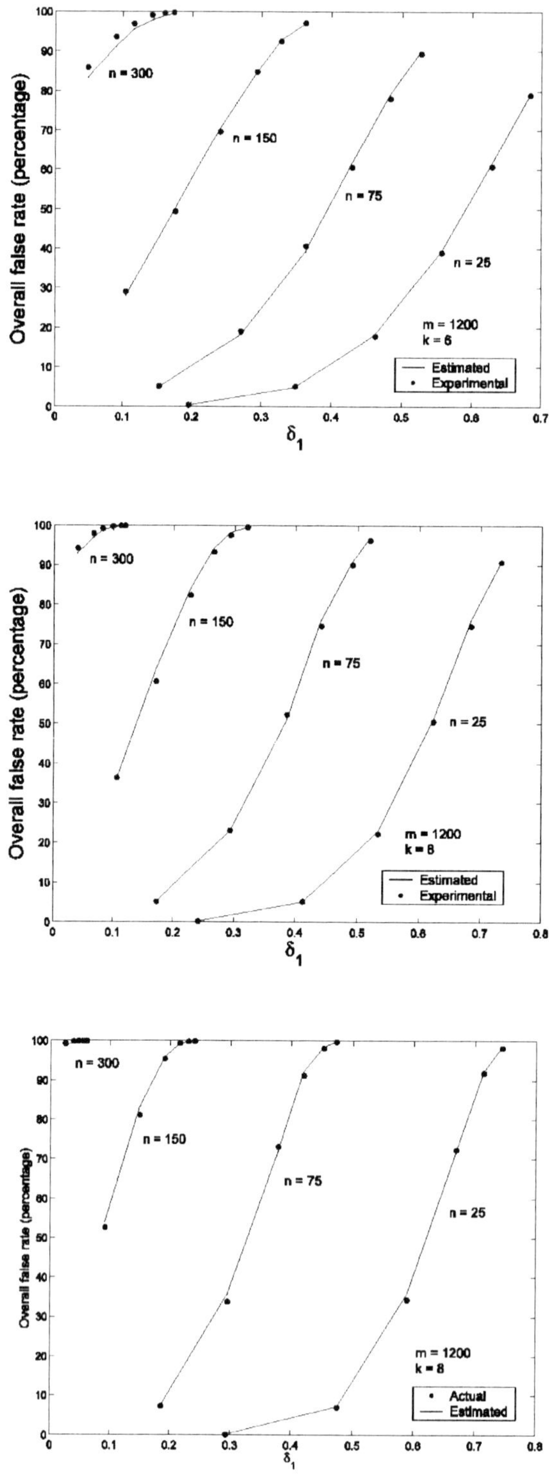

Table 2. Overall false rate comparisons under optimum initial operation state when k is 6 and 8 respectively. 100 new objects are added on each host and then a set of existing objects are deleted from each host. The number of deleted objects increases from 10 to 100 with a step size of 10. (m = 1200) In the first group, initially Initially n = 150 and m/n = 8; in the second group, n = 100 and m/n = 12 initially.

			$f_{overall}$ **(percentage)**	
k	δ_0	δ_1	Estimated	Experimental
6	0.0100	0.1705	46.2259	45.2200
6	0.0227	0.1657	42.4850	40.6880
6	0.0347	0.1627	38.7101	37.2420
6	0.0458	0.1582	34.9268	33.8460
6	0.0593	0.1545	31.3748	30.4540
6	0.0715	0.1497	27.8831	27.3700
6	0.0837	0.1445	24.5657	24.8000
6	0.0938	0.1392	21.2719	22.5560
6	0.1045	0.1340	18.2490	20.4520
6	0.1165	0.1300	15.5103	18.7540
8	0.0123	0.2375	30.9531	29.6280
8	0.0255	0.2275	25.7946	23.6280
8	0.0413	0.2180	21.0943	18.0000
8	0.0552	0.2123	16.7982	14.6720
8	0.0658	0.2043	12.9800	12.0040
8	0.0772	0.1965	9.7307	9.7320
8	0.0920	0.1900	7.1016	7.7520
8	0.1075	0.1848	4.9936	6.1280
8	0.1237	0.1788	3.4031	4.8400
8	0.1377	0.1732	2.2034	3.8160

$$E(f_{host}^{-}) = 1 - \prod_{j=1, j \neq i}^{\gamma} (1 - \hat{f}_j^{-}) \qquad (15)$$

where f_i^{+}, $\hat{f}_j^{-}$ and $\hat{f}_j^{+}$ are given in Theorem 2, 3 and 4 respectively.

The probability that Host i fails a membership lookup can be expressed as follows:

$$E(f_{host}) = E(f_{host}^{+} + f_{host}^{-} - f_{host}^{+} f_{host}^{-}) \qquad (16)$$

In practice, we can use the overall false rate of a BF replica to trigger updating process and use the overall false rate of all BFs on a host to evaluate the whole systems. In a typical distributed environment with many nodes, the updating of a Bloom filter replica $\hat{B}_i$ stored on node j can be triggered by either the home node i or the node j. Since many nodes hold the replica of B_i, it is more efficient to let the home node i to initiate the updating process of all replicas of B_i. Otherwise, the procedure of checking whether an updating is needed would be performed by all other nodes, wasting both network and CPU resources. Accordingly, we can only use the overall false rate of a BF replica $E(f_{overall})$ as the updating criteria. On the other hand, $E(f_{host})$ can be used to evaluate the overall efficiency of all BFs stored on the same host.

EXPERIMENTAL VALIDATION

This section validates our theoretical framework developed in this chapter by comparing the analytical results produced by our models with experimental results obtained through real experiments.

We begin by examining a single BF replica. Initially the Bloom filter replica $\hat{B}$ is exactly the same as B. Then we artificially change B by randomly inserting new objects into B or randomly deleting existing objects from B repeatedly. For each specific modification made to B, we calculate the corresponding δ_1 and δ_0 and use 100,000 randomly generated objects to test the memberships against $\hat{B}$. Since the actual objects represented in B are known in the experiments, the false negative and positive rates can be easily measured.

Figure 8 compares analytical and real false negative rates, obtained from the theoretic models and from experiments respectively, by plotting the false negative rate in $\hat{B}$ as a function of δ_1, a measure of update threshold, for different numbers of hashing functions ($k = 6$ and $k = 8$) when the initial number of objects in B are 25, 75, 150 and 300 respectively. Since the false negative rates are independent of δ_0, only object deletions are performed in B.

Table 1 compares the analytical and real false positive rates of $\hat{B}$ when k is 6 and 8 respectively. In these experiments, both object deletions and additions are performed in B while $\hat{B}$ remains unaltered. It is interesting that the false positive rates of $\hat{B}$ is kept around some constant for a specific $\hat{n}$ although the objects in B changes in the real experiments. It is true that if the number of objects in B increases or decreases, the false positive rate in $\hat{B}$ should decrease or increase accordingly before the changes of B is propagated to $\hat{B}$. However, due to the fact that n is far less than the total object number in the universe U, the change of the false positive rate in $\hat{B}$ is too small to be perceptible. These tests are made accordant with the real scenarios of BF applications in distributed systems. In such real applications, the number of possible objects is usually very large and thus BFs are deployed to efficiently reduce the network and network communication requirements. Hence, in these experiments the number of objects used to test $\hat{B}$ is much larger than the number of objects in B or $\hat{B}$ (100,000 random objects are tested). Under such large size of testing samples, the influence of the modification in B on the false positive rate of $\hat{B}$ is difficult to be observed.

We also simulated the lookup problem in a distributed system with 5 hosts. Figure 9 shows the comparisons of the analytical and experimental average overall false rates on each host. In these experiments, we only added new objects without deleting any existing items so that δ_0 is kept zero. The experiments presented in Table 2 considers both the deletion and addition of objects on each host when the initial state of BF on each host is optimized, this is, the number of hash functions is the optimal under the ratio between m and the initial number of objects n. This specific setting aims to emulate the real application where m/n and k are usually optimally or sub-optimally matched by dynamically adjusting the BF length m (Hong & Tao, 2003) or designing the BF length according to the average number of objects (Ledlie et al., 2002; Li et al., 2000; Little et al., 2002; Matei & Ian, 2002; Zhu et al., 2004). All the analytical results have been very closely matched by their real (experimental) counterparts consistently, strongly validating our theoretical models.

Figure 10. In an environment of two servers, the figures show the overall false rate on one server when the initial number of elements in one server are 25 and 150 respectively. The ratio of bits per element is 8 and 6 hash functions are used. The rate for element addition and deletion are respectively 5 and 2 per time unit on each server.

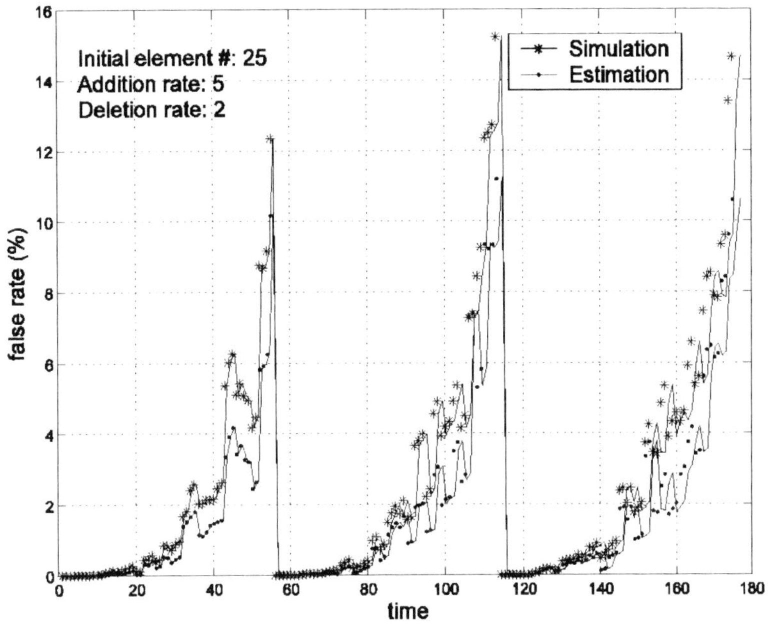

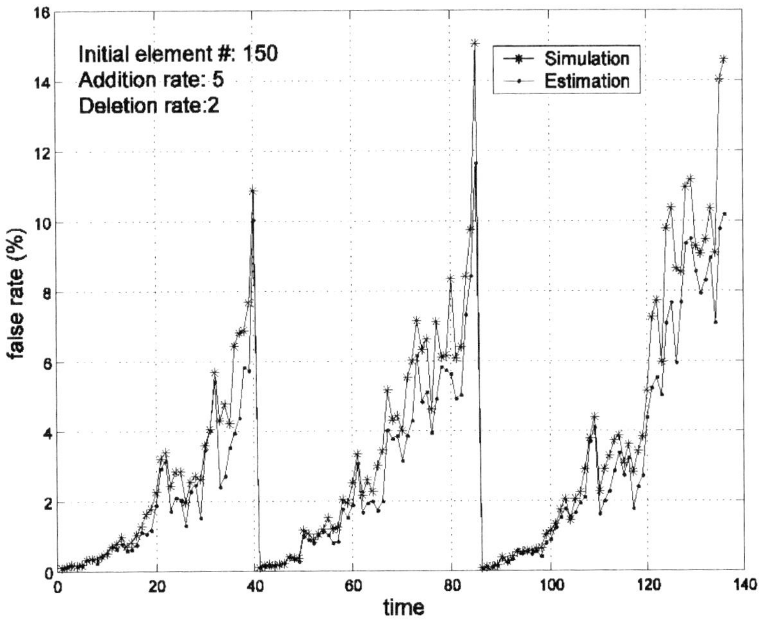

REPLICA UPDATE PROTOCOL

To reduce the false rate caused by staleness, the remote Bloom filter replica needs to be periodically updated. An update process is typically triggered if the percentage of dirty bits in a local BF exceeds some threshold. While a small threshold causes large network traffic and a large threshold increases the false rate, this tradeoff is usually reached by a trial-and-error approach that runs numerous (typically a large number of) trials in real experiments or simulations. For example, in the summery cache study (Li et al., 2000), it is recommended that if 10 percent of bits in a BF are dirty, then the BF propagates its changes to all replicas. However, this approach has the following disadvantages.

1. It cannot directly control the false rate. To keep the false rate under some target value, complicated simulations or experiments have to be conducted to adjust the threshold for dirty bits. If the target false rate changes, this tedious process has to be repeated to find a "golden" threshold.
2. It treats all dirty bits equally and does not distinguish the zero-dirty bits from the one-dirty bits. In fact, as shown in previous sections, the dirty one bits and the dirty zero bits exert different impacts on the false rates.
3. It does not allow flexible update control. In many applications, the penalty of a false positive and a false negative are significantly different. For example, in summery cache (Li et al., 2000), a false positive occurs if a request is not a cache hit on some web proxy when the corresponding Bloom filter replica confirms so. The penalty of a false positive is a waste of query message to this local web proxy. A false negative happens if a request can be hit in a local web proxy but the Bloom filter replica mistakenly indicates otherwise. The penalty of a false negative is a round-trip delay in retrieving information from a remote web server through the Internet. Thus, the penalty of a false negative is much larger than that of a false positive. The updating protocols based on the percentage of dirty bits do not allow one to place more weight on the false negative rate, thus limiting the flexibility and efficiency of the updating process.

Based on the theoretic models presented in the previous sections, an updating protocol that directly controls the false rate is designed in this chapter. In a distributed system with γ nodes where each node has a local BF to represent all local elements, each node is responsible for automatically updating its BF replicas. Each node estimates the false rate of its remote BF replica and if the false rate exceeds some desire false rate, as opposed to a predetermined threshold on the percentage of dirty bits in the conventional updating approaches, a updating process is triggered. To estimate the false rate of remote BF replica $\hat{B}$, each node has to record the number of elements stored locally (n), in addition to a copy of remote BF replica $\hat{B}$. This copy is essentially the local BF B when the last updating is made. It is used to calculate the percentage of dirty one bits (δ_1) and the dirty zero bits (δ_0). Compared with the conventional updating protocols based on the total percentage of dirty bits, this protocol only needs to record one more variable (n), thus it does not significantly increase the maintenance overhead.

This protocol allows more flexible updating protocols that consider the penalty difference between a false positive and a false negative. The overall false rate can be a weighted sum of the false positive rate and the false negative rate, shown as follows:

$$E(f_{overall}) = w^{+}E(f^{+}) + w^{-}E(f^{-}) \tag{17}$$

where w^+ and w^- are the weights. The values of w^+ and w^- depends on the applications and also the application environments.

We prove the effectiveness of this update protocol through event driven simulations. In this simulation, we made the following assumptions.

1. Each item is randomly accessed. This assumption may not be realistic in some real workloads, in which an item has a greater than equal chance of being accessed again once it has been accessed. Though all previous theoretic studies on Bloom filters assume a workload with uniform access spectrum, further studies are needed to investigate the impact of this assumption.
2. Each local node deletes or adds items at a constant rate. In fact, the deletion and addition rate changes dynamically throughout the lifetime of applications. This simplifying assumption is employed just to prove our concept while keeping our experiments manageable in the absence of a real trace or benchmark.
3. The values of w^+ and w^- are 1. Their optimal values depend on the nature of the applications and environments.

We simulate a distributed system with two nodes where each node keeps a BF replica of the other. We assume the addition and deletion are 5 and 2 per time unit respectively and our desired false rate is 10%. Figure 10 shows the estimated false rate and the measured false rate of node 1 throughout the deletion, addition and updating processes. Due to the space limitation, the false rate on node 2, which is similar to node 1, is not shown in this chapter. In addition, we have changed the addition rate and deletion rates. Simulation results consistently indicate that our protocol is accurate and effective in control the false rate.

RELATED WORK

Standard Bloom filters (Bloom, 1970) have inspired many extensions and variants, such as the Counting Bloom filters (Li et al., 2000), compressed Bloom filters (Michael, 2002), the space-code Bloom filters (Kumar et al., 2005), the spectral Bloom filters (Saar & Yossi, 2003), time-decaying Bloom filters (Cheng et al., 2005), and the Bloom filter state machine (Bonomi et al., 2006). The counting Bloom filters are used to support the deletion operation and handle a set that is changing over time (Li et al., 2000). Time-decaying Bloom filters maintains the frequency count for each item stored in the Bloom filters and the values of these frequency count decay with time (Cheng et al., 2005). Multi-Dimension Dynamic Bloom Filters (MDDBF) supports representation and membership queries based on the multi-attribute dimension (Guo et al., 2006). Its basic idea is to represent a dynamic set A with a dynamic $s \times m$ bit matrix, in which there are s standard Bloom filters and each Bloom filter has a length of m bits. A novel Parallel Bloom Filters (PBF) and an additional hash table has been developed to maintain multiple attributes of items and verify the dependency of multiple attributes, thereby significantly decreasing false positives (Hua & Xiao, 2006).

Bloom filters have significant advantages in space saving and fast query operations and thus have been widely applied in many distributed computer applications, such as aiding longest prefix matching (Dharmapurikar et al., 2006), and packet classification (Baboescu & Varghese, 2005). Extended Bloom filter provides better throughput performance for router applications based on hash tables by using a small amount of multi-port on-chip memory (Song et al., 2005). Whenever space is a concern, a Bloom filter can be an excellent alternative to storing a complete explicit list.

In many distributed applications, BFs are often replicated to multiple hosts to support membership query without contacting other hosts. However, these replicas might become stale since the changes of BFs usually cannot be propagated instantly to all replicas in order to reduce the update overhead. As a result, the BF replicas may return false negatives. This observation motivates the research presented in this chapter.

CONCLUSION

Although false negatives do not occur in standard BF, this chapter shows that the staleness in a BF replica can produce false negative. We presents the theoretical analysis of the impact of staleness existing in many distributed BF applications on the false negative and false positive rates, and developed an adaptive update control mechanism that accurately and efficiently maintains a desirable level of false rate for a given application. To the best of our knowledge, we are the first to derive accurate closed-form expressions that incorporate the staleness into the analysis of the false negative and positive rates of a single BF replica, to develop the analytical models of the overall false rates of BF arrays that have been widely used in many distributed systems, and to develop an adaptively controlled update process that accurately maintains a desirable level of false rate for a given application. We have validated our analysis by conducting extensive experiments. The theoretical analysis presented not only provides system designers with significant theoretical insights into the development and deployment of BFs in distributed systems, but also are useful in practice for accurately determining when to trigger the processes of updating BF replicas in order to keep the false rates under some desired values, or, equivalently, minimize the frequency of updates to reduce update overhead.

ACKNOWLEDGMENT

This work was partially supported by a faculty startup grant of University of Maine, and National Science Foundation Research Grants (CCF #0621493, CCF #0754951, CNS #0723093, DRL #0737583, CNS #0619430, CCF #0621526).

REFERENCES

Baboescu, F., & Varghese, G. (2005). Scalable packet classification. *IEEE/ACM Trans. Netw.*, *13*(1), 2–14.

Bloom, H. B. (1970). Space/time trade-offs in hash coding with allowable errors. *Communications of the ACM*, *13*(7), 422–426. doi:10.1145/362686.362692

Bonomi, F., Mitzenmacher, M., Panigrah, R., Singh, S., & Varghese, G. (2006). *Beyond bloom filters: from approximate membership checks to approximate state machines*. Paper presented at the Proceedings of the 2006 conference on Applications, technologies, architectures, and protocols for computer communications.

Broder, A., & Mitzenmacher, M. (2003). *Network Applications of Bloom Filters: A Survey. Internet Mathematics, 1*(4), 485–509.

Cheng, K., Xiang, L., Iwaihara, M., Xu, H., & Mohania, M. M. (2005). *Time-Decaying Bloom Filters for Data Streams with Skewed Distributions*. Paper presented at the Proceedings of the 15th International Workshop on Research Issues in Data Engineering: Stream Data Mining and Applications.

Dharmapurikar, S., Krishnamurthy, P., & Taylor, D. E. (2006). Longest prefix matching using bloom filters. *IEEE/ACM Trans. Netw., 14*(2), 397–409.

Ghose, F., Grossklags, J., & Chuang, J. (2003). *Resilient Data-Centric Storage in Wireless Ad-Hoc Sensor Networks*. Proceedings the 4th International Conference on Mobile Data Management (MDM'03), (pp. 45-62).

Guo, D., Wu, J., Chen, H., & Luo, X. (2006). *Theory and Network Applications of Dynamic Bloom Filters*. Paper presented at the INFOCOM 2006. 25th IEEE International Conference on Computer Communications.

Hailong, C., & Jun, W. (2004). *Foreseer: a novel, locality-aware peer-to-peer system architecture for keyword searches*. Paper presented at the Proceedings of the 5th ACM/IFIP/USENIX International Conference on Middleware.

Hong, T., & Tao, Y. (2003). *An Efficient Data Location Protocol for Self.organizing Storage Clusters*. Paper presented at the Proceedings of the 2003 ACM/IEEE conference on Supercomputing.

Hua, Y., & Xiao, B. (2006). A Multi-attribute Data Structure with Parallel Bloom Filters for Network Services. *Proceedings of 13th International Conference of High Performance Computing (HiPC)*,(pp. 277-288).

Hua, Y., Zhu, Y., Jiang, H., Feng, D., & Tian, L. (2008). Scalable and Adaptive Metadata Management in Ultra Large-Scale File Systems. *Proceedings of the 28th International Conference on Distributed Computing Systems (ICDCS 2008)*.

James, K. M. (1983). A second look at bloom filters. *Communications of the ACM, 26*(8), 570–571. doi:10.1145/358161.358167

John, K., David, B., Yan, C., Steven, C., Patrick, E., & Dennis, G. (2000). OceanStore: an architecture for global-scale persistent storage. *SIGPLAN Not., 35*(11), 190–201. doi:10.1145/356989.357007

Kumar, A., Xu, J., & Zegura, E. W. (2005). *Efficient and scalable query routing for unstructured peer-to-peer networks*. Paper presented at the Proceedings INFOCOM 2005, 24th Annual Joint Conference of the IEEE Computer and Communications Societies.

Ledlie, J., Serban, L., & Toncheva, D. (2002). *Scaling Filename Queries in a Large-Scale Distributed File System*. Harvard University, Cambridge, MA.

Lee, L. G. (1982). Designing a Bloom filter for differential file access. *Communications of the ACM, 25*(9), 600–604. doi:10.1145/358628.358632

Li, F., Pei, C., Jussara, A., & Andrei, Z. B. (2000). Summary cache: a scalable wide-area web cache sharing protocol. *IEEE/ACM Trans. Netw., 8*(3), 281–293.

Little, M. C., Shrivastava, S. K., & Speirs, N. A. (2002)... *The Computer Journal, 45*(6), 645–652. doi:10.1093/comjnl/45.6.645

Luk, M., Mezzour, G., Perrig, A., & Gligor, V. (2007). MiniSec: A Secure Sensor Network Communication Architecture. *Proceedings of IEEE International Conference on Information Processing in Sensor Networks (IPSN)*, (pp. 479-488).

Matei, R., & Ian, F. (2002). *A Decentralized, Adaptive Replica Location Mechanism*. Paper presented at the Proceedings of the 11th IEEE International Symposium on High Performance Distributed Computing.

McIlroy, M. (1982). Development of a Spelling List. *Communications, IEEE Transactions on [legacy, pre - 1988], 30*(1), 91-99.

Michael, M. (2002). Compressed bloom filters. *IEEE/ACM Trans. Netw., 10*(5), 604–612.

Mohan, A., & Kalogeraki, V. (2003). *Speculative routing and update propagation: a kundali centric approach.* Paper presented at the IEEE International Conference on Communications, 2003.

Pai-Hsiang, H. (2001). *Geographical region summary service for geographical routing*. Paper presented at the Proceedings of the 2nd ACM international symposium on Mobile ad hoc networking and computing.

Rhea, S. C., & Kubiatowicz, J. (2002). *Probabilistic location and routing.* Paper presented at the IEEE INFOCOM 2002, Twenty-First Annual Joint Conference of the IEEE Computer and Communications Societies Proceedings.

Saar, C., & Yossi, M. (2003). *Spectral bloom filters*. Paper presented at the Proceedings of the 2003 ACM SIGMOD international conference on Management of data.

Song, H., Dharmapurikar, S., Turner, J., & Lockwood, J. (2005). *Fast hash table lookup using extended bloom filter: an aid to network processing*. Paper presented at the Proceedings of the 2005 conference on Applications, technologies, architectures, and protocols for computer communications.

Zhu, Y., & Jiang, H. (2006). *False Rate Analysis of Bloom Filter Replicas in Distributed Systems*. Paper presented at the Proceedings of the 2006 International Conference on Parallel Processing.

Zhu, Y., Jiang, H., & Wang, J. (2004). *Hierarchical Bloom filter arrays (HBA): a novel, scalable metadata management system for large cluster-based storage*. Paper presented at the Proceedings of the 2004 IEEE International Conference on Cluster Computing.

Zhu, Y., Jiang, H., Wang, J., & Xian, F. (2008). *HBA: Distributed Metadata Management for Large Cluster-Based Storage Systems. IEEE Transactions on Parallel and Distributed Systems, 19*(6), 750–763. doi:10.1109/TPDS.2007.70788

KEY TERMS AND DEFINITIONS

Bloom Filter: A Bloom filter is a space-efficient data structure that supports membership queries. It consists of a bit array and all bits are initially set to 0. It uses a fix number of predefined independent hash functions. For each element, all hashed bits are set to 1. To check whether an element belongs to the set represented by a Bloom filter, one simply checks all bits pointed by the hash functions are 1. If not, the element is not in the set. If yes, the element is consider as a member.

Bloom Filter Array: A Bloom filter array, consisted of multiple Bloom filters, represents multiple sets. It is a space-efficient data structure to evaluate whether an element is within these sets and which set this element belongs to if yes.

Bloom Filter Replica: A Bloom filter replica is a replication of a Bloom filter. In a distributed environment, the original and replicated Bloom filters are typically stored on different servers for improved performance and fault tolerance. A Bloom filter replica will generate both false positives and false negatives.

Bloom Filter Update Protocol: When the set that a Bloom filter represents is changed over time, the corresponding Bloom filter replica becomes out-dated. In order to reduce the probability that the Bloom filter replica reports the membership incorrectly, the replica needs to be updated frequently. The Bloom filter update protocol determines when a Bloom filter replica needs to be updated.

Distributed Membership Query: Membership query is one fundamental function that reports where the target data, resource, or service is located. The membership query can be performed by a centralized server or by a group of distributed server. The latter approach has a stronger scalability and is referred as distributed memory query.

False Negative: A false negative happens when an element is a member of the set that a Bloom filter represents but the Bloom filter mistakenly reports it is not. A standard Bloom filter has no false negatives. However, in a distributed system, a Bloom filter replica can generate false negatives when the replica is not timely updated.

False Positive: A false positive happens when an element is not a member of the set that a Bloom filter represents but the Bloom filter mistakenly reports it is. The probability of false positives can be very slow when the Bloom filter is appropriately designed.

Chapter 35
Image Partitioning on Spiral Architecture

Qiang Wu
University of Technology, Australia

Xiangjian He
University of Technology, Australia

ABSTRACT

Spiral Architecture is a relatively new and powerful approach to image processing. It contains very useful geometric and algebraic properties. Based on the abundant research achievements in the past decades, it is shown that Spiral Architecture will play an increasingly important role in image processing and computer vision. This chapter presents a significant application of Spiral Architecture for distributed image processing. It demonstrates the impressive characteristics of spiral architecture for high performance image processing. The proposed method tackles several challenging practical problems during the implementation. The proposed method reduces the data communication between the processing nodes and is configurable. Moreover, the proposed partitioning scheme has a consistent approach: after image partitioning each sub-image should be a representative of the original one without changing the basic object, which is important to the related image processing operations.

INTRODUCTION

Image processing is a traditional area in computing science which has been used widely in many applications including the film industry, medical imaging, industrial manufacturing, weather forecasting etc. With the development of new algorithms and the rapid growth of application areas, a key issue emerges and attracts more and more challenging research in digital image processing. That issue is the dramatically increasing computation workload in image processing. The reasons can be classified into three groups: relatively low-power computing platform, huge image data to be processed and the nature of image-processing algorithms.

DOI: 10.4018/978-1-60566-661-7.ch035

Inefficient computing is a relative concept. The microcomputer has been powerful enough in the last decade to make personal image processing practically feasible to the individual researcher for inexpensive image processing (Miller, 1993; Schowengerdt & Mehldau, 1993). In recent years, although such systems still functionally satisfy the requirements of most general purpose image-processing needs, the limited computing capacity in a standalone processing node has become inadequate to keep up with the faster growth of image-processing applications in such practical areas as real-time image processing and 3D image rendering.

The huge amount of image data is another issue which has been faced by many image-processing applications today. Many applications such as computer graphics, rendering photo realistic images and computer-animated films consume the aggregate power of whole farms of workstations (Oberhuber, 1998). Although the common sense of what is "large" to the image data being processed has changed over time, expression in Megabytes or Gigabytes is observed from the application point of view (Goller, 1999). Over the past few decades, the image to be processed has become larger and larger. Consequently, the issue of how to decrease the processing time despite the growth of image data becomes an urgent point in digital image processing.

Moreover, the nature of the traditional image-processing algorithms is another issue which reduces the processing speed. In digital image processing, the elementary image operators can be differentiated between point image operators, local imageoperators and global image operators (Braunl, Feyrer, Rapf, & Reinhardt, 2001). The main characteristic of point operator is that a pixel in the output image depends only on the corresponding pixel in the input image. Point operators are used to copy an image from one memory location to another, in arithmetic and logic operations, table lookup and image composition (Nicolescu & Jonker, 2002). Local operators create a destination pixel based on criteria that depend on the source pixel and the values of the pixels in some "neighbourhood" surrounding it. They are used widely in low-level image processing such as image enhancement by sharpening, blurring and noise removal. Global operators create a destination pixel based on the entire image information. A representative example of an operator within this class is the Discrete Fourier Transform (DFT). Compared with point operators, local operators and global operator are more computationally intensive.

As a consequence of the above, image processing-related tasks involve the execution of a large number of operations on large sets of structured data. The processing power of the typical desktop workstation can therefore become a severe bottleneck in many image-processing applications. Thus, it may make sense to perform image processing on multiple workstations or on a parallel processing system. Actually, many image-processing tasks exhibit a high degree of data locality and parallelism, and map quite readily to specialized massively parallel computing hardware (Chen, Lee, & Cho, 1990; Siegel, Armstrong, & Watson, 1992; Stevenson, Adams, Jamieson, & Delp, April, 1993).

For several image-processing applications, a number of existing programs have been optimized for execution on parallel computer architectures (Pitas, 1993). The parallel approach, as an alternative to replace the original sequential processing, promises many benefits to the development of image processing. Gloller and Leberl (Goller & Leberl, 2000) implemented shape-from-shading, stereo matching, re-sampling, gridding and visualization of terrain models, which are all compute-intensive algorithms in radar image processing, in such a manner that they execute either on a parallel machine or on a cluster of workstations which connects many computing nodes together via a local area network. Other typical applications of image processing on parallel computing platform can be seen in the field of remote image processing such as the 3D object mediator (Kok, Pabst, & Afsarmanseh, April, 1997), internet-based distributed 3D rendering and animation (Lee, Lee, Lu, & Chen, 1997), remote image-processing systems design using an IBM PC as front-end and a transputer network as back-end (Wu & Guan, 1995), telemedicine projects (Marsh, 1997), satellite image processing (Hawick et al., 1997) and the general approach for remote execution of software (Niederl & Goller, Jan, 1998).

Many parallel image-processing tasks map quite readily to specialized massively parallel computing hardware. However, specific parallel machines require a significant investment but may only be needed for a short time. Accessing such systems is difficult and requires in-depth knowledge of the particular system. Alternatively, the users must turn to supercomputers, which may be unacceptable for many customers. These three aspects are the main reasons why parallel computing has not been widely adopted for computer vision and image processing.

Clusters of workstations have been proposed as a cheap alternative to parallel machines. Driven by advances in network technology, cluster management systems are becoming a viable and economical parallel computing platform for the implementation of parallel processing algorithms. Moreover, the utilization of workstation clusters can yield many potential benefits, such as performance and reliability. It can be expected that workstation clusters can take over computing intensive tasks from supercomputers.

Offsetting the many advantages mentioned above, the main disadvantages of clusters of workstation are high communication latency and irregular load patterns on the computing nodes. The system performance mainly depends on the amount and structure of communication between processing nodes. Thus, many coarse-grained parallel algorithms perform well, while fine-grained data decomposition methods like the ones in the Parallel Image-Processing Toolkit (PIPT) (Squyres, Lumsdaine, & Stevenson, 1995) require such a high communication bandwidth that execution on the cluster may even be slower than on a single workstation. Moreover, the coexistence of parallel and sequential jobs that is typical when interactive users work on the cluster makes scheduling and mapping a hard problem (Arpaci et al., May, 1995).

Thus, taking care of the intercommunication required for processing is an important issue for distributed processing. For instance, if a particular processor is processing a set of rows, it needs information about the rows above and below its first and last rows, when row partitioning is effected (Bharadwaj, Li., & Ko, 2000; Siegel, Siegel, & Feather, 1982). The additional information must be exchanged between the corresponding nodes. It can be done by two approaches in general. In the first approach, explicit communication is built up on-demand between the processors (Siegel et al., 1992) and is carried out concurrently with the main processes. In another approach, the required data is over-supplied to the respective processor at the distribution phase (Siegel et al., 1982). In many cases, the second approach is a natural choice for the architecture that is considered, although it introduces additional data transfer.

The facts revealed above is a key problem related to information partitioning. In term of the applications of image processing, it is defined as the problem of image data partitioning. Most image partitioning techniques can be classified into two groups: fine-grained decomposition and coarse-grained decomposition (Squyres et al., 1995). A fine-grained decomposition-based image-processing operation will assign an output pixel per processor and assign the required windowed data for each output pixel to the processor. Thus, each processor will perform the necessary processing for its output pixel. A coarse-grained decomposition will assign large contiguous regions of the output image to each of a small number of processors. Each processor will perform the appropriate window based operations to its own region of the image. Appropriate overlapping regions of the image will be assigned in order to properly accommodate the processing at the image boundaries.

There are some difficulties as a consequence of the general data partitioning. The first one is the extra communication required between the processors, which has been mentioned above. This is inevitable when a processor participating in the parallel computation needs some additional information pertaining to the data residing in other processors (Bertsekas & Tsitsiklis, 1989; Siegel et al., 1992) for processing its share of the data. Another difficulty is that the number of processors available and the size of the input image may vary in the different applications, so the sizes of sub-images for distribution and the number of processors for a specific operation cannot be arbitrarily determined in the early stages.

This chapter presents a highly efficient image partitioning method which is based on a special image architecture, Spiral Architecture. Using Spiral Architecture on a cluster of workstations, a new uniform image partitioning scheme is derived in order to reduce many overhead components that otherwise penalize time performance. With such scheme, uniform sub-images can be produced, which are near copies rather than different portions of the original image. Each sub-image can then be processed by the different processing nodes individually and independently. Moreover, this image-partitioning method provides a possible stereo method to deal with many traditional image-processing tasks simultaneously. Because each partitioned sub-image contains the main features of the original image, i.e. a representation of the original image, the different tasks can execute on the different processing nodes in parallel without interfering with each other.

This method is a closed-form solution. In each application, the number of partitions can be decided based on the practical requirements and the practical system conditions. A formula is derived to build the relation between the number of partitions and the multiplier in Spiral Multiplication which is used to achieve image partitioning.

The organization of this chapter is as follows. Spiral Architecture and its special mathematic operations are introduced on the section of Related Work which is followed by the detailed explanation of image partitioning on Spiral Architecture. In this section, several problems and the solutions are discussed regarding the implementation of image segmentation on the new architecture. Finally, the experimental results and conclusion are presented.

RELATED WORK

Spiral Architecture

Traditionally, almost all image processing and image analysis is based on the rectangular architecture, which is a collection of rectangular pixels in the column-row arrangement. However, rectangular architecture is not historically the only one used in image-processing research. Another architecture used often is the Spiral Architecture. Spiral Architecture is inspired from anatomical considerations of primate vision (Schwartz, 1980). The cones on the retina possess the hexagonal distribution feature as shown in Figure 1.

The cones, with the shape of hexagons, are arranged in a spiral cluster. Each unit is a set of seven hexagons (Sheridan, Hintz, & Alexander, 2000). That is, each pixel has six neighbouring pixels. This arrangement is different from the 3×3 rectangular vision unit in Rectangular Architecture, where each pixel has eight neighbouring pixels. A collection of hexagonal pixels represented using spiral architecture is shown as Figure 2. The origin point is normally located on the centre of Spiral Architecture. In Spiral Architecture any pixel has only six neighbour pixels which have the same distance to the central hexagon of the seven-hexagon unit of vision. From research on the geometry of the cones in the pri-

Figure 1. Distribution of Cones on the Retina (from (He, 1998))

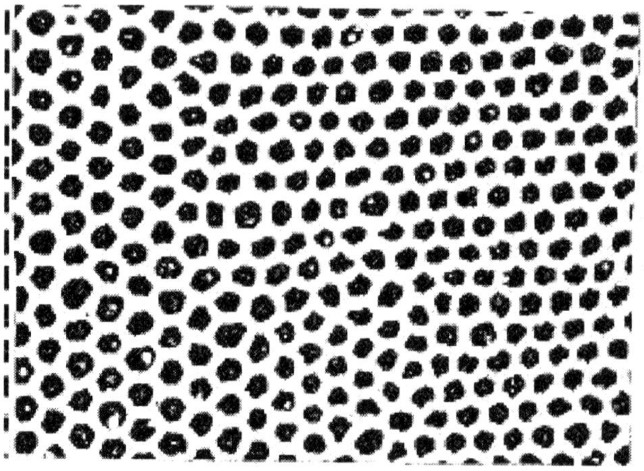

Figure 2. A collection of hexagonal cells

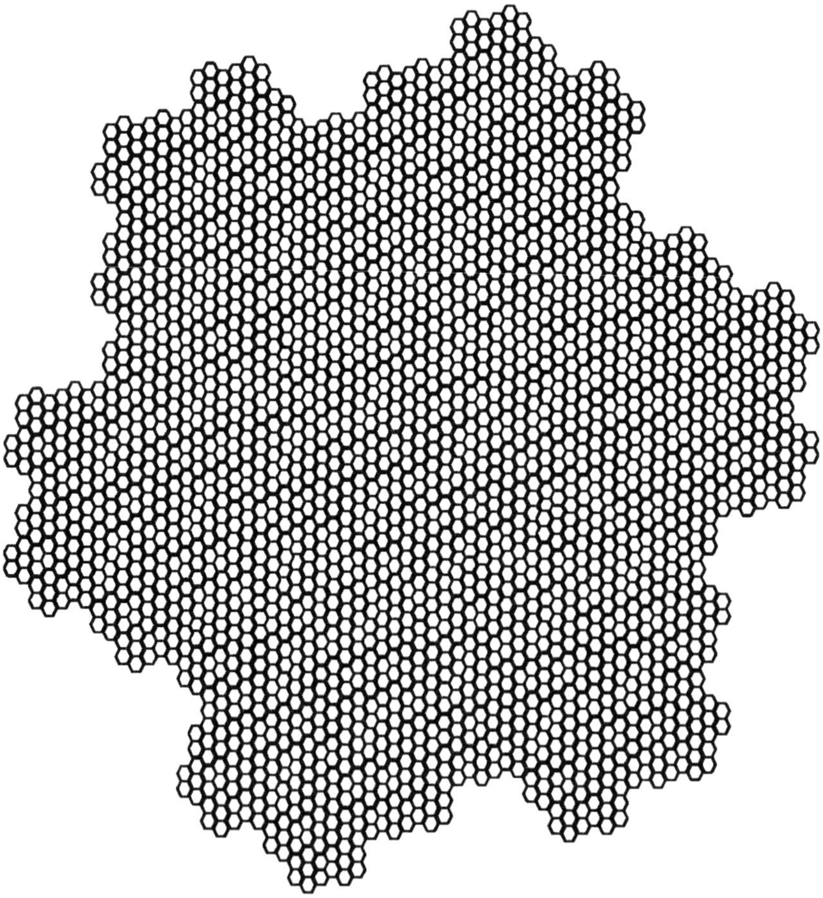

Figure 3. A labelled cluster of seven hexagons

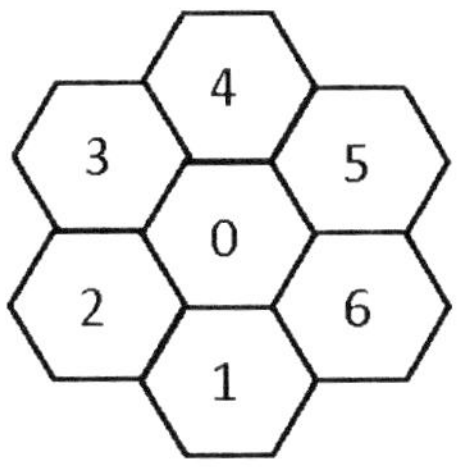

mate's retina it can be concluded that the cones' distribution is distinguished by its potential powerful computation abilities.

Spiral Addressing

It is obvious that the hexagonal pixels on Figure 2 cannot be labelled in column-row order as in rectangular architecture. Instead of labelling the pixel with a pair of numbers (x, y), each pixel is labelled with a unique number.

Addressing proceeds in a recursive manner. Initially, a collection of seven hexagons are labelled as shown in Figure 3. Such a cluster of seven hexagons dilates so that six more clusters of seven hexagons are placed around the original cluster. The addresses of the centres of the additional six clusters are obtained by multiplying the adjacent address in Figure 3 by 10 (See Figure 4.)

In each new cluster, the other pixels are labelled consecutively from the centre as shown in Figure 3. Dilation can then repeat to grow the architecture in powers of seven with unique assigned addresses. The hexagons thus tile the plane in a recursive modular manner along a spiral direction (Alexander,

Figure 4. Dilation of the cluster of seven hexagons

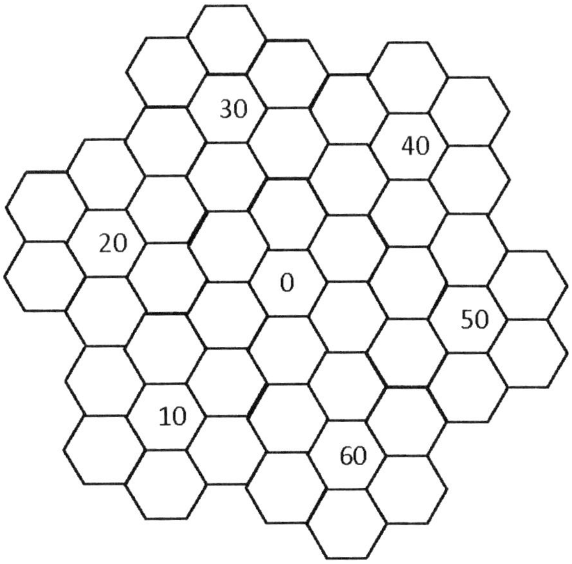

1995). It eventuates that spiral address in fact is a base-seven number. A cluster with size of 7^3 with the corresponding addresses is shown in Figure 5.

Mathematical Operations on Spiral Architecture

Spiral Architecture contains very useful geometric and algebraic properties, which can be interpreted in terms of a mathematical object, the Euclidean ring. Two algebraic operations have been defined on Spiral Architecture: Spiral Addition and Spiral Multiplication. The neighbouring relation among the pixels on Spiral Architecture can be expressed uniquely by these two operations. Spiral Addition and Spiral Multiplication will be used together to achieve uniform and complete image partitioning which is very important to distributed image processing.

Figure 5. Hexagons with labelled addresses on Spiral Architecture (He, 1998)

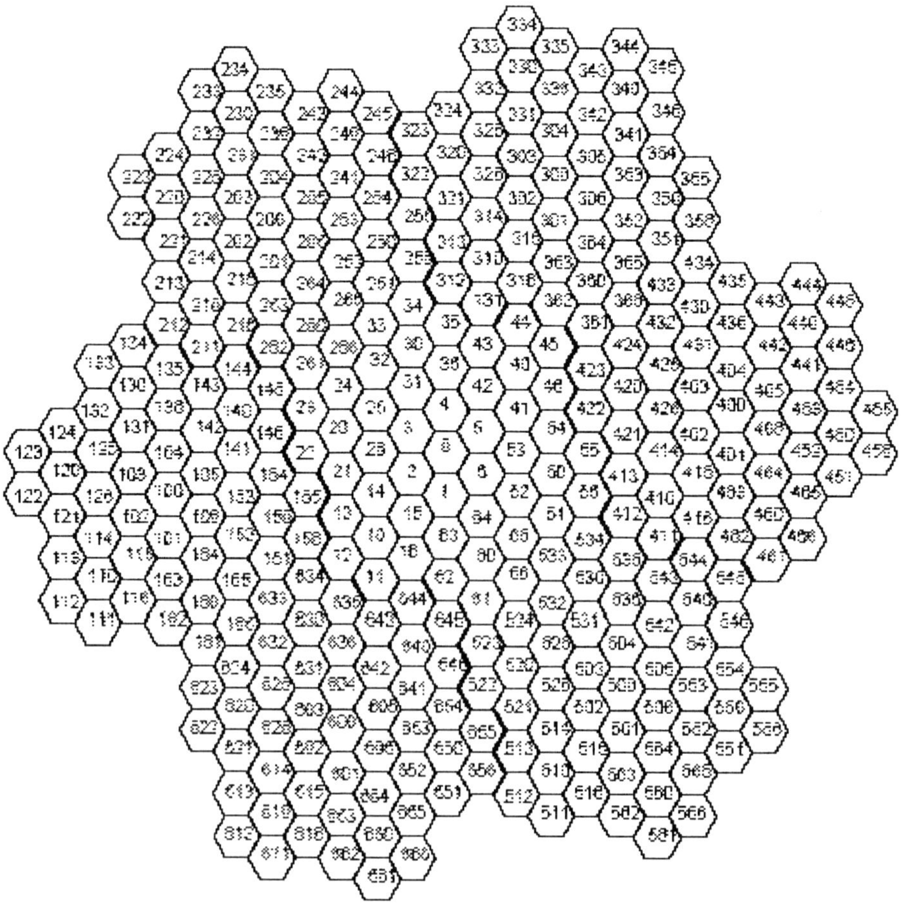

Spiral Addition

Spiral Addition is an arithmetic operation with closure properties defined on the spiral address space so that the result of Spiral Addition will be an address in the same finite set on which the operation is performed (Sheridan, 1996). In addition, Spiral Addition incorporates a special form of modularity.

To develop Spiral Addition, a scalar form of Spiral Addition is defined first as shown in Table 1.

A procedure for Spiral Addition based on the Spiral Counting principle (Sheridan, 1996) is defined. For the convenience of our explanation, a common naming convention is followed. Any number $X = (X_n X_{n-1} \ldots X_1)\ \forall X_i \in \{0, 1, \ldots 6\}$, where X_i is a digit of number X. Let $a = (a_n a_{n-1} \ldots a_1)$ and $b = (b_n b_{n-1} \ldots b_1)$ be two spiral addresses. Then the result of Spiral Addition of them is worked out as follows.

1. $scale = 1$; $result = 0$;
2. $OP1 = (OP1_n OP1_{n-1} \ldots OP1_1) = (a_n a_{n-1} \ldots a_1)$ $OP2 = (OP2_n OP2_{n-1} \ldots OP2_1) = (b_n b_{n-1} \ldots b_1)$
3. $C = OP1 + OP2_1 = (C_n C_{n-1} \ldots C_1)$ (Spiral Addition). Here, the carry rule is applied. For Spiral Addition between two single-digit addresses, it follows the rules as shown in Table 1;
4. $result = result + scale \times C_1$, $scale = scale \times 10$ (Here, "+" and "×" mean normal mathematical addition and mathematical multiplication respectively);
5. $CA = OP1$; $CB = OP2$;
6. $OP1 = (CB_n CB_{n-1} \ldots CB_2) = (OP1_{n-1} OP1_{n-2} \ldots OP1_1)$ $OP2 = (C_n C_{n-1} \ldots C_2) = (OP2_{n-1} OP2_{n-2} \ldots OP2_1)$
7. Repeatedly apply steps 3 through 6 until $OP1 = 0$;
8. $result = result + scale \times OP2$ (Here, "+" and "×" mean normal mathematical addition and mathematical multiplication respectively);
9. Return *result*.

For example, for Spiral Addition 26+14, the procedure is shown below. In the demonstration, numbering "*a.b*" like "3.2" means "Step 3 and 2nd time" as mentioned above:

1. $scale = 1$; $result = 0$;
2. $OP1 = (2\ 6)$; $OP2 = (1\ 4)$;

Table 1. Scalar Spiral Addition (Sheridan, 1996)*

	0	**1**	**2**	**3**	**4**	**5**	**6**
0	0	1	2	3	4	5	6
1	1	63	15	2	0	6	64
2	2	15	14	26	3	0	1
3	3	2	26	25	31	4	0
4	4	0	3	31	36	42	5
5	5	6	0	4	42	41	53
6	6	64	1	0	5	53	52

* Bold type shows the scalar spiral address; normal type shows the results of Spiral Addition between the corresponding spiral addresses in the first row and the first column respectively.

3.1 $C = 26 + 4 = (2\ 5)$;
4.1 *result* = 0 + 1 × 5 = 5; *scale* = 1 × 10 = 10;
5.1 *CA* = 26; *CB* = 14;
6.1 *OP*1 = 1; *OP*2 = 2;
3.2 $C = 1 + 2 = (1\ 5)$;
4.2 *result* = 5 + 10 × 5 = 55; *scale* = 10 × 10 = 100;
5.2 *CA* = 1; *CB* = 2;
6.2 *OP*1 = 0; *OP*2 = 1;
7. *OP*1 = 0;
8. *result* = 55 + 100 × 1 = 155;
9. Return 155.

To guarantee that all the pixels are still located within the original image area after Spiral Addition (Sheridan et al., 2000), a modulus operation is defined on the spiral address space. From Figure 5, it is shown that the spiral address is a base-seven number, so modular operations based on such a number system must execute accordingly. Suppose $spiral\_address_{max}$ stands for the maximum spiral address in the given Spiral Architecture area, the modulus number is

$$\text{modulus} = spiral\_address_{max} + 1 \tag{1}$$

where + is Spiral Addition.

Then, the modular operation on spiral addressing system can be performed as follows. First, the address number and the corresponding modulus number are converted to their decimal formats and work out the result of the modulus operation in the decimal number system. Then, the result in decimal format is converted to its corresponding base-seven spiral address again.

In addition, an Inverse Spiral Addition exists on spiral address space. That means for any given spiral address x there is a unique spiral address $\overline{x}$ in the same image area, which satisfies the condition $x + \overline{x} = 0$, where sign "+" stands for Spiral Addition. The procedure for computing the inverse value of a spiral address can be summarized briefly as follows.

According to Table 1, it is shown that the inverse values of the seven basic spiral addresses, 0, 1, 2, 3, 4, 5 and 6, are 0, 4, 5, 6, 1, 2 and 3 respectively. So the inverse value $\overline{p}$ of any spiral address $p = (p_n\ p_{n-1} \cdots p_1)$ can be computed as:

$$\overline{p} = \left(\overline{p}_n\ \overline{p}_{n-1}\ \cdots\ \overline{p}_1\right) \tag{2}$$

Furthermore, Spiral Addition meets the requirement of a bijective mapping. That is, each pixel in the original image maps one-to-one to each pixel in the output image after Spiral Addition.

Spiral Multiplication

Spiral Multiplication is also an arithmetic operation with closure properties defined on the spiral addressing system so that the resulting product will be a spiral address in the same finite set on which the operation is performed. In addition, like Spiral Addition, Spiral Multiplication incorporates a special form of modularity.

For basic Spiral Multiplication, a scalar form is defined as Table 2.

The same naming convention is followed as in the last section in the Spiral Addition explanation. Multiplication of address a by the scalar $\alpha(\alpha \in \{0, 1, \ldots 6\})$ is obtained by applying scalar multiplication to each digital component of a according to the above scalar form, and denoted by:

$$\alpha \times (a) = (\alpha a_n \, \alpha a_{n-1} \ldots \alpha a_1) \text{ where}$$

$$a = (a_n \, a_{n-1} \ldots a_1) \; \forall a_i \in \{0, 1, \ldots, 6\} \tag{3}$$

If the address in Spiral Multiplication is a common address like,

$$b = (b_n \, b_{n-1} \ldots b_1) \; \forall b_i \in \{0, 1, \ldots, 6\} \tag{4}$$

then

$$a \times b = \sum_{i=1}^{n} a \times b_i \times_{nml} 10^{i-1} \tag{5}$$

where $\sum$ denotes Spiral Addition, $\times$ denotes Spiral Multiplication and $\times_{nml}$ denotes normal mathematical multiplication. A carry rule is required in Spiral Addition to handle the addition of numbers composed of more than one digit.

For example, to compute the Spiral Multiplication of 26×14, the procedure is shown below:

Table 2. Scalar Spiral multiplication (Sheridan, 1996)*

	0	**1**	**2**	**3**	**4**	**5**	**6**
0	0	0	0	0	0	0	0
1	0	1	2	3	4	5	6
2	0	2	3	4	5	6	1
3	0	3	4	5	6	1	2
4	0	4	5	6	1	2	3
5	0	5	6	1	2	3	4
6	0	6	1	2	3	4	5

* Bold type shows the scalar spiral address; normal type shows the results of Spiral Multiplication between the corresponding spiral addresses on the first row and the first column respectively.

$26 \times 14 = 26 \times 4 \times_{nml} 1 + 26 \times 1 \times_{nml} 10$

$= (2 \times 4\ 6 \times 4) \times_{nml} 1 + (2 \times 1\ 6 \times 1) \times_{nml} 10$

$= 53 \times_{nml} 1 + 26 \times_{nml} 10$

$= 33$

In the above demonstration, the Spiral Addition procedure is omitted.

Similarly to Spiral Addition, a modulus operation on the spiral address space is defined in order to guarantee that all the pixels are still located within the original Spiral area after Spiral Multiplication. Furthermore the transformation through Spiral Multiplication defined on spiral address space is a bi-jective mapping. That is, each pixel in the original image maps one-to-one to each pixel in the output image after Spiral Multiplication.Modulus Multiplication is shown as follows:Let p be the product of two elements a,b. That is,

$$p = a \times b \tag{6}$$

where a and b are two spiral addresses

If $p \geq (modulus)$, then

if a is a multiple of 10

$$p = (p + (p \div (\text{modulus})))\text{mod}(\text{modulus}) \tag{7}$$

otherwise,

$$p = p\ \text{mod}(\text{modulus}), \tag{8}$$

where

$modulus = \text{spiral\_address}_{max} + 1$

and + is Spiral Addition. (9)

Finally, another point relative to Spiral multiplication is the existence of a multiplicative inverse. Given a spiral address a, there should be another address b, such that $a \times b = 1$ (Spiral Multiplication), denoted by a^{-1}, i.e., $b = a^{-1}$.

Two cases must be considered to find out the inverse value for a spiral address. Here, it is assumed that spiral address 0 has no valid inverse value.

Case 1: *a* is Not a Multiple of 10

Let us assume $a = (a_n\, a_{n-1} \ldots a_1)\ \forall\, a_i \in \{0, 1, \ldots, 6\}$ and the inverse value $b = (b_n\, b_{n-1} \ldots b_1)\ \forall\, b_i \in \{0, 1, \ldots, 6\}$. In general, it is easy to get the inverse values for the basic spiral addresses 1, 2, 3, 4, 5 and 6. They are 1, 6, 5, 4, 3 and 2 respectively. So the inverse value, *b*, can be constructed successfully by the following formula,

$$\begin{aligned} b_1 &= a_1^{-1} \\ b_2 &= -\left(a_2 b_1\right) \times b_1 \\ &\vdots \\ b_n &= -\left(\sum_{i=0}^{n-2} a_{n-i} \times b_{i+1}\right) \times b_1 \end{aligned} \tag{10}$$

Case 2: *a* is a Multiple of 10

$a = k \times 10^m\ (m < n)$

$$\text{modulus} = 10^n = spiral\_address_{\max} + 1 \tag{11}$$

k^{-1} can be obtained by Equation (10). Then, the inverse value of a is,

$$a^{-1} = k^{-1} \times 10^{n-m} \text{ (Spiral Multiplication)} \tag{12}$$

Mimicking Spiral Architecture

In order to implement the idea of Spiral Architecture on the applications for image processing, it is inevitable to use mimic Spiral Architecture based on the existing rectangular image architecture because of lack of mature devices for capturing image and for displaying image based on hexagonal image architecture. Mimic Spiral Architecture plays an important role in image processing applications on Spiral Architecture. It forwards the image data between image processing algorithms on Spiral Architecture and rectangular image architecture for display purpose (see Figure 6). Such mimic Spiral Architecture must retain the symmetrical properties of hexagonal grid system. In addition, mimic Spiral Architecture does not degrade the resolution of the original image.

For a given picture represented on rectangular architecture, if it is re-represented on Spiral Architecture on which each hexagonal grid has the same area size as square grid on rectangular architecture, the image resolution is retained.

In order to work out the size of hexagonal gird, the length of the side in a square grid is defined as

Figure 6. Image processing on mimic Spiral Architecture

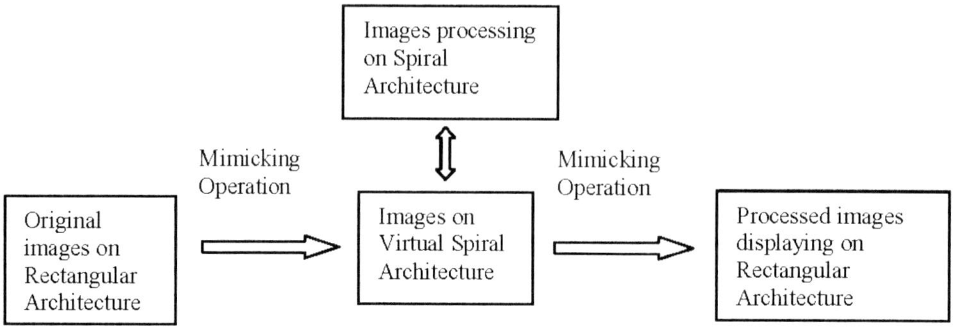

Figure 7. A square grid and a hexagonal grid which have the same size of area

Figure 8. Relation between mimic hexagonal grid and the connected square grid. s_i is the size of overlap area

(a) One mimic hexagonal grid and its four connected square grids

(b) One square grid and its three connected mimic hexagonal grids

1 unit length. Namely, the area of a square grid is 1 unit area. Then, for a hexagonal grid which has the same area size as square grid, the distance from the centre to the side in a hexagonal grid is 0.537 (see Figure 7).

In order to work out the grey value of a hexagonal gird, the relations between the hexagonal grid and its connected square grid must be investigated. The purpose is to find out the different contribution of each connected square grid's grey value to the referenced hexagonal grid (see Figure 8).

Let N denote the number of square grids which are connected to a particular hexagonal grid. s_i denotes the size of overlap area between square grid i, one of connected square grid, and the hexagonal grid. Because the size of grid is 1 unit area (see Figure 7), the percentage of overlap area in a referenced hexagonal grid is,

$$p_i = s_i / 1 \times 100\% = s_i \tag{13}$$

Let gh denote the grey value of hexagonal grid, and gs denote the grey value of square grid. Thus, the grey value of hexagonal grid is calculated as the weighted average of the grey values of the connected square grids as,

$$gh = \sum_{i=1}^{N} p_i \bullet gs_i. \tag{14}$$

On the other hand, the reverse operation must be considered in order to map the images from virtual Spiral Architecture to rectangular architecture after image processing on Spiral Architecture (see Figure 6). After image processing on Spiral Architecture, the grey values of virtual hexagonal grids have been changed. Thus, the aim is to calculate the grey values of square grid from the connected hexagonal grids (see Figure 8.b). The same way as Equation (14) is used to calculate the grey value of square grid. However, p_i stands for the percentage of overlap area in a referenced square grid (see Figure 8.b). Supposing there are M virtual hexagonal grids connected to a particular square grid, the square grid's grey value is,

$$gs = \sum_{i=1}^{M} p_i \bullet gh_i. \tag{15}$$

Using Equation (14) and (15), the grey values of grids can be calculated easily as long as p_i can be calculated. Wu et al. (Wu, He, & Hintz, 2004) proposed a practically achievable method for easily calculating the relation between mimic Spiral Architecture and the connected square grid on digital images.

IMAGE PARTITIONING ON SPIRAL ARCHITECTURE

A novel image partitioning method is proposed for distributed image processing based on Spiral Architecture. Using this method each processing node will be assigned a uniform partitioned sub-image that contains all the representative information, so each processing node can deal with the assigned information independently without data exchanges between the processing nodes. The first requirement for such a partitioning scheme is that it should be configurable according to the number of partition required. Second, the partitioning has a consistent approach: after image partitioning each sub-image should be a representative of the original one without changing the basic object features. Finally, the partitioning should be fast without introducing extra cost to the system.

General Image Partitioning on Spiral Architecture

Under the traditional rectangular image architecture there are three basic image partitioning, row partitioning, column partitioning and block partitioning (Bharadwaj et al., 2000; Koelbel, Loveman, Schreiber,

Jr., & Zosel, 1994). Compared with rectangular image architecture, Spiral Architecture does not arrange the pixels row-wise, column-wise or in normal rectangular blocks. Instead, each pixel is positioned by a unique Spiral Address along the spiral rotation direction shown in Figure 9. The traditional partitioning methods are infeasible except for block partitioning. For example, the image on Figure 9 can be partitioned into seven parts evenly with seven sub-data sets like [0, 1, …, 6], [10, 11, …, 16], [20, 21, …, 26], [30, 31, …, 36], [40, 41, …, 46], [50, 51, …, 56], [60, 61, …, 66], where numbers in the brackets are the spiral addresses of the pixels of Figure 9. That is, Spiral Architecture can split the original picture into $M\,(M = 7^n, n = 1,2,\ldots)$ parts. Based on Spiral addressing scheme, the continually consecutive hexagonal pixels are grouped together. Inside of each part, the total number of pixel is also a power of seven. The index of the partitioned sub-area is consistent with the spiral addressing system. Thus the pixels on the different sub-areas can be identified immediately. A real example of image segmentation based on the partition scheme above is show on Figure 10.

From Figure 10, it is seen that such partition scheme simply splits the original image area into the equal size pieces but does not consider the image contents inside. For global image processing operation such as global Gaussian processing using distributed processing system, each node may process one segment of original image. During processing, the nodes have to exchange necessary information between them. Such kind of local communication will be a disadvantage. It will become greater as the number of partitions increase.

Uniform Image Partitioning on Spiral Architecture

In Spiral Architecture, two algebraic operations have been defined, Spiral Addition and Spiral Multiplication. After an image is projected onto Spiral Architecture, each pixel on the image is associated with a particular hexagon and its Spiral address. The two operations mentioned above can then be used to define

Figure 9. Pixel arrangement on Spiral Architecture

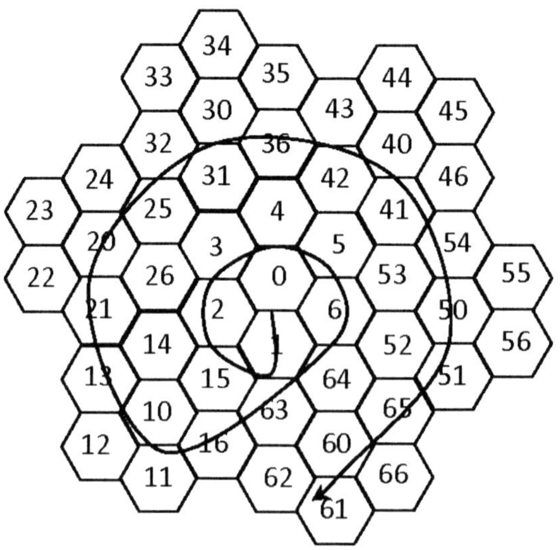

Figure 10. Simple equal size image partitioning on Spiral Architecture

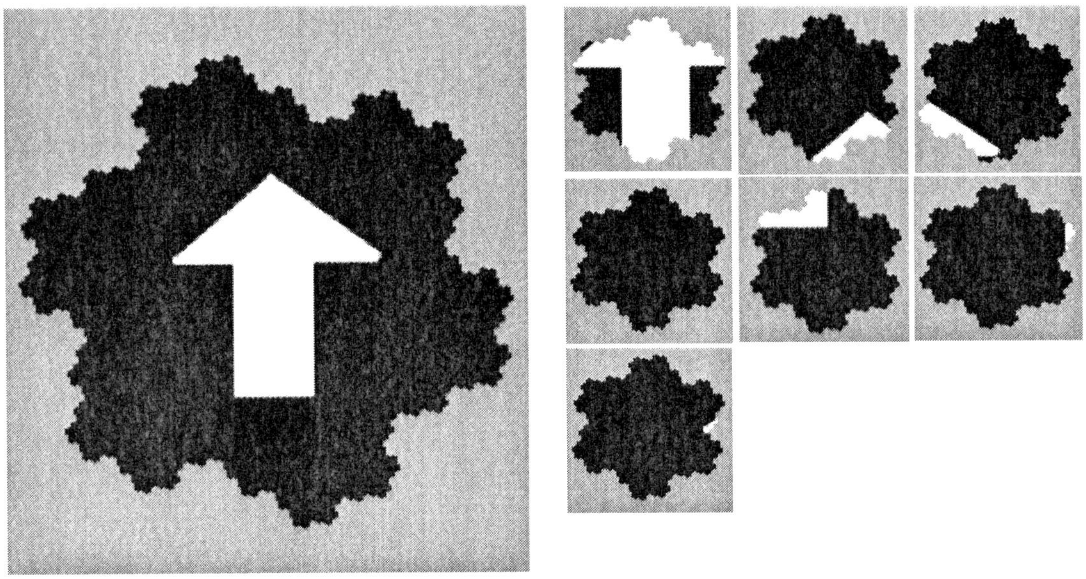

a) Original image

b) Equal-size image partitioning

two transformations on the spiral address space: image translation and rotating image partitioning. In our research, Spiral Multiplication is applied to achieve uniform image partitioning which is capable of balancing workload among the processing nodes and achieves zero data exchange between the nodes.

From Figure 10, it is seen that simple image segmentation will result in much network overhead for node synchronization and algorithm programming. In Spiral Architecture, after an image is multiplied by a specific Spiral Address, the original image is partitioned into several parts. Each part is a near copy of the original image. Each copy results from a unique sampling of the input image. Each sample is mutually exclusive and the collection of all such samples represents a partitioning of the input image. As the scaling in effect represents the viewing of the image at a lower resolution, each copy has less information. However, as none of the individual light intensities have been altered in any way, the scaled images in total still hold all of the information contained in the original one (Sheridan, 1996). Consequently, the sub-images can be processed independently by the corresponding processing nodes without requiring data exchange between them.

Figure 11 shows an example of image partitioning with Spiral Multiplication. The original image has 16807 hexagon pixels. The multiplier used in Spiral Multiplication is 10000[1]. With the novel uniform image partitioning on Spiral Architecture, task parallelism can be achieved. An application containing complicated image processing often requires processing results in the different aspects such as histogram, edge map and spectrum distribution. Under the proposed image partitioning, all these tasks can be dealt with independently on the assigned sub-images. Such a parallel processing scheme increases the system efficiency. Moreover, because each node possesses less information than the original image, processing time will be shortened dramatically. Detailed demonstration will be shown in the experiment section.

There are two points still existing in the above partitioning method that must be resolved before it is utilized in practical applications. First, it is known that the uniform image partitioning is simply achieved by Spiral Multiplication. However, the relation between the multiplier and the number of partitions has not been described yet. This is an important point in practical systems, since it must be able to determine the number of partitions according to the image to be processed and the practical system performance. Second, a complete sub-image may not be obtained when the multiplier used in Spiral Multiplication is a general spiral address. For example, when the spiral address is 55555, the original image is partitioned into several parts, but only the middle part holds the complete information of the original image. Other sub-images are scattered on different areas (see Figure 12). It would be necessary to collect the corresponding scattered parts together to form a complete sub-image before it is delivered to the corresponding node for distributed processing.

In the following sections, solutions are proposed to deal with the two points mentioned above.

Computing the Number of Partitions

It is necessary to determine the relation between the multiplier and the number of partitions. Further, the relation should be static, so for any given multiplier, the number of partitions is determined uniquely when the corresponding Spiral Multiplication is executed. From the aspect of a distributed processing application, the number of partitions often needs to be decided according to the image to be processed and the performance of the system platform before the processing procedure commences. With the help of a static relation between the multiplier and the partitioning number, it can be known that what multiplier to use in Spiral Multiplication in order to partition the image into the specific parts.

In the work, it was found that it is unable to find such a relation between the Spiral Address and the partitioning number directly. In order to achieve this goal, the Spiral Architecture is refined with the help of the structure proposed in (He, 1998). This redefined architecture originally was used to find the spiral address for image rotation on Spiral Architecture. In this chapter, it will be used to construct the relation between the multiplier (spiral address) which is used in the Spiral Multiplication for a particular

Figure 11. Seven part (near copies) image partitioning on Spiral Architecture

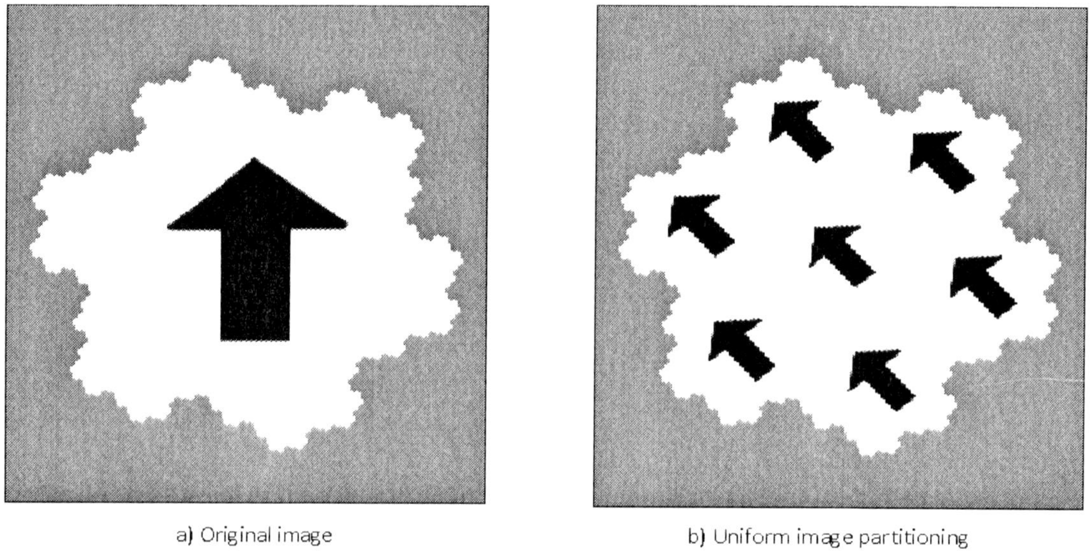

Figure 12. Spiral Multiplication by a common Spiral Address 55555

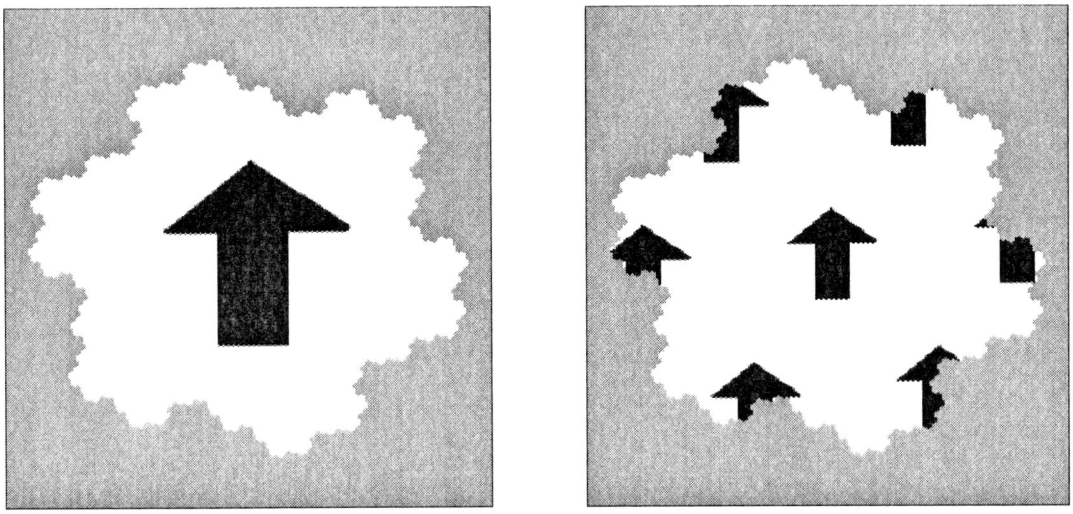

a) Original image

b) Incomplete image partitioning

image partitioning and the number of partitions. The newly refined architecture contains three parameters to identify each of its hexagonal pixels. Then, every spiral address will be mapped into a set of three parameters. The refined Spiral Architecture is shown in Figure 13.

The original Spiral Architecture is divided into six regions, which are denoted by $r = 1, 2, \ldots, 6$. In each region, the pixels are grouped into the different levels denoted by $l = 0, 1, \ldots$ along the radial direction. On each level, each pixel is regarded as an item denoted by i, where $i = 0, 1, \ldots, l$ clockwise, as shown in Figure 13. Each pixel can then be located uniquely by the three parameters, (r, l, i), in addition to the Spiral Address within Spiral Architecture.

Based on the theory of Spiral Multiplication, every spiral address value x has a unique inverse value y for an image of a given size. They should meet the condition,

Figure 13. Redefined Spiral architecture

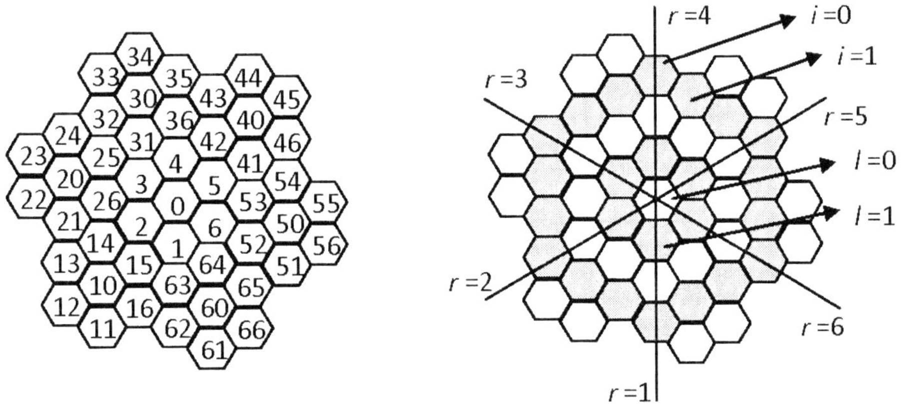

$$(x \times y) \bmod N = 1 \tag{16}$$

where N is determined by the size of the image. Suppose the maximum spiral address of an image is a_{max}, then $N = a_{max} + 1$ (Spiral Addition).

In order to find the relation between the multiplier and the number of partitions, the second step is to work out the inverse value of the multiplier with Equation (16), which is also a spiral address. This can be done instantly using the principles of Spiral Multiplication. Then, the parameter (r, l, i) corresponding to the inverse value of the multiplier can be found in the refined Spiral Architecture as shown in Figure 13. In a practical application, a table is made to map each spiral address to its corresponding parameter (r, l, i) beforehand.

Naturally, there are no mathematical modules which yield the relation between multiplier and number of partitions. In this research, an inductive method is followed to exploit the principle. The number of partitions is counted manually after the image is transformed by Spiral Multiplication with a particular multiplier. For example, the number of partitions is counted manually when the inverse values of the multiplier are 0, 1, 2, 14, 15, 63 whose corresponding parameters in the refined Spiral Architecture are (0, 0, 0), (1, 1, 0), (1, 1, 1), (1, 2, 2), (1, 2, 1), (1, 2, 0). The numbers of partitions are 0, 1, 1, 4, 3, 4 respectively. In the work, more similar tests were made manually in order to reveal the relationship between the multiplier and the number of partitions. Based on the inductive method, the following formula is derived:

$$PNumber(r,l,i) = [l^2 - i(l-1) + i(i-1)] \,, \qquad where$$
$$r = 1,\ 2,\ \ldots,\ 6;$$
$$l = 0,\ 1,\ 2,\ \ldots\ ;\ \text{and}$$
$$i = 0,\ 1,\ \ldots,\ l. \tag{17}$$

Then, the above formula is tested by a special image partitioning whose multiplier for Spiral Multiplication and numbers of partitions are known. Initially, it is known that, for an image of 49 hexagonal pixels, it will be partitioned into seven near copies (See Figure 11) through Spiral Multiplication with the multiplier 10. In this case, the inverse value of 10 is also 10 according to the principles of Spiral Multiplication. From the refined Spiral Architecture, it is known that the corresponding parameters are (1, 3, 2).

They are substituted in Equation (17). The number of partitions is calculated, and is seven, as expected.

It is found that the number of partitions is only determined by the parameters l and i. That means the partitioning number is only related to the level number and the item number of the inverse value of the multiplier. The rotation angle is the only difference among the images transformed by Spiral Multiplication with different multipliers that correspond to the same parameters l and i, but different values of r. The angle difference is a multiple of 60 degrees. This point will be analysed in detail in the next section.

In addition, every point on the border of two adjoining regions on the refined Spiral Architecture (See Figure 13) has two different sets of parameters, because it strides over two regions with different region numbers and different item numbers. Its corresponding number of partitions is identical, however, regardless of which set of parameters are substituted into Equation (17). For example, address 14 has the parameters (1, 2, 2) and (2, 2, 0), but the corresponding number of partitions is 4 if the inverse value of the multiplier used by the Spiral Multiplication for image partitioning is 4.

Using the formula derived above, an image can be partitioned into as many parts as required, which are subsampled copies of the original image in Spiral Architecture. This image partitioning method is thus controllable and manageable according to the required precision and the capacity of processing nodes on the network for distributed image processing.

Unfortunately, using Spiral Multiplication cannot partition the original image into any number of sub-images. For example, it is impossible to find a multiplier which can partition an image into two parts by Spiral Multiplication. Thus, in practical applications, the approximate number of partitions must be found to meet the requirements. The reason is that uniform image partitioning on Spiral Architecture is the result of Spiral Multiplication. The new positions of the pixels are determined uniquely by the principle of Spiral Multiplication. The relation of the pixel positions before and after Spiral Multiplication is a one-to-one mapping. Ordinary mathematical multiplication is defined on a continuous domain. However, Spiral Multiplication is actually a kind of address counting operation which is a procedure for pixel repositioning. Consequently, it cannot be guaranteed that a multiplier (spiral address) can be found to partition the input image into any number of parts. From the mathematical view, it cannot always guaranteed an integral solution of the multivariate formula as:

$l^2 - i(l-1) + i(i-1) - PNumber = 0$, *where*

$l = 0, 1, 2,...$; and

$i = 0, 1, ..., l,$ (18)

Complete Image Partitioning in Spiral Architecture

With the formula developed in the previous section, a Spiral Multiplier can be decided to partition the original image into the required number of near copies. The number of partitions can be found to match practical requirements by an adaptive method such as Divisible Load Theory (DLT) (Bharadwaj et al., 2000).

However, it is found that when the number of partitions is not a power of seven such as 7, 49 or 343 only one sub-image in the middle of the image area is a complete sub-image, while the other sub-images are segmented into several fragments scattered to different positions in the original image area. For example, an image multiplied by a common spiral address 55555 gives the results shown in Figure 12. With the exception of the middle sub-image, the other three sub-images are each split into two fragments. This is unacceptable for distributed processing. Obviously, two problems must be resolved before distributing the data to the processing nodes. One is that the corresponding fragments that belong to the same sub-image must be identified. Another problem is that all the corresponding fragments must be moved together to become a complete sub-image.

In this research, it is found that the boundaries of the different sub-image areas could be detected by investigating the neighbouring relation of the spiral addresses between the reference point and its six adjacent points: the neighbouring relation of spiral addresses along the boundary is different from the neighbouring relation within the sub-image area. All the points belonging to the same sub-image area

Figure 14. Seven hexagon cluster with six addends of Spiral Addition

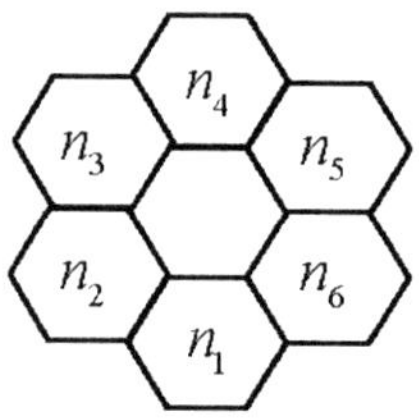

have a consistent relation. Consistency is destroyed only across a boundary between two different sub-image areas. Moreover, it is shown that the consistency can be expressed by Spiral Addition.

Figure 14 shows a seven-hexagon cluster. The six numbers $n_1, n_2, \ldots, n_6$ shown are addends for Spiral Addition, to be used later. The values of these addends are different under different Spiral Multiplications with the appropriate multipliers for the required image partitioning. The details of the method to calculate the addends will be explained later. Here, it is assumed these addends have been already given. Then, after image partitioning, all the points of the original image will move to new positions in the new image. In the output partitioned image, if a point's original spiral address on the input image before partitioning is given, its six neighbouring points' original spiral addresses will be determined by Spiral Addition with the addends as shown in Figure 14. For example, suppose a point's spiral address on the original image is x and the original address of its neighbouring point below is y, corresponding to the position labelled n_1 in Figure 14. If $y = x + n_1$, these two points are in the same sub-image. Otherwise, these two points are in different sub-images and they both stay on the boundaries of the sub-images. Here, "+" stands for Spiral Addition including modular operation if necessary.

Definition 4.1. *A point is defined as an inside point, i.e. a point within a sub-image area, if the relation between the point's address x and its six neighbouring points' addresses y_i for $i \in \{1, 2, \ldots, 6\}$ satisfies Equation (19); otherwise it is defined as an adjoining point, i.e. a point on the boundary between two sub-image areas.*

$$y_i = x + n_i,\ i \in \{1, 2, \ldots, 6\} \tag{19}$$

Addition in Equation (19) is Spiral Addition including any necessary modular operation (See Section 1.1) rather than normal mathematical addition.

Now, the remaining question is how to compute the addends n_i, for $i \in \{1, 2, 3, 4, 5, 6\}$. During image partitioning, the values of addends are determined by Spiral Multiplication, which achieves the corresponding image partitioning. In other words, once the number of image partitions is determined, the multiplier used in Spiral Multiplication is determined as explained in the previous section. The values of addends as shown in Figure 14 are then fixed. Whether the point is an *inside point* or an *adjoining point* is determined by the condition mentioned above. In fact, the values of addends in Figure 14 are the original spiral addresses of the six points surrounding the centre of the image. An example is given below.

Figure 15 shows the computation results of the Spiral Multiplication with multiplier "23" on an image of 49 points. As shown in the figure, all the points move to unique new positions. Based on the above explanation, the addends n_i, $i \in \{1, 2, 3, 4, 5, 6\}$, are 15, 26, 31, 42, 53 and 64 respectively. The point with address "15" is an *inside point* because the relation between its address and its six neighbouring points' addresses meet the condition shown in Equation (19). The point with address "25" is an *adjoining point* because some of its neighbouring points cannot meet the address relation of Equation (19). For example, its upper neighbouring point's original address is "24". The corresponding addend used for Spiral Addition in Equation (19) is $n_4 = 42$. According to Equation (19) if the point of address "25" is an *inside point*, the original address of the neighbouring point above it should be "30", i.e, 25+42 = 30 (Spiral Addition) rather than "24". So the point of address "25" is an *adjoining point*. This checking procedure proceeds on each point as follows:

1. Initialize sub-image number *sn* = 1;
2. Choose any unchecked point on the image as the next point to be checked;
3. Label this point as *sn*;
4. Label all the unchecked neighbouring points which meet the condition in Equation (19) as *sn*;
5. Store the neighbouring points just labelled in step 4 temporarily in a buffer;
6. Choose any one of the neighbouring points which was just labelled in step 4 as the next point to be checked;
7. Repeat steps 3 to 6 until no unchecked neighbouring points can be found in step 4;
8. Choose any one of the unchecked points stored in the buffer as the next point to be checked;
9. Repeat steps 3 to 8 until no unchecked point can be found in the buffer;
10. Clear the buffer and set *sn*= *sn* + 1;

Figure 15. Relocation of points after Spiral Multiplication with multiplier "23"

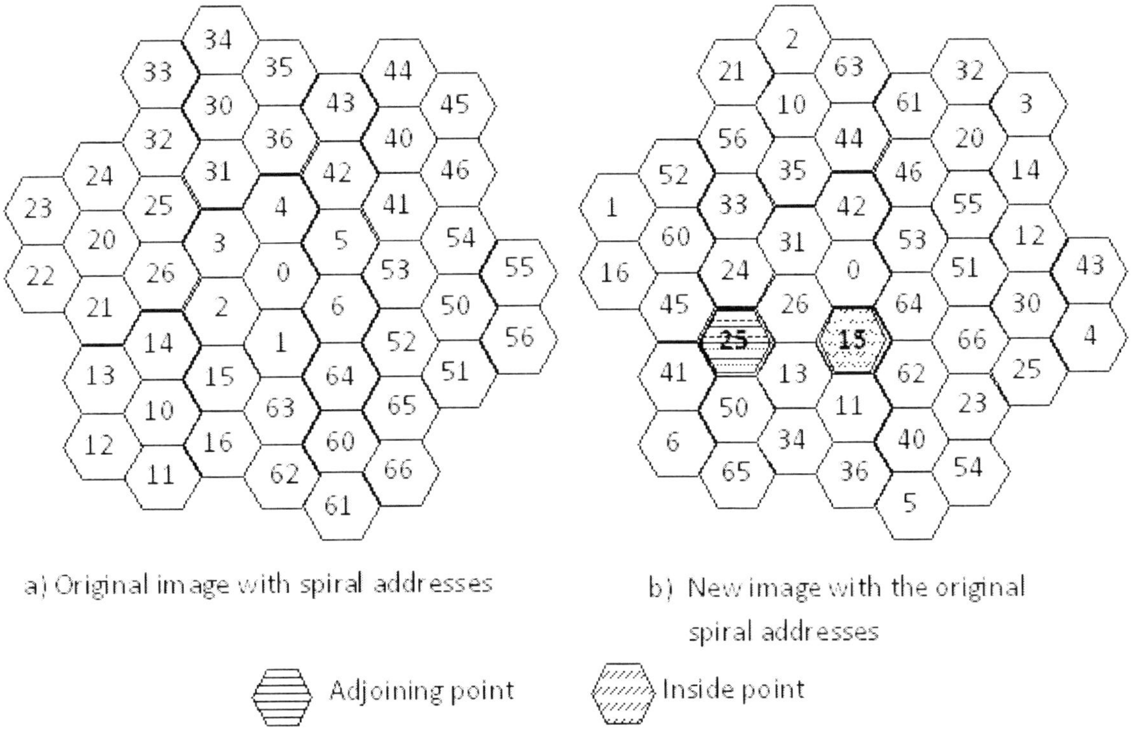

Figure 16. Three labelled sub-image areas after image partitioning

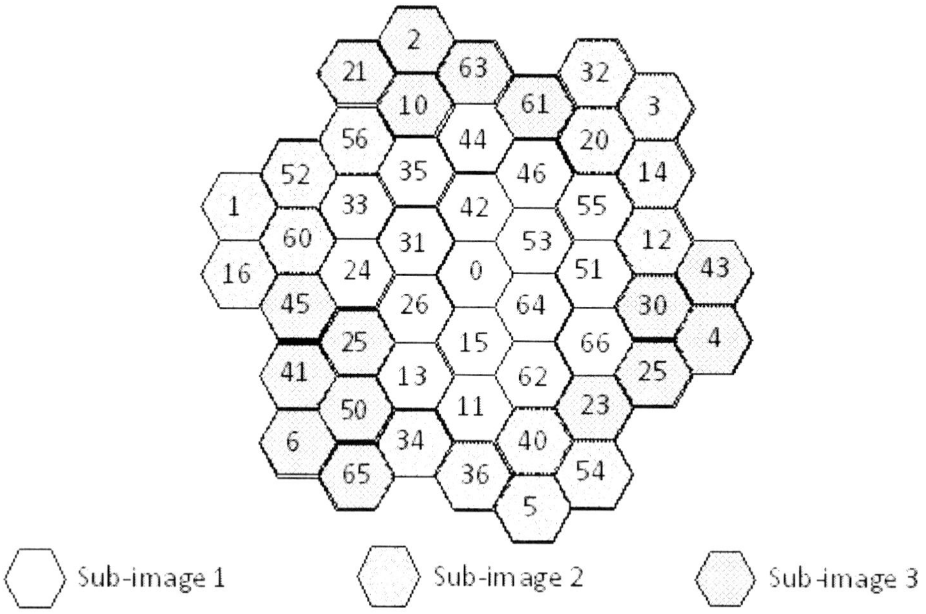

11. Repeat steps 2 to 10 until no unchecked point can be found on the image.

Then, all the points will be labelled by an area number. The fragments corresponding to the same sub-image are found as shown in Figure 16.

The last requirement is to collect the corresponding fragments together to form a complete sub-image. Actually, suppose the number of partitions is not the power of seven. After image partitioning in Spiral Architecture all the sub-images are incomplete partitioned images except the middle one. It is known that Spiral Addition with a common addend will move each point to a new position and guarantee one-to- one mapping between the input image and the output image without changing the object shape, so it is a good technique to collect fragments of the sub-image. Moreover, from Figure 16 it is observed that all the sub-images have similar sizes and the sub-image in the middle area is always a complete sub-image. There is a special case: when the number of partitions is a power of seven, all the sub-images have exactly the same size. This fact confirms that if the pixels in an incomplete sub-image can be moved into the middle sub-image area properly, this sub-image will be restored successfully.

Since Spiral Addition is a consistent operation, if the point that was closest to the point with spiral address "0" on the original image is moved, other points will be automatically located to corresponding positions without changing the object shape in the image. Such movement is achieved using Spiral Addition as mentioned above. This operation is performed on each sub-image that has been given an area number in the previous step, and then all the incomplete sub-images will be restored one by one.

Let us call the point which was closest to the point with spiral address "0" before image partitioning the relative centre of the sub-image. The addend of Spiral Addition for restoring the incomplete sub-image is computed as follows.

Figure 17. Four-part complete image partitioning in Spiral Architecture

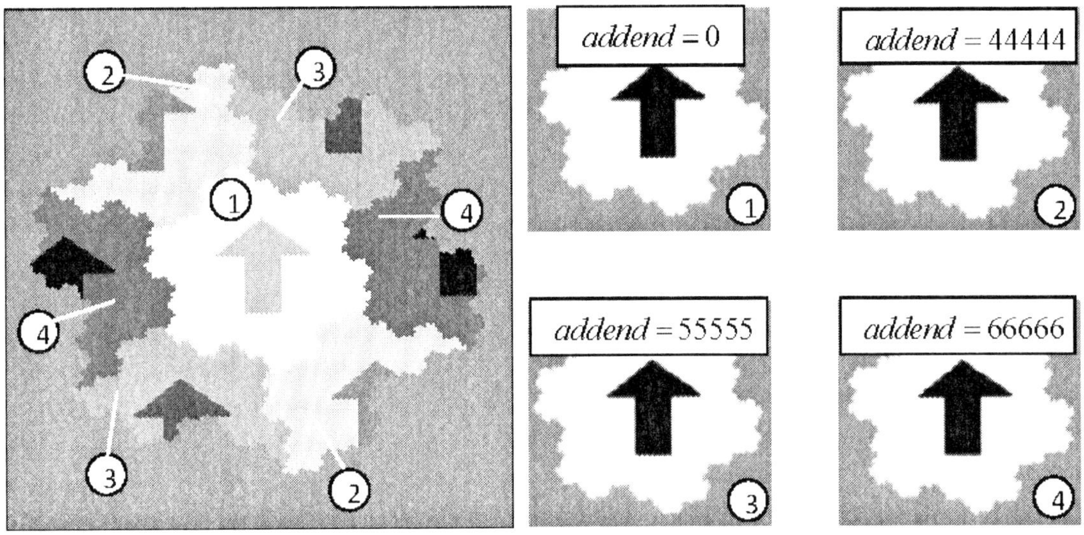

a) Four labelled sub-images after image partitioning

b) Four complete sub-images after fragment collecting with Spiral Addition using different addends

Suppose the spiral address of the relative centre of the sub-image is x after image partitioning. Then the addend of Spiral Addition for collecting the fragments of sub-images is the inverse value of x, $\overline{x}$, which is computed according to the principles of Spiral Addition. As a result, the relative centre is moved to the point of spiral address "0" and other points in the fragments are moved to corresponding positions to produce a complete sub-image.

Figure 17 gives an examples showing the procedure mentioned above. The original images contain 16807 points. They are partitioned into four parts with multiplier 55555 and three parts with multiplier 56123 respectively. The separated sub-image areas are shown using different illuminations and labelled using different area numbers. Finally, the fragments of incomplete sub-images were collected together to produce a complete partitioned sub-image. The addends used in Spiral Addition for fragment collection are also shown on each sub-image. The complete sub-images so obtained can be distributed to different nodes for further processing.

Figure 18 gives another example which shows image portioning to 3 parts on Spiral Architecture. The relevant addends are shown on the pictures.

EXPERIMENTS

In order to demonstrate the advanced performance provided by distributed processing based on special image partitioning on Spiral Architecture, global Gaussian processing for image blurring is chosen as a testing algorithm. Gaussian processing is an algorithm used widely in image processing for several applications such as edge detection, image denoising, and image blurring. It can be mathematically explained as,

Figure 18. Three-part complete image partitioning on Spiral Architecture

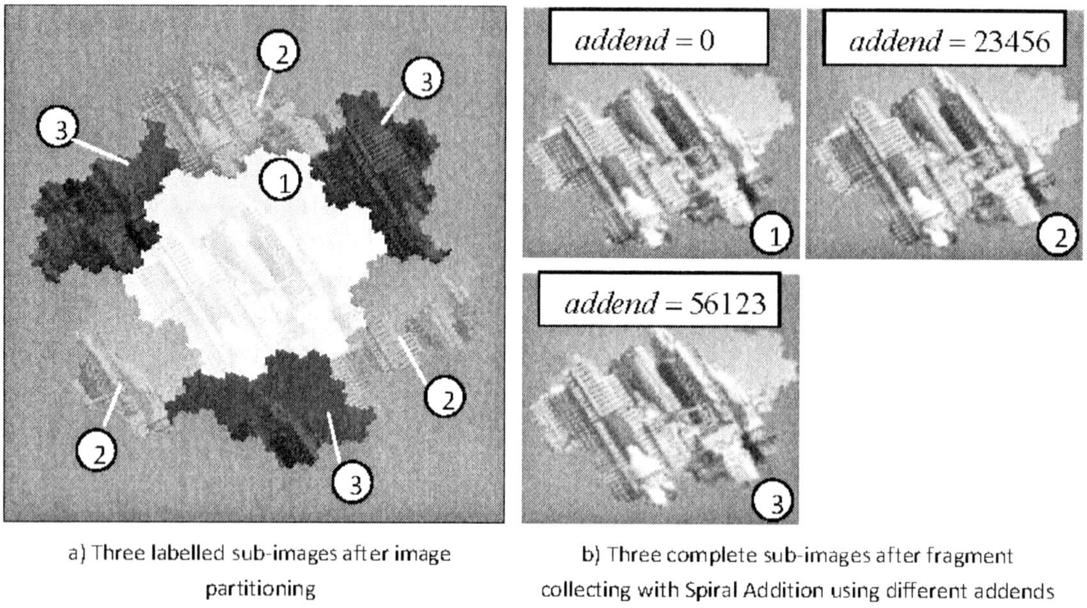

Figure 19. Prototype of distributed system topology

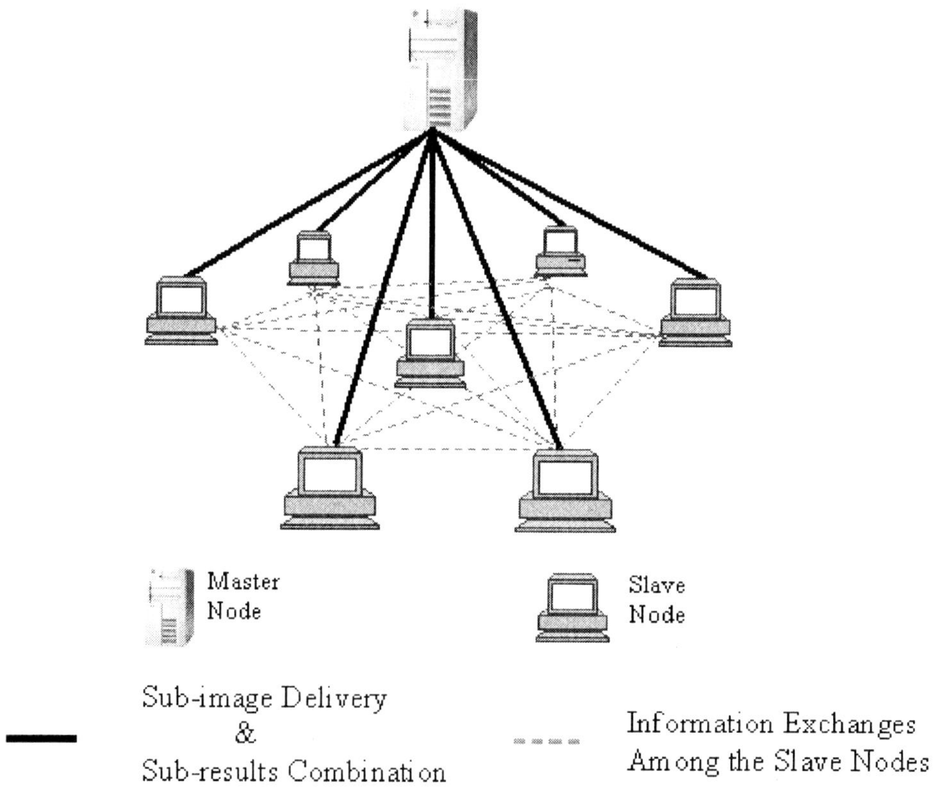

$$L(x,y;t) = g(x,y;t) * f(x,y)$$
$$= \iint_{\sigma} f(u,v)\frac{1}{2\pi t}e^{-\frac{(x-u)^2+(y-v)^2}{2t}}dudv. \qquad (20)$$

where f maps the coordinates of the pixel (x, y) to a value representing the light intensity, i.e. $f : \Re^2 \to \Re$. $g(\bullet)$ is the Gaussian kernel. $L(\bullet)$ represents the image after Gaussian processing. t is called the 'coarseness scale' and $t > 0$. σ stands for a set of points on the image area which participate in the Gaussian convolution. For global Gaussian processing, σ stands for the whole area of original image. As t increases the signal which is L becomes gradually smoother.

In our work, partitioning approach is implemented on a cluster of workstations shown as Figure 19. One of the computers acts as a master computer (master node) and the remaining seven computers are used as slave computers (slave nodes). In the early phase of the processing, the master node is responsible for initial data partitioning and data delivery to the slave nodes. The data is then processed on the slave nodes. Depending on the image partition scheme, the slave nodes may or may not need to exchange data (denoted by dash line on Figure 19). For the scheme of simple image partitioning shown on Figure 10, data exchange between slave nodes is inevitable since each part does not represent the information of the whole image. During the procedure of global Gaussian processing, each slave node must obtain necessary pixel information which is located on other parts to complete the computation of Equation (20). On the other hand, if uniform image partitioning scheme based on Spiral Architecture is chosen (see Figure 11), each slave node can carry out the necessary processing independently without data exchange between nodes because each node possesses a near copy of the original image. The individual processing result will be sent to the master node where the relatively simple process is carried out to combine the individual result together to produce the final result of global Gaussian processing. Thus, the dash lines presented on Figure 19 can be removed.

A three-level algorithm is designed, which consists of a parent process, seven child processes and seven remote processes. The parent process and the seven child processes reside on the master computer. Each slave node executes one of the remote processes. The parent process is mainly responsible for data management and process management, including data communication, command delivery, data manipulation, child process creation, process monitoring and process synchronization. Each remote process completes all the detail work on the data block assigned by the master node.

Three techniques are applied for data communication between the processes. They are *Share Memory*, *Message Queues* and *Sockets*. The former two are used for the data exchanges between the parent processes and the child processes. The latter is used for Client-Server communication between the child processes and the remote processes, and between the remote processes if required.

In the experiments, two approaches are used to achieve distributed processing. One used a single CPU with multiple processes. Another used multiple computers in a network, where each of them had one process to deal with the assigned sub-image. The test bed consists of eight computers (Ultra Sun-Workstations, of which each has a SPARC-based CPU with clock rate being approximately 333.6 MHz).

The experimental results based on simple data partitioning (see Figure 10) is shown on Figure 20, where the data communication between slave nodes are necessary.

In the figures, "1 Process/1 Node" actually is sequential processing, where only one computer and one process deal with the task. "7 Processes/1 Node" uses one CPU with multiple processes, as mentioned above. Finally, "7 Processes/7 Nodes" means that seven computers on a network are used to achieve distributed processing and each of them has only one process to process the assigned sub-image, the second approach mentioned above. As shown in the figure, distributed processing speeds up the data processing for the case shown, but this is not always true. For an image of 2401 pixels, processing based on a single CPU with multiple processes will take more time than sequential processing, because the CPU will require more extra time to deal with process management, so the time cost exceeds the time saved by distributed processing.

This situation becomes more serious when the pixel number decreases to 343. Besides the extra cost for process or node management, data communication becomes a significant issue during the procedure.

The total processing time is divided into data-processing time and non-data-processing time, including the time for data exchange, process management and sub-task synchronization. The statistical results for processing times are shown in Figure 21. The components of processing time under the different situations based on simple image partitioning. It shows that the fraction of time for data processing decreases as the size of the image decreases. The reason is that when the size of the image decreases, the system requires less time for data processing. This part of the time decreases dramatically. However, the non-data-processing time decreases relatively more slowly. The reason is that the time for process management does not change when the number of child process stays fixed. In addition, the throughput of data I/O is determined by the system I/O performance. The response of a high-speed hard disk to an image of 1MBytes and an image of 100KBytes is almost the same, so when the size of the image decreases, the time cost for data I/O through the hard disk does not change much. The situation is the same for data communication on high-speed Local Area Network (LAN).

Moreover, Figure 10. Simple Equal Size Image Partitioning on Spiral Architecture shows that after equal-size image partitioning, processing nodes do not receive equal effective object information. Some nodes contain much more object information, while some nodes do not contain any effective object information. Consequently, some nodes finish their assigned tasks earlier than other nodes. The processing times on each node may range from one second to several minutes. The nodes with less object information must therefore wait for the nodes with more object information before they can receive new commands and update information for the next sub-task from the master node. That is another reason that sequential processing is sometimes faster than distributed processing.

As discussed above, if uniform image partitioning scheme (see Figure 11) is chosen, system overheads and the complexities of program design will be greatly reduced because there will no data communication between slave nodes.

The same task, global Gaussian processing as in the previous section, is now carried out again here based on the new partitioning scheme. Some statistics for processing time are shown in Figure 22 and Figure 23.

Obviously, the computing complexity has been both reduced and nicely partitioned without discarding any information for distributed processing. In addition, as shown in Figure 23, most of the processing time is the cost of data processing. This processing system is clearly highly efficient. If the percentage of data processing time in the total processing time is used as the index of system efficiency, the new partitioning scheme improves the system efficiency about 2% from 96.94% to 98.73% compared to the same processing approach, "7 Processes/7 Nodes", using the simple partitioning scheme.

Figure 20. Image processing time based on simple image partitioning

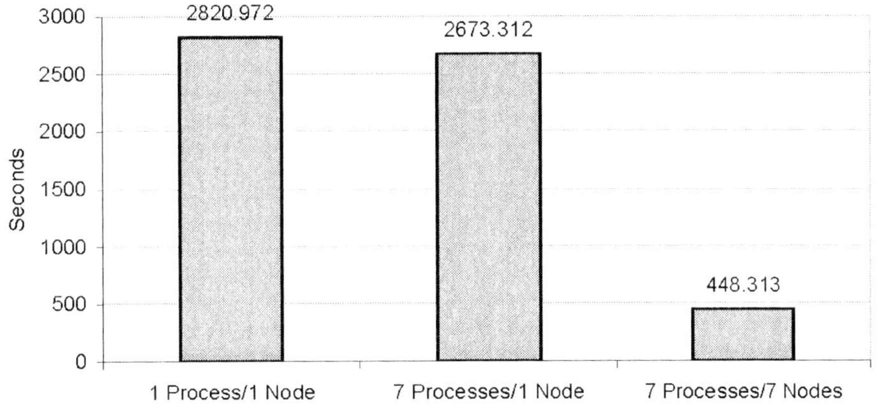

a) Image of 16807 pixels

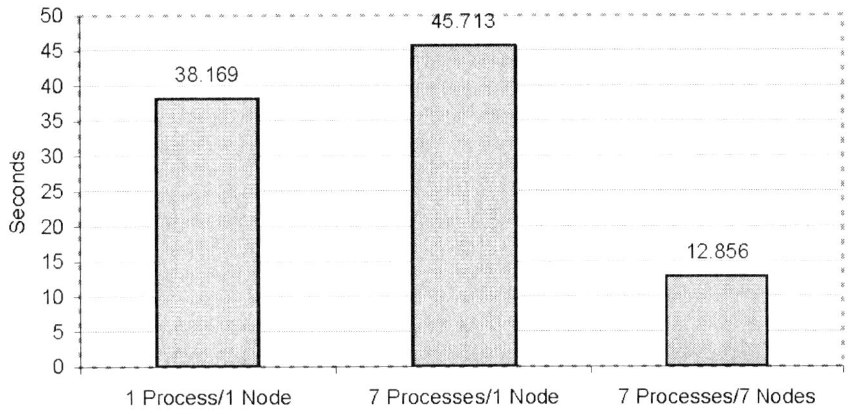

b) Image of 2401 pixels

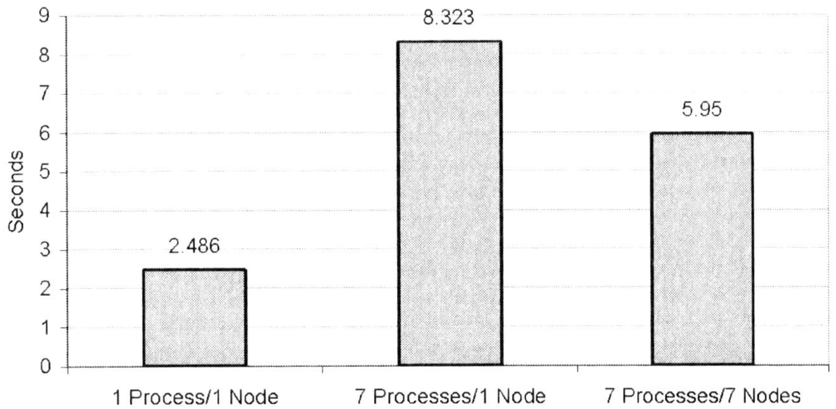

c) Image of 343 pixels

Figure 21. The components of processing time under the different situations based on simple image partitioning

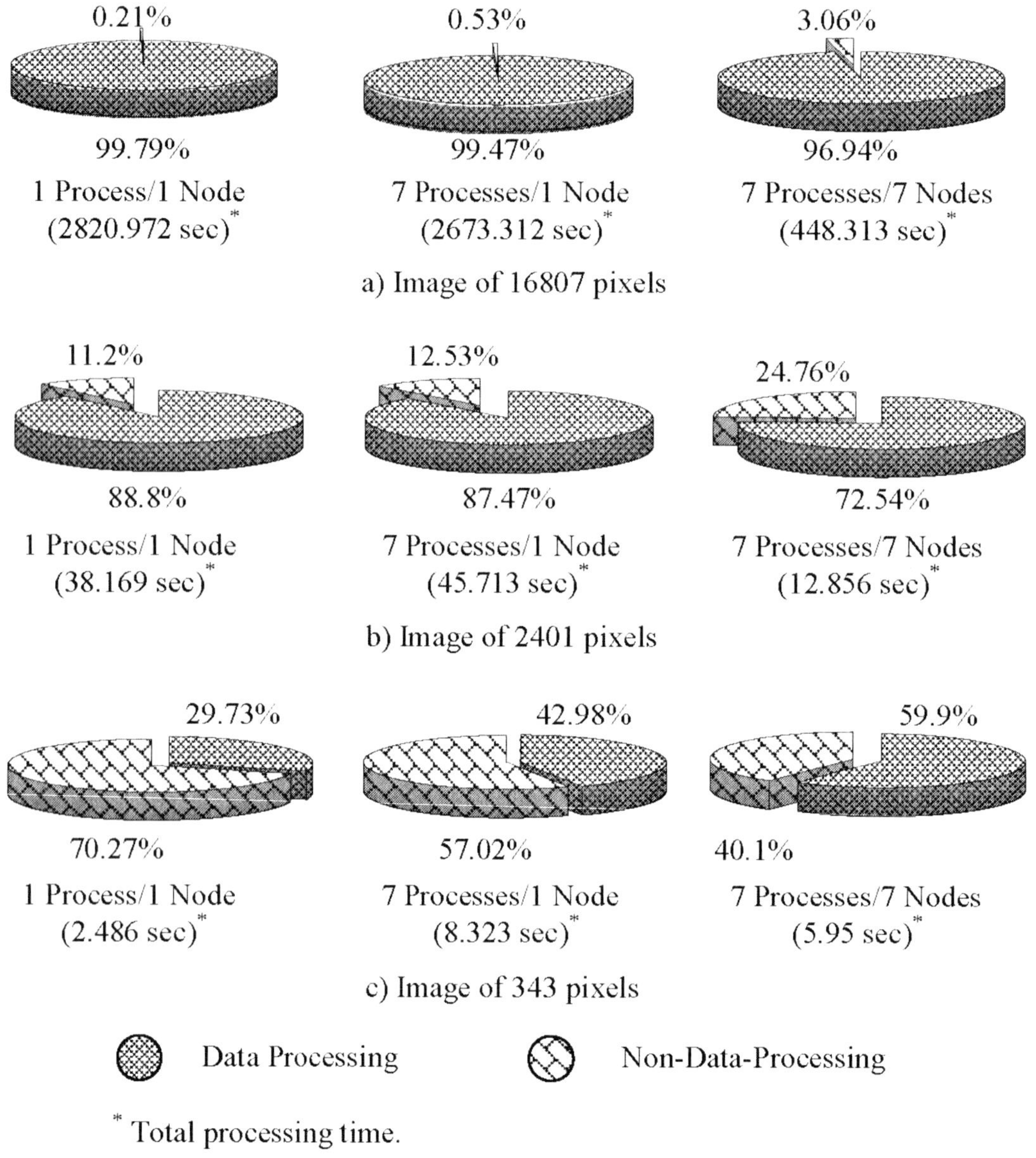

CONCLUSION

This chapter presents an application of Spiral Architecture to image partitioning which is important for distributed image processing. Based on the principle of Spiral Multiplication, a new image partitioning scheme is proposed. Using Spiral Multiplication an image can be partitioned into a few parts. Each part is an exclusive sampling of the original image and contains representative information from all areas of the original image. Consequently, each sub-image can be viewed as a near copy of the original im-

Figure 22. Processing time comparison based on the normal equal-size partitioning and uniform partitioning on Spiral Architecture (Image of 16807 points)

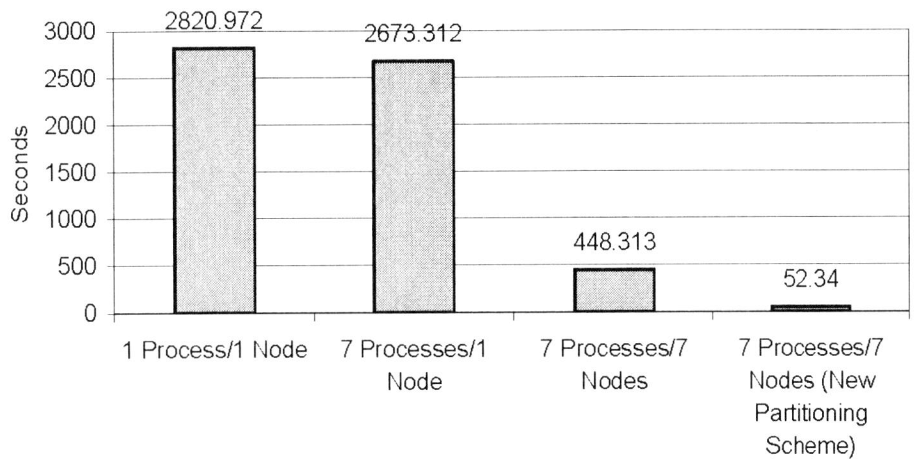

Figure 23. The components of the processing time under the different partitioning scheme

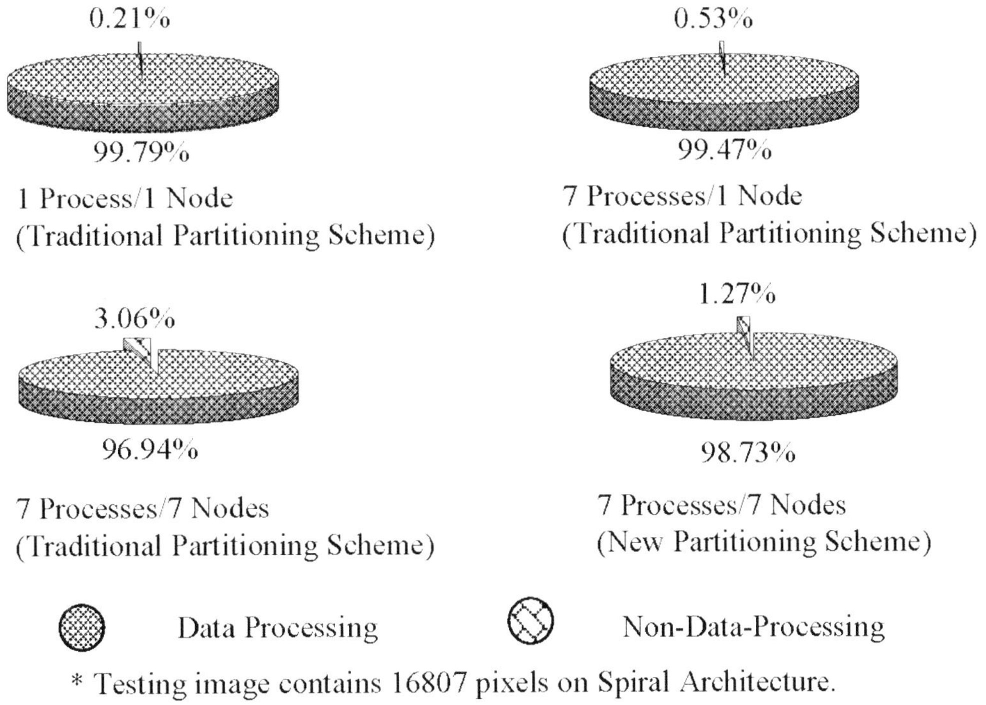

age. In distributed processing based on such an image partitioning scheme, each node will process the assigned sub-image independently without the data exchange normally required. This should speed up processing very much.

In a practical system, the number of partitions is determined by the application requirement, the image to be processed and the system performance. However, the relation between the partitioning number and the multiplier (spiral address) used in Spiral Multiplication was not known. In this chapter, an equation was built up to describe this relationship, so the number of partitions can be worked out for the given multiplier and vice versa as required.

Unfortunately, complete sub-images can be obtained by Spiral Multiplication only when the partitioning number is a power of seven. In other words, when the number of image partitions is some other value like 4 and 5, all the sub-images except one are split into a few fragments and scattered to different positions. It was impossible to tell which fragments belonged to which sub-image, an unacceptable flaw for parallel image processing. In this chapter, the neighbouring relation of the points is found out and explicitly expressed after Spiral Multiplication using Spiral Addition. The different sub-image areas are identified. Then, the points on the different sub-image areas are labelled. Finally, the fragments corresponding to the same sub-images are collected together to produce the complete sub-images. Such complete sub-images can be distributed to the different nodes for further processing.

REFERENCES

Alexander, D. (1995). *Recursively Modular Artificial Neural Network.* Doctoral Thesis, Macquire University, Australia, Sydney, Australia.

Arpaci, R. H., Dusseau, A. C., Vahdat, A. M., Liu, L. T., Anderson, T. E., & Patterson, D. A. (May, 1995). *The interaction of parallel and sequential workloads on a network of workstations.* Paper presented at the 1995 ACM SIGMETRICS Conference on Measurement and Modeling of Computer Systems.

Bertsekas, D. P., & Tsitsiklis, J. N. (1989). *Parallel and Distributed Computation: Numerical Methods.* Englewood Cliffs, NJ: Prentice Hall.

Bharadwaj, V., Li, X., & Ko, C. C. (2000). *Efficient partitioning and scheduling of computer vision and image processing data on bus networks using divisible load analysis. Image and Vision Computing, 18,* 919–938. doi:10.1016/S0262-8856(99)00085-2

Braunl, T., Feyrer, S., Rapf, W., & Reinhardt, M. (2001). *Parallel Image Processing.* Berlin: Springer-Verlag.

Chen, C. M., Lee, S. Y., & Cho, Z. H. (1990). A Parellel Implementation of 3D CT Image Reconstruction on HyperCube Multiprocessor. *IEEE Transactions on Nuclear Science, 37*(3), 1333–1346. doi:10.1109/23.57385

Goller, A. (1999). *Parallel and Distributed Processing of Large Image Data Sets.* Doctoral Thesis, Graz University of Technology, Graz, Austria.

Goller, A., & Leberl, F. (2000). *Radar Image Processing with Clusters of Computers.* Paper presented at the IEEE Conference on Aerospace.

Hawick, K. A., James, H. A., Maciunas, K. J., Vaughan, F. A., Wendelborn, A. L., Buchhorn, M., et al. (1997). *Geostationary-satellite Imagery Application on Distributed, High-Performance Computing.* Paper presented at the High Performance Computing on the Information Superhighway: HPC Asia'97.

He, X. (1998). *2D -Object Recognition With Spiral Architecture.* Doctoral Thesis, University of Technology, Sydney, Sydney, Australia.

Koelbel, C. H., Loveman, D. B., & Schreiber, R. S., Jr. G. L. S., & Zosel, M. E. (1994). *The High Performance Fortran Handbook*. Cambridge, MA: MIT Press.

Kok, A. J. F., Pabst, J. L. v., & Afsarmanseh, H. (April, 1997). *The 3D Object Mediator: Handling 3D Models on Internet.* Paper presented at the High-Performance Computing and Networking, Vienna, Austria.

Lee, C., Lee, T.-y., Lu, T.-c., & Chen, Y.-t. (1997). A World-wide Web Based Distributed Animation Environment. *Computer Networks and ISDN Systems, 29,* 1635–1644. doi:10.1016/S0169-7552(97)00078-0

Marsh, A. (1997). *EUROMED - Combining WWW and HPCN to Support Advanced Medical Imaging.* Paper presented at the High-Performance Computing and Networking, Vienna, Austria.

Miller, R. L. (1993). High Resolution Image Processing on Low-cost Microcomputer. *International Journal of Remote Sensing, 14*(4), 655–667. doi:10.1080/01431169308904366

Nicolescu, C., & Jonker, P. (2002). A Data and Task Parallel Image Processing Environment. *Parallel Computing, 28,* 945–965. doi:10.1016/S0167-8191(02)00105-9

Niederl, F., & Goller, A. (Jan, 1998). *Method Execution On A Distributed Image Processing Backend.* Paper presented at the 6th EUROMICRO Workshop on Parallel and Distributed Processing, Madrid, Spain.

Oberhuber, M. (1998). *Distributed High-Performance Image Processing on the Internet.* Doctoral Thesis, Graz University of Technology, Austria.

Pitas, I. (1993). *Parallel Algorithm for Digital Image Processing, Computer Vision and Neural Network.* Chichester, UK: John Wiley & Sons.

Schowengerdt, R. A., & Mehldau, G. (1993). Engineering a Scientific Image Processing Toolbox for the Macintosh II. *International Journal of Remote Sensing, 14*(4), 669–683. doi:10.1080/01431169308904367

Schwartz, E. (1980). Computational Anatomy and Functional Architecture of Striate Cortex: A Spatial Mapping Approach to Perceptual Coding. *Vision Research, 20,* 645–669. doi:10.1016/0042-6989(80)90090-5

Sheridan, P. (1996). *Spiral Architecture for Machine Vision.* Doctoral Thesis, University of Technology, Sydney.

Sheridan, P., Hintz, T., & Alexander, D. (2000). Pseudo-invariant Image Transformations on a Hexagonal Lattice. *Image and Vision Computing, 18*(11), 907–917. doi:10.1016/S0262-8856(00)00036-6

Siegel, H. J., Armstrong, J. B., & Watson, D. W. (1992). Mapping Computer-Vision-Related Tasks onto Reconfigurable Parallel-Processing Systems. *IEEE Computer, 25*(2), 54–63.

Siegel, L. J., Siegel, H. J., & Feather, A. E. (1982). Parallel Processing Approaches to Image Correlation. *IEEE Transactions on Computers*, *31*(3), 208–218. doi:10.1109/TC.1982.1675976

Squyres, J. M., Lumsdaine, A., & Stevenson, R. L. (1995). *A Cluster-based Parallel Image Processing Toolkit.* Paper presented at the IS&T Conference on Image and Video Processing, San Jose, CA.

Stevenson, R. L., Adams, G. B., Jamieson, L. H., & Delp, E. J. (1993, April). Parallel Implementation for Iterative Image Restoration Algorithms on a Parallel DSP Machine. *The Journal of VLSI Signal Processing*, *5*, 261–272. doi:10.1007/BF01581300

Wu, D. M., & Guan, L. (1995). A Distributed Real-Time Image Processing System. *Real-Time Imaging*, *1*(6), 427–435. doi:10.1006/rtim.1995.1044

Wu, Q., He, X., & Hintz, T. (2004, June 21-24). *Virtual Spiral Architecture.* Paper presented at the International Conference on Parallel and Distributed Processing Techniques and Applications, Las Vegas, Nevada, USA.

KEY TERMS AND DEFINITIONS

Distributed Processing: Distributed processing refer to a special computer system which is capable of running a program simultaneously on multiple nodes such as computers and processors. These nodes are connected to each other and managed by sophisticated software which detects idle notes and parcels out programs to utilize them.

Image Partitioning: For distributed processing purpose, image partitioning is to efficiently segment the images into multiple parts. Each part is sent to a computing node and processed simultaneously.

Spiral Architecture: Spiral Architecture is a special image architecture where the image is displayed by a set of hexagonal pixels. These pixels with the shape of hexagons are arranged in a spiral cluster. Each unit is a set of seven hexagons. That is, each pixel has six neighbouring pixels.

Spiral Addressing: Spiral Addressing is a special addressing scheme which is used to uniquely identify each pixel on Spiral Architecture. The addressing number in fact is a base-seven number. Such kind of addressing labels all pixel in a recursive modular manner along a spiral direction.

Spiral Addition: Spiral Addition is an arithmetic operation with closure properties defined on the spiral address space. Applying spiral addition on the image labelled by spiral address can achieve image transfer on Spiral Architecture.

Spiral Multiplication: Spiral Multiplication is an arithmetic operation with closure properties defined on the spiral address space. Applying spiral multiplication on the image labelled by spiral address can achieve image rotation on Spiral Architecture.

ENDNOTE

[1] This is a base 7 number. Unless specified otherwise, spiral addresses, addends used in Spiral Addition and multipliers used in Spiral Multiplication are base 7 numbers in the following sections.

Chapter 36
Scheduling Large-Scale DNA Sequencing Applications

Sudha Gunturu
Oklahoma State University, USA

Xiaolin Li
Oklahoma State University, USA

Laurence Tianruo Yang
St. Francis Xavier University, Canada

ABSTRACT

This chapter studies a load scheduling strategy with near-optimal processing time that is designed to explore the computational characteristics of DNA sequence alignment algorithms, specifically, the Needleman-Wunsch Algorithm. Following the divisible load scheduling theory, an efficient load scheduling strategy is designed in large-scale networks so that the overall processing time of the sequencing tasks is minimized. In this study, the load distribution depends on the length of the sequence and number of processors in the network and, the total processing time is also affected by communication link speed. Several cases have been considered in the study by varying the sequences, communication and computation speeds, and number of processors. Through simulation and numerical analysis, this study demonstrates that for a constant sequence length as the numbers of processors increase in the network the processing time for the job decreases and minimum overall processing time is achieved.

INTRODUCTION

Large-scale network-based computing has attracted tremendous efforts from both academia and industry because it is scalable, flexible, extendable, and economic with wide-spread applications across many disciplines in science and engineering. To address scalability issues for an important class of applications, researchers proposed a divisible load scheduling theory (DLT). These applications are structured as large numbers of independent tasks with low granularity (Bharadwaj. V., Ghose.D ., & Thomas Robertazzi. G ., 2003). They are thus amenable to embarrassingly parallelism, typically in master-slave fashion.

DOI: 10.4018/978-1-60566-661-7.ch036

Such applications are called divisible load because a scheduler may divide the computation time among worker processes arbitrarily, both in terms of task and task sizes. Scheduling the tasks of a parallel application on the resources of a distributed computing platform efficiently is critical for achieving optimal performance (Bharadwaj. V., Ghose. D., & Mani.V ., 1995)

The load distribution problem in distributed computing networks, consisting of a number of processors interconnected through communication links, has attracted a great deal of attention (Sameer Bataineh, Te-Yu Hsiung, & Thomas Robertazzi, 1994). Divisible Load Theory (DLT) is a methodology that is involved in the linear and continuous modeling of partitioning the computation and communication loads for parallel processing (Robertazzi,T.G, 2003). DLT is primarily used for handling large scale processing on network based systems.

The DLT paradigm has demonstrated numerous applications such as edge detection in image processing, file compression, joining operations in relational databases, graph coloring and genetic searches (Wong Han Min., & Bharadwaj Veeravalli, 2005). Some more examples of real divisible applications include searching for pattern in text, audio, graphic files, database and measurement processing, data retrieval systems, some linear algebra algorithms, and simulations (Maciej Drozdowski., & Marcin Lawenda., 2005).

Over the past few decades research in the field of molecular biology has made advancement that is coupled with advances in genomic technologies. This has led to an explosive growth in the biological information generated, in turn, led to the requirement for computerized databases to store, organize, and index the data and for specialized tools to view and analyze the data.

In this chapter a parallel strategy is designed to explore the computational characteristics of the Needleman-Wunsch algorithm that are used for biological sequence comparisons proposed in the literature. In designing the strategy the load is partitioned among the processors of the network using the DLT paradigm (Bharadwaj. V., Ghose. D., & Mani.V ., 1995).

Two commonly used algorithms for sequence alignment are the Needleman-Wunsch Algorithm and Smith-Waterman Algorithm where the former is employed for Global Alignment and the latter is used for Local Alignment. The complexity of the Needleman-Wunsch Algorithm and Smith-Waterman Algorithm to align sequence of length x is given by $O(x^2)$ (Wong Han Min., & Bharadwaj Veeravalli, 2005).

The algorithm used in this study is the Needleman-Wunsch Algorithm. The way that has been adopted in this study to for parallelizing the Needleman-Wunsch Algorithm is by computing the matrix elements in diagonal fashion by using a Multiple Instruction Multiple Data Systems.

Divisible Load Theory is employed for handling the sequence alignment. The objective is to minimize the total processing time for sequence alignment. The partition of the load depends primarily on the matrix that is generated by the Needleman-Wunsch Algorithm. The network has been studied for variable link speed and constant link speed.

RELATED WORK

The merging of the two rapid advancing technologies of molecular biology and computer science resulted in a new informatics science, namely bio informatics (Wong Han Min., & Bharadwaj Veeravalli, 2005). Over the past few years, the interest and research in the area of biotechnology has increased drastically. This area of study deals primarily with the methodologies of operating on molecular biological information. The present days of molecular biology is characterized by collection of large volumes of data.

Information science when applied to biology produced a field called the "Bioinformatics". The areas of bioinformatics and computational biology involve the use of techniques and concepts including applied mathematics, informatics, statistics, computer science, artificial intelligence, chemistry, and biochemistry to solve biological problems usually on the molecular level. The terms of bioinformatics and computational biology are often interchangeable. Research in computational biology often overlaps with systems biology. Major research efforts in the field include sequence alignment, gene finding, genome assembly, protein structure alignment, protein structure prediction, prediction of gene expression and protein-protein interactions, and the modeling of evolution. The area of bioinformatics more clearly refers to the creation and advancement of algorithms, computational and statistical techniques, and also includes the theory to solve formal and practical problems arising from the management and analysis of biological data. Computational biology refers to hypothesis-driven investigation of a specific biological problem using computers, carried out with experimental or simulated data, with the primary goal of discovery and the advancement of biological knowledge. In other words, bioinformatics is concerned with the information while computational biology is concerned with the hypotheses. The most common operations on biological data include sequence analysis, protein structures predications, genome sequence alignment, phylogeny tree construction, pathway research and sequence database placement. One of the most basic and important application of bio informatics task is to find a set of homologies for a given sequence because the sequences are often related to the functions, if they are similar (Felix Autenrieth., Barry Isralewitz ., Zaida Luthey-Schulten., Anurag Sethi., & Taras Pogorelov., 2000) (Jones., Neil C., & Pavel A. Penvzner., 2004).

The different bio informatics applications like sequence analysis, protein structures predications, genome sequence alignment, and phylogeny tree construction are distributed in different individual projects and they require high performance computational environments. Biologists use a tool called the BLAST for performing research (Altschul., Gish W., Miller W., Myers., & Lipman, 1990).This tool is a database search, in other words this is described as a Google for biological sequences. This tool provides a method for searching a nucleotide and protein database. This BLAST is designed in such a way that it can detect local and global alignment. Sequence Alignment is often used in biological analysis. This sequence alignment between any two newly discovered biological sequences can be aligned with the algorithms present in the literature and the similarity can be determined. This sequence alignment can be useful in understanding the function, structure and origin of the new gene. In sequence alignment two sequences are compared with the residues of one another while taking the positions of the residues into account. Residues in the sequence can be inserted, deleted or substituted to achieve maximum similarity or optimal alignment . For example, GenBank is growing at an exponential rate up to over 100 million of sequences [1] (Wong Han Min., & Bharadwaj Veeravalli, 2005) (Benson D.A ., Karsch-Mizrachi I., Lipman D. J ., Ostell J., Rapp B. A., & Wheller D.L., 2000). To meet the growing needs a wide variety of heuristics methods have been proposed for aligning the sequences such as FASTP, FASTA,BLAST, and FLASH (Yap T.K ., Frieder O., & Martino R.L ., 1998).

The NIH Biomedical Information Science and Technology Initiative Consortium that was held on July 17, 2000 has agreed on formal definitions for bioinformatics and computational biology. They also recognized that there is no definition that could completely eliminate the overlap of the variations in interpretation by different individuals and organizations. One of the definition proposed by them are as follows:

- Bioinformatics: Research, development, or application of computational tools and approaches for expanding the use of biological, medical, behavioral or health data, including those to acquire, store, organize, archive, analyze, or visualize such data (Michael Huerta ., Florence Haseltine., &Yuan Liu ., 2000).
- Computational Biology: The development and application of data-analytical and theoretical methods, mathematical modeling and computational simulation techniques to the study of biological, behavioral, and social systems (Michael Huerta ., Florence Haseltine., &Yuan Liu ., 2000).

The areas of bioinformatics and computational biology use mathematical tools to extract useful information from data produced by high-throughput biological techniques such as genome sequencing. One of the most common representative problems in bioinformatics is the assembly of high-quality genome sequences from fragmentary "shotgun" DNA sequencing. Other common problems include the study of gene regulation using data from micro arrays or mass spectrometry (Cristianini N., & Hahn M., 2006).

"Sequence Analysis" in biology can be explained by subjecting a DNA or peptide sequence to sequence alignment, sequence databases, repeated sequence searches, or other bioinformatics methods on a computer (Felix Autenrieth., Barry Isralewitz ., Zaida Luthey-Schulten., Anurag Sethi., & Taras Pogorelov, 2000). Sequence analysis in molecular biology and bioinformatics is an automated, computer-based examination of characteristically fragments, for example a DNA-strand. It basically includes five biologically relevant topics: (1) This is used for the comparison of sequences in order to find similar sequences (sequence alignment). (2) In identification of gene-structures, reading frames, distributions of introns and exons and regulatory elements. (3) Used for prediction of protein structures. (4) Used for genome mapping. (5) Comparison of homologous sequences to construct a molecular phylogeny.

Similarity detection is often used in biological analysis. This is widely used when a new gene sequence and unknown gene sequence can give significant understanding on the function, structure and origin of the new gene. While comparing two gene sequences, which is also known as aligning two sequences residues form, one sequence is compared with the residues of the other, in which the position of the residues is taken into consideration. The different operations that can be performed are insertion, deletion and substitution of residues in other sequence.

Many algorithms have been proposed in the literature for comparing two biological sequences for similarities. The most popular algorithms in aligning the DNA are the Needleman-Wunsch algorithm. For protein alignment it's the Smith-Waterman algorithm. In the sequence comparison a combination of the DLT approach and the algorithms are used in order to align the sequences accurately. In this chapter a load scheduling strategy is designed for large scale networks for sequence alignment and it has been observed that as the number of processors increases in the network results in a minimal computation time.

PROBLEM FORMULATION

The Needleman-Wunsch algorithm is one of the algorithms that perform a global alignment on two sequences (called X and Y here). This algorithm finds its application in bioinformatics to align protein or nucleotide sequences (Vladimir Likic, 2000). The algorithm was first proposed by Saul Needleman and Christian Wunsch in 1970 (Walter B.Goad, 1987).The Needleman-Wunsch algorithm is an example

Figure 1. Needleman-Wunsch algorithm after the generation of S matrix

	G	T	C	A	G	T	C
G	1	0	0	0	1	0	0
C	0	0	1	0	0	0	1
C	0	0	1	0	0	0	1
T	0	1	0	0	0	1	0
C	0	0	1	0	0	0	1

of dynamic programming, and was the first application of dynamic programming to biological sequence comparison. The algorithm can be explained in the following steps

1. Initialize the matrix S=0
2. Fill in the matrix S with 1 if it is a match and 0 if it is a mismatch
3. Compute score from right hand bottom based on the formula M[i,j]=S[i, j]+Max{M[i+1:x],M[j+1:y]}
4. Trace back from the left-top corner, and select the maximum value from the adjacent column and row, and so on. For example let us consider two sequences GTCAGTC and GCCTC. In order to align these sequences we first need to construct the matrix as shown in figures

The Needleman-Wunsch Algorithm as well as some of the characteristics of the S and M matrices that are generated by the algorithm are explained as follows. In aligning two biological sequences that are denoted as Seq X and Seq Y of length x and y, respectively, the algorithm generates two matrices represented by S and M as shown in Figure 1 and Figure 2. The matrices S and M are related to each other with the equation M[i,j]=S[i, j]+Max {[M[i+1: x],M[j+1: y]]} for the range 1 <= p <= x, 1 <= q <= y where $S_{p,q}$ and $M_{p,q}$ represents the pth row and q^{th} column of the matrices S and M respectively.

Figure 2. Needleman-Wunsch algorithm after the generation of M matrix

	G	T	C	A	G	T	C
G	4	3	2	2	3	1	0
C	4	3	3	2	2	1	1
C	2	2	3	2	2	1	1
T	1	2	1	1	1	2	0
C	0	0	1	0	1	0	1

Figure 3. Single level tree network

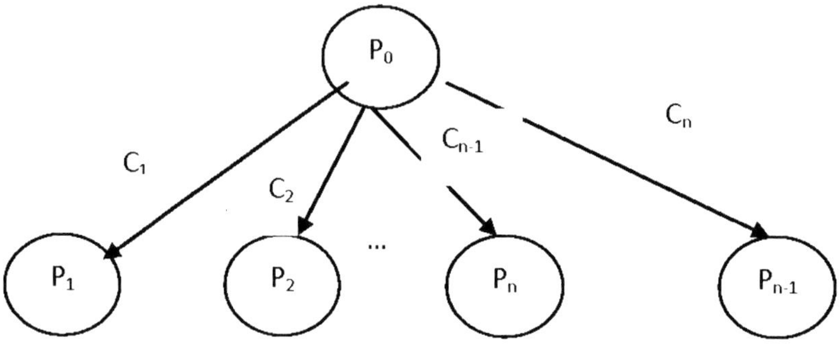

The network under consideration is a simple single level tree network (SLTN) which is shown in Figure 3, the root node can communicate only with one child at a time. The approach to the problem can be described in a series of steps. The first step is create a simple SLTN with a fixed number of nodes and apply divisible load theory on the same network. Further the number of nodes in the system is increased and DLT technique is applied. The two biological sequences are given to the network and the Needleman-Wunsch algorithm gives the alignment. The final aim of this chapter will include the computation time involved in processing the job. From the results it can be observed that by applying DLT technique the computation time decreases drastically.

The objective is to design a strategy such that the processing time or the computation time for the alignment of the two biological sequences is a minimum. The two biological sequences are considered to be of length x and y. These sequences may vary from 1 character to 1000's of characters. In the results section however the sequences are varied from length of 100 to 1000.

We assume that all the processors in the network $P_1, P_2, \ldots\ldots, P_m$ already have Sequence x and Sequence y in their local memories, or they can be initialized in this way. To carry the process of sequence alignment in a multiprocessor environment one of the way will be by keeping a copy of the sequences in the local memory.

LOAD SCHEDULING STRATEGIES AND ANALYSIS

The distribution strategy for the S matrix is given by a matrix consisting of 0's and 1's so it does not have any special kind of distribution. The M matrix is partitioned into sub matrices like $M_{p,q}$ where p= 1,2,...m and q= 1,2,...z where each portion of Seq x and Seq y is contained in one particular cell of the matrix M. This assignment can be explained as shown in the Figure 4. The distribution pattern is as shown in figures 4 and 5.

According to the Needleman-Wunsch Algorithm the last row will be calculated first. So the last row is given to the first processor or the root node of the system. In accordance with the Needleman-Wunsch Algorithm the timing diagram is as shown in Figure 6.

The generalized equations are as shown below. The two sequences can be divided into a number of smaller parts. This can be explained from the example given below. Let us consider that sequence Seq x and Seq y are where,Seq x = GCCTCSeq y = GCTAC

Figure 4. Illustration of the computational dependency of the element (p,q) in the M matrix

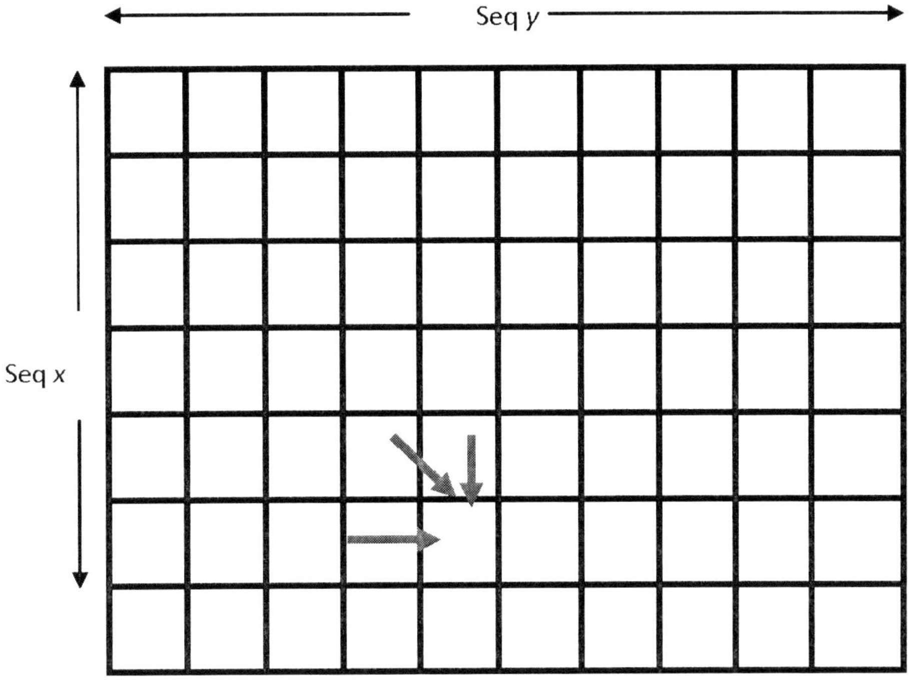

The length of Seq x is 5 and length of Seq y is 5. There for the total length should be 5. From the above example we can write the generalized equations as shown in equation (1).

$$x_1 + x_2 + x_3 + \ldots\ldots + x_{n-1} + x_n = x$$
$$y_1 + y_2 + y_3 + \ldots\ldots + y_{n-1} + y_n = y \qquad (1)$$

From the timing diagram we can derive the generalized equation for the load on each processor is given in the equation (2).

$$\sum_{n=2}^{m} x_n = x_{n-1} y_{n-1} E_{n-1} - 2C_{n-1} x_{n-1} / y_n E_n \qquad (2)$$

The load that is given to the first processor or the root node is given by equation (3).

$$x_1 = x / [1 + \sum_{n=2}^{m} [y_1 E_1 - 2C_1] / y_n E_n] \qquad (3)$$

The total completion time for the alignment of the two sequences can be given by

Figure 5. Illustration of Load Distribution

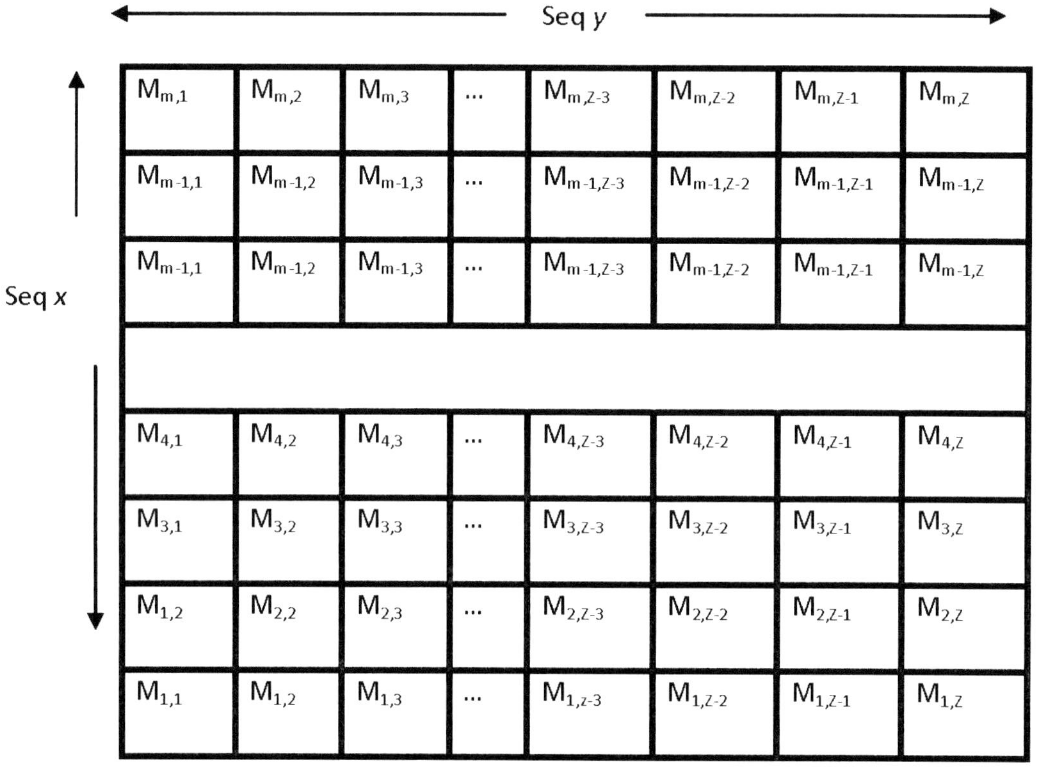

$$T(m) = xyE_1 + \Sigma \sum_{i=2}^{m} E_i + 2C(m-1) \quad (4)$$

To enhance the understanding of the performance of Needleman-Wunsch Algorithm and divisible load strategy a single machine has been used (Wong Han Min., & Bharadwaj Veeravalli, 2005). Therefore the speedup, can be given bySpeedup= T(1)/ T(m) (5)where T(m) is the processing time of our strategy on a system using m-processors. T(1) is the processing time using a single processor and is given byT(1)=xyE$_1$ (6)

RESULTS AND DISCUSSION

This section presents the evaluation of the results of load scheduling for sequence alignment technique. The results have been tabulated for the single level tree network that has constant link speed and also variable link speed. In the experimental results the sequence lengths have been varied from 100 to 1000 characters.

Figure 6. Timing diagram

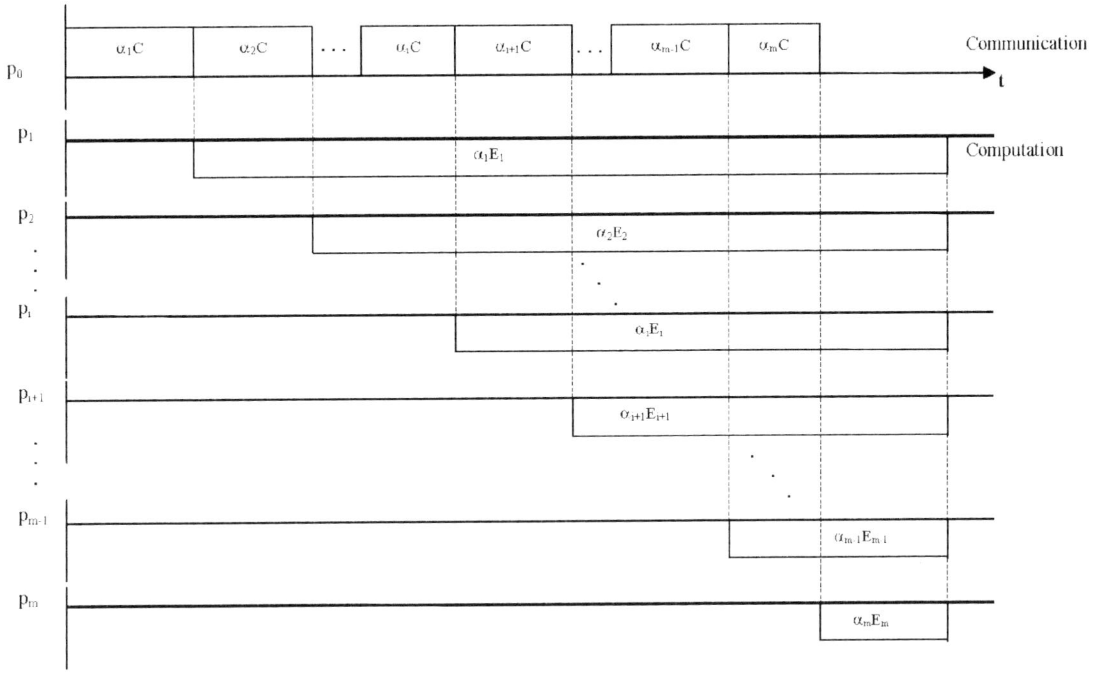

Figure 7. Variable link speed

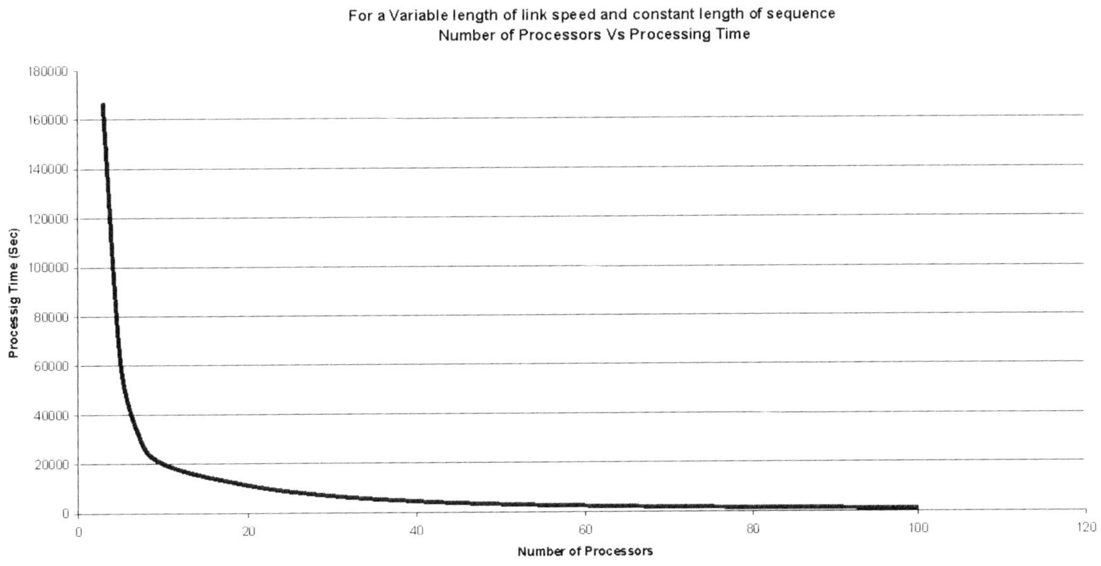

Figure 8. Variable link speed 3-D graph

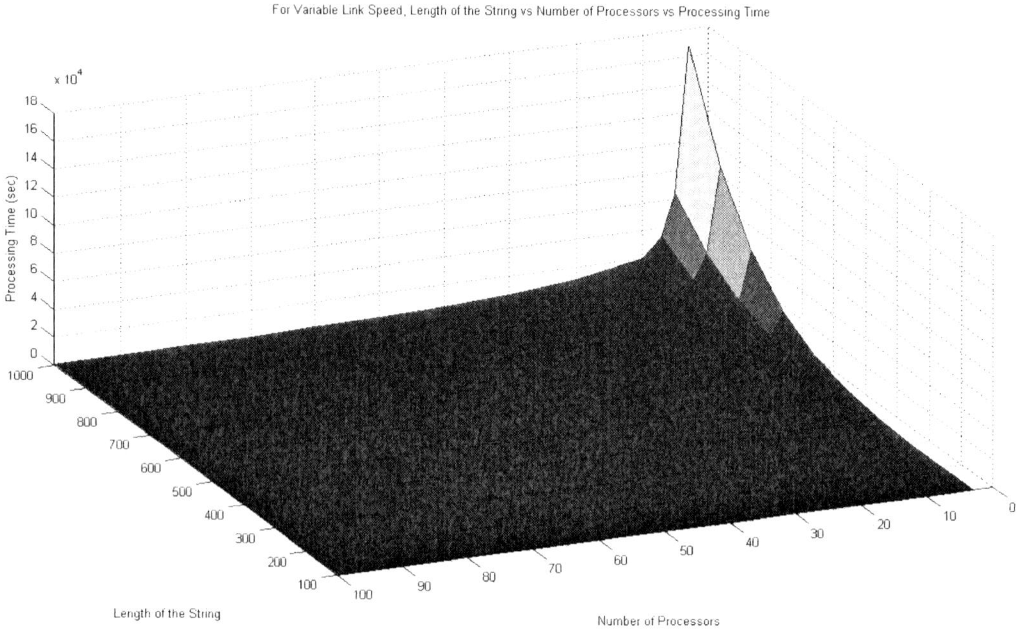

Table 1. Processing time variations for variable link speed

Number of processors	Processing Time (Sec)
3	166915.49
5	62671.53
7	33498.78
10	20163.56
20	11250.11
30	6804.34
40	4493.82
50	3186.41
60	2387.78
70	1868.71
80	1514.16
90	1262.08
100	1076.88

Figure 9. Graph for Variable Link Speed

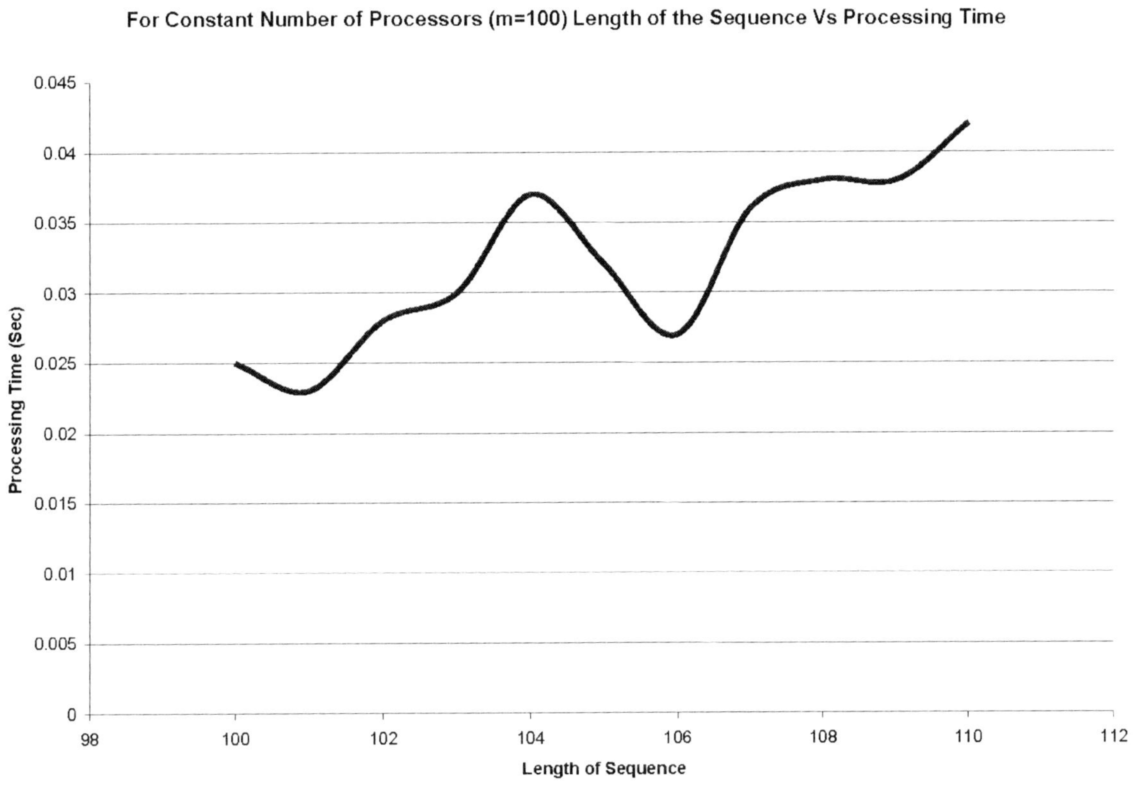

Variable Link Speed

This section briefly discusses about how does the processing time changes when the link speed has been varied. The graphs have been plotted for two ranges of link speed variations. Experiments have been conducted for variable link speed where link speed has been varied from 1-10 nanoseconds and 1-100 nanoseconds. From the graphs it can be observed that the processing time depends on the communication link speed C. In other words, the higher the link speed of the network the faster is the job processing. The link speed has been varied using the Random Generator method in java. The results and the tabulated values are as shown in the Figure 7, Figure 8 and Table 1.

The tabular column related to the table present below represents the graph for "Number of Processors Vs Processing time" with X-axis as the number of processors and Y-axis as the Processing Time. This graph has been plotted for a constant sequence length of 1000. From the figure 7 it has been observed that for a constant sequence length as the number of processors increase the computation time decreases This also reemphasizes the definition of DLT that as more number of processors are added into the network the processing time decreases.

Figure 8 demonstrates the 3-D representation of how the processing time varies with respect to the length of the sequence and number of processors. From the 3-D graph of the single processor tree network it can be observed that keeping the length of the sequence constant as the number of processors increase the processing time decreases. On the other hand it can also be observed that as the numbers of

Figure 10. Graph for constant link speed

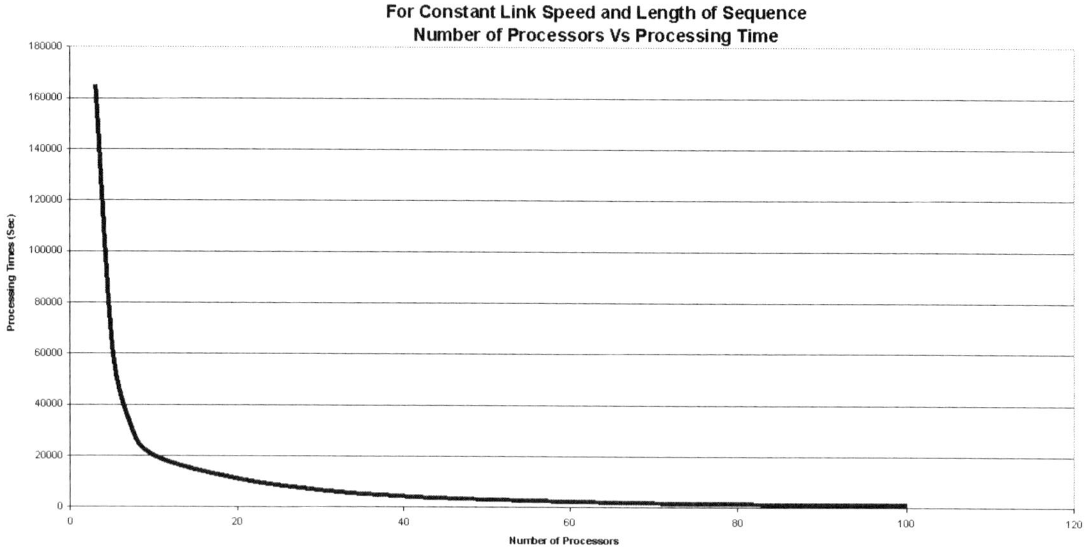

processors are kept constant and the length of sequences increases and the computation time increases. As discussed in the Problem Formulation chapter, the speedup has been calculated and the values are tabulated as shown for a constant sequence length of 1000.

Figure 9 represents the graph for "Length of sequence Vs Processing Time" for a constant number

Figure 11. 3-D graph for constant link speed

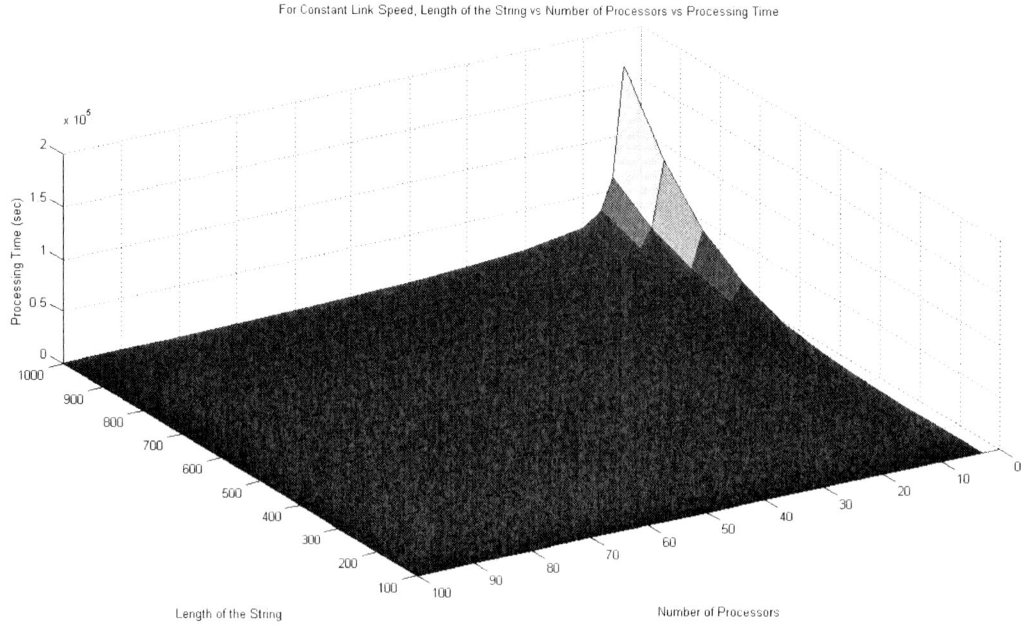

Table 2. Processing time variations for constant link speed

Number of processors	Processing Time (Sec)
3	165000
5	62500
7	33400
10	20100
20	11200
30	6790
40	4480
50	3170
60	2380
70	1864
80	1511
90	1250
100	1074

of processors (m=100), in which X-axis represents the length of sequence and Y-axis represents the Processing Time. According to divisible load theory for a constant number of processors as the length of sequence increases the processing time increases because each processors in the system has more load on it. But from the graph we can say that the processing time is not constantly increasing. This can be attributed to the communication link, as the processing time is dependent on the communication link speed. From the results it can be concluded the greater the communication link speed the lesser the processing time for the sequences.

Constant Link Speed

The variation of the processing time vary when the link speed has been varied. In the graphs shown below in Figure 10 and Figure 11, the link speed(C) has been taken as 5 nanoseconds. The results have been discussed as shown below.

Figure 10 represents the graph for "Number of Processors Vs Processing time" with X-axis as the number of processors and Y-axis as the Processing Time. This graph has been plotted for a constant sequence length of 1000. From the graph it has been observed that for a constant sequence length as the number of processors increase the computation time decreases This adds strength to the definition of DLT that as more number of processors are added into the network the processing time decreases

Figure 11 demonstrates the 3-D representation of how the processing time varies with respect to the length of the sequence and number of processors. From the 3-D graph of the single processor tree network it has been observed that keeping the length of the sequence constant as the number of processors increase the processing time decreases. On the other hand it has also been observed that as the numbers of processors are kept constant and the length of sequences increases the computation time increases. As discussed in the Methodology chapter, the speedup has been calculated and the values are tabulated as shown for a constant sequence length of 1000.

Figure 12. Number of processors vs. processing time for a constant length of sequence

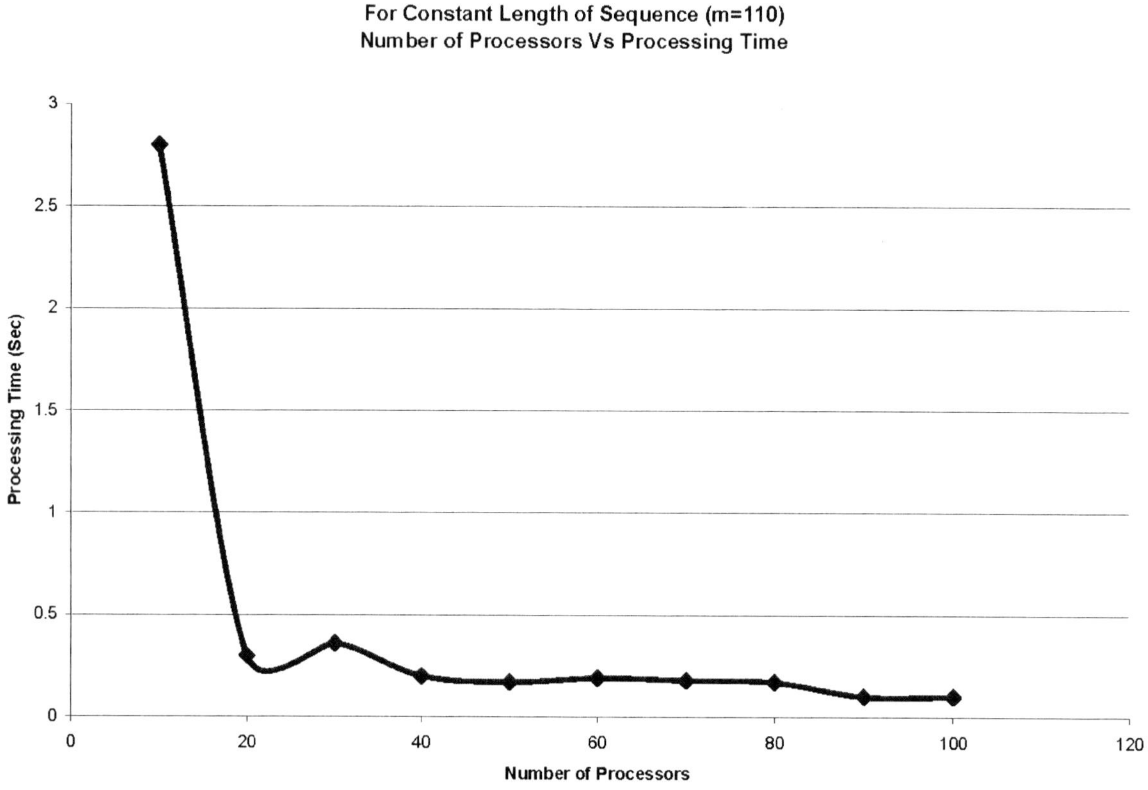

Figure 12 represents the graph for "Number of Processors Vs Processing Time" for a constant length of sequence, in which X-axis represents the number of processors and Y-axis represents the Processing Time. According to divisible load theory for a constant length of sequence as the number of processors increases the processing time should decrease, as more number of processors is being added to the system the load should be distributed among all of them. But from the graph it can be observed that the processing time is not constantly decreasing. This can be attributed to the communication link speed, as the processing time is dependent on the communication link speed. The greater the communication link speed, the lesser the processing time

CONCLUSION

This chapter presented a method for the alignment of two biological sequences following divisible load scheduling paradigm (DLT). A parallel solution in a single level tree network has been proposed and the communication delays are assumed to be non zero. We adopted the Needleman-Wunsch algorithm for aligning two biological sequences. Following Divisible Load Theory (DLT) we can determine the number of residues that should be assigned to each processor in the network.

The approach presented in this chapter is as follows. First we had a matrix S which is a matrix of order x*y where x is the length of the first sequence and y is the length of the second sequence. Then we derived the M matrix which will give the final values and depending on that we can align the sequences. We derived the equations that will determine the size of the sub matrices according to the processor speeds where here it is assumed that all processors have equal speeds and the communication speeds are varied. With these constraints the equations have been derived and the graphs have been plotted.

We evaluated the performance by varying the communication link speed from 10-100 nanoseconds and for a constant link speed of 5 nanoseconds. First, we considered the performance of our strategy when the communication link has been maintained at a constant value of 5 nanoseconds. The results clearly demonstrated that the processing time decreased constantly for a constant number of processors for a constant length of sequence. Then the communication link speed has been varied from 10-100 nanoseconds and the performance has been observed. From the graph it can be observed that for a variable link speed the computation time decreases for a constant length of sequence. In certain cases the behavior of the graph was not uniform; this explains that the communication link plays a major role in the processing time of the sequence alignment.

Extensions to this work can be deriving solutions that will further decrease the computation speed. This can be achieved by applying multi-installment strategy and performing the analysis using the Needleman-Wunsch Algorithm. The same problem of aligning biological sequences can be applied to various types of networks. The alignment of biological sequences can be solved using the Sellers algorithm (Michael Huerta, Florence Haseltine, and Yuan Liu, 2000) and the load distribution strategy. Further work can also be carried out on aligning multiple sequences with various types of clustering strategies. The same strategy of aligning sequences can be further extended to aligning multiple sequences using the algorithm like Berger-Munson algorithm (Berger M.P., & Munson P. J., 1991).

REFERENCES

Altschul, G. W., M. W, Myers., & Lipman. (1990). Basic local alignment search tool. *Journal of Molecular Biology*, *215*(3), 403–410.

Autenrieth., F., Isralewitz, B., Luthey-Schulten., Z., Sethi, A. & Pogorelov, T. *Bioinformatics and Sequence Alignment*.

Bataineh, S., Hsiung, T.-Y., & Robertazzi, T. (1994). Closed form solutions for bus and tree networks of processors load sharing a divisible job. *Institute of Electrical and Electronic Engineers*, *43*(10), 1184–119.

Benson, D. A., Karsch-Mizrachi, I., Lipman, D. J., Ostell, J., Rapp, B. A., & Wheller, D. L. (2000, October). Genbank. *Nucleic Acids Research*, *28*(1), 15–18. doi:10.1093/nar/28.1.15

Berger, M. P., & Munson, P. J. (1991). A novel randomized iteration strategy for aligning multiple protein sequences. *Computer Applications in the Biosciences*, *7*, 479–484.

Bharadwaj, V., Ghose, D., & Mani, V. (1995, April). Multi-installment load distribution in tree network with delays. *Institute of Electrical and Electronic Engineers*, *31*(2), 555–567.

Bharadwaj, V., Ghose, D., & Robertazzi, T. G. (2003, January). Divisible load theory: A new paradigm for load scheduling in distributed systems. *Cluster Computing*, *6*(1), 7–17. doi:10.1023/A:1020958815308

Cristianini, N., & Hahn, M. (2006). *Introduction to Computational Genomics*. Cambridge, UK: Cambridge University Press.

Drodowski, M., Lawenda, M., & Guinand, F. (2006). Scheduling multiple divisible loads. *International Journal of High Performance Computing Applications*, *20*(1), 19–30. doi:10.1177/1094342006061879

Drozdowski, M., & Lawenda, M. (2005). *On Optimum Multi-installment Divisible Load Processing in Heterogeneous Distributed Systems*, (LNCS 3648, pp. 231–240). Berlin: Springer.

Fourment, M., & Gillings, M. R. (2008, February). A comparison of common programming languages used in bioinformatics. *Bioinformatics (Oxford, England)*, 9.

Goad, W. B. (1987). Sequence analysis. *Los Alamos Science*, (Special Issue), 288–291.

Huerta, M. Haseltine, F., & Liu, Y. (2004, July). *Nih working definition of bioinformatics and computational biology.*

Jones, N. C. & Penvzner, P.A. (2004, August). *An Introduction to Bioinformatics Algorithms.*

Likic, V. (2000). *The needleman-wunsch algorithm for sequence alignment*. The University of Melbourne, Australia.

Min, W. H., & Veeravalli, B. (2005, December). Aligning biological sequences on distributed bus networks: a divisible load scheduling approach. *Institute of Electrical and Electronic Engineering*, *9*(4), 489–501.

Robertazzi, T. (2003). Ten reasons to use divisible load theory. *Institute of Electrical and Electronic Engineering*, *36*(5), 63–68.

Trelles, Andrade, & Valencia, Zapata, & Carazo. (1998, June). Computational space reduction and parallelization of a new clustering approach for large groups of sequences. *Bioinformatics (Oxford, England)*, *14*(5), 439–451. doi:10.1093/bioinformatics/14.5.439

Yap, T., Frieder, O., & Martino, R. (1998, March). Parallel computation in biological sequence analysis. *Institute of Electrical and Electronic Engineers*, *9*(3), 283–294.

KEY TERMS AND DEFINITIONS

Bioinformatics: Bioinformatics is the application of information technology to the field of molecular biology. *Bioinformatics* entails the creation and advancement of databases, algorithms, computational and statistical techniques, and theory to solve formal and practical problems arising from the management and analysis of biological data.

Cluster Computing: A computer cluster is a group of linked computers, working together closely so that in many respects they form a single computer. The components of a cluster are commonly, but not always, connected to each other through fast local area networks. Clusters are usually deployed to improve performance and/or availability over that provided by a single computer, while typically being much more cost-effective than single computers of comparable speed or availability.

Computational Biology: Computational biology refers to hypothesis-driven investigation of a biological problem using computers, carried out with experimental or simulated data, with the primary goal of discovery and the advancement of biological knowledge.

Computer Networks: A computer network is a group of interconnected computers. Networks may be classified according to a wide variety of characteristics.

Divisible Load Theory: Divisible load theory is a methodology involving the linear and continuous modeling of partitionable computation and communication loads for parallel processing

Parallel Computing: Parallel computing is a form of computation in which many calculations are carried out simultaneously, operating on the principle that large problems can often be divided into smaller ones, which are then solved concurrently .

Sequence Alignment: In bioinformatics, a sequence alignment is a way of arranging the primary sequences of DNA, RNA, or protein to identify regions of similarity that may be a consequence of functional, structural, or evolutionary relationships between the sequences.

ENDNOTE

1 http://www.ncbi.nlm.nih.gov/Genbank/

Chapter 37
Multi-Core Supported Deep Packet Inspection

Yang Xiang
Central Queensland University, Australia

Daxin Tian
Tianjin University, China

ABSTRACT

Network security applications such as intrusion detection systems (IDSs), firewalls, anti-virus/spyware systems, anti-spam systems, and security visualisation applications are all computing-intensive applications. These applications all heavily rely on deep packet inspection, which is to examine the content of each network packet's payload. Today these security applications cannot cope with the speed of broadband Internet that has already been deployed, that is, the processor power is much slower than the bandwidth power. Recently the development of multi-core processors brings more processing power. Multi-core processors represent a major evolution in computing hardware technology. While two years ago most network processors and personal computer microprocessors had single core configuration, the majority of the current microprocessors contain dual or quad cores and the number of cores on die is expected to grow exponentially over time. The purpose of this chapter is to discuss the research on using multi-core technologies to parallelize deep packet inspection algorithms, and how such an approach will improve the performance of deep packet inspection applications. This will eventually provide a security system the capability of real-time packet inspection thus significantly improve the overall status of security on current Internet infrastructure.

1. INTRODUCTION

Current Internet is facing many serious attacks such as financial frauds, viruses and worms, distributed denial of service attacks, spyware, and spam. Although many network security applications such as intrusion detection systems (IDS), anti-virus/spam systems, and firewalls have been proposed to control

DOI: 10.4018/978-1-60566-661-7.ch037

the attacks, securing distributed systems and networks is still extremely challenging. There are unknown threats and zero day attacks (exploits released before the vendor patch is released to the public) appearing everyday, which place an impractical burden on network security systems. The key question here is can we have real time solutions to identify and eliminate attacks without excessive security and management overhead overburdening the networks and computer systems? To deal with the rapidly evolving threats today and more intelligent and automatic threats in the future, we urgently need new methods that support network security applications, at all times and in real time, without causing performance penalty to normal network and system operations.

A multi-core processor combines two or more independent cores into a single package composed of a single integrated circuit (called a die), or more dies packaged together (Intel, 2007). Multi-core processors represent a major evolution in computing hardware technology. While two years ago most network processors and personal computer microprocessors had single core configuration, the majority of the current microprocessors contain dual or quad cores and the number of cores on die is expected to grow exponentially over time (Johnson & Welser, 2005). As the price of multi-core processors keeps falling, multi-core will eventually provide affordable processing power to support the real-time requirement of network security applications.

Multi-core provides a network security application with more processing power from the hardware perspective. However, there are still significant software design challenges that must be overcome. Today the difficulty is not in building multi-core hardware, but programming it in a way that lets applications benefit from the continued growth in CPU performance (Sutter & Larus, 2005). From the server or router side, if the network security software is not fast enough, it can be very difficult to process every incoming packet then it would slow down the traffic. From the client side, it can also be very difficult to run network security applications without any interruption to normal applications because those computing-intensive applications significantly slow down other simultaneously running applications.

Taking advantage of the full power of multi-core processor requires an in-depth approach to realize the speedups by parallelizing the traditional deep packet inspection applications. In this chapter we discuss the research direction of using multi-core processors to support real-time deep packet inspection applications. Section 2 introduces the related work in the parallel approaches to enhance the performance of deep packet inspection applications. Section 3 presents our new system architecture of using multi-core to support deep packet inspection applications. Section 4 presents the basic packet-level parallelization and flow-level parallelization. Section 5 presents a new parallel string matching algorithm. Benefits of using multi-core are discussed in Section 6. Section 7 concludes this chapter.

2. RELATED WORK

2.1 Development of Multi-Core Processors

In 1965, Gordon Moore observed an exponential growth in the number of transistors per integrated circuit and predicted that this trend would continue - a prediction today known as Moore's Law (Moore, 1965). In reality, the doubling of transistors every couple of years has been maintained for almost 40 years. However, scaling up the processor's frequency has been more difficult because of several constraints revealed recently. First, memory speeds are not increasing as quickly as processor's logic speeds. Now the processor takes more clock cycles to access memory than before. The wasted clock cycles can nullify the benefits of frequency increases in the processor. Second, manufacture difficulty has shown that smaller and denser transistors on chips need to be threaded together with ever-increasing lengths of wire interconnects. As these interconnects stretch from hundreds to thousands of meters in length on a single processor, path delays can offset the speed increases of the transistors. Finally, the power density problem has become an unsustainable problem. The number of transistors per chip has significantly increased in recent years. The power consumption and generated heat have been a serious problem for processors.

Instead of developing chips that can run faster, processor designers are adding more cores and more cache to provide comparable or better performance at lower power. Additional transistors are being leveraged to create more diverse capability, such as virtualization technology or security features as opposed to driving to higher clock speeds. Multi-core processors are clocked at slower speeds and supplied with lower voltage to yield greater performance per watt.

The development of multi-core processors has a significant impact on software applications. To take advantage of multi-core, software requires migration to a multi-threaded software model and necessitates incremental validation and performance tuning. Although kernel or system threads managed by the operating system can enhance the application performance, it is essential to have multiple user threads maintained by programmers to improve the performance of traditional applications.

2.2 Parallel Network Security Applications on Multi-Core Processors

As the Internet traffic volumes and rates continue to race forward, it has become difficult for network security applications to process network packets in real-time. Many network security applications nowadays can process network packets at Mbps level. However, most network backbones and many local network interfaces operate at Gbps level. To improve the performance of the network security applications, most previous research focus on parallelism with the hardware approaches such as ASICs and FPGAs (Dharmapurikar, Krishnamurthy, Sproull, & Lockwood, 2004; Hayes & Luo, 2007; Liu, Zheng, Liu, Zhang, & Liu, 2006; Piyachon & Luo, 2006; Villa, Scarpazza, & Petrini, 2008). They require highly deliberate and customized programming, which is directly at odds with the pressing need to perform diverse, increasingly sophisticated forms of analysis. In (Paxson et al., 2006) the authors argued that it is time to fundamentally rethink the nature of using hardware to support network security applications.

Previously, efforts in multi-core software design has been primarily on simultaneous multithreading (SMT) (Eggers et al., 1997; Tullsen, Lo, Eggers, & Levy, 1999) at a low level, which permits multiple independent threads of execution to better utilize the resources provided by microprocessor architectures. Most of current research is still focused on automatically mapping general-purpose applications onto multi-core systems with instruction, data, or thread level parallelization techniques (Sohi, Breach, & Vijaykumar, 1995; Taylor et al., 2004; Yan & Zhang, 2007) or relying on virtualization technologies such as VMware (WMware, 2008). Most of them are essentially extensions of utilizing shared-memory multiprocessors and can only execute coarse-grained threads. Network security applications have their own unique behavioral characteristics such as frequent memory or disk access, complex data structures, and high bandwidth and high speed requirements. There is a distinct mismatch between current multi-core hardware development and high performance demand from network security applications. There has been very little preliminary research done in this area (Paxson, Sommer, & Weaver, 2007; Qi et al., 2007). In short, there is an imperative need for specifically re-designing network security applications from a software perspective based on multi-core hardware architecture.

2.3 Parallel Deep Packet Inspection

Deep packet inspection refers to the process of checking packet payload and header in a network device. The applications of deep packet inspection include, for example, network security applications that filter out packets containing certain malicious Internet worms or computer viruses; content-based billing systems that analyze media files and bill the receiver based on the material transferred over the network; and content forwarding applications that look at the hypertext transport protocol headers and distribute the requests among the servers for load balancing (Dharmapurikar et al., 2004). Contrastingly, shallow packet inspection refers to the process of only checking packet header in a network device. Deep packet inspection requires much more processing power than shallow packet inspection.

Most deep packet inspection applications have a common requirement for string matching. For example, the presence of a string of certain byte sequences in packet payloads can identify the presence of a virus, such as the well-known Internet worms Nimda, Code Red, and Slammer. One requirement of deep packet inspection applications is that the applications must be able to detect strings of different lengths starting at arbitrary locations in the packet payload because the location of such strings in the packet payload and their length is normally unknown. The other requirement of deep packet inspection applications is that they must be able to process network packets at line speed, otherwise it will causes the delay of network traffic, or the incompleteness of deep packet inspection.

Dharmapurikar (Dharmapurikar et al., 2004) described a technique based on Bloom filters for detecting predefined signatures (a string of bytes) in the packet payload. A Bloom filter is a data structure for representing a set of strings in order to support membership queries. It used parallel hardware Bloom filters to isolate all packets that potentially contain predefined signatures. Another independent process eliminates false positives produced by Bloom filters. The authors implemented a prototype system in a Xilinx XCV2000E FPGA, using the Field-Programmable Port Extender (FPX) platform.

Finite state machine approach is another popular method in deep packet inspection. Tripp (Tripp, 2006) described a finite state machine approach to string matching for an intrusion detection system. By splitting the search strings into multiple interleaved substrings and by combining the outputs from the individual finite state machines in an appropriate way it can perform string matching in parallel across multiple finite state machines. A VHDL model of a string matching engine based on the above ideas has been developed on a Xilinx XC2V250-6 FPGA and tested via simulation. This implementation is capable of matching up to 27 search strings in parallel, depending on the length of the strings.

3. SYSTEM DESIGN

The idea of using multi-core processors to enhance the performance of network security applications is promising. However, the research in this area is just emerging and thus requires intensive exploration. It faces many challenges such as

- How can we actually use multi-core to continue running the network security applications while keeping the overall system performance?
- How can we efficiently partition and distribute the workload of network security applications between the different cores in the multi-core processor?
- How can we split network data and solve the data dependency problem?

Figure 1. System architecture of using multi-core processors to support deep packet inspection

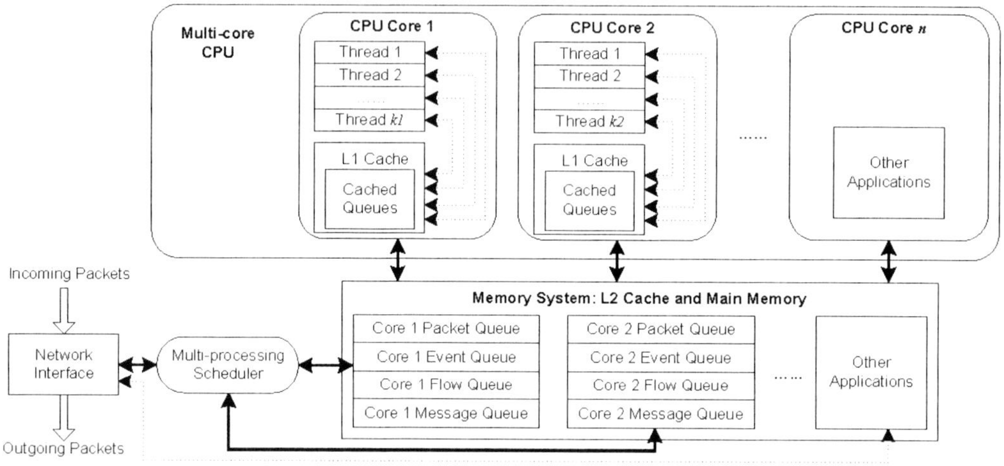

- As multi-core uses shared off-chip memory, how can we smartly utilize the memory then it will bring less memory access latencies?
- How can we synchronize and coordinate different threads of the applications when it is parallelized on multi-core?

To best solve these challenges, we propose the new system architecture as in figure 1. The essential ability of this architecture is that it can process network packets in parallel and thus meet the real-time requirement. As is shown in the figure, the multi-processing scheduler coordinates and distributes the workload to different cores. The information from packets, events, flows, and messages are processed in the multi-core processor in parallel. The processor has spare cores to run other applications.

As is illustrated in Figure 1, the proposed architecture must be able to process network packets at line speed. In another words, it must keep its performance in normal applications, such as forwarding packets in a router. To fully utilize the potential of multi-core, this system architecture will use different level of parallelization such as instruction-level parallelization, memory parallelization, loop-level parallelization, and fine-grained thread-level parallelization. High performance can be achieved through interaction between algorithms, strategies, and architectural design, from high-level decisions on data allocation and task partitioning to low-level micro-architectural decisions on instruction selection and scheduling. For each network security application, we also need to identify what the potential bottlenecks are and how to possibly avoid them. The potential bottlenecks could be packet processing, data normalization, data correlation, pattern generation, and pattern matching in such a parallel computing environment.

4. PACKET-LEVEL AND FLOW-LEVEL PARALLELIZATIONS

As the instance of the aforementioned multi-core based deep packet inspection architecture, we test two levels of parallelization on multi-core: packet level and flow-level parallelization. As current network traffic speeds and volume are increasing at an exponential rate, the processing speed required by a deep

Figure 2. Experiment environment

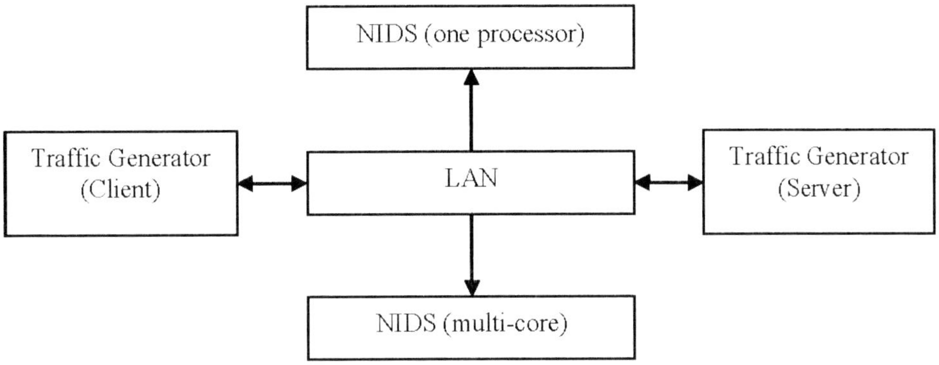

packet inspection application is high. In this experiment, we evaluate the performance of multi-core parallel deep packet inspection methods based on Snort (Roesch, 1999), an open source intrusion detection system. The test environment is shown in Figure 2. To simulate the large volumes of network traffic, network traffic generator is used to test the capability of the intrusion detection system Snort to handle continuous high traffic loads. We use TG2.0 (McKenney, Lee, & Denny, 2008) to generate high volumes of network traffic. A dual-core computer with a 2.26GHz Intel Pentium processor and 512MB RAM is used in the experiment. The network adaptors used are 10/100M PCI Ethernet adaptors.

We first use the packet-level parallelization to evaluate the multi-core supported intrusion detection system's performance on deep packet inspection. The TG's client is set to open a UDP socket to send packets to the TG server waiting at 192.168.10.1 and port 4322, with packet data length being 576 and packet number is 2000. On the multi-core system, the odd number packets are processed by one core and the even number packets are processed by another core. The detailed procedure is specified in the basic algorithm as follows.

The testing results under different inter-packet transmission time (0.02 seconds equals 1/0.02=50 packets/sec) is shown in Figure 4, and the dropping rate (the percentage of dropped packets in all packets) is shown in Figure 5. Because the system needs to capture the incoming packets from the network adapter and analyze these packets for possible attacks, depending on the packet capturing and analyzing

Figure 3. Algorithm of packet-level parallelization

```
Algorithm 1: Packet-level parallelization
 n: the number of parallel threads;
        int i=0; all the threads start;
        While (true)
        {
                get a packet from the network interface;
                i++;
                if (i>n)
                        i=1;
                send the packet to the ith thread;
        }
```

Figure 4. The number of packet analyzed on packet-level parallelization

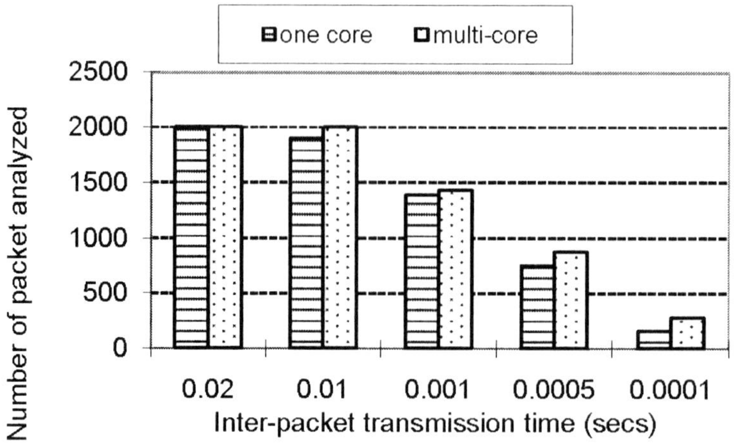

speed (processing speed), and the speed of incoming packets (network speed), the system may be able to process all incoming packets, or have to drop some packets. If the processing speed is slower than the network speed (this may happen when the system is under heavy load), the system may drop some packets thus may lose some useful information, which will increase false positive and false negative rate. The figures show the trend that if the system is parallelized at packet-level by using more than one core, the dropping rate can be slightly decreased. The number of analyzed packets thus can also be slightly increased. This proves that multi-core can increase the processing speed of the whole system.

For packet-level parallelization to be practical, no resource should actually share common information across separate packets. Although deep packet inspection applications like Snort receive input packet-by-packet, they must aggregate distinct packets into flows such as TCP streams to prevent an attacker from disguising malicious communications by breaking the data up across several packets. Since packets

Figure 5. Dropping rate on packet-level parallelization

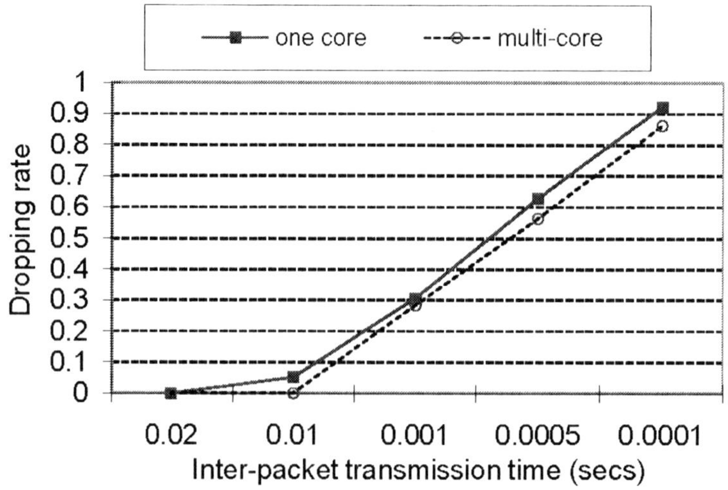

Figure 6. Algorithm of flow-level parallelization

```
Algorithm 2: Flow-level parallelization
 n: the number of parallel threads;
        all the threads start;
        While (true)
        {
                get a packet from the network interface;
                read the source address, destination address, source port, destination port;
                if (these arguments' value is same to one record maintained by one thread)
                        if (the packet's sequence number is continue with the record)
                                send the packet to that thread;
                        else
                        send the packet to the thread which has least load;
        }
```

from one flow will not affect the states of another flow, different flows can be processed by independent processing threads with no constraints on ordering. To test the flow-level parallelization performance on multi-core, we conduct another experiment based on flow-level parallelization.

One TG's client is set to open a UDP socket to send packets to the TG server waiting at 192.168.10.1 and port 4322, with packet data length being 576 and packet number is 1000, another TG's client is set to open a UDP socket to send packets to the TG server waiting at 10.10.10.1 and port 5322, with packet data length being 576 and packet number is 1000. The two Snorts running on the multi-core processor are set to one analyzes the packets relative to the 192.168.10.0 class C network, and another analyzes the 10.10.10.0 class C network. The detailed procedure is specified in algorithm 2 in Figure 6.

The testing results are shown in Figure 7 and Figure 8. From the experiments we find that the flow-level parallelization based on multi-core has higher speed to analyze packets than single-core system. However, the double core system does not achieve double speedups. The experiment proves that the parallel strategies can improve the deep packet inspection performance. From the comparison between packet-level parallelization and flow-level parallelization we also find that flow-based parallelization has similar performance speedups as packet-level parallelization. However, it is a practical solution to meaningfully examine each packet in real deep packet inspection applications.

5. PARALLEL STRING-MATCHING

In the above experiments we find that the parallel algorithms at packet-level and flow-level running on multi-core can minimize the number of dropped packets thus potentially increase the detection rate. In this chapter we do not discuss the detection rate measurement because it does not depend on just the parallel algorithms employed but also the intelligent algorithms used, such as neural networks, finite state machine, and so on. The improvement of performance on detection rate brought by multi-core can be found in our other papers (Chonka, Zhou, Knapp, & Xiang, 2008; Tian & Xiang, 2008).

Parallel deep packet inspection applications face the following challenges: distributed network traffic over several hosts while avoiding overloading any of the cores; the traffic distribution scheme should

Figure 7. The number of packet analyzed on flow-level parallelization

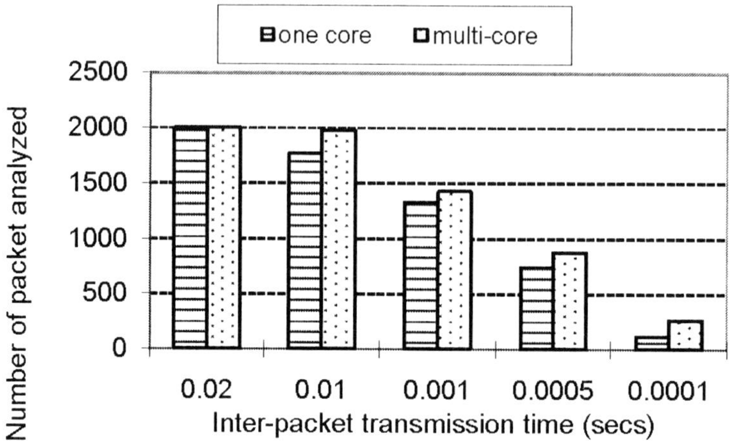

not negatively impact the application's ability to perform packet inspection. The deep packet inspection applications must be able to check the incoming payload against a rule set which contains the threat signatures. However, given the growing number of rules, these applications are becoming more difficult to perform inspections in real-time without fast string matching mechanisms. In this section, we evaluate another parallel mechanism which pays more attention on fast multiple string matching.

Currently many string matching algorithms have been widely used in different applications. It is used in data filtering and data mining to find selected patterns, for example, from a stream of newsfeed; it is used in security applications to detect certain suspicious keywords, for example, in Snort; it is used in DNA searching by translating an approximate search to a search for a large number of exact patterns, and so on. Among them, Aho-Corasick algorithm (Aho & Corasick, 1975) is a linear-time algorithm for this problem, based on an automata approach. The drawback of this automata approach is the large amount of memory space it requires. Aho-Corasick algorithm and its extensions deal well with regular

Figure 8. Dropping rate on flow-level parallelization

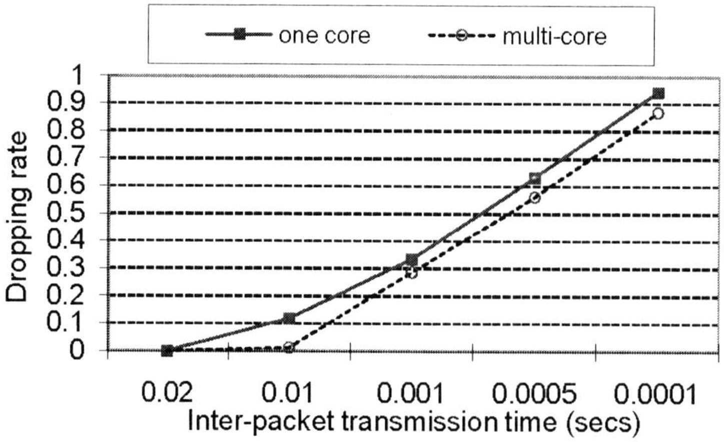

Figure 9. Algorithm of parallel string matching

```
Algorithm 3: Parallel string matching
 n: the number of parallel threads;
        participate the whole rule set into n subsets;
        send ith subset to ith thread to build the automaton;
        While (true)
        {
                get a packet from the network interface;
                read the packet load and send it to each thread;
                each thread search patterns in the payload;
        }
```

expression matching, but if the keyword set is larger, they are not practical because of its large number of states.

Aho-Corasick algorithm constructs a trie with suffix tree-like set of links from each node representing a string (e.g. *abc*) to the node corresponding to the longest proper suffix (e.g. *bc* if it exists, else *c* if that exists, else the root). It also contains links from each node to the longest suffix node that corresponds to a dictionary entry; thus all of the matches may be enumerated by following the resulting linked list. It then uses the trie at runtime, moving along the input and keeping the longest match, using the suffix links to make sure that computation is linear. For every node that is in the dictionary and every link along the dictionary suffix linked list, an output is generated.

Parallel string matching offers a scalable method for inspecting packets in a high speed network environment. But these parallel methods typically distribute the arriving packets evenly across the array of processors, each having a copy of the complete policy. Given the rising number of rules, for example the Snort contains more than thousands of rules, it follows that, for each packet, much more signature strings need to be checked against the payload of the packet. To the multiple string matching algorithms, such as Aho-Corasick algorithm, it not only requires a significant amount of memory for the state machine and preprocessing, but also increases content matching time, thus can not be sufficient for the high speed networks.

In this experiment we first partition the pattern string sets into small sets, then build the Aho-Corasick automatons on each small set, and last run the matching algorithm in parallel. The detailed procedure is specified in algorithm 3 in Figure 9 and Figure 10.

We evaluate the performance of the parallel string matching algorithm and compare it with the original Aho-Corasick algorithm. To test the performance of the parallel string matching algorithm, the size of pattern set is 1000, and the length of each pattern is from 3 to 33 characters; the size of the test data is 3953KB. The original and parallel Aho-Corasick algorithms run on the Linux OS. We test the performance under different set numbers. If the set number is *k*, we partition the pattern set into *k* groups and each group contains 1000/*k* strings. The results are shown in Table 1, Table 2, Table 3, and Table 4.

In each table, the state number reflects the amount of the consumed memory. As the multi-core supports thread level parallelization, using multiple threads can significant reduce the consumed time for string matching. Parallel mechanisms can also reduce the time for automaton building. The total state numbers of parallel algorithms are shown in Figure 11. The speed of one parallel algorithm is decided by the pattern string set *i* which finishes the searching process lastly. Total time comparison is shown

Figure 10. The progress of parallel Aho-Corasick algorithm

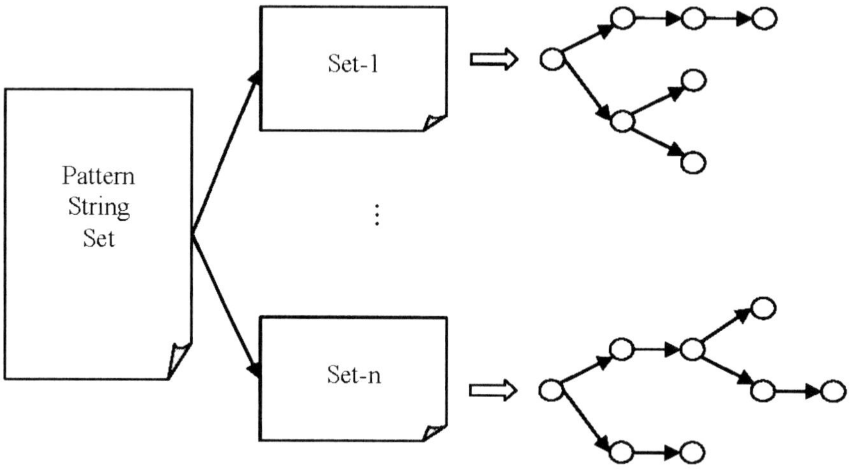

Table 1. One thread algorithm

	Automaton Building	String Matching	State Number	Total Time
Thread 1	404.86ms	12756.67ms	3519	13161.53ms

Table 2. Two parallel threads algorithm

	Automaton Building	String Matching	State Number	Total Time
Thread 1	79.49ms	8013.18ms	3060	8092.67ms
Thread 2	102.46ms	7405.39ms	3509	7507.85ms

Table 3. Four parallel threads algorithm

	Automaton Building	String Matching	State Number	Total Time
Thread 1	41.24ms	2843.80ms	2216	2885.04ms
Thread 2	72.14ms	2811.93ms	2978	2884.07ms
Thread 3	59.34ms	2942.18ms	2224	3001.52ms
Thread 4	57.83ms	2568.61ms	3211	2626.44ms

Table 4. Eight parallel threads algorithm

	Automaton Building	String Matching	State Number	Total Time
Thread 1	18.13ms	1538.62ms	1073	1556.75ms
Thread 2	16.04ms	1415.35ms	1347	1431.39ms
Thread 3	18.56ms	1294.76ms	1448	1313.32ms
Thread 4	39.85ms	1624.30ms	1749	1664.15ms
Thread 5	18.26ms	1454.73ms	1175	1472.99ms
Thread 6	33.98ms	1611.35ms	1390	1645.33ms
Thread 7	18.37ms	1439.90ms	1402	1458.27ms
Thread 8	21.98ms	1276.07ms	2004	1298.05ms

Figure 11. The total state numbers

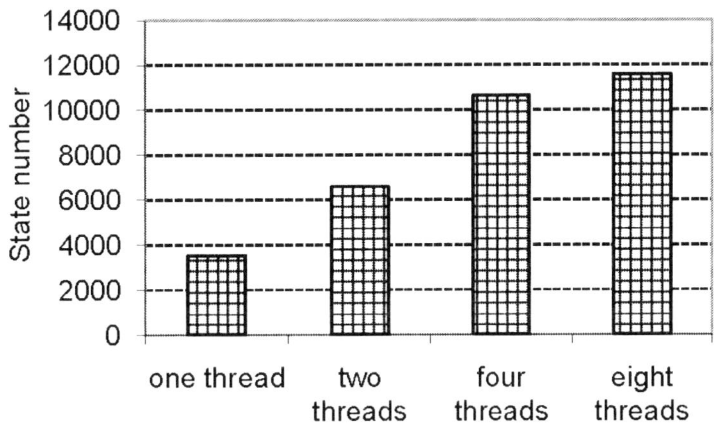

Figure 12. The total time

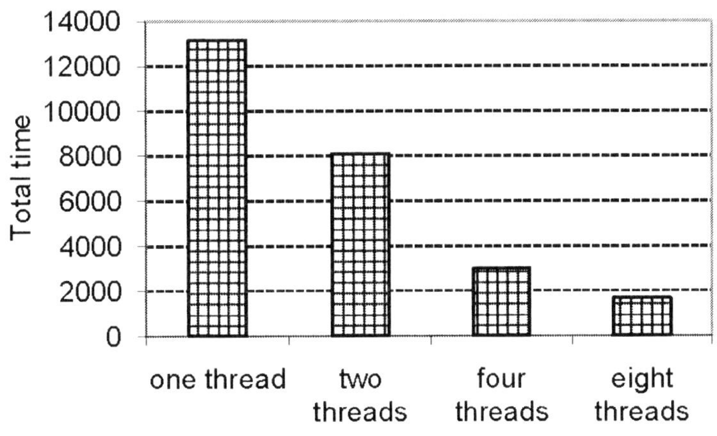

in Figure 12. From the results we find that this multi-core supported parallel mechanism can speed up Aho-Corasick string matching algorithm significantly.

6. DEEPER THINKING OF USING MULTI-CORE

From the above evaluation results we find there are many benefits to use multi-core to support deep packet inspection applications. We summarize the benefits of using multi-core supported system architecture in deep packet inspection applications as high performance, comprehensive, intelligent, and scalable.

Firstly, traditional deep packet inspection applications are based on serial or very limited parallel execution of packet processing (Dharmapurikar et al., 2004). For example, traditional single-threaded network-based intrusion detection systems log activities that it finds to a safeguarded database and detects if the events match any malicious event recorded in the knowledge base. It must read packet level information and process it on the processor in serial. Traditional anti-virus systems and network visualizes also heavily rely on serially reading packets, files, or logged data. The serial execution performance largely depends on the clock frequency of a single CPU, which has not been improved much in recent years. Therefore, they cannot process large amount of packets in real-time. If we can parallelize them at application level instead of relying on operating system level parallelization, then the workload of network security applications can be distributed to different cores to achieve high performance, in terms of latency, throughput, and CPU utilization.

Secondly, multi-core supported deep packet inspection applications can provide comprehensive protection against different threats. Currently, if a router performs deep packet inspection, for example, to check a certain virus signature in the packet's payload, its forwarding capability will be significantly affected. Most network providers cannot afford to slow down traffic to perform such security operations. Another fact is that current computer systems can only separately run a single network security application at a time because these computing-intensive network security applications exclusively occupy CPU time. With the support from multi-core and application level parallelization, these computing tasks can be divided into many threads and distributed to different cores for processing. Thus if we have enough cores, the network security applications will then be virtually invisible to users because other applications still have free cores to perform their tasks. This enables comprehensive protection as it can integrate as many modules (such as intrusion detection module, anti-virus module, and anti-spam module) as necessary.

Thirdly, with the support from multi-core, deep packet inspection applications will have greatly improved intelligence compared to traditional applications because we can employ many computing-intensive methods to perform packet inspection and classification and anomaly detection. In (Xiang & Zhou, 2006) we have tested the performance of using neural network to detect attack packets with the aid of packet marking schemes. It has advantages such as high detection rate and low false positive rate because it relies on more intelligent method rather than signature matching. However, it also has the limitation of long training time, thus it cannot provide real-time protection. How to improve the performance of the intrusion detection system by utilizing the power of multi-core becomes critical to have a high-intelligent deep packet inspection application.

Lastly, multi-core supported deep packet inspection applications are scalable. They can be used on not only network level devices but also end host level devices. As we know, pure network-based security applications cannot fully capture the profile of each end host. Therefore in order to achieve the best protection, security checks must be performed on both network processing devices and end hosts. Many tasks that must be done on infrastructure level computing nodes before can now be moved to the far end of personal computers, which not only alleviate the load of the information infrastructure but also make the security check more meaningful. On the other side, many tasks that must be done on end host level before can now be performed at the infrastructure level, such as checking virus signatures, which can effectively prevent the propagation of malicious codes from reaching the end hosts. They are also customizable according to their scalability for different requirements because switching different parallel applications on or off becomes easy with the support from multi-core.

7. CONCLUSION

In this chapter we present new multi-core supported deep packet inspection architecture and an instance of the architecture. Leveraging the power of multi-core processors can be the answer to many yet-unsolved but crucial challenges in deep packet inspection applications such as isolated security environment, real-time attack detection and attack packets filtering, and real-time visualization of network monitoring. It enables sophisticated and stateful network processing rich in semantics and context as a routine capability provided by a network's routers. The use of multi-core will support flexible recompilation of security software but rather than redesign of hardware. It will provide significant benefits to the security of future distributed networks and systems.

REFERENCES

Aho, A. V., & Corasick, M. J. (1975). Efficient string matching: An aid to bibliographic search. *Communications of the ACM, 18*(6), 333–340. doi:10.1145/360825.360855

Amarasinghe, S. (2007). *Multicore programming primer and programming competition.* A course at MIT, Cambridge, MA.

Chonka, A., Zhou, W., Knapp, K., & Xiang, Y. (2008). Protecting information systems from ddos attack using multicore methodology. *Proceedings of IEEE 8th International Conference on Computer and Information Technology.*

Dharmapurikar, S., Krishnamurthy, P., Sproull, T. S., & Lockwood, J. W. (2004). Deep packet inspection using parallel bloom filters. *IEEE Micro, 24*(1), 52–61. doi:10.1109/MM.2004.1268997

Eggers, S., Emer, J., Levy, H., Lo, J., Stamm, R., & Tullsen, D. (1997). Simultaneous multithreading: A platform for next-generation processors. *IEEE Micro, 17*(5), 12–19. doi:10.1109/40.621209

Hayes, C. L., & Luo, Y. (2007). Dpico: A high speed deep packet inspection engine using compact finite automata. *Proceedings of ACM/IEEE ANCS*, (pp. 195-203).

Intel (2007). *Intel® multi-core: An overview.*

Johnson, C., & Welser, J. (2005). Future processors: Flexible and modular. *Proceedings of 3rd IEEE/ACM/IFIP International Conference on Hardware/Software Codesign and System Synthesis,* (pp. 4-6).

Liu, H., Zheng, K., Liu, B., Zhang, X., & Liu, Y. (2006). A memory-efficient parallel string matching architecture for high-speed intrusion detection. *IEEE Journal on Selected Areas in Communications, 24*(10), 1793–1804. doi:10.1109/JSAC.2006.877221

McKenney, P. E., Lee, D. Y., & Denny, B. A. (2008). Traffic generator software release notes.

Moore, G. (1965). Cramming more components onto integrated circuits. *Electronics Magazine, 38*(8).

Paxson, V., Asanović, K., Dharmapurikar, S., Lockwood, J., Pang, R., Sommer, R., et al. (2006). Rethinking hardware support for network analysis and intrusion prevention. *Proceedings of the 1st conference on USENIX Workshop on Hot Topics in Security.*

Paxson, V., Sommer, R., & Weaver, N. (2007). An architecture for exploiting multi-core processors to parallelize network intrusion prevention. *Proceedings of IEEE Sarnoff Symposium.*

Piyachon, P., & Luo, Y. (2006). Efficient memory utilization on network processors for deep packet inspection. *Proceedings of ACM/IEEE ANCS*, (pp. 71-80).

Qi, Y., Xu, B., He, F., Yang, B., Yu, J., & Li, J. (2007). Towards high-performance flow-level packet processing on multi-core network processors. *Proceedings of 3rd ACM/IEEE Symposium on Architecture for Networking and Communications Systems,* (pp. 17-26).

Roesch, M. (1999). Snort - lightweight intrusion detection for networks. *Proceedings of 13th USENIX LISA Conference*, (pp. 229-238).

Sohi, G. S., Breach, S. E., & Vijaykumar, T. N. (1995). Multiscalar processors. *Proceedings of 22nd Annual International Symposium on Computer Architecture*, (pp. 414-425).

Sutter, H., & Larus, J. (2005). Software and the concurrency revolution. *ACM Queue; Tomorrow's Computing Today*, *3*(7), 54–62. doi:10.1145/1095408.1095421

Taylor, M. B., Lee, W., Miller, J., Wentzlaff, D., Bratt, I., Greenwald, B., et al. (2004). Evaluation of the raw microprocessor: An exposed-wire-delay architecture for ilp and streams. *Proceedings of 31st Annual International Symposium on Computer Architecture*, (pp. 2-13).

Tian, D., & Xiang, Y. (2008). A multi-core supported intrusion detection system. *Proceedings of IFIP International Conference on Network and Parallel Computing.*

Tripp, G. (2006). A parallel "string matching engine" for use in high speed network intrusion detection systems. *Journal in Computer Virology*, *2*(1), 21–34. doi:10.1007/s11416-006-0010-4

Tullsen, D., Lo, J., Eggers, S., & Levy, H. (1999). Supporting fine-grain synchronization on a simultaneous multithreaded processor. *Proceedings of the 5th International Symposium on High Performance Computer Architecture*, (p. 54).

Villa, O., Scarpazza, D. P., & Petrini, F. (2008). Accelerating real-time string searching with multicore processors. *IEEE Computer*, *41*(4), 42–50.

WMware. (2008).

Xiang, Y., & Zhou, W. (2006). Protecting information infrastructure from ddos attacks by mark-aided distributed filtering (madf). *International Journal of High Performance Computing and Networking*, *4*(5/6), 357–367. doi:10.1504/IJHPCN.2006.013491

Yan, J., & Zhang, W. (2007). Hybrid multi-core architecture for boosting single-threaded performance. *ACM SIGARCH Computer Architecture News*, *35*(1), 141–148. doi:10.1145/1241601.1241603

KEY TERMS AND DEFINITIONS

Deep Packet Inspection: Deep Packet Inspection (DPI) is a form of computer network packet filtering that examines the data and/or header part of a packet as it passes an inspection point, searching for protocol non-compliance, viruses, spam, intrusions or predefined criteria to decide if the packet can pass or if it needs to be routed to a different destination, or for the purpose of collecting statistical information. This is in contrast to shallow packet inspection which just checks the header portion of a packet.

High-Performance Security Systems: High-performance security systems refer to the software or hardware systems that perform security functions at high performance in terms of processing speed, data, or throughput.

Intrusion Detection: Intrusion detection is the act of detecting actions that attempt to compromise the confidentiality, integrity or availability of a resource.

Multi-Core: Multi-core represents a major evolution in the development of processor. A multi-core processor (or chip-level multiprocessor, CMP) combines two or more independent cores (normally a CPU) into a single package composed of a single integrated circuit (IC), called a die, or more dies packaged together.

Network Security: Network security consists of the provisions made in an underlying computer network infrastructure, policies adopted by the network administrator to protect the network and the network-accessible resources from unauthorized access and consistent and continuous monitoring and measurement of its effectiveness (or lack) combined together.

Parallel Algorithms: Parallel algorithms are algorithms that can be executed a piece at a time on many different processing devices, and then put back together again at the end to get the correct result.

Router: Router is a networking device whose software and hardware are usually tailored to the tasks of routing and forwarding information.

Chapter 38
State-Carrying Code for Computation Mobility

Hai Jiang
Arkansas State University, USA

Yanqing Ji
Gonzaga University, USA

ABSTRACT

Computation mobility enables running programs to move around among machines and is the essence of performance gain, fault tolerance, and system throughput increase. State-carrying code (SCC) is a software mechanism to achieve such computation mobility by saving and retrieving computation states during normal program execution in heterogeneous multi-core/many-core clusters. This chapter analyzes different kinds of state saving/retrieving mechanisms for their pros and cons. To achieve a portable, flexible and scalable solution, SCC adopts the application-level thread migration approach. Major deployment features are explained and one example system, MigThread, is used to illustrate implementation details. Future trends are given to point out how SCC can evolve into a complete lightweight virtual machine. New high productivity languages might step in to raise SCC to language level. With SCC, thorough resource utilization is expected.

INTRODUCTION

The way in which scientific and engineering research is conducted has radically changed in the past two decades. Computers have been used widely for data processing, application simulation and performance analysis. As application programs' complexity increases dramatically, powerful supercomputers are on demand. Due to the cost/performance ratio, computer clusters are commonly utilized and treated as virtual supercomputers. Such computing environments can be easily acquired for scientific and engineering applications.

For each individual computer node, multi-core/many-core architecture is becoming popular in the computer industry. In the near future, hundreds and thousands of cores might be placed inside of computer

DOI: 10.4018/978-1-60566-661-7.ch038

nodes on server-clusters. Multi-core clusters are promising high performance computing platforms where multiple processes can be generated and distributed across participating machines and the multithreading technique can be applied to take advantage of multi-core architecture on each node. This hybrid distributed/shared memory infrastructure fits the natural layout of computer clusters.

Since computer clusters for high performance computing can change their configurations dynamically, i.e., computing nodes can join or leave the systems at runtime, the ability of re-arranging running jobs is on demand to exploit the otherwise wasted resources. Such dynamic rescheduling can optimize the execution of applications, utilize system resource effectively, and improve the overall system throughput. Since computation mobility, i.e., the ability of moving computations around, is one of the essences to this dynamic scheduling, it has become indispensable to scalable computing for the following outstanding features:

- Load Balancing: Evenly distributing workloads over multiple cores/processors can improve the whole computation's performance. For scientific applications, computations are partitioned into multiple tasks running on different processors/computers. In addition to variant computing powers, multiple users and programs share the computation resources in non-dedicated computing environments where load imbalance occurs frequently even though the workload was initially distributed evenly. Therefore, dynamically and periodically adjusting workload distribution is required to make sure that all running tasks at different locations finish their execution at the same time in order to minimize total idle time. Such load reconfiguration needs to transfer tasks from one location to another.
- Load Sharing: From the system's point of view, load sharing typically increases the throughput of computer clusters. Studies have indicated that a large fraction of workstations could be unused for a large fraction of time. Scalable computing systems seek to exploit otherwise idle cores/processors and improve the overall system efficiency.
- Data Locality: Sharing resources includes two approaches: moving data to computation or moving computation to data. Current applications favor data migration as in FTP, web, and Distributed Shared Memory (DSM) systems. However, when computation sizes are much smaller than data sizes, the code or computation migration might be more efficient. Communication frequency and volume will be minimized by converting remote data accesses into local ones. In data intensive computing, when client-server and RPC (Remote Procedure Call) infrastructure are not available, computation migration is an effective approach to accessing massive remote data.
- Fault Tolerance: Before a computer system crashes, local computations/jobs should be transferred to other machines without losing most existing computing results. Computation migration and checkpointing are effective approaches.

Computation migration feature has existed in some batch schedulers and task brokers, such as Condor (Bricker, Litzkow, & Livny, 1992), LSF (Zhou, Zheng, Wang, & Delisle, 1993) and LoadLeveler (IBM Corporation, 1993). However, they can only work at a coarse granularity (process) level and in homogeneous environments. So far, there is no effective task/computation migration solution in heterogeneous environments. This has become the major bottleneck in dynamic schedulers and obstacle for scalable computing to achieve high performance and effective resource utilization.

State-Carrying Code (SCC) is a software mechanism that intends to provide the ability of moving computations around. It allows programs to contain both normal statements for application execution and special primitives inserted by the SCC precompiler for portable computation state construction. Such a program can stop on one machine, generate its computation state, and then restart on another machine. SCC brings mobility to applications and addresses some critical issues including computation granularity, virtualization level, computation/data locality, distributed synchronization, distributed data sharing, and highly efficient data conversion.

The objective of this chapter is to introduce the relevant backgrounds, design strategies and limitations of SCC as well as its uses for computation mobility in heterogeneous environments. The next section discusses the related research and their limitations. Then the strategies and design of SCC are introduced to show how to support heterogeneous computation migration to take advantage of multi-core architecture. The future work and conclusion are given at the end.

Computation Mobility

Computation mobility concerns the movement of a computation starting at one node and continuing execution at another network node in distributed systems. Such computation relocation requires the movement of both programs and execution contexts. How to construct and reload the execution contexts at runtime is the essence of computation mobility.

Sometimes data mobility might imply computation mobility when data is closely bound to computations and both of them have to be moved around together. In fact, such a scenario indicates the data-computes rule: a computation only works on its own data.

Computation mobility enabled systems can be classified by their computation granularities and implementation levels. Candidates for computation units could be processes, threads, and user defined objects. The engine of computation mobility is optionally placed at data, language, application, library, virtual machine, kernel, and platform levels. A variety of research activities have been reported in the literature.

Process Migration

Process migration concerns the construction of process states. A process is an operating system abstraction representing an instance of a running computer program. Each process contains its own address space, program counter, stack, and heaps. All these dynamic factors form the process state which is normally buried in operating systems.

Kernel-level process migration is supported by some distributed or networked operating systems. Some operating systems such as MOSIX (Barak & La'adan, 1998), Sprite (Douglis & Ousterhout, 1991), Mach (Accetta, et al., 1986), Locus (Walker, Popek, English, Kline, & Thiel, 1992), and OSF/1 (Zajcew, Roy, Black, & Peak, 1993) migrate the whole process images whereas others like Accent (Rashid & Robertson, 1981) and V Kernel (Theimer, Lantz, & Cheriton, 1985) apply "Copy-On-Reference" and "precopying" techniques to shorten the process freeze time. These operating systems can access process states efficiently and support preemptive migration at virtually any point. Thus, they provide good transparency and flexibility to end users. However, this approach brings much complexity into kernels and process images cannot be shared between different operating systems. Inability to provide a heterogeneous solution presents a severe drawback of this approach.

User-level process migration as in Condor (Bricker, Litzkow, & Livny, 1992) and Libckpt (Plank, Beck, Kinsley, & Li, 1995) achieves similar results without the kernel modification. Normally user libraries are used and linked to the application at compile-time. Process state is constructed through library calls. Since system calls are invoked in library calls to fetch process images from the kernel, this approach only works on homogeneous platforms.

Application-level approach supports process migration in a heterogeneous environment since the process state can be replicated in user programs. The Tui system (Smith & Hutchinson, 1998), MigThread (Jiang & Chaudhary, 2004), SNOW (Chanchio & Sun, 2001), Porch (Ramkumar & Strumpen, 1997), PREACHES (Ssu, Yao, & Fuchs, 1999), and Process Introspection (Ferrari, Chapin, & Grimshaw, 1997) apply source-to-source transformation to convert programs into semantically equivalent source programs for saving and recovering process states across binary incompatible machines. Such an approach deliberately sacrifices transparency and reusability although pre-compilers/preprocessors are usually available to improve transparency to a certain degree.

Since the original process states are buried in operating systems and no proper system calls are provided to fetch them easily, most process migration systems are not being widely used in open systems. One solution is to duplicate process states in user space as in application or language approaches. The state replicas are used instead for migration in heterogeneous environments.

Thread Migration

Threads are flows of control in running programs. One process might contain multiple threads which share the same address space including text and data segments. However, each thread has its own stack and heap.

Thread migration enables fine-grained computation adjustment in parallel computing. As multithreading becomes a popular programming practice, thread migration is increasingly important in fine-tuning high-end computing to fit dynamic and non-dedicated environments. Different threads can be migrated to utilize different resources for load balancing and load sharing. The core of thread migration is about transferring thread state and necessary data from the local heap to the destination.

Current thread migration research focuses on updating internal self-referential pointers in stacks and heaps. Three approaches exist in the literature. The first approach uses language and compiler support to maintain enough type information and identify pointers as in MigThread (Jiang & Chaudhary, 2004) and Arachne (Dimitrov & Rego, 1998). The second approach requires scanning the stacks at run-time to detect and translate the possible pointers dynamically. The representative implementation of this is Ariadne (Mascarenhas & Rego, 1995). Since some pointers in stack cannot possibly be detected (Itzkovitz, Schuster, & Shalev, 1998), the resumed execution can be incorrect. The third approach is the most popular one. It necessitates the partitioning of the address space and reservation of unique virtual addresses for the stack of each thread so that the internal pointers maintain the same values. A common solution is to preallocate memory space for threads on all machines and restrict each thread to migrate to its corresponding location on other machines. This "iso-address" solution requires a large address space and is not scalable since there are limitations on stacks and heaps (Itzkovitz, Schuster, & Shalev, 1998). Such systems include Millipede (Itzkovitz, Schuster, & Shalev, 1998), Amber (Chase, Amador, Lazowska, Levy, & Littlefield, 1996), UPVM system (Casa, Konuru, Prouty, Walpole, & Otto, 1994), PM2 (Antoniu & Boung, 2001), Nomad system (Milton, 1998), and the one proposed by Cronk et al (Cronk & Mehrotra, 1997).

Based on the location, threads can be classified as kernel-, user-, and language-level threads. Kernel-level threads exist in operating systems and can be scheduled onto processors directly. User-level threads are defined and scheduled by libraries in user space. Language-level threads are defined in a programming language. For example, Java threads are defined in the Java language and implemented in the Java Virtual Machine (JVM). According to thread types, migration systems have to fetch thread states from different places and port them to different platforms. To our knowledge, only MigThread (Jiang & Chaudhary, 2004) and Jessica2 (Zhu, Wang, & Lan, 2002) can support heterogeneous thread migration. MigThread achieves this by defining its own data conversion scheme whereas Jessica2 relies on modified JVMs.

Checkpointing

Checkpointing is the saving of computation state, usually in stable storage, so that it may be reconstructed later. Therefore, the major difference between migration and checkpointing is the medium: memory-to-memory vs. memory-to-file transfer. Checkpointing may use most migration strategies.

Libckpt (Plank, Beck, Kinsley, & Li, 1995), PREACHES (Ssu, Yao, & Fuchs, 1999), Porch (Ramkumar & Strumpen, 1997), CosMic (Chung, 1997), and other user-directed checkpointing systems save process states in stable storage, such as magnetic disks. The memory exclusion technique has been employed effectively in incremental checkpointing, where pages are not checkpointed when they are clean. The technique, "compiler-assisted checkpointing," uses compiler/preprocessor to ensure correct memory exclusion calls for better performance.

For message passing and shared address space parallel computing applications, CoCheck (Stellner, 1996) and C^3 (Bronevetsky, Marques, Schulz, Pingali, & Stodghill, 2004) manage to get clear-cut checkpoints which can be treated as computation states for migration. Hence, from the computation state's point of view, migration and checkpointing systems are equivalent.

Virtual Machines

To enable code portability in heterogeneous environments, Virtual Machine (VM) techniques are widely used, for example in JVM (Lindholm & Yellin, 1999), VMware (VMware Inc., 1999), and Xen (Barham, et al., 2003). They present the image of a dedicated raw machine to each user. Virtual machines allow the configuration of an entire operating system to be independent from that of the physical resource; it is possible to completely represent a VM "guest" machine by its virtual state and instantiate it in any VM "host." Therefore, VMs provide stable computing environments to programs.

Some migration systems, such as Jessica2 (Zhu, Wang, & Lan, 2002), can work on top of process VMs to enable the migration in heterogeneous environments. Process VMs are used to interpret computation states to hide low-level architecture variety. Since such process VMs play a role as data converter and provide uniform platforms, states can be fetched in a unique way and heterogeneity issue is resolved smoothly (Zhu, Wang, & Lan, 2002).

However, VMs do not support efficient computation mobility since they always have difficulties in distinguishing useful resources. A safe way is to wrap up the whole abstract view of the underlying physical machine. Obviously, the efficiency drops dramatically and VMs themselves are not portable across different physical hosts.

Mobile Agents

A mobile agent is a software object, representing an autonomous computation that can travel in a network to perform tasks on behalf of its creator. It has the ability to interact with its execution environment, and to act asynchronously and autonomously upon it. The code is their object-oriented context, and most existing mobile agent systems, including Charm++ (Kale & Krishnan, 1998), Emerald (Jul, Levy, Hutchinson, & Blad, 1998), Telescript (White, 1996) and IBM Aglets (Lange & Oshima, 1998), implement their agents in object-oriented languages such as Java and Telescript.

Mobile agents demand a different coding environment, including new language constructs, programming styles, compilers, and execution platforms. Although current mobile agent systems are intended for general applications and have demonstrated some progress in Internet/mobile computing, it is still not clear how they will perform for computation-intensive and high performance computing applications with object-oriented technology.

Deployment of SCC

State-Carrying Code (SCC) takes advantage of multi-core SMP architecture, virtualizes computations, and achieves better application performance in heterogeneous environments. Computation mobility is the essential tool. All existing packages have indicated the fact that computation migration performance is mainly affected by computing units and the location of computation states. SCC provides a flexible, portable, practical, and efficient solution to computation mobility.

Granularity

The term granularity refers to the size of computation units which can move around individually. Normally it indicates the flexibility that mobility systems can provide.

Since Virtual Machines can only dump the whole system images, they support coarse-grained mobility. All computations on the VMs will be transferred together and they cannot be distinguished explicitly. In this case, sequential and parallel jobs are treated as the same. This extreme migration case is efficient only when all VM's local jobs need to leave the current machine. VMs provide the virtually stable platform for applications. However, VMs themselves are not portable over various physical machines. In VM migration, applications are not aware of the movement, but obviously such coarse-grained migration incurs high overhead and inflexibility.

From the traditional operating systems' point of view, processes are the basic computational abstraction. All sequential computations are executed on just a single process. In parallel computing, the overall jobs need to be decomposed into multiple tasks. In multi-process parallel applications such as those using MPI (Message Passing Interface), tasks are assigned to processes for parallel execution. In such cases, processes are treated as computation units. Compared to VM migration, process migration has its advantages in reducing overheads significantly without worrying about the execution environment. It can also manipulate individual or partial applications. Parallel jobs with multiple processes can be reconfigured dynamically. Different implementations of process migration exhibit various degrees of transparency to programmers.

To reduce the heavy inter-process context switch overhead, many modern parallel computing applications adopt multi-threading techniques. Each process may contain multiple threads to share the same address space. Former multi-processed applications can be replaced by multi-threaded counterparts. Otherwise, former processes are further partitioned into multiple local threads to achieve finer task decomposition. Synchronization overhead among computation units is further reduced. Sequential applications can be viewed as single-threaded instances whereas parallel ones consist of multiple threads. Once threads are used as computation units, thread migration can move sequential jobs and entire or partial parallel computations. Since process migration treats multi-threaded applications as a whole, it will either move the whole computation or perform no migration at all. Such "all-or-nothing" scenarios do not exist in thread migration. However, since some thread libraries are invisible to operating systems, the difficulty of implementing thread migration is higher than process migration.

Charm++ (Kale & Krishnan, 1998), Emerald (Jul, Levy, Hutchinson, & Blad, 1998), and other mobile agent systems provide mechanisms at the language level to migrate the user defined objects/agents. However, new languages and compilers expose everything to programmers. Therefore, many legacy systems have to be re-deployed. Transparency is the major drawback so that most systems have given up this approach.

Multi-core architecture has been widely adopted. To take advantage of the extra computing cores, applications need to be implemented with multiple processes or threads. Normally they need to exchange or share data with each other. Thus multi-threading is the preferred selection. Also, all modern operating systems have been multi-threaded. Threads in applications can be mapped onto kernel threads naturally.

SCC follows this multi-threading trend and threads will be the basic units of computation mobility although processes can be handled.

Positioning Computation States

The main issue in SCC and all other migration systems is how to retrieve computation states quickly and precisely. Then the current computation can be stopped on the current machine and resumed on a new machine based on its state. Computation states are buried or recreated at data, language, application, library, thread virtual machine, kernel, and platform virtual machine levels, as shown in Figure 1. However, not all of them are suitable to user threads whose states consist of the execution contexts in kernel and the thread contexts in thread libraries.

Platform Virtual Machine approach provides execution platforms such as VMware (VMware Inc., 1999), and Xen (Barham, et al., 2003). These VMs can only deal with the whole environment, not the fine-grained tasks such as threads.

Kernel-level approach is the most effective and transparent method for process migration. However, it cannot deal with user threads and does not work in heterogeneous environments.

Thread Virtual Machine approach can only provide execution platform for running threads, such as Jessica2 (Zhu, Wang, & Lan, 2002) in JVM (Lindholm & Yellin, 1999) which needs to be modified to support Java thread migration. However, the requirement of distributing and installing the modified JVMs makes applications only work in closed computer clusters.

User-level approach provides computation mobility function in user libraries (Bricker, Litzkow, & Livny, 1992) (Plank, Beck, Kinsley, & Li, 1995). Unique library calls will be translated into different system calls to fetch execution contexts inside operating systems. Normally it is not straightforward to convert computation states from one system to another.

Application-level approach constructs computation states inside the source code for better portability

Figure 1. Implementation levels of computation mobility.

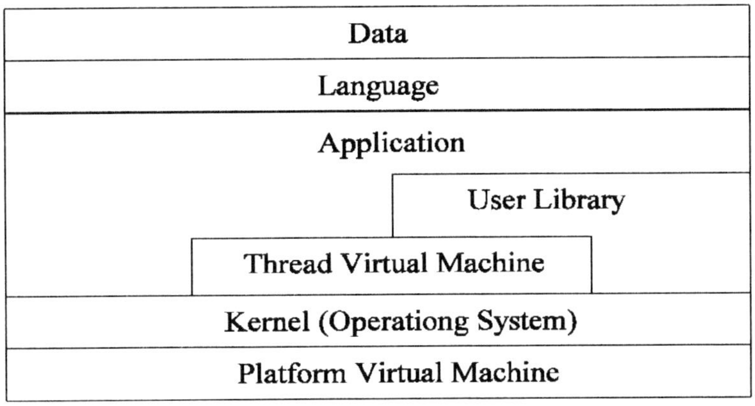

and heterogeneity (Smith & Hutchinson, 1998) (Jiang & Chaudhary, 2004) (Chanchio & Sun, 2001). Normally pre-compilers/preprocessors are provided for code transformation without programmers' involvement. Computation units, such as processes or threads, are defined according to applications. Flexibility is another major advantage of this approach.

Language-level approach requires new languages and compilers (Kale & Krishnan, 1998) (Jul, Levy, Hutchinson, & Blad, 1998). It is hard to persuade programmers to learn new languages. Sometimes data-level approach is applicable in regular scientific applications where computation states can be represented by pure variable sets.

Due to the required characteristics in computer clusters, SCC selects the application-level approach for portability, flexibility, heterogeneity and scalability.

Issues in Application-level Approach

There are two major issues in application-level thread migration:

- Availability of Source Code

The major restriction of the application-level approach is the requirement of source code. Since thread states need to be replicated in the programs, applications with only executable code cannot be transformed for mobility. However, for high performance computing, users are normally also the programmers. Most time the source code is available.

To get rid of this restriction, migration engine will have to be buried at lower levels, such as user, kernel and platform virtual machine levels. However, as we discussed before, approaches at those levels will not be able to utilize multi-core architecture effectively and performance improvement will be limited. Therefore, application-level approach is the better choice if the source code is available.

- Associated Overheads

In some fields, such as Internet Computing and Mobile Agents, prompt state construction is the key

Figure 2. The Infrastructure of SCC.

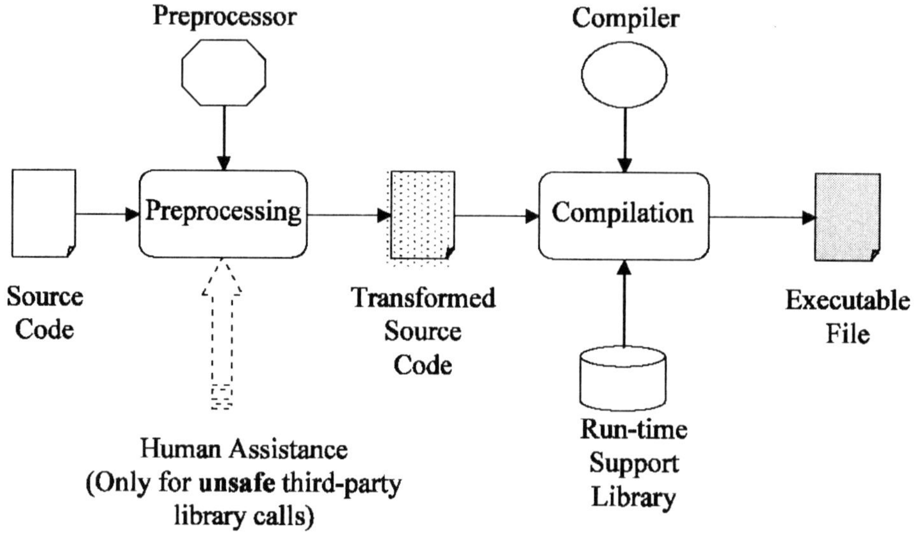

issue so that computations (agents) can start and stop quickly. However, in the application-level approach, the overhead of constructing computation states is relatively higher. Therefore, it is not suitable for Internet/Agent computing.

SCC aims at high-end computing where the most overhead lies in the scientific computing or business data processing (mainly the floating pointing operations or data searching). The cost to set up a state replica in the program is ignorable. Many Grand Challenging problems in Computational Physics, Computational Chemistry, and Bioinformatics have exhibited such characteristic. The work in MigThread (Jiang & Chaudhary, 2004) has demonstrated such phenomena.

Infrastructure

SCC suggests supporting both process and thread migration at application level. Among many existing application-level process migration systems, MigThread (Jiang & Chaudhary, 2004) covers the most features required by SCC and supports thread migration to take advantage of multi-core architecture. In this chapter, MigThread is used as an example to demonstrate major features in SCC.

SCC consists of two parts: a preprocessor (pre-compiler) and a run-time support module. The preprocessor is designed to transform user's source code into a format from which the run-time support module can construct the computation state precisely and efficiently. The run-time support module constructs, transfers, and restores computation states dynamically as well as provides other run-time safety checks, as shown in Figure 2 . Most of the time, user assistance is not required unless the preprocessor encounters unsolvable third-party library calls. Manual support is a necessity for this case.

The preprocessor of MigThread is similar to the ones in other SCC systems and conducts the following tasks:

- Information Collection: Collect related stack and heap data for future state construction. The stack

Figure 3. The original function.

```
foo(int arg1, int *arg2)
{
  double   lcl1;
  double **lcl2;
            .
            .
            .
  MTh_checkpoint();
            .
            .
            .
}
```

data includes globally shared variables, local variables, function parameters, and program counters, etc. whereas the heap data contains dynamically allocated memory segments.

- Tag Definition: Create tags for heterogeneous data blocks.
- Position Labeling: Detect and label potential migration points.
- Control Dispatching: Insert switch statements to orchestrate execution flows.
- Safety Protection: Detect and overcome unsafe cases; seek human assistance/instruction for third-party library calls; and leave other unresolved cases to the run-time support module.

Its run-time support module consists of a thread record list (including globally shared data), a stack management module, a memory block management module, and a pointer-casting closure. Since activation frames in the stack are arranged in last-in-first-out (LIFO) order, stacks are maintained in linked lists. Meanwhile, heaps and PC Closures are maintained in red-black trees for random accesses.

The run-time support module is activated through primitives inserted by the preprocessor at compile time. It is required to link this run-time support library with user's applications in the final compilation. During the execution, its task list includes:

- Stack Maintenance: Keep a user-level stack of activation frames for each thread.
- Tag Generation: Fill out tag contents which are platform-dependent.
- Heap Maintenance: Keep a user-level memory management subsystem for dynamically allocated memory blocks.
- Migration: Construct, transfer, and restore computation state.
- Data Conversion: Translate computation states for destination platforms.
- Safety Protection: Detect and recover remaining unsafe cases.
- Pointer Updating: Identify and update pointers after migration or checkpointing.

State Construction

The state data typically consists of the process data segment, stack, heap and register contents. In SCC, the computation state is in a platform-independent format to reduce migration restrictions. Therefore,

SCC does not rely on any type of thread library or operating system.

State construction is done by both the preprocessor and the run-time support module. The preprocessor collects globally shared variables, stack variables, function parameters, program counters, and dynamically allocated memory regions, into certain pre-defined data structures. Since the virtual address spaces might be different, pointers are marked at compile time and updated at runtime. In many SCC systems such as the Tui system (Smith & Hutchinson, 1998) and SNOW (Chanchio & Sun, 2001), related variables are collected at the migration points to reduce the size of actual computation states. However, due to pointer arithmetic operations, related variables are not always detected correctly.

Figure 4. The transformed function in MigThread.

```
MTh_foo(int MTh_rank, int arg1,
        int *arg2)
{
  struct MThV_t {                         (1)
      void    *MThP;
      int     stepno;

      int     arg1;
      double  lcl1;
  } MThV;

  struct MThP_t {
      int     *arg2;
      double **lcl2;
  } MThP;
  char MThV_heter[60];
  char MThP_heter[41];

  int MTh_so4 = sizeof(double);
  int MTh_so3 = sizeof(int);
  int MTh_so1 = sizeof(struct MThP_t);
  int MTh_so0 = sizeof(struct MThV_t);
  int MTh_so2 = sizeof(void *);

  MThV.MThP = (void *)&MThP;              (2)
  MThV.stepno = 0;
  MThP.arg2 = NULL;
  MThP.lcl2 = NULL;
  MThV.arg1 = arg1;
  MThP.arg2 = arg2;

  if (MTh_reg(MTh_rank, "MTh_foo",
          (void *)&MThV, MTh_so0,
          (void *)&MThP, MTh_so1)
      == 0) {

    sprintf(MThV_heter,
 "(%d,-1)(%d,0)(%d,1)(%d,0)(%d,1)(%d,0)
 (%d,1)(%d,0)", MTh_so2,
 (long)&MThV.stepno-(long)&MThV.MThP-
 MTh_so2, MTh_so3,(long)&MThV.arg1-
 (long)&MThV.stepno-MTh_so3,
 MTh_so3,(long)&MThV.lcl1-
 (long)&MThV.arg1- MTh_so3,
 MTh_so4,(long)&MThV+MTh_so0-
 (long)&MThV.lcl1-MTh_so4);

    sprintf(MThP_heter,
 "(%d,-1)(%d,0)(%d,-1)(%d,0)",
 MTh_so2,(long)&MThP.lcl2-
 (long)&MThP.arg2-MTh_so2,
 MTh_so2,(long)&MThP+MTh_so1-
 (long)&MThP.lcl2-MTh_so2);

    MTh_heter_reg("MTh_foo",
          MThV_heter, MThP_heter);
    MTh_reg(MTh_rank, "MTh_foo",
          (void *)&MThV, MTh_so0,
          (void *)&MThP, MTh_so1);
  }
  switch(MThV.stepno) {                   (3)
    case 0:
        break;
    case 1:
        goto MTh_step_1;
        break;
    default:
        break;
  }
        .
        .
    MThV.stepno = 1;                      (4)
    MThV_checkpoint(MTh_rank);
MTh_step_1:   ;
        .
        .
}
```

Figure 5. Tag definition and generation in MigThread.

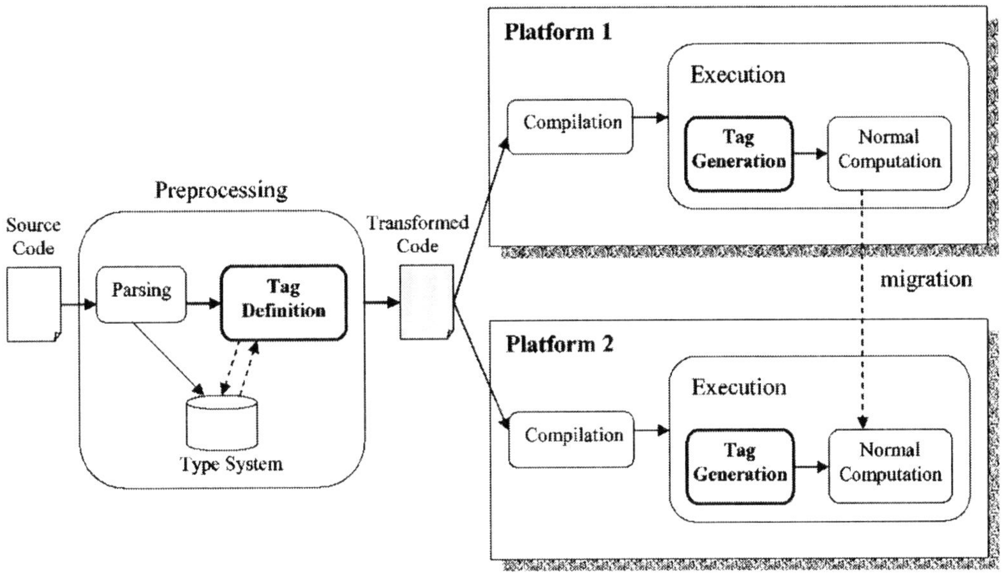

MigThread puts variables in two predefined structures to speed up the state construction process. This speedy way can discover the hidden variables although it might be over-conservative. Figures 3 and 4 show this process in MigThread. A simple function *foo()* is defined in Figure 3. In MigThread, the preprocessor transforms the function and generates a corresponding *MTh_foo()* shown in Figure 4. Non-pointer variables are collected in *MThV* whereas pointers are gathered in *MThP* (as shown in area 1). In thread stacks, each function's activation frame contains *MThV* and *MThP* to record the current function's computation states.

The program counter (PC) is a register that contains the memory address of the current execution point within a program. Its content is represented as a series of integer values. In MigThread, it is declared as *MThV.stepno* in each affected function. Since all possible positions for migration have been detected at compile-time (as shown in area 4), different integer values of *MThV.stepno* correspond to different adaptation points. In the transformed code, after the function initialization in area 2, a **switch** statement is inserted to dispatch execution to each labeled point according to the value of *MThV.stepno* as shown in area 3. The **switch** and **goto** statements help control jump to resumption points quickly.

SCC also supports user-level memory management for heaps. Eventually, all computation state related contents, including stacks and heaps, are moved out to the user space and handled by SCC directly for portability.

Data Conversion Schemes

Computation states can be transformed into pure data. If different platforms use different data formats, the computation states constructed on one platform need to be interpreted by another. Thus, data conversion is unavoidable. Some application-level migration systems only work in homogeneous systems without the data conversion issue. Many SCC systems adopt symmetric data conversion approach which can be easily implemented. Both the sender and receiver need to convert data to and from an intermediate (universal) data format. Special compilers (Smith & Hutchinson, 1998) or data representation libraries such as XDR (Srinivasan, 1995) are employed. In open and homogeneous systems, data conversion will still have to be conducted twice although it is not necessary at all (in closes systems, they can be eliminated).

MigThread (Jiang & Chaudhary, 2004) adopt asymmetric data conversion method to perform data conversion only on the receiver side. This approach is more flexible in open systems. Data conversion is only conducted when necessary, i.e., senders and receivers are on different platforms. The module in MigThread is called Coarse-Grain Tagged "receiver makes it right" (CGT-RMR). This tagged RMR version scheme can tackle data alignment and padding physically, convert data structures as a whole, and eventually generate a lighter workload compared to existing standards. It accepts ASCII character sets, handles byte ordering, and adopts IEEE 754 floating-point standard because of its dominance in the market. Since CGT-RMR in MigThread converts variables as a whole, in most cases it is faster than the ones in other SCC systems.

In MigThread, programmers do not need to worry about data formats. The preprocessor parses the source code, sets up type systems, transforms source code, and communicates with the run-time support module through inserted primitives. With helps from the type system, CGT-RMR can analyze data types, flatten down aggregate types recursively, detect padding patterns, and define tags as in Figure 5. But the actual tag contents can be set only at run-time and they may not be the same on different platforms. Since all of the tedious tag definition work has been performed by the preprocessor, the programming style becomes extremely simple. Also, with global control, low-level issues such as data conversion status can be conveyed to upper-level scheduling modules. Therefore, easy coding style and performance gains come from the preprocessor. CGT-RMR is very efficient in handling large data chunks which are common in migration and checkpointing (Jiang & Chaudhary, 2004).

Tags in CGT-RMR are used to describe data types and their paddings so that data conversion routines can handle aggregate types as well as common scalar types. Tags are defined and generated for these structures as well as dynamically allocated memory blocks in the heap. At compile time, it is still too early to determine the content of the tags. The preprocessor defines rules to calculate structure members' sizes and variant padding patterns, and inserts **sprintf()** to glue partial results together. The actual tag generation has to take place at run-time when the **sprintf()** statement is executed. Only one statement is issued for each data type regardless of whether it is a scalar or aggregate type. The flattening procedure is accomplished by MigThread's preprocessor during tag definition instead of the encoding/decoding process at run-time. Hence, programmers are freed from this responsibility. In MigThread, all memory segments for predefined data structures are represented in a "tag-block" format. The process/thread stack becomes a sequence of these structures and their tags. Memory blocks in heaps are also associated with such tags to express the actual layout in memory space. Therefore, the computation state physically consists of a group of memory segments associated with their own tags in a "tag-segment" pair format.

State Restoration

To support open systems, if symmetric data conversion scheme is adopted, both sides need to convert data. But with the asymmetric one, the senders do not need to perform data conversion. Only the receivers have to convert the computation state, i.e., data, as required. Normally variables are converted one by one. MigThread can do this block by block. Since activation frames in stacks are re-run and heaps are recreated, a new set of segments in "tag-block" format is available on the new platform. MigThread first compares architecture tags by **strcmp()**. If they are identical and the blocks have the same sizes, the platforms remain unchanged and the old segment contents are simply copied over by **memcpy()** to the new architectures. This enables prompt processing between homogeneous platforms while symmetric conversion approaches still suffer data conversion overhead on both ends.

If platforms have been changed, conversion routines are applied on all memory segments. For each segment, a "walk-through" process is conducted against its corresponding old segment from the previous platform. In these segments, according to their tags, memory blocks are viewed to alternately consist of scalar type data and padding slots. The high-level conversion unit is data slots rather than bytes in order to achieve portability. The "walk-through" process contains two index pointers pointing to a pair of matching scalar data slots in both blocks. The contents of the old data slots are converted and copied to the new data slots if byte ordering changes, and then the index pointers are moved down to the next slots. In the mean time, padding slots are skipped over. In MigThread, data items are expressed in "scalar type data - padding slots" pattern to support heterogeneity.

Safety Issues

Some SCC systems such as the Tui system (Smith & Hutchinson, 1998) and SNOW (Chanchio & Sun, 2001) declare that they only work with programs written in type safe languages or substrates whereas others assume so. Most migration safety issues can be eliminated by the "type safety" requirement, but not all of them. MigThread can detect and handle more migration "unsafe" features, including pointer casting, pointers in unions, library calls, and incompatible data conversion (Jiang & Chaudhary, 2004). Then computation states will be precisely constructed to make those programs eligible for migration. Programmers are free to code in any programming style.

Pointer casting does not mean the cast between different pointer types, but the cast to/from integral types, such as integer, long, or double. The problem is that pointers might hide in integral type variables. The central issue is to detect those integral variables containing pointer values (or memory addresses) so that they could be updated during state restoration. Casting could be direct or indirect.

Pointer arithmetic and operations may cause harmful pointer casting which is the most difficult safety issue. In MigThread, an intra-procedural, flow-insensitive, and context-insensitive pointer inference algorithm was proposed to detect hidden pointers created by unsafe pointer casting, regardless of whether it is applied in pointer assignments or memcpy() library calls. The static analysis at compile time and dynamic checks at run-time work together to trace and recover unsafe pointer uses.

Library calls bring difficulties to all migration schemes since it is hard to determine what is going on inside the library code. It is even harder for application-level schemes because they work on the source code and "memory leakage" might happen in the libraries. Without the source code of libraries, it is difficult to intercept all memory allocations because of the "blackbox" effect. The current version of MigThread provides a user interface to specify the syntax of certain library calls so that the preprocessor can know how to insert proper primitives for memory management and pointer tracing.

Another unsafe factor is the incompatible data conversion. Between incompatible platforms, if data items are converted from higher precision formats to lower precision formats, precision loss may occur. Detecting incompatible data formats and conveying this low-level information up to the scheduling module can help move computations back or to proper nodes.

In MigThread, the pointer inference algorithm, a friendly user interface, and the data conversion scheme

CGT-RMR work together to eliminate unsafe factors to qualify almost all programs for migration.

Adaptation Point Analysis

An adaptation point is a location in a program where a thread/process can be migrated or checkpointed correctly. The locations of adaptation points for computation migration are critical since the distance between two consecutive adaptation points determines the migration scheme's sensitivity and overheads. If two adaptation points are too far apart, applications might be insensitive to the dynamic situation. But if they are too close, the related overheads with constructing, saving, and retrieving computation states will slow down the actual computation.

Several methods have been proposed in the literature regarding how to insert adaptation points. The first approach is that adaptation points are inserted by users or initiated at a barrier (Abdel-Shafi, Speight, & Bennet, 1999). This method is straightforward, but it brings undue burden on inexperienced programmers who do not know the structure and workload of their applications. And for some large and complex applications where many developers are involved, it is very difficult to insert adaptation points by users.

Some automatic adaptation point placement methods were proposed in order to overcome the disadvantage of the above approach. SNOW handles migration points by counting the number of floating point operations. That is, it inserts a migration point after a certain number of floating point operations. Since we do not always know the upper bound of a loop at compile time, this scheme cannot determine the count of operations inside a loop. Furthermore, this scheme is not applicable to non-scientific applications where most operations may not be floating point operations. Actually, it might be difficult to adopt a quantitative method because of pipelining, caches, and compiler optimizations. Therefore, such approach might be inaccurate under many circumstances.

The adaptation point placement approach in (Li, Stewart, & Fuchs, 1994) inserts potential adaptation points inside loops. It uses a counter to determine when checkpointing actually occurs. The counter is initially set to a value, called "reduction factor," and it is reduced by one for each loop. When the counter is equal to zero, the program does actual checkpointing. This scheme can only insert potential adaptation points at certain sparse points. With many small loops or loops with unknown upper bounds, checkpointing might not take place for a long time. Therefore, this method is fine with checkpointing, but if it is applied to migration, it will be insensitive to dynamic environment since migration is only allowed at sparse points.

MigThread aggressively inserts a lot of potential adaptation points into users' programs using its preprocessor. That is, it inserts at least one potential adaptation point into each nested loop, subroutine or branch. Whether a potential adaptation point will be actually activated is decided by a scheduler (or server) which determines the actual adaptation intervals according to the dynamic environment or using any existing optimal adaptation interval estimation methods, e.g Young's Law (Young, 1974). When an actual migration or checkpoint is needed, the scheduler sends a signal to users' programs in order to set a flag that controls each potential adaptation point. This approach can tolerate more adaptation points, and thus the applications can be more sensitive to their dynamic situations.

Library and system calls can cause problems to all application-level migration approaches since no source code is available to insert potential adaptation points at the higher level. However, to achieve better portability of the application-level approach, it is reasonable to give up the sensitivity during the third-party library call procedures. Luckily, the execution time of most library calls is relatively short.

For some parallel applications where relaxed memory consistency models are used, Migthread first inserts a pseudo-barrier primitive to synchronize computation progress of multiple threads/processes across different machines. If an actual migration is scheduled, real barrier operation will be activated to synchronize both computation progress and data copies. Therefore, migration can take place with consistent states.

Communication States

Networking applications set up communication channels by certain protocols such as TCP/IP. During and after migration, messages and those channels themselves need to be handled properly. If migration happens in a closed system using a distributed or networked operating system, the OS can re-establish communication seamlessly. The kernel-level approach is always efficient and transparent. However, portability is not supported.

Some SCC systems such as SNOW (Chanchio & Sun, 2001) proposed a new communication protocol above the regular TCP/IP and UDP/IP layers to deal with message channels in user space. This "connection-aware" protocol can reconstruct communication channels after migration. However, it only works within a closed PVM (Parallel Virtual Machine) system since the modified PVM library should be installed on all participating computers. This "closed-system" restriction is too strict for generic systems which have ports opened to communicate with outside applications.

In open systems, resetting the communication layout is difficult since we do not have the full control of the whole system. To achieve portability, system call wrappers can be used again to forward data to shadow-threads. The performance may not be as good as in kernel-level and VM-level approaches. Portability gain is very attractive in heterogeneous distributed systems.

Future Trends

SCC adopts the application-level thread/process migration approach. To achieve the complete high-level virtual machine abstraction, many features need to be enhanced or added. For example, communication states need to be improved to support open systems properly. Some future trends are listed to indicate possible research directions.

Resource Access Transparency

Most SCC systems focus on code and execution state migration. In fact, the most difficult task is to access original system resources seamlessly. Such resources include data in memory, files in secondary storage, signals, communication connections, and even databases. Communication states are the example for connection migration. Modified communication primitives can tear down and set up connections transparently. However, this requires a new communication library.

One possible solution is to install proxy server at the original node before any migration. To access old resources such as printers and databases, requests are sent back so that the proxy server can perform the local access and send back the results. However, this "leftover residue" method might slow down the performance because of the introduction of communication channels.

Data in memory could be shared by multiple threads. After thread migration, such data will be shared across threads on multiple machines. To achieve such distributed sharing, Distributed Shared Memory

(DSM) might be applied and a distributed lock mechanism needs to be implemented. This is similar to cache coherence or page/object-based DSM.

Resources in secondary storage such as files can be accessed by migrated computations through global references or copies. If the resources are supported by global naming, they can be accessed anywhere. Otherwise, copying them to the new destination can enable local access to hide the remote access after the migration.

Different resources require different strategies. SCC should be able to set up support accordingly.

Migration Policy

More and more researchers have realized the benefit of moving computations to data over the traditional way of moving data to computations. SCC needs to analyze the data and computation locality. Then it activates data/computation migration to minimize communication frequency and volume. Tasks and their required data are distributed nearby since local accesses are much faster than remote ones. Such a task-data relationship needs to be identified during the task mapping period. More importantly, it should be adjusted dynamically. An SCC scheduler should be implemented to detect communication patterns and orchestrate data/computation migration according to the predefined migration policy.

The migration policy is set up based on the size of data and computations. Its details need to be exploited further.

New Languages

SCC adopts the application-level approach. It exhibits several disadvantages. Firstly, it needs to handle different kinds of thread libraries. Secondly, the source-to-source translation might not be able to handle all programming styles, i.e., migration safety issues will appear. Finally, SCC has to deal with different kinds of libraries which might handle stacks or heaps directly or indirectly.

To support all migration features smoothly, powerful new programming languages might be the future direction. As part of DARPA's High Productivity Computing Systems (HPCS) program, several programming languages are being developed. The representative ones include IBM's X10 (Charles, et al., 2005), Sun Microsystems's Fortess (Allen, et al., 2008), and Cray's Chapel (Cray Inc., 2005). They all support parallel and distributed computing over multi-core clusters. However, computation mobility is not the significant feature of these on-going languages. If these languages take it as one of their main goals, programmers can take advantage of all features together without having to face the difficulty of combining multiple modules from different vendors. With the support from corresponding compilers on different platforms, these languages can deploy more new portable features easily.

With the new language, SCC can be raised to the language level. The integrated package with computation mobility and other new features might attract more programmers. At least up to now, no new language has been planned to tackle issues in SCC because of the difficulties.

CONCLUSION

This chapter points out the benefits of computation mobility in performance improvement, fault tolerance and throughput increase. To enable computation mobility, the key issue is to construct moveable computation states during application execution. Their granularity and position in software determine the solution's portability and flexibility. The eventual goal is to support computation mobility in heterogeneous environments and take advantage of multi-core/many-core clusters.

State-carrying code (SCC) is a software mechanism to achieve the above-mentioned computation mobility. Applications replicate their states at high level during their normal execution. Whenever the computation needs to be moved between different platforms, its computation state can be constructed easily. Since multithreading is widely used in multi-core architecture, threads are chosen as the basic computing units. Therefore, SCC adopts application-level thread migration to achieve computation mobility in heterogeneous systems.

Deployment and major features of SCC are explained. MigThread and several other existing systems are used to demonstrate the implementation strategies. Some future trends are given to indicate how SCC can encapsulate computation states further and evolve into a lightweight virtual machine. New high productivity languages can even upgrade SCC to language level. After the much richer system resources such as cores are exploited thoroughly in clusters, performance gain and high availability are expected.

REFERENCES

Abdel-Shafi, H., Speight, E., & Bennet, J. K. (1999). Efficient user-level thread migration and checkpointing on Windows NT clusters. *Proceedings of the 3rd USENIX Windows NT Research Symposium*, (pp. 1-10).

Accetta, M., Baron, R., Bolosky, W., Golub, D., Rashid, R., Tevanian, A., et al. (1986). March: A New Kernel Foundation for UNIX Development. *Proceedings of the the Summer USENIX Confernce*, (pp. 93-112).

Allen, E., Cadthase, D., Hallett, J., Luchangco, V., Maessen, J., Ryu, S., et al. (2008). *The fortress language specification, version 1.0.* Santa Clara, CA: Sun Microsystems.

Antoniu, G., & Boung, L. (2001). Dsm-pm2: A portable implementation platform for multi-threaded dsm consistency protocols. *Proceedings of the 6th international workshop on high-level parallel programming models and supportive environments.*

Barak, A., & La'adan, O. (1998). The mosix multicomputer operating system for high per-formance cluster computing. *Journal of Future Generation Computer System, 13*(4-5), 361–372. doi:10.1016/S0167-739X(97)00037-X

Barham, P., Dragovic, B., Fraser, K., Hand, S., Harris, T., Ho, A., et al. (2003). Xen and the art of virtualization. *Proceedings of the ACM symposium on operating systems principles.*

Bricker, A., Litzkow, M., & Livny, M. (1992). *Condor Technical Summary, Version 4.1b.* Madison, WI: University of Wisconsin - Madison.

Bronevetsky, G., Marques, D., Schulz, M., Pingali, K., & Stodghill, P. (2004). Application-level checkpointing for shared memory programs. *Proceedings of 11th international conference on architectural support for programming languages and operating systems.*

Casa, J., Konuru, R., Prouty, R., Walpole, J., & Otto, S. (1994). Adaptive Load Migration Systems for PVM. *Proceedings of supercomputing*, (pp. 390-399). Washington D.C.

Chanchio, K., & Sun, X. H. (2001). Communication state transfer for the mobility of con-curent heterogeneous computing. *Proceedings of the 2001 international conference on parallel processing.*

Charles, P., Grothoff, C., Saraswat, V., Donawa, C., Kielstra, A., Ebcioglu, K., et al. (2005). X10: an object-oriented approach of non-uniform cluster computing. *Proceedings of 20th annual ACM sigplan conference on object oriented programming, systems, languages, and applications*, (pp. 519-538).

Chase, J. S., Amador, F. F., Lazowska, E. D., Levy, H. M., & Littlefield, R. J. (1996). The amber systems: Parallel programming on a network of multiprocessors. *Proceedings of acm symposium on operating system principles.*

Chung, P. E. (1997). Checkpointing in cosmic: a user-level process migration environment. *Proceedings of Pacific Rim International Symposium on Fault-Tolerant Systems.*

Corporation, I. B. M. (1993). *IBM Load Leveler: User's Guide.*

Cray Inc. (2005). *The Chapel language specification, version 0.4.*

Cronk, M. H., & Mehrotra, P. (1997). Thread migration in the presence of pointers. *Proceedings of the mini-track on multithreaded systems, 30th hawaii interantional conference on system science.*

Dimitrov, B., & Rego, V. (1998). Arachne: A portable threads system supporting migrant threads on heterogeneous network farms. *IEEE Transactions on Parallel and Distributed Systems*, *9*(5), 459–469. doi:10.1109/71.679216

Douglis, F., & Ousterhout, J. K. (1991). Transparent process migration: Design alternatives and the sprite implementation. *Software, Practice & Experience*, *21*(8), 757–785. doi:10.1002/spe.4380210802

Ferrari, A. J., Chapin, S. J., & Grimshaw, A. S. (1997). *Process introspection: A heterogeneous checkpoint/restart mechanism based on automatic code modification,* (Technical Report: CS-97-05). University of Virginia, Charlottesville, VA.

Itzkovitz, A., Schuster, A., & Shalev, L. (1998). Thread migration and its applications in distributed shared memory systems. *Journal of Systems and Software*, *42*(1), 71–87. doi:10.1016/S0164-1212(98)00008-9

Jiang, H., & Chaudhary, V. (2004). Process/thread migration and checkpointing in heterogeneous distributed systems. *Proceedings of the 37th Hawaii International Conference on System Sciences,* Hawaii, USA.

Jul, E., Levy, H., Hutchinson, N., & Blad, A. (1998). Fine-grained mobility in the emerald system. *ACM Transactions on Computer Systems*, *6*(1), 109–133. doi:10.1145/35037.42182

Kale, L. V., & Krishnan, S. (1998). Charm++: Parallel Programming with Message-Driven Objects. In G. V. Wilson, & P. Lu, *Parallel programming using c++* (pp. 175-213). Cambridge, MA: MIT Press.

Lange, D., & Oshima, M. (1998). Mobile agents with java: The aglet api. *World Wide Web (Bussum)*, *1*(3). doi:10.1023/A:1019267832048

Li, C.-C. J., Stewart, E. M., & Fuchs, W. K. (1994). Compiler assisted full checkpointing. *Software, Practice & Experience*, *24*, 871–886. doi:10.1002/spe.4380241002

Lindholm, T., & Yellin, F. (1999). *The jave(tm) virtual machine specification (2nd Ed.).* New York: Addison Wesley.

Mascarenhas, E., & Rego, V. (1995). *Ariadne: Architecture of a portable threads system supporting mobile process,* (Tech. Rep. No. CSD-TR 95-017). Dept. of Computer Sciences, Purdue University, Southbend, IN.

Milton, S. (1998). *Thread migration in distributed memory multicomputers,* (Tech. Rep. No. TR-CS-98-01). Dept. of Comp Sci & Comp Sciences Lab, Australia National University, Acton, Australia.

Plank, J. S., Beck, M., Kinsley, G., & Li, K. (1995). Libckpt: Transparent checkpointing under unix. *Usenix winter technical conference*, (pp. 213-223).

Ramkumar, B., & Strumpen, V. (1997). Portable checkpointing for heterogenous architectures. *Symposium on fault-tolerent computing*, (pp. 58-67).

Rashid, R. F., & Robertson, G. (1981). Accent: A communication oriented network operating system kernel. *Proceedings of the eighth acm symposium on operating systems principles*, (pp. 64-75).

Smith, P., & Hutchinson, N. C. (1998). Heterogeneous process migration: The tui system. *Software, Practice & Experience*, *28*(6), 611–639. doi:10.1002/(SICI)1097-024X(199805)28:6<611::AID-SPE169>3.0.CO;2-F

Srinivasan, R. (1995). *XDR: External Data Representation Standard* (Tech. Rep. No. RFC 1832).

Ssu, K., Yao, B., & Fuchs, W. K. (1999). An adaptive checkpointing protocol to bound recovery time with message logging. *Symposium on reliable distributed systems*, (pp. 244-252).

Stellner, G. (1996). Cocheck: Checkpointing and process migration for mpi. *Proceedings of 10th international parallel processing symposium.*

Theimer, M. M., Lantz, K. A., & Cheriton, D. R. (1985). Preemptable remote execution facilities for the v-system. *SIGOPS Oper. Syst. Rev.*, *19*(5), 2–12. doi:10.1145/323627.323629

VMware Inc. (1999). *VMware virtual platform.*

Walker, B., Popek, G., English, R., Kline, C., & Thiel, G. (1992). The locus distributed operating system. *Ditributed Computing Systems: Concepts and Structures, 17*(5).

White, J. E. (1996). Telescript technology: Mobile agents. *Journal of Software Agents.*

Young, J. W. (1974). A first order approximation to the optimum checkpoint interval. *Communications of the ACM, 17*, 530–531. doi:10.1145/361147.361115

Zajcew, R., Roy, P., Black, D., & Peak, C. (1993). An osf/l unix for massively parallel multi-computers. *Proceedings of the winter 1993 conference*, (pp. 449-468).

Zhou, S., Zheng, X., Wang, J., & Delisle, P. (1993). Utopia: a load sharing facility for large, heterogeneous distributed computer systems. *Software, Practice & Experience*, *23*(12), 1305–1336. doi:10.1002/spe.4380231203

Zhu, W., Wang, C.-L., & Lan, F. (2002). Jessica2: a distributed java virtual machine with trans-parent thread migration support. *Proc. of IEEE international conference on cluster computing.*

KEY TERMS AND DEFINITIONS

Computation Mobility: The ability to move a running program from one machine to another

Computation States: The required information to indicate the execution progress, including register contents, stacks, and heaps, etc.

Data Conversion: The function to translate data from one format to another

Migration Safety: The necessary features of a program to enable its mobility

State-Carrying Code: Transformed programs which can acquire the running state in order to stop and restart the execution

Thread/Process Migration: The feature to move a running thread/process from one machine to another

Virtualization: The abstraction of system resources where computations can be executed for portability

Compilation of References

3GPP TS 23.234 V7.5.0 (2007). *3GPP system to WLAN interworking, 3GPP Specification*. Retrieved May 1, 2008, from http://www.3gpp.org, 2007.

A Blueprint for the Open Science Grids. (2004, December). Snapshot v0.9.

Abawajy, J. (2004). Placement of file replicas in data grid environments. In *Proceedings of international conference on computational science* (Vol. 3038, pp. 66-73).

Abdel-Shafi, H., Speight, E., & Bennet, J. K. (1999). Efficient user-level thread migration and checkpointing on Windows NT clusters. *Proceedings of the 3rd USENIX Windows NT Research Symposium*, (pp. 1-10).

Abdennadher, N., & Boesch, R. (2005). Towards a peer-to-peer platform for high performance computing. In HPCASIA'05 *Proceedings of the Eighth International Conference in High-Performance Computing in Asia-Pacific Region*, (pp. 354-361). Los Alamitos, CA: IEEE Computer Society. Retrieved from http://doi.ieeecomputersociety.org/10.1109/HPCASIA.2005.98

Abdennadher, N., & Boesch, R. (2006, August). A scheduling algorithm for high performance peer-to-peer platform. In W. Lehner, N. Meyer, A. Streit, & C. Stewart (Eds.), *Coregrid Workshop, Euro-Par 2006* (p. 126-137). Dresden, Germany: Springer.

Aberer, K., Cudr-Mauroux, P., Datta, A., Despotovic, Z., Hauswirth, M., & Punceva, M. (2003). P-Grid: A self-organizing structured p2p system. *SIGMOD Record*, *32*(3), 29–33. doi:10.1145/945721.945729

Abramson, D., Buyya, R., & Giddy, J. (2002). A computational economy for grid computing and its implementation in the Nimrod-G resource broker. *Future Generation Computer Systems*, *18*(8), 1061–1074. doi:10.1016/S0167-739X(02)00085-7

Accetta, M., Baron, R., Bolosky, W., Golub, D., Rashid, R., Tevanian, A., et al. (1986). March: A New Kernel Foundation for UNIX Development. *Proceedings of the the Summer USENIX Confernce*, (pp. 93-112).

ACR-NEMA. (2005). *DICOM (Digital Image and Communications in Medicine)*. Retrieved June 15th, 2008, from http://medical.nema.org/

Adabala, S., Chadha, V., Chawla, P., Figueiredo, R., Fortes, J., & Krsul, I. (2005, June). From virtualized resources to virtual computing Grids: the In-VIGO system. *Future Generation Computer Systems*, *21*(6), 896–909. doi:10.1016/j.future.2003.12.021

Adamy, U., & Erlebach, T. (2004). *Online coloring of intervals with bandwidth* (LNCS Vol. 2909, pp. 1–12). Berlin: Springer.

Adiga, N. R., et al. (2002). An overview of the BlueGene/L supercomputer. In *Proceedings of the Supercomputing Conference (SC'2002), Baltimore MD, USA*, (pp. 1–22).

Adjie-Winoto, W., Schwartz, E., Blakrishnan, H., & Lilley, J. (1999). The design and implementation of an intentional naming system. *Operating Systems Review*, *34*(5), 186–201. doi:10.1145/319344.319164

Adler, M., Halperin, E., Karp, R. M., & Vazirani, V. (2003, June). A stochastic process on the hypercube with applications to peer-to-peer networks. In *Proc. of STOC*.

Adve, S. V., & Hill, M. D. (1993). A Unified Formalization of Four Shared-Memory Models. *IEEE Transactions on Parallel and Distributed Systems*, *4*(6), 613–624. doi:10.1109/71.242161

Afgan, E., Velusamy, V., & Bangalore, P. (2005). Grid resource broker using application benchmarking. *European Grid Conference*, (LNCS 3470, pp. 691-701). Amsterdam: Springer Verlag.

Agarwal, A., Bianchini, R., Chaiken, D., Johnson, K. L., Kranz, D., Kubiatowicz, J., et al. (1995). The MIT Alewife machine: architecture and performance. In *Proceedings of the 22nd Annual International Symposium on Computer Architecture* (ISCA'95), S. Margherita Ligure, Italy, (pp. 2-13). New York: ACM Press.

Agarwal, A., Lim, B.-H., Kranz, D., & Kubiatowicz, J. (1990). *April: a processor architecture for multiprocessing*. In Proceedings of the 17th Annual International Symposium on Computer Architecture (ISCA'90), (pp. 104-114), Seattle, WA: ACM Press.

Agarwal, S., Chuah. C. N., & Katz, R. H. (2003). *OPCA: Robust Inter-domain Policy Routing and Traffic Control*, OPENARCH.

Agrawal, D. P., & Zeng, Q.-A. (2006). *Introduction to wireless and mobile systems* (2nd Ed.). Florence, KY: Thomson.

Aho, A. V., & Corasick, M. J. (1975). Efficient string matching: An aid to bibliographic search. *Communications of the ACM*, *18*(6), 333–340. doi:10.1145/360825.360855

Akenine-Moller, T., & Haines, E., (2002, July). *Real-time rendering* (2nd Ed.). Wellesley, MA: A. K. Peters Publishing Company.

Akyildiz, I., Mohanty, S., & Xie, J. (2005). A ubiquitous mobile communication architecture for next-generation heterogeneous wireless systems. *IEEE Radio Communications*, *43*(6), 29–36. doi:10.1109/MCOM.2005.1452832

Alam, S. R., Meredith, J. S., & Vetter, J. S. (2007, Sept.) Balancing productivity and performance on the cell broadband engine. *IEEE Annual International Conference on Cluster Computing*.

Aldinucci, M., Danelutto, M., & Teti, P. (2003). An advanced environment supporting structured parallel programming in Java. *Future Generation Computer Systems*, *19*(5), 611–626. doi:10.1016/S0167-739X(02)00172-3

Aldwairi, M., Conte, T., & Franzon, P., (2005) Configurable string matching hardware for speeding up intrusion detection. *ACM SIGARCH Computer Architecture News*, *33*(1).

Alexander, D. (1995). *Recursively Modular Artificial Neural Network*. Doctoral Thesis, Macquire University, Australia, Sydney, Australia.

Alexandrov, A. D., Ibel, M., Schauser, K. E., & Scheiman, C. (1997, April). SuperWeb: Towards a global web-based parallel computing infrastructure. In *Proceedings of the 11th IEEE International Parallel Processing Symposium (IPPS)*.

Alexandrov, A. Ionescu, M. F. Schauser, K. E. & Scheiman, C. (1995). LogGP: Incorporating long messages into the LogP model. In *Proceedings of the seventh annual ACM symposium on Parallel algorithms and architectures,* (pp. 95–105). New York: ACM Press.

ALF for Cell BE Programmer's Guide and API Reference. Retrieved from http://www01.ibm.com/chips/techlib/techlib.nsf/techdocs/41838EDB5A15CCCD002573530063D465

ALF for Hybrid-x86 Programmer's Guide and API Reference. Retrieved from http://www01.ibm.com/chips/techlib/techlib.nsf/techdocs/389BBE99638335B80025735300624044

Ali, A., McClatchey, R., Anjum, A., Habib, I., Soomro, K., Asif, M., et al. (2006). From grid middleware to a grid operating system. In *Proceedings of the Fifth International Conference on Grid and Cooperative Computing,* (pp. 9-16). China: IEEE Computer Society.

Alima, L. O., El-Ansary, S., Brand, P., & Haridi, S. (2003). DKS (N, k, f): A Family of Low Communication, Scalable and Fault-tolerant Infrastructures for P2P Applications. In *Proceedings of the 3rd IEEE Intl. Symp. on Cluster Computing and the Grid* (pp. 344-350). New York: IEEE Computer Society Press.

Allcock, W. (2003, Mar). *GridFTP protocol specification.* Global Grid Forum Recommendation GFD.20.

Allen, E., Cadthase, D., Hallett, J., Luchangco, V., Maessen, J., Ryu, S., et al. (2008). *The fortress language specification, version 1.0.* Santa Clara, CA: Sun Microsystems.

Allen, E., Chase, D., Hallett, J., Luchangco, V., Maessen, J.-W., Ryo, S., et al. (2008). *The Fortress language specification, Version 1.0.* Santa Clara, CA: Sun Microsystems, Inc.

Allen, G., Davis, K., Dolkas, K. N., Doulamis, N. D., Goodale, T., Kielmann, T., et al. (2003). Enabling applications on the grid: A Gridlab overview. *International Journal of High Performance Computing Applications: Special issue on Grid Computing: Infrastructure and Applications.*

Alshwede, R., Cai, N, Li, S.-Y. R., & Yeung, R. W. (2000). Network information flow: Single Source. *IEEE Transactions on information theory,* (submitted for publication).

Altintas, I., Berkley, C., Jaeger, E., Jones, M., Ludascher, B., & Mock, S. (2004). Kepler: an extensible system for design and execution of scientific workflows. In *Proceedings of the 16th International Conference on Scientific and Statistical Database Management (SSDBM),* Santorini Island, Greece.

Altschul, G. W., M. W, Myers., & Lipman. (1990). Basic local alignment search tool. *Journal of Molecular Biology, 215*(3), 403–410.

Alverson, R., Callahan, D., Cummings, D., Koblenz, B., Porterfield, A., & Smith, B. (1990) *The Tera computer system.* In Proceedings of the 4th International Conference on Supercomputing (ICS'90), (pp. 1-6). Amsterdam: ACM Press.

Amarasinghe, S. (2007). *Multicore programming primer and programming competition.* A course at MIT, Cambridge, MA.

Amazon Elastic Compute Cloud (2007). Retrieved from www.amazon.com/ec2

Amazon Elastic Compute Cloud. (2008, November). Retrieved from http://www.amazon.com/ec2

Ambastha, N., Beak, I., Gokhale, S., & Mohr, A. (2003). A cache-based resource location approach for unstructured P2P network architectures. *Graduate Research Conference*, Department of Computer Science, Stony Brook University, NY.

Ammann, P., Jajodia, S., & Ray, I. (1997). Applying formal methods to semantic-based decomposition of transactions. [TODS]. *ACM Transactions on Database Systems, 22*(2), 215–254. doi:10.1145/249978.249981

Ancilotti, P., Lazzerini, B., & Prete, C. A. (1990). A distributed commit protocol for a multicomputer system. *IEEE Transactions on Computers, 39*(5), 718–724. doi:10.1109/12.53589

Anderson, D. P. (2004). BOINC: A system for public-resource computing and storage. In Grid'04 *Proceedings of the Fifth IEEE/ACM International Workshop on Grid Computing*, (pp. 4-10). Los Alamitos, CA: IEEE Computer Society. Retrieved from http://dx.doi.org/10.1109/GRID.2004.14

Anderson, D. P., Cobb, J., Korpela, E., Lebofsky, M., & Werthimer, D. (2002). SETI@home: An experiment in public-resource computing. *Communications of the ACM, 45*(11), 56-61. New York: ACM Press. Retrieved from http://doi.acm.org/10.1145/581571.581573

Anderson, D., & Fedak, G. (2006). The computational and storage potential of volunteer computing. In *Proceedings of The IEEE International Symposium on Cluster Computing and The Grid (CCGRID'06)*.

Andrade, N., Brasileiro, F., Cirne, W., & Mowbray, M. (2007). Automatic Grid assembly by promoting collaboration in peer-to-peer Grids. *Journal of Parallel and Distributed Computing, 67*(8), 957–966. doi:10.1016/j.jpdc.2007.04.011

Andrade, N., Cirne, W., Brasileiro, F., & Roisenberg, R. (2003, October). OurGrid: An approach to easily assemble grids with equitable resource sharing. In JSSPP'03 *Proceedings of the 9th Workshop on Job Scheduling Strategies for Parallel Processing* (LNCS). Berlin/Heidelberg, Germany: Springer. doi: 10.1007/10968987

Androutsellis-Theotokis, S., & Spinellis, D. (2004). A survey of peer-to-peer content distribution technologies. *ACM Computing Surveys, 36*(4), 335–371. doi:10.1145/1041680.1041681

Andrzejak, A., Domingues, P., & Silva, L. (2006). Predicting Machine Availabilities in Desktop Pools. In *IEEE/IFIP Network Operations and Management Symposium* (pp. 225–234).

Andrzejak, A., Kondo, D., & Anderson, D. P. (2008). Ensuring collective availability in volatile resource pools via forecasting. In *19th Ifip/Ieee Distributed Systems: Operations And Management (DSOM 2008)*. Samos Island, Greece.

Anfinson, J., & Luk, F. T. (1988, December). A Linear Algebraic Model of Algorithm-Based Fault Tolerance. *IEEE Transactions on Computers, 37*(12), 1599–1604. doi:10.1109/12.9736

Antoniu, G., & Boung, L. (2001). Dsm-pm2: A portable implementation platform for multi-threaded dsm consistency protocols. *Proceedings of the 6th international workshop on high-level parallel programming models and supportive environments*.

Antoniu, G., Bougé, L., Hatcher, P., MacBeth, M., McGuigan, K., & Namyst, R. (2001). The Hyperion system: Compiling multithreaded Java bytecode for distributed execution. *Parallel Computing, 27*(10), 1279–1297. doi:10.1016/S0167-8191(01)00093-X

Araujo, F., Domingues, P., Kondo, D., & Silva, L. M. (2008, April). Using cliques of nodes to store desktop grid checkpoints. In *Coregrid Integration Workshop*, Crete, Greece.

Aridor, Y., Factor, M., & Teperman, A. (1999). *cJVM: A Single System Image of a JVM on a Cluster*. Paper presented at the Proceedings of the 1999 International Conference on Parallel Processing.

Aridor, Y., Factor, M., Teperman, A., Eilam, T., & Schuster, A. (2000). Transparently obtaining scalability for Java applications on a cluster. *Journal of Parallel and Distributed Computing, 60*(10), 1159–1193. doi:10.1006/jpdc.2000.1649

ARM. (2008). *ARM Achieves 10 Billion Processor Milestone*. Retrieved March 10, 2008, from http://www.arm.com/news/19720.html

Arpaci, R. H., Dusseau, A. C., Vahdat, A. M., Liu, L. T., Anderson, T. E., & Patterson, D. A. (May, 1995). *The interaction of parallel and sequential workloads on a network of workstations*. Paper presented at the 1995 ACM SIGMETRICS Conference on Measurement and Modeling of Computer Systems.

Arpaci-Dusseau, R. H., Arpaci-Dusseau, A. C., Vahdat, A., Liu, L. T., Anderson, T. E., & Patterson, D. A. (1995). The interaction of parallel and sequential workloads on a network of workstations. *SIGMETRICS*, (pp. 267-278).

Asanovic, K., Bodik, R., Catanzaro, B. C., Gebis, J. J., Husbands, R., Keutzer, K., et al. (2006, Dec). *The Landscape of Parallel Computing Research: A View from Berkeley* (Tech. Rep. No. UCB/EECS-2006-183). EECS Department, University of California, Berkeley.

ASF. (2002). *The Apache Tomcat Connector*. Retrieved June 18, 2008, from http://tomcat.apache.org/connectors-doc/

Audsley, N. C., Burns, A., Richardson, M. F., Tindall, K., & Wellings, A. (1993). *Applying New Scheduling Theory to Static Priority Pre-emptive Scheduling. Software Engineering Journal, 8*(5).

Australian Partnership for Advanced Computing (APAC) Grid. (2005). Retrieved from http://www.apac.edu.au/programs/GRID/index.html.

Autenrieth., F., Isralewitz, B., Luthey-Schulten., Z., Sethi, A. & Pogorelov, T. *Bioinformatics and Sequence Alignment*.

Awduche, D.O., Chiu, A., Elqalid, A., Widjaja, I., & Xiao, X. (2002). *A Framework for Internet Traffic Engineering* [draft 2]. Retrieved from IETF draft database.

Azar, Y. Broder, A., et al. (1994). Balanced allocations. *In Proc. of STOC* (pp. 593–602).

Baboescu, F., & Varghese, G. (2005). Scalable packet classification. *IEEE/ACM Trans. Netw., 13*(1), 2–14.

Bader, D. A., & Agarwal, V. (2007, Dec). FFTC: Fastest fourier transform on the ibm cell broadband engine. In *14th IEEE international conference on high performance computing (hipc 2007)* Goa, India, (pp. 18–21).

Badia, R. M., Labarta, J. S., Sirvent, R. L., Perez, J. M., Cela, J. M., & Grima, R. (2003). Programming grid applications with GRID superscalar. *Journal of Grid Computing, 1*, 151–170. doi:10.1023/B:GRID.0000024072.93701.f3

Bailey, D., Barszcz, E., Barton, J. T., Browning, D. S., Carter, R. L., & Dagum, L. (1991). The NAS parallel benchmarks. *The International Journal of Supercomputer Applications, 5*(3), 63–73.

Baker, M., Buyya, R., & Laforenza, D. (2002). Grids and grid technologies for wide-area distributed computing. *Software* [SPE]. *Practice and Experience, 32*, 1437–1466. doi:10.1002/spe.488

Baker, S. (2007). Google and the wisdom of clouds. *Business Week, Dec. 13*. Retrieved from www.businessweek.com/magazine/content/07_52/b4064048925836.htm

Bal, H. E., & Haines, M. (1998). Approaches for integrating task and data parallelism. *IEEE Concurrency, 6*(3), 74–84. doi:10.1109/4434.708258

Balasubramanian, V., & Banerjee, P. (1990). Compiler-Assisted Synthesis of Algorithm-Based Checking in Multiprocessors. *IEEE Transactions on Computers, C-39*, 436–446. doi:10.1109/12.54837

Balaton, Z., Gombas, G., Kacsuk, P., Kornafeld, A., Kovacs, J., & Marosi, A. C. (2007, March 26-30). Sztaki desktop grid: a modular and scalable way of building large computing grids. In *Proceedings of the 21st International Parallel And Distributed Processing Symposium*, Long Beach, CA.

Balazinska, M., Balakrishnan, H., & Stonebraker, M. (2004, March). Contract-based load management in federated distributed systems. In *1st Symposium on Networked Systems Design and Implementation (NSDI)* (pp. 197-210). San Francisco: USENIX Association.

Balazinska, M., Blakrishnan, H., & Karger, D. (2002). INS/Twine: a scalable peer-to-peer architecture for intentional resource discovery. In *Pervasive 2002*, Zurich, Switzerland, August. Berlin: Springer Verlag.

Baldassari, J., Finkel, D., & Toth, D. (2006, November 13-15). Slinc: A framework for volunteer computing. In *Proceedings of the 18th Iasted International Conference On Parallel And Distributed Computing And Systems (PDCS 2006)*. Dallas, TX.

Baldridge, K., Biros, G., Chaturvedi, A., Douglas, C. C., Parashar, M., How, J., et al. (2006, January). *National Science Foundation DDDAS Workshop Report*. Retrieved from http://www.dddas.org/nsf-workshop-2006/wkshpreport.pdf.

Ban, B. (1997). *JGroups - A Toolkit for Reliable Multicast Communication*. Retrieved June 18, 2008, from http://www.jgroups.org/javagroupsnew/docs/index.html

Banerjee, P., Rahmeh, J. T., Stunkel, C. B., Nair, V. S. S., Roy, K., & Balasubramanian, V. (1990). Algorithm-based fault tolerance on a hypercube multiprocessor. *IEEE Transactions on Computers*, *C-39*, 1132–1145. doi:10.1109/12.57055

Bangerth, W., Matossian, V., Parashar, M., Klie, H., & Wheeler, M. (2005). An autonomic reservoir framework for the stochastic optimization of well placement. *Cluster Computing*, *8*(4), 255–269. doi:10.1007/s10586-005-4093-3

Banks, T. (2006). *Web services resource framework (WSRF)*. Organization for the Advancement of Structured Information Standards (OASIS).

Barak, A., & La'adan, O. (1998). The mosix multicomputer operating system for high per-formance cluster computing. *Journal of Future Generation Computer System*, *13*(4-5), 361–372. doi:10.1016/S0167-739X(97)00037-X

Barak, A., Guday, S., & R., W. (1993). *The MOSIX Distributed Operating System, Load Balancing for UNIX* (Vol. 672). Berlin: Springer-Verlag.

Baratloo, A., Karaul, M., Kedem, Z., & Wyckoff, P. (1996). Charlotte: Metacomputing on the Web. In *Proceeidngs of the 9th International Conference On Parallel And Distributed Computing Systems (PDCS-96)*.

Barham, P., Dragovic, B., Fraser, K., Hand, S., Harris, T., Ho, A., et al. (2003). Xen and the art of virtualization. In *19th ACM Symposium on Operating Systems Principles (SOSP '03)* (pp. 164–177). New York: ACM Press.

Barrett, R., Berry, M., Chan, T. F., Demmel, J., Donato, J., Dongarra, J., et al. (1994). *Templates for the Solution of Linear Systems: Building Blocks for Iterative Methods, 2nd Edition*., Philadelphia, PA: SIAM.

Barua, S., Thulasiram, R. K., & Thulasiraman, P. (2005, Aug.). High performance computing for a financial application using fast Fourier transform. In *Euro-par parallel processing* (p. 1246-1253). Lisbon, Portugal.

Bassi, A., Beck, M., Fagg, G., Moore, T., Plank, J. S., & Swany, M. (2002). The Internet BackPlane Protocol: A Study in Resource Sharing. In *Second ieee/acm international symposium on cluster computing and the grid*, Berlin, Germany.

Bataineh, S., Hsiung, T.-Y., & Robertazzi, T. (1994). Closed form solutions for bus and tree networks of processors load sharing a divisible job. *Institute of Electrical and Electronic Engineers*, *43*(10), 1184–119.

Baude, F., Caromel, D., Huet, F., & Vayssiere, J. (2000, May). Communicating mobile active objects in java. In R. W. Marian Bubak Hamideh Afsarmanesh & B. Hetrzberger (Eds.), *Proceedings of HPCN Europe 2000* (Vol. 1823, p. 633-643). Berlin: Springer. Retrieved from http://www-sop.inria.fr/oasis/Julien.Vayssiere/publications/18230633.pdf

BBC. (2005). *SMEF- Standard Media Exchange Framework*. Retrieved June 15th, 2008, from http://www.bbc.co.uk/guidelines/smef/.15th June, 2008.

BEinGRID. (2008). *Business experiments in grids*. Retrieved from www.beingrid.com

Belalem, G., & Slimani, Y. (2006). A hybrid approach for consistency management in large scale systems. *In Proceedings of the international conference on networking and services* (pp. 71–76).

Belalem, G., & Slimani, Y. (2007). Consistency management for data grid in optorsim simulator. In *Proceedings of the international conference on multimedia and ubiquitous engineering* (pp. 554–560).

Bell, W. H., Cameron, D. G., Carvajal-Schiaffino, R., Millar, A. P., Stockinger, K., & Zini, F. (2003). Evaluation of an economy-based file replication strategy for a data grid. In *Proceedings of the 3rd IEEE/ACM international symposium on cluster computing and the grid*.

Bell, W., Cameron, D., Capozza, L., Millar, P., Stockinger, K., & Zini, F. (2003). Optorsim - A grid simulator for studying dynamic data replication strategies. *International Journal of High Performance Computing Applications*, *17*, 403–416. doi:10.1177/10943420030174005

Bellavista, P., & Corradi, A. (2007). *The Handbook of Mobile Middleware*. New York: Auerbach publications.

Beltrame, F., Maggi, P., Melato, M., Molinari, E., Sisto, R., & Torterolo, L. (2006, February 2-3). SRB Data grid and compute grid integration via the enginframe grid portal. In *Proceedings of the 1st SRB Workshop*, San Diego, CA. Retrieved from www.sdsc.edu/srb/Workshop/SRB-handout-v2.pdf

Ben Hassen, S., Bal, H. E., & Jacobs, C. J. H. (1998). A task- and data-parallel programming language based on shared objects. [TOPLAS]. *ACM Transactions on Programming Languages and Systems*, *20*(6), 1131–1170. doi:10.1145/295656.295658

Bender, T. (1982). *Community and Social Change in America*. Baltimore, MD: The Johns Hopkins University Press.

Benjelloun, O., Sarma, A. D., Halevy, A. Y., Theobald, M., & Widom, J. (2008). Databases with uncertainty and lineage. *The VLDB Journal*, *17*(2), 243–264. doi:10.1007/s00778-007-0080-z

Benkert, K. Gabriel, E. & Resch, M. M. (2008). *Outlier Detection in Performance Data of Parallel Applications*. In the 9th IEEE International Workshop on Parallel Distributed Scientific and Engineering Computing (PDESC), Miami, Florida, USA.

Benson, D. A., Karsch-Mizrachi, I., Lipman, D. J., Ostell, J., Rapp, B. A., & Wheller, D. L. (2000, October). Genbank. *Nucleic Acids Research*, *28*(1), 15–18. doi:10.1093/nar/28.1.15

Berezin, Y. A., & Vshivkov, V. A. (1980). *The method of particles in rarefied plasma dynamic*. Novosibirsk, Russia: Nauka (Science).

Berger, M. P., & Munson, P. J. (1991). A novel randomized iteration strategy for aligning multiple protein sequences. *Computer Applications in the Biosciences*, *7*, 479–484.

Berman, F., Casanova, H., Chien, A. A., Cooper, K. D., Dail, H., & Dasgupta, A. (2005). New Grid scheduling and rescheduling methods in the GrADS project. *International Journal of Parallel Programming*, *33*(2-3), 209–229. doi:10.1007/s10766-005-3584-4

Berman, F., Chien, A., Cooper, K., Dongarra, J., Foster, I., & Gannon, D. (2001). The grads project: Software support for high-level grid application development. *International Journal of High Performance Computing Applications*, *15*(4), 327–344. doi:10.1177/109434200101500401

Berman, F., Fox, G., & Hey, T. (Eds.). (2003). *Grid computing making the global infrastructure a reality*. New York: Wiley Series in Communication Networking & Distributed Systems.

Berman, F., Wolski, R., Casanova, H., Cirne, W., Dail, H., & Faerman, M. (2003). Adaptive computing on the Grid using AppLeS. *IEEE Transactions on Parallel and Distributed Systems*, *14*(4), 369–382. doi:10.1109/TPDS.2003.1195409

Berman, F., Wolski, R., Figueira, S., Schopf, J., & Shao, G. (1996). Application-Level Scheduling on Distributed Heterogeneous Networks. In *Proc. of supercomputing'96*, Pittsburgh, PA.

Berriman, G. B., Good, J. C., & Laity, A. C. (2003). Montage: A grid enabled image mosaic service for the national virtual observatory. In F. Ochsenbein (Ed.), *Astronomical Data Analysis Software and Systems XIII*, (pp. 145-167). Livermore, CA: ASP press.

Bertossi, A. A., Pinotti, M. C., Rizzi, R., & Gupta, P. (2004). Allocating servers in infostations for bounded simultaneous requests. *Journal of Parallel and Distributed Computing*, *64*, 1113–1126. doi:10.1016/S0743-7315(03)00118-7

Bertsekas, D. P., & Tsitsiklis, J. N. (1989). *Parallel and Distributed Computation: Numerical Methods*. Englewood Cliffs, NJ: Prentice Hall.

Bharadwaj, V., Ghose, D., & Mani, V. (1995, April). Multi-installment load distribution in tree network with delays. *Institute of Electrical and Electronic Engineers*, *31*(2), 555–567.

Bharadwaj, V., Ghose, D., & Robertazzi, T. G. (2003, January). Divisible load theory: A new paradigm for load scheduling in distributed systems. *Cluster Computing, 6*(1), 7–17. doi:10.1023/A:1020958815308

Bharadwaj, V., Li, X., & Ko, C. C. (2000). *Efficient partitioning and scheduling of computer vision and image processing data on bus networks using divisible load analysis. Image and Vision Computing, 18*, 919–938. doi:10.1016/S0262-8856(99)00085-2

Bhatt, S. N., Chung, F. R. K., Leighton, F. T., & Rosenberg, A. L. (1997). An optimal strategies for cycle-stealing in networks of workstations. *IEEE Transactions on Computers, 46*(5), 545–557. doi:10.1109/12.589220

Bhowmick, S. Eijkhout, V. Freund, Y. Fuentes, E. & Keyes, D. (in press). Application of Machine Learning in Selecting Sparse Linear Solver. Submitted for publication to the *International Journal on High Performance Computing Applications.*

Bienkowski, M., Korzeniowski, M., & auf der Heide, F. M. (2005). Dynamic load balancing in distributed hash tables. In *Proc. of IPTPS.*

BIRN. (2008). *Biomedical informatics research network.* Retrieved from www.nbirn.net/index.shtm

Bishop, P., & Warren, N. (2002). *JavaSpaces in Practice.* New York: Addison Wesley.

Black, F., & Scholes, M. (1973). The Pricing of Options and Corporate Liabilities. *The Journal of Political Economy, 81*(3). doi:10.1086/260062

Blackford, L. S., Choi, J., Cleary, A., Petitet, A., & Whaley, R. C. Demmel, et al. (1996). ScaLAPACK: a portable linear algebra library for distributed memory computers - design issues and performance. In *Supercomputing '96: Proceedings of the 1996 ACM/IEEE conference on Supercomputing (CDROM)*, (p. 5).

Blair, G. S., Coulson, G., & Blair, L. DuranLimon, H., Grace, P., Moreira, R., & Parlavantzas, N. (2002). Reflection, self-awareness and self-healing in OpenORB. In *WOSS '02 Proceedings of the First Workshop on Self-Healing Systems,* (pp. 9-14).

Bloom, H. B. (1970). Space/time trade-offs in hash coding with allowable errors. *Communications of the ACM, 13*(7), 422–426. doi:10.1145/362686.362692

Bluetooth (2008). Retrieved November 2008 from www.bluetooth.com

Boghosian, B., Coveney, P., Dong, S., Finn, L., Jha, S., Karniadakis, G. E., et al. (2006, June). Nektar, SPICE and vortonics: Using federated Grids for large scale scientific applications. In *IEEE Workshop on Challenges of Large Applications in Distributed Environments (CLADE).* Paris: IEEE Computing Society.

BOINC. (2008). *Berkeley Open Infrastructure for Network Computing.* Retrieved March 10, 2008 from http://boinc.berkeley.edu

BOINCstats. (2008). *Seti@home Project Statistics.* Retrieved March 10, 2008, from http://boincstats.com/stats/project_graph.php?pr=sah

Bojadziew, G., & Bojadziew, M. (1997). *Fuzzy Logic for Business, Finance, and Management Modeling,* (2nd Ed.). Singapore: World Scientific Press.

Boley, D. L., Brent, R. P., Golub, G. H., & Luk, F. T. (1992). Algorithmic fault tolerance using the lanczos method. *SIAM Journal on Matrix Analysis and Applications, 13,* 312–332. doi:10.1137/0613023

Bolosky, W., Douceur, J., Ely, D., & Theimer, M. (2000). Feasibility of a Serverless Distributed file System Deployed on an Existing Set of Desktop PCs. In *Proceedings of sigmetrics.*

Bonomi, F., Mitzenmacher, M., Panigrah, R., Singh, S., & Varghese, G. (2006). *Beyond bloom filters: from approximate membership checks to approximate state machines.* Paper presented at the Proceedings of the 2006 conference on Applications, technologies, architectures, and protocols for computer communications.

Boyd, C. (2008, March/April). Data-parallel computing. *ACM Queue; Tomorrow's Computing Today, 6*(2). doi:10.1145/1365490.1365499

Boyer, R., & Moore, J. (1977). A fast string searching algorithm. *Communications of the ACM*, *20*(10), 762–777. doi:10.1145/359842.359859

Boyle, P. P. (1986). Option Valuing Using a Three Jump Process. *International Options Journal*, *3*(2).

Brandes, T. (1999). Exploiting advanced task parallelism in high performance Fortran via a task library. In *Euro-Par '99: Proceedings of the 5th International Euro-Par Conference on Parallel Processing* (pp. 833–844). London: Springer-Verlag.

Braun, T., Feyrer, S., Rapf, W., & Reinhardt, M. (2001). *Parallel Image Processing*. Berlin: Springer-Verlag.

Brecht, T., Sandhu, H., Shan, M., & Talbot, J. (1996). Paraweb: towards world-wide supercomputing. In *Ew 7: Proceedings of the 7th workshop on acm sigops european workshop* (pp. 181–188). New York: ACM.

Bricker, A., Litzkow, M., & Livny, M. (1992). *Condor Technical Summary, Version 4.1b.* Madison, WI: University of Wisconsin - Madison.

Brighten Godfrey, P., & Stoica, I. (2005). Heterogeneity and load balance in distributed hash tables. *In Proc. of IEEE INFOCOM.*

Broder, A., & Mitzenmacher, M. (2003). *Network Applications of Bloom Filters: A Survey. Internet Mathematics*, *1*(4), 485–509.

Bronevetsky, G., Marques, D., Schulz, M., Pingali, K., & Stodghill, P. (2004). Application-level checkpointing for shared memory programs. *Proceedings of 11th international conference on architectural support for programming languages and operating systems.*

Brune, M., Gehring, J., Keller, A., & Reinefeld, A. (1999). Managing clusters of geographically distributed high-performance computers. *Concurrency (Chichester, England)*, *11*(15), 887–911. doi:10.1002/(SICI)1096-9128(19991225)11:15<887::AID-CPE459>3.0.CO;2-J

Bruneo, D., Scarpa, M., Zaia, A., & Puliafito, A. (2003). Communication paradigms for mobile grid users. In *CCGRID 03* (p. 669).

Bulhões, P. T., Byun, C., Castrapel, R., & Hassaine, O. (2004, May). *N1 Grid Engine 6 Features and Capabilities* [White Paper]. Phoenix, AZ: Sun Microsystems.

Burnett, I. (2006). *MPEG-21: Digital Item Adaptation - Coding Format Independence*, Chichester, UK. Retrieved 15th June, 2008, from http://www.ipsi.fraunhofer.de/delite/projects/mpeg7/Documents/mpeg21-Overview4318.htm#_Toc523031446.

Burns, J., & Gaudiot, J.-L. (2002). SMT layout overhead and scalability. *IEEE Transactions on Parallel and Distributed Systems*, *13*(2), 142–155. doi:10.1109/71.983942

Butt, A. R., Johnson, T. A., Zheng, Y., & Hu, Y. C. (2004). Kosha: A Peer-to-Peer Enhancement for the Network File System. In *Proceeding of International Symposium On Supercomputing SC'04.*

Butt, A. R., Zhang, R., & Hu, Y. C. (2003). A self-organizing flock of condors. In SC '03 *Proceedings of the ACM/IEEE Conference on Supercomputing*, (p. 42). Los Alamitos, CA: IEEE Computer Society. Retrieved from http://doi.ieeecomputersociety.org/10.1109/SC.2003.10031

Buyya, R., Abramson, D., & Giddy, J. (2000). Nimrod/G: An architecture for a resource management and scheduling system in a global computational grid. In *Proceedings of the 4th International Conference on High Performance Computing in the Asia-Pacific Region.* Retrieved from www.csse.monash.edu.au/~davida/nimrod/nimrodg.htm

Buyya, R., Abramson, D., & Giddy, J. (2000, June). An economy driven resource management architecture for global computational power grids. In *7th International Conference on Parallel and Distributed Processing Techniques and Applications (PDPTA 2000).* Las Vegas, AZ: CSREA Press.

Buyya, R., Abramson, D., & Venugopal, S. (2005). The Grid Economy. *IEEE Journal.*

Buyya, R., Giddy, J., & Abramson, D. (2000). An evaluation of Economy-based Resource Trading and Scheduling on Computational Power Grids for Parameter Sweep Applications. *Proceedings of the 2nd Workshop on Active Middleware Services, Pittsburgh, PA.*

Buyya, R., Yeo, C. S., & Venugopal, S. (2008, September). Market-oriented cloud computing: vision, hype, and reality for delivering it services as computing utilities. In HPCC'08 *Proceedings of the 10th IEEE International Conference on High Performance Computing and Communications*. Los Alamitos, CA: IEEE CS Press.

Byers, J. Considine, J., & Mitzenmacher, M. (2003, Feb.). Simple load balancing for distributed hash tables. *In Proc. of IPTPS.*

Cabrera, F., Copel, G., & Coxetal, B. (2002). *Web Services Transaction* (WS- Transaction). Retrieved from http://www.ibm.com/developerworks/library/ws-transpec.

Caesar, M., & Rexford, J. (2005, March). *BGP routing policies in ISP networks*, (Tech. Rep. UCB/CSD-05-1377). U. C. Berkeley, Berkeley, CA.

Camiel, N., London, S., Nisan, N., & Regev, O. (1997, April). The PopCorn Project: Distributed computation over the Internet in Java. In *Proceedings of the 6th international world wide web conference.*

Cannataro, M., & Talia, D. (2003). Towards the next-generation grid: A pervasive environment for knowledge-based computing. In *Proceedings of the International Conference on Information Technology: Computers and Communications* (pp.437-441), Italy.

Cannon, L. E. (1969). *A cellular computer to implement the kalman filter algorithm*. Ph.D. thesis, Montana State University, Bozeman, MT.

Cao, J., Jarvis, S. A., Saini, S., Kerbyson, D. J., & Nudd, G. R. (2002). ARMS: An agent-based resource management system for grid computing. *Science Progress*, *10*(2), 135–148.

Cappello, F., Djilali, S., Fedak, G., Herault, T., Magniette, F., & Néri, V. (2004). Computing on large scale distributed systems: Xtremweb architecture, programming models, security, tests and convergence with grid. *Future Generation Computer Science (FGCS).*

Cappello, P., Christiansen, B., Ionescu, M., Neary, M., Schauser, K., & Wu, D. (1997). Javelin: Internet-Based Parallel Computing Using Java. In *Proceedings of the sixth acm sigplan symposium on principles and practice of parallel programming.*

Carlsson C. & Fullér, R. (2003). A Fuzzy Approach to Real Option Valuation. *Journal of Fuzzy Sets and Systems, 39.*

Caromel, D., di Costanzo, A., & Mathieu, C. (2007). Peer-to-peer for computational Grids: Mixing clusters and desktop machines. *Parallel Computing, 33*(4–5), 275–288. doi:10.1016/j.parco.2007.02.011

Casa, J., Konuru, R., Prouty, R., Walpole, J., & Otto, S. (1994). Adaptive Load Migration Systems for PVM. *Proceedings of supercomputing*, (pp. 390-399). Washington D.C.

Casanova, H., Legrand, A., & Quinson, M. SimGrid: a Generic Framework for Large-Scale Distributed Experimentations. In *Proceedings of the 10th ieee international conference on computer modelling and simulation (uksim/eurosim'08).*

Casanova, H., Legrand, A., Zagorodnov, D., & Berman, F. (2000, May). Heuristics for Scheduling Parameter Sweep Applications in Grid Environments. In *Proceedings of the 9th heterogeneous computing workshop (hcw'00)* (pp. 349–363).

Casanova, H., Obertelli, G., Berman, F., & Wolski, R. (2000, Nov.). The AppLeS Parameter Sweep Template: User-Level Middleware for the Grid. In *Proceedings of supercomputing 2000 (sc'00).*

Castro, M., Costa, M., & Rowstron, A. (2004). Performance and Dependability of Structured Peer-to-Peer Overlays. In *Proceedings of the 2004 Intl. Conf. on Dependable Systems and Networks* (pp. 9-18). New York: IEEE Computer Society Press.

Castro, M., Druschel, P., Hu, Y. C., & Rowstron, A. (2002). Topology-aware routing in structured peer-to-peer overlay networks. In *Future Directions in Distributed Computing*.

Catlett, C., Beckman, P., Skow, D., & Foster, I. (2006, May). Creating and operating national-scale cyberinfrastructure services. *Cyberinfrastructure Technology Watch Quarterly*, *2*(2), 2–10.

Cazorla, F. J., Ramirez, A., Valero, M., & Fernandez, E. (2004). Dcache Warn: an I-fetch policy to increase SMT efficiency. In *Proceedings of the 18th International Parallel & Distributed Processing Symposium* (IPDPS'04), (pp. 74-83). Santa Fe, NM: IEEE Computer Society Press.

Cazorla, F. J., Ramirez, A., Valero, M., & Fernandez, E. (2004). Dynamically controlled resource allocation in SMT processors. In *Proceedings of the 37th Annual IEEE/ACM International Symposium on Microarchitecture* (MICRO'04), (pp. 171-182). Portland, OR: IEEE Computer Society Press.

CDO2. (2008). *CDOSheet for pricing and risk analysis*. Retrieved from www.cdo2.com

Chaarawi, M. Squyres, J. Gabriel, E. & Feki, S. (2008). A Tool for Optimizing Runtime Parameters of Open MPI. Accepted for publications in *EuroPVM/MPI, September 7-10*, Dublin, Ireland.

Chamberlain, B. L., Callahan, D., & Zima, H. P. (2007). Parallel programmability and the chapel language. *International Journal of High Performance Computing Applications*, *21*(3), 291–312. doi:10.1177/1094342007078442

Chanchio, K., & Sun, X. H. (2001). Communication state transfer for the mobility of con-curent heterogeneous computing. *Proceedings of the 2001 international conference on parallel processing*.

Chandy, M., Foster, I., Kennedy, K., Koelbel, C., & Tseng, C.-W. (1994). Integrated support for task and data parallelism. *The International Journal of Supercomputer Applications*, *8*(2), 80–98.

Chang, R., & Chang, J. (2006). Adaptable replica consistency service for data grids. In *Proceedings of the third international conference on information technology: New generations* (ITNG'06) (pp. 646–651).

Chang, R., & Chen, P. (2007). Complete and fragmented replica selection and retrieval in data grids. *Future Generation Computer Systems*, *23*(4), 536–546. doi:10.1016/j.future.2006.09.006

Chang, R., Chang, J., & Lin, S. (2007). Job scheduling and data replication on data grids. *Future Generation Computer Systems*, *23*(7), 846–860. doi:10.1016/j.future.2007.02.008

Chang, R., Wang, C., & Chen, P. (2005). Replica selection on co-allocation data grids. In *Proceedings of the second international symposium on parallel and distributed processing and applications* (Vol. 3358, pp. 584–593).

Chao, C.-H. (2006, April). An Interest-based architecture for peer-to-peer network systems. In *Proceedings of the International Conference* AINA.

Chapman, B. M., Mehrotra, P., van Rosendale, J., & Zima, H. P. (1994). A software architecture for multidisciplinary applications: integrating task and data parallelism. In *CONPAR 94 - VAPP VI: Proceedings of the Third Joint International Conference on Vector and Parallel Processing* (pp. 664–676). London: Springer-Verlag.

Chapman, B., Haines, M., Mehrota, P., Zima, H., & van Rosendale, J. (1997). Opus: A coordination language for multidisciplinary applications. *Science Progress*, *6*(4), 345–362.

Charles, P., Grothoff, C., Saraswat, V., Donawa, C., Kielstra, A., Ebcioglu, K., et al. (2005). X10: An object-oriented approach to non-uniform cluster computing. In *OOPSLA '05 Proceedings of the 20th annual ACM SIGPLAN Conference on Object Oriented Programming, Systems, Languages, and Applications* (pp. 519–538). New York: ACM.

Chase, J. S., Amador, F. F., Lazowska, E. D., Levy, H. M., & Littlefield, R. J. (1996). The amber systems: Parallel programming on a network of multiprocessors. *Proceedings of acm symposium on operating system principles.*

Chase, J. S., Irwin, D. E., Grit, L. E., Moore, J. D., & Sprenkle, S. E. (2003). Dynamic virtual clusters in a Grid site manager. In *12th IEEE International Symposium on High Performance Distributed Computing (HPDC 2003)* (p. 90). Washington, DC: IEEE Computer Society.

Chaubal, Ch. (2003). *Sun grid engine, enterprise edition—Software configuration guidelines and use cases.* Sun Blueprints, Retrieved from www.sun.com/blueprints/0703/817-3179.pdf

Chawathe, Y., Ratnasamy, S., Breslau, L., Lanham, N., & Shenker, S. (2003). Making gnutella-like p2p systems scalable. In *Proceedings of the 2003 Conference on Applications, Technologies, Architectures, and Protocols for Computer Communications* (pp. 407-418).

Chen, C. M., Lee, S. Y., & Cho, Z. H. (1990). A Parellel Implementation of 3D CT Image Reconstruction on HyperCube Multiprocessor. *IEEE Transactions on Nuclear Science, 37*(3), 1333–1346. doi:10.1109/23.57385

Chen, C.-H., & Lee, C.-Y. (1999). A cost effective lighting processor for 3D graphics application. *Proceedings of International Conference on Image Processing, 2*, 792–796.

Chen, D. J., & Huang, T. H. (1992). Reliability analysis of distributed systems based on a fast reliability algorithm. *IEEE Transactions on Parallel and Distributed Systems, 3*(2), 139–154. doi:10.1109/71.127256

Chen, D. J., Chen, R. S., & Huang, T. H. (1997). A heuristic approach to generating file spanning trees for reliability analysis of distributed computing systems. *Computers and Mathematics with Applications, 34*(10), 115–131. doi:10.1016/S0898-1221(97)00210-1

Chen, T., Raghavan, R., Dale, J. N., & Iwata, E. (2007, Sept.). Cell Broadband Engine Architecture and its first implementation-A performance view. IBM. Journal of Research and Development (Srinagar), 51(5), 559–572.

Chen, W., Liu, J., & Huang, H. (2004). An adaptive scheme for vertical handoff in wireless overlay networks. *IEEE International Conference on Parallel and Distributed Systems* (ICPADS) (pp. 541-548). Washington, DC: IEEE.

Chen, Z., & Dongarra, J. (2005). Condition numbers of gaussian random matrices. *SIAM Journal on Matrix Analysis and Applications, 27*(3), 603–620. doi:10.1137/040616413

Cheng, A. H., & Joung, Y. J. (2006). Probabilistic file indexing and searching in unstructured peer-to-peer networks. *Computer Networks, 50*(1), 106–127. doi:10.1016/j.comnet.2005.12.008

Cheng, K., Xiang, L., Iwaihara, M., Xu, H., & Mohania, M. M. (2005). *Time-Decaying Bloom Filters for Data Streams with Skewed Distributions.* Paper presented at the Proceedings of the 15th International Workshop on Research Issues in Data Engineering: Stream Data Mining and Applications.

Chervenak, A. (2002). Giggle: A framework for constructing scalable replica location services. In *Proceedings of the IEEE supercomputing* (pp. 1–17).

Chervenak, A., Foster, L., Kesselman, C., Salisbury, C., & Tueckem, S. (2000). The data grid: Towards an architecture for the distributed management and analysis of large scientific data sets. *Journal of Network and Computer Applications, 23*(3), 187–200. doi:10.1006/jnca.2000.0110

Chien, A., Calder, B., Elbert, S., & Bhatia, K. (2003). Entropia: Architecture and performance of an enterprise desktop grid system. *Journal of Parallel and Distributed Computing, 63*, 597–610. doi:10.1016/S0743-7315(03)00006-6

Chinese National Grid (CNGrid) Project Web Site. (2007). Retrieved from http://www.cngrid.org/

Chiueh, T., & Deng, P. (1996). Evaluation of checkpoint mechanisms for massively parallel machines. In *FTCS*, (pp. 370–379).

Choi, S., & Yeung, D. (2006). Learning-based SMT processor resource distribution via hill-climbing. In *Proceedings of the 33rd Annual International Symposium on Computer Architecture* (ISCA'06), (pp. 239-251), Boston: IEEE Computer Society Press.

Chonka, A., Zhou, W., Knapp, K., & Xiang, Y. (2008). Protecting information systems from ddos attack using multicore methodology. *Proceedings of IEEE 8th International Conference on Computer and Information Technology.*

Chow, A. C., Gossum, G. C., & Brokenshire, D. A. (2005). A programming example: Large fft on the cell broadband engine. In *Gspx. tech. conf. proc. of the global signal processing expo.*

Chrysanthis, P. K., & Ramamriham, K. (1994). Synthesis of extended transaction models using ACTA. *ACM Transactions on Database Systems, 19*(3), 450–491. doi:10.1145/185827.185843

Chrysanthis, P., & Ramamriham, K. (Eds.). (1992). ACTA: The SAGA continues. *Transactions Models for Advanced Database Applications.* San Francisco: Morgan Kaufmann.

Chu, D., & Humphrey, M. (2004, November 8). *Bmobile ogsi.net: Grid computing on mobile devices.* In Grid computing workshop (associated with supercomputing 2004), Pittsburgh, PA.

Chu, E., & George, A. (2000). *Inside the fft black box: Serial and parallel fast Fourier transform algorithms.* Boca Raton, FL: CRC Press LLC.

Chu, X., Nadiminti, K., Jin, C., Venugopal, S., & Buyya, R. (2007, December). Aneka: Next-generation enterprise grid platform for e-science and e-business applications, e-Science'07: In *Proceedings of the 3rd IEEE International Conference on e-Science and Grid Computing,* Bangalore, India (pp. 151-159). Los Alamitos, CA: IEEE Computer Society Press. For more information, see http://doi.ieeecomputersociety.org/10.1109/E-SCIENCE.2007.12

Chung, P. E. (1997). Checkpointing in cosmic: a user-level process migration environment. *Proceedings of Pacific Rim International Symposium on Fault-Tolerant Systems.*

Ciancarini, P. (1996). Coordination Models and Languages as Software Integrators. *SCM Comput. Surv., 28*(2), 300–302. doi:10.1145/234528.234732

Ciarpaglini, S., Folchi, L., Orlando, S., Pelagatti, S., & Perego, R. (2000). Integrating task and data parallelism with taskHPF. In H. R. Arabnia (Ed.). *Proceedings of the International Conference on Parallel and Distributed Processing Techniques and Applications, PDPTA 2000.* Las Vegas, NV: CSREA Press.

Cirne, W., Brasileiro, F., Andrade, N., Costa, L., Andrade, A., & Novaes, R. (2006, September). Labs of the world, unite!!! *Journal of Grid Computing, 4*(3), 225–246. doi:10.1007/s10723-006-9040-x

Clarke, B., & Humphrey, M. (2002, April 19). Beyond the "device as portal": Meeting the requirements of wireless and mobile devices in the legion grid computing system. *In 2nd International Workshop On Parallel And Distributed Computing Issues In Wireless Networks And Mobile Computing* (associated with ipdps 2002), Ft. Lauderdale, FL.

CloudCamp. (2008). Retrived from http://www.cloudcamp.com/

CNGrid GOS Project Web site. *(2007).* Retrieved from http://vega.ict.ac.cn

Coffman, E. G., Galambos, G., Martello, S., & Vigo, D. (1999). Bin-packing approximation algorithms: Combinatorial analysis. In D. Z. Du & P. M. Pardalos, (Ed.), *Handbook of Combinatorial Optimization,* (pp. 151–207). Dondrecht, the Netherlands: Kluwer.

CoG Toolkit (n.d.). Retrieved from http://www.cogkit.org/

Cohen, B. (2002). *BitTorrent Protocol 1.0.* Retrieved from BitTorrent.org.

Cohen, B. (2003). Incentives build robustness in BitTorrent. In *Workshop on economics of peer-to-peer systems*, Berkeley, CA.

Condor Team. (2006). CondorVersion 6.4.7 Manual. Retrieved October 18, 2006, from www.cs.wisc.edu/condor/manual/v6.4

Corbat, F. J., & Vyssotsky, V. A. (1965). Introduction and overview of the multics system. *FJCC, Proc. AFIPS, 27*(1), 185–196.

Coronato, A., & Pietro, G. D. (2007). Mipeg: A middleware infrastructure for pervasive grids. *Journal of Future Generation Computer Systems.*

Corporation, I. B. M. (1993). *IBM Load Leveler: User's Guide.*

Corradi, A., Leonardi, L., & Zambonelli, F. (1997). Performance comparison of load balancing policies based on a diffusion scheme. *In Proc. of the Euro-Par'97* (LNCS Vol. 1300). Springer: Germany.

Costa, F., Silva, L., Fedak, G., & Kelley, I. (2008, in press). Optimizing the Data Distribution Layer of BOINC with BitTorrent. In *2nd workshop on desktop grids and volunteer computing systems (pcgrid 2008)*, Miami, FL.

Cotroneo, D., Migliaccio, A., & Russo, S. (2007). The Esperanto Broker: a communication platform for nomadic computing systems. *Software, Practice & Experience, 37*(10), 1017–1046. doi:10.1002/spe.794

Cotton, W., Pielke, R., Walko, R., Liston, G., Tremback, C., & Jiang, H. (2003). RAMS 2001: Current status and future directions. *Meteorology and Atmospheric Physics, 82*(1-4), 5–29. doi:10.1007/s00703-001-0584-9

Coulson, G., Grace, P., Blair, G., Duce, D., Cooper, C., & Sagar, M. (2005, April). *A middleware approach for pervasive grid environments.* In Uk-ubinet/ uk e-science programme workshop on ubiquitous computing and e-research.

Cox, J. C., Ross, S., & Rubinstein, M. (1979). Option Pricing: A Simplified Approach. *Journal of Financial Economics, 3*(7).

Cray Inc. (2005). *The Chapel language specification, version 0.4.*

Cristianini, N., & Hahn, M. (2006). *Introduction to Computational Genomics.* Cambridge, UK: Cambridge University Press.

Cronk, M. H., & Mehrotra, P. (1997). Thread migration in the presence of pointers. *Proceedings of the mini-track on multithreaded systems, 30th hawaii interantional conference on system science.*

Culler, D. E., Singh, J. P., & Gupta, A. (1998) *Parallel computer architecture: a hardware/software approach,* (1st edition). San Francisco: Morgan Kaufmann.

Culler, D., & Karp, R. Patterson, D. Sahay, A. Schauser, K. E. Santos, E. Subramonian, R. & von Eicken, T. (1993). LogP: Towards a realistic model of parallel computation. In *Proceedings of the fourth ACM SIGPLAN symposium on Principles and practice of parallel programming,* (pp. 1–12). New York: ACM Press.

Czajkowski, K., Fitzgerald, S., Foster, I., & Kesselman, C. (2001). Grid information services for distributed resource sharing. *10th International Symposium on High Performance Distributed Computing* (pp. 181-194). San Francisco: IEEE Computer Society Press.

Dabek, F., Kaashoek, M. F., Karger, D., Morris, R., & Stoica, I. (2001). Wide-Area Cooperative Storage with CFS. In *Proceedings of the 11th ACM Symp. on Operating Systems Principles* (pp. 202-215). New York: ACM Press.

Dabek, F., Zhao, B., Druschel, P., Kubiatowicz, J., & Stoica, I. (2003). Towards a common API for structured peer-to-peer overlays. In IPTPS03 *Proceedings of the 2nd International Workshop on Peer-to-Peer Systems,* (pp. 33-44). Heidelberg, Germany: SpringerLink. doi: 10.1007/b11823

Dai, Y. S., & Levitin, G. (2006). Reliability and performance of tree-structured grid services . *IEEE Transactions on Reliability, 55*(2), 337–349. doi:10.1109/TR.2006.874940

Dai, Y. S., Pan, Y., & Zou, X. K. (2006). A hierarchical modelling and analysis for grid service reliability. *IEEE Transactions on Computers.*

Dai, Y. S., Xie, M., & Poh, K. L. (2002), Reliability analysis of grid computing systems. *IEEE Pacific Rim International Symposium on Dependable Computing (PRDC2002),* (pp. 97-104). New York: IEEE Computer Press.

Dai, Y. S., Xie, M., & Poh, K. L. (2005). Markov renewal models for correlated software failures of multiple types. *IEEE Transactions on Reliability, 54*(1), 100–106. doi:10.1109/TR.2004.841709

Dai, Y. S., Xie, M., & Poh, K. L. (2006).Availability modeling and cost optimization for the grid resource management system. IEEE Transactions on Systems, Man, and Cybernetics. Part A . *Systems and Humans: a Publication of the IEEE Systems, Man, and Cybernetics Society., 38*(1), 170.

Dai, Y. S., Xie, M., Poh, K. L., & Liu, G. Q. (2003). A study of service reliability and availability for distributed systems. *Reliability Engineering & System Safety, 79*(1), 103–112. doi:10.1016/S0951-8320(02)00200-4

Dai, Y. S., Xie, M., Poh, K. L., & Ng, S. H. (2004). A model for correlated failures in *N*-version programming. *IIE Transactions, 36*(12), 1183–1192. doi:10.1080/07408170490507729

Dalal, S., Temel, S., & Little, M. (2003). Coordinating business transactions on the Web. *IEEE Internet Computing, 7*(1), 30–39. doi:10.1109/MIC.2003.1167337

Dang, N. N., & Lim, S. B. (2007). Combination of replication and scheduling in data grids. *International Journal of Computer Science and Network Security, 7*(3).

Dang, V. D. (2004). *Coalition Formation and Operation in Virtual Organisations.* PhD thesis, Faculty of Engineering, Science and Mathematics, School of Electronics and Computer Science, University of Southampton, Southampton, UK.

Das, S. K., Harvey, D. J., & Biswas, R. (2001). Parallel processing of adaptive meshes with load balancing. *IEEE Transactions on Parallel and Distributed Systems, 12*(12), 1269–1280. doi:10.1109/71.970562

Davies, N., Friday, A., & Storz, O. (2004). Exploring the grid's potential for ubiquitous computing. *IEEE Pervasive Computing / IEEE Computer Society [and] IEEE Communications Society, 3*(2), 74–75. doi:10.1109/MPRV.2004.1316823

Davis, C. (2007). *Could Android open door for cellphone Grid computing?* Retrieved March 10, 2008, from http://www.google-phone.com/could-android-open-door-for-cellphone-grid-computing-12217.php

de Assunção, M. D., & Buyya, R. (2008, December). Performance analysis of multiple site resource provisioning: Effects of the precision of availability information [Technical Report]. In *International Conference on High Performance Computing (HiPC 2008)* (Vol. 5374, pp. 157–168). Berlin/Heidelberg: Springer.

de Assunção, M. D., Buyya, R., & Venugopal, S. (2008, June). InterGrid: A case for internetworking islands of Grids. [CCPE]. *Concurrency and Computation, 20*(8), 997–1024. doi:10.1002/cpe.1249

De Roure, D., Jennings, N., & Shadbolt, N. (2005, March). The semantic grid: Past, present, and future. *Proceedings of the IEEE, 93*(3), 669–681. doi:10.1109/JPROC.2004.842781

De Roure, M., & Surridge, D. (2003). Interoperability challenges in Grid for industrial applications. *GGF9 Semantic Grid Workshop,* Chicago.

Dean, J., & Ghemawat, S. (2004). MapReduce: Simplified Data Processing on Large Clusters. In *Osdi'04: Sixth symposium on operating system design and implementation,* (pp. 137–150). San Francisco, CA.

DECI. (2008). *DEISA extreme computing initiative.* Retrieved from www.deisa.eu/science/deci

Deelman, E., Blythe, J., Gil, Y., Kesselman, C., Mehta, G., Patil, S., et al. (2004). Pegasus: Mapping scientific workflows onto the grid. In M. Dikaiakos (Ed.), *AxGrids 2004*, (LNCS 3165, pp. 11-20). Berlin: Springer Verlag.

DEISA. (2008). *Distributed European infrastructure for supercomputing applications*. Retrieved from www.deisa.eu

Demers, A., Keshav, S., & Shenker, S. (1989). Analysis and Simulation of a Fair Queuing Algorithm. *Proceedings of ACM SIGCOMM*.

Deng, Z., Liu, J.W.S., Zhang, L., Mouna, S., & Frei, A. (1999). An Open Environment for Real-Time Applications. *Real-Time Systems Journal, 16*(2/3).

DESHL. (2008*). DEISA services for heterogeneous management layer*. http://forge.nesc.ac.uk/projects/deisa-jra7/

Desprez, F., & Vernois, A. (2006). Simultaneous scheduling of replication and computation for data-intensive applications on the grid. *Journal of Grid Computing, 4*(1), 66–74. doi:10.1007/s10723-005-9016-2

D-Grid (2008). Retrieved from www.d-grid.de/index.php?id=1&L=1

Dharmapurikar, S., & Lockwood, J. (2006, October). Fast and Scalable Pattern Matching for Network Intrusion Detection Systems. *Communication of the IEEE Journal, 24*(10).

Dharmapurikar, S., Krishnamurthy, P., & Taylor, D. E. (2006). Longest prefix matching using bloom filters. *IEEE/ACM Trans. Netw., 14*(2), 397–409.

Dharmapurikar, S., Krishnamurthy, P., Sproull, T. S., & Lockwood, J. W. (2004). Deep packet inspection using parallel bloom filters. *IEEE Micro, 24*(1), 52–61. doi:10.1109/MM.2004.1268997

Dheepak, R., Ali, S., Sengupta, S., & Chakrabarti, A. (2005). Study of scheduling strategies in a dynamic data grid environment. In *Distributed Computing - IWDC 2004* (Vol. 3326). Berlin: Springer.

Diaz, M., Rubio, B., Soler, E., & Troya, J. M. (2002). A border-based coordination language for integrating task and data parallelism. *Journal of Parallel and Distributed Computing, 62*(4), 715–740. doi:10.1006/jpdc.2001.1814

Diaz, M., Rubio, B., Soler, E., & Troya, J. M. (2003). Domain interaction patterns to coordinate HPF tasks. *Parallel Computing, 29*(7), 925–951. doi:10.1016/S0167-8191(03)00064-4

Diaz, M., Rubio, B., Soler, E., & Troya, J. M. (2004). SBASCO: Skeleton-based scientific components. In *Proceedings of the 12th Euromicro Workshop on Parallel, Distributed and Network-Based Processing (PDP 2004)* (pp. 318–325). Washington, DC: IEEE Computer Society.

Dikaiakos, M. D. (2007). Grid benchmarking: vision, challenges, and current status. [New York: Wiley InterScience.]. *Concurrency and Computation, 19*, 89–105. doi:10.1002/cpe.1086

Dimitrakos, T., Golby, D., & Kearley, P. (2004, October). Towards a trust and contract management framework for dynamic virtual organisations. In *eChallenges*. Vienna, Austria.

Dimitrov, B., & Rego, V. (1998). Arachne: A portable threads system supporting migrant threads on heterogeneous network farms. *IEEE Transactions on Parallel and Distributed Systems, 9*(5), 459–469. doi:10.1109/71.679216

Ding, Q., Chen, G. L., & Gu, J. (2002). A unified resource mapping strategy in computational grid environments. *Journal of Software, 13*(7), 1303–1308.

Dixit, K. M. (1991). The SPEC benchmarks. *Parallel Computing, 17*(10-11), 1195–1209. doi:10.1016/S0167-8191(05)80033-X

Dixit, S., & Wu, T. (2004). *Content Networking in the Mobile Internet*. New York: John Wiley & Sons.

Dixon, C., Bragin, T., Krishnamurthy, A., & Anderson, T. (2006, September). Tit-for-Tat Distributed Resource Allocation [Poster]. *The ACM SIGCOMM 2006 Conference*.

Domenici, A., Donno, F., Pucciani, G., & Stockinger, H. (2006). Relaxed data consistency with CONStanza. In *Proceedings of the sixth IEEE international symposium on cluster computing and the grid* (pp. 425–429).

Domenici, A., Donno, F., Pucciani, G., Stockinger, H., & Stockinger, K. (2004, Nov). *Replica consistency in a Data Grid. Nuclear Instruments and Methods in Physics Research, 534*, 24–28. doi:10.1016/j.nima.2004.07.052

Domingues, P., Araujo, F., & Silva, L. M. (2006, December). A dht-based infrastructure for sharing checkpoints in desktop grid computing. In *Conference on e-science and grid computing (escience '06),* Amsterdam, The Netherlands.

Donegan, B., Doolan, D. C., & Tabirca, S. (2008). Mobile Message Passing using a Scatternet Framework. *International Journal of Computers, Communications & Control, 3*(1), 51–59.

Dong, X., Halevy, A. Y., & Yu, C. (2007). Data integration with uncertainty. In *Vldb '07: Proceedings of the 33rd International Conference on Very Large Data Bases* (pp. 687–698). VLDB Endowment.

Dongarra, J. J., & Eijkhout, V. (2003). Self-Adapting Numerical Software for Next-Generation Applications. *International Journal of High Performance Computing Applications, 17*(2), 125–131. doi:10.1177/1094342003017002002

Dongarra, J., Foster, I., Fox, G., Gropp, W., Kennedy, K., Torczon, L., & White, A. (2003). *Sourcebook of parallel computing.* San Francisco: Morgan Kaufmann Publishers.

Dongarra, J., Luszczek, P., & Petitet, A. (2003, August). The LINPACK Benchmark: past, present and future. *Concurrency and Computation, 15*(9), 803–820. doi:10.1002/cpe.728

Dongarra, J., Meuer, H., & Strohmaier, E. (2004). TOP500 Supercomputer Sites, 24th edition. In *Proceedings of the Supercomputing Conference (SC'2004), Pittsburgh PA.* New York: ACM.

Doolan, D. C., Tabirca, S., & Yang, L. T. (2006). Mobile Parallel Computing. *In Proceedings of the Fifth International Symposium on Parallel and Distributed Computing (ISPDC 06),* (pp. 161-167).

Dorigo, M. (1992). *Optimization, learning and natural algorithms* (Tech. Rep.). Ph.D. Thesis, Politecnico di Milano, Milan, Italy.

Dorta, A. J., González, J. A., Rodriguez, C., & de Sande, F. (2003). LLC: A parallel skeletal language. *Parallel Processing Letters, 13*(3), 437–448. doi:10.1142/S0129626403001409

Dorta, A. J., López, P., & de Sande, F. (2006). Basic skeletons in LLC. *Parallel Computing, 32*(7-8), 491–506. doi:10.1016/j.parco.2006.07.001

Douglis, F., & Ousterhout, J. K. (1991). Transparent process migration: Design alternatives and the sprite implementation. *Software, Practice & Experience, 21*(8), 757–785. doi:10.1002/spe.4380210802

Draves, S. (2005, March). The electric sheep screen-saver: A case study in aesthetic evolution. In *3rd european workshop on evolutionary music and art.*

Drodowski, M., Lawenda, M., & Guinand, F. (2006). Scheduling multiple divisible loads. *International Journal of High Performance Computing Applications, 20*(1), 19–30. doi:10.1177/1094342006061879

Drozdowski, M., & Lawenda, M. (2005). *On Optimum Multi-installment Divisible Load Processing in Heterogeneous Distributed Systems,* (LNCS 3648, pp. 231–240). Berlin: Springer.

Duan, R., Prodan, R., & Fahringer, T. (2006). Run-time optimization for Grid workflow applications. *International Conference on Grid Computing.* Barcelona, Spain: IEEE Computer Society Press.

Dumitrescu, C., & Foster, I. (2004). Usage policy-based CPU sharing in virtual organizations. In *Proceedings of the fifth IEEE/ACM international workshop on grid computing* (pp. 53–60).

Dumitrescu, C., & Foster, I. (2004). Usage policy-based CPU sharing in virtual organizations. In *5th IEEE/ACM International Workshop on Grid Computing (Grid 2004)* (pp. 53–60). Washington, DC: IEEE Computer Society.

Dumitrescu, C., & Foster, I. (2005, August). GRUBER: A Grid resource usage SLA broker. In J. C. Cunha & P. D. Medeiros (Eds.), *Euro-Par 2005* (Vol. 3648, pp. 465–474). Berlin/Heidelberg: Springer.

Dumitrescu, C., Raicu, I., & Foster, I. (2005). DI-GRUBER: A distributed approach to Grid resource brokering. In *2005 ACM/IEEE Conference on Supercomputing (SC 2005)* (p. 38). Washington, DC: IEEE Computer Society.

Dumitrescu, C., Wilde, M., & Foster, I. (2005, June). A model for usage policy-based resource allocation in Grids. In *6th IEEE International Workshop on Policies for Distributed Systems and Networks* (pp. 191–200). Washington, DC: IEEE Computer Society.

Dümmler, J., Kunis, R., & Rünger, G. (2007). A scheduling toolkit for multiprocessor-task programming with dependencies. In *Proceedings of the 13th International Euro-Par Conference* (pp. 23–32). Berlin: Springer.

Dümmler, J., Kunis, R., & Rünger, G. (2007). A comparison of scheduling algorithms for multiprocessor tasks with precedence constraints. In *Proceedings of the 2007 High Performance Computing & Simulation (HPCS'07) Conference* (pp. 663–669). ECMS.

Dümmler, J., Rauber, T., & Rünger, G. (2007). Communicating multiprocessor-tasks. In *Proceedings of the 20th International Workshop on Languages and Compilers for Parallel Computing (LCPC 2007).* Berlin: Springer.

Dümmler, J., Rauber, T., & Rünger, G. (2008). A transformation framework for communicating multiprocessor-tasks. In *Proceedings of the 16th Euromicro International Conference on Parallel, Distributed and Network-Based Processing (PDP 2008)* (pp. 64–71). New York: IEEE Computer Society.

Dümmler, J., Rauber, T., & Rünger, G. (2008). Mapping algorithms for multiprocessor tasks on multi-core clusters. In *Proceedings of the 37th International Conference on Parallel Processing (ICPP08).* New York: IEEE Computer Society.

Duvvuri, V., Shenoy, P., & Tewari, R. (2000). Adaptive leases: A strong consistency mechanism for the World Wide Web. *In Proceedings of IEEE INFOCOM* (pp. 834–843).

Edelman, A. (1988). Eigenvalues and condition numbers of random matrices. *SIAM Journal on Matrix Analysis and Applications, 9*(4), 543–560. doi:10.1137/0609045

Eggers, S. J., Emer, J. S., Levy, H. M., Lo, J. L., Stamm, R. L., & Tullsen, D. M. (1997). Simultaneous multithreading: a platform for next-generation processors. *IEEE Micro, 17*(5), 12–19. doi:10.1109/40.621209

Elias, J. A., & Moldes, L. N. (2002). Behaviour of the fast consistency algorithm in the set of replicas with multiple zones with high demand. In *Proceedings of symposium in informatics and telecommunications.*

Elias, J. A., & Moldes, L. N. (2002). A demand based algorithm for rapid updating of replicas. In *Proceedings of IEEE workshop on resource sharing in massively distributed systems* (pp. 686– 691).

Elias, J. A., & Moldes, L. N. (2003). Generalization of the fast consistency algorithm to a grid with multiple high demand zones. *In Proceedings of international conference on computational science* (*ICCS 2003*) (pp. 275–284).

El-Moursy, A., & Albonesi, D. H. (2003). Front-end policies for improved issue efficiency in SMT processors. In *Proceedings of the 9th International Symposium on High-Performance Computer Architecture* (HPCA'03), (pp. 31-40). Anaheim, CA: IEEE Computer Society Press.

Elmroth, E., & Gardfjäll, P. (2005, December). Design and evaluation of a decentralized system for Grid-wide fairshare scheduling. In *1st IEEE International Conference on e-Science and Grid Computing* (pp. 221–229). Melbourne, Australia: IEEE Computer Society Press.

Enabling Grids for E-sciencE (EGEE) project. (2005). Retrieved from http://public.eu-egee.org.

EnginFrame. (2008). *Grid and cloud portal*. Retrieved from www.nice-italy.com

Epema, D. H. J., Livny, M., van Dantzig, R., Evers, X., & Pruyne, J. (1996). A worldwide flock of condors: Load sharing among workstation clusters. *Future Generation Computer Systems*, *12*(1), 53–65. doi:10.1016/0167-739X(95)00035-Q

ERCIM. (2005). Multimedia Informatics. *ERCIM News, 62*.

Erl, T. (2005). *Service-Oriented Architecture (SOA): Concepts, Technology, and Design*. Upper Saddle River, NJ: Prentice Hall.

Evans, J. J. Hood, C. S.& Gropp, W. D. (2003). Exploring the Relationship Between Parallel Application Run-Time Variability and Network Performance. In *Proceedings of the Workshop on High-Speed Local Networks (HSLN), IEEE Conference on Local Computer Networks (LCN)*, (pp. 538-547).

Factor, M., Schuster, A., & Shagin, K. (2003). *JavaSplit: a runtime for execution of monolithic Java programs on heterogenous collections of commodity workstations*. Paper presented at the Proceedings of the IEEE International Conference on Cluster Computing.

Fagg, G. E., & Dongarra, J. (2000). FT-MPI: Fault tolerant MPI, supporting dynamic applications in a dynamic world. In *PVM/MPI 2000*, (pp. 346–353).

Fagg, G. E., Gabriel, E., Bosilca, G., Angskun, T., Chen, Z., Pjesivac-Grbovic, J., et al. (2004). Extending the MPI specification for process fault tolerance on high performance computing systems. In *Proceedings of the International Supercomputer Conference*, Heidelberg, Germany.

Fagg, G. E., Gabriel, E., Chen, Z., Angskun, T., Bosilca, G., & Pjesivac-Grbovic, J. (2005). Process faulttolerance: Semantics, design and applications for high performance computing. [Winter.]. *International Journal of High Performance Computing Applications*, *19*(4), 465–477. doi:10.1177/1094342005056137

Fahringer, T., Prodan, R., Duan, R., Hofer, J., Nadeem, F., Nerieri, F., et al. (2006). ASKALON: A development and grid computing environment for scientific workflows. In I. J. Taylor, E. Deelman, D. G. Ganon, & M. Shields (Eds.), *Workflows for e-Science* (p. 530). Berlin: Springer Verlag.

Faraj, A. Patarasuk, P. & Yuan, X. (2007). A Study of Process Arrival Patterns for MPI Collective Operations. *International Conference on Supercomputing*, (pp.168-179).

Faraj, A. Yuan, X. & Lowenthal, D. (2006). STAR-MPI: self tuned adaptive routines for MPI collective operations. In *ICS '06: Proceedings of the 20th Annual International Conference on Supercomputing*, (pp. 199-208). New York: ACM Press.

Fasttrack product description. (2001). http://www.fasttrack.nu/index.html.

Fedak, G., & Germain, C. N'eri, V., & Cappello, F. (2001, May). XtremWeb: A Generic Global Computing System. In *Proceedings of the ieee international symposium on cluster computing and the grid (ccgrid'01)*.

Fedak, G., Germain, C., Neri, V., & Cappello, F. (2002, May). XtremWeb: A generic global computing system. In CCGRID'01: *Proceeding of the First IEEE Conference on Cluster and Grid Computing, workshop on Global Computing on Personal Devices*, Brisbane, (pp. 582-587). Los Alamitos, CA: IEEE Computer Society. Retrieved from http://doi.ieeecomputersociety.org/10.1109/CCGRID.2001.923246

Fedak, G., He, H., & Cappello, F. (2008, November). BitDew: A Programmable Environment for Large-Scale Data Management and Distribution. In *Proceedings of the acm/ieee supercomputing conference* (sc'08), Austin, TX.

Federation, M. D. The Biomedical Informatics Research Network (2003). In I. Foster & C. Kesselman (Eds.), *The grid, blueprint for a new computing infrastructure* (2nd ed.). San Francisco: Morgan Kaufmann.

Femando, R., Harris, M., Wloka, M., & Zeller, C. (2004). Programming graphics hardware. In *Tutorial on EUROGRAPHICS*. NVIDIA Corporation.

Fernandess, Y., & Malkhi, D. (2006). On Collaborative Content Distribution using Multi-Message Gossip. In *Proceedings of the international parallel and distributed processing symposium*. Rhodes Island, Greece: IEEE.

Ferrari, A. J., Chapin, S. J., & Grimshaw, A. S. (1997). *Process introspection: A heterogeneous checkpoint/restart mechanism based on automatic code modification*, (Technical Report: CS-97-05). University of Virginia, Charlottesville, VA.

Fink, S. J. (1998). *A programming model for block-structured scientific calculations on smp clusters. Doctoral* thesis, University of California, San Diego, CA.

Fischer, L. (Ed.). (2004). *Workflow Handbook 2004*. Lighthouse Point, FL: Future Strategies Inc.

Fisk, A. (2003). *Gnutella dynamic query protocol v. 0.1*. Retrieved from http://www9.limewire.com/developer/dynamic query.html.

Folding@home, (2008). *Client statistics by OS*. Retrieved March 10, 2008, from http://fah-web.stanford.edu/cgi-bin/main.py?qtype=osstats

Fontán, J., Vázquez, T., Gonzalez, L., Montero, R. S., & Llorente, I. M. (2008, May). OpenNEbula: The open source virtual machine manager for cluster computing. In *Open Source Grid and Cluster Software Conference – Book of Abstracts*. San Francisco.

Foster, I. (2000). Internet computing and the emerging grid. *Nature*. Retrieved from www.nature.com/nature/webmatters/grid/grid.html

Foster, I. (2002). The grid: A new infrastructure for 21st century science. *Physics Today*, *55*, 42–47. doi:10.1063/1.1461327

Foster, I. (2002). *What is the Grid? A three point checklist*. Retrieved from http://www-fp.mcs.anl.gov/~foster/Articles/WhatIsTheGrid.pdf

Foster, I. (2006). Globus toolkit version 4: Software for service-oriented systems. In *Proceedings of the international conference on network and parallel computing* (pp. 2–13).

Foster, I. Kesselman, & C., Tuecke, S. (2002). *The anatomy of the Grid: Enabling scalable virtual organizations*. Retrieved from www.globus.org/alliance/publications/papers/anatomy.pdf

Foster, I. T., & Chandy, K. M. (1995). Fortran M: A language for modular parallel programming. *Journal of Parallel and Distributed Computing*, *26*(1), 24–35. doi:10.1006/jpdc.1995.1044

Foster, I. T., & Iamnitchi, A. (2003). On death, taxes, and the convergence of peer-to-peer and grid computing. *2735*, 118-128.

Foster, I., & Kesselman, C. (1997). Globus: A metacomputing infrastructure toolkit. *International Journal of Supercomputer Applications and High Performance Computing*, *11*(2), 115–128. doi:10.1177/109434209701100205

Foster, I., & Kesselman, C. (1999). *The Grid: Blueprint for a New Computing Infrastructure*. San Francisco: Morgan Kaufmann Publishers, Inc.

Foster, I., & Kesselman, C. (2003). *The Grid 2: Blueprint for a new computing infrastructure*. San Francisco: Morgan-Kaufmann.

Foster, I., & Kesselman, C. (2004). *The Grid: Blueprint for a future computing infrastructure* (2 Ed.). San Francisco: Morgan Kaufmann.

Foster, I., Freeman, T., Keahey, K., Scheftner, D., Sotomayor, B., & Zhang, X. (2006, May). Virtual clusters for Grid communities. In *6th IEEE International Symposium on Cluster Computing and the Grid (CCGRID 2006)* (pp. 513–520). Washington, DC: IEEE Computer Society.

Foster, I., Kesselman, C., & Nick, J. (2002). Grid services for distributed system integration. *IEEE Computer, 35*(6), 37–46.

Foster, I., Kesselman, C., & Tuecke, S. (2001). The anatomy of the the grid: Enabling scalable virtual organization. *The International Journal of Supercomputer Applications, 15*(3), 200–222.

Foster, I., Kesselman, C., Nick, J. M., & Tuecke, S. (2002). Grid services for distributed system integration. *Computer, 35*(6), 37–46. doi:10.1109/MC.2002.1009167

Foster, I., Kesselman, C., Nick, J., & Tuecke, S. (2002). *The physiology of the grid: An open grid services architecture for distributed systems integration.* Retrieved from citeseer.nj.nec.com/foster02physiology.html

Foster, I., Kesselman, C., Tsudik, G., & Tuecke, S. (1998). A security Architecture for Computational Grids. *ACM Conference on Computer and Communications Security.*

Foster, I., Kohr, D. R., Krishnaiyer, R., & Choudhary, A. (1996). Double standards: Bringing task parallelism to HPF via the message passing interface. In *Proceedings of the 1996 ACM/IEEE Conference on Supercomputing* (pp. 36-36). New York: IEEE Computer Society.

Fourment, M., & Gillings, M. R. (2008, February). A comparison of common programming languages used in bioinformatics. *Bioinformatics (Oxford, England)*, 9.

Fowler, M. (2008, November). Inversion of control containers and the dependency injection pattern. Retrieved from http://www.martinfowler.com/articles/injection.html

Fox, F., & Gannon, D. (2001). Computational grids. *Computing in Science & Engineering, 3*(4), 74–77. doi:10.1109/5992.931906

Fox, G. C., Johnson, M., Lyzenga, G., Otto, S. W., Salmon, J., & Walker, D. (1988). *Solving Problems on Concurrent Processors: Vol. 1.* Englewood Cliffs, NJ: Prentice-Hall.

Fox, G., Hiranandani, S., Kennedy, K., Koelbel, C., Kremer, U., Tseng, C.-W., et al. (1990). *Fortran D Language Specification* (No. CRPC-TR90079), Houston, TX.

Fox, G., Williams, R., & Messina, P. (1994). *Parallel computing works!* San Francisco: Morgan Kaufmann Publishers.

FreePastry. (2008, November). Retrieved from http://freepastry.rice.edu/FreePastry

Frey, J., Mori, T., Nick, J., Smith, C., Snelling, D., Srinivasan, L., & Unger, J. (2005). *The open grid services architecture, Version 1.0.* Retrieved from www.ggf.org/ggf_areas_architecture.htm

Frey, J., Tannenbaum, T., Livny, M., Foster, I. T., & Tuecke, S. (2001, August). Condor-G: A computation management agent for multi-institutional Grids. In *10th IEEE International Symposium on High Performance Distributed Computing (HPDC 2001)* (pp. 55–63). San Francisco: IEEE Computer Society.

Frigo, M., & Johnson, S. (2005). The Design and Implementation of FFTW3. *Proceedings of the IEEE, 93*(2), 216–231. doi:10.1109/JPROC.2004.840301

Fritsch, D., Klinec, D., & Volz, S. (2000). NEXUS positioning and data management concepts for location aware applications. In the *2nd International Symposium on Telegeoprocessing* (Nice-Sophia-Antipolis, France), (pp. 171-184).

Fu, S., Xu, C. Z., & Shen, H. (April 2008). Random choices for Churn resilient load balancing in peer-to-peer networks. *Proc. of IEEE International Parallel and Distributed Processing Symposium.*

Fu, Y., Chase, J., Chun, B., Schwab, S., & Vahdat, A. (2003). SHARP: An architecture for secure resource peering. In *19th ACM Symposium on Operating Systems Principles (SOSP 2003)* (pp. 133–148). New York: ACM Press.

Furmento, N., Hau, J., Lee, W., Newhouse, S., & Darlington, J. (2003). *Implementations of a service-oriented architecture on top of jini, jxta and ogsa.* In Proceedings of uk e-science all hands meeting.

Gabriel, E. Fagg, G. Bosilca, G. Angskun, T. Dongarra, J. J. Squyres, J. M., et al. (2004). Open MPI: Goals, Concept, and Design of a Next Generation MPI Implemention. In D. Kranzlmueller, P. Kacsuk, J. J. Dongarra (Eds.), *Recent Advances in Parallel Virtual Machine and Message Passing Interface*, (LNCS, Vol. 3241, pp. 97-104). Berlin: Springer.

Gabriel, E., & Huang, S. (2007). Runtime optimization of application level communication patterns. In *Proceedings of the 2007 International Parallel and Distributed Processing Symposium, 12th International Workshop on High-Level Parallel Programming Models and Supportive Environments*, (p. 185).

Gaddah, A., & Kunz, T. (2003). *A survey of middleware paradigms for mobile computing. Carleton University and Computing Engineering* [Research Report]. Retrieved June 15th, 2008, from http://www.sce.carleton.ca/wmc/middleware/middleware.pdf

Gao, L. (2001). On inferring autonomous system relationships in the Internet. *IEEE/ACM Transactions on networking, 9*(6), December.

Garbacki, P., Biskupski, B., & Bal, H. (2005). Transparent fault tolerance for grid application. In P. M. Sloot (Ed.) *Advances in Grid Computing - EGC 2005*, (pp. 671-680). Berlin: Springer Verlag.

Garcés-Erice, L., Biersack, E. W., Felber, P. A., Ross, K. W., & Urvoy-Keller, G. (2003). Hierarchical Peer-to-Peer Systems. In *Proceedings of the 9th Intl. Euro-Par Conf.* (pp. 1230-1239). Berlin: Springer-Verlag.

Garcia-Molina, H., & Salem, K. (1987). SAGAS. In *Proceedings of ACM SIGMOD'87, International Conference on Management of Data, 16*(3), 249-259.

Garey, M. R., & Johnson, D. S. (1979). *Computers and Intractability.* San Francisco: Freeman.

GAT. (2005). *Grid application toolkit*. www.gridlab.org/WorkPackages/wp-1/

Gelenbe, E. (1979). On the optimum checkpoint interval. *Journal of the ACM, 26*(2), 259–270. doi:10.1145/322123.322131

Gentzsch (2008). Top 10 rules for building a sustainable Grid. In *Grid thought leadership series*. Retrieved from www.ogf.org/TLS/?id=1

Gentzsch, W. (2002). Response to Ian Foster's "What is the Grid?" *GRIDtoday,* August 5. Retrieved from www.gridtoday.com/02/0805/100191.html

Gentzsch, W. (2004). Enterprise resource management: Applications in research and industry. In I. Foster & C. Kesselman (Eds.), *The Grid 2: Blueprint for a new computing infrastructure* (pp. 157 – 166). San Francisco: Morgan Kaufmann Publishers.

Gentzsch, W. (2004). Grid computing adoption in research and industry. In A. Abbas (Ed.), *Grid computing: A practical guide to technology and applications* (pp. 309 – 340). Florence, KY: Charles River Media Publishers.

Gentzsch, W. (2007). *Grid initiatives: Lessons learned and recommendations*. RENCI Report. Retrieved from www.renci.org/publications/reports.php

Gentzsch, W. (Ed.). (2007). *A sustainable Grid infrastructure for Europe, Executive Summary of the e-IRG Open Workshop on e-Infrastructures*, Heidelberg, Germany. Retrieved from www.e-irg.org/meetings/2007-DE/workshop.html

GEONgrid. (2008). Retrieved from www.geongrid.org

Georgakopoulos, D., Hornick, M., & Sheth, A. (1995). An overview of workflow management: From process modeling to workflow automation infrastructure. *Distributed and Parallel Databases, 3*(2), 119–153. doi:10.1007/BF01277643

Ghare, G., & Leutenegger, L. (2004, June). Improving Speedup and Response Times by Replicating Parallel Programs on a SNOW. In *Proceedings of the 10th workshop on job scheduling strategies for parallel processing.*

Ghinita, G., & Teo, Y. M. (2006). An adaptive stabilization framework for distributed hash tables. In *Proceedings of the 20th IEEE Intl. Parallel and Distributed Processing Symp.* New York: IEEE Computer Society Press.

Ghodsi, A., Alima, L. O., & Haridi, S. (2005). Low-bandwidth topology maintenance for robustness in structured overlay networks. In *Proceedings of 38th Hawaii Intl. Conf. on System Sciences* (p. 302). New York: IEEE Computer Society Press.

Ghodsi, A., Alima, L. O., & Haridi, S. (2005). Symmetric replication for structured peer-to-peer systems. In *Proceedings of the 3rd Intl. Workshop on Databases, Information Systems and Peer-to-Peer Computing* (p. 12). Berlin: Spinger-Verlag.

Ghormley, D., Petrou, D., Rodrigues, S., Vahdat, A., & Anderson, T. (1998, July). GLUnix: A global layer unix for a network of workstations. *Software, Practice & Experience, 28*(9), 929. doi:10.1002/(SICI)1097-024X(19980725)28:9<929::AID-SPE183>3.0.CO;2-C

Ghose, F., Grossklags, J., & Chuang, J. (2003). *Resilient Data-Centric Storage in Wireless Ad-Hoc Sensor Networks*. Proceedings the 4th International Conference on Mobile Data Management (MDM'03), (pp. 45-62).

Gill, P. E. Murray, W. & Wright, M. H. (1993). *Practical Optimization*. London: Academic Press Ltd.

Gilmont, T., Legat, J.-D., & Quisquater, J.-J. (1999). Enhancing the security in the memory management unit. In *Proceedings of the 25th EuroMicro Conference* (EUROMICRO'99). *1*, 449-456. Milan, Italy: IEEE Computer Society Press.

Gkantsidis, C., & Rodriguez, P. (2005, March). Network Coding for Large Scale Content Distribution. In *Proceedings of ieee/infocom 2005*, Miami, USA.

gLite - Lightweight Middleware for Grid Computing. (2005). Retrieved from http://glite.web.cern.ch/glite.

Globus: Grid security infrastructure (GSI) (n.d.). Retrieved from http://www.globus.org/security/

Globus: The grid resource allocation and management (GRAM) (n.d.). Retrieved from http://www.globus.org/toolkit/docs/3.2/gram/

Goad, W. B. (1987). Sequence analysis. *Los Alamos Science*, (Special Issue), 288–291.

Goderis, D. et al. (2001, July). *Service Level Specification Semantics and parameters: draft-tequila-sls-01.txt* [Internet Draft].

Godfrey, B., Lakshminarayanan, K., Surana, S., Karp, R., & Stoica, I. (2004). Load balancing in dynamic structured p2p systems. In *Proceedings of INFOCOM* (pp. 2253- 2262). New York: IEEE Press.

Godfrey, B., Lakshminarayanan, K., Surana, S., Karp, R., & Stoica, I. (2006). Load balancing in dynamic structured P2P systems. *Performance Evaluation, 63*(3).

Godfrey, P. B., & Stoica, I. (2005). Heterogeneity and load balance in distributed hash tables. In *Proceedings of INFOCOM* (pp. 596-606). New York: IEEE Press.

Goldberg, & D. E. (1989). *Genetic algorithm: In search, optimization and machine learning*. New York: Addison-Wesley.

Golding, R. A. (1992, Dec). *Weak-consistency group communication and membership* (Tech. Rep.). Computer and Information Sciences, University of California, Ph.D. Thesis.

Goller, A. (1999). *Parallel and Distributed Processing of Large Image Data Sets*. Doctoral Thesis, Graz University of Technology, Graz, Austria.

Goller, A., & Leberl, F. (2000). *Radar Image Processing with Clusters of Computers*. Paper presented at the IEEE Conference on Aerospace.

Golub, G. H., & Van Loan, C. F. (1989). *Matrix Computations*. Baltimore, MD: The John Hopkins University Press.

Golumbic, M. C. (1980). *Algorithmic Graph Theory and Perfect Graphs*. New York: Academic Press.

Gong, L. (2001, June). JXTA: A network programming environment. *IEEE Internet Computing, 5*(3), 88-95. Los Alamitos, CA: IEEE Computer Society. Retrieved from http://doi.ieeecomputersociety.org/10.1109/4236.93518

Gontmakher, A., Mendelson, A., Schuster, A., & Shklover, G. (2006) *Speculative synchronization and thread management for fine granularity threads*. In Proceedings of the 12th International Symposium on High-Performance Computer Architecture (HPCA'06), (pp. 278-287). Austin, TX: IEEE Computer Society Press.

Gonzalez-Castano, F. J., Vales-Alonso, J., Livny, M., Costa-Montenegro, E., & Anido-Rifo, L. (2003). Condor grid computing from mobile handheld devices. *SIGMOBILE Mobile Comput. Commun. Rev.*, *7*(1), 117–126. doi:10.1145/881978.882005

Gonzalo, C., & García-Martín, M.-A. (2006). *The 3G IP Multimedia Subsystem (IMS): Merging the Internet and the Cellular Worlds*. New York: Wiley.

Goodale, T., Jha, S., Kaiser, H., Kielmann, T., Kleijer, P., Merzky, A., et al. (2008). *A simple API for Grid applications (SAGA). Grid Forum Document GFD.90. Open Grid Forum*. Retrieved from www.ogf.org/documents/GFD.90.pdf

Goodman, D. J., Borras, J., Mandayam, N. B., & Yates, R. D. (1997). INFOSTATIONS: A new system model for data and messaging services. *Proceedings of the 47th IEEE Vehicular Technology Conference (VTC)*, Phoenix, AZ, (Vol. 2, pp. 969–973).

Google (2008). *Google App Engine*. Retrieved from http://code.google.com/appengine/

Google App Engine. (2008, November). Retrieved from http://appengine.google.com

Google Groups. (2008). *Cloud computing*. Retrieved from http://groups.google.ca/group/cloud-computing

Govindaraju, M., Krishnan, S., Chiu, K., Slominski, A., Gannon, D., & Bramley, R. (2002, June). *Xcat 2.0: A component-based programming model for grid web services* (Tech. Rep. No. Technical Report-TR562). Dept. of C.S., Indiana Univ., South Bend, IN.

Graboswki, P., Lewandowski, B., & Russell, M. (2004). Access from j2me-enabled mobile devices to grid services. In *Proceedings of Mobility Conference* 2004, Singapore.

Grama, A., Gupta, A., Kumar, V., & Karypis, G. (2003). *Introduction to parallel computing*. Upper Saddle River, NJ: Pearson Education Limited.

Grassi, V., Donatiello, L., & Iazeolla, G. (1988). Performability evaluation of multicomponent fault tolerant systems. *IEEE Transactions on Reliability*, *37*(2), 216–222. doi:10.1109/24.3744

Graupner, S., Kotov, V., Andrzejak, A., & Trinks, H. (2002, August). *Control Architecture for Service Grids in a Federation of Utility Data Centers* (Technical Report No. HPL-2002-235). Palo Alto, CA: HP Laboratories Palo Alto.

Gray, A. A., Arabshahi, P., Lamassoure, E., Okino, C., & Andringa, J.. (2004). *A Real Option Framework for Space Mission Design*. Technical report, VNational Aeronautics and Space Administration NASA.

Gray, J. (1981). The transaction concept: Virtues and limitations. In *Proceedings of the 7th International Conference on VLDB*, (pp.144-154).

Grelck, C., Scholz, S.-B., & Shafarenko, A. V. (2007). Coordinating data parallel SAC programs with S-Net. In *Proceedings of the 21th International Parallel and Distributed Processing Symposium (IPDPS 2007)* (pp. 1–8). New York: IEEE.

Grid Computing, I. B. M. *(n.d.)*. Retrieved from http://www-1.ibm.com/grid/

Grid Engine. (2001). *Open source project*. Retrieved from http://gridengine.sunsource.net/

Grid Interoperability Now Community Group (GIN-CG). (2006). Retrieved from http://forge.ogf.org/sf/projects/gin.

GridFTP (n.d.). Retrieved from http://www.globus.org/toolkit/docs/4.0/data/gridftp/

GridSphere (2008). Retrieved from www.gridsphere.org/gridsphere/gridsphere

GridWay. (2008). *Metascheduling technologies for the grid*. Retrieved from www.gridway.org/

Grigg, A. (2002). *Researvation-Based Timing Analysis – A Partitioned Timing Analysis Model for Distributed Real-Time Systems* (YCST-2002-10). York, UK: University of York, Dept. of Computer Science.

Grigoras, D. (2005). Service-oriented Naming Scheme for Wireless Ad Hoc Networks. In the *Proceedings of the NATO ARW "Concurrent Information Processing and Computing"*, July 3-10 2003, Sinaia, Romania, 2005, (pp. 60-73). Amsterdam: IOS Press

Grigoras, D., & Riordan, M. (2007). Cost-effective mobile ad hoc networks management. *Future Generation Computer Systems*, *23*(8), 990–996. doi:10.1016/j.future.2007.04.001

Grigoras, D., & Zhao, Y. (2007). *Simple Self-management of Mobile Ad Hoc Networks.* Proc of the 9th IFIP/IEEEInternational Conference on Mobile and Wireless Communication Networks, 19-21 September 2007, Cork, Ireland.

Grimme, C., Lepping, J., & Papaspyrou, A. (2008, April). Prospects of collaboration between compute providers by means of job interchange. In *Job Scheduling Strategies for Parallel Processing* (Vol. 4942, p. 132-151). Berlin / Heidelberg: Springer.

Grimshaw, A. S., & Wulf, W. A. (1997). The legion vision of a worldwide virtual computer. *Communications of the ACM*, *40*(1), 39–45. doi:10.1145/242857.242867

Grit, L. E. (2005, October). *Broker Architectures for Service-Oriented Systems* [Technical Report]. Durham, NC: Department of Computer Science, Duke University.

Grit, L. E. (2007). *Extensible Resource Management for Networked Virtual Computing.* PhD thesis, Department of Computer Science, Duke University, Durham, NC. (Adviser: Jeffrey S. Chase)

Gschwind, M., Hofstee, H.P., Flachs, B., Hopkins M., Watambe, Y., & Yamazaki, T., (2006). Synergistic Processing in Cell's Multicore Architecture. *IEEE Computer Society*, 0272-1732/06.

GSI (Globus Security Infrastructure). Retrieved from http://www.globus.org/Security/

Guiffaut, C., & Mahdjoubi, K. (2001, April). A Parallel FDTD Algorithm Using the MPI Library. *IEEE Antennas andPropagation Magazine, 43*(No. 2), 94–103.

Gummadi, K., Gummadi, R., Gribble, S., Ratnasamy, S., Shenker, S., & Stoica, I. (2003). The impact of dht routing geometry on resilience and proximity. In *Proceedings of ACM SIGCOMM* (pp. 381-394). New York: ACM Press.

Guo, D., Wu, J., Chen, H., & Luo, X. (2006). *Theory and Network Applications of Dynamic Bloom Filters.* Paper presented at the INFOCOM 2006. 25th IEEE International Conference on Computer Communications.

Guo, S.-F., Zhang, W., Ma, D., & Zhang, W.-L. (2004, Aug.). Grid mobile service: using mobile software agents in grid mobile service. Machine learning and cybernetics, 2004. In *Proceedings of 2004 International Conference on, 1,* 178-182.

Gupta, A., Sahin, O. D., Agarwal, D., & El Abbadi, A. (2004). Meghdoot: Content-based publish/subscribe over peer-to-peer networks. In Middleware'04 *Proceedings of the 5th ACM/IFIP/USENIX International Conference on Middleware*, (pp. 254-273). Heidelberg, Germany: SpringerLink. doi: 10.1007/b101561.

Gupta, I., Birman, K., Linga, P., Demers, A., & Renesse, R. V. (2003). Kelips: Building an efficient and stable P2P DHT through increased memory and background overhead. In *Proceedings of the 2nd Intl. Workshop on Peer-to-Peer Systems* (pp. 160-169). Berlin: Springer-Verlag.

Gustafson, J. (1988). Reevaluating Amdahl's law. *Communications of the ACM, 31,* 532–533. doi:10.1145/42411.42415

Haahr, M., Cunningham, R., & Cahill, V. (1999). Supporting CORBA applications in a mobile environment. In *MobiCom '99: Proceedings of the 5th Annual ACM/IEEE International Conference on Mobile Computing and Networking,* (pp. 36-47).

Hailong, C., & Jun, W. (2004). *Foreseer: a novel, locality-aware peer-to-peer system architecture for keyword searches*. Paper presented at the Proceedings of the 5th ACM/IFIP/USENIX International Conference on Middleware.

Haji, M. H., Gourlay, I., Djemame, K., & Dew, P. M. (2005). A SNAP-based community resource broker using a three-phase commit protocol: A performance study. *The Computer Journal*, *48*(3), 333–346. doi:10.1093/comjnl/bxh088

Hakami, S. (1999). Optimum location of switching centers and the absolute centers and medians of a graph. *Operations Research*, *12*, 450–459. doi:10.1287/opre.12.3.450

Halsall, F. (2000). *Multimedia Communications: Applications, Networks, Protocols and Standards (Hardcover)*. New York: Addison Wesley.

Hammond, L., Hubbert, B. A., Siu, M., Prabhu, M. K., Chen, M., & Olukotun, K. (2000). The Stanford Hydra CMP. *IEEE Micro*, *20*(2), 71–84. doi:10.1109/40.848474

Hammond, L., Nayfeh, B. A., & Olukotun, K. (1997). A single-chip multiprocessor. *IEEE Computer*, *30*(9), 79–85.

Hammond, L., Wong, V., Chen, M., Carlstrom, B. D., Davis, J. D., & Hertzberg, B. (2004). Transactional Memory Coherence and Consistency. *SIGARCH Comput. Archit. News*, *32*(2), 102. doi:10.1145/1028176.1006711

Harte, L., Wiblitzhouser, A., & Pazderka, T. (2006). *Introduction to MPEG; MPEG-1, MPEG-2 and MPEG-4*. Fuquay Varina, NC: Althos Publishing.

Harvey, N. J., Jones, M. B., Saroiu, S., Theimer, M., & Wolman, A. (2003). SkipNet: A scalable overlay network with practical locality properties. In *Proceedings of the 4th USENIX Symp. on Internet Technologies and Systems* (pp. 113-126). USENIX Association.

Hawick, K. A., James, H. A., Maciunas, K. J., Vaughan, F. A., Wendelborn, A. L., Buchhorn, M., et al. (1997). *Geostationary-satellite Imagery Application on Distributed, High-Performance Computing*. Paper presented at the High Performance Computing on the Information Superhighway: HPC Asia'97.

Hayes, B. (2007). Computing in a parallel universe. *American Scientist*, 95.

Hayes, C. L., & Luo, Y. (2007). Dpico: A high speed deep packet inspection engine using compact finite automata. *Proceedings of ACM/IEEE ANCS*, (pp. 195-203).

He, X. (1998). *2D -Object Recognition With Spiral Architecture*. Doctoral Thesis, University of Technology, Sydney, Sydney, Australia.

He, X., & Sun, X. (2005). Incorporating data movement into grid task scheduling. In *Proceedings of grid and cooperative computing* (pp. 394–405).

He, X., Sun, X., & Laszewski, G. (2003). QoS guided Min-Min heuristic for grid task scheduling. *Journal of Computer Science and Technology, Special Issue on Grid Computing, 18* (4).

Heien, E., Fujimoto, N., & Hagihara, K. (2008). Computing low latency batches with unreliable workers in volunteer computing environments. In *Pcgrid*.

Heine, F., Hovestadt, M., Kao, O., & Keller, A. (2005). Provision of fault tolerance with grid-enabled and SLA-aware resource management systems. In G. R. Joubert (Ed.) *Parallel Computing: Current and Future Issues of High End Computing*, (pp. 105-112), NIC-Directors.

Heine, F., Hovestadt, M., Kao, O., & Keller, A. (2005). SLA-aware job migration in grid environments. In L. Grandinetti (Ed.), *Grid Computing: New Frontiers of High Performance Computing* (345-367). Amsterdam, The Netherland: Elsevier Press.

Hennessy, J., & Patterson, D. (2006). *Computer architecture: a quantitative approach* (4th Ed.). San Francisco: Morgan Kaufmann.

Hey, T., & Trefethen, A. E. (2002). The UK e-science core programme and the Grid. *Future Generation Computer Systems*, *18*(8), 1017–1031. doi:10.1016/S0167-739X(02)00082-1

Heymann, E., Fernandez, A., Senar, M. A., & Salt, J. (2003). The EU-Crossgrid approach for grid application scheduling. *European Grid Conference*, (LNCS 2970, pp. 17-24). Amsterdam: Springer Verlag.

High Performance Fortran Forum. (1993). *High performance Fortran language specification, version 1.0* (No. CRPC-TR92225). Center for Research on Parallel Computation, Rice University, Houston, TX.

High Performance Fortran Forum. (1997). *High performance Fortran language specification 2.0*. Center for Research on Parallel Computation, Rice University, Houston, TX.

Hill, M. D., & Marty, M. R. (2008, July). Amdahl's Law in the Multicore Era. *HPCA 2008, IEEE 14th International Symposium* (pp.187).

Hingne, V., Joshi, A., Finin, T., Kargupta, H., & Houstis, E. (2003). Towards a pervasive grid. In *International parallel and distributed processing symposium* (ipdps'03) (p. 207).

Hinton, G., Sager, D., Upton, M., Boggs, D., Carmean, D., Kyker, A., & Roussel, P. (2001). The microarchitecture of the Pentium 4 processor. *Intel® Technology Journal*, *5*(1), 1-13.

Ho, T., Medard, M., Koetter, R., Karger, D. R., Effros, M., Shi, J., & Leong, B. (2006, October). A random linear network coding approach to multicast. *IEEE Transactions on Information Theory*, *52*(10). doi:10.1109/TIT.2006.881746

Hockney, R., & Berry, M. (1994). PARKBENCH report: public international benchmarks for parallel computers. *Science Progress*, *3*(2), 101–146.

Hockney, R., & Eastwood, J. (1981). *Computer simulation using particles*. London: McGraw-Hill, Inc.

Hoefler, T. Lichei, A. & Rehm, W. (2007). Low-Overhead LogGP Parameter Assessment for Modern Interconnect Networks. *Proceedings of the IPDPS*, Long Beach, CA, March 26-30. New York: IEEE.

Hong, T., & Tao, Y. (2003). *An Efficient Data Location Protocol for Self.organizing Storage Clusters*. Paper presented at the Proceedings of the 2003 ACM/IEEE conference on Supercomputing.

Hopper, R. (2002). *P/Meta - metadata exchange scheme*. Retrieved June 15th, 2008, from http://www.ebu.ch/trev_290-hopper.pdf

Hoschek, W., Jaen-Martinez, J., Samar, A., Stockinger, H., & Stockinger, K. (2000). *Data management in an international data grid project. grid computing - GRID 2000* (pp.333-361). UK.

Hovestadt, M. (2003). Scheduling in HPC resource management systems: Queuing vs. planning. In D. Feitelson (Ed.), *Job Scheduling Strategies for Parallel Processing*, (pp.1-20). Berlin: Springer Verlag.

Hsiao, H.-C., & King, C.-T. (2003). A tree model for structured peer-to-peer protocols. In *Proceedings of the 3rd IEEE Intl. Symp. on Cluster Computing and the Grid* (pp. 336-343). New York: IEEE Computer Society Press.

Hua, Y., & Xiao, B. (2006). A Multi-attribute Data Structure with Parallel Bloom Filters for Network Services. *Proceedings of 13th International Conference of High Performance Computing (HiPC)*,(pp. 277-288).

Hua, Y., Zhu, Y., Jiang, H., Feng, D., & Tian, L. (2008). Scalable and Adaptive Metadata Management in Ultra Large-Scale File Systems. *Proceedings of the 28th International Conference on Distributed Computing Systems (ICDCS 2008)*.

Huang, A. (2003) *Hacking the Xbox: an introduction to reverse engineering*, (1st Ed.). San Francisco: No Starch Press.

Huang, J., & Lilja, D. J. (1999). Exploiting basic block value locality with block reuse. *Proceedings of 5th International Symposium on High-Performance Computer Architecture* (HPCA'99), (pp. 106-114). Orlando, FL: IEEE Computer Society Press.

Huang, K.-H., & Abraham, J. A. (1984). Algorithm-based fault tolerance for matrix operations. *EEE Transactions on Computers*, *C-33*, 518–528. doi:10.1109/TC.1984.1676475

Huang, R., Casanova, H., & Chien, A. A. (2006, April). Using virtual Grids to simplify application scheduling. In *20th International Parallel and Distributed Processing Symposium (IPDPS 2006)*. Rhodes Island, Greece: IEEE.

Huang, S. (2007). *Applying Adaptive Software Technologies for Scientific Applications.* Master Thesis, Department of Computer Science, University of Houston, Houston, TX.

Huedo, E., Montero, R. S., & Llorente, I. M. (2004). A framework for adaptive execution in Grids. *Software, Practice & Experience*, *34*(7), 631–651. doi:10.1002/spe.584

Huerta, M. Haseltine, F., & Liu, Y. (2004, July). *Nih working definition of bioinformatics and computational biology.*

Hull, J. C. (2006). *Options, Futures, and Other Derivatives* (6th Edition). Upper Saddle River, NJ: Prentice Hall.

Hunold, S., Rauber, T., & Rünger, G. (2004). Multilevel hierarchical matrix-matrix multiplication on clusters. In *Proceedings of the 18th International Conference of Supercomputing (ICS'04)* (pp. 136–145). New York: ACM.

Hunold, S., Rauber, T., & Rünger, G. (2008). Combining building blocks for parallel multi-level matrix multiplication. *Parallel Computing*, *34*(6-8), 411–426. doi:10.1016/j.parco.2008.03.003

Huston, G. (n.d.). Peering and settlements Part-1. *The Internet protocol journal.* San Jose, CA: CISCO Systems.

Hwang, J., & Arvamudham, P. (2004). Middleware services for P2P computing in wireless grid networks. *IEEE Internet Computing*, 8(4)40–46. doi:10.1109/MIC.2004.19

Hwang, S., & Kesselman, C. (2003). GridWorkflow: A flexible failure handling framework for the Grid. In B. Lowekamp (Ed.), *12th IEEE International Symposium on High Performance Distributed Computing*, (pp. 126—131). New York: IEEE press.

Iamnitchi, A., Doraimani, S., & Garzoglio, G. (2006). Filecules in High-Energy Physics: Characteristics and Impact on Resource Management. In *proceeding of 15th ieee international symposium on high performance distributed computing hpdc 15,* Paris.

Iamnitchi, A., Foster, I. T., & Nurmi, D. (2002). A peer-to-peer approach to resource location in grid environments. In *Hpdc* (p. 419).

IBM. (2007). *Blue Gene*. Retrieved March 10, 2008, from http://domino.research.ibm.com/comm/research_projects.nsf/pages/bluegene.index.html

Information Services. *(n.d.).* Retrieved from http://www.globus.org/toolkit/mds/

Intel (2007). *Intel® multi-core: An overview.*

Intel News Release. (2006). *New dual-core Intel® Itanium® 2 processor doubles performance, reduces power consumption.* Santa Clara, C: Author.

Iosevich, V., & Schuster, A. (2005). Software Distributed Shared Memory: a VIA-based implementation and comparison of sequential consistency with home-based lazy release consistency: Research Articles. *Software, Practice & Experience*, *35*(8), 755–786. doi:10.1002/spe.656

Iosup, A., & Epema, D. H. (2006). GRENCHMARK: A framework for analyzing, testing, and comparing grids. *International Conference on Cluster Computing and the Grid* (pp. 313-320). Singapore: IEEE Computer Society Press.

Iosup, A., & Epema, D. H. (2007). Build-and-test workloads for Grid middleware: Problem, analysis, and applications. *International Conference on Cluster Computing and the Grid* (pp. 205-213). Rio de Janeiro, Brazil: IEEE Computer Society Press.

Iosup, A., Epema, D. H. J., Tannenbaum, T., Farrellee, M., & Livny, M. (2007, November). Inter-operating Grids through delegated matchmaking. In *2007 ACM/IEEE Conference on Supercomputing (SC 2007)* (pp. 1–12). New York: ACM Press.

Irwin, D., Chase, J., Grit, L., Yumerefendi, A., Becker, D., & Yocum, K. G. (2006, June). Sharing networked resources with brokered leases. In *USENIX Annual Technical Conference* (pp. 199–212). Berkeley, CA: USENIX Association.

Ishikawa, Y., Matsuda, M., Kudoh, T., Tezuka, H., & Sekiguchi, S. (2003). The design of a latency-aware mpi communication library. In *Proceedings of swopp03*.

ISO/IEC. (1995). *SMDL (Standard Music Description Language) Overview*. Retrieved June 15th, 2008, from http://xml.coverpages.org/gen-apps.html#smdl

ISO/IEC. (2003). *MPEG-7 Overview*. Retrieved June 15th, 2008, from http://www.chiariglione.org/mpeg/standards/mpeg-7/mpeg-7.htm.

Itzkovitz, A., Schuster, A., & Shalev, L. (1998). Thread migration and its applications in distributed shared memory systems. *Journal of Systems and Software*, *42*(1), 71–87. doi:10.1016/S0164-1212(98)00008-9

Iwata, T., & Kurosawa, K. (2003). OMAC: One-Key CBC MAC. In *10th International Workshop on Fast Software Encryption* (FSE'03), (LNCS Vol. 2887/2003, pp. 129-153), Lund, Sweden. Berlin/Heidelberg: Springer.

Jacob, B., Ferreira, L., Bieberstein, N., Gilzean, C., Girard, J.-Y., Strachowski, R., & Yu, S. (2003). *Enabling applications for Grid computing with Globus. IBM Redbook*. Retrieved from www.redbooks.ibm.com/abstracts/sg246936.html?Open

Jain, R. K. (1991). *The Art of Computer Systems Performance Analysis: Techniques for Experimental Design, Measurement, Simulation, and Modeling*. New York: Wiley.

James, K. M. (1983). A second look at bloom filters. *Communications of the ACM*, *26*(8), 570–571. doi:10.1145/358161.358167

Jamin, S., Jin, C., Jin, Y., Raz, D., Shavitt, Y., & Zhang, L. (2000). On the placement of Internet instrumentation. *In Proc. of INFOCOM*.

Jarvis, S. A., & Nudd, G. R. (2005, February). Performance-based middleware for Grid computing. *Concurrency and Computation: Practactice and Experience*, *17*(2-4), 215–234. doi:10.1002/cpe.925

Jayram, T. S., Kimbrel, T., Krauthgamer, R., Schieber, B., & Sviridenko, M. (2001). Online server allocation in server farm via benefit task systems. *Proceedings of the ACM Symposium on Theory of Computing (STOC'01)*, Crete, Greece, (pp. 540–549).

Jean, K., Galis, A., & Tan, A. (2004). Context-aware grid services: Issues and approaches. In *Computational science– iccs 2004: 4th international conference Krak'ow, Poland, June 6–9, 2004, proceedings, part iii* (LNCS Vol. 3038, p. 1296). Berlin: Springer.

Jennings, C., Lowekamp, B., Rescorla, E., Baset, S., & Schulzrinne, H. (2008). *REsource LOcation And Discovery (RELOAD)*. Retrieved June 15th, 2008, from http://tools.ietf.org/id/draft-bryan-p2psip-reload-04.txt.

Jha, S., Kaiser, H., El Khamra, Y., & Weidner, O. (2007, Dec. 10-13). Design and implementation of network performance aware applications using SAGA and Cactus. *3rd IEEE Conference on eScience and Grid Computing*, (pp. 143- 150). Bangalore, India.

Jiang, H., & Chaudhary, V. (2004). Process/thread migration and checkpointing in heterogeneous distributed systems. *Proceedings of the 37th Hawaii International Conference on System Sciences,* Hawaii, USA.

Jiang, J. L., Yang, G. W., & Shi, M. L. (2006). Transaction Model for Service Grid Environment and Implementation Considerations. In *Proceedings of IEEE International Conference on Web Services* (pp. 949 – 950).

Jiang, S., O'Hanlon, P., & Kirstein, P. (2004). Moving grid systems into the ipv6 era. In *Proceedings of Grid And Cooperative Computing 2003* (LNCS 3033, pp. 490–499). Heidelberg, Germany: Springer-Verlag.

Jiang, X.-F., Zheng, H.-W., Macian, C., & Pascual, V. (2008). *Service Extensible P2P Peer Protocol.* Retrieved June 15th, 2008, from http://tools.ietf.org/id/draft-jiang-p2psip-sep-01.txt

Jin, H., Xiong, M., Wu, S., & Zou, D. (2006). Replica Based Distributed Metadata Management in Grid Environment. *Computational Science* (LNCS 3944, pp. 1055-1062). Berlin: Springer-Verlag.

John, K., David, B., Yan, C., Steven, C., Patrick, E., & Dennis, G. (2000). OceanStore: an architecture for global-scale persistent storage. *SIGPLAN Not., 35*(11), 190–201. doi:10.1145/356989.357007

Johnson, C., & Welser, J. (2005). Future processors: Flexible and modular. *Proceedings of 3rd IEEE/ACM/IFIP International Conference on Hardware/Software Codesign and System Synthesis,* (pp. 4-6).

Johnson, R. (2002). *Spring Framework - a full-stack Java/JEE application framework*. Retrieved June 18, 2008, from http://www.springframework.org/

Joisha, P. G., & Banerjee, P. (1999). PARADIGM (version 2.0): A new HPF compilation system. In *IPPS '99/SPDP '99: Proceedings of the 13th International Symposium on Parallel Processing and the 10th Symposium on Parallel and Distributed Processing* (pp. 609–615). Washington, DC: IEEE Computer Society.

Jones, N. C. & Penvzner, P.A. (2004, August). *An Introduction to Bioinformatics Algorithms.*

JSR166. (2004). *Java concurrent utility package in J2SE 5.0* (JDK1.5). Retrieved June 24, 2008, from http://java.sun.com/j2se/1.5.0/docs/api/java/util/concurrent/package-summary.html

Jul, E., Levy, H., Hutchinson, N., & Blad, A. (1998). Fine-grained mobility in the emerald system. *ACM Transactions on Computer Systems, 6*(1), 109–133. doi:10.1145/35037.42182

Jung, E. B., Choi, S.-J., Baik, M.-S., Hwang, C.-S., Park, C.-Y., & Young, S. (2005). Scheduling scheme based on dedication rate in volunteer computing environment. In *Third international symposium on parallel and distributed computing (ispdc 2005),* Lille, France.

Kaashoek, M. F., & Karger, D. R. (2003). Koorde: A simple degree-optimal distributed hash table. In *Proceedings of the 2nd Intl. Workshop on Peer-to-Peer Systems* (pp. 98-107). Berlin: Springer-Verlag.

Kale, L. V., & Krishnan, S. (1998). Charm++: Parallel Programming with Message-Driven Objects. In G. V. Wilson, & P. Lu, *Parallel programming using c++* (pp. 175-213). Cambridge, MA: MIT Press.

Kalogeraki, V., Gunopulos, D., & Zeinalipour-Yazti, D. (2002). A local search mechanism for peer-to-peer networks. In *Proceedings of the Eleventh International Conference on Information and Knowledge Management* (pp. 300-307).

Kang, D.-S. (2004) *Speculation-aware thread scheduling for simultaneous multithreading.* Doctoral Dissertation, University of Southern California, Los Angeles, CA.

Kang, D.-S., Liu, C., & Gaudiot, J.-L. (2008). The impact of speculative execution on SMT processors. [IJPP]. *International Journal of Parallel Programming, 36*(4), 361–385. doi:10.1007/s10766-007-0052-3

Kangasharju, J. (2002). *Implementing the Wireless CORBA Specification.* PhD Disertation, Computer Science Department, University of Helsinki, Helsinki, Finland. Retrieved June 15th, 2008, from http://www.cs.helsinki.fi/u/jkangash/laudatur-jjk.pdf

Karger, D. R., & Ruhl, M. (2004). Diminished chord: A protocol for heterogeneous subgroup. In *Proceedings of the 3rd Intl. Workshop on Peer-to-Peer Systems* (pp. 288-297). Berlin: Springer-Verlag.

Karger, D. R., & Ruhl, M. (2004). Simple, efficient load balancing algorithms for peer-to-peer systems. In *Proceedings of the 3rd Intl. Workshop on Peer-to-Peer Systems* (pp. 131-140). Berlin: Springer-Verlag.

Karger, D., Lehman, E., Leighton, T., Levine, M., et al. (1997). Consistent hashing and random trees: Distributed caching protocols for relieving hot spots on the World Wide Web. *In Proc. of STOC* (pp 654–663).

Karonis, N. T., Toonen, B., & Foster, I. (2003). MPICH-G2: A Grid-enabled implementation of the message passing interface. [JPDC]. *Journal of Parallel and Distributed Computing, 63*, 551–563. doi:10.1016/S0743-7315(03)00002-9

Karp, R. M. (1992). Online algorithms versus offline algorithms: How much is it worth to know the future? In J. van Leeuwen, (Ed.), *Proceedings of the 12th IFIP World Computer Congress. Volume 1: Algorithms, Software, Architecture*, (pp. 416–429). Amsterdam: Elsevier.

Katzy, B., Zhang, C., & Löh, H. (2005). Virtual organizations: Systems and practices. In L. M. Camarinha-Matos, H. Afsarmanesh, & M. Ollus (Eds.), (p. 45-58). New York: Springer Science+Business Media, Inc.

Keahey, K., Foster, I., Freeman, T., & Zhang, X. (2006). Virtual workspaces: Achieving quality of service and quality of life in the Grids. *Science Progress, 13*(4), 265–275.

Kedrinskii, V. K., Vshivkov, V. A., Dudnikova, G. I., Shokin, Yu. I., & Lazareva, G. G. (2004). Focusing of an oscillating shock wave emitted by a toroidal bubble cloud. *Journal of Experimental and Theoretical Physics, 98*(6), 1138–1145. doi:10.1134/1.1777626

Keleher, P., Cox, A. L., & Zwaenepoel, W. (1992). *Lazy release consistency for software distributed shared memory*. Paper presented at the Proceedings of the 19th annual international symposium on Computer architecture.

Keleher, P., Cox, A. L., Dwarkadas, S., & Zwaenepoel, W. (1994). *TreadMarks: Distributed Shared Memory on Standard Workstations and Operating Systems*. Paper presented at the Proceedings of Winter 1995 USENIX Conference.

Kelly, W., Roe, P., & Sumitomo, J. (2002). G2: A grid middleware for cycle donation using. net. In *Proceedings of the 2002 International Conference on Parallel and Distributed Processing Techniques and Applications.*

Kephart, J. O., & Chess, D. M. (2003). The vision of autonomic computing. Computer *IEEE Computer Society, 36*(1), 41–50.

Kertész, A., Farkas, Z., Kacsuk, P., & Kiss, T. (2008, April). Grid enabled remote instrumentation. In F. Davoli, N. Meyer, R. Pugliese, & S. Zappatore (Eds.), *2nd International Workshop on Distributed Cooperative Laboratories: Instrumenting the Grid (INGRID 2007)* (pp. 303–312). New York: Springer US.

Kesselman, C., & Foster, I. (1998). *The Grid: Blueprint for a new computing infrastructure*. San Francisco: Morgan Kaufmann Publishers.

Kessler, C. W., & Löwe, W. (2007). A framework for performance-aware composition of explicitly parallel components. In [Jülich/Aachen, Germany: IOS Press.]. *Proceedings of the International Conference ParCo, 2007*, 227–234.

Khanna, G., Vydyanathan, N., Catalyurek, U., Kurc, T., Krishnamoorthy, S., Sadayappan, P., et al. (2006).Task scheduling and file replication for data-intensive jobs with batch-shared I/O. In *Proceedings of high-performance distributed computing* (*HPDC*) (pp. 241–252).

Kielmann, T. Hofman, R. F. H. Bal, H. E. Plaat, A. & Bhoedjang, R. A. F. (1999). MagPIe: MPI's collective communication operations for clustered wide area systems. *ACM SIGPLAN Symposium on Principles and Practice of Parallel Programming (PPoPP'99), 34*(8),131-140.

Kim, J.-S., Nam, B., Keleher, P. J., Marsh, M. A., Bhattacharjee, B., & Sussman, A. (2006). Resource discovery techniques in distributed desktop grid environments. In *Grid* (pp. 9-16).

Kim, K. H., & Buyya, R. (2007, September). Fair resource sharing in hierarchical virtual organizations for global Grids. In *8th IEEE/ACM International Conference on Grid Computing (Grid 2007)* (pp. 50–57). Austin, TX: IEEE.

Kim, S., & Weissman, J. B. (2004). A genetic algorithm based approach for scheduling decomposable data grid applications. In *Proceedings of international conference on parallel processing* (Vol. 1, pp. 405–413).

Kim, Y. (1996, June). *Fault Tolerant Matrix Operations for Parallel and Distributed Systems*. Ph.D. dissertation, University of Tennessee, Knoxville.

Knuth, D. E. (1975). *The art of computer programming. Volume 1: Fundamental Algorithms*. Reading, MA: Addison Wesley.

Koelbel, C. H., Loveman, D. B., & Schreiber, R. S., Jr. G. L. S., & Zosel, M. E. (1994). *The High Performance Fortran Handbook*. Cambridge, MA: MIT Press.

Koetter, R., & Medard, M. (2003, October). An algebraic approach to network coding. *IEEE/ACM Transactions on Networking (TON), 11*(5), 782 – 795.

Kok, A. J. F., Pabst, J. L. v., & Afsarmanseh, H. (April, 1997). *The 3D Object Mediator: Handling 3D Models on Internet.* Paper presented at the High-Performance Computing and Networking, Vienna, Austria.

Kondo, D., Araujo, F., Malecot, P., Domingues, P., Silva, L. M., & Fedak, G. (2006). *Characterizing result errors in internet desktop grids* (Tech. Rep. No. INRIA-HALTech Report 00102840), INRIA, France.

Kondo, D., Chien, A. A., & Casanova, H. (2007). Scheduling task parallel applications for rapid turnaround on enterprise desktop grids. *Journal of Grid Computing, 5*(4), 379–405. doi:10.1007/s10723-007-9063-y

Kondo, D., Chien, A., & H., C. (2004, November). Rapid Application Turnaround on Enterprise Desktop Grids. In *Acm conference on high performance computing and networking, sc2004.*

Kondo, D., Fedak, G., Cappello, F., Chien, A. A., & Casanova, H. (2006, December). On Resource Volatility in Enterprise Desktop Grids. In *Proceedings of the 2nd IEEE International Conference On E-Science And Grid Computing (eScience'06)* (pp. 78–86). Amsterdam, Netherlands.

Kondo, D., Taufer, M., Brooks, C., Casanova, H., & Chien, A. (2004, April). Characterizing and evaluating desktop grids: An empirical study. In *Proceedings of the International Parallel and Distributed Processing Symposium (IPDPS'04).*

Koskela, T., Kassinen, O., Korhonen, J., Ou, Z., & Ylianttila, M. (2008). Peer-to-Peer Community Management using Structured Overlay Networks. In *the Proc. of International Conference on Mobile Technology, Applications and Systems*, September 10-12, Yilan, Taiwan.

Koufaty, D., & Marr, D. (2003). Hyperthreading technology in the Netburst microarchitecture. *IEEE Micro, 23*(2), 56–65. doi:10.1109/MM.2003.1196115

Kowaliski, C. (2008). NVIDIA CEO talks down CPU-GPU hybrids, Larrabee. *The Tech Report,* April 11th. Retrieved from http://techreport.com/discussions.x/14538

Kraeva, M. A., & Malyshkin, V. E. (1997). Implementation of PIC method on MIMD multicomputers with assembly technology. In *Proc. of the High Performance Computing and Networking Europe 1997 Int. Conference.* (LNCS, Vol.1255), (pp. 541-549). Berlin: Springer Verlag.

Kraeva, M. A., & Malyshkin, V. E. (1999). Algorithms of parallel realization of PIC method with assembly technology. In *Proceedings of 7th High Performance Computing and Networking Europe,* (LNCS Vol. 1593), (pp. 329-338). Berlin: Springer Verlag.

Kraeva, M. A., & Malyshkin, V. E. (2001). Assembly technology for parallel realization of numerical models on MIMD-multicomputers. *International Journal on Future Generation Computer Systems, Elsevier Science, 17*(6), 755–765. doi:10.1016/S0167-739X(00)00058-3

Krafzig, D., Banke, K., & Slama, D. (2005). *Enterprise SOA: Service-Oriented Architecture Best Practices*. Upper Saddle River, NJ: Prentice Hall.

Krauter, K., Buyya, R., & Maheswaran, M. (2002). A taxonomy and survey of grid resource management systems for distributed computing. *Software, Practice & Experience*, *32*(2), 135–164. doi:10.1002/spe.432

Krishna, V. & Perry, M. (2007). *Efficient mechanism Design*.

Krishnan, S., & Gannon, D. (2004). Xcat3: A framework for cca components as ogsa services. In *Proceedings of Hips 2004, 9th International Workshop on High-Level Parallel Programming Models and Supportive Environments*.

Kubiatowicz, J., Bindel, D., Chen, Y., Eaton, P., Geels, D., Gummadi, R., et al. (2000). OceanStore: An Architecture for Global-Scale Persistent Storage. In *Proceedings of the 9th Intl. Conf. on Architectural Support for Programming Languages and Operating Systems* (pp. 190-201). New York: ACM Press.

Kühnemann, M., Rauber, T., & Rünger, G. (2004). A source code analyzer for performance prediction. In *Proceedings of IPDPS'04 Workshop on Massively Parallel Processing (WMPP'04*. New York: IEEE.

Kuksheva, E. A., Malyshkin, V. E., Nikitin, S. A., Snytnikov, A. V., Snytnikov, V. N., & Vshivkov, V. A. (2005). Supercomputer simulation of self-gravitating media. *International Journal on Future Generation Computer Systems*, *21*(5), 749–758. doi:10.1016/j.future.2004.05.019

Kumar, A. (2000). An efficient SuperGrid protocol for high availability and load balancing. *IEEE Transactions on Computers*, *49*(10), 1126–1133. doi:10.1109/12.888048

Kumar, A., Xu, J., & Zegura, E. W. (2005). *Efficient and scalable query routing for unstructured peer-to-peer networks*. Paper presented at the Proceedings INFOCOM 2005, 24th Annual Joint Conference of the IEEE Computer and Communications Societies.

Kumar, R., Tullsen, D. M., & Jouppi, N. P. (2006). Core Architecture Optimization for Heterogeneous Chip Multiprocessors. In *Proceedings of the 15th International Conference on Parallel Architecture and Compilation Techniques (pact 2006)* (pp. 23-32).

Kumar, V. K. P., Hariri, S., & Raghavendra, C. S. (1986). Distributed program reliability analysis. *IEEE Transactions on Software Engineering*, *SE-12*, 42–50.

Kumary, R. Tullsen D.M., Ranganathan, P., Jouppi, N.P., & Farkas, K.I., (2004). Single-ISA Heterogeneous Multi-Core Architecture for Multithreaded Workload Performance. In *Proceedings of the 31st International Symposium on Computer Architecture (ISCA'04)*, June, 2004.

Kurkovsky, S. Bhagyavati, Ray, A., & Yang, M. (2004). *Modeling a grid-based problem solving environment for mobile devices*. In *ITCC* (2) (p. 135). New York: IEEE Computer Society.

Kwok, T. T.-O., & Kwok, Y.-K. (2007). *Design and Evaluation of Parallel String Matching Algorithms for Network Intrusion Detection Systems* (NPC 2007), (LNCS 4672, pp. 344-353). Berlin: Springer.

Lamehamedi, H., & Szymanski, B. shentu, Z., & Deelman, E. (2002). Data replication strategies in grid environments. In *Proceedings of the fifth international conference on algorithms and architectures for parallel processing* (pp. 378–383).

Lamehamedi, H., Szymanski, B., Shentu, Z., & Deelman, E. (2003). Simulation of dynamic data replication strategies in data grids. *In Proceedings of the international parallel and distributed processing symposium* (pp. 10–20).

Landers, M., Zhang, H., & Tan, K.-L. (2004). PeerStore: Better performance by relaxing in peer-to-peer backup. In *Proceedings of the 4th Intl. Conf. on Peer-to-Peer Computing* (pp. 72-79). New York: IEEE Computer Society Press.

Lange, D., & Oshima, M. (1998). Mobile agents with java: The aglet api. *World Wide Web (Bussum)*, *1*(3). doi:10.1023/A:1019267832048

Laszewski, G. v., Foster, I., & Gawor, J. (2000). Cog kits: A bridge between commodity distributed computing and high-performance grids. In *ACM 2000 Conference on java grande* (p.97 - 106). San Francisco, CA: ACM Press.

Laure, E. (2001). OpusJava: A Java framework for distributed high performance computing. *Future Generation Computer Systems, 18*(2), 235–251. doi:10.1016/S0167-739X(00)00094-7

Laure, E., Mehrotra, P., & Zima, H. P. (1999). Opus: Heterogeneous computing with data parallel tasks. *Parallel Processing Letters, 9*(2). doi:10.1142/S0129626499000256

Lawler, E. L., Lenstra, J. K., Rinnooy Kan, A. H. G., & Shmoys, H. (1993). *Sequencing and Scheduling: Algorithms and Complexity*. Amsterdam: North-Holland.

Ledlie, J., Serban, L., & Toncheva, D. (2002). *Scaling Filename Queries in a Large-Scale Distributed File System*. Harvard University, Cambridge, MA.

Lee, C. (2003). Grid programming models: Current tools, issues and directions. In G. F. Fran Berman, T. Hey, (Eds.), *Grid computing* (pp. 555–578). New York: Wiley Press.

Lee, C., Lee, T.-y., Lu, T.-c., & Chen, Y.-t. (1997). A World-wide Web Based Distributed Animation Environment. *Computer Networks and ISDN Systems, 29*, 1635–1644. doi:10.1016/S0169-7552(97)00078-0

Lee, L. G. (1982). Designing a Bloom filter for differential file access. *Communications of the ACM, 25*(9), 600–604. doi:10.1145/358628.358632

Lee, S., Ren, X., & Eigenmann, R. (2008). Efficient content search in ishare, a p2p based internet-sharing system. In *PCGRID*.

Lee, S.-W., & Gaudiot, J.-L. (2003). Clustered micro-architecture simultaneous multithreading. In *9th International Euro-Par Conference on Parallel Processing* (Euro-Par'03), (LNCS Vol. 2790/2004, pp. 576-585), Klagenfurt, Austria. Berlin/Heidelberg: Springer.

Lee, Y. C., & Zomaya, A. Y. (2006). Data sharing pattern aware scheduling on grids. In *Proceedings of International Conference on Parallel Processing*, (pp. 365–372).

Legrand, I., Newman, H., Voicu, R., Cirstoiu, C., Grigoras, C., Toarta, M., et al. (2004, September-October). Monalisa: An agent based, dynamic service system to monitor, control and optimize Grid based applications. In *Computing in High Energy and Nuclear Physics (CHEP)*, Interlaken, Switzerland.

Lei, M., & Vrbsky, S. V. (2006). A data replication strategy to increase data availability in data grids. In *Proceedings of the international conference on grid computing and applications* (pp. 221–227).

Leslie, M., Davies, J., & Huffman, T. (2006). replication strategies for reliable decentralised storage. In *Proceedings of the 1st Workshop on Dependable and Sustainable Peer-to-Peer Systems* (pp. 740-747). New York: IEEE Computer Society Press.

Leutenegger, S., & Sun, X. (1993). Distributed computing feasibility in a non-dedicated homogeneous distributed system. In *Proceedings of SC'93*, Portland, OR.

Levitin, G., Dai, Y. S., & Ben-Haim, H. (2006). Reliability and performance of star topology grid service with precedence constraints on subtask execution. *IEEE Transactions on Reliability, 55*(3), 507–515. doi:10.1109/TR.2006.879651

Levitin, G., Dai, Y. S., Xie, M., & Poh, K. L. (2003). Optimizing survivability of multi-state systems with multi-level protection by multi-processor genetic algorithm. *Reliability Engineering & System Safety, 82*, 93–104. doi:10.1016/S0951-8320(03)00136-4

Li, C.-C. J., Stewart, E. M., & Fuchs, W. K. (1994). Compiler assisted full checkpointing. *Software, Practice & Experience, 24*, 871–886. doi:10.1002/spe.4380241002

Li, F., Pei, C., Jussara, A., & Andrei, Z. B. (2000). Summary cache: a scalable wide-area web cache sharing protocol. *IEEE/ACM Trans. Netw., 8*(3), 281–293.

Li, J., Stribling, J., Gil, T. M., Morris, R., & Kaashoek, M. F. (2004). Comparing the performance of distributed hash tables under churn. In *Proceedings of the 3rd Intl. Workshop on Peer-to-Peer Systems* (pp. 87-99). Berlin: Springer-Verlag.

Li, J., Stribling, J., Morris, R., & Kaashoek, M. F. (2005). Bandwidth-efficient management of dht routing tables. In *Proceedings of 2nd Symp. on Networked Systems Design and Implementation* (pp. 99-114). USENIX Association.

Li, S.-Y. R., Yeung, R. W., & Cai, N. (2003, Feb.). Linear network coding. *IEEE Transactions on Information Theory, 49*(2), 371–381. doi:10.1109/TIT.2002.807285

Li, X., & Gaudiot, J.-L. (2006). Design trade-offs and deadlock prevention in transient fault-tolerant SMT processors. In *Proceedings of 12th Pacific Rim International Symposium on Dependable Computing* (PRDC'06), (pp. 315-322). Riverside, CA: IEEE Computer Society Press.

Li, Z. Zhang, Duan, Z., Gao, L.& Hou, Y.T.(2000). Decoupling QoS control from Core routers: A Novel bandwidth broker architecture for scalable support of guaranteed services. *Proc. OfSIGCOMM'00*, Stockholm, Sweden, (pp. 71-83).

Li, Z., & Mohapatra, P. (2004, January). QoS Aware routing in Overlay networks (QRON). *IEEE Journal on Selected Areas in Communications, 22*(1).

Li, Z., Sun, L., & Ifeachor, E. (2005). Challenges of mobile ad-hoc grids and their applications in e-healthcare. In *Proceedings of Second International Conference on Computational Intelligence in Medicine And Healthcare* (cimed' 2005).

Li, Z., Xu, X., Hu, W., & Tang, Z. (2006). Microarchitecture and performance analysis of Godson-2 SMT processor. In *Proceedings of the 24th International Conference on Computer Design* (ICCD'06), (pp. 485-490). San Jose, CA: IEEE Computer Society Press.

Liang, D., & Tripathi, S. (1996). Performance analysis of longlived transaction processing systems with rollbacks and aborts. *IEEE Transactions on Knowledge and Data Engineering, 8*(5), 802–815. doi:10.1109/69.542031

Likic, V. (2000). *The needleman-wunsch algorithm for sequence alignment.* The University of Melbourne, Australia.

Lin, M. S., Chang, M. S., Chen, D. J., & Ku, K. L. (2001). The distributed program reliability analysis on ring-type topologies. *Computers & Operations Research, 28*, 625–635. doi:10.1016/S0305-0548(99)00151-3

Lin, Y., Liu, P., & Wu, J. (2006). Optimal placement of replicas in data grid environments with locality assurance. In *Proceedings of the 12th International Conference on Parallel and Distributed Systems* (*ICPADS*'06), *01*, 465–474.

Lindholm, T., & Yellin, F. (1999). *The jave(tm) virtual machine specification (2nd Ed.).*New York: Addison Wesley.

Litchfield, S. (2008). *A detailed comparison of Seires 60 (S60) Symbian smartphones.* Retrieved March 10, 2008, from http://3lib.ukonline.co.uk/s60history.htm

Litke, A., Skoutas, D., & Varvarigou, T. (2004). Mobile grid computing: Changes and challenges of resource management in a mobile grid environment. In *Proceedings of Practical Aspects of Knowledge Management* (PAKM 2004), Austria.

Little, M. C., Shrivastava, S. K., & Speirs, N. A. (2002)... *The Computer Journal, 45*(6), 645–652. doi:10.1093/comjnl/45.6.645

Litzkow, M. J., Livny, M., & Mutka, M. W. (1988, June). Condor – a hunter of idle workstations. In *8th International Conference of Distributed Computing Systems* (pp. 104–111). San Jose, CA: Computer Society.

Liu, C., & Gaudiot, J.-L. (2008). Resource sharing control in simultaneous multithreading microarchitectures. In *Proceedings of the 13th IEEE Asia-Pacific Computer Systems Conference* (ACSAC'08), (pp. 1-8). Hsinchu, Taiwan: IEEE Computer Society Press.

Liu, C., Qian, D., Liu, Y., Li, Y., & Wang, C. (2006). RSVP Context Extraction in IP Mobility Environments. *Vehicular Technology Conference, 2006, VTC 2006-Spring, IEEE 63rd,* (Vol. 2, pp. 756-760).

Liu, G. Q., Xie, M., Dai, Y. S., & Poh, K. L. (2004). On program and file assignment for distributed systems. *Computer Systems Science and Engineering, 19*(1), 39–48.

Liu, H., Zheng, K., Liu, B., Zhang, X., & Liu, Y. (2006). A memory-efficient parallel string matching architecture for high-speed intrusion detection. *IEEE Journal on Selected Areas in Communications, 24*(10), 1793–1804. doi:10.1109/JSAC.2006.877221

Liu, L.-L., Liu, Q., Natsev, A., Ross, K. A., Smith, J. R., & Varbanescu, A. L. (2007, July). Digital media indexing on the cell processor. In *16th international conference on parallel architecture and compilation techniques,* Beijing, China (pp. 425–425).

Liu, S., & Gaudiot, J.-L. (2007). Synchronization mechanisms on modern multi-core architectures. In *Proceedings of the 12th Asia-Pacific Computer Systems Architecture Conference* (ACSAC'07), (LNCS Vol. 4697/2007), (pp. 290-303), Seoul, Korea. Berlin/Heidelberg: Springer.

Liu, S., & Gaudiot, J.-L. (2008). The potential of fine-grained value prediction in enhancing the performance of modern parallel machines. *In Proceedings of the 13th IEEE Asia-Pacific Computer Systems Conference* (ACSAC'08), (pp. 1-8). Hsinchu, Taiwan: IEEE Computer Society Press.

Liu, X., Li, V., & Zhang, P. (2006). *Joint radio resource management through vertical handoffs in 4G networks IEEE GLOBECOM* (pp. 1-5). Washington, DC: IEEE.

Livny, M., & Raman, R. (1998). High-throughput resource management. In *The Grid: Blueprint for a new computing infrastructure* (pp. 311-338). San Francisco: Morgan-Kaufmann

Loan, C. V. (1992). *Computational frameworks for the fast Fourier transform.* Philadelphia, PA: Society for Industrial and Applied Mathematics.

Locke, C. D., Vogel, D. R., & Mesler, T. J. (1991). Building A Predictable Avionics Platform in Ada. In *Proceedings of IEEE Real-Time Systems Symposium.*

Lodygensky, O., Fedak, G., Cappello, F., Neri, V., Livny, M., & Thain, D. (2003). XtremWeb & Condor: Sharing resources between Internet connected condor pools. In *Proceedings of CCGRID'2003, Third International Workshop On Global And Peer-To-Peer Computing (GP2PC'03)* (pp. 382–389). Tokyo, Japan.

Loo, B. T., Huebsch, R., Stoica, I., & Hellerstein, J. M. (2004). The case for a hybrid p2p search infrastructure. In *Proceedings of the 3rd Intl. Workshop on Peer-to-Peer Systems* (pp. 141-150). Berlin: Springer-Verlag.

Lopez, J., Aeschlimann, M., Dinda, P., Kallivokas, L., Lowekamp, B., & O'Hallaron, D. (1999, June). Preliminary report on the design of a framework for distributed visualization. In *Proceedings of the international conference on parallel and distributed processing techniques and applications (PDPTA'99)* (pp. 1833–1839). Las Vegas, NV.

Lovas, R., Dózsa, G., Kacsuk, P., Podhorszki, N., & Drótos, D. (2004). Workflow support for complex Grid applications: Integrated and portal solutions. In M. Dikaiakos (Ed.): *AxGrids 2004,* (LNCS 3165, pp. 129-138). Berlin: Springer Verlag.

Ludtke, S., Baldwin, P., & Chiu, W. (1999). EMAN: Semiautomated software for high-resolution single-particle reconstruction. *Journal of Structural Biology, 128,* 146–157. doi:10.1006/jsbi.1999.4174

Luk, F. T., & Park, H. (1986). An analysis of algorithm-based fault tolerance techniques. *SPIE Adv. Alg. and Arch. for Signal Proc., 696,* 222–228.

Luk, M., Mezzour, G., Perrig, A., & Gligor, V. (2007). MiniSec: A Secure Sensor Network Communication Architecture. *Proceedings of IEEE International Conference on Information Processing in Sensor Networks (IPSN),* (pp. 479-488).

Luther, A., Buyya, R., Ranjan, R., & Venugopal, S. (2005). Peer-to-peer grid computing and a. NET-based alchemi framework. high performance computing: Paradigm and Infrastructure. In M. Guo, (Ed.). New York: Wiley Press. Retrieved from www.alchemi.net

Luther, A., Buyya, R., Ranjan, R., & Venugopal, S. (2005, June). Alchemi: A. NET-based enterprise grid computing system, In ICOMP'05 *Proceedings of the 6th International Conference on Internet Computing*, Las Vegas, USA.

Lv, C., Cao, P., Cohen, E., Li, K., & Shenker, S. (2002). Search and replication in unstructured peer-to-peer networks. In *Proceedings of the 2002 ACM SIGMETRICS international conference on Measurement and modeling of computer systems* (pp.258-259).

Ma, M. J. M., Wang, C. L., & Lau, F. C. M. (2000). JESSICA: Java-enabled single-system-image computing architecture. *Journal of Parallel and Distributed Computing*, *60*(10), 1194–1222. doi:10.1006/jpdc.2000.1650

Mahadevan, U., & Ramakrishnan, S. (1994) *Instruction scheduling over regions: A framework for scheduling across basic blocks*. In *Proceedings of the 5th International Conference on Compiler Construction* (CC'94), Edinburgh, (LNCS Vol. 786/1994, pp. 419-434). Berlin/Heidelberg: Springer.

Malécot, P., Kondo, D., & Fedak, G. (2006, June). Xtremlab: A system for characterizing internet desktop grids. In *Poster in the 15th ieee international symposium on high performance distributed computing hpdc'06*. Paris, France.

Malyshkin V.E., Sorokin S.B., & K.G.Chauk (2008, May). Fragmented numerical algorithms for the library parallel standard subroutines. Accepted to publication in *Siberian Journal of Numerical Mathematics*, Novosibirsk, Russia.

Malyshkin, V. (2006). How to create the magic wand? Currently implementable formulation of the problem. In *New Trends in Software Methodologies, Tools and Techniques, Proceedings of the Fifth SoMeT_06, 147*, 127-132.

Malyshkin, V. E. (1995). Functionality in ASSY system and language of functional programming. In *Proceedings of the First Aizu International Symposium on Parallel Algorithms/Architecture Synthesis*. (pp. 92-97). Aizu-Wakamatsu, Japan: IEEE Comp. Soc. Press.

MandelbrotSet. (2008, November). Retrieved from http://mathworld.wolfram.com/MandelbrotSet.html.

Manku, G. (2004). Balanced binary trees for ID management and load balance in distributed hash tables. *In Proc. of PODC*.

March, V., Teo, Y. M., & Wang, X. (2007). DGRID: A DHT-based resource indexing and discovery scheme for computational grids. In *Proceedings of the 5th Australasian Symp. on Grid Computing and e-Research* (pp. 41-48). Australian Computer Society, Inc.

March, V., Teo, Y. M., Lim, H. B., Eriksson, P., & Ayani, R. (2005). Collision detection and resolution in hierarchical peer-to-peer systems. In *Proceedings of the 30th IEEE Conf. on Local Computer Networks* (pp. 2-9). New York: IEEE Computer Society Press.

Marcuello, P., & Gonzalez, A. (1999) *Exploiting speculative thread-level parallelism on a SMT processor*. In *Proceedings of the 7th International Conference on High-Performance Computing and Networking* (HPCN Europe'99), Amsterdam, the Netherlands, (LNCS Vol. 1593/1999, pp. 754-763) Berlin/Heidelberg: Springer.

Marr, D.T., Binns, F., Hill, D.L., Hinton, G., Koufaty, D.A, Miller, J.A., & Upton, M. (2002). Hyper-threading technology architecture and microarchitecture. *Intel® Technology Journal*, *6*(1), 4-15.

Marsh, A. (1997). *EUROMED - Combining WWW and HPCN to Support Advanced Medical Imaging*. Paper presented at the High-Performance Computing and Networking, Vienna, Austria.

Mascarenhas, E., & Rego, V. (1995). *Ariadne: Architecture of a portable threads system supporting mobile process*, (Tech. Rep. No. CSD-TR 95-017). Dept. of Computer Sciences, Purdue University, Southbend, IN.

Mason, R., & Kelly, W. (2005). G2-p2p: A fully decentralized fault-tolerant cycle-stealing framework. In R. Buyya, P. Coddington, and A. Wendelborn, (Eds.), In *AusGrid'05 Australasian Workshop on Grid Computing and e-Research*, Newcastle, Australia, (Vol. 44 of CRPIT, pp. 33-39).

Matei, R., & Ian, F. (2002). *A Decentralized, Adaptive Replica Location Mechanism*. Paper presented at the Proceedings of the 11th IEEE International Symposium on High Performance Distributed Computing.

Mathe, J., Kuntner, K., Pota, S., & Juhasz, Z. (2003). The use of jini technology in distributed and grid multimedia systems. In *MIPRO 2003, Hypermedia and Grid Systems* (p. 148-151). Opatija, Croatia.

Matjaz, B. J. (2008). *BPEL and Java*. Retrieved June 15th, 2008, from http://www.theserverside.com/tt/articles/article.tss?l=BPELJava

Matossian, V., Bhat, V., Parashar, M., Peszynska, M., Sen, M., & Stoffa, P. (2005). Autonomic oil reservoir optimization on the grid. [John Wiley and Sons.]. *Concurrency and Computation*, *17*(1), 1–26. doi:10.1002/cpe.871

Mattson, T., Sanders, B., & Massingill, B. (2004). *Patterns for parallel programming*. New York: Addison-Wesley.

Maymounkov, P., & Mazières, D. (2002). Kademlia: A Peer-to-peer Information System Based on the XOR Metric. In *Proceedings of the 1st international workshop on peer-to-peer systems (iptps'02)* (pp. 53–65).

McGinnis, L., Wallom, D., & Gentzsch, W. (Eds.). (2007). *2nd International Workshop on Campus and Community Grids*. retrieved from http://forge.gridforum.org/sf/go/doc14617?nav=1

McIlroy, M. (1982). Development of a Spelling List. *Communications, IEEE Transactions on [legacy, pre - 1988]*, *30*(1), 91-99.

McKenney, P. E., Lee, D. Y., & Denny, B. A. (2008). Traffic generator software release notes.

McKnight, L., Howison, J., & Bradner, S. (2004, July). Wireless grids, distributed resource sharing by mobile, nomadic and fixed devices. *IEEE Internet Computing*, *8*(4), 24–31. doi:10.1109/MIC.2004.14

McNair, J., & Fang, Z. (2004). Vertical handoffs in fourth-generation multinetwork environments. *IEEE Wireless Communications.*, *11*(3), 8–15. doi:10.1109/MWC.2004.1308935

Merlin, J. H., Baden, S. B., Fink, S., & Chapman, B. M. (1999). Multiple data parallelism with HPF and KeLP. *Future Generation Computer Systems*, *15*(3), 393–405. doi:10.1016/S0167-739X(98)00083-1

Merton, R. C. (1973). Theory of Real Option Pricing. *The Bell Journal of Economics and Management Science*, *4*(1). doi:10.2307/3003143

Message Passing Interface Forum. (1994). MPI: A Message Passing Interface Standard. (Technical Report ut-cs-94-230), University of Tennessee, Knoxville, TN.

Messig, M., & Goscinski, A. (2007). Autonomic system management in mobile grid environments. In *Proceedings of the Fifth Australasian Symposium on ACSW Frontiers* (ACSW' 07), (pp. 49–58). Darlinghurst, Australia: Australian Computer Society, Inc.

Metz, C. (2001). Interconnecting ISP networks. *IEEE Internet Computing*, *5*(2), 74–80. doi:10.1109/4236.914650

Meyer, J. (1980). On evaluating the performability of degradable computing systems. *IEEE Transactions on Computers*, *29*, 720–731. doi:10.1109/TC.1980.1675654

Michael, M. (2002). Compressed bloom filters. *IEEE/ACM Trans. Netw.*, *10*(5), 604–612.

Microsoft Live Mesh. (2008, November). Retrieved from http://www.mesh.com.

Migliaccio, A. (2006). *The Design and Development of a Nomadic Computing Middleware: the Esperanto Broker*. PhD Dissertation, Department of Computer and System Engineering, Federico II, University of Naples, Naples, Italy.

Migliardi, M., & Sunderam, V. (1999). The harness metacomputing framework. In *Proceedings of Ninth Siam Conference on Parallel Processing for Scientific Computing*. San Antonio, TX: SIAM.

Miller, R. L. (1993). High Resolution Image Processing on Low-cost Microcomputer. *International Journal of Remote Sensing, 14*(4), 655–667. doi:10.1080/01431169308904366

Milton, S. (1998). *Thread migration in distributed memory multicomputers,* (Tech. Rep. No. TR-CS-98-01). Dept. of Comp Sci & Comp Sciences Lab, Australia National University, Acton, Australia.

Min, W. H., & Veeravalli, B. (2005, December). Aligning biological sequences on distributed bus networks: a divisible load scheduling approach. *Institute of Electrical and Electronic Engineering, 9*(4), 489–501.

Mislove, A., & Druschel, P. (2004). Providing administrative control and autonomy in structured peer-to-peer overlays. *Proceedings of the 3rd Intl. Workshop on Peer-to-Peer Systems* (pp. 162-172). Berlin: Springer-Verlag.

Mitzenmacher, M. (1997). On the analysis of randomized load balancing schemes. *In Proc. of SPAA.*

Mohamed, H. H., & Epema, D. H. (2005). Experiences with the KOALA co-allocating scheduler in multiclusters. *International Conference of Cluster Computing and the Grid* (pp. 784-791). Cardiff, UK: IEEE Computer Society Press.

Mohamed, H., & Epema, D. (in press). KOALA: A co-allocating Grid scheduler. *Concurrency and Computation.*

Mohan, A., & Kalogeraki, V. (2003). *Speculative routing and update propagation: a kundali centric approach.* Paper presented at the IEEE International Conference on Communications, 2003.

Mondal, A., Goda, K., & Kitsuregawa, M. (2003). Effective load-balancing of peer-to-peer systems. In *Proc. of IEICE DEWS DBSJ Annual Conference.*

Montero, R. S., Huedo, E., & Llorente, I. M. (2008, September/October). Dynamic deployment of custom execution environments in Grids. In *2nd International Conference on Advanced Engineering Computing and Applications in Sciences (ADVCOMP '08)* (pp. 33–38). Valencia, Spain: IEEE Computer Society.

Montgomery, D. C. (2004). *Design and analysis of experiments* (6 ed.). New York: Wiley.

Moore, G. E. (1965). Cramming more components onto integrated circuits. *Electronics Magazine, 38*(8).

Motwani, R., & Raghavan, P. (1995). *Randomized Algorithms.* New York: Cambridge University Press.

MRML. (2003). *MRML- Multimedia Retrieval Markup Language.* Retrieved June 15th, 2008, from http://www.mrml.net/

Murphy, A. L., Picco, G. P., & Roman, G. (2001). LIME: a middleware for physical and logical mobility. *21st International Conference on Distributed Computing Systems,* (pp. 524-533).

Mutka, M. W., & Livny, M. (1987). Profiling workstations' available capacity for remote execution. In *Proceedings of performance-87, the 12th ifip w.g. 7.3 international symposium on computer performance modeling, measurement and evaluation.* Brussels, Belgium.

Mutka, M., & Livny, M. (1991, July). The available capacity of a privately owned workstation environment. *Performance Evaluation, 4*(12).

Mutz, A., Wolski, R., & Brevik, J. (2007). Eliciting honest value information in a batch-queue environment. *In The 8th IEEE/ACM Int' Conference on Grid Computing (Grid 2007) Austin, Texas, USA.*

Myers, D. S., Bazinet, A. L., & Cummings, M. P. (2008). Expanding the reach of grid computing: combining globus- and boinc-based systems. In *Grids for Bioinformatics and Computational Biology.* New York: Wiley.

MyGrid. (2008). Retrieved from www.mygrid.org.uk

N'takpé. T., & Suter, F. (2006). Critical path and area based scheduling of parallel task graphs on heterogeneous platforms. In *Proceedings of the Twelfth International Conference on Parallel and Distributed Systems (IC-PADS)* (pp. 3–10), Minneapolis, MN.

N'takpé. T., Suter, F., & Casanova, H. (2007). A comparison of scheduling approaches for mixed-parallel applications on heterogeneous platforms. In *6th International Symposium on Parallel and Distributed Computing* (pp. 35–42). Hagenberg, Austria: IEEE Computer Press.

Nabrzyski, J., Schopf, J. M., & Weglarz, J. (2003). *Grid Resource Management*. Amsterdam: Kluwer Publishing.

Nakada, H., Matsuoka, S., Seymour, K., Dongarra, J., Lee, C., & Casanova, H. (2003). *Gridrpc: A remote procedure call api for grid computing.*

Nam, M., Choi, N., Seok, Y., & Choi, Y. (2004). WISE: Energy-efficient interface selection on vertical handoff between 3G networks and WLANs. *IEEE PIMRC 2004, 1*, (pp. 692-698). Washington, DC: IEEE.

Nanda, P. (2008, January). *A three layer policy based architecture supporting Internet QoS*. Ph.D. thesis, University of Technology, Sydney, Australia.

Naor, M., & Wieder, U. (June 2003). Novel Architectures for P2P applications: The continuous-discrete approach. *In Proc. SPAA.*

National e-Science Centre. (2005). Retrieved from http://www.nesc.ac.uk.

NEESgrid. (2008). Retrieved from www.nees.org/

Nelson, B. J. (1981). *Remote Procedure Call.* Palo Alto, CA: Xerox - Palo Alto Research Center.

Nemirovsky, M. D., Brewer, F., & Wood, R. C. (1991). DISC: dynamic instruction stream computer. In *Proceedings of the 24th Annual International Symposium on Microarchitecture* (MICRO'91), Albuquerque, NM (pp. 163-171). New York: ACM Press.

Nesargi, S., & Prakash, R. (2002). *MANETconf: Configuration of Hosts in a Mobile Ad Hoc Network.* In Proceedings of the IEEE Infocom 2002, New York, June 2002.

Neuroth, H., Kerzel, M., & Gentzsch, W. (Eds.). (2007). *German Grid Initiative D-Grid.* Göttingen, Germany: Universitätsverlag Göttingen Publishers. Retrieved from www.d-grid.de/index.php?id=4&L=1

Ni, J., & Lin, C. Chen, Z., & Ungsunan, P. (2007, September). A Fast Multi-pattern Matching Algorithm for Deep Packet Inspection on a Network Processor. In *Proceedings of International Conference on Parallel Processing (ICPP 2007)*(p.16).

Nickolls, J., Buck. I, & Garland, M., (2008). Scalable Parallel Programming with CUPA. *ACM QUEUE*, March/April, *6*(2), 40-53

Nicolescu, C., & Jonker, P. (2002). A Data and Task Parallel Image Processing Environment. *Parallel Computing, 28*, 945–965. doi:10.1016/S0167-8191(02)00105-9

Niederl, F., & Goller, A. (Jan, 1998). *Method Execution On A Distributed Image Processing Backend.* Paper presented at the 6th EUROMICRO Workshop on Parallel and Distributed Processing, Madrid, Spain.

Nieuwpoort, R. V. v., Maassen, J., Wrzesinska, G., Hofman, R., Jacobs, C., & Kielmann, T. (2005). Ibis: a flexible and efficient Java-based Grid programming environment. Concurrency and Computation, 17(7/8), 1079-1108.

Nieuwpoort, R. V. v., Maassen, J., Wrzesinska, G., Kielmann, T., & Bal, H. E. (2004). Satin: Simple and efficient Java-based grid programming. *Journal of Parallel and Distributed Computing Practices.*

Nisan, N., London, S., Regev, O., & Camiel, N. (1998). Globally distributed computation over the internet - the popcorn project. In *International conference on distributed computing systems 1998* (p. 592). New York: IEEE Computer Society.

Norman, T. J., Preece, A., Chalmers, S., Jennings, N. R., Luck, M., & Dang, V. D. (2004). Agent-based formation of virtual organisations. *Knowledge-Based Systems, 17*, 103–111. doi:10.1016/j.knosys.2004.03.005

Oaks, S., Traversat, B., & Gong, L. (2002). *JXTA in a Nutshell*. Sebastopol, CA: O'Reilly Media, Inc.

Oberhuber, M. (1998). *Distributed High-Performance Image Processing on the Internet*. Doctoral Thesis, Graz University of Technology, Austria.

ObjectWeb. (2004). *RUBBoS: Bulletin Board Benchmark*. Retrieved June 19, 2008, from http://jmob.objectweb.org/rubbos.html

ObjectWeb. (2005). *TPC-W Benchmark* (Java Servlets version). Retrieved June 19, 2008, from http://jmob.objectweb.org/tpcw.html

OGF. (2008). *Open Grid Forum*. Retrieved from www.ogf.org

Oh, J., Lee, S., & Lee, E. (2006). An adaptive mobile system using mobile grid computing in wireless network. In *Computational Science And Its Applications - ICCSA 2006* (LNCS Vol. 3984, pp. 49-57). Berlin: Springer.

Olukotun, K., & Hammond, L., (September 2005). The Future of Microprocessors. *ACM Queue*, September, *3*(7), 26-29

OMG. (2002). *Wireless Access and Terminal Mobility in CORBA Specification*. Retrieved June 15th, 2008, from http://www.info.fundp.ac.be/~ven/CIS/OMG/new%20documents%20from%20OMG%20on%20CORBA/corba%20wireless.pdf

Open Science Grid. (2005). Retrieved from http://www.opensciencegrid.org

Open Source Metascheduling for Virtual Organizations with the Community Scheduler Framework (CSF) (Tech. Rep.) (2003, August). Ontario, Canada: Platform Computing.

OpenPBS. *The portable batch system software*. (2005). Veridian Systems, Inc., Mountain View, CA. Retrieved from http://www.openpbs.org/scheduler.html

Oram, A. (2001). *Peer-to-Peer: Harnessing the power of disruptive technologies*. O'Reilly.

Orlando, S., & Perego, R. (1999). COLTHPF, A run-time support for the high-level co-ordination of HPF tasks. *Concurrency (Chichester, England), 11*(8), 407–434. doi:10.1002/(SICI)1096-9128(199907)11:8<407::AID-CPE435>3.0.CO;2-0

Orlando, S., Palmerini, P., & Perego, R. (2000). Coordinating HPF programs to mix task and data parallelism. In *Proceedings of the 2000 ACM Symposium on Applied Computing (SAC'00)* (pp. 240–247). New York: ACM Press.

Otebolaku, A., Adigun, M., Iyilade, J., & Ekabua, O. (2007). On modeling adaptation in context-aware mobile grid systems. In *Icas '07: Proceedings of the Third International Conference on Autonomic And Autonomous Systems* (p. 52). Washington, DC: IEEE Computer Society.

Otoo, E., Rotem, D., & Romosan, A. (2004). Optimal File-Bundle Caching Algorithms for Data-Grids. In *Sc '04: Proceedings of the 2004 acm/ieee conference on supercomputing* (p. 6). Washington, DC: IEEE Computer Society.

p2psip working group. (2008). *Peer-to-Peer Session Initiation Protocol Specification*. Retrieved June 15th, 2008, from http://www.ietf.org/html.charters/p2psip-charter.html

Padala, P., & Wilson, J. N. (2003). GridOS: Operating system services for grid architectures. In *High Performance Computing* (pp. 353-362). Berlin: Springer.

Padala, P., Shin, K. G., Zhu, X., Uysal, M., Wang, Z., Singhal, S., et al. (2007, March). Adaptive control of virtualized resources in utility computing environments. In *2007 Conference on EuroSys (EuroSys 2007)* (pp. 289-302). Lisbon, Portugal: ACM Press.

Pai-Hsiang, H. (2001). *Geographical region summary service for geographical routing*. Paper presented at the Proceedings of the 2nd ACM international symposium on Mobile ad hoc networking and computing.

Pairot, C., Garcia, P., Rallo, R., Blat, J., & Gomez Skarmeta, A. F. (2005). The Planet Project: collaborative educational content repositories on structured peer-to-peer grids. *CCGrid 2005, IEEE International Symposium on Cluster Computing and the Grid,* (Vol. 1, pp. 35-42).

Palankar, M., Onibokun, A., Iamnitchi, A., & Ripeanu, M. (2007). Amazon S3 for Science Grids: a Viable Solution? *Poster: 4th USENIX mposium on Networked Systems Design and Implementation (NSDI'07).*

Pantry, S., & Griffiths, P. (1997). *The Complete Guide to Preparing and Implementary Service Level Agreements* (1st Ed.). London: Library Association Publishing.

Parashar, M., & Browne, J. (2005, Mar). Conceptual and implementation models for the grid. *Proceedings of the IEEE, 93*(3), 653–668. doi:10.1109/JPROC.2004.842780

Parashar, M., & Hariri, S. (Eds.). (2006). *Autonomic computing: Concepts, infrastructure and applications.* Boca Raton, FL: CRC Press.

Parashar, M., & Lee, C. A. (2005, March). Scanning the issue: Special isssue on grid-computing. In *Proceedings of the IEEE, 93* (3), 479-484. Retrieved from http://www.caip.rutgers.edu/TASSL/Papers/proc-ieee-intro-04.pdf

Parashar, M., Matossian, V., Klie, H., Thomas, S. G., Wheeler, M. F., Kurc, T., et al. (2006). Towards dynamic data-driven management of the ruby gulch waste repository. In V. N. Alexandrox & et al. (Eds.), *Proceedings of the Workshop on Distributed Data Driven Applications and Systems, International Conference on Computational Science 2006* (ICCS 2006) (Vol. 3993, pp. 384–392). Berlin: Springer Verlag.

Parekh, A.K. & Gallager, R.G. (1994). A Generalised Processor Sharing Approach to Flow Control in Integrated Services Networks. *IEEE Transactions on Networking 2*(2).

Park, H.-S., Yoon, S.-H., Kim, T.-Y., Park, J.-S., Do, M., & Lee, J.-Y. (2003). *Vertical handoff procedure and algorithm between IEEE 802.11 WLAN and CDMA cellular network* (LNCS, pp.103-112). Berlin: Springer.

Park, S., Kim, J., Ko, Y., & Yoon, W. (2003). Dynamic data grid replication strategy based on Internet hierarchy. In *Proceedings of the second international workshop on grid and cooperative computing* (*GCC*'2003).

Park, S.-M., Ko, Y.-B., & Kim, J.-H. (2003, December). Disconnected operation service in mobile grid computing. In *First International Conference on Service Oriented Computing* (ICSOC'2003), Trento, Italy.

Pascual, V., Matuszewski, M., Shim, E., Zheng, H., & Song, Y. (2008). *P2PSIP Clients.* Retrieved June 15th, 2008, from http://tools.ietf.org/id/draft-pascual-p2psip-clients-01.txt

Patel, J., Teacy, L. W. T., Jennings, N. R., Luck, M., Chalmers, S., & Oren, N. (2005). Agent-based virtual organisations for the Grids. *International Journal of Multi-Agent and Grid Systems, 1*(4), 237–249.

Patterson, D.A., & Hennessy, J.L. *Computer Organization and Design* (3rd Ed.).

Pavlidou, F. N. (1994). Two-dimensional traffic models for cellular mobile systems. *IEEE Transactions on Communications, 42*(234), 1505–1511. doi:10.1109/TCOMM.1994.582831

Paxson, V., & Sommer, R. (2007). An Architecture Exploiting Multi-Core Processors to Parallelize Network Intrusion Prevention. In . *Proceedings of IEEE Sarnoff Symposium, 3*(7), 26–29.

Paxson, V., Asanović, K., Dharmapurikar, S., Lockwood, J., Pang, R., Sommer, R., et al. (2006). Rethinking hardware support for network analysis and intrusion prevention. *Proceedings of the 1st conference on USENIX Workshop on Hot Topics in Security.*

Pedroso, J., Silva, L., & Silva, J. (1997, June). Web-based metacomputing with JET. In *Proc. of the acm ppopp workshop on java for science and engineering computation.*

Pelagatti, S. (2003). Task and Data Parallelism in P3L. In F. A. Rabhi & S. Gorlatch (Eds.), *Patterns and skeletons for parallel and distributed computing* (pp.155–186). London: Springer-Verlag.

Pelagatti, S., & Skillicorn, D. B. (2001). Coordinating programs in the network of tasks model. *Journal of Systems Integration*, *10*(2), 107–126. doi:10.1023/A:1011228808844

Pennebaker, W. B., & Mitchell, J. L. (1992). *JPEG: Still Image Data Compression Standard (Digital Multimedia Standards)*. Berlin: Springer.

Perez, C. E. (2003). *Open Source Distributed Cache Solutions Written in Java*. Retrieved June 24, 2008, from http://www.manageability.org/blog/stuff/distributed-cache-java

Perez, J.M., Bellens, P., Badia, R.M., & Labarta, J. (2007, August). CellSs: Programming the Cell/ B.E. made easier. *IBM Journal of R& D, 51*(5).

Pericas, M., Cristal, A., Cazorla, F. J., Gonzalez, R., Jimenez, D. A., & Valero, M. (2007). A Flexible Heterogeneous Multi-Core Architecture. In *Proceedings of the 16th International Conference on Parallel Architecture and Compilation Techniques*, (pp. 13 -24).

Perkins, C. (2003). *RTP: Audio and Video for the Internet*. New York: Addison-Wesley.

Persistence of Vision Raytracer. (2008, November). Retrieved from http://www.povray.org

Peterson, L., Muir, S., Roscoe, T., & Klingaman, A. (2006, May). *PlanetLab Architecture: An Overview* (Tech. Rep. No. PDN-06-031). Princeton, NJ: PlanetLab Consortium.

Petrini, F. Kerbyson, D. J. & Pakin, S. (2003). The Case of the Missing Supercomputer Performance: Achieving Optimal Performance on the 8,192 Processors of ASCI Q. *Proceedings of the 2003 ACM/IEEE Conference on Supercomputing*.

P-GRADE. (2003). *Parallel grid run-time and application development environment*. Retrieved from www.lpds.sztaki.hu/pgrade/

Pham, H. (2000). *Software reliability*. Singapore: Springer-Verlag.

Phan, T., Huang, L., & Dulan, C. (2002). Challenge: integrating mobile wireless devices into the computational grid. In *Mobicom '02: Proceedings of the 8th annual international conference on mobile computing and networking* (pp. 271–278). New York: ACM Press.

Pierson, J.-M. (2006, June). *A pervasive grid, from the data side* (Tech. Rep. No. RR-LIRIS-2006-015). LIRIS UMR 5205 CNRS/INSA de Lyon/Universit Claude Bernard Lyon 1/Universit Lumire Lyon 2/Ecole Centrale de Lyon. Retrieved from http://liris.cnrs.fr/publis/?id=2436

Pitas, I. (1993). *Parallel Algorithm for Digital Image Processing, Computer Vision and Neural Network*. Chichester, UK: John Wiley & Sons.

Piyachon, P., & Luo, Y. (2006). Efficient memory utilization on network processors for deep packet inspection. *Proceedings of ACM/IEEE ANCS*, (pp. 71-80).

Pjesivac-Grbovic, J., Bosilca, G., Fagg, G. E., Angskun, T., & Dongarra, J. J. (2007). MPI Collective Algorithm Selection and Quadtree Encoding. *Parallel Computing*, *33*(9), 613–623. doi:10.1016/j.parco.2007.06.005

PlanetLab Europe. (2008). Retrieved from http://www.planet-lab.eu/.

Plank, J. S. (1997, September). A tutorial on Reed-Solomon coding for fault-tolerance in RAID-like systems. *Software, Practice & Experience*, *27*(9), 995–1012. doi:10.1002/(SICI)1097-024X(199709)27:9<995::AID-SPE111>3.0.CO;2-6

Plank, J. S., & Li, K. (1994). Faster checkpointing with *n*+1 parity. In *FTCS*, (pp. 288–297).

Plank, J. S., & Thomason, M. G. (2001, November). Processor allocation and checkpoint interval selection in cluster computing systems. *Journal of Parallel and Distributed Computing*, *61*(11), 1570–1590. doi:10.1006/jpdc.2001.1757

Plank, J. S., Beck, M., Kinsley, G., & Li, K. (1995). Libckpt: Transparent checkpointing under unix. *Usenix winter technical conference*, (pp. 213-223).

Plank, J. S., Kim, Y., & Dongarra, J. (1997). Fault-tolerant matrix operations for networks of workstations using diskless checkpointing. *Journal of Parallel and Distributed Computing, 43*(2), 125–138. doi:10.1006/jpdc.1997.1336

Plank, J. S., Li, K., & Puening, M. A. (1998). Diskless checkpointing. *IEEE Transactions on Parallel and Distributed Systems, 9*(10), 972–986. doi:10.1109/71.730527

Polak, S., Slota, R., Kitowski, J., & Otfinowski, J. (2001). XML-based Tools for Multimedia Course Preparation. *Archiwum Informatyki Teoretycznej i Stosowanej, 13*, 3–21.

Portal, C. H. R. O. N. O. S. (2004). Retrieved from http://portal.chronos.org/gridsphere/gridsphere

PortoResearch. (2008). *Slicing Up the Mobile Services Revenue Pie*. Retrieved March 10, 2008, from http://www.portioresearch.com/slicing_pie_press.html

PPDG. (2006). *From fabric to physics* (Tech. Rep.). The Particle Physics Data Grid.

PRACE. (2008). *Partnership for advanced computing in Europe*. Retrieved from www.prace-project.eu/

Preston, R. P., Badeau, R. W., Bailey, D. W., Bell, S. L., Biro, L. L., Bowhill, W. J., et al. (2002). Design of an 8-wide superscalar RISC microprocessor with simultaneous multithreading. In *Digest of Technical Papers of the 2002 IEEE International Solid-State Circuits Conference* (ISSCC'02), San Francisco, CA (Vol. 1, pp. 334-472). New York: IEEE Press.

Proactive (2005). *Proactive manual REVISED 2.2.*, Proactive, INRIA. Retrieved from http://www-sop.inria.fr/oasis/Proactive/

Prodan, R., & Fahringer, T. (2008, March). overhead analysis of scientific workflows in grid environments. *Transactions on Parallel and Distributed Systems, 19*(3), 378–393. doi:10.1109/TPDS.2007.70734

Pro-MPEG. (2005). *Material eXchange Format (MXF)*. Retrieved 15th June, 2008, from http://www.pro-mpeg.org.

Pruyne, J., & Livny, M. (1996). A Worldwide Flock of Condors: Load Sharing among Workstation Clusters. *Journal on Future Generations of Computer Systems, 12*.

Qi, Y., Xu, B., He, F., Yang, B., Yu, J., & Li, J. (2007). Towards high-performance flow-level packet processing on multi-core network processors. *Proceedings of 3rd ACM/IEEE Symposium on Architecture for Networking and Communications Systems*, (pp. 17-26).

Qiu, D., & Srikant, R. (2004). Modeling and performance analysis of bittorrent-like peer-to-peer networks. *Computer Communication Review, 34*(4), 367–378. doi:10.1145/1030194.1015508

Quan, D. M. (Ed.). (2008). *A Framework for SLA-aware execution of Grid-based workflows*. Saabbrücken, Germany: VDM Verlag.

Quan, D. M., & Altmann, J. (2007). Business model and the policy of mapping light communication grid-based workflow within the SLA Context. In *Proceedings of the International Conference of High Performance Computing and Communication (HPCC07)*, (pp. 285-295). Berlin: Springer Velag.

Quan, D. M., & Altmann, J. (2007). Mapping a group of jobs in the error recovery of the Grid-based workflow within SLA context. In L. T. Yang (Ed.), *Proceedings of the 21st International Conference on Advanced Information Networking and Applications (AINA 2007)*, (pp. 986-993). New York: IEEE press.

Quasy, H. M. (2004). *Middleware for Communications*. Chichester, UK: John Wiley Sons ltd.

Quoitin, B., & Bonaventure, O. (2005). A Co-operative approach to Inter-domain traffic engineering. *1st Conference on Next Generation Internet Networks Traffic Engineering* (NGI 2005), Rome, Italy, April 18-20th.

Quoitin, B., Uhlig, S., Pelsser, C., Swinnen, L., & Bonaventure, O. (2003). *Internet traffic engineering with BGP: Quality of Future Internet Services*. Berlin: Springer

Raasch, S. E., & Reinhardt, S. K. (1999). Applications of thread prioritization in SMT processors. In *Proceedings of the 3rd Workshop on Multithreaded Execution and Compilation* (MTEAC'99), Orlando, FL.

Raasch, S. E., & Reinhardt, S. K. (2003). The impact of resource partitioning on SMT processors. In *Proceedings of the 12th International Conference on Parallel Architectures and Compilation Techniques* (PACT'03), (pp. 15–25). New Orleans, LA: IEEE Computer Society.

Radulescu, A., & van Gemund, A. J. C. (2001). A low-cost approach towards mixed task and data parallel scheduling. In *Proceedings of the International Conference on Parallel Processing (ICPP'01)*(pp. 69–76). New York: IEEE Computer Society.

Radulescu, A., Nicolescu, C., van Gemund, A. J. C., & Jonker, P. (2001). CPR: Mixed task and data parallel scheduling for distributed systems. In *Proceedings of the 15th International Parallel and Distributed Processing Symposium (IPDPS'01)* (pp. 39-46). New York: IEEE Computer Society.

Rahman, R. M., Barker, K., & Alhajj, R. (2005). Replica selection in grid environment: A data-mining approach. In *Proceedings of the ACM symposium on applied computing* (pp. 695–700).

Rahman, R. M., Barker, K., & Alhajj, R. (2005). Replica placement in data grid: A multi-objective approach. In *Proceedings of the international conference on grid and cooperative computing* (pp. 645–656).

Rahman, R. M., Barker, K., & Alhajj, R. (2005). Replica placement in data grid: Considering utility and risk. In *Proceedings of the international conference on information technology: Coding and computing* (*ITCC*'05) (Vol. 1, pp. 354–359).

Raicu, I., Zhao, Y., Dumitrescu, C., Foster, I., & Wilde, M. (2007). Falkon: a fast and light-weight task execution framework. In *Ieee/acm supercomputing.*

Ramakrishnan, L., Irwin, D., Grit, L., Yumerefendi, A., Iamnitchi, A., & Chase, J. (2006). Toward a doctrine of containment: Grid hosting with adaptive resource control. In *2006 ACM/IEEE Conference on Supercomputing (SC 2006)* (p. 101). New York: ACM Press.

Raman, R., Livny, M., & Solomon, M. H. (1998). Matchmaking: Distributed resource management for high throughput computing. In *Hpdc* (p. 140).

Raman, R., Livny, M., & Solomon, M. H. (1999). Matchmaking: An extensible framework for distributed resource management. *Cluster Computing*, *2*(2), 129–138. doi:10.1023/A:1019022624119

Ramaswamy, S. (1996). *Simultaneous exploitation of task and data parallelism in regular scientific computations.* Doctoral thesis, University of Illinois at Urbana-Champaign.

Ramaswamy, S., Sapatnekar, S., & Banerjee, P. (1997). A framework for exploiting task and data parallelism on distributed memory multicomputers. *IEEE Transactions on Parallel and Distributed Systems*, *8*(11), 1098–1116. doi:10.1109/71.642945

Ramaswamy, S., Simons, B., & Banerjee, P. (1996). Optimizations for efficient array redistribution on distributed memory multicomputers. *Journal of Parallel and Distributed Computing*, *38*(2), 217–228. doi:10.1006/jpdc.1996.0142

Ramjee, R., Li, L., La Porta, T., & Kasera, S. (2002). IP paging service for mobile hosts. *Wireless Networks*, *8*, 427–441. doi:10.1023/A:1016534027402

Ramkumar, B., & Strumpen, V. (1997). Portable checkpointing for heterogenous architectures. *Symposium on fault-tolerent computing*, (pp. 58-67).

Ranganathan, K., & Foster, I. (2001). Design and evaluation of dynamic replication strategies for a high performance data grid. *In Proceedings of the international conference on computing in high energy and nuclear physics* (pp. 260-263).

Ranganathan, K., & Foster, I. (2002). Decoupling computation and data scheduling in distributed data intensive applications. In *Proceedings of the 11th international symposium for high performance distributed computing (HPDC)* (pp. 352–358).

Ranganathan, K., & Foster, I. (2003). Simulation studies of computation and data scheduling algorithms for data grids. *Journal of Grid Computing, 1*(1), 53–62. doi:10.1023/A:1024035627870

Ranganathan, K., & Foster, I. T. (2001). Identifying dynamic replication strategies for a high-performance data grid. In *Proceedings of the International Workshop on Grid Computing (GRID'*2001) (pp. 75–86).

Ranganathan, K., Iamnitchi, A., & Foster, I. (2002). Improving data availability through dynamic model-driven replication in large peer-to-peer communities. In *Proceedings of the 2nd IEEE/ACM international symposium on cluster computing and the grid (CCGRID'*02) (pp. 376–381).

Ranjan, R. (2007, July). Coordinated resource provisioning in federated grids. Doctoral thesis, The University of Melbourne, Australia.

Ranjan, R., Buyya, R., & Harwood, A. (2005, September). A case for cooperative and incentive-based coupling of distributed clusters. In *7th IEEE International Conference on Cluster Computing*. Boston, MA: IEEE CS Press.

Ranjan, R., Harwood, A., & Buyya, R. (2006, September). SLA-based coordinated superscheduling scheme for computational Grids. In *IEEE International Conference on Cluster Computing (Cluster 2006)* (pp. 1–8). Barcelona, Spain: IEEE.

Ranjan, R., Harwood, A., & Buyya, R. (2008). Coordinated load management in peer-to-peer coupled federated grid systems. (Technical Report GRIDS-TR-2008-2). Grid Computing and Distributed Systems Laboratory, The University of Melbourne, Australia. doi: http://www.gridbus.org/reports/CoordinatedGrid2007.pdf

Ranjan, R., Harwood, A., & Buyya, R. (2008, July). Peer-to-peer resource discovery in global grids: A tutorial. IEEE Communication Surveys and Tutorials (COMST), 10(2), 6-33. New York: IEEE Communications Society Press. doi:doi:10.1109/COMST.2008.4564477

Ranjan, R., Rahman, M., & Buyya, R. (2008, May). A decentralized and cooperative workflow scheduling algorithm. In *8th IEEE International Symposium on Cluster Computing and the Grid (CCGRID 2008)*. Lyon, France: IEEE Computer Society.

Rao, A., Lakshminarayanan, K., Surana, S., Karp, R., & Stoica, I. (2003). Load Balancing in structured P2P systems. *Proceedings of the 2nd Intl. Workshop on Peer-to-Peer Systems* (pp. 68-79). Berlin: Springer-Verlag.

Rashid, R. F., & Robertson, G. (1981). Accent: A communication oriented network operating system kernel. *Proceedings of the eighth acm symposium on operating systems principles*, (pp. 64-75).

Ratnasamy, S., Francis, P., Handley, M., Karp, R., & Schenker, S. (2001). A scalable content-addressable network. In SIGCOMM'01 *Proceedings of the 2001 Conference on Applications, Technologies, Architectures, and Protocols for Computer Communications*, (pp. 161-172). New York: ACM Press. Retrieved from http://doi.acm.org/10.1145/ 383059.383072

Ratnasamy, S., Handley, M., Karp, R., & Shenker, S. (2002). Topologically aware overlay construction and server selection. In *Proc. of INFOCOM.*

Ratnasamy, S., Stoica, I., & Shenker, S. (2002). Routing algorithms for DHTs: Some open questions. *Proceedings the 1st Intl. Workshop on Peer-to-Peer Systems* (pp. 45-52). Berlin: Springer-Verlag.

Rauber, T., & Rünger, G. (1996). The compiler TwoL for the design of parallel implementations. In *Proceedings of the 1996 Conference on Parallel Architectures and Compilation Techniques(PACT'96)*(pp. 292-301). Washington, DC: IEEE Computer Society.

Rauber, T., & Rünger, G. (1999). Compiler support for task scheduling in hierarchical execution models. *Journal of Systems Architecture*, *45*(6-7), 483–503. doi:10.1016/S1383-7621(98)00019-8

Rauber, T., & Rünger, G. (1999). Parallel execution of embedded and iterated Runge-Kutta methods. *Concurrency (Chichester, England)*, *11*(7), 367–385. doi:10.1002/(SICI)1096-9128(199906)11:7<367::AID-CPE430>3.0.CO;2-G

Rauber, T., & Rünger, G. (1999). Scheduling of data parallel modules for scientific computing. In *Proceedings of the 9th SIAM Conference on Parallel Processing for Scientific Computing (PPSC), SIAM(CD-ROM)*, San Antonio, TX.

Rauber, T., & Rünger, G. (2000). A transformation approach to derive efficient parallel implementations. *IEEE Transactions on Software Engineering*, *26*(4), 315–339. doi:10.1109/32.844492

Rauber, T., & Rünger, G. (2005). TLib - A library to support programming with hierarchical multi-processor tasks. *Journal of Parallel and Distributed Computing*, *65*(3), 347–360.

Rauber, T., & Rünger, G. (2006). A data re-distribution library for multi-processor task programming. *International Journal of Foundations of Computer Science*, *17*(2), 251–270. doi:10.1142/S0129054106003814

Rauber, T., & Rünger, G. (2007). Mixed task and data parallel executions in general linear methods. *Science Progress*, *15*(3), 137–155.

Rauber, T., Reilein-Ruß, R., & Rünger, G. (2004). Group-SPMD programming with orthogonal processor groups. *Concurrency and Computation: Practice and Experience . Special Issue on Compilers for Parallel Computers*, *16*(2-3), 173–195.

Rauber, T., Reilein-Ruß, R., & Rünger, G. (2004). On compiler support for mixed task and data parallelism. In G. R. Joubert, W. E. Nagel, F. J. Peter, & W. V. Walter (Eds.), *Parallel Computing: Software Technology, Algorithms, Architectures & Applications. Proceedings of 12th International Conference on Parallel Computing (ParCo'03)* (pp. 23–30). New York: Elsevier.

Rauber, T., Rünger, G., & Wilhelm, R. (1995). Deriving optimal data distributions for group parallel numerical algorithms. In *Proceedings of the Conference on Programming Models for Massively Parallel Computers (PMMP'94)* (pp. 33–41). Washington, DC: IEEE Computer Society.

Ray, E. (2003). *Learning XML*. Sebastopol, CA: O'Reilly Media, Inc.

Reed, D. A. (2003). Grids: The teragrid, and beyond. *IEEE Computer*, *36*(1), 62–68.

Reilein-Ruß, R. (2005). *Eine komponentenbasierte Realisierung der TwoL Spracharchitektur*. PhD Thesis, TU Chemnitz, Fakultät für Informatik, Chemnitz, Germany.

Reinhardt, S., & Mukherjee, S. (2000). Transient fault detection via simultaneous multithreading. In *ACM SIGARCH Computer Architecture News: Special Issue: Proceedings of the 27th Annual International Symposium on Computer Architecture* (ISCA'00), (pp. 25-36). Vancouver,Canada: ACM Press

Rekhter, Y. & Li, T. (2002, January). *A border gateway protocol 4 (BGP-4): draft-ietf-idr-bgp4-17.txt* [Internet draft, work in progress].

Replica Location Service (RLS) (n.d.). Retrieved from http://www.globus.org/toolkit/docs/4.0/data/rls/

Reuters (2007). *Global cellphone penetration reaches 50 pct*. Retrieved March 10, 2008, from http://investing.reuters.co.uk/news/articleinvesting.aspx?type=media&storyID=nL29172095

Revees, C. (1993). *Moderm heuristic techniques for combinatorial problems*. Oxford, UK: Oxford Blackwell Scientific Publication.

Rhea, S. C., & Kubiatowicz, J. (2002). *Probabilistic location and routing.* Paper presented at the IEEE INFOCOM 2002, Twenty-First Annual Joint Conference of the IEEE Computer and Communications Societies Proceedings.

Rhea, S. C., Eaton, P. R., Geels, D., Weatherspoon, H., Zhao, B. Y., & Kubiatowicz, J. (2003). Pond: The oceanstore prototype. In *Fast.* Rodriguez, A., Gonzalez, A., & Malumbres, M. P. Performance evaluation of parallel mpeg-4 video coding algorithms on clusters of workstations. *International Conference on Parallel Computing in Electrical Engineering (PARELEC'04)*, 354-357.

Rhea, S., Geels, D., Roscoe, T., & Kubiatowicz, J. (2004). Handling Churn in a DHT. *Proceedings of the USENIX* (pp. 127-140). USENIX Association.

Rhea, S., Godfrey, B., Karp, B., Kubiatowicz, J., Ratnasamy, S., Shenker, S., et al. (2005). OpenDHT: A public DHT service and its uses. In *Proceedings of ACM SIGCOMM* (pp. 73-84). New York: ACM Press.

Ricci, R., Oppenheimer, D., Lepreau, J., & Vahdat, A. (2006, January). Lessons from resource allocators for large-scale multiuser testbeds. *SIGOPS Operating Systems Review*, *40*(1), 25–32. doi:10.1145/1113361.1113369

Richardson, I., & Richardson, I. E. G. (2003). *H.264 and MPEG-4 Video Compression: Video Coding for Next Generation Multimedia.* Chichester, UK: Wiley.

Ripeanu, M., Foster, I., & Iamnitchi, A. (2002). Mapping the gnutella network: properties of large-scale peer-to-peer systems and implications for system design. *IEEE Internet Computing*, *6*(1), 50-57.

Robertazzi, T. (2003). Ten reasons to use divisible load theory. *Institute of Electrical and Electronic Engineering*, *36*(5), 63–68.

Rodriguez, B. (2002). *EDLXML serialization.* Retrieved 15th June, 2008, from download.sybase.com/pdfdocs/prg0390e/prsver39edl.pdf

Roesch, M. (1999). Snort - lightweight intrusion detection for networks. *Proceedings of 13th USENIX LISA Conference*, (pp. 229-238).

Roman, M., Kon, F., & Campbell, R. (2001). Reflective Middleware: From your Desk to your Hand. *IEEE Communications Surveys, 2*(5).

Roure, D. D. (2003). *Semantic grid and pervasive computing.* http://www.semanticgrid.org/GGF/ggf9/gpc/

Rowstron, A., & Druschel, P. (2001). Pastry: Scalable, decentralized object location, and routing for large-scale peer-to-peer systems. In Middleware'01 *Proceedings of the IFIP/ACM International Conference on Distributed Systems Platforms*, (pp. 329-350). Heidelberg, Germany: SpringerLink. doi: 10.1007/3-540-45518-3

Rowstron, A., & Druschel, P. (2001). Pastry: Scalable, distributed object location and routing for large-scale peer-to-peer systems. In *Proceedings of IFIP/ACM Intl. Conf. on Distributed Systems Platforms* (pp. 329-350). Berlin: Springer-Verlag.

Rowstron, A., & Druschel, P. (2001, November). Pastry: Scalable, distributed object location and routing for large-scale peer-to-peer systems. In *Proceedings of the 18th ifip/acm international conference on distributed systems platforms (middleware 2001),* Heidelberg, Germany.

Rowstron, A., & Druschel, P. Pastry. (2001). Scalable, decentralized object location and routing for large-scale peer-to-peer systems. *In Proc. of the 18th IFIP/ACM Int'l Conf. on Distributed Systems Platforms (Middleware).*

Rubio-Montero, A., Huedo, E., Montero, R., & Llorente, I. (2007, March). Management of virtual machines on globus Grids using GridWay. In *IEEE International Parallel and Distributed Processing Symposium (IPDPS 2007)* (pp. 1–7). Long Beach, USA: IEEE Computer Society.

Ruth, P., Jiang, X., Xu, D., & Goasguen, S. (2005, May). Virtual distributed environments in a shared infrastructure. *IEEE Computer, 38*(5), 63–69.

Ruth, P., McGachey, P., & Xu, D. (2005, September). VioCluster: Virtualization for dynamic computational domain. In *IEEE International on Cluster Computing (Cluster 2005)* (pp. 1–10). Burlington, MA: IEEE.

Ruth, P., Rhee, J., Xu, D., Kennell, R., & Goasguen, S. (2006, June). Autonomic live adaptation of virtual computational environments in a multi-domain infrastructure. In *3rd IEEE International Conference on Autonomic Computing (ICAC 2006)* (pp. 5-14). Dublin, Ireland: IEEE.

Saar, C., & Yossi, M. (2003). *Spectral bloom filters*. Paper presented at the Proceedings of the 2003 ACM SIGMOD international conference on Management of data.

Saara Väärtö, S. (Ed.). (2008). Advancing science in Europe. DEISA – Distributed European Infrastructure for Supercomputing Applications. *EU FP6 Project*. Retrieved from www.deisa.eu/press/DEISA-AdvancingScienceInEurope.pdf

SAGA. (2006). *SAGA implementation home page* Retrieved from http://fortytwo.cct.lsu.edu:8000/SAGA

Sahai, A., Graupner, S., Machiraju, V., & Moorsel, A. (2003). Specifying and monitoring guarantees in commercial grids through SLA. In F. Tisworth (Ed.), *Proceeding of the 3rd IEEE/ACM CCGrid2003*, (pp.292—300). New York: IEEE press.

Sairamesh, J., Stanbridge, P., Ausio, J., Keser, C., & Karabulut, Y. (2005, March). *Business Models for Virtual Organization Management and Interoperability* (Deliverable A - WP8&15 WP - Business & Economic Models No. V.1.5). Deliverable document 01945 prepared for TrustCom and the European Commission.

Saito, Y., & Levy, H. M. (2000). Optimistic replication for internet data services. *In Proceedings of international symposium on distributed computing* (pp. 297–314).

Saito, Y., & Shapiro, M. (2005). Optimistic replication. *ACM Computing Surveys*, *37*(1), 42–81. doi:10.1145/1057977.1057980

Saleh, O., & Hefeeda, M. (2006). Modeling and caching of peer-to-peer traffic. In *Proc. of 14th IEEE International Conference on Network Protocols (ICNP'06)*, (pp. 249-258).

Salkintzis, A. K. (2004). Interworking techniques and architectures for WLAN-3G integration toward 4G mobile data networks. *IEEE Wireless Communications*, *11*(3), 50–61. doi:10.1109/MWC.2004.1308950

Salkintzis, A. K., Fords, C., & Pazhyannur, R. (2002). WLAN-GPRS integration for next generation mobile data networks. *IEEE Wireless Communications*, *9*(5), 112–124. doi:10.1109/MWC.2002.1043861

Salsano, S. (2001 October). *COPS usage for Diffserv resource allocation (COPS-DRA)* [Internet Draft].

Samet, H. (2008, November). *The design and analysis of spatial data structures*. New York: Addison-Wesley Publishing Company.

Sanders, R. (2008). *SETI@home looking for more volunteers*. Retrieved 10 March, 2008, from http://www.berkeley.edu/news/media/releases/2008/01/02_setiahome.shtml

Santos-Neto, E., Cirne, W., Brasileiro, F., & Lima, A. (2004). Exploiting Replication and Data Reuse to Efficiently Schedule Data-intensive Applications on Grids. In *Proceedings of the 10th workshop on job scheduling strategies for parallel processing.*

Santos-Neto, E., Cirne, W., Brasileiro, F., & Lima, A. (2004). Exploiting replication and data reuse to efficiently schedule data-intensive applications on grids. In *Proceedings of 10th workshop on job scheduling strategies for parallel processing* (Vol. 3277, pp. 210–232).

Sarmenta, L. F. G. (2002). Sabotage-tolerance mechanisms for volunteer computing systems. *Future Generation Computer Systems*, *18*(4), 561–572. doi:10.1016/S0167-739X(01)00077-2

Sarmenta, L. F. G., & Hirano, S. (1999). Bayanihan: Building and studying volunteer computing systems using Java. *Future Generation Computer Systems*, *15*(5/6), 675-686.

Saroiu, S., et al. (2002). A Measurement Study of Peer-to- Peer File Sharing Systems. In *Proc. of MMCN*.

Scales, D. J., & Gharachorloo, K. (1997). *Towards transparent and efficient software distributed shared memory.* Paper presented at the Proceedings of the sixteenth ACM symposium on Operating systems principles.

Schiffmann, W., Sulistio, A., & Buyya, R. (2007). Using Revenue management to Determine Pricing of Reververvations. *Proc. 3rd International Conference on e-Science and Grid Computing (eScience 2007) Bangalore, India, December 10-13.*

Schilit, B., Adams, N., & Want, R. (1994). Context-aware computing applications. In *Proceedings of Mobile Computing Systems and Applications,* (pp. 85-90).

Schintke, F., & Reinefeld, A. (2003). Modeling replica availability in large data grids. *Journal of Grid Computing, 1*(2), 219–227. doi:10.1023/B:GRID.0000024086.50333.0d

Schirrmeister, F. (2007). *Multi-core Processors: Fundamentals, Trends, and Challenges, Embedded Systems Conference,* (pp. 6-15).

Schowengerdt, R. A., & Mehldau, G. (1993). Engineering a Scientific Image Processing Toolbox for the Macintosh II. *International Journal of Remote Sensing, 14*(4), 669–683. doi:10.1080/01431169308904367

Schüller, F., Qin, J., Nadeem, F., Prodan, R., Fahringer, T., & Mayr, G. (2006). Performance, scalability and quality of the meteorological grid workflow MeteoAG. In *Austrian Grid Symposium.* Innsbruck, Austria: OCG Verlag.

Schwartz, E. (1980). Computational Anatomy and Functional Architecture of Striate Cortex: A Spatial Mapping Approach to Perceptual Coding. *Vision Research, 20,* 645–669. doi:10.1016/0042-6989(80)90090-5

Schwarz, K., Blaha, P., & Madsen, G. K. (2002). Electronic structure calculations of solids using the WIEN2k package for material sciences. *Computer Physics Communications, 147*(71).

Schwiegelshohn, U., & Yahyapour, R. (1999). Resource allocation and scheduling in metasystems. In *7th International Conference on High-Performance Computing and Networking (HPCN Europe '99)* (pp. 851–860). London, UK: Springer-Verlag.

Schwiegelshohn, U., & Yahyapour, R. (2000). Fairness in parallel job scheduling. *Journal of Scheduling, 3*(5), 297–320. doi:10.1002/1099-1425(200009/10)3:5<297::AID-JOS50>3.0.CO;2-D

Seiler, L., Carmean, D., Sprangle, E., Forsyth, T., Abrash, M., & Dubey, P. (2008). Larabee: a many-core x86 architecture for visual computing. [TOG]. *ACM Transactions on Graphics, 27*(3). doi:10.1145/1360612.1360617

Seltzer, M. I., Krinsky, D., & Smith, K. A. (1999). The case for application-specific benchmarking. *Workshop on Hot Topics in Operating Systems* (pp. 102-109). Rio Rico, AZ: IEEE Computer Society Press.

Sensor Networks. Retrieved from http://www.sensornetworks.net.au/network.html

SETIstats. (2008). *Seti@home Project Statistics.* Retrieved March 10, 2008, from http://boincstats.com/stats/project_graph.php?pr=bo

Seymour, K., Nakada, H., Matsuoka, S., Dongarra, J., Lee, C., & Casanova, H. (2002). Overview of GridRPC: A remote procedure call API for Grid computing. In *Proceedings of the Third International Workshop on Grid Computing,* Baltimore, MD (LNCS 2536, pp. 274–278). Berlin: Springer.

Sfiligoi, K. O., Venekamp, G., Yocum, D., Groep, D., & Petravick, D. (2007). *Addressing the Pilot security problem with gLExec* (Tech. Rep. No. FERMILAB-PUB-07-483-CD). Fermi National Laboratory, Batavia, IL.

Shankland, S. (2007). *Sun starts bidding adieu to mobile-specific Java.* Retrieved March 10, 2008, from http://www.news.com/8301-13580_3-9800679-39.html?part=rss&subj=news&tag=2547-1_3-0-20

SHARCNET. (2008). *Shared Hierarchical Academic Research Computing Network* (SHARCNET).

ShareGrid Project. (2008, November). Retrieved from http://dcs.di.unipmn.it/sharegrid.

Shen, H., & Xu, C. (2006,April). Hash-based proximity clustering for load balancing in heterogeneous DHT networks. In *Proc. of IPDPS.*

Shen, H., & Xu, C.-Z. (2007). Locality-aware and Churn-resilient load balancing algorithms in structured peer-to-peer networks. [TPDS]. *IEEE Transactions on Parallel and Distributed Systems, 18*(6), 849–862. doi:10.1109/TPDS.2007.1040

Shen, H., Xu, C., & Chen, G. (2006). Cycloid: A scalable constant-degree P2P overlay network. *Performance Evaluation, 63*(3), 195–216. doi:10.1016/j.peva.2005.01.004

Shen, J. P., & Lipasti, M. (2004). *Modern Processor Design: Fundamentals of Superscalar Processors* (1st Ed.).

Shen, W., & Zeng, Q.-A. (2007). Cost-function-based network selection strategy in heterogeneous wireless networks. *IEEE International Symposium on Symposium on Ubiquitous Computing and Intelligence (UCI-07).* Washington, DC: IEEE.

Shen, W., & Zeng, Q.-A. (2008). Cost-function-based network selection strategy in integrated heterogeneous wireless and mobile networks. To appear in *IEEE Transactions on Vehicle Technology.*

Sheridan, P. (1996). *Spiral Architecture for Machine Vision.* Doctoral Thesis, University of Technology, Sydney.

Sheridan, P., Hintz, T., & Alexander, D. (2000). Pseudo-invariant Image Transformations on a Hexagonal Lattice. *Image and Vision Computing, 18*(11), 907–917. doi:10.1016/S0262-8856(00)00036-6

Shi, W., Lee, H.-H., Ghosh, M., & Lu, C. (2004). Architectual support for high speed protection of memory integrity and confidentiality in multiprocessor systems. In *Proceedings of the 13th International Conference on Parallel Architectures and Computation Techniques* (PACT'04), Antibes Juan-les-Pins, France (pp.123-134). New York: IEEE Computer Society.

Shin, C.-H., & Gaudiot, J.-L. (2006). Adaptive dynamic thread scheduling for simultaneous multithreaded architectures with a detector thread. *Journal of Parallel and Distributed Computing, 66*(10), 1304–1321. doi:10.1016/j.jpdc.2006.06.003

Shin, C.-H., Lee, S.-W., & Gaudiot, J.-L. (2003). Dynamic scheduling issues in SMT architectures. In *Proceedings of the 17th International Symposium on Parallel and Distributed Processing* (IPDPS'03), Nice, France, (p. 77b). New York: IEEE Computer Society.

Shirts, M., & Pande, V. (2000). Screen savers of the world, unite! *Science, 290,* 1903–1904. doi:10.1126/science.290.5498.1903

Shoch, J. F., & Hupp, J. A. (1982). 03). The "worm" programs - early experience with a distributed computation. *Communications of the ACM, 3*(25).

Shoykhet, A., Lange, J., & Dinda, P. (2004, July). *Virtuoso: A System For Virtual Machine Marketplaces* [Technical Report No. NWU-CS-04-39]. Evanston/Chicago: Electrical Engineering and Computer Science Department, Northwestern University.

Siagri, R. (2007). Pervasive computers and the GRID: The birth of a computational exoskeleton for augmented reality. In *6th Joint Meeting of the European Software Engineering Conference and the ACM SIGSOFT Symposium on The foundations of software engineering* (pp.1-4), Croatia.

Siddiqui, M., Villazón, A., & Fahringer, T. (2006). Grid capacity planning with negotiation-based advance reservation for optimized QoS. In *2006 ACM/IEEE Conference on Supercomputing (SC 2006)* (pp. 21–21). New York: ACM.

Siddiqui, M., Villazon, A., Hoffer, J., & Fahringer, T. (2005). GLARE: A Grid activity registration, deployment, and provisioning framework. *Supercomputing Conference.* Seattle, WA: IEEE Computer Society Press.

Siegel, H. J., Armstrong, J. B., & Watson, D. W. (1992). Mapping Computer-Vision-Related Tasks onto Reconfigurable Parallel-Processing Systems. *IEEE Computer, 25*(2), 54–63.

Siegel, L. J., Siegel, H. J., & Feather, A. E. (1982). Parallel Processing Approaches to Image Correlation. *IEEE Transactions on Computers, 31*(3), 208–218. doi:10.1109/TC.1982.1675976

Silagadze, Z. (1997). Citations and the Mandelbrot-Zipf's law. *Complex Systems, 11*, 487–499.

Silva, L. M., & Silva, J. G. (1998). An experimental study about diskless checkpointing. In *EUROMICRO'98*, (pp. 395–402).

SIMDAT. (2008). *Grids for industrial product development*. Retrieved from www.scai.fraunhofer.de/about_simdat.html

Simmonds, A., & Nanda, P. (2002). Resource Management in Differentiated Services Networks. In C McDonald (Ed.), *Proceedings of 'Converged Networking: Data and Real-time Communications over IP,' IFIP Interworking 2002*, Perth, Australia, October 14 - 16, (pp. 313 – 323). Amsterdam: Kluwer Academic Publishers.

Singh, M. P., & Vouk, M. A. (1997). *Scientific workflows: Scientific computing meets transactional workflows*. Retrieved January 13, 2006 from http://www.csc.ncsu.edu/faculty/mpsingh/papers/databases/workflows / sciworkflows.html

Sinharoy, B., Kalla, R. N., Tendler, J. M., Eickemeyer, R. J., & Joyner, J. B. (2005). Power5 system microarchitecture. *IBM Journal of Research and Development, 49*(4/5), 505–521.

Sips, H. J., & van Reeuwijk, C. (2004). An integrated annotation and compilation framework for task and data parallel programming in Java. In *Parallel Computing (PARCO): Software Technology, Algorithms, Architectures and Applications* (pp. 111–118). New York: Elsevier.

Skillicorn, D. B. (1999). *The network of tasks model*, (TR1999-427). Queen's University, Kingston, Canada.

Smallen, S., Casanova, H., & Berman, F. (2001, Nov.). Tunable on-line parallel tomography. In *Proceedings of Supercomputing'01, Denver, CO.*

Smarr, L., & Catlett, C. E. (1992, June). Metacomputing. *Communications of the ACM, 35*(6), 44–52. doi:10.1145/129888.129890

SMIL/ W3C. (2005). *SMIL- Synchronized Multimedia Integration Language.* Retrieved June 15th, 2008 from http://www.w3.org/AudioVideo/

Smith, B. J. (1981). Architecture and applications of the HEP multiprocessor computer system. In *SPIE Proceedings of Real Time Signal Processing IV, 298*, 241-248.

Smith, P., & Hutchinson, N. C. (1998). Heterogeneous process migration: The tui system. *Software, Practice & Experience, 28*(6), 611–639. doi:10.1002/(SICI)1097-024X(199805)28:6<611::AID-SPE169>3.0.CO;2-F

SMPTE. (2004). *Metadata dictionary registry of metadata element descriptions*. Retrieved June 15th, 2008, from http://www.smpte-ra.org/mdd/rp210-8.pdf

Snavely, A., & Weinberg, J. (2006). Symbiotic space-sharing on SDSC's datastar system. *Job Scheduling Strategies for Parallel Processing.* (LNCS 4376, pp.192-209). St. Malo, France: Springer Verlag.

Snytnikov, V. N., Vshivkov, V. A., Kuksheva, E. A., Neupokoev, E. V., Nikitin, S. A., & Snytnikov, A. V. (2004). Three-dimensional numerical simulation of a nonstationary gravitating n-body system with gas. *Astronomy Letters, 30*(2), 124–138. doi:10.1134/1.1646697

SOAP/W3C. (2003). *SOAP Version 1.2 Part 1: Messaging Framework*. Retrieved June 15th, 2008, from Http://www.w3.org/TR/2003/REC-soap12-part1-20030624/

Soh, H., Shazia Haque, S., Liao, W., & Buyya, R. (2006). Grid programming models and environments. In Yuan-Shun Dai, et al. (Eds.) *Advanced parallel and distributed computing* (pp. 141–173). Hauppauge, NY: Nova Science Publishers.

Sohi, G. S., Breach, S. E., & Vijaykumar, T. N. (1995). Multiscalar processors. *Proceedings of 22nd Annual International Symposium on Computer Architecture*, (pp. 414-425).

Song, H., Dharmapurikar, S., Turner, J., & Lockwood, J. (2005). *Fast hash table lookup using extended bloom filter: an aid to network processing*. Paper presented at the Proceedings of the 2005 conference on Applications, technologies, architectures, and protocols for computer communications.

Song, Q., & Jamalipour, A. (2005). Network selection in an integrated wireless LAN and UMTS environment using mathematical modeling and computing techniques. *IEEE Wireless Communications*, *12*(3), 42–48. doi:10.1109/MWC.2005.1452853

Song, Y., Jiang, X., Zheng, H., & Deng, H. (2008). *P2PSIP Client Protocol*. Retrieved June 15th, 2008, from http://tools.ietf.org/id/draft-jiang-p2psip-sep-01.txt.

Sonnek, J. D., Nathan, M., Chandra, A., & Weissman, J. B. (2006). Reputation-based scheduling on unreliable distributed infrastructures. In *ICDCS* (p. 30).

Spooner, D. P., Jarvis, S. A., Cao, J., Saini, S., & Nudd, G. R. (2003). Local grid scheduling techniques using performance prediction. In S. Govan (Ed.), *IEEE Proceedings - Computers and Digital Techniques Vol 150*, (pp. 87-96). New York: IEEE Press.

Spring.NET. (2008, November). Retrieved from http://www.springframework.net.

Squyres, J. M., Lumsdaine, A., & Stevenson, R. L. (1995). *A Cluster-based Parallel Image Processing Toolkit*. Paper presented at the IS&T Conference on Image and Video Processing, San Jose, CA.

SRB (Storage Resource Broker) (n.d.). Retrieved from http://www.sdsc.edu/srb/index.php/Main_Page

Srinivasan, R. (1995). *XDR: External Data Representation Standard* (Tech. Rep. No. RFC 1832).

Srinivasan, S. H. (2005). Pervasive wireless grid architecture. In *Proceedings of The Second Annual Conference on Wireless On-demand Network Systems and Services* (pp.83-88), Switzerland.

Ssu, K., Yao, B., & Fuchs, W. K. (1999). An adaptive checkpointing protocol to bound recovery time with message logging. *Symposium on reliable distributed systems*, (pp. 244-252).

Steen, van M., Homburg, P., & Tanenbaum, A. S. (1999). Globe: a wide area distributed system. *Concurrency, IEEE [See also IEEE Parallel & Distributed Technology]*, *7*, 70-78.

Stellner, G. (1996). Cocheck: Checkpointing and process migration for mpi. *Proceedings of 10th international parallel processing symposium.*

Stemm, M., & Katz, R. H. (1998). Vertical handoffs in wireless overlay networks. *ACM Mobile Networking (MONET)* [New York: ACM.]. *Special Issue on Mobile Networking in the Internet*, *3*(4), 335–350.

Stets, R., Dwarkadas, S., Hardavellas, N., Hunt, G., Kontothanassis, L., & Parthasarathy, S. (1997). Cashmere-2L: software coherent shared memory on a clustered remote-write network. *SIGOPS Oper. Syst. Rev.*, *31*(5), 170–183. doi:10.1145/269005.266675

Stevenson, R. L., Adams, G. B., Jamieson, L. H., & Delp, E. J. (1993, April). Parallel Implementation for Iterative Image Restoration Algorithms on a Parallel DSP Machine. *The Journal of VLSI Signal Processing*, *5*, 261–272. doi:10.1007/BF01581300

Stoica, I., Morris, R., Karger, D., Kaashoek, M. F., & Balakrishnan, H. (2001). Chord: A scalable peer-to-peer lookup service for Internet applications. In *Proceedings of ACM SIGCOMM* (pp. 149-160). New York: ACM Press.

Stone, N. (2004). *GWD-I: An architecture for grid checkpoint recovery services and a GridCPR API.* Retrieved October 15, 2006 from http://gridcpr.psc.edu/GGF/docs/draft-ggf-gridcpr-Architecture-2.0.pdf

Storz, O., Friday, A., & Davies, N. (2003, October). Towards 'ubiquitous' ubiquitous computing: an alliance with 'the grid'. In *Proceedings of the First Workshop On System Support For Ubiquitous Computing Workshop* (UBISYS 2003) in association with Fifth International Conference On Ubiquitous Computing, Seattle, WA. Retrieved from http://ciae.cs.uiuc.edu/ubisys/papers/alliance-w-grid.pdf

Stuart, W., & Koch, T. (2000). *The Dublin Core Metadata Initiative: Mission, Current Activities, and Future Directions*, (Vol. 6). Retrieved June 15th, 2008, from http:/www/dlib.org/dlib/december00/weibel/12weibel.html

Su, M. El-kady, I., Bader, D. A., & Lin, S. (2004, August). A Novel FDTD Application Featuring OpenMP-MPI Hybrid Parallelization. In *33rd international conference on parallel processing(icpp)* Montreal, Canada, (pp. pp. 373–379).

Subhlok, J., & Vondran, G. (1995). Optimal mapping of sequences of data parallel tasks. *ACM SIGPLAN Notices*, *30*(8), 134–143. doi:10.1145/209937.209951

Subhlok, J., & Yang, B. (1997). A new model for integrated nested task and data parallel programming. In *Proceedings of the 6th ACM SIGPLAN symposium on Principles and Practice of Parallel Programming* (pp. 1–12). New York: ACM Press.

Sun, M., Sun, J., Lu, E., & Yu, C. (2005). Ant algorithm for file replica selection in data grid. In *Proceedings of the first international conference on semantics, knowledge, and grid* (*SKG 2005*) (pp. 64–66).

Sun, Y., & Xu, Z. (2004). Grid replication coherence protocol. In *Proceedings of the 18th international parallel and distributed processing symposium* (pp. 232–239).

SunGrid. (2005). *Sun utility computing*. Retrieved from www.sun.com/service/sungrid/

SURA Southeastern Universities Research Association. (2007). *The Grid technology cookbook: Programming concepts and challenges*. Retrieved from www.sura.org/cookbook/gtcb/

Suter, F., Desprez, F., & Casanova, H. (2004). From heterogeneous task scheduling to heterogeneous mixed parallel scheduling. In *Proceedings of the 10th International Euro-Par Conference (Euro-Par'04),* (LNCS: Vol. 3149, pp. 230–237). Pisa, Italy: Springer.

Sutter, H., & Larus, J. (2005). Software and the concurrency revolution. *ACM Queue; Tomorrow's Computing Today*, *3*(7), 54–62. doi:10.1145/1095408.1095421

Svirskas, A., Arevas, A., Wilson, M., & Matthews, B. (2005, October). Secure and trusted virtual organization management. *ERCIM News* (63).

Taesombut, N., & Chien, A. (2004). Distributed virtual computer (dvc): Simplifying the development of high performance grid applications. In *Workshop on Grids and Advanced Networks (GAN '04), IEEE Cluster Computing and the Grid (ccgrid2004) Conference*, Chicago.

Taflove, A., & Hagness, S. (2000). *Computational Electrodynimics: The Finite-Difference Time-Domain Method, second edition*. Boston: Artech House.

Tai, A., Meyer, J., & Avizienis, A. (1993). Performability enhancement of fault-tolerant software. *IEEE Transactions on Reliability*, *42*(2), 227–237. doi:10.1109/24.229492

Tanenbaum, A. S., & Steen, M. V. (2008). *Distributed Systems: Principles and Paradigms*. Upper Saddle River, NJ: Prentice Hall.

Tang, F. L., Li, M. L., & Huang, Z. X. (2004). Real-time transaction processing for autonomic Grid applications. *Engineering Applications of Artificial Intelligence*, *17*(7), 799–807. doi:10.1016/S0952-1976(04)00122-8

Tang, M., Lee, B., Tang, X., & Yeo, C. K. (2005). Combining data replication algorithms and job scheduling heuristics in the data grid. In *Proceedings of European conference on parallel computing* (pp. 381–390).

Tang, M., Lee, B., Yeo, C., & Tang, X. (2005). Dynamic replication algorithms for the multi-tier data grid. *Future Generation Computer Systems*, *21*(5), 775–790. doi:10.1016/j.future.2004.08.001

Tang, M., Lee, B., Yeo, C., & Tang, X. (2006). The impact of data replication on job scheduling performance in the data grid. *Future Generation Computer Systems, 22*(3), 254–268. doi:10.1016/j.future.2005.08.004

Tang, X., & Xu, J. (2005). QoS-aware replica placement for content distribution. *IEEE Transactions on Parallel and Distributed Systems, 16*(10), 921–932. doi:10.1109/TPDS.2005.126

Tanin, E., Harwood, A., & Samet, H. (2007). Using a distributed quadtree index in peer-to-peer networks. [Heidelberg, Germany: SpringerLink.]. *The VLDB Journal, 16*(2), 165–178. doi:. doi:10.1007/s00778-005-0001-y

Taubman, D., & Marcellin, M. (2001). *JPEG2000: Image Compression Fundamentals, Standards and Practice.* Berlin: Springer.

Taufer, M., Anderson, D., Cicotti, P., & III, C. L. B. (2005). Homogeneous redundancy: a technique to ensure integrity of molecular simulation results using public computing. In *Proceedings of The International Heterogeneity In Computing Workshop.*

TAVERNA. (2008). *The Taverna Workbench 1.7.* Retrieved from http://taverna.sourceforge.net/

Taylor, I., Shields, M., Wang, I., & Philp, R. (2003). Distributed p2p computing within triana: A galaxy visualization test case. In *International Parallel and Distributed Processing Symposium (IPDPS'03).* Nice, France: IEEE Computer Society Press.

Taylor, M. B., Lee, W., Miller, J., Wentzlaff, D., Bratt, I., Greenwald, B., et al. (2004). Evaluation of the raw microprocessor: An exposed-wire-delay architecture for ilp and streams. *Proceedings of 31st Annual International Symposium on Computer Architecture*, (pp. 2-13).

Tendler, J. M., Dodson, J. S. Jr, Fields, J. S., Le, H., & Sinharoy, B. (2002). Power4 system microarchitecture. *IBM Journal of Research and Development, 46*(1), 5–25.

Teo, Y. M., & Mihailescu, M. (2008). Collision avoidance in hierarchical peer-to-peer systems. In *Proceedings of 7th Intl. Conf. on Networking* (pp. 336-341). New York: IEEE Computer Society Press.

Terzis, A., Wang, L., Ogawa, J. & Zhang, L. (1999, December). *A two tier resource management model for the Internet, Global Internet*, (pp. 1808 – 1817).

Thain, D., & Livny, M. (2004). Building reliable clients and services. In *The grid2* (pp. 285–318). San Francisco: Morgan Kaufman.

Thain, D., Tannenbaum, T., & Livny, M. (2002). *Condor and the grid.* John Wiley & Sons Inc.

Thatte, S. (2003). *BPEL4WS, business process execution language for web services.* Retrieved June 15th, 2008, from http://xml.coverpages.org/ni2003-04-16-a.html

The EU Data Grid Project (n.d.). Retrieved from http://www.eu-datagrid.org/.

The Globus Alliance (n.d.). Retrieved from http://www.globus.org/

The seti@home project. Retrieved from http://setiathome.ssl.berkeley.edu/

The TrustCoM Project. (2005). Retrieved from http://www.eu-trustcom.com.

Theimer, M. M., Lantz, K. A., & Cheriton, D. R. (1985). Preemptable remote execution facilities for the v-system. *SIGOPS Oper. Syst. Rev., 19*(5), 2–12. doi:10.1145/323627.323629

Theiner, D., & Rutschmann, P. (2005). An inverse modelling approach for the estimation of hydrological model parameters. (I. Publishing, Ed.) *Journal of Hydroinformatics.*

Thistle, M. R., & Smith, B. J. (1988). A processor architecture for Horizon. In *Proceedings of the 1988 ACM/IEEE conference on Supercomputing* (SC'88), Orlando, FL, (pp. 35-41). New York: IEEE Computer Society Press.

Thomasian, A. (1997). A performance comparison of locking methods with limited wait depth. *IEEE Transactions on Knowledge and Data Engineering*, *9*(3), 421–434. doi:10.1109/69.599931

Thornton, J. E. (1970). *Design of a computer - the Control Data 6600*. Upper Saddle River, NJ: Scott Foresman & Co.

Thulasiraman, P., Khokhar, A., Heber, G., & Gao, G. (2004, Jan.). A fine-grain load adaptive algorithm of the 2d discrete wavelet transform for multithreaded architectures. [JPDC]. Journal of Parallel and Distributed Computing, 64(1), 68–78. doi:10.1016/j.jpdc.2003.06.003doi:10.1016/j.jpdc.2003.06.003

Thulasiraman, P., Theobald, K. B., Khokhar, A. A., & Gao, G. R. (2000, July). Multithreaded algorithms for the fast Fourier transform. In *Acm symposium on parallel algorithms and architectures* Winnipeg, Canada, (p. 176-185).

Tian, D., & Xiang, Y. (2008). A multi-core supported intrusion detection system. *Proceedings of IFIP International Conference on Network and Parallel Computing.*

Tian, R., Xiong, Y., Zhang, Q., Li, B., Zhao, B. Y., & Li, X. (2005). Hybrid Overlay Structure Based on Random Walks. In *Proceedings of the 4th Intl. Workshop on Peer-to-Peer Systems* (pp. 152-162). Berlin: Springer-Verlag.

Tirado-Ramos, A., Tsouloupas, G., Dikaiakos, M. D., & Sloot, P. M. (2005). Grid resource selection by application benchmarking: A computational haemodynamics case study. *International Conference on Computational Science.* (LNCS 3514, pp. 534-543). Atlanta, GA: Springer Verlag.

TOP500. (2007). *TOP 500 Supercomputer Sites, Performance Development, November 2007.* Retrieved March 10, 2008 from http://www.top500.org/lists/2007/11/performance_development

Trelles, Andrade, & Valencia, Zapata, & Carazo. (1998, June). Computational space reduction and parallelization of a new clustering approach for large groups of sequences. *Bioinformatics (Oxford, England)*, *14*(5), 439–451. doi:10.1093/bioinformatics/14.5.439

TRIANA. (2003). *The Triana Project*. Retrieved from www.trianacode.org/

Tripp, G. (2006). A parallel "string matching engine" for use in high speed network intrusion detection systems. *Journal in Computer Virology*, *2*(1), 21–34. doi:10.1007/s11416-006-0010-4

Tsaregorodtsev, A., Garonne, V., & Stokes-Rees, I. (2004). Dirac: A scalable lightweight architecture for high throughput computing. In *Fifth IEEE/ACM International Workshop On Grid Computing (Grid'04).*

Tseng, Y-C., Shen, C-C. & Chen, W-T. (2003). Integrating Mobile IP with ad hoc networks. *IEEE Computer*, May, 48-55.

Tsouloupas, G., & Dikaiakos, M. D. (2007). GridBench: A tool for the interactive performance exploration of Grid infrastructures. *Journal of Parallel and Distributed Computing*, *67*(9), 1029–1045. doi:10.1016/j.jpdc.2007.04.009

Tsoumakos, D., & Rousseopoulos, N. (2006). Analysis and comparison of p2p search methods. In *Proceedings of the 1st International Conference on Scalable Information Systems (INFOSCALE 2006)*, No. 25.

Tuck, N., & Tullsen, D. M. (2005). Multithreaded value prediction. In *Proceedings of the 11th International Symposium on High-Performance Computer Architecture* (HPCA'05), (pp. 5-15), San Francisco: IEEE Computer Society.

Tullsen, D. M., & Brown, J. A. (2001). Handling long-latency loads in a simultaneous multithreading processor. In *Proceedings of the 34th Annual ACM/IEEE International Symposium on Microarchitecture* (MICRO'01), (pp. 318–327). Austin, TX: IEEE Computer Society.

Tullsen, D. M., Eggers, S. J., & Levy, H. M. (1995). Simultaneous multithreading: maximizing on-chip parallelism. In *Proceedings of the 22nd Annual International Symposium on Computer Architecture* (ISCA'95), Santa Margherita Ligure, Italy (pp. 392-403). New York: ACM Press.

Tullsen, D. M., Eggers, S. J., Emer, J. S., Levy, H. M., Lo, J. L., & Stamm, R. L. (1996). Exploiting choice: instruction fetch and issue on an implementable simultaneous multithreading processor. In *Proceedings of the 23rd Annual International Symposium on Computer Architecture* (ISCA'96), Philadelphia, (pp. 191–202). New York: ACM Press.

Tullsen, D. M., Lo, J. L., Eggers, S. J., & Levy, H. M. (1999). Supporting fine-grained synchronization on a simultaneous multithreading processor. In *Proceedings of the 5th International Symposium on High Performance Computer Architecture* (HPCA'99), Orlando, FL (pp. 54-58). New York: IEEE Computer Society.

Turner, D., & Chen, X. (2002). Protocol-dependent message-passing performance on linux clusters. *Proceedings of the 2002 IEEE International Conference on Linux Clusters, pp. 187-194.* New York: IEEE Computer Society.

TV-Anytime. (2005). *TV-Anytime*. Retrieved June 15th, 2008, from http://www.tv-anytime.org

UDDI. (2004). *UDDI Version 3.0.2.* Retrieved June 15th, 2008, from http://www.Oasis-Open.org/committees/uddi-spec/doc/spec/v3/uddi-v3.0.2-20041019.Htm

Uhlig, S., Bonaventure, O., & Quoitin, B. (2003). Internet traffic engineering with minimal BGP configuration. *18th International Teletraffic Congress.*

Unicore (n.d.). Retrieved from http://unicore.sourceforge.net

UNICORE. (2008). *UNiform Interface to COmputing Resources*. Retrieved from www.unicore.eu/

Ururahy, C., & Rodriguez, N. (2004). Programming and coordinating grid environments and applications. In *Concurrency and computation: Practice and experience.*

Vakali, A., & Pallis, G. (2003). Content Delivery Networks: Status and Trends. *IEEE Internet Computing*, (November 6): 68–74. doi:10.1109/MIC.2003.1250586

Valkovskii, V. A., & Malyshkin, V. E. (1988). *Synthesis of parallel programs and systems on the basis of computational models*. Novosibirsk, Russia: Nauka.

van der Houwen, P. J., & Messina, E. (1999). Parallel Adams methods. *Journal of Computational and Applied Mathematics*, *101*(1-2), 153–165. doi:10.1016/S0377-0427(98)00214-3

van der Houwen, P. J., & Sommeijer, B. P. (1991). Iterated Runge-Kutta methods on parallel computers. *SIAM Journal on Scientific and Statistical Computing*, *12*(5), 1000–1028. doi:10.1137/0912054

Van der Wijngaart, R. F., & Frumkin, M. A. (2004). Evaluating the information power Grid using the NAS Grid benchmarks. *International Parallel and Distributed Processing Symposium.* Santa Fe, NM: IEEE Computer Society Press.

van der Wijngaart, R. F., & Jin, H. (2003). *The NAS parallel benchmarks, multi-zone versions* (No. NAS-03-010). NASA Ames Research Center, Sunnydale, CA.

van Reeuwijk, C., Kuijlman, F., & Sips, H. J. (2003). Spar: A set of extensions to Java for scientific computation. *Concurrency and Computation*, *15*, 277–299. doi:10.1002/cpe.659

Vanneschi, M. (2002). The programming model of ASSIST, an environment for parallel and distributed portable applications. *Parallel Computing*, *28*(12), 1709–1732. doi:10.1016/S0167-8191(02)00188-6

Vanneschi, M., & Veraldi, L. (2007). Dynamicity in distributed applications: Issues, problems and the ASSIST approach. *Parallel Computing*, *33*(12), 822–845. doi:10.1016/j.parco.2007.08.001

Vazhkudai, S. (2003, Nov). Enabling the co-allocation of grid data transfers. In *Proceedings of the fourth international workshop on grid computing* (pp. 41–51).

Vazhkudai, S., & Ma, X. V. F., Strickland, J., Tammineedi, N., & Scott, S. (2005). Freeloader:scavenging desktop storage resources for scientific data. In *Proceedings of Supercomputing 2005 (SC'05)*, Seattle, WA.

Vazhkudai, S., & Syed, J., & Maginnis T. (2002). PODOS - The design and implementation of a performance oriented Linux cluster. *Future Generation Computer Systems*, *18*(3), 335–352. doi:10.1016/S0167-739X(01)00055-3

Vazhkudai, S., Tuecke, S., & Foster, I. (2001). Replica selection in the globus data grid. *In Proceedings of the first IEEE/ACM international conference on cluster computing and the grid* (*CCGRID* 2001) (pp. 106–113).

Vázquez-Poletti, J. L., Huedo, E., Montero, R. S., & Llorente, I. M. (2007). A comparison between two grid scheduling philosophies: EGEE WMS and Grid Way. *Multiagent and Grid Systems*, *3*(4), 429–439.

Vecchiola, C., & Chu, X. (2008). *Aneka tutorial series on developing task model applications.* (Technical Report). Grid Computing and Distributed Systems Laboratory, The University of Melbourne, Australia.

Veldema, R., Hofman, R. F. H., Bhoedjang, R., & Bal, H. E. (2001). *Runtime optimizations for a Java DSM implementation*. Paper presented at the Proceedings of the 2001 joint ACM-ISCOPE conference on Java Grande.

Venugopal, S., & Buyya, R. (2005, Oct). A deadline and budget constrained scheduling algorithm for escience applications on data grids. In *Proceedings of the 6th international conference on algorithms and architectures for parallel processing* (ICA3PP-2005) (pp. 60–72).

Venugopal, S., Buyya, R., & Ramamohanarao, K. (2006). A taxonomy of data grids for distributed data sharing, management, and processing. *ACM Computing Surveys*, *1*, 1–53.

Venugopal, S., Buyya, R., & Winton, L. (2004). A grid service broker for scheduling distributed data-oriented applications on global grids. *Proceedings of the 2nd workshop on Middleware for grid computing*, Toronto, Canada, (pp. 75–80). Retrieved from www.Gridbus.org/broker

Venugopal, S., Nadiminti, K., Gibbins, H., & Buyya, R. (2008). Designing a resource broker for heterogeneous Grids. *Software, Practice & Experience*, *38*(8), 793–825. doi:10.1002/spe.849

Villa, O., Scarpazza, D. P., & Petrini, F. (2008). Accelerating real-time string searching with multicore processors. *IEEE Computer*, *41*(4), 42–50.

VMware Inc. (1999). *VMware virtual platform.*

Voss, M. J., & Eigenmann, R. (2000). ADAPT: Automated De-coupled Adaptive Program Transformation. *International Conference on Parallel Processing,* Toronto, Canada, (pp. 163).

Vshivkov, V. A., Nikitin, S. A., & Snytnikov, V. N. (2003). Studying instability of collisionless systems on stochastic trajectories. *JETP Letters*, *78*(6), 358–362. doi:10.1134/1.1630127

Vuduc, R., Demel, J., & Bilmes, J. A. (2004). Statistical Models for Empirical Search-Based Performance Tuning. *International Journal of High Performance Computing Applications*, *18*(1), 65–94. doi:10.1177/1094342004041293

Vydyanathan, N., Krishnamoorthy, S., Sabin, G., Çatalyürek, Ü. V., Kurç, T. M., Sadayappan, P., et al. (2006). An integrated approach for processor allocation and scheduling of mixed-parallel applications. In *Proceedings of the 2006 International Conference on Parallel Processing (ICPP'06)* (pp. 443–450). New York: IEEE.

Vydyanathan, N., Krishnamoorthy, S., Sabin, G., Çatalyürek, Ü. V., Kurç, T. M., Sadayappan, P., et al. (2006). Locality conscious processor allocation and scheduling for mixed parallel applications. In *Proceedings of the 2006 IEEE International Conference on Cluster Computing, September 25-28, 2006, Barcelona, Spain.* New York: IEEE.

Wachter, H., & Reuter, A. (Eds.). (1992). Contracts: A means for Extending Control Beyond Transaction Boundaries. *Advanced Transaction Models for New Applications.* San Francisco: Morgan Kaufmann.

Waldburger, M., & Stiller, B. (2006). Toward the mobile grid:service provisioning in a mobile dynamic virtual organization. In. Proceedings of the IEEE International Conference on Computer Systems and Applications, 2006, (pp.579–583).

Waldvogel, M., & Rinaldi, R. (2002). Efficient topology-aware overlay network. In *Proc. of HotNets-I.*

Walker, B., Popek, G., English, R., Kline, C., & Thiel, G. (1992). The locus distributed operating system. *Ditributed Computing Systems: Concepts and Structures, 17*(5).

Walker, D. W. (1990). Characterising the parallel performance of a large-scale, particle-in-cell plasma simulation code. *International Journal on Concurrency: Practice and Experience.*, *2*(4), 257–288. doi:10.1002/cpe.4330020402

Wall, D. W. (1991). Limits of instruction-level parallelism. In *Proceedings of the 4th International Conference on Architectural Support for Programming Languages and Operating Systems,* Santa Clara, CA (ASPLOS-IV), (pp. 176-188). New York: ACM Press.

Wang, C., Hsu, C., Chen, H., & Wu, J. (2006). Efficient multi-source data transfer in data grids. In *Proceedings of the sixth IEEE international symposium on cluster computing and the grid* (CCGRID'06) (pp. 421–424).

Wang, C., Xiao, L., Liu, Y., & Zheng, P. (2004). Distributed caching and adaptive search in multilayer P2P networks. *In International Conference on Distributed Computing Systems (ICDCS'04)* (pp. 219-226).

Wang, H., Katz, R., & Giese, J. (1999). Policy-enabled handoffs across heterogeneous wireless networks. *Mobile Computing Systems and Applications (PWMCSA),* (pp. 51-60).

Wang, H., Liu, P., & Wu, J. (2006). A QoS-aware heuristic algorithm for replica placement. *Journal of Grid Computing*, 96–103.

Wang, J., Zeng, Q.-A., & Agrawal, D. P. (2003). Performance analysis of a preemptive and priority reservation handoff scheme for integrated service-based wireless mobile networks. *IEEE Transactions on Mobile Computing, 2*(1), 65–75. doi:10.1109/TMC.2003.1195152

Wang, T., Vonk, J., Kratz, B., & Grefen, P. (2008). A survey on the history of transaction management: from flat to grid transactions. *Distributed and Parallel Databases, 23*(3), 235–270. doi:10.1007/s10619-008-7028-1

Wang, Y., Scardaci, D., Yan, B., & Huang, Y. (2007). Interconnect EGEE and CNGRID e-infrastructures through interoperability between gLite and GOS middlewares. In *International Grid Interoperability and Interoperation Workshop (IGIIW 2007) with e-Science 2007* (pp. 553–560). Bangalore, India: IEEE Computer Society.

Wang, Z., Yu, B., Chen, Q., & Gao, C. (2005). Wireless grid computing over mobile ad-hoc networks with mobile agent. In *Skg '05: Proceedings of the first international conference on semantics, knowledge and grid* (p. 113). Washington, DC: IEEE Computer Society.

Wasson, G., & Humphrey, M. (2003). Policy and enforcement in virtual organizations. In *4th International Workshop on Grid Computing* (pp. 125–132). Washington, DC: IEEE Computer Society.

Watt, A. Lilley Chris, & J., Daniel. (2003). *SVG Unleashed.* Indianapolis, IN: SAMS.

Wei, B., Fedak, G., & Cappello, F. (2005). scheduling independent tasks sharing large data distributed with BitTorrent. In *The 6th IEEE/ACM International Workshop On Grid Computing, 2005,* Seattle, WA.

Weiser, M. (1991, February). The computer for the 21st century. *Scientific American, 265*(3), 66–75.

Wesner, S., Dimitrakos, T., & Jeffrey, K. (2004, October). Akogrimo - the Grid goes mobile. *ERCIM News,* (59), 32-33.

West, E. A., & Grimshaw, A. S. (1995). Braid: Integrating task and data parallelism. In *Proceedings of the Fifth Symposium on the Frontiers of Massively Parallel Computation (Frontiers'95)* (p. 211). New York: IEEE Computer Society.

Whaley, R. C., & Petite, A. (2005). Minimizing development and maintenance costs in supporting persistently optimized BLAS. *Software, Practice & Experience, 35*(2), 101–121. doi:10.1002/spe.626

White Paper, A. M. D. (2008). *The industry-changing impact of accelerated computing.*

White, J. E. (1996). Telescript technology: Mobile agents. *Journal of Software Agents.*

Wieczorek, M., Prodan, R., & Fahringer, T. (2005). Scheduling of scientific workflows in the ASKALON Grid environment. *SIGMOD Record, 09.*

WiFi (2008). Retrieved November 2008 from http://www.ieee802.org/11/

Wikipedia, *Gauss-Jordan elimination.* Retrieved from http://en.wikipedia.org/wiki/Gauss-Jordan_elimination

Wikipedia, *Max-flow min-cut theorem.* Retrieved from http://en.wikipedia.org/wiki/Max-flow_min-cut_theorem

Wilkinson, T. (1998). Kaffe - a clean room implementation of the Java virtual machine. Retrieved 2002, from http://www.kaffe.org/

Williams, S., Shalf, J., Oliker, L., Kamil, S., Husbands, P., & Yelick, K. (2006, May). The Potential of the Cell Processor for Scientific Computing. In *Computing frontiers (cf'06)* Ischia, Italy (pp. 9–20).

Winkler, P., & Zhang, L. (2003). Wavelength assignment and generalized interval graph coloring. In *Proceedings of the ACM-SIAM Symposium on Discrete Algorithms (SODA'03)*, Baltimore, MD, (pp. 830–831).

Witten, I. H., & Frank, E. (2005). *Data Mining: Practical Machine Learning Tools and Techniques* (2nd Ed.). San Francisco: Morgan Kaufmann.

Woeginger, G. J. (1997). There is no asymptotic PTAS for two-dimensional vector packing. *Information Processing Letters, 64*, 293–297. doi:10.1016/S0020-0190(97)00179-8

Wolski, R. (2003). Experiences with predicting resource performance on-line in computational grid settings. *ACM SIGMETRICS Performance Evaluation Review, 30*(4), 41–49. doi:10.1145/773056.773064

Wong, S.-W., & Ng, K.-W. (2006). Security support for mobile grid services framework. In *Nwesp'06: Proceedings of the international conference on next generation web services practices* (pp.75–82). Washington, DC: IEEE Computer Society.

World Wide Web Consortium (W3C). (n.d.). *Web services activity.* Retrieved from http://www.w3.org/2002/ws/

WSDL/W3C. (2005). *WSDL: Web Services Description Language (WSDL) 1.1.* Retrieved June 15th, 2008, from http://www.w3.org/TR/wsdl.

Wu, D. M., & Guan, L. (1995). A Distributed Real-Time Image Processing System. *Real-Time Imaging, 1*(6), 427–435. doi:10.1006/rtim.1995.1044

Wu, G., Chu, C. W., Wine, K., Evans, J., & Frenkiel, R. (1999). WINMAC: A novel transmission protocol for infostations. *Proceedings of the 49th IEEE Vehicular Technology Conference (VTC)*, Houston, TX, (Vol. 2, pp. 1340–1344).

Wu, Q., He, X., & Hintz, T. (2004, June 21-24). *Virtual Spiral Architecture.* Paper presented at the International Conference on Parallel and Distributed Processing Techniques and Applications, Las Vegas, Nevada, USA.

Wyckoff, P., McLaughry, S. W., Lehman, T. J., & Ford, D. A. (1998). T Spaces. *IBM Systems Journal, 37*, 454–474.

Xiang, Y., & Zhou, W. (2006). Protecting information infrastructure from ddos attacks by mark-aided distributed filtering (madf). *International Journal of High Performance Computing and Networking, 4*(5/6), 357–367. doi:10.1504/IJHPCN.2006.013491

Xie, M. (1991). *Software reliability modeling*. Hackensack, NJ: World Scientific Publishing Company.

Xie, M., Dai, Y. S., & Poh, K. L. (2004). *Computing systems reliability: Models and analysis*. New York: Kluwer Academic Publishers.

Xu, C. (2005). *Scalable and Secure Internet Services and Architecture*. Boca Raton, FL: Chapman & Hall/ CRC Press.

Xu, J. (2003). On the fundamental tradeoffs between routing table size and network diameter in peer-to-peer networks. In *Proceedings of INFOCOM* (pp. 2177-2187). New York: IEEE Press.

Xu, M., Sabouni, A., Thulasiraman, P., Noghanian, S., & Pistorius, S. (2007, Sept.). Image Reconstruction using Microwave Tomography for Breast Cancer Detection on Distributed Memory Machine. In *International conference on parallel processing (icpp)* XiAn, China (p. 1-8).

Xu, Y., Liu, H., & Zeng, Q.-A. (2005). Resource management and Qos control in multiple traffic wireless and mobile Internet systems. [WCMC]. *Wiley's Journal of Wireless Communications and Mobile Computing*, *2*(1), 971–982. doi:10.1002/wcm.360

Xu, Z., Mahalingam, M., & Karlsson, M. (2003). Turning heterogeneity into an advantage in overlay routing. In *Proc. of INFOCOM*.

Xu, Z., Min, R., & Hu, Y. (2003). HIERAS: A DHT based hierarchical p2p routing algorithm. In *Proceedings of the 2003 Intl. Conf. on Parallel Processing* (pp. 187-194). New York: IEEE Computer Society Press.

Xu, Z., Tang, C., & Zhang, Z. (2003). Building topology-aware overlays using global soft-state. *In Proc. of ICDCS*.

Yamamoto, W., & Nemirovsky, M. (1995). Increasing superscalar performance through multistreaming. In *Proceedings of the IFIP WG10.3 Working Conference on Parallel Architectures and Compilation Techniques* (PACT'95), (pp. 49-58). Limassol, Cyprus: IFIP Working Group on Algol.

Yamin, A., Augustin, I., Barbosa, J., da Silva, L., Real, R., & Cavalheiro, G. (2003). Towards merging context-aware, mobile and grid computing. *International Journal of High Performance Computing Applications*, *17*(2), 191–203. doi:10.1177/1094342003017002008

Yan, C., Rogers, B., Englender, D., Solihin, Y., & Prvulovic, M. (2006). Improving cost, performance, and security of memory encryption and authentication. In *Proceedings of 33rd Annual International Symposium on Computer Architecture* (ISCA'06), (pp. 179-190). Boston: IEEE Computer Society Press.

Yan, J., & Zhang, W. (2007). Hybrid multi-core architecture for boosting single-threaded performance. *ACM SIGARCH Computer Architecture News*, *35*(1), 141–148. doi:10.1145/1241601.1241603

Yang, B., & Garcia-Molina, H. (2002). Improving search in peer-to-peer networks. In *Proceedings of the 22nd International Conference on Distributed Computing Systems* (ICDCS'02) (pp. 5).

Yang, B., & Xie, M. (2000). A study of operational and testing reliability in software reliability analysis. *Reliability Engineering & System Safety*, *70*, 323–329. doi:10.1016/S0951-8320(00)00069-7

Yang, C., Yang, I., Chen, C., & Wang, S. (2006). Implementation of a dynamic adjustment mechanism with efficient replica selection in data grid environments. In *Proceedings of the ACM symposium on applied computing* (pp. 797–804).

Yang, H. T., Wang, Z. H., & Deng, Q. H. (2008). Scheduling optimization in coupling independent services as a Grid transaction. *Journal of Parallel and Distributed Computing*, *68*(6), 840–854. doi:10.1016/j.jpdc.2008.01.004

Yang, Y. G., Jin, H., & Li, M. L. (2004). Grid computing in China. *Journal of Grid Computing*, *2*(2), 193–206. doi:10.1007/s10723-004-4201-2

Yap, T., Frieder, O., & Martino, R. (1998, March). Parallel computation in biological sequence analysis. *Institute of Electrical and Electronic Engineers*, *9*(3), 283–294.

Yau, D. K. Y., & Lam, S. S. (1996). Adaptive Rate-Controlled Scheduling for Multimedia Applications. In *Proceedings of ACM Multimedia Conference.*

Yavatkar, R., Pendarakis, D., & Guerin, R. (2000, January). *A framework for policy based admission control*, (RFC 2753).

Yeager, K. C. (1996). The MIPS R10000 superscalar microprocessor. *IEEE Micro*, *16*(2), 28–40. doi:10.1109/40.491460

Yee, K. (1966, May). Numerial solution of initial boundary value problems involving maxwell's equations in isotropic media. IEEE Transactions on Antennas and Propagation, AP-14(8), 302–307.

Yeh, C.-H., Parhami, B., Varvarigos, E. A., & Lee, H. (2002, July). VLSI layout and packaging of butterfly networks. In *Acm symposium on parallel algorithms and architectures* Winnipeg, Canada (pp. 196–205).

Yeo, C. S., & Buyya, R. (2007). Integrated Risk Analysis for a Commercial Computing Service. *Proceedings of the 21st IEEE International Parallel and Distributed Processing Symposium (IPDPS 2007, IEEE CS Press, Los Alamitos, CA, USA).*

Yinglian, X. O'Hallaron D. (2002). Locality in search engine queries and its implications for caching. In *Proceedings of the IEEE Infocom* (pp. 1238-1247).

Young, J. W. (1974). A first order approximation to the optimal checkpoint interval. *Communications of the ACM*, *17*(9), 530–531. doi:10.1145/361147.361115

Yu, W., & Cox, A. (1997). Java/DSM: A Platform for Heterogeneous Computing. *Concurrency (Chichester, England)*, *9*(11), 1213–1224. doi:10.1002/(SICI)1096-9128(199711)9:11<1213::AID-CPE333>3.0.CO;2-J

Yu, W., Mittra, R., Su, T., Liu, Y., & Yang, X. (2006). *Parallel Finite-Difference Time-Domain Method.* Boston: Artech House publishers.

Zajcew, R., Roy, P., Black, D., & Peak, C. (1993). An osf/1 unix for massively parallel multi-computers. *Proceedings of the winter 1993 conference*, (pp. 449-468).

Zander, J. (2000). Trends and challenges in resource management future wireless networks. In *Proceedings of the IEEE Wireless Communications and Networks Conference (WCNC)*, Chicago, (Vol. 1, pp. 159–163).

Zegura, E. Calvert, K. et al. (1996). How to model an Internetwork. *In Proc. of INFOCOM.*

Zhang, G., & Parashar, M. (2003). Dynamic context-aware access control for grid applications. In *4th international workshop on grid computing* (grid 2003), (pp. 101 – 108). Phoenix, AZ: IEEE Computer Society Press. Retrieved from citeseer.ist.psu.edu/zhang03dynamic.html

Zhang, Q., Guo, C., Guo, Z., & Zhu, W. (2003). Efficient mobility management for vertical handoff between WWAN and WLAN. *IEEE Communications Magazine*, *41*(11), 102–108. doi:10.1109/MCOM.2003.1244929

Zhang, X. Y., Zhang, Q., Zhang, Z., Song, G., & Zhu, W. (2004). A construction of locality-aware overlay network: mOverlay and its performance. *IEEE Journal on Selected Areas in Communications*, *22*(1), 18–28. doi:10.1109/JSAC.2003.818780

Zhang, X., Freschl, J. L., & Schopf, J. M. (2003, June). A performance study of monitoring and information services for distributed systems. In HPDC'03: Proceedings of the Twelfth International Symposium on High Performance Distributed Computing, (pp. 270-281). Los Alamitos, CA: IEEE Computer Society Press.

Zhao, B. Y., Duan, Y., Huang, L., Joseph, A., & Kubiatowicz, J. (2003). Brocade: landmark routing on overlay networks. In *Proceedings of the 2nd Intl. Workshop on Peer-to-Peer Systems* (pp. 34-44). Berlin: Springer-Verlag.

Zhao, B. Y., Kubiatowicz, J., & Oseph, A. D. (2001). *Tapestry: An infrastructure for fault-tolerant wide-area location and routing* (Tech. Rep. UCB/CSD-01-1141). University of California at Berkeley, Berkeley, CA.

Zhao, S., & Lo, V. (2001, May). Result Verification and Trust-based Scheduling in Open Peer-to-Peer Cycle Sharing Systems. In *Proceedings of Ieee Fifth International Conference on Peer-To-Peer Systems.*

Zhou, D., & Lo, V. M. (2006). Wavegrid: A scalable fast-turnaround heterogeneous peer-based desktop grid system. In *IPDPS*.

Zhou, J., Ou, Z., Rautiainen, M., & Ylianttila, M. (2008b). P2P SCCM: Service-oriented Community Coordinated Multimedia over P2P. In *Proceedings of 2008 IEEE International Conference on Web Services*, Beijing, China, September 23-26, (pp. 34-40).

Zhou, J., Rautiainen, M., & Ylianttila, M. (2008a). Community coordinated multimedia: Converging content-driven and service-driven models. In *proceedings of 2008 IEEE International Conference on Multimedia & Expo*, June 23-26, 2008, Hannover, Germany.

Zhou, S., Zheng, X., Wang, J., & Delisle, P. (1993). Utopia: a load sharing facility for large, heterogeneous distributed computer systems. *Software, Practice & Experience*, *23*(12), 1305–1336. doi:10.1002/spe.4380231203

Zhou, X., Kim, E., Kim, J. W., & Yeom, H. Y. (2006). ReCon: A fast and reliable replica retrieval service for the data grid. *In Proceedings of IEEE international symposium on cluster computing and the grid* (pp. 446–453).

Zhou, Y., Iftode, L., & Li, K. (1996). Performance evaluation of two home-based lazy release consistency protocols for shared virtual memory systems. *SIGOPS Oper. Syst. Rev.*, *30*(SI), 75-88.

Zhu, F., & McNair, J. (2004). Optimizations for vertical handoff decision algorithms. *IEEE Wireless Communications and Network Conference (WCNC)*, (pp. 867-872).

Zhu, W., Wang, C. L., & Lau, F. C. M. (2002). *JESSICA2: A Distributed Java Virtual Machine with Transparent Thread Migration Support*. Paper presented at the Proceedings of the IEEE International Conference on Cluster Computing.

Zhu, Y., & Hu, Y. (2005). Efficient, proximity-aware load balancing for DHT-based P2P systems. *Proc. of IEEE TPDS*, *16*(4).

Zhu, Y., & Jiang, H. (2006). *False Rate Analysis of Bloom Filter Replicas in Distributed Systems*. Paper presented at the Proceedings of the 2006 International Conference on Parallel Processing.

Zhu, Y., Jiang, H., & Wang, J. (2004). *Hierarchical Bloom filter arrays (HBA): a novel, scalable metadata management system for large cluster-based storage*. Paper presented at the Proceedings of the 2004 IEEE International Conference on Cluster Computing.

Zhu, Y., Jiang, H., Wang, J., & Xian, F. (2008). *HBA: Distributed Metadata Management for Large Cluster-Based Storage Systems*. *IEEE Transactions on Parallel and Distributed Systems*, *19*(6), 750–763. doi:10.1109/TPDS.2007.70788

Zilka, A. (2006). *Terracotta - JVM Clustering, Scalability and Reliability for Java*. Retrieved June 19, 2008, from http://www.terracotta.org

About the Contributors

Kuan-Ching Li received the PhD and MS degrees in Electrical Engineering and Licenciatura in Mathematics from the University of São Paulo, Brazil. After he received his PhD, he was a postdoctoral scholar in the University of California – Irvine (UCI) and University of Southern California (USC). His main research interests include cluster and grid computing, parallel software design, and life science applications. He has authored over 60 research papers and book chapters, and co-editor of book entitled "Handbook of Research on Scalable Computing Technologies" published by IGI Global and volumes of LNCS and LNAI published by Springer. He has served as Guest Editor of a number of journal special issues, including The Journal of Supercomputing (TJS), International Journal of Ad Hoc and Ubiquitous Computing (IJAHUC), and International Journal of Computer Applications in Technology (IJCAT). In addition, he has served on the steering, organizing, and program committees of several conferences and workshops, including Conference co-chair of CSE'2008 (Sao Paulo, Brazil) and Program co-chair of APSCC'2008 (Yilan, Taiwan), AINA'2008 (Okinawa, Japan). He is a senior member of the IEEE.

Ching-Hsien Hsu received the B.S. and Ph.D. degrees in Computer Science from Tung Hai University and Feng Chia University, Taiwan, in 1995 and 1999, respectively. He is currently an associate professor of the department of Computer Science and Information Engineering at Chung Hua University, Taiwan. Dr. Hsu's research interest is primarily in parallel and distributed computing, grid computing, P2P computing, RFID and services computing. Dr. Hsu has published more than 80 academic papers in journals, books and conference proceedings. He was awarded as annual outstanding researchers by Chung Hua University in 2005, 2006 and 2007 and got the excellent research award in 2008. He is serving in a number of journal editorial boards, including International Journal of Communication Systems, International Journal of Computer Science, International Journal of Grid and High Performance Computing, International Journal of Smart Home and International Journal of Multimedia and Ubiquitous Engineering.

Laurence T. Yang is a professor at Department of Computer Science of St Francis Xavier University, Canada. His research includes high performance computing and networking, embedded systems, ubiquitous/pervasive computing and intelligence. He has published around 300 papers (including around 80+ international journal papers such as IEEE and ACM Transactions) in refereed journals, conference proceedings and book chapters in these areas. He has been involved in more than 100 conferences and workshops as a program/general/steering conference chair and more than 300 conference and workshops as a program committee member. He served as the vice-chair of IEEE Technical Committee of Supercomputing Applications (TCSA) until 2004, currently is the chair of IEEE Technical Committee of Scalable Computing (TCSC), the chair of IEEE Task force on Ubiquitous Computing and Intelligence. In addition, he is the editors-in-chief of several international journals and few book series. He is serving as an editor for numerous international journals. He has been acting as an author/co-author or an editor/co-editor of 25 books from Kluwer, Springer, IGI, Nova Science, American Scientific Publishers and John Wiley & Sons. He has won 5 Best Paper Awards (including the IEEE 20th International Conference on Advanced Information Networking and Applications (AINA-06)) and 1 Best Paper Nomination in 2007; as well as a Distinguished Achievement Award, 2005; Canada Foundation for Innovation Award, 2003.

Jack Dongarra holds an appointment at the University of Tennessee and holds the title of Distinguished Research Staff at Oak Ridge National Laboratory (ORNL), Turing Fellow at the University of Manchester. He was awarded the IEEE Sid Fernbach Award in 2004 for his contributions in the application of high performance computers using innovative approaches and in 2008 he was the recipient of the IEEE Medal of Excellence in Scalable Computing. He is a Fellow of the AAAS, ACM, and the IEEE and a member of the National Academy of Engineering.

Hans P. Zima is a Principal Scientist at the Jet Propulsion Laboratory, California Institute of Technology, and a Professor Emeritus of the University of Vienna, Austria. He received his Ph.D. degree in Mathematics and Astronomy from the University of Vienna in 1964. His major research interests have been in the fields of high-level programming languages, compilers, and advanced software tools. In the early 1970s, while working in industry, he designed and implemented one of the first high-level real-time languages for the German Air Traffic Control Agency. During his tenure as a Professor of Computer Science at the University of Bonn, Germany, he contributed to the German supercomputer project "SUPRENUM", leading the design of the first Fortran-based compilation system for distributed-memory architectures (1989). After his move to the University of Vienna, he became the chief designer of the Vienna Fortran language (1992) that provided a major input for the High Performance Fortran de-facto standard. From 1997 to 2007, Dr. Zima headed the Priority Research Program "Aurora", a ten-year program funded by the Austrian Science Foundation. His research over the past years focused on the design of the "Chapel" programming language in the framework of the DARPA-sponsored HPCS project "Cascade". More recently, Dr. Zima has become involved in the design of space-borne fault-tolerant high capability computing systems. Dr. Zima is the author or co-author of about 200 publications, including 4 books.

* * *

David Allenotor has a B.Sc. and M.Sc. in Computer Science, University of Benin 1996 and 2000. He also has M.Sc. in Computer Science, University of Manitoba, Canada. 2005. At present he is a Ph.D. candidate in Department of Computer Science, University of Manitoba, Canada and a member of the Computational Finance Derivatives Lab (CFD). His interest and field is Grid Computing, Cloud Computing, applications fuzzy logic to Computational Finance Derivatives, and Modeling of Financial Engineering problems.

Jörn Altmann is Associate Professor at the International University of Bruchsal, Germany, where he heads the group of Computer Networks and Distributed Systems. Dr. Altmann received his B.Sc. degree, his M.Sc. degree (1993), and his Ph.D. (1996) from the University of Erlangen-Nürnberg, Germany. Dr. Altmann's current research centers on the economics of Internet services and Internet infrastructures, integrating economic models into distributed systems. In particular, he focuses on capacity planning, network topologies, and resource allocation.

Carlos Eduardo Rodrigues Alves is an Associate Professor of the Computer Science Department of São Judas Tadeu University. He obtained his Ph.D. in Computer Science at the Institute of Mathematics and Statistics of the University of São Paulo in 2002. He was a graduate of the Instituto Tecnológico de Aeronática where he finished both his undergraduate course in Electronics Engineering and his M.Sc. degree in Electrical and Computer Engineering. His research interests are the design of efficient sequential and parallel algorithms.

Marcos Dias de Assunção is a PhD candidate at the University of Melbourne, Australia. His PhD thesis is on peering and resource allocation across Grids. He has previously obtained a masters degree on network management at the Federal University of Santa Catarina, Brazil. The current topics of his interest include Grid scheduling, virtual machines, and network virtualisation.

Alan A. Bertossi got the Laurea Degree in Computer Science from the University of Pisa (Italy) in 1979. Currently, he is a Professor of Computer Science at the Department of Computer Science of the University of Bologna (Italy). His main research interests are the design and analysis of algorithms for high-performance, parallel, distributed, wireless, fault-tolerant, and real-time systems. He has published 45 refereed papers on international archival journals, as well as several other papers in conference proceedings, book chapters, and encyclopedias. He served as a guest coeditor for special issues of international journals, mainly on algorithms for wireless networks. Since 2000, he has been in the editorial board of Information Processing Letters.

Rajkumar Buyya is an Associate Professor and Reader of Computer Science and Software Engineering; and Director of the Grid Computing and Distributed Systems (GRIDS) Laboratory at the University of Melbourne, Australia. Dr. Buyya has authored/co-authored over 250 publications. He has co-authored three books: Microprocessor x86 Programming, BPB Press, New Delhi, 1995, Mastering C++, Tata McGraw Hill Press, New Delhi, 1997, and Design of PARAS Microkernel. The books on emerging topics that he edited include, High Performance Cluster Computing (Prentice Hall, USA, 1999), High Performance Mass Storage and Parallel I/O (IEEE and Wiley Press, USA, 2001), Content Delivery Networks (Springer, Germany, 2008), and Market Oriented Grid and Utility Computing (Wiley Press, USA, 2009).

Edson Norberto Caceres is a Professor of the Department of Computer Science and Statistics of the Federal University of Mato Grosso do Sul, where he has been a former Pro-Rector of Undergraduate Stuties. He hold a PhD in Computer Science obtained at the Federal University of Rio de Janeiro in 1992. His research interests include the design of parallel algorithms, especially graph algorithms. He is the Director of Education of the Brazilian Computer Society. In addition to belonging to the Federal University of Mato Grosso do Sul since the early eighties, currenly he is also with the Brazilian Ministery of Education as the General Coordinator of Student Relations.

Franck Cappello holds a Senior Researcher position at INRIA. He leads the Grand-Large project at INRIA, focusing on High Performance issues in Large Scale Distributed Systems. He has initiated the XtremWeb (Desktop Grid) and MPICH-V (Fault tolerant MPI) projects. He was the director of the Grid5000 project from its beginning and until 2008 and is the scientific director of ALADDIN/Grid5000, the new 4 years INRIA project aiming to sustain the Grid5000 infrastructure. He has contributed to more than 50 Program Committees. He is editorial board member of the international Journal on Grid Computing, Journal of Grid and Utility Computing and Journal of Cluster Computing. He is a steering committee member of IEEE HPDC and IEEE/ACM CCGRID. He is the Program co-Chair of IEEE CCGRID'2009 and System Software area co-chair of SC'2009 and was the General Chair of IEEE HPDC'2006.

Jih-Sheng Chang received his B.E. degree from the Department of Computer Science and Information Engineering, I-Shou University, Kaohsiung, Taiwan in 2002 and his M.S. degree from the Department of Computer Science and Information Engineering, National Dong Hwa University, Hualien, Taiwan in 2004. He is a Ph.D. candidate at the Department of Computer Science and Information Engineering at National Dong Hwa University currently. His academic research interests focuses on wireless network technology and grid computing.

Ruay-Shiung Chang received his B.S.E.E. degree from National Taiwan University in 1980 and his Ph.D. degree in Computer Science from National Tsing Hua University in 1988. He is now a professor in the Department of Computer Science and Information Engineering, National Dong Hwa University. His research interests include Internet, wireless networks, and grid computing. Dr. Chang is a member of ACM, a senior member of IEEE, and a founding member of ROC Institute of Information and Computing Machinery. Dr. Chang also served on the advisory council for the Public Interest Registry (www.pir.org) from 2004/5 to 2007/4.

Jinjun Chen received his Ph.D. degree in Computer Science and Software Engineering from Swinburne University of Technology, Melbourne, Australia, in 2007. He is currently a Lecturer in Centre for Complex Systems and Services in the Faculty of Information and Communication Technologies at Swinburne University of Technology, Melbourne, Australia. His research interests include: Scientific Workflow Management and Applications, Workflow Management and Applications in Web Service or SOC Environments, Workflow Management and Applications in Grid (Service)/Cloud Computing Environments, Software Verification and Validation in Workflow Systems, QoS and Resource Scheduling in Distributed Computing Systems such as Cloud Computing, Service Oriented Computing (SLA, Negotiation, Engineering, Composition), Semantics and Knowledge Management, Cloud Computing.

Zizhong Chen received a B.S. degree in mathematics from Beijing Normal University, P. R. China, in 1997, and M.S. and Ph.D. degrees in computer science from the University of Tennessee, Knoxville, in 2003 and 2006, respectively. He is currently an assistant professor of computer science at Colorado School of Mines. His research interests include high performance computing, parallel, distributed, and grid computing, fault tolerance and reliability, numerical algorithms and software, and computational science and engineering. The goal of his research is to develop techniques, design algorithms, and build software tools for computational science applications to achieve both high performance and high reliability on a wide range of computational platforms.

Shang-Feng Chiang was graduate students at the Department of Electrical Engineering, National Taiwan University.

Kuo Chiang and Ruo-Jian Yu were research assistants at the Department of Electrical Engineering, National Taiwan University.

Kenneth Chiu is an assistant professor at SUNY Binghamton. His interests are in the areas of scientific data management, web services, and grid computing. He has served as program co-chair for IEEE e-Science 2007, and as workshops chair for e-Science 2008. He is involved in a number of multi-disciplinary projects with domain scientists, and he is PI or co-PI on five research/education awards from the NSF or DOE, five of which are still active. He received his A.B. from Princeton University and his Ph.D. from Indiana University, both in computer science.

Yuanshun Dai is currently an assistant professor with the Department of Electrical Engineering and Computer Science and the Department of Industrial and Information Engineering at the University of Tennessee, Knoxville. He was the program chair of the 12th IEEE Pacific Rim Symposium on Dependable Computing (PRDC 06). He was also the general chair of the IEEE Symposium on Dependable Autonomic and Secure Computing (DASC) in 2005, 2006, 2007. He was an Associate Editor of IEEE Transactions on Reliability. His research interests are dependability, security, grid computing, and autonomic computing. He published over 60 papers and 5 books.

F. Dehne received a M.C.S. degree (Dipl. Inform.) from the RWTH Aachen University, Germany in 1983 and a Ph.D. (Dr. Rer. Nat.) from the University of Würzburg, Germany in 1986. In 1986 he joined the School of Computer Science at Carleton University in Ottawa, Canada as an Assistant Professor. He was appointed Associate Professor and Professor of Computer Science in 1990 and 1997, respectively. From 2000 to 2003 and 2006 to 2008 he served as Director of the School of Computer Science. His current research interests are in the areas of Parallel Computing, Coarse Grained Parallel Algorithms, Parallel Computational Geometry, Parallel Data Warehousing & OLAP, and Parallel Bioinformatics. He is a Senior Member of the IEEE, member of the ACM Symposium on Parallel Algorithms and Architectures Steering Committee, and former Vice-Chair of the IEEE Technical Committee on Parallel Processing. He is an Editorial Board member for IEEE Transaction on Computers, Information Processing Letters, Journal of Bioinformatics Research and Applications, and Int. Journal of Data Warehousing and Mining.

Evgueni Dodonov is currently finishing his PhD research at the University of São Paulo, Brazil. He completed his Master degree at Federal University of São Carlos in 2004, and worked in the computer industry for several years. His research interests include autonomic computing, file systems, process behavior evaluation and distributed programming.

Daniel C. Doolan is a lecturer in the School of Computing, Robert Gordon University, Scotland. His main research interest is in Mobile and Parallel Computing. He has published over 40 articles in the areas of mobile multimedia and parallel computation.

Dou Wanchun received his Ph.D. degree in Mechanical and Electronic Engineering from Nanjing University and Scientific and Technology, Nanjing, P.R. China, in 2001. He is currently a full professor in Department of Computer Scientific and Technology at Nanjing University, Nanjing, P.R. China. His research interests include: Scientific Workflow Management and Applications, Workflow Management and Applications in Web Service, QoS and Resource Scheduling in Distributed Computing Systems.

Jörg Dümmler received his Master degree in Computer Science from the Chemnitz University of Technology in 2004 and is pursuing doctoral research since then. His research interest include scheduling and mapping of mixed parallel applications, parallel programming models for distributed memory platforms and transformation tools for the development of parallel applications.

M. Rasit Eskicioglu received his B.Sc. in Chemical Engineering from Istanbul Technical University, Turkey, M.Sc. in Computer Engineering from Middle East Technical University, Turkey, and Ph.D. in Computing Science from University of Alberta, Canada. His research interests are mainly in the systems area, including operating systems, cluster and grid computing, high-speed network interconnects, and mobile networks. He has investigated ways to make software DSM systems more efficient and scalable using high-speed, programmable interconnects. Currently he is looking at wireless sensor networks and their applications to real world problems, such as environmental monitoring. Dr. Eskicioglu is currently an associate professor in Computer Science Department, at the University of Manitoba, Canada. He is a member of ACM and senior member of IEEE.

Thomas Fahringer received his Ph.D. in 1993 from the Vienna University of Technology. Between 1990 and 1998, Fahringer worked as Assistant Professor at the University of Vienna, where he was promoted as Associate Professor in 1998. Since 2003, Fahringer is a Full Professor in Computer Science at the Institute of Computer Science, University of Innsbruck, where he is leading a research group developing the ASKALON Grid application development and computing environment. Fahringer's main research interests include software architectures, programming paradigms, compiler technology, performance analysis, and prediction for parallel and distributed Grid systems. Fahringer is currently coordinating the IST-034601 edutain@grid project and is involved in numerous Austrian (SFB Aurora, Austrian Grid) and European Grid (EGEE, CoreGrid, K-Wf Grid, ASG) projects. He is the author of over 100 papers, including two books, 20 journal articles, and two best paper awards (ACM and IEEE).

Tore Ferm received his Bachelor of Computer Science Degree from Sydney University in 2004. He is currently working in the Telecommunication industry in Sydney, Australia.

Gilles Fedak received its PhD degree from University Paris-XI in 2003. He is currently junior INRIA researcher at the LIP Laboratory. He is mainly interested in research around Desktop Grids. He has designed several Desktop Grid middleware, most notably XtremWeb (Desktop Grid) and BitDew (Data Management).

Edgar Gabriel is an Assistant Professor in the Department of Computer Science at the University of Houston, Texas, USA. He got his PhD and Dipl.-Ing. in mechanical engineering from the University of Stuttgart. His research interests are Message Passing Systems, High Performance Computing, Parallel Computing on Distributed Memory Machines, and Grid Computing

Jean-Luc Gaudiot received his Diplôme d'Ingénieur from the École Supérieure d'Ingénieurs en Electrotechnique et Electronique, Paris, France in 1976 and the M.S. and Ph.D. degrees in Computer Science from the University of California, Los Angeles in 1977 and 1982, respectively. He is currently a Professor and Chair of the Electrical Engineering and Computer Science Department at the University of California, Irvine. His research interests include multithreaded architectures, fault-tolerant multi-processors, and implementation of reconfigurable architectures. He has published over 170 journal and conference papers. Dr. Gaudiot is a Fellow of IEEE and AAAS.

Wolfgang Gentzsch is dissemination advisor for the DEISA Distributed European Initiative for Supercomputing Applications, and a member of the Board of Directors of the Open Grid Forum. Before, he was Chairman of the German D-Grid Initiative; managing director of MCNC Grid and Data Center Services in Durham; adjunct professor of computer science at Duke University; and visiting scientist at RENCI Renaissance Computing Institute at UNC Chapel Hill in North Carolina. At the same time, he was a member of the US President's Council of Advisors for Science and Technology. Before he joined Sun in Menlo Park, CA, in 2000, as the senior director of Grid Computing, he was the President, CEO, and CTO of start-up companies Genias and Gridware, and a professor of mathematics and computer science at the University of Applied Sciences in Regensburg, Germany. Gentzsch studied mathematics and physics at the Technical Universities in Aachen and Darmstadt, Germany.

Lin Guan is a Lecturer in the Department of Computer Science at Loughborough University, UK. Her research interests include performance modeling/evaluation of computer networks, Quality of Service (QoS) analysis and enhancement, such as congestion control mechanisms with QoS constraints, mobile computing and wireless networks.

Sudha Gunturu received B.Tech degree in Computer Science and Engineering, from Jawaharlal Nehru Technological University, Hyderabad, India., in 2005. Currently, she is pursuing her MS degree in the Computer Science Department of Oklahoma State University, Stillwater, OK. Her research interests include bioinformatics, scheduling computational loads in parallel and distributed systems and grid computing.

Minyi Guo received his Ph.D. degree in computer science from University of Tsukuba, Japan. Before 2000, Dr. Guo had been a research scientist of NEC Corp., Japan. He is now a full professor at Department of Computer Science and Engineering, Shanghai Jiao Tong University, China. His research interests include pervasive computing, parallel and distributed processing, parallelizing compilers and software engineering. He is a member of the ACM, IEEE, IEEE Computer Society, and IEICE.

Phalguni Gupta received the Doctoral degree from the Indian Institute of Technology Kharagpur, India in 1986. He works in the field of data structures, sequential algorithms, parallel algorithms, on-line algorithms. From 1983 to 1987, he was in the Image Processing and Data Product Group of the Space Applications Centre (ISRO), Ahmedabad, India and was responsible for software for correcting image data received from Indian Remote Sensing Satellite. In 1987, he joined the Department of Computer Science and Engineering, Indian Institute of Technology Kanpur, India. Currently he is a Professor in the department. He is responsible for several research projects in the area of image processing, graph theory and network flow. Dr. Gupta is a member of the Association for Computing Machinery (ACM).

Peter Graham is an Associate Professor in the Computer Science Department and Associate Dean (Research) for the Faculty of Science at the University of Manitoba. He is also an adjunct scientist at TRLabs, Winnipeg. His current research interests include large-scale parallel and distributed systems, pervasive computing, and mobile computing. He is a member of the ACM, IEEE and USENIX.

Alan Grigg is a senior researcher in the Systems Engineering Research Centre at Loughborough University, UK, a BAE Systems funded position. His research interests include real-time embedded systems design, analysis and implementation issues around scheduling, communication and reconfiguration.

Dan Grigoras is Senior Lecturer in the Department of Computer Science of National University of Ireland, Cork, where he leads the Mobile and Cluster Computing Group. His main research interests are in Mobile Networking and Parallel Computing, especially MANET management, middleware services, mobile applications design, load balancing and load sharing. He published one book, co-edited seven others and 44 papers in journals and proceedings of conferences. He is also involved in many conferences and workshops.

Xiangjian He is an Associate Professor at the Faculty of Engineering and Information Technology, University of Technology, Sydney, Australia. In the previous few years, he has received many research grants including four Australian National Grants for research in the fields of computing and telecommunication. His current research interests include multi-scale computing, computer vision, and network security and QoS. More information can be found at http://www-staff.it.uts.edu.au/~sean/

Yong J. Jang received the B.S. degree from the School of Electrical and Electronic Engineering in Yonsei University in March, 2008. He is in the master degree program from the School of Electrical and Electronic Engineering in Yonsei University. Yong's research interest includes multi-processor system and SOC design.

Hai Jiang is an Assistant Professor in the Department of Computer Science at Arkansas State University. He received his Ph. D. in Computer Science from Wayne State University, Detroit, Michigan in December, 2003. His current research interests include Parallel Computing, Distributed Systems, High Performance Computing and Communication, Modeling and Simulation, and System Security. He is a member of the IEEE, the IEEE Computer Society, and the ACM. His personal web page is at http://www.csm.astate.edu/~hjiang.

Hong Jiang received B.Sc. and M.A.Sc. in Computer Engineering in 1982 from Huazhong University of Science and Technology and in 1987 from University of Toronto; and PhD in Computer Science in 1991 from Texas A&M University. Since 1991 he has been at the University of Nebraska-Lincoln, where he is Professor in Computer Science and Engineering. His present research interests are computer architecture, parallel I/O, parallel/distributed computing, cluster and Grid computing, performance evaluation, real-time systems, middleware, and distributed systems for distance education. He has over 150 publications in major journals and international Conferences in these areas and his research has been supported by NSF, DOD and the State of Nebraska.

Yanqing Ji received his Ph.D. in Computer Engineering from Wayne State University, Detroit, Michigan, in 2007. He is currently an Assistant Professor in the Department of Electrical and Computer Engineering at Gonzaga University, Spokane, Washington. His research interests include parallel and distributed systems, application-level thread migration/checkpointing, multi-agent systems, and their biomedical applications. His website is at: http://barney.gonzaga.edu/~ece/yji.html.

Derrick Kondo received his PhD in Computer Science from the University of California at San Diego, and his BS from Stanford University. Currently, he is a research scientist at INRIA Rhône-Alpes in the MESCAL team. His interests lie in the area of volunteer computing and desktop grids. In particular, he leads research on the measurement and characterization of Internet distributed systems, their simulation and modelling, and resource management. He founded and continues to serve as co-chair of the Workshop on Volunteer Computing and Desktop Grids (PCGrid), and also co-chaired the BOINC 2008 workshop on volunteer computing and distributed thinking. He is serving as guest co-editor of a special issue in 2009 of the Journal of Grid Computing on volunteer computing and desktop grids.

King Tin Lam received his B.Eng. degree in Electrical and Electronic Engineering and M.Sc. degree in Computer Science both from the University of Hong Kong in 2001 and 2006 respectively. He worked in the IT Department of the Hongkong and Shanghai Banking Corporation for five years between graduations of the two degrees. Mr. Lam is currently a full-time Ph.D. candidate in the Department of Computer Science at the University of Hong Kong. His research interests include distributed Java virtual machines for cluster computing, software transactional memory and server clustering technologies.

Xiaobin Li received the B.S. degree in electrical engineering from Chongqing University, China, in 1990 and the M.S and the Ph.D. degree in electrical and computer engineering from the University of California, Irvine, in 2001 and 2005, respectively. He is now a senior engineer of Enterprise Microprocessor Group at Intel Corporation, where he is developing XEON microprocessors. His research interests are in the fault-tolerant computing and the power and thermal management.

Xiaolin Li is currently an assistant professor in Computer Science Department at Oklahoma State University (OSU), USA, and director of Scalable Software Systems Laboratory (S3Lab,http://s3lab.cs.okstate.edu/). He received the Ph.D. degree in Computer Engineering from Rutgers University, USA. His research interests include distributed systems, sensor networks, network security, and bioinformatics. He is in the executive committee of IEEE Technical Committee of Scalable Computing (TCSC) and the coordinator of Sensor Networks. He has been a TPC chair for several international conferences and workshops and is on the editorial board of three international journals. He regularly reviews NSF grant proposals as a panelist. He is a member of IEEE and ACM.

Chen Liu received his B.E. degree in Electrical Engineering from University of Science and Technology of China in 2000. He received the M.S. degree in Electrical Engineering from the University of California, Riverside in 2002 and the Ph.D. degree in Electrical and Computer Engineering from the University of California, Irvine in 2008. He currently works as an Assistant Professor in the Department of Electrical and Computer Engineering at Florida International University. His current research interests are high-performance microprocessor design and multi-thread multi/many-core architecture.

Shaoshan Liu is currently a Ph.D. candidate in Computer Architecture at the University of California, Irvine. He received the B.S. degree in Computer Engineering, M.S. in Computer Engineering, and M.S. in Biomedical Engineering in 2005, 2006, and 2007 respectively, all from the University of California, Irvine. His research interests include high performance parallel computer systems, runtime systems, and biomedical engineering. He has been with Intel Research as a member of the Managed Runtime Optimization (MRO) lab, and Broadcom Corporation as a Device Verification and Test (DVT) engineer.

Paul Malécot is Ph.D. candidate in computer science from LRI, Paris South University (France) under the direction of Franck Cappello and Gilles Fedak. He is a member of the INRIA Grand-Large project. His research interests includes the characterization of volunteer desktop computing platforms.

Victor Malyshkin received his M.S. degree in Mathematics from the State University of Tomsk (1970), Ph.D. degree in Computer Science from the Computing Center of the Russian Academy of Sciences (1984), Doctor of Sciences (Dr.h.) degree from the State University of Novosibirsk (1993). From 1970 he had a job in software industry. In 1979 he jointed the Computing Center RAS where he is presently the head of Supercomputer Software Department. He also found the Chair of Parallel Computing Technologies at the State Technical University of Novosibirsk and the Chair bof Parallel Computing in the Novosibirsk State (Classical) University.. He is one of the organizers of the PaCT (Parallel Computing Technologies) series of international conferences that held each odd year. He published over 100 scientific papers on parallel and distributed computing, parallel program synthesis, supercomputer software and applications, parallel implementation of the large scale numerical models. His current research interests include parallel computing technologies; parallel programming languages and systems; methods of parallel implementation of the large scale numerical models; dynamic load balancing; methods, algorithms and tools for parallel program synthesis.

Verdi March is a Research Fellow at the Department of Computer Science, National University of Singapore, and a Research Scientist at the Asia-Pacific Science & Technology Center (APSTC), Sun Microsystems Inc.. He completed his PhD from the Department of Computer Science, NUS, in 2007. He received his BSc in Computer Science from the University of Indonesia in 2000. Verdi is currently leading the HPC research projects in APSTC. His main research interest includes the performance analysis of HPC systems, and distributed systems such as grid computing and peer-to-peer computing.

Rodrigo Fernandes de Mello is currently a faculty member at the Institute of Mathematics and Computer Sciences, Department of Computer Science, University of São Paulo, São Carlos, Brazil. He completed his PhD degree at the University of São Paulo, São Carlos in 2003. His research interests include autonomic computing, load balancing, scheduling and bio-inspired computing.

Marian Mihailescu is pursuing a PhD in Computer Science at the Department of Computer Science, National University of Singapore. He received his BSc in Computer Science in 2005 from the Polytechnic University of Bucharest, Romania. His main research interests include grid computing, peer-to-peer systems, resource allocation and game theory, with a focus on pricing mechanisms.

Farrukh Nadeem received his Master's degree in Computer Science from Punjab University of College of Information Technology, Lahore, Pakistan, in 2002. Currently he is employed as a Ph.D. student at the Institute of Computer Science, University of Innsbruck, Austria, where he is working in area of performance modeling and prediction for high performance Grid computing. Nadeem is the author of over 10 scientific papers and co-author of two book chapters.

Priyadarsi Nanda is a Lecturer at School of Computing and Communications in the Faculty of Engineering and IT at the University of Technology Sydney (UTS), Australia. He has a wide ranging career in teaching, research, industry and consultancy. He received B.Eng. degree in Computer Engineering from Shivaji University, India, M.Eng. degree in Computer and Telecommunication from University of Wollongong, Australia and PhD in Computing Science from University of Technology, Sydney, Australia in 1990, 1996 and 2008 respectively. Details of his research and teaching are available at http://www-staff.it.uts.edu.au/~pnanda/

Doohwan. Oh has received the B.S. degree in of Kyung Hee University in 2007. Doohwan is in the master degree program from the School of Electrical and Electronic Engineering, Yonsei University. His research interest includes ASIC designs and SOC (system on a chip) development.

Zhonghong Ou received his M.Sc degree in electronic engineering from Beijing University of Posts and Telecommunications, Beijing, in 2005. He is now pursuing his PhD degree at both Beijing University of Posts and Telecommunications, China and University of Oulu, Finland. His current research interests span the fields of P2PSIP systems, hierarchical P2P networks, routing algorithms, and protocols.

Manish Parashar is Professor of Electrical and Computer Engineering at Rutgers University, , where he also is Director of the NSF Center for Autonomic Computing and The Applied Software Systems Laboratory and director of the Applied Software Systems Laboratory (TASSL). He received a BE degree in Electronics and Telecommunications from Bombay University, India and MS and Ph.D. degrees in Computer Engineering from Syracuse University. His research interests include autonomic computing, parallel & distributed computing (including peer-to-peer and Grid computing), scientific computing, and software engineering. Manish has received the IBM Faculty Award (2008), Rutgers University Board of Trustees Award for Excellence in Research (2004-2005), the NSF CAREER Award (1999), TICAM, University of Texas at Austin, Distinguished Fellowship (1999-2001), Enrico Fermi Scholarship, Argonne National Laboratory (1996). He is a senior member of IEEE/IEEE Computer Society and ACM. For more information please visit http://www.ece.rutgers.edu/~parashar/.

Jean-Marc Pierson: Since September 2006, Jean-Marc Pierson serves as a University Professor in Computer Science at the University Paul Sabatier, Toulouse 3 (France). Jean-Marc Pierson received his PhD from the ENS-Lyon, France in1996. He was an Associate Professor at the University Littoral Cote-d'Opale (1997-2001) in Calais, then at INSA-Lyon (2001-2006). He is a member of the IRIT Laboratory. His main interests are related to large-scale distributed systems, funded by several projects in Grids and Pervasive environments, with applications in biomedical informatics. He serves on several PCs in the Grid and Pervasive computing area. His researches focus on security, cache and replica management, monitoring and more recently energy aware distributed systems. For more information, please visit http://www.irit.fr/~Jean-Marc.Pierson/

M. Cristina Pinotti received the Laurea degree in Computer Science from the University of Pisa (Italy) in 1986. Currently, she is a Professor of Computer Science at the University of Perugia. She spent visiting periods at the University of North Texas and at the Old Dominion University (USA). Her research interests are the design and analysis of algorithms for wireless networks, sensor networks, parallel and distributed systems, and special purpose architectures. She has published about 50 refereed papers on international journals, conferences, and workshops. She has been a guest coeditor for special issues of international journals. She is in the editorial board of the International Journal of Parallel, Emergent and Distributed Systems.

Radu Prodan received his Master's degree in Computer Science from the Technical University of Cluj-Napoca, Romania, in 1997. Between 1998 and 2001 he served as Research Assistant in Switzerland at ETH Zurich, University of Basel and the Swiss Centre for Scientific Computing. In 2001 he joined the Institute for Software Science, University of Vienna, where he earned his Ph.D. in 2004 from the Vienna University of Technology. Prodan is currently an assistant professor at the Institute of Computer Science, University of Innsbruck. He is interested in distributed software architectures, compiler technology, performance analysis, and scheduling for parallel and Grid computing. Prodan participated in several national and European projects and is currently workpackage leader in the IST-034601 edutain@grid project. He is the author of over 50 papers, including one book, over 10 journal articles, and one IEEE best paper award.

Dang Minh Quan is senior researcher at the School of Information Technology at the International University in Bruchsal. Dr. Quan received his Eng. degree (2001), his M.Sc. degree (2003) from Hanoi University of Technology, VietNam, and his Ph.D. (2006) from the University of Paderborn, Germany. Dr. Quan's current research focuses on High Performance Computing, and Grid computing. In particular, he put special focus on supporting management of SLA-based workflows in the Grid.

Rajiv Ranjan is a post doctoral research fellow in the Grids laboratory, Department of Computer Science and Software Engineering, the University of Melbourne. Dr. Ranjan has authored/co-authored more than 15 papers, which are published in well reputed international conferences, journals, and edited books. His current research interest includes design, development, and implementation of algorithms, software frameworks, and middleware services for realizing autonomic Grid and Cloud computing systems. In particular, he researches on next generation decentralized protocols, data indexing algorithms, and fault-tolerant scheduling heuristics for autonomic management of applications in large scale Grid and Cloud computing environment.

Thomas Rauber received his Master degree, his PhD degree, and the Habilitation in Computer Science from the University des Saarlandes (Saarbrücken) in 1986, 1990, and 1996 respectively. From 1996 to 2002, he has been professor for computer science at the Martin-Luther-University Halle-Wittenberg. He joined the University Bayreuth in 2002 where he holds the chair for parallel and distributed systems. His research interest include parallel and distributed algorithms, programming environments for parallel and distributed systems, compiler optimizations and performance prediction.

Mika Rautiainen is currently working as a post-doctoral researcher at the University of Oulu. He received his M.Sc (eng.) and Dr. Tech. degrees from the Department of Electrical and Information Engineering, University of Oulu, Finland, in 2001 and 2006, respectively. His research interests include content-based multimedia management and retrieval systems, pattern recognition, and digital image and video processing and understanding.

Ala Rezmerita is a Ph.D. student in the Cluster and Grid group of the LRI laboratory at Paris-South University and is a member of the Grand-Large team of INRIA. She has obtained a Master in computer science in 2005 from the French University of Paris 7 – Denis Diderot. Her research interests include parallel and distributed computing, grid middleware and Desktop Grid.

Romeo Rizzi was born in 1967. He received the Laurea degree in Electronic Engineering from the Politecnico di Milano in 1991, and in 1997 he received a Ph.D. in Computational Mathematics and Informatics from the University of Padova, Italy. Afterwards, he held Post-Doc and other temporary positions at research centers like CWI (Amsterdam, Holland), BRICS (Aarhus, Denmark) and IRST (Trento, Italy). In March 2001, he became an Assistant Professor at the University of Trento. Since 2005, he is with the University of Udine, as an Associated Professor. He is fond of combinatorial optimization and algorithms and has a background in operations research.

Won W. Ro received the B.S. degree in Electrical Engineering from Yonsei University, Seoul, Korea, in 1996. He received the M.S. and Ph.D. degrees in Electrical Engineering from the University of Southern California in 1999 and 2004, respectively. He also worked as a research scientist in Electrical Engineering and Computer Science Department in University of California, Irvine. Dr. Ro has worked as an Assistant Professor in the Department of Electrical and Computer Engineering of the California State University, Northridge. He also worked as a college intern in Apple Computer Inc. and as a contract software engineer in ARM Inc. His current research interest includes high-performance microprocessor design, compiler optimization, and embedded system designs. (http://escal.yonsei.ac.kr)

Gudula Rünger received her Master degree and her PhD degree in mathematics from the University of Cologne in 1985 and 1989, respectively, and the Habilitation in Computer Science from the University des Saarlandes (Saarbrücken) in 1996. From 1997 to 2000, she has been professor for computer science at the University Leipzig. Since 2000 she is full professor at the Technical University of Chemnitz. Her research interest include parallel applications, parallel programming languages and libraries, scientific computing, software tools for mixed programming models, as well as algorithmic and parallel adaptivity.

Haiying Shen received the BS degree in Computer Science and Engineering from Tongji University, China in 2000, and the MS and Ph.D. degrees in Computer Engineering from Wayne State University in 2004 and 2006, respectively. She is currently an Assistant Professor in the Department of Computer Science and Computer Engineering of the University of Arkansas. Her research interests include distributed and parallel computer systems and networks, with an emphasis on peer-to-peer networks, wireless networks, resource management in cluster and grid computing, and data processing. She has been a PC member of many conferences, and a member of IEEE and ACM.

Wei Shen is currently a Ph.D. candidate at the University of Cincinnati, USA. He received his B.E. degree from Anhui Normal University, China, in 1997, and an M. E. degree from Nanjing University of Posts and Telecommunications in 2001, both in electrical engineering. His current research interests include resource and mobility management of wireless and mobile networks, QoS provision, and the next generation heterogeneous wireless networks.

Mohammad Shorfuzzaman is a PhD student in the Department of Computer Science, University of Manitoba (UofM), Canada. He received his B.Sc.Engg. (Bachelor of Science and Engineering) in Computer Science and Engineering from Bangladesh University of Engineering and Technology, Bangladesh in 2001 and M.Sc. degree in Computer Science from University of Manitoba in 2005. Prior to his current study in UofM, he worked as a Lecturer in Asian University of Bangladesh for one year. His research interests include distributed systems and in particular Grid computing.

Siang Wun Song is a Professor of the Department of Computer Science, University of Sao Paulo, Brazil, where has been a former dean of the Institute of Mathematics and Statistics. He holds a PhD in Computer Science obtained at Carnegie Mellon University in 1981. He was on the editorial boards of Parallel Computing, and Parallel and Distributed Computing Practices. He is currently on the editorial boards of Parallel Processing Letters, Scalable Computing: Practice and Experience, and Journal of the Brazilian Computer Society. His area of interest is the design of parallel algorithms.

Jun-Zhao Sun received his Dr. Eng. degree in computer science in 1999 from the Harbin Institute of Technology in China. He has been a senior researcher at the Department of Electrical and Information Engineering, University of Oulu in Finland since 2000. From 2006 he works as an academy research fellow for the Academy of Finland. His research interests are in mobile and pervasive computing, wireless sensor networks, context awareness, middleware, and mobility management.

Sabin Tabirca is lecturer in the Department of Computer Science of National University of Ireland, Cork. His main research interest is in Mobile Multimedia with an emphasis on visualisation and graphics. He has published more than 130 articles in the areas of HPC computing and Mobile Multimedia.

Feilong Tang received his Ph.D degree in Computer Science and Technology from Shanghai Jiao Tong University (SJTU), China in 2005. Now, he works with the Department of Computer Science and Engineering, Shanghai Jiao Tong University. His research interests focus on grid and pervasive computing, distributed transaction processing, wireless sensor networks, and distributed computing.

Yong Meng Teo is an Associate Professor with the Department of Computer Science at the National University of Singapore, and an Associate Senior Scientist at the Asia-Pacific Science & Technology Center, Sun Microsystems Inc. He heads the Computer Systems Research Laboratory and the Information Technology Unit. He was a Fellow of the Singapore-Massachusetts Institute of Technology Alliance from 2002-2006. He received his MSc and PhD in Computer Science from the University of Manchester, UK, in 1987 and 1989. His main research interest is in parallel and distributed systems covering the organization, programming models, networking and performance of multi-core, grid and peer-to-peer systems. Current projects include peer-to-peer networks, performance analysis of large systems, fault-tolerant consensus in distributed systems and component-based modeling and simulation.

Parimala Thulasiraman received B.Eng. (Honors) and M.A.Sc. degrees in Computer Engineering from Concordia University, Montreal, Canada and obtained her Ph.D. from University of Delaware, Newark, DE, USA after finishing most of her formalities in McGill University, Montreal, Canada. She is now an Associate Professor with the Department of Computer Science, University of Manitoba, Winnipeg, MB, Canada. The focus of her research is on parallel and algorithms for applications such as computational biology, computational finance, medical imaging or computational medicine on advanced architectures. Over the past few years, she has been working on distributed algorithms for mobile networks using nature inspired algorithms such as Ant Colony Optimization techniques. She has published several papers in the above areas in leading journals and conferences and has graduated many students. Parimala has organized conferences as local chair, program chair and tutorial chair. She has has been serving as a reviewer and program committee member for many conferences. She has also been a reviewer for many leading journals. She is a member of the ACM and IEEE societies.

Ruppa K. Thulasiram (Tulsi) is an Associate Professor with theDepartment of Computer Science, University of Manitoba, Winnipeg, Manitoba. He received his Ph.D., from Indian Institute of Science, Bangalore, India and spent years at Concordia University, Montreal, Canada; Georgia Institute of Technology, Atlanta; and University of Delaware as Post-doc, Research Staff and Research Faculty before taking up the position with University of Manitoba. Tulsi has undergone training in Mathematics, Applied Science, Aerospace Engineering, Computer Science and Finance during various stages of his schooling and post doctoral positions. Tulsi's current primary research interests is in the emerging area of Computational Finance. Tulsi has developed a curriculum for cross-disciplinary computational finance course at University of Manitoba and currently teaching this at both graduate and undergraduate level. He has trained and graduated many students in this area.His research interests include Scientific and Grid Computing, Bio-inspired algorithms for Finance, M-Commerce Applications, and Mathematical Finance, where he has been training many graduate students. He has published number of papers in the areas of High Temperature Physics, Gas Dynamics, Scientific Computing and Computational Finance in leading journals and conferences and has own best and distinguished paper awards in prominent conferences. Tulsi has been serving in many conference technical committees related to parallel and distributed computing, Neural Networks, Computational Finance as program chair, general chair etc and has been a reviewer for many conferences and journals. He is a member of the ACM and IEEE societies.

Daxin Tian received the BS, MS.and Ph.D (Hons) degrees, in computer science, from the Jilin University, Changchun, China, in July 2002, July 2005, and December 2007, respectively. His research interests include network security, intrusion detection system, neural network, machine learning.

Sameer Tilak is an assistant research scientist at the University of California, San Diego. He is involved in the design and development of the cyberinfrastructure for a number of large-scale sensor-based environmental observing system initiatives including the Global Lake Ecological Observatory Network (GLEON) and the Coral Reef Environmental Observatory Network (CREON). He received his Ph.D. and M.S. in computer science from SUNY Binghamton in 2005 (degree conferred: January 2006) and 2002 respectively. He received his M.S. in computer science from the University of Rochester in 2003. His research interests include wireless networks (specifically ad-hoc and sensor networks), grid computing, stream data management, and parallel discrete-event simulation. He has served as a TPC member for numerous conferences and workshops including IEEE Percom 2009, DCOSS (2008-2009), IEEE LCN (2007-2009), IEEE SECON 2009, ACM-IEEE MSWiM 2008, IEEE SenseApp (2007-2009) and IEEE e-Science 2007.

Cho-Li Wang received his Ph.D. degree in Computer Engineering from University of Southern California in 1995. He is currently an associate professor of the Department of Computer Science at the University of Hong Kong. Dr. Wang's research interests mainly focus on distributed Java virtual machines on clusters, Grid middleware, and software systems for pervasive/mobile computing. Dr. Wang is serving in a number of editorial boards, including IEEE Transaction on Computers (TC), Multiagent and Grid Systems (MAGS), and the International Journal of Pervasive Computing and Communications (JPCC). He is the regional coordinator (Hong Kong) of IEEE Technical Committee on Scalable Computing (TCSC).

Sheng-De Wang was born in Taiwan in 1957. He received the B.S. degree from National Tsing Hua University, Hsinchu, Taiwan, in 1980, and the M. S. and the Ph. D. degrees in electrical engineering from National Taiwan University, Taipei, Taiwan, in 1982 and 1986, respectively. Since 1986 he has been on the faculty of the department of electrical engineering at National Taiwan University, Taipei, Taiwan, where he is currently a professor. From 1995 to 2001, he also served as the director of computer operating group of computer and information network center, National Taiwan University. He was a visiting scholar in Department of Electrical Engineering, University of Washington, Seattle during the academic year of 1998-1999. From 2001 to 2003, He has been served as the Department Chair of Department of Electrical Engineering, National Chi Nan University, Puli, Taiwan for the 2-year appointment. His research interests include parallel and distributed computing, embedded systems, and intelligent systems. Dr. Wang is a member of the Association for Computing Machinery and IEEE computer societies. He is also a member of Phi Tau Phi Honor society.

Yang Xiang is currently with School of Management and Information Systems, Central Queensland University. His research interests include network and system security, and wireless systems. He has served or is serving as PC Chair for the The 11th IEEE International Conference on High Performance Computing and Communications (HPCC 09), The 3rd IEEE International Conference on Network and System Security (NSS 09), and The 14th IEEE International Conference on Parallel and Distributed Systems (ICPADS 08). He has served as or is serving as guest editor for ACM Transactions on Autonomous and Adaptive Systems, Journal of Network and Computer Applications, and Concurrency and Computation: Practice and Experience.

Meilian Xu is a PhD student in the University of Manitoba. She received her M.Sc degree in Computer Science from Peking University and B.E. degree in Computer Science from East China Normal University in China. Her research interest is high performance computing and parallel algorithm design for applications such as medical imaging on parallel systems, focusing on multi-core architectures such as Cell Broadband Engine architecture. She has published several papers in leading conferences in this direction. She is a member of the ACM and IEEE societies.

Jaeyoung Yi received the B.S. degree in Mathematics department and Computer Science department from Yonsei University in March, 2008. Currently, she is in the master degree program of the School of Electrical and Electronic Engineering, Yonsei University. Jaeyoung's research interest includes multi-processor system on a chip architectures.

Mika Ylianttila is a professor and adjunct professor in computer science and information networks at the Information Processing laboratory and Research Manager at the MediaTeam Oulu research group at the University of Oulu, Finland. His research interests include mobile applications and services, protocol design and performance, and communication and middleware architectures. He is a senior member of IEEE.

Jiehan Zhou is currently working as a research scientist at MediaTeam, Information Processing laboratory, University of Oulu. He obtained his PhD in manufacturing and automation from the Huazhong University of Science and Technology, Wuhan, China in 2000. He did 2-year postdoctoral research In CIMS, Department of Automation, Tsinghua University, Beijing, China. He worked in VTT/Oulu Finland and INRIA/Sophia Antipolis France for a 18-month ERCIM fellowship. His current research interests include middleware, community coordinated multimedia, service-oriented computing, ontology engineering, semantic Web, and protocol engineering.

Yifeng Zhu received BSc in electrical engineering in 1998 from the Huazhong University of Science and Technology, China, and the MS and PhD degrees in computer science from the University of Nebraska, Lincoln, in 2002 and 2005, respectively. He is currently an assistant professor in Electrical and Computer Engineering at University of Maine. His research interests include parallel I/O storage systems, supercomputing, energy aware memory systems, and wireless sensor networks. He served as the program chair of IEEE NAS'09 and IEEE SNAPI'07, the guest editor of a special issue of the International Journal of High Performance Computing and Networking. He received Best Paper Award at IEEE CLUSTER'07.

Albert Y. Zomaya currently holds the Chair of High Performance Computing and Networking in the School of Information Technologies at Sydney University. He is the author/co-author of seven books, more than 300 papers, and the editor of eight books and eight conference proceedings. He serves as an associate editor for 16 leading journals. Professor Zomaya is the recipient of the Meritorious Service Award (in 2000) and the Golden Core Recognition (in 2006), both from the IEEE Computer Society. He is a Chartered Engineer (CEng), a Fellow of the American Association for the Advancement of Science, the IEEE, the Institution of Engineering and Technology (U.K.), and a Distinguished Engineer of the ACM.

Index

A

B

C

D

E

F

G

H

I

N

O

P

Q

R

S

T

U

V

W

X